Peugeot Scooters
Service and Repair Manual

by Phil Mather

Models covered
(5751-368)

V-Clic. 2008-on
Speedfight 3 50. 2009-on
Speedfight 3 125. 2014-on
Vivacity 3 50. 2008-on
Vivacity 3 125. 2010-on
Kisbee 50. 2010-on
Kisbee 100. 2013-on
Tweet 50. 2012-on
Tweet 125/150. 2010-on

Includes R, RS, Iceblade, Silversport, Sportline, Sixties and Team versions

© Haynes Publishing 2014

ABCDE
FGHIJ
KLMNO
PQRST

A book in the **Haynes Service and Repair Manual Series**

ISBN 978 0 85733 751 1

British Library Cataloguing in Publication Data
A catalogue record for this book is available from the British Library

Printed in the USA

Haynes Publishing
Sparkford, Yeovil, Somerset BA22 7JJ, England

Haynes North America, Inc
861 Lawrence Drive, Newbury Park, California 91320, USA

Haynes Publishing Nordiska AB
Box 1504, 751 45 Uppsala, Sweden

Printed using 33-lb Resolute Book 65 4.0 from Resolute Forest Products Calhoun, TN mill. Resolute is a member of World Wildlife Fund's Climate Savers programme committed to significantly reducing GHG emissions. This paper uses 50% less wood fibre than traditional offset. The Calhoun Mill is certified to the following sustainable forest management and chain of custody standards: SFI, PEFC and FSC Controlled Wood.

Contents

LIVING WITH YOUR SCOOTER

Introduction

Pre-ride checks

MAINTENANCE

Routine maintenance and servicing

Contents

French Flair

Peugeot has had a significant part to play in the development of the motorcycle. The Grand Bi penny farthing established Peugeot as a producer of quirky and innovative designs, which from 1886 were in production at the Beaulieu plant in the south of France. Bicycle production soon moved on to motorcycle production and in 1901 a 1.5 horsepower trike was launched which used a Swiss-made 200cc engine.

The company developed as a manufacturer of single and V-twin engines, using its experise to build engines for other motorcycle manufacturers. A Peugeot V-twin engined Norton won the first TT in 1907. Many racing success followed during the 1920s, particularly with the dohc 494cc twin which had bevel gear driven cams. The factory were producing motorcycles from 198cc to 746cc through the war years and achieved great success with the P515 495 cc engined machine which took 9 world records. All this was of course running alongside a mass-market car production programme which started in 1929 and bicycle production – all products bearing the iconic Peugeot lion.

After WWII Peugeot concentrated on the lightweight motorcycle market and developed a range of two-stroke engined cycle-motor models. A significant breakthrough into the moped and scooter markets was made in 1955 with the launch of the S55 and S57 scooters. Mass market production was the way forward, and Peugeot again showed its innovative side in being the first manufacturer to fit plastic bodywork on the 1982 SC/SX scooter range.

Small capacity Peugeot mopeds and scooters sold well in the home market and the French were very loyal to the Peugeot brand, however the scooter which really put Peugeot on the map outside of France was the Speedfight. Twist and Go 50cc and 100cc two-stroke engined models were produced in massive numbers during the second half of the 90s and very quickly the company was a leading player in many European markets and a serious competitor for the established Italian and Japanese brands. The Trekker model with its rugged looks and commutor style Vivacity followed on the back of the established Speedfight.

Ten years later and the competition was coming not from the established manufacturers in Europe and Japan, but from Chinese brands. Like many, Peugeot switched production from its factories in France to manufacturing plants in China enabling a competitively priced product. When you consider that the PSA Peugeot Citroën group has an interest in the Chinese Jinan Qingqi company you can see how this might work.

Production in the far east wasn't for all models though, many of the larger engined scooters are still made at the Beaulieu-Mandeure plant near the Swiss border of France. Of the models covered in this manual, the engine units for the Tweet range, Vivacity 50 4T and Speedfight 125 are sourced from the Sym company in Taiwan, and all others are from Jinan Qingqi in China.

Maxi scooters, or touring scooters, are a more recent development, with the Peugeot Satelis 250, 300 and 500, and 3-wheeled Metropolis 400 offering riders better performance, weather protection and storage capacity, and a greater level of comfort.

Peugeot have been active in the alternative power market too, with their first two-wheeler, the Scoot'Elec going on sale in 1996. This all electric scooter was based on the existing two-stroke engined Zenith model and had a range of 25 miles. An improved electric scooter, the E-Vivacity, was released in 2011 with lithium-ion batteries instead of the nickel-cadmium units on the Scoot'Elec. The E-Vivacity is a capable urban commuter with a range of 50 to 60 miles.

Acknowledgements

Our thanks are due to Scootertech of Bristol, Bransons of Yeovil and Zöe Hawes who supplied project machines. Also to 3X Motorcycles for technical assistance. We would like to thank NGK Spark Plugs (UK) Ltd for supplying the colour spark plug condition photographs, the Avon Rubber Company for supplying information on tyre fitting and Draper Tools Ltd for some of the workshop tools shown.

About this Manual

The aim of this manual is to help you get the best value from your scooter. It can do so in several ways. It can help you decide what work must be done, even if you choose to have it done by a dealer; it provides information and procedures for routine maintenance and servicing; and it offers diagnostic and repair procedures to follow when trouble occurs.

We hope you use the manual to tackle the work yourself. For many simpler jobs, doing it yourself may be quicker than arranging an appointment to get the scooter into a dealer and making the trips to leave it and pick it up. More importantly, a lot of money can be saved by avoiding the expense the shop must pass on to you to cover its labour and overhead costs. An added benefit is the sense of satisfaction and accomplishment that you feel after doing the job yourself.

References to the left or right side of the scooter assume you are sitting on the seat, facing forward.

We take great pride in the accuracy of information given in this manual, but manufacturers make alterations and design changes during the production run of machines about which they do not inform us. No liability can be accepted by the authors or publishers for loss, damage or injury caused by any errors in, or omissions from, the information given.

Frame and engine numbers

The frame serial number, or VIN (Vehicle Identification Number) as it is often known, is stamped into the frame behind the kick panel. It also appears on the VIN plate. The engine number is stamped into the lower left-hand side of the crankcase or the upper surface of the transmission casing. Both of these numbers should be recorded and kept in a safe place so they can be furnished to law enforcement officials in the event of a theft.

The frame and engine numbers should also be kept in a handy place (such as with your driving licence) so they are always available when purchasing or ordering parts for your scooter.

The procedures in this manual identify models by their model name e.g. Speedfight, and if necessary by their engine size e.g. Vivacity 125, or by engine type e.g. air-cooled (a/c) or liquid-cooled (l/c), two-stroke (2T) or four stroke (4T).

It is sometimes necessary to differentiate between variants of a model during its production run e.g. Tweet RS, or by production year (e.g. 2010 Kisbee). The model code and production year are on the VIN plate.

Buying spare parts

When ordering replacement parts, it is essential to identify exactly the model for which the parts are required. While in some cases it is sufficient to identify the machine by its title e.g. 'Vivacity125', any modifications made to components mean that it is usually essential to identify the scooter by its year of production, or better still by its frame or engine number.

To be absolutely certain of receiving the correct part, not only is it essential to have the scooter engine or frame number to hand, but it is also useful to take the old part for comparison (where possible). Note that where a modified component has superseded the original, a careful check must be made that

Model name	Engine No. prefix	Production years
V-Clic 50	139QMB-E	2008-on
Speedfight 3 50 a/c	B1E40QMB	2009-on
Speedfight 3 50 l/c	B1E4QMB	2009-on
Speedfight 3 125	XS1P52QMI-3B	2014-on
Vivacity 3 50 2T	B1E400MB	2008-on
Vivacity 3 50 4T	XS1P37QMA-2	2008-on
Vivacity 3 125	152QMI	2010-on
Kisbee 50	139QMB-E	2010-on
Kisbee 100	150QMG-A	2013-on
Tweet 50	XS1P37QMA-2	2012-on
Tweet 125	XS1P52QMI-4	2010-on
Tweet 150	XS1P57QMJ-2	2010-on

there are no related parts which have also been modified and must be used to enable the replacement to be correctly refitted; where such a situation is found, purchase all the necessary parts and fit them, even if this means replacing apparently unworn items.

Purchase replacement parts from an authorised Peugeot dealer or someone who specialises in scooter parts; they are more likely to have the parts in stock or can order them quickly from the importer. Pattern parts may be available for certain components; if used, ensure these are of recognised quality brands which will perform as well as the original.

Expendable items such as lubricants, spark plugs, bearings, bulbs and tyres can usually be obtained at lower prices from accessory shops, motor factors or from specialists advertising in the national motorcycle press.

The frame number is stamped into the frame behind the kick panel

The VIN plate is fixed to the frame usually behind the kick panel...

...but may be found under the floor board panel

The engine number is stamped into the crankcase...

...or the transmission casing

Professional mechanics are trained in safe working procedures. However enthusiastic you may be about getting on with the job at hand, take the time to ensure that your safety is not put at risk. A moment's lack of attention can result in an accident, as can failure to observe simple precautions.

There will always be new ways of having accidents, and the following is not a comprehensive list of all dangers; it is intended rather to make you aware of the risks and to encourage a safe approach to all work you carry out on your bike.

Asbestos

● Certain friction, insulating, sealing and other products - such as brake pads, clutch linings, gaskets, etc. - contain asbestos. Extreme care must be taken to avoid inhalation of dust from such products since it is hazardous to health. If in doubt, assume that they do contain asbestos.

Fire

● Remember at all times that petrol is highly flammable. Never smoke or have any kind of naked flame around, when working on the vehicle. But the risk does not end there - a spark caused by an electrical short-circuit, by two metal surfaces contacting each other, by careless use of tools, or even by static

electricity built up in your body under certain conditions, can ignite petrol vapour, which in a confined space is highly explosive. Never use petrol as a cleaning solvent. Use an approved safety solvent.
● Always disconnect the battery earth terminal before working on any part of the fuel or electrical system, and never risk spilling fuel on to a hot engine or exhaust.
● It is recommended that a fire extinguisher of a type suitable for fuel and electrical fires is kept handy in the garage or workplace at all times. Never try to extinguish a fuel or electrical fire with water.

Fumes

● Certain fumes are highly toxic and can quickly cause unconsciousness and even death if inhaled to any extent. Petrol vapour comes into this category, as do the vapours from certain solvents such as trichloro-ethylene. Any draining or pouring of such volatile fluids should be done in a well ventilated area.
● When using cleaning fluids and solvents, read the instructions carefully. Never use materials from unmarked containers - they may give off poisonous vapours.
● Never run the engine of a motor vehicle in an enclosed space such as a garage. Exhaust fumes contain carbon monoxide which is extremely poisonous; if you need to run the

engine, always do so in the open air or at least have the rear of the vehicle outside the workplace.

The battery

● Never cause a spark, or allow a naked light near the vehicle's battery. It will normally be giving off a certain amount of hydrogen gas, which is highly explosive.
● Always disconnect the battery ground (earth) terminal before working on the fuel or electrical systems (except where noted).

Electricity

● When using an electric power tool, inspection light etc., always ensure that the appliance is correctly connected to its plug and that, where necessary, it is properly grounded (earthed). Do not use such appliances in damp conditions and, again, beware of creating a spark or applying excessive heat in the vicinity of fuel or fuel vapour. Also ensure that the appliances meet national safety standards.
● A severe electric shock can result from touching certain parts of the electrical system, such as the spark plug wires (HT leads), when the engine is running or being cranked, particularly if components are damp or the insulation is defective. Where an electronic ignition system is used, the secondary (HT) voltage is much higher and could prove fatal.

Remember...

✗ **Don't** start the engine without first ascer-taining that the transmission is in neutral.

✗ **Don't** suddenly remove the pressure cap from a hot cooling system - cover it with a cloth and release the pressure gradually first, or you may get scalded by escaping coolant.

✗ **Don't** attempt to drain oil until you are sure it has cooled sufficiently to avoid scalding you.

✗ **Don't** grasp any part of the engine or exhaust system without first ascertaining that it is cool enough not to burn you.

✗ **Don't** allow brake fluid or antifreeze to contact the machine's paintwork or plastic components.

✗ **Don't** siphon toxic liquids such as fuel, hydraulic fluid or antifreeze by mouth, or allow them to remain on your skin.

✗ **Don't** inhale dust - it may be injurious to health (see Asbestos heading).

✗ **Don't** allow any spilled oil or grease to remain on the floor - wipe it up right away, before someone slips on it.

✗ **Don't** use ill-fitting spanners or other tools which may slip and cause injury.

✗ **Don't** lift a heavy component which may

be beyond your capability - get assistance.

✗ **Don't** rush to finish a job or take unverified short cuts.

✗ **Don't** allow children or animals in or around an unattended vehicle.

✗ **Don't** inflate a tyre above the recommended pressure. Apart from overstressing the carcass, in extreme cases the tyre may blow off forcibly.

✔ **Do** ensure that the machine is supported securely at all times. This is especially important when the machine is blocked up to aid wheel or fork removal.

✔ **Do** take care when attempting to loosen a stubborn nut or bolt. It is generally better to pull on a spanner, rather than push, so that if you slip, you fall away from the machine rather than onto it.

✔ **Do** wear eye protection when using power tools such as drill, sander, bench grinder etc.

✔ **Do** use a barrier cream on your hands prior to undertaking dirty jobs - it will protect your skin from infection as well as making the dirt easier to remove afterwards; but make sure your hands aren't left slippery. Note that long-term contact with used engine oil can be a health hazard.

✔ **Do** keep loose clothing (cuffs, ties etc. and long hair) well out of the way of moving

mechanical parts.

✔ **Do** remove rings, wristwatch etc., before working on the vehicle - especially the electrical system.

✔ **Do** keep your work area tidy - it is only too easy to fall over articles left lying around.

✔ **Do** exercise caution when compressing springs for removal or installation. Ensure that the tension is applied and released in a controlled manner, using suitable tools which preclude the possibility of the spring escaping violently.

✔ **Do** ensure that any lifting tackle used has a safe working load rating adequate for the job.

✔ **Do** get someone to check periodically that all is well, when working alone on the vehicle.

✔ **Do** carry out work in a logical sequence and check that everything is correctly assembled and tightened afterwards.

✔ **Do** remember that your vehicle's safety affects that of yourself and others. If in doubt on any point, get professional advice.

● If in spite of following these precautions, you are unfortunate enough to injure yourself, seek medical attention as soon as possible.

Engine oil level check – four-stroke engine

The correct oil
● Engines place great demands on their oil. It is very important that the correct oil is used.
● Always top up with a good quality motorcycle/scooter oil of the specified type and viscosity and do not overfill the engine. Do not use oil designed for use in car engines.

Oil type	API grade SL/SJ
Oil viscosity	SAE 5W-40 Synthetic

Scooter care:
● If you have to add oil frequently, check the engine joints, oil seals and gaskets for oil leakage. If not, the engine could be burning oil, in which case there will be white smoke coming out of the exhaust (see *Fault Finding*).

Before you start:
✔ Support the scooter on its centrestand on level ground.
✔ Check the oil level when the engine is cold.
✔ If the engine is hot wait at least ten minutes after stopping it before checking the level to get a true reading.

1 Unscrew the oil filler cap/level dipstick (arrowed) from the right-hand side of the engine and wipe the dipstick clean.

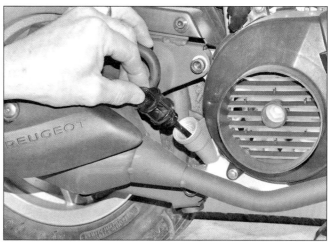

2 Insert the dipstick into the filler neck and rest the cap on top of the filler neck – do not screw it in.

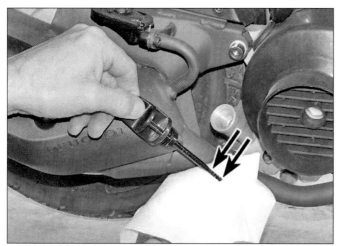

3 Remove the dipstick and check the oil mark – it should lie between the MAX and MIN extent of the hatched area (arrowed).

4 If the level is on or below the MIN line, top up the engine with the recommended grade and type of oil to bring the level almost up to the upper line. **Do not overfill.**

Engine oil level check – two-stroke engine

The correct oil

● A two-stroke engine burns oil during the combustion process, with the oil being held in a tank and pumped into the engine whilst it is running. Most oil tanks hold about 1 litre of two-stroke oil and it is vitally important to keep the oil tank topped-up to avoid lubrication failure. The level will fall at a gradual rate, in line with use of the scooter.

● Don't rely on the oil warning light to tell you that the oil needs topping-up. Get into the habit of checking the oil level at the same time as you fill up with fuel.

● If the engine is run without oil, even for a short time, serious engine damage and engine seizure will occur. It is advised that a bottle of two-stroke oil is carried in the scooter's storage compartment.

● Use a good quality semi-synthetic two-stroke oil to API TC JASO FC standard. Choose a product which is designed for scooter or motorcycle use and is suitable for oil injection (autolube) systems.

Scooter care:

● Although the oil level in the tank will fall in line with scooter usage, if the rate of oil consumption increases, check for any sign of oil leakage between the tank and pump.

Before you start:

✔ Make sure you have a supply of the correct oil available.

✔ Support the scooter on its centrestand on level ground.

1 The oil tank is located underneath the seat at the rear of the storage compartment. Remove the filler cap to check the oil level.

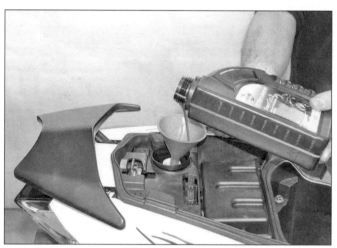

2 If the level is low, top-up with the recommended grade and type of oil, then replace the filler cap securely.

Legal and safety checks

Lighting and signalling

● Take a minute to check that the headlight, tail light, brake light, instrument lights and turn signals all work correctly.

● Check that the horn sounds when the button is pushed.

● A working speedometer graduated in mph is a statutory requirement in the UK.

Safety

● Check that the throttle grip rotates smoothly and snaps shut when released, in all steering positions.

● Check that stand return springs hold the stand(s) securely up when retracted.

● Check that both brakes work correctly when applied and free off when released.

Fuel

● This may seem obvious, but check that you have enough fuel to complete your journey. Do not wait until the fuel gauge or warning light tells you that the level in the tank is low before filling up.

● If you notice signs of leakage you must rectify the cause immediately.

● Ensure you use the correct grade unleaded petrol, minimum 95 octane (RON) – 95 octane is the standard rating for premium unleaded in the UK.

Coolant level check (liquid-cooled models)

> ⚠️ **Warning: Do not remove the cap from the reservoir when the engine is hot. Scalding hot coolant and steam may be blown out under pressure, which could cause serious injury. When the engine has cooled slowly remove the cap allowing any residual pressure to escape.**
>
> ⚠️ **Warning: DO NOT leave open containers of coolant about, as it is poisonous.**

Scooter care:

● Use only the specified coolant mixture. It is important that anti-freeze is used in the system all year round, and not just in the winter. Do not top-up the system with water only, as the coolant will become too diluted.

● Do not overfill the reservoir tank. The coolant level should be just below the MAX level line. Any surplus should be siphoned or drained off to prevent the possibility of it being expelled when the engine is hot.

● If the coolant level falls steadily, check the system for leaks (see Chapter 1). If no leaks are found and the level continues to fall, it is recommended that the machine is taken to a Peugeot dealer for a pressure test.

Before you start:

✔ The coolant reservoir is located behind the radiator grille.
✔ Make sure you have a supply of premix coolant available or prepare some yourself (a mixture of 50% distilled water and 50% corrosion inhibited ethylene glycol anti-freeze is needed).
✔ Support the scooter on its centrestand on level ground.
✔ Check the coolant level when the engine is cold.

1 Remove the coolant reservoir cover (see Chapter 9).

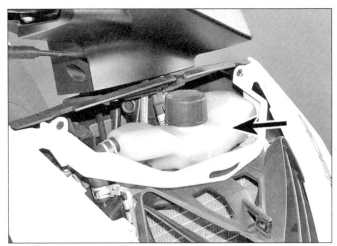

2 Check the level of coolant in the reservoir – it should be just below the level of the filler neck (arrowed).

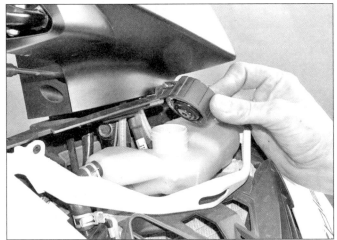

3 If the level is low, slowly unscrew the reservoir cap – if you hear a hissing sound (indicating there is still pressure in the system), wait until it stops before fully removing the cap.

4 Top-up with the specified coolant mixture, using a funnel if required. **Do not overfill**. Fit the reservoir cap and install the reservoir cover.

Brake fluid level check

Before you start:
✔ Support the scooter on its centrestand on level ground. Turn the handlebars until the brake reservoir is as level as possible – remember to check both reservoirs if your scooter is equipped with a rear disc brake.

✔ Make sure you have a supply of DOT 4 brake fluid.
✔ If topping-up is required wrap a rag around the reservoir to ensure that any spillage does not come into contact with painted or plastic surfaces. If any fluid is spilt, wash it off immediately with cold water.

> ⚠ **Warning:** Brake fluid can harm your eyes and damage painted surfaces, so use extreme caution when handling and pouring it and cover surrounding surfaces with rag. Do not use fluid that has been standing open for some time, as it absorbs moisture from the air which can cause a dangerous loss of braking effectiveness.

Scooter care:
● The fluid in the brake master cylinder reservoir(s) will drop as the brake pads wear. If the fluid level is low check the brake pads for wear (see Chapter 1), and replace them with new ones if necessary before topping the reservoir up (see Chapter 8).
● If the reservoir requires repeated topping-up this is an indication of a fluid leak somewhere in the system, which should be investigated immediately.
● Check for signs of fluid leakage from the brake hoses and components – if found, rectify immediately.
● Check the operation of the brakes before riding the machine. If there is evidence of air in the system (a spongy feel to the lever), bleed the brake as described in Chapter 8.

1 Check the fluid level in the window in the reservoir body (arrowed) – the fluid level must be visible in the window.

2 If the window is not clearly visible, remove the front handlebar cover for access (see Chapter 9).

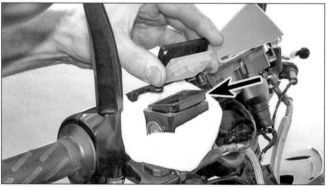

3 If the fluid level is below the top of the window, or is not visible, remove the front handlebar cover, then undo the reservoir cover screws and remove the cover, diaphragm plate (if fitted) and diaphragm (arrowed).

4 Top up with new clean DOT 4 hydraulic fluid, until the level is up to the top of the window. Do not overfill and take care to avoid spills (see **Warning** above).

5 Wipe any moisture out of the diaphragm with a clean cloth or paper towel.

6 Ensure that the diaphragm is correctly seated before fitting the diaphragm plate and cover. Secure the cover with its screws, then fit the handlebar cover.

Tyre checks

The correct pressures:
● The tyres must be checked when **cold**, not immediately after riding. Note that low tyre pressures may cause the tyre to slip on the rim or come off. High tyre pressures will cause abnormal tread wear and unsafe handling.
● Use an accurate pressure gauge. Many forecourt gauges are wildly inaccurate. If you buy your own, spend as much as you can justify on a quality gauge.
● Proper air pressure will increase tyre life and provide maximum stability and ride comfort.
● Refer to the table for the correct tyre pressures for your model.

Tyre care:
● Check the tyres carefully for cuts, tears, embedded nails or other sharp objects and excessive wear. Operation of the scooter with excessively worn tyres is extremely hazardous, as traction and handling are directly affected.
● Check the condition of the tyre valve and ensure the dust cap is in place.
● Pick out any stones or other objects which may have become embedded in the tyre tread. If left, they could eventually penetrate through the casing and cause a puncture. If there are any nails or metal shards check for any air leakage from the hole after removing them (a dab of soapy water over the hole will bubble up if any air is leaking), and also check the tyre pressure a few hours later. Any puncture, however slow, must be dealt with.
● If tyre damage is apparent, or unexplained loss of pressure is experienced, seek the advice of a tyre fitting specialist without delay.

	Front	Rear
V-Clic, Speedfight 50, Vivacity 50	26 psi (1.8 Bar)	29 psi (2.0 Bar)
Kisbee 50, Tweet 50	23 psi (1.6 Bar)	26 psi (1.8 Bar)
Kisbee 100, Speedfight 125	26 psi (1.8 Bar)	29 psi (2.0 Bar)
Vivacity 125	26 psi (1.8 Bar)	32 psi (2.2 Bar)
Tweet 125/150	25 psi (1.75 Bar)	33 psi (2.25 Bar)

Tyre tread depth:
● At the time of writing, UK law requires that for machines over 50cc tread depth must be at least 1 mm over 3/4 of the tread breadth all the way around the tyre, with no bald patches. For machines with an engine size not greater than 50cc UK law states that tread depth may be less than 1 mm if the tread pattern is clearly visible across the whole of the tread breadth all the way around the tyre. Refer to the tyre tread legislation in your country.

● Many riders, however, consider 2 mm tread depth minimum to be a safer limit. Peugeot recommend that the tyres are renewed when they wear down to the 1.6 mm wear indicators in the tread grooves. Identify the location marking(s) (usually an arrow, a triangle or the letters TWI) on the tyre sidewall to locate the indicator bars and replace the tyre if the tread has worn down to the bars.

1 Remove the dust cap from the valve and do not forget to fit it after checking the pressure.

2 Check the tyre pressures when the tyres are **cold**.

3 Measure tread depth at the centre of the tyre using a tread depth gauge.

4 Tyre tread wear indicator bar location marking (in this case the letters TWI)…

5 …and indicator bar (arrowed) in the tread groove.

Suspension and steering checks

● Check that the front and rear suspension operates smoothly without binding.

● Check that the steering moves smoothly from lock-to-lock.

Chapter 1
Routine maintenance and servicing

Contents

Degrees of difficulty

Easy, suitable for novice with little experience	**Fairly easy,** suitable for beginner with some experience	**Fairly difficult,** suitable for competent DIY mechanic	**Difficult,** suitable for experienced DIY mechanic	**Very difficult,** suitable for expert DIY or professional

Introduction

1 This Chapter is designed to help the home mechanic maintain his/her scooter for safety, economy, long life and peak performance.

2 Deciding where to start or plug into a service schedule depends on several factors. If the warranty period on your scooter has just expired, and if it has been maintained according to the warranty standards, you will want to pick up routine maintenance as it coincides with the next mileage or calendar interval. If you have owned the machine for some time but have never performed any maintenance on it, or if you have just purchased a used scooter and have no knowledge of its history or maintenance record, then you should carry out all checks and perform all necessary procedures in one big service to ensure that nothing is overlooked, then start the regular maintenance schedule from that point. If you have just had a major engine overhaul, then you will want to start the schedule from the beginning as with a new machine.

3 Before beginning any maintenance or repair, clean your scooter thoroughly, especially around the suspension, brakes, engine and gearbox covers. Cleaning will help ensure that dirt does not contaminate the working parts and will allow you to detect wear and damage that could otherwise easily go unnoticed.

4 Certain maintenance information is sometimes printed on decals attached to the scooter. If the information on the decals differs from that included here, use the information on the decal.

Note 1: *Pre-ride checks are listed at the beginning of this manual. Always perform the pre-ride inspection at every maintenance interval (in addition to the procedures listed).*

Note 2: *The intervals listed below are the intervals recommended by the manufacturer.*

Note 3: *An initial (one-off) service should be performed by a Peugeot dealer after the first 325 miles (500 km) from new. Thereafter, the scooter should be serviced according to the intervals specified in the service schedules which follow.*

V-Clic

Model identification

Engine . . . . . . .49.58cc air-cooled, 2v four-stroke, code 139QMB-E
Gearbox . . . . Variable speed automatic, belt driven
Ignition . . . . Capacitor discharge ignition (CDI)
Fuel system. . . . . Carburettor
Front suspension . . . . Telescopic forks
Rear suspension. . . . . .Swingarm and monoshock
Front brake . . . . .Hydraulic disc
Rear brake. . . . . .Drum
Tyre size 3.50/10
Overall length . . . . .1660 mm
Overall width. . . . . .700 mm
Overall height . . . . .1070 mm
Wheelbase. . . . . .1200 mm
Kerb weight. . . . . .79 kg
Fuel tank capacity . . . . 6.3 litres

Servicing specifications and lubricants

Drive belt width (service limit). . . . . 16.3 mm
Spark plug type. . . . . .NGK CR7HSA
Spark plug electrode gap . . . . 0.6 to 0.8 mm
Idle speed . . . . .1500 to 1700 rpm
Valve clearances (engine COLD). 0.10 mm
Fuel . . . . .Petrol (unleaded) 95 to 98 octane
Engine oil type . . . . .SAE 5W-40 synthetic. API SJ
Engine oil capacity. . . . . approx 0.8 litre
Gearbox oil . . . . SAE 80W-90 API GL3 gear oil
Gearbox oil capacity . . . . .120 ml
Brake fluid. . . . . DOT 4

Torque settings

Engine oil drain plug . . . . 30 Nm
Gearbox oil drain plug . . . . 12 Nm
Spark plug . . . . .18 Nm

Service schedule – V-Clic

Note 1: Always perform the Pre-ride checks before every service interval – see the beginning of this Manual.
Note 2: Initial one-off services are carried out by the Peugeot dealer at the first 500 km and 1000 km (after 1 month and 4 months) from new.

Normal riding conditions	Section number	**Every** 5000 km (3000 miles)	**Every** 10,000 km (6000 miles)	**Every** 20,000 km (12,000 miles)
Hard riding conditions (intensive urban riding, short journeys with a cold engine, door-to-door deliveries or in an ambient temperature over 30ºC)	Section number	**Every** 2500 km (1500 miles)	**Every** 5000 km (3000 miles)	**Every** 10,000 km (6000 miles)
Time intervals		Every year	Every 2 years	Every 4 years
Air filter and drive belt cover filter	1	Clean		renew
Battery	2	check		
Brake pads and shoes	3	check		
Brake system*	4	check		
Cooling fan and cowling	5	check		
Engine oil (check level every 1000 km/600 m)	6	change		
Engine oil strainer	6	clean		
Throttle cable	7	check		
Idle speed	8	check		
Fuel system	9	check		
Fuel hose**	9	check		
Fuel in-line filter	9			renew
Drive belt	10	check	renew	
Variator and rollers	11	check	renew rollers	
Clutch bearing	12		lubricate	
Kickstarter mechanism	13		lubricate	
Valve clearances	14		check	
Spark plug	15	renew		
Gearbox oil	17		change	
Headlight aim	18	check		
Stand and brake lever pivots	19	lubricate		
Nuts and bolts tightness	20	check		
Steering head bearings	21	check		
Suspension	22	check		fork oil change
Wheels and tyres	23	check		

* The brake fluid must be changed every 2 years, irrespective of mileage.
** The fuel hose must be changed every 4 years, irrespective of mileage.

Speedfight 3 50

Model identification

Engine
    Air-cooled model . . . . 49.9cc two-stroke, code B1E40QMB
    Liquid-cooled model . . . . . . .49.9cc two-stroke, code B1E4QMB
Gearbox . . . . Variable speed automatic, belt driven
Ignition . . . . Capacitor discharge ignition (CDI)
Fuel system. . . . . Carburettor
Front suspension . . . . Telescopic forks
Rear suspension. . . . . .Swingarm and monoshock
Front brake . . . . Hydraulic disc
Rear brake
    Air-cooled model . . . . Drum
    Liquid-cooled model . . . . Hydraulic disc
Tyre size 130/60-13
Overall length . . . . .1895 mm
Overall width. . . . . .700 mm
Overall height . . . . .1120 mm
Wheelbase. . . . . .1290 mm
Kerb weight
    Air-cooled version . . . . .97 kg
    Liquid-cooled version. . . . . .100 kg
Fuel tank capacity . . . . .8.0 litres

Servicing specifications and lubricants

Drive belt width (service limit). . . . . 15.5 mm
Spark plug type
    Air-cooled engine (unrestricted) . . . . NGK BR7HS
    Air-cooled engine (restricted) . . . . .NGK BR5HS
    Liquid-cooled engine . . . . NGK CR7EB
Spark plug electrode gap . . . . 0.6 to 0.7 mm
Idle speed
    Air-cooled engine (unrestricted) . . . . .1800 rpm
    Air-cooled engine (restricted) . . . . .1200 rpm
    Liquid-cooled engine . . . . .1800 rpm
Fuel .Petrol (unleaded) 95 to 98 octane
Engine oil type . . . . . .Semi-synthetic API TC JASO FC two-stroke oil
Engine oil tank capacity. approx 1.1 litre
Gearbox oil . . . . SAE 80W-90 API GL4 gear oil
Gearbox oil capacity . . . . .120 ml
Brake fluid. . . . . DOT 4
Coolant capacity. . . . . 1.3 litres

Torque settings

Cylinder head nuts . . . . 12 to 15 Nm
Spark plug . . . . .20 Nm

Service schedule – Speedfight 3 50

Note 1: *Always perform the Pre-ride checks before every service interval – see the beginning of this Manual.*
Note 2: *An initial one-off service is carried out by a Peugeot dealer at the first 500 km (after 1 month) from new.*

Normal riding conditions	Section number	**Every** 10,000 km (6000 miles)	**Every** 20,000 km (12,000 miles)
Hard riding conditions (*intensive urban riding, short journeys with a cold engine, door-to-door deliveries or in an ambient temperature over 30ºC*)	Section number	**Every** 5000 km (3000 miles)	**Every** 10,000 km (6000 miles)
Time intervals		Every 2 years	Every 4 years
Air filter	1	renew	
Battery	2	check	
Brake pads and shoes	3	check	
Brake system*	4	check	
Cooling system**	5	check	
Engine oil hoses and in-line oil filter	6	check	
Throttle cable	7	check	
Idle speed and fuel system	8	check	
Fuel hose***	9	check	
Fuel in-line filter	9		renew
Drive belt	10	renew	
Variator and rollers	11	check	renew rollers
Clutch bearing – lubricate	12	lubricate	
Kickstarter mechanism	13	lubricate	
Spark plug	15	renew	
Engine top-end and exhaust	16	de-coke	
Headlight aim	18	check	
Stand and brake lever pivot points	19	lubricate	
Nuts and bolts tightness	20	check	
Steering head bearings	21	check	
Suspension	22	check	
Wheels and tyres	23	check	

* *The brake fluid must be changed every 2 years, irrespective of mileage.*
** *The coolant must be renewed every 5 years, irrespective of mileage.*
*** *The fuel hose must be renewed every 5 years, irrespective of mileage.*

Speedfight 3 125

Model identification

Engine ... 124.6cc air-cooled 2v four-stroke, code XS1P52QMI-3B
Gearbox . . . . Variable speed automatic, belt driven
Ignition . . . . Capacitor discharge ignition (CDI)
Fuel system . . . . Carburettor
Front suspension . . . . Telescopic forks
Rear suspension . . . . Swingarm and monoshock
Front brake . . . . Hydraulic disc
Rear brake . . . . Hydraulic disc
Tyre size 130/60-13
Overall length . . . . 1895 mm
Overall width . . . . .700 mm
Overall height . . . . 1120 mm
Wheelbase . . . . 1290 mm
Kerb weight . . . . 121 kg
Fuel tank capacity . . . . 7.5 litres

Servicing specifications and lubricants

Drive belt width (service limit) . . . . 18.0 mm
Spark plug type . . . . NGK CR7HSA
Spark plug electrode gap . . . . 0.7 to 0.8 mm
Idle speed . . . . 1700 to 1900 rpm
Valve clearances (engine COLD) . . . . 0.12 mm
Fuel . . . . Petrol (unleaded) 95 to 98 octane
Engine oil type . . . . SAE 5W-40 synthetic. API SJ
Engine oil capacity . . . . approx 0.9 litre
Gearbox oil . . . . SAE 80W-90 API GL4 gear oil
Gearbox oil capacity . . . . 180 ml
Brake fluid . . . . DOT 4

Torque settings

Engine oil drain plug . . . . 20 Nm
Engine oil strainer cap . . . . 15 Nm
Gearbox oil drain plug . . . . 10 Nm
Gearbox oil filler plug . . . . 10 Nm
Spark plug . . . . 12 Nm

Service schedule – Speedfight 3 125

Note 1: Always perform the Pre-ride checks before every service interval – see the beginning of this Manual.
Note 2: Initial one-off services are carried out by the Peugeot dealer at the first 500 km and 1000 km (after 1 month and 6 months) from new.

Normal riding conditions	Section number	Every 5000 km (3000 miles)	Every 10,000 km (6000 miles)	Every 20,000 km (12,000 miles)
Hard riding conditions (*intensive urban riding, short journeys with a cold engine, door-to-door deliveries or in an ambient temperature over 30°C*)	Section number	Every 2500 km (1500 miles)	Every 5000 km (3000 miles)	Every 10,000 km (6000 miles)
Time intervals		Every year	Every 2 years	Every 4 years
Air filter	1		renew	
Battery	2	check		
Brake pads	3	check		
Brake system*	4	check		
Cooling fan and cowling	5	check		
Engine oil (check level every 1000 km/600 m)	6	change		
Engine oil strainer	6	clean		
Throttle cable	7	check		
Idle speed	8		check	
Fuel system	9		check	
Fuel hose**	9	check		
Fuel filter	9			renew
Drive belt	10	renew		
Variator and rollers	11	check	renew	
Clutch bearing	12		lubricate	
Kickstarter mechanism	13		lubricate	
Valve clearances	14	check		
Spark plug	15	renew		
Gearbox oil	17	change		
Headlight aim	18	check		
Stand and brake lever pivots	19	lubricate		
Nuts and bolts tightness	20	check		
Steering head bearings	21	check		
Suspension	22	check		fork oil change
Wheels and tyres	23	check		

* The brake fluid must be changed every 2 years, irrespective of mileage.
** The fuel hose must be changed every 5 years, irrespective of mileage.

Vivacity 50 (with two-stroke engine)

Model identification

Engine	49.9cc air-cooled two-stroke, code B1E40QMB
Gearbox	Variable speed automatic, belt driven
Ignition	Capacitor discharge ignition (CDI)
Fuel system	Carburettor
Front suspension	Telescopic forks
Rear suspension	Swingarm and monoshock
Front brake	Hydraulic disc
Rear brake	Drum
Tyre size	120/70-12
Overall length	1923 mm
Overall width	670 mm
Overall height	1170 mm
Wheelbase	1337 mm
Kerb weight	96 kg
Fuel tank capacity	8.5 litres

Servicing specifications and lubricants

Drive belt width (service limit)	15.5 mm
Spark plug type	NGK BR7HS
Spark plug electrode gap	0.6 mm
Idle speed	1800 rpm
Fuel	Petrol (unleaded) 95 to 98 octane
Engine oil type	Semi-synthetic API TC JASO FC two-stroke oil
Engine oil tank capacity	approx 1.3 litre
Gearbox oil	SAE 80W-90 API GL4 gear oil
Gearbox oil capacity	120 ml
Brake fluid	DOT 4

Torque settings

Spark plug	20 Nm

Service schedule – Vivacity 50 (with two-stroke engine)

Note 1: *Always perform the Pre-ride checks before every service interval – see the beginning of this Manual.*
Note 2: *An initial one-off service is carried out by a Peugeot dealer at the first 500 km (after 1 month) from new.*

Normal riding conditions	Section number	**Every** 10,000 km (6000 miles)	**Every** 20,000 km (12,000 miles)
Hard riding conditions (intensive urban riding, short journeys with a cold engine, door-to-door deliveries or in an ambient temperature over 30ºC)	Section number	**Every** 5000 km (3000 miles)	**Every** 10,000 km (6000 miles)
Time intervals		Every 2 years	Every 4 years
Air filter	1	renew	
Battery	2	check	
Brake pads and shoes	3	check	
Brake system*	4	check	
Cooling fan and cowling	5	clean	
Engine oil hose and in-line oil filter	6	check	
Throttle cable	7	check	
Idle speed and fuel system	8	check	
Fuel hose**	9	check	
Fuel filter	9		renew
Drive belt	10	renew	
Variator and rollers	11	check	renew rollers
Clutch bearing – lubricate	12	lubricate	
Kickstarter mechanism	13	lubricate	
Spark plug	15	renew	
Engine top-end and exhaust	16	de-coke	
Headlight aim	18	check	
Stand and pivot points	19	lubricate	
Nuts and bolts tightness	20	check	
Steering head bearings	21	check	
Suspension	22	check	
Wheels and tyres	23	check	

* *The brake fluid must be changed every 2 years, irrespective of mileage.*
** *The fuel hose must be renewed every 5 years, irrespective of mileage.*

Vivacity 50 Sixties (with four-stroke engine) and Vivacity 125

Vivacity 50 Sixties

Vivacity 125

Model identification

Engine
   50cc . . . . 49.5cc air-cooled 2v four-stroke, code XS1P37QMA-2
   125ccc . . . . . . .124.6cc air-cooled 2v four-stroke, code P152QMI-A
Gearbox . . . . Variable speed automatic, belt driven
Ignition . . . . Capacitor discharge ignition (CDI)
Fuel system . . . . Carburettor
Front suspension . . . . Telescopic forks
Rear suspension . . . . .Swingarm and monoshock
Front brake . . . . .Hydraulic disc
Rear brake . . . . .Drum
Tyre size 120/70-12
Overall length . . . . 1923 mm (50cc), 2006 mm (125cc)
Overall width . . . . .670 mm
Overall height . . . . .1170 mm
Wheelbase . . . . 1353 mm (50cc), 1390 mm (125cc)
Kerb weight . . . . .95 kg (50cc), 110 kg (125cc)
Fuel tank capacity . . . . 8.5 litres (50cc), 7.5 litres (125cc)

Servicing specifications and lubricants

Drive belt width (service limit) . . . . 17.2 mm
Spark plug type and gap
   50cc . . . . .NGK CR6HSA, 0.6 mm
   125cc . . . . .NGK CR7HSA, 0.7 mm
Idle speed
   50cc . . . . 2000 to 2200 rpm
   125cc . . . . 1500 to 1700 rpm
Valve clearances (engine COLD)
   50cc . . . . 0.05 mm (intake), 0.10 mm (exhaust)
   125cc . . . . .0.10 mm (intake and exhaust)
Fuel .Petrol (unleaded) 95 to 98 octane
Engine oil type . . . . SAE 5W-40 synthetic. API SL/SJ
Engine oil capacity
   50cc . . . . approx 0.7 litre
   125cc . . . . approx 0.9 litre
Gearbox oil . . . . SAE 80W-90 API GL4 gear oil
Gearbox oil capacity
   50cc . . . . .90 ml
   125cc . . . . .100 ml
Brake fluid . . . . DOT 4

Torque settings

Engine oil drain plug . . . . .20 Nm
Engine oil strainer cap . . . . .15 Nm
Gearbox oil drain plug . . . . .10 Nm (50cc), 23 Nm (125cc)
Gearbox oil filler plug . . . . .10 Nm (50cc), 23 Nm (125cc)
Spark plug . . . . .12 Nm (50cc), 15 Nm (125cc)
Valve cover bolts . . . . .10 Nm (125cc)

Service schedule – Vivacity 50 Sixties (with four-stroke engine) and Vivacity 125

Note 1: *Always perform the Pre-ride checks before every service interval – see the beginning of this Manual.*
Note 2: *Initial one-off services are carried out by the Peugeot dealer at the first 500 km and 1000 km (after 1 month and 6 months) from new.*

Normal riding conditions	Section number	Every 5000 km (3000 miles)	Every 10,000 km (6000 miles)	Every 20,000 km (12,000 miles)
Hard riding conditions (*intensive urban riding, short journeys with a cold engine, door-to-door deliveries or in an ambient temperature over 30°C*)	Section number	**Every** 2500 km (1500 miles)	**Every** 5000 km (3000 miles)	**Every** 10,000 km (6000 miles)
Time intervals		Every year	Every 2 years	Every 4 years
Air filter	1		renew or clean	
Battery	2	check		
Brake pads and shoes	3	check		
Brake system*	4	check		
Cooling fan and cowling	5	check		
Engine oil (check level every 1000 km/600 m)	6	change		
Engine oil strainer	6	clean		
Throttle cable	7	check		
Idle speed	8		check	
Fuel system	9		check	
Fuel hose**	9	check		
Fuel filter	9			renew
Drive belt	10	check	renew	
Variator and rollers	11	check	renew	
Clutch bearing	12		lubricate	
Kickstarter mechanism	13		lubricate	
Valve clearances	14	check		
Spark plug	15	renew		
Gearbox oil	17	change		
Headlight aim	18	check		
Stand and lever pivots	19	lubricate		
Nuts and bolts tightness	20	check		
Steering head bearings	21	check		
Suspension	22	check		fork oil change
Wheels and tyres	23	check		

* The brake fluid must be changed every 2 years, irrespective of mileage.
** The fuel hose must be changed every 5 years, irrespective of mileage.

Kisbee

Kisbee 50

Kisbee 100

Model identification

Engine	
50cc	49cc air-cooled 2v four-stroke, code 139QMB-E
100cc	102cc air-cooled 2v four-stroke, code 150QMG-A
Gearbox	Variable speed automatic, belt driven
Ignition	Capacitor discharge ignition (CDI)
Fuel system	Carburettor
Front suspension	Telescopic forks
Rear suspension	Swingarm and monoshock
Front brake	Hydraulic disc
Rear brake	Drum
Tyre size	
50cc	110/70-12
100cc	100/90-10
Overall length	1849 mm (50cc), 1803 mm (100cc)
Overall width	667 mm
Overall height	1156 mm (50cc), 1123 mm (100cc)
Wheelbase	1256 mm
Kerb weight	95 kg (50cc), 97 kg (100cc)
Fuel tank capacity	6.8 litres

Servicing specifications and lubricants

Drive belt width (service limit)	
50cc	16.3 mm
100cc	17.0 mm
Spark plug type	NGK CR7HSA
Spark plug electrode gap	
50cc	0.6 to 0.7 mm
100cc	0.7 to 0.8 mm
Idle speed	1700 to 1900 rpm
Valve clearances (engine COLD)	
50cc	0.10 mm
100cc	0.13 mm
Fuel	Petrol (unleaded) 95 to 98 octane
Engine oil type	SAE 5W-40 synthetic. API SL/SJ
Engine oil capacity	approx 0.8 litre
Gearbox oil	SAE 80W-90 API GL4 gear oil
Gearbox oil capacity	120 ml
Brake fluid	DOT 4

Torque settings

50cc	
Engine oil drain plug	30 Nm
Gearbox oil drain plug and filler plug	12 Nm
Spark plug	18 Nm
100cc	
Engine oil drain plug	20 Nm
Engine oil strainer cap	15 Nm
Gearbox oil drain plug and filler plug	10 Nm
Spark plug	12 Nm

Service schedule – Kisbee

Note 1: Always perform the Pre-ride checks before every service interval – see the beginning of this Manual.
Note 2: Initial one-off services are carried out by the Peugeot dealer at the first 500 km and 1000 km (after 1 month and 6 months) from new.

Normal riding conditions	Section number	Every 5000 km (3000 miles)	Every 10,000 km (6000 miles)	Every 20,000 km (12,000 miles)
Hard riding conditions (*intensive urban riding, short journeys with a cold engine, door-to-door deliveries or in an ambient temperature over 30ºC*)	Section number	**Every** 2500 km (1500 miles)	**Every** 5000 km (3000 miles)	**Every** 10,000 km (6000 miles)
Time intervals		Every year	Every 2 years	Every 4 years
Air filter	1		clean	
Drive belt cover filter (Kisbee 100)	1		clean	
Battery	2	check		
Brake pads and shoes	3	check		
Brake system*	4	check		
Cooling fan and cowling	5	check		
Engine oil (check level every 1000 km/600 m)	6	change		
Engine oil strainer	6	clean		
Throttle cable	7	check		
Idle speed	8		check	
Fuel system	9		check	
Fuel hose**	9	check		
Fuel filter	9			renew
Drive belt	10	check	renew	
Variator and rollers	11	check	renew	
Clutch bearing	12		lubricate	
Kickstarter mechanism	13		lubricate	
Valve clearances	14	check		
Spark plug	15	renew		
Gearbox oil	17	change		
Headlight aim	18	check		
Stand and lever pivots	19	lubricate		
Nuts and bolts tightness	20	check		
Steering head bearings	21	check		
Suspension	22	check		fork oil change
Wheels and tyres	23	check		

* The brake fluid must be changed every 2 years, irrespective of mileage.
** The fuel hose must be changed every 5 years, irrespective of mileage.

Tweet

Model identification

Engine
    Tweet 50 . . . . . 49.5cc air-cooled 2v four-stroke, code XS1P37QMA-2
    Tweet 125 . . . . . 124.6cc air-cooled 2v four-stroke, code XS1P52QMI-4
    Tweet 150 . . . . 150.6cc air-cooled 2v four-stroke, code XS1P57QMJ-2
Gearbox . . . . Variable speed automatic, belt driven
Ignition . . . . Capacitor discharge ignition (CDI)
Fuel system . . . . Carburettor
Front suspension . . . . Telescopic forks
Rear suspension
    Tweet 50 . . . . Swingarm and monoshock
    Tweet 125/150 . . . . Swingarm and twin shocks
Front brake . . . . Hydraulic disc
Rear brake
    Tweet 50 . . . . Drum
    Tweet 125/150 . . . . Hydraulic disc
Front tyre size 90/80-16
Rear tyre size
    Tweet 50 . . . . 90/80-16
    Tweet 125/150 . . . . 110/70-16
Overall length . . . . .2000 mm
Overall width . . . . .690 mm
Overall height . . . . .1125 mm
Wheelbase . . . . .1330 mm
Kerb weight
    Tweet 50 . . . . .97 kg
    Tweet 125/150 . . . . 106 kg
Fuel tank capacity . . . . 5.7 litres

Servicing specifications and lubricants

Drive belt width (service limit)
    Tweet 50 . . . . 17.2 mm
    Tweet 125/150 . . . . 17.5 mm
Spark plug type
    Tweet 50 . . . . NGK CR6HSA
    Tweet 125/150 . . . . NGK CR7HSA
Spark plug electrode gap . . . . 0.7 to 0.8 mm
Idle speed . . . . 1500 to 1700 rpm
Valve clearances (engine COLD) . . . . 0.12 mm
Fuel . . . . Petrol (unleaded) 95 to 98 octane
Engine oil type . . . . SAE 5W-40 synthetic. API SL/SJ
Engine oil capacity . . . . approx 0.7 litre
Gearbox oil . . . . SAE 80W-90 API GL4 gear oil
Gearbox oil capacity . . . . .90 ml
Brake fluid . . . . DOT 4

Torque settings

Engine oil drain plug . . . . 20 Nm
Engine oil strainer cap . . . . 15 Nm
Gearbox oil drain plug . . . . 10 Nm
Gearbox oil filler plug . . . . 10 Nm
Spark plug . . . . 12 Nm

Service schedule – Tweet

Note 1: Always perform the Pre-ride checks before every service interval – see the beginning of this Manual.
Note 2: Initial one-off services are carried out by the Peugeot dealer at the first 500 km and 1000 km (after 1 month and 6 months) from new.

Normal riding conditions	Section number	Every 5000 km (3000 miles)	Every 10,000 km (6000 miles)	Every 20,000 km (12,000 miles)
Hard riding conditions (*intensive urban riding, short journeys with a cold engine, door-to-door deliveries or in an ambient temperature over 30°C*)	Section number	**Every** 2500 km (1500 miles)	**Every** 5000 km (3000 miles)	**Every** 10,000 km (6000 miles)
Time intervals		Every year	Every 2 years	Every 4 years
Air filter	1		renew	
Battery	2	check		
Brake pads and shoes	3	check		
Brake system*	4	check		
Cooling fan and cowling	5	check		
Engine oil (check level every 1000 km/600 m)	6	change		
Engine oil strainer	6	clean		
Throttle cable	7	check		
Idle speed	8		check	
Fuel system	9		check	
Fuel hose**	9	check		
Fuel filter	9			renew
Drive belt	10	renew (125/150cc)	renew (50cc)	
Variator and rollers	11	check	renew	
Clutch bearing	12		lubricate	
Kickstarter mechanism	13		lubricate	
Valve clearances	14	check		
Spark plug	15	renew		
Gearbox oil	17	change		
Headlight aim	18	check		
Stand and lever pivots	19	lubricate		
Nuts and bolts tightness	20	check		
Steering head bearings	21	check		
Suspension	22	check		fork oil change
Wheels and tyres	23	check		

* The brake fluid must be changed every 2 years, irrespective of mileage.
** The fuel hose must be changed every 5 years, irrespective of mileage.

1.1 Loosen the air hose clip (arrowed)

1.2b Undo the cover screws...

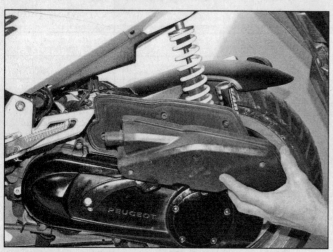

1.2b ...and remove the cover

1.3 Ease out the filter element

Note: *Refer to the model specifications at the beginning of this Chapter for service intervals*

1 Air filters

Engine air filter

Speedfight, V-Clic and Vivacity 50 two-stroke

1 Loosen the clip securing the intake air hose at the front of the air filter cover and disconnect the hose (see illustration).
2 Undo the cover screws and remove the cover (see illustrations).
3 Remove the filter element carefully, noting how it fits (see illustration).
4 If the element is damaged or torn a new one must be fitted. Otherwise, wash the element in hot soapy water, then rinse out the soap. Gently squeeze out the excess water –

DO NOT wring it out – then dry the element with an absorbent towel and short blasts of compressed air if available.
5 When dry, lay the element in a clean tray and soak it in air filter oil (see illustration). Air filter oil is available from dealers – always follow the instructions on the container. Gently

squeeze out any excess liquid, then allow the element to drip-dry for a while.
6 Clean the inside of the filter housing and the cover. Make sure the rubber seal is in good condition and properly seated (see illustration). Renew the seal if it is damaged, deformed or deteriorated.

1.5 Soak the element in air filter oil

1.6 Check the condition of the housing seal

7 Fit the filter element, making sure it is properly seated on the support pegs **(see illustration 1.3)**.

8 Fit the filter cover and secure it with its screws **(see illustrations 1.2a)**.

9 Reconnect the intake air hose and tighten the clip securely.

Vivacity 50 four-stroke and Tweet

10 On Vivacity models, loosen the clip securing the intake air hose at the front of the air filter cover and disconnect the hose.

11 Undo the cover screws and remove the cover. Note that on Tweet models access to one of the screws is through a hole in the side panel and the fuel filter is secured by a tab on the top edge of the cover **(see illustrations)**.

12 Lift out the filter element. On Tweet models, undo the screws securing the element **(see illustrations)**.

13 Clean the inside of the filter housing and the cover. Make sure the rubber seal is in good condition and properly seated. Renew the seal

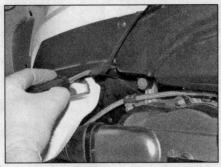
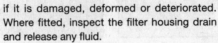

1.11a Access the front cover screw through the side panel

1.11b Unclip the fuel filter from the tab (arrowed)

if it is damaged, deformed or deteriorated. Where fitted, inspect the filter housing drain and release any fluid.

14 Fit the new filter element, making sure it is properly seated. On Tweet models, tighten the mounting screws securely.

15 Fit the filter cover and secure it with its

screws. On Tweet models, don't forget to secure the fuel filter **(see illustration 1.11b)**.

16 On Vivacity models, reconnect the intake air hose and tighten the clip securely.

Kisbee and Vivacity 125

17 Undo the cover screws and remove the cover **(see illustrations)**.

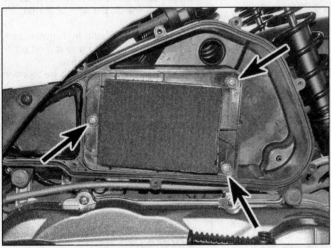

1.12a Undo the screws...

1.12b ...and remove the filter element

1.17a Undo the screws...

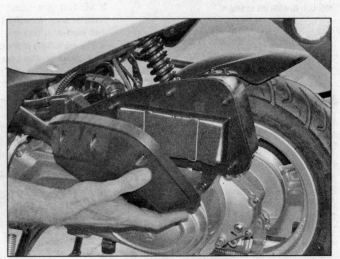

1.17b ...and remove the cover

1.18 Lift out the filter element

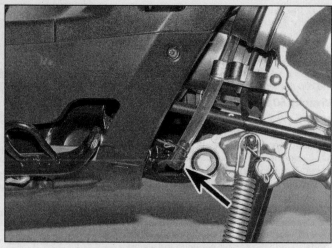

1.21 Release the filter housing drain plug

18 Lift out the filter element **(see illustration)**. Where fitted, unclip the foam cover from the paper filter element.

19 If the foam cover is damaged or torn a new one must be fitted. Otherwise wash the foam in hot soapy water, then rinse out the soap. Gently squeeze out the excess water – DO NOT wring it out – then dry the foam with an absorbent towel.

20 Light dust can be removed from the filter element by blowing compressed air through from the inside. If the element is very dirty a new one must be fitted. **Note:** *Always renew the filter element at the specified service interval.*

21 Clean the inside of the filter housing and the cover. Make sure the rubber seal is in good condition and properly seated. Renew the seal if it is damaged, deformed or deteriorated. Inspect the filter housing drain and release any fluid **(see illustration)**.

22 Install the foam cover.

23 Install the filter element, making sure it is properly seated, then fit the filter cover and secure it with its screws.

Drive belt cover air filter

24 Certain models are fitted with a filter at the front of the drive belt cover. Loosen the clip and ease the filter off **(see illustrations)**.

25 Remove the foam filter. Check the condition of the filter and replace it with a new one if it is damaged.

26 If required, wash the foam in hot soapy water, then rinse out the soap. Gently squeeze out the excess water – DO NOT wring it out – then dry the foam with an absorbent towel.

27 Install the new or cleaned filter in a reverse of the removal procedure.

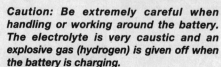

2 Battery

Caution: Be extremely careful when handling or working around the battery. The electrolyte is very caustic and an explosive gas (hydrogen) is given off when the battery is charging.

1 Refer to Chapter 10, Section 3, for access to the battery.

2 Ensure that the battery terminals and leads are tight and clean.

3 Models are fitted with either a sealed, maintenance-free (MF) battery, or a traditional wet lead-acid battery.

4 The condition of the battery can be assessed by measuring the open-circuit voltage with a multimeter.

5 The level of the electrolyte in a traditional

battery will fall gradually in use and will require topping-up with distilled water. It is essential to maintain the level of the electrolyte above the lower level line on the side of the battery **(see illustration)**.

6 If the machine is not in regular use, disconnect the battery and give it a refresher charge every month to six weeks.

7 Full details of battery care can be found in Chapter 10.

 Warning: Do not attempt to open a maintenance-free battery as resulting damage will mean that it will be unfit for further use.

3 Brake pads and shoes

Disc brake pad wear check

1 Some brake pads have wear indicators, either in the form of cut-outs in the face of the friction material, or in the form of a groove in the side of the friction material **(see illustration 3.2)**. The wear indicators should be plainly visible, but note that an accumulation of road dirt and brake dust could make them difficult to see.

1.24a Loosen the clip (arrowed)...

1.24b ...and ease off the filter

2.5 Keep electrolyte level above the lower line

3.2 Check the condition of the brake pads (arrowed)

3.3 Measure the thickness of the friction material

2 Follow the procedure in Chapter 8 to displace the appropriate brake caliper to check the condition of the brake pads **(see illustration)**.

3 If the indicators aren't visible, measure the amount of friction material remaining on each pad backing plate. Peugeot specify a minimum thickness of 1.5 mm for the friction material, and anything less than 1 mm is critical **(see illustration)**.

4 On twin piston calipers also check that the pads are wearing evenly – uneven wear is indicative of a sticking piston, in which case the caliper should be overhauled (see Chapter 8).

5 If the pads are dirty or if you are in doubt as to the amount of friction material remaining, remove them for inspection. If the pads are excessively worn, check the condition of the brake disc.

6 If the pads are worn to or beyond the wear indicator, or to the minimum thickness specified, they must be replaced with new ones without delay. Ideally, it is best to fit new pads before they become this worn.

7 Refer to Chapter 8 for details of pad removal and installation.

Drum brake shoe and drum wear check

8 Make sure the amount of rear brake lever freeplay is correct (see Section 4).

9 As the brake shoes wear and the freeplay is adjusted to compensate, the wear indicator on the rear brake arm moves closer to the wear limit mark on the brake backplate **(see illustration)**.

10 Have an assistant apply the brake, or tie the lever to the handlebar so the brake is applied, and check the position of the wear indicator **(see illustration)**. If the indicator has reached the line replace the brake shoes with new ones (see Chapter 8).

11 With the wheel removed check the condition of the drum lining (see Chapter 8).

4 Brake system

1 A routine check of the brake system will ensure that any problems are discovered and remedied before the rider's safety is jeopardised.

2 Make sure all brake fasteners, including the reservoir cover screws, brake hose banjo bolts and caliper mounting bolts are tight.

3 Make sure the brake light operates when each brake lever is pulled in. The brake light switches are not adjustable. If they fail to operate properly, check them (see Chapter 10).

Brake levers

4 Check the brake levers for looseness, rough action, excessive play and other damage. Replace any worn or damaged parts with new ones (see Chapter 8).

5 The lever pivots should be lubricated periodically to reduce wear and ensure safe and trouble-free operation. In order for the lubricant to be applied where it will do the most good, the lever should be removed (see Chapter 8). However, if an aerosol lubricant is being used, it can be applied to the pivot joint gaps and will usually work its way into the areas where friction occurs **(see illustration)**. A calcium complex grease, which is available as an aerosol spray, is recommended. If motor oil or light grease is being used, apply it sparingly as it may attract dirt (which could cause the controls to bind or wear at an accelerated rate).

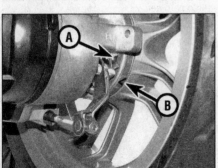

3.9 Drum brake shoe wear indicator (A) and limit mark (B) – air-cooled Speedfight shown

3.10 Drum brake shoe wear indicator (A) and limit mark (B) – Kisbee 100 shown

4.5 Lubricate the brake lever pivots

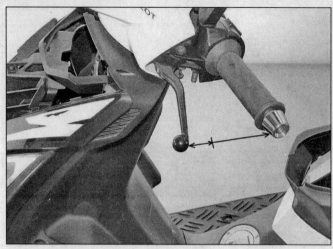
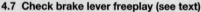

4.7 Check brake lever freeplay (see text)

4.8 To adjust lever freeplay turn the adjuster nut as required

Lever freeplay

6 Where a disc brake is fitted, if the lever action is spongy (i.e. the lever does not come up hard and can travel all the way to the handlebar) first check the fluid level (see *Pre-ride checks*), then bleed the brakes (see Chapter 8).

7 Where a drum brake is fitted, check the amount of free travel in the brake lever before the brake comes on – it should be about 1/3 of the distance between the end of the lever and the handlebar, but you may prefer slightly less **(see illustration)**. Make sure freeplay is not excessive to ensure efficient braking, but also that there is sufficient freeplay to allow the wheel to turn freely with the lever at rest.

8 To adjust the amount of free travel, first support the scooter on its centrestand. Turn the adjuster nut on the end of the cable as required until the freeplay is correct – to reduce freeplay in the lever, turn the nut clockwise; to increase freeplay, turn the nut anti-clockwise **(see illustration)**. Make sure the nut is set so its cut-out seats around the pivot bush in the arm. After adjustment turn the rear wheel and check that there is no brake drag.

Disc brake

Brake hoses

Note: *For a complete check of all brake hose and pipe connections, especially on models with a rear disc brake, remove the body covers and panels as required according to model for access (see Chapter 9).*

9 Twist and flex each hose looking for cracks, bulges and seeping fluid **(see illustration)**. Check extra carefully where the hose connects to the banjo fittings as this is a common area for hose failure **(see illustration)**.

10 Inspect the banjo fittings – if they are rusted, cracked or damaged, fit new hoses.

11 Inspect the banjo union connections for leaking fluid **(see illustration)**. If they leak when tightened securely, refer to Chapter 8 and fit new sealing washers, then bleed the system.

12 Flexible hydraulic hoses will deteriorate with age and should be replaced with new ones every three years or so regardless of their apparent condition (see Chapter 8).

Brake fluid

13 The fluid level in the master cylinder reservoir(s) should be checked before riding the machine (see *Pre-ride checks*).

14 Brake fluid will degrade over a period of time. Peugeot recommends that it should be changed every 2 years, or whenever a new master cylinder or caliper is fitted. Refer to the brake bleeding and fluid change section in Chapter 8.

Brake caliper and master cylinder seals

15 Brake system seals will deteriorate over a period of time and lose their effectiveness. Old master cylinder seals will cause sticky operation of the brake lever; old caliper seals will cause the pistons to stick, and both could cause fluid to leak out. Corrosion build-up in the caliper, particularly due to exposure to road salt, can also lead to seal failure.

16 Check the brake master cylinder(s) and caliper(s) for improper action and signs of leaking fluid.

17 Unfortunately caliper and master cylinder rebuild kits are not available from Peugeot, so if problems are found a new caliper or master cylinder must be fitted (see Chapter 8).

Drum brake

Brake cable

18 The rear wheel should spin freely when the brake lever is at rest. If the brake is binding,

4.9a Inspect the brake hose carefully

4.9b Check the hose-to-banjo fitting connection

4.11 Check the banjo union connections

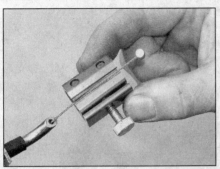

4.22a Fit the cable into the adapte ...

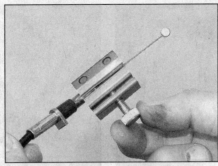

4.22b ...and tighten the screw to seal it in...

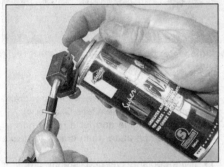

4.22c ...then apply the lubricant using the nozzle provided inserted in the hole in the adapter

4.25 Fully unscrew the nut and draw the cable out

first check that the lever is moving freely and that there is the correct amount of freeplay (see Steps 4,5, 7 and 8).

19 Disconnect the cable from the left-hand brake lever and the arm on the brake drum (see Chapter 8). Check that the inner cable slides smoothly in the outer cable. If the action is stiff, inspect along the length of the outer cable for splits and kinks, and at both the ends of the inner cable for fraying. Replace the cable with a new one if necessary (see Chapter 8).

20 If there are no signs of damage, lubricate the cable (see Steps 21 and 22). If the cable is

still stiff after lubrication, replace it with a new one (see Chapter 8).

21 The cable should be lubricated periodically to ensure safe and trouble-free operation. Dedicated cable lubricants in aerosol form are available and are easy to apply using a pressure adapter, available cheaply from dealers.

22 To lubricate the cable, first disconnect it from the lever. Attach the adapter and follow the procedure shown **(see illustrations)**.

23 Reconnect the cable and adjust the freeplay (see Step 8).

24 If the handlebar lever and brake cable are in

good condition but the brake is still binding, check the operation of the brake cam (see below).

Brake cam

25 To check the operation of the brake cam, first unscrew the adjuster nut and disconnect the cable from the brake arm **(see illustration)**. Note the fitting of the bush in the arm and the cable return spring where fitted, and make sure the spring is not deformed.

26 Apply the brake using hand pressure on the arm and ensure that the arm returns to the rest position when it is released. If the brake arm is binding in the backplate, follow the procedure in Chapter 8 to remove the brake shoes and inspect the brake arm return spring, the brake cam and the springs on the brake shoes.

27 Apply a smear of copper grease to the bearing surfaces of the cam and its shaft before reassembly. Adjust the lever freeplay on completion (see Steps 7 and 8).

Caution: Do not apply too much copper grease otherwise there is a risk of it contaminating the brake drum and shoe linings.

5 Cooling system

> **Warning: The engine must be cool before beginning this procedure.**

Liquid-cooled engines (Speedfight models)

1 Check the coolant level (see *Pre-ride checks*).

2 Follow the procedure in Chapter 9 to remove the headlight panel, floor panel, kick panel and left and right-hand front and belly panels to expose the radiator and the coolant hoses between it and the engine **(see illustration)**.

3 Check the entire cooling system for evidence of leaks. Examine each coolant hose along its entire length – squeeze the hoses at various points and look for cracks, abrasions and other damage **(see illustration)**. The

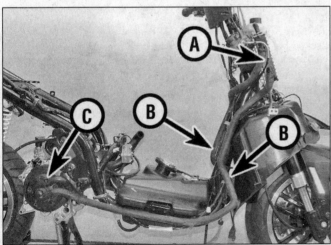

5.2 Radiator (A), coolant hoses (B) and water pump (C)

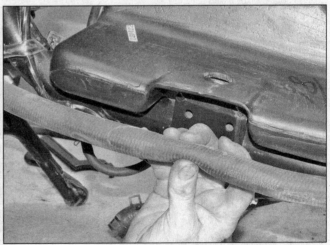

5.3 Squeeze the hoses to check their condition

5.4 Check all hose connections and hose clips

5.5 Check the water pump for leakage

hoses should feel firm, yet pliable, and return to their original shape when released. If they are hard or perished, replace them with new ones (see Chapter 4).

4 Check each cooling system joint. Ensure that the hoses are pushed fully onto their unions and that the hose clips are tight **(see illustration)**.

5 Check the underside of the water pump for evidence of leakage **(see illustration)**. If coolant is leaking from the pump the internal seals will have failed and a new pump will have to be fitted – individual components are not available (see Chapter 4).

6 Check the radiator for leaks and other damage **(see illustration)**. Leaks in the radiator leave tell-tale scale deposits or coolant stains on the outside of the core below the leak. If leaks are noted, remove the radiator (see Chapter 4) and have it repaired or replace it with a new one.

Caution: Do not use a liquid leak stopping compound to try to repair leaks.

7 Inspect the radiator fins for dirt and insects which will impede the flow of air through the radiator. If the fins are dirty, remove the radiator (see Chapter 4) and clean it using water or low pressure compressed air directed through the fins from the back. If the fins are bent or distorted, straighten them carefully with a screwdriver. If airflow is restricted by bent or damaged fins over more than 30% of the radiator's surface area, fit a new radiator.

8 Check the condition of the coolant in the coolant reservoir. If it is rust-coloured or if accumulations of scale are visible, drain, flush and refill the system with new coolant (see Chapter 4). **Note:** *Peugeot recommends draining and refilling the cooling system with fresh coolant every 5 years.*

9 Check the antifreeze content of the coolant with an antifreeze hydrometer. Sometimes coolant looks like it's in good condition, but is too weak to offer adequate protection. If the

hydrometer indicates a weak mixture, drain, flush and refill the system (see Chapter 4).

10 Start the engine and let it reach normal operating temperature, then check for leaks again.

11 If the coolant level consistently drops or overheating occurs, and no evidence of leaks can be found, replace the reservoir cap with a new one. If this fails to cure the problem have the system pressure-checked by a dealer.

Air-cooled engines

12 On air-cooled models a fan mounted on the alternator rotor forces air into the cowling fitted around the cylinder and cylinder head.

13 Check that the air intake in the alternator cover on the right-hand side of the engine is unobstructed and that the cover and cowling sections are correctly fitted together and secure **(see illustration)**. If any sections are missing the engine will not be cooled adequately.

5.6 Check the radiator for leaks and damage

5.13 Ensure the alternator cover (A) and engine cowling (B) are correctly fitted

5.14 Check the fan for broken vanes and make sure the mounting bolts are tight

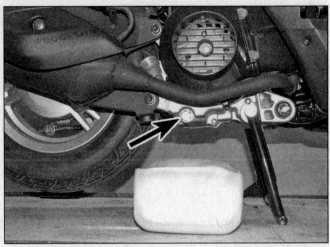

6.2 Place a drain tray below the drain plug (arrowed)

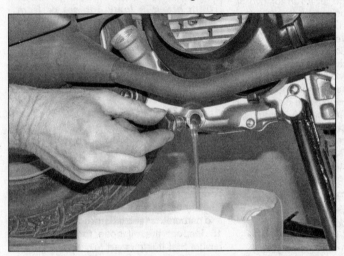

6.4a Draining the engine oil – Kisbee 100 shown

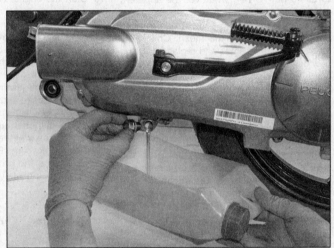

6.4b Draining the engine oil – Tweet 125 shown

14 Remove the alternator cover (see the appropriate Chapter 2 for your scooter) and check the fan **(see illustration)**. If any of the vanes are broken replace the fan with a new one. Make sure the fan screws are tight.

6 Engine oil system

Four stroke engines

⚠️ *Warning: Be careful when draining the oil, as the exhaust pipe, the engine, and the oil itself can cause severe burns. To avoid getting oil over your hands it is best to wear some disposable latex or nitrile gloves, cheaply available from most chemists and hardware stores.*

1 Consistent routine oil changes are the single most important maintenance procedure you can perform. The oil not only lubricates the internal parts of the engine, but it also acts as a coolant, a cleaner, a sealant and a protector. Because of these demands, the oil takes a terrific amount of abuse and should be replaced often with new oil of the recommended grade and type. Saving a little money on the difference in cost between a good oil and a cheap oil won't pay off if the engine is damaged.

Caution: Do not run the engine in an enclosed space such as a garage or workshop.

2 Before changing the oil, warm up the engine so the oil will drain easily. Stop the engine and turn the ignition OFF, and wait for a few minutes to allow the oil to drain to the bottom of the engine. Support the scooter on its centrestand and position a clean drain tray under the oil drain plug in the bottom of the crankcase **(see illustration)**. Note: *The location of the drain plug varies from model to model and on some engines a combined drain plug and strainer is fitted – if in doubt, check in your owner's handbook.*

3 Unscrew the oil filler cap to vent the crankcase and to act as a reminder that there is no oil in the engine.

4 Unscrew the oil drain plug and allow the oil to flow into the drain tray **(see illustrations)**. Discard the drain plug sealing washer as a new one must be fitted.

5 Unscrew the oil strainer plug and remove the spring and strainer **(see illustrations)**.

6.5a Remove the plug, spring...

6.5b ...and strainer – Kisbee 100 shown

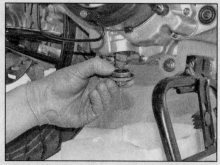

6.5c Plug, spring and strainer – Tweet 125 shown

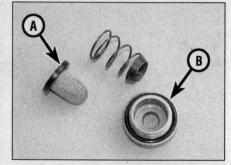

6.5d Location of strainer seal (A) and plug O-ring (B)

Note which way round the spring and strainer are fitted. Check the condition of the O-ring on the strainer plug and replace it with a new one if it is damaged or deformed – it is a good idea to use a new O-ring whatever the apparent condition of the old one (see illustration).

6 Clean the strainer in solvent and remove any debris caught in the mesh. Check the mesh for splits or holes and replace it with a new one if necessary.

7 When the oil has completely drained, fit a new sealing washer on the drain plug, then fit the plug and tighten it to the torque setting specified at the beginning of this Chapter. Do not overtighten the plug as damage to the threads will result.

8 Fit a new O-ring into the groove in the strainer plug and lubricate it with a smear of engine oil. Fit the strainer into the engine with the seal innermost, then fit the spring with the tighter wound coils against the inside of the plug (see illustrations 6.5d, b and a). Tighten the plug to the specified torque setting. Do not overtighten the plug as damage to the threads will result.

9 Refill the engine to the correct level using the recommended type and amount of oil (see Pre-ride checks). Make sure the O-ring

on the underside of the filler cap is in good condition and properly seated. Fit a new one if necessary. Wipe it clean and smear new oil onto it. Fit the cap and tighten it by hand.

10 Start the engine and let it run for two or three minutes. Shut it off, wait a few minutes, then check the oil level. If necessary, top-up the oil to the correct level.

11 Check around the drain and strainer plugs for leaks and ensure they are tightened to the specified torque.

12 The old oil drained from the engine cannot be re-used and should be disposed of properly. Check with your local refuse disposal company, disposal facility or environmental agency to see whether they will accept the used oil for recycling. Don't pour used oil into drains or onto the ground to soak away, as this is likely to pollute your local environment.

OIL CARE FOLLOW THE CODE

Note: It is illegal and anti-social to dump oil down the drain. To find the location of your local oil recycling bank in the UK, call 03708 506 506 or visit www.oilbankline.org.uk

HAYNES HiNT *Check the old oil carefully – if it is very metallic coloured, then the engine is experiencing wear from break-in (new engine) or from insufficient lubrication. If there are flakes or chips of metal in the oil, then something is drastically wrong internally and the engine will have to be disassembled for inspection and repair.*

Two-stroke engines

13 Check the oil level in the tank regularly and top-up as necessary – see Pre-ride checks.

14 At the specified service interval, or if oil leakage is evident, remove the storage compartment and the seat cowling (see Chapter 9) to access the oil hose, filter, pump and carburettor (see illustrations).

15 Inspect the oil hose for damage and ensure that it is pushed fully onto its unions and that the securing clips are firm. If any clips have corroded replace them with new ones.

16 Examine the in-line oil filter (see

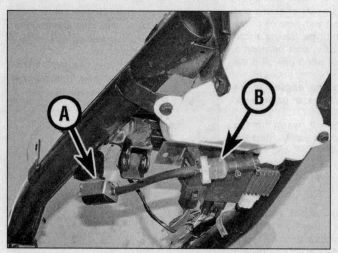

6.14a Location of the oil pump (A) and filter (B)

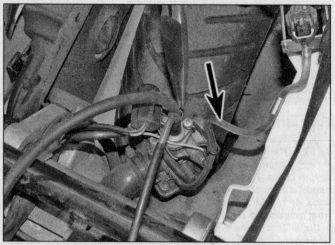

6.14b Oil hose (arrowed) to the carburettor

illustration). If there is any sediment inside, a new filter should be fitted. Ensure the new filter is installed correctly – there is a direction-of-flow arrow on the filter body. Connect the filter to the hose from the oil tank first and allow the filter to fill with oil before connecting the hose to the oil pump. **Note:** *Follow the procedure in the relevant engine Chapter for your model to bleed any air from the oil system before starting the engine.*

7 Throttle

1 Ensure the throttle twistgrip rotates easily from fully closed to fully open with the handlebars turned at various angles, and that the twistgrip returns automatically to the fully closed position when released.
2 If the throttle sticks, this is probably due to a cable fault. Follow the procedure in Chapter 5 and disconnect the cable at the twistgrip end, then lubricate it using a pressure adapter and aerosol cable lubricant **(see illustrations 4.22a, b and c).**
3 If the throttle action is still stiff, remove the storage compartment, handlebar cover(s), kick panel and floor panel as required to access the cable along its length and check

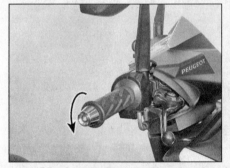

7.4 Check and adjust throttle twistgrip freeplay

6.16 Note how the filter is fitted and the hoses are secured

for a trapped or damaged section. If required, follow the procedure in Chapter 5 and install a new cable.
4 With the throttle operating smoothly, make sure there is a small amount of freeplay in the cable, measured in terms of the amount of twistgrip rotation before the throttle opens – Peugeot do not specify an amount but generally there should be at least 2 mm and no more than 5 mm freeplay **(see illustration).**
5 To adjust the freeplay, first pull back the boot on the cable adjuster at the handlebar end **(see illustration).** Loosen the locknut on the adjuster, then turn the adjuster until the specified amount of freeplay is evident. Tighten the locknut and replace the boot.

7.5 Throttle cable adjuster locknut (arrowed)

6 If the adjuster has reached its limit a new cable will have to be fitted (see Chapter 5).
7 Start the engine and check the idle speed. If the idle speed is too high, this could be due to incorrect adjustment of the cable. Loosen the locknut and turn the adjuster in – if the idle speed falls as you do, there is insufficient freeplay in the cable. Reset the adjuster (see Step 5). Turn the handlebars from side to side and check that the idle speed does not change as you do. If it does, the throttle cable is routed incorrectly. Correct the problem before riding the scooter.

8 Idle speed

1 Although idle speed (engine running with the throttle twistgrip closed) is specified in engine revolutions per minute (rpm), for scooters not fitted with a tachometer it is sufficient to ensure that at idle the engine speed is steady and does not falter, and that it is not so high that the automatic transmission engages.
2 The idle speed should be adjusted when it is obviously too high or too low. Before adjusting the idle speed, make sure the air filter is clean (see Section 1), the throttle cable is correctly adjusted (see Section 7) and check the spark plug gap (see Section 15). On four-stroke engines, the valve clearances must be correct to achieve a satisfactory idle speed (see Section 14).
3 The engine should be at normal operating temperature, which is usually reached after 10 to 15 minutes of stop-and-go riding. Support the scooter upright with the rear wheel clear off the ground.

⚠ ***Warning: Do not allow exhaust gases to build up in the work area; either perform the check outside or use an exhaust gas extraction system***

4 The idle speed adjuster is located on the carburettor **(see illustrations).** Remove the storage compartment and, on Speedfight

8.4a Idle speed adjuster screw – two-stroke engine

8.4b Idle speed adjuster screw – four-stroke engine

models, the rear cover for access (see Chapter 9). **Note:** *The air filter must remain connected to the carburettor during this procedure.*

5 With the engine running, turn the screw clockwise to increase idle speed, and anti-clockwise to decrease it. Snap the throttle open and shut a few times, then recheck the idle speed. If necessary, repeat the adjustment procedure.

6 If a smooth, steady idle can't be achieved, the fuel/air mixture may be incorrect or the carburettor may need cleaning (see Chapter 5). Ensure that the clamps securing the air filter housing duct to the carburettor, and the one securing the carburettor to the intake manifold, are tight.

7 If a satisfactory idle speed still cannot be achieved, check the ignition system (see Chapter 6).

8 With the idle speed correctly adjusted, recheck the throttle cable freeplay (see Section 7).

9 Fuel system

⚠️ *Warning: Petrol is extremely flammable, so take extra precautions when you work on any part of the fuel system. Don't smoke or allow open flames or bare light bulbs near the work area, and don't work in a garage where a natural gas-type appliance is present. If you spill any fuel on your skin, rinse it off immediately with soap and water. When you perform any kind of work on the fuel system, wear safety glasses and have a fire extinguisher suitable for a Class B type fire (flammable liquids) on hand.*

1 Remove the storage compartment (see Chapter 9).

2 Referring to Chapter 5 to confirm the location of the fuel system components, remove the appropriate body panels to access the fuel tank, fuel pump, in-line filter (if fitted) and hoses.

3 Check the fuel tank, fuel tap, the fuel hoses (including vacuum hoses), pump and carburettor, and the hose connections between each component for signs of leakage, deterioration or damage **(see illustrations)**. **Note:** *Fuel system components vary from model to model; refer to Chapter 5 for full details.* Replace any hoses that are cracked or deteriorated, or where hose connections show signs of leakage. Make sure the hoses are secure on the union at each end.

4 If there is evidence of leakage from around the fuel tap or pump body, a new component must be fitted (see Chapter 5).

5 Renew the in-line fuel filter at the specified service interval **(see illustration)**.

6 Cleaning of the fuel strainer in the carburettor is advised after a particularly high mileage has been covered or if fuel starvation is suspected **(see illustration)**.

7 Fuel starvation can also be caused by

9.3a Check that the fuel pump connections are secure – Speedfight shown

9.3b Check fuel tap is secure in the fuel tank – Kisbee 100 shown

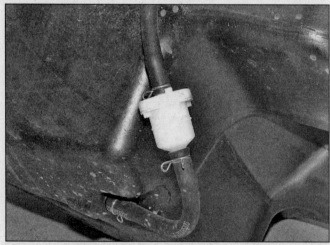
9.5 Note the location of the inline fuel filter

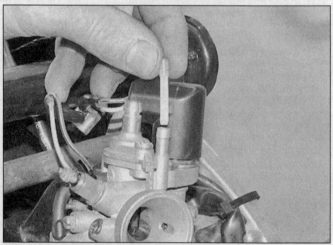
9.6 Location of the carburettor fuel strainer – two-stroke engine

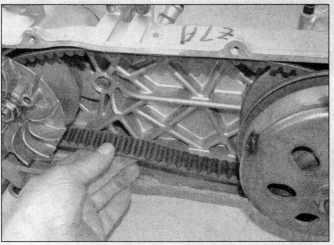

10.2 Check the condition of the belt...

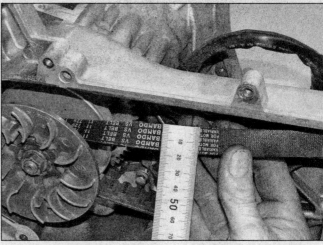

10.3 ...and measure its width as shown

a blocked tank vent in the filler neck or obstructed vent hose. Check and clean as required, and if necessary fit a new hose.

8 If the fuel gauge is believed to be faulty, check the operation of the gauge and sensor (see Chapter 5).

10 Drive belt

1 Remove the drive belt cover (see Chapter 3).

2 Check along the entire length of the belt for cracks, splits, frays and damaged teeth and replace the belt with a new one if any damage is found **(see illustration)**.

3 The edges of the belt will gradually wear away – black dust inside the casing is evidence of belt wear. Measure the width of the outer face of the belt and compare the result with the specification at the beginning of this Chapter **(see illustration)**.

4 If the drive belt has worn below the service limit, has fraying or is cracked, or is contaminated with oil or grease, it must be replaced with a new one (see Chapter 3). **Note:** *If there is any doubt about the condition of the drive belt, replace it with a new one just in case – a broken belt could cause severe damage to engine or gearbox components.* The belt must be renewed at the specified service interval, irrespective of condition.

5 In the event of premature belt wear, the cause should be investigated (see Chapter 3).

6 Oil or grease inside the casing is evidence that a crankshaft, gearbox shaft or clutch assembly seal has failed. Trace the source of the leak and fit a new seal.

7 Clean any dust from inside the casing before installing the drive belt cover.

11 Variator and rollers

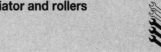

Check

1 Refer to Chapter 3 and remove the drive pulley and variator components.

2 Inspect the rollers and ramp guides for wear and replace them with new ones if necessary, or at the specified service interval.

12 Clutch bearing

Check

1 Remove the drive belt cover (see Chapter 3).

2 Grasp the clutch assembly firmly with both hands and try to rock it from side to side. There should be no freeplay between the clutch and the gearbox input shaft.

3 If there is freeplay, follow the procedure in Chapter 3 to remove the clutch assembly.

13.3 Inspect the kickstart mechanism for wear – Tweet 125 shown

Before disassembling the assembly, check for up and down movement on the input shaft – if the shaft bearings are worn there will be freeplay in the shaft.

4 If the shaft bearings are good it is likely the clutch centre bearings are worn and a new clutch pulley assembly will have to be fitted.

13 Kickstart mechanism

Check

1 Remove the drive belt cover (see Chapter 3).

2 There are several different variations of the kickstart mechanism – refer to the information in Chapter 3.

3 Inspect the ratchet mechanism and the teeth on the kickstart gears for wear and damage **(see illustration)**. Take great care when releasing the kickstart return spring as this is under considerable tension when fitted. Check the teeth on the kickstart driven gear on the centre of the variator pulley.

4 Lubricate the components with a light smear of grease and take care not to get any grease on the variator drive pulley, clutch driven pulley or drive belt.

14 Valve clearances (four-stroke engines)

1 The engine must be completely cold for this maintenance procedure.

2 Remove the storage compartment, seat cowling and centre cover panel as appropriate for your scooter (see Chapter 9) to gain

14.2 Engine valve cover – Kisbee 100 shown

14.5a Location of the static timing mark – Kisbee 100 shown

14.5b Location of the static timing mark – Tweet 125 shown

14.6a Note alignment of the timing marks (arrowed)

access to the engine valve cover **(see illustration)**.

3 Remove the spark plug (see Section 15).

4 Remove the alternator cover (see the appropriate part of Chapter 2 for your engine type). On Vivacity and Tweet 50 models, unscrew the valve inspection caps and remove the camshaft sprocket cover. On all other models remove the valve cover.

5 The valve clearances are checked with the piston at top dead centre (TDC) on its compression stroke (both valves are closed and a small clearance can be felt at each rocker arm). Turn the engine clockwise using a socket on the alternator rotor nut until the line next to the T mark on the alternator rotor aligns with the static timing mark on the crankcase **(see illustrations)**.

6 Check that the timing mark on the camshaft sprocket is correctly aligned. On Vivacity and Tweet 50 models, the mark on the camshaft sprocket should align with the mark on the outside edge of the inspection aperture. On V-Clic and Kisbee 50, and Tweet and Vivacity

125 models, the two short lines on the gear should align with the gasket surface of the cylinder head **(see illustration)**. On Kisbee 100 models the line on the gear (with the numbering the right way up) should align with the gasket surface of the cylinder head **(see illustration)**. If the mark on the rotor aligns but the mark on the camshaft sprocket does not, turn the engine clockwise one full turn (360°) –

all marks will now be aligned and there should now be some freeplay in each rocker arm (i.e. they are not contacting the valve stems).

7 With the engine in this position, check the clearance of each valve by inserting a feeler gauge of the same thickness as the correct valve clearance (refer to the Specifications for your model) in the gap between the rocker arm and the valve stem **(see illustration)**. The

14.6b Note alignment of the timing mark (arrowed)

14.7 Checking the intake valve clearance

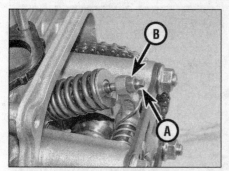

14.8 Valve clearance adjuster (A) and locknut (B)

intake valve is uppermost in the cylinder head and the exhaust valve is below. The feeler gauge should be a firm sliding fit – you should feel a slight drag when you pull the gauge out.

8 If the gap (clearance) is either too wide or too narrow, slacken the locknut on the adjuster in the rocker arm **(see illustration)**. Turn the adjuster using a small spanner or pliers until the gap is as specified and the feeler gauge is a firm sliding fit, then hold the adjuster still and tighten the locknut. Recheck the clearance after tightening the locknut.

9 When the clearances are correct install the components in the reverse order of removal, checking the condition of any gaskets or seals and fitting new ones where necessary.

15 Spark plug

1 Make sure your spark plug socket is the correct size (16 mm hex for four-stroke engines and 20.8 mm hex for two-stroke engines) before attempting to remove the plug – a suitable one is supplied in the scooter's tool kit.

2 Remove the storage compartment (see Chapter 9).

3 On Vivacity models, locate the spark plug cap on the right-hand side of the engine cowling. Pull the plug cap and seal out from the top of the cowling and unscrew the spark plug.

4 On liquid-cooled Speedfight models, the spark plug is located in the top of the cylinder head – pull off the plug cap to access the plug **(see illustrations)**. On air-cooled Speedfight models, pull the plug cap and seal out from the top of the engine cowling **(see illustrations)**. Unscrew the spark plug.

5 On V-Clic models, remove the centre cover panel (see Chapter 9). Pull off the plug cap and unscrew the spark plug.

6 On Kisbee models, pull the plug cap and seal out from the top of the engine cowling

15.4a Pull off the cap (arrowed)...

15.4b ...to access the spark plug – liquid-cooled Speedfight

15.4c Pull off the cap and seal...

15.4d ...to access the spark plug – air-cooled Speedfight

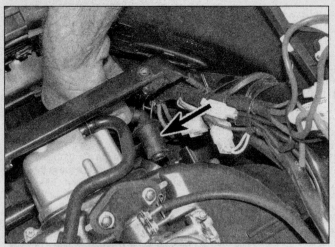

15.6a Pull out the cap and seal...

15.6b ...ease out the access panel...

15.6c ...use a plug socket and extension...

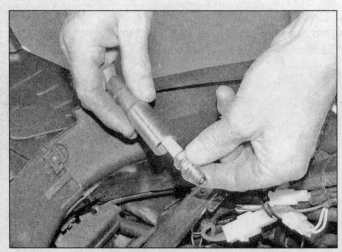

15.6d ...to unscrew the spark plug – Kisbee

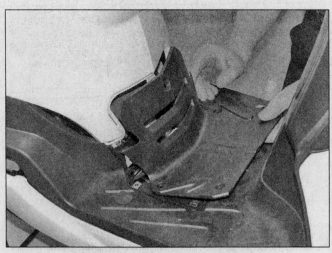

15.7a Remove the battery access panel...

15.7b ...then pull out the cap and seal – Tweet

0.6–0.7mm

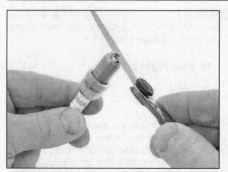

15.9a Using a feeler gauge to measure the electrode gap

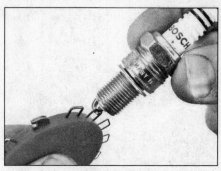

15.9b Using a wire-type gauge to measure the electrode gap

15.9c Adjusting the spark plug gap

(see illustration). Ease out the access panel and use a plug socket and extension bar to unscrew the plug (see illustrations).

7 On Tweet models, remove the battery access panel, then pull the plug cap and seal out from the top of the engine cowling (see illustrations). Unscrew the spark plug.

8 Check the condition of the plug electrodes, referring to the spark plug reading chart at the end of this manual if signs of contamination are evident.

9 Clean the plug with a wire brush. Examine the tips of the electrodes; if a tip has rounded off, the plug is worn. Measure the gap between the side and centre electrodes using a feeler gauge or a wire type gauge (see illustrations). The gap should be as given in the Specifications at the beginning of this chapter; if necessary either adjust the gap by bending the side electrode, or fit a new plug (see illustration).

10 Check the threads, the washer and the ceramic insulator body for cracks and other damage.

11 If the plug is worn or damaged, or if any deposits cannot be cleaned off, replace the plug with a new one. If in any doubt as to the condition of the plug replace it with a new one – the expense is minimal. At the specified service interval, whatever the condition of the existing spark plug, fit a new one.

12 Thread the plug into the cylinder head until the washer seats. Since the cylinder head is made of aluminium, which is soft and easily damaged, thread the plug as far as possible by hand. Once the plug is finger-tight, the job can be finished with the tool supplied or a socket drive. If a new plug is being installed, tighten it by 1/2 a turn after the washer has seated. If the old plug is being reused, tighten it by 1/8 to 1/4 turn after the washer has seated, or if a torque wrench can be applied, tighten the spark plug to the torque setting specified at the beginning of the Chapter. Otherwise tighten it according to the instructions on the box. Do not over-tighten it.

13 Fit the spark plug cap, making sure it locates correctly onto the plug. If a seal is fitted, make sure it locates correctly into the engine cowling.

14 Install any access panels or bodywork in the reverse order of removal.

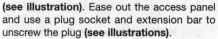

HAYNES HiNT *Stripped plug threads in the cylinder head can be repaired with a Heli-Coil insert – see 'Tools and Workshop Tips' in the Reference section.*

16 Engine de-coke (two-stroke engine)

Caution: If the machine is continually ridden on short journeys which do not allow the engine to reach and maintain its normal operating temperature, the engine and exhaust system may need decarbonising more frequently.

1 Using a semi-synthetic two-stroke oil greatly reduces carbon build-up in the engine and exhaust system. Before removing the engine for a full service, remove the exhaust system and check the inside of the header pipe and the cylinder exhaust port for carbon. If there are only light deposits the service interval can be extended.

2 Loss of power, increased fuel consumption, smokey exhaust and running-on when the ignition is cut are all symptoms of a coked engine. If all other service items are up-to-date, a de-coke will be necessary.

3 The recommended procedure for de-coking is to remove the cylinder head, cylinder and piston and clean off carbon deposits and gum.

4 Clean the inside of the cylinder head with wire wool and a suitable solvent (see illustration). Use a plastic scraper to remove hard deposits but take care not to gouge the soft aluminium. Small scratches can be removed with fine emery cloth. Pay particular attention to remove all carbon from around the spark plug hole. Do not, under any circumstances, use a wire brush mounted in a drill motor – the brush will erode the aluminium of the head.

5 The top of the piston can be cleaned with a hand-held wire brush and finished-off with fine emery cloth (see illustration). Once the piston rings have been removed, use a piston ring groove cleaning tool to remove any carbon deposits from the ring grooves. If a tool is not available, a piece broken off an old ring will do the job. Be very careful to remove only the carbon deposits. Do not remove any metal or damage the ring locating pins and do not nick or gouge the sides of the ring grooves. Once the carbon has been removed, wash the piston with a suitable solvent and dry it thoroughly.

6 Use the same materials to clean the cylinder exhaust port, again taking care not to damage the surface of the metal. The inside of the exhaust header pipe should also be cleaned.

7 Full details of engine removal and disassembly are described in Chapter 2 (refer to the relevant Chapter for your engine). Engine top-end disassembly should be done in the following general order with reference to the appropriate Sections.

16.4 Clean carbon from the inside of the cylinder head

16.5 Clean the top of the piston and the ring grooves (arrowed)

● Remove the exhaust system (see Chapter 5)
● Remove the engine cowling
● Remove the cylinder head
● Remove the cylinder
● Remove the piston
● Remove the piston rings

8 After cleaning and checking, reassemble the components in the reverse order of removal using new gaskets for the cylinder base, cylinder head and exhaust manifold.

9 Oily carbon deposits inside the exhaust header pipe can be scraped out using an old knife or hacksaw blade.

17 Gearbox oil

Check

1 Unless there is evidence that oil is leaking from the gearbox, either on the underside of the gearbox casing or inside the transmission housing, there is no need to check the gearbox oil level between oil change intervals.

2 Oil leaks can be caused by a failed gearbox shaft seal or by a damaged gearbox housing gasket (see Chapter 3). A gearbox oil leak must be rectified immediately to avoid damage to the gearbox components and the possibility of a gearbox seizure. **Note:** *The gearbox oil filler plug is not a level plug – only ever put the specified amount of oil into the gearbox.*

Oil change

Note: *Changing the gearbox oil on Speedfight 50 and Vivacity 50 two-stroke models is not a service item and there is no facility for doing this on these scooters.*

3 Place the scooter on its centrestand on level ground.

4 Clean around the oil filler plug and drain plug **(see illustration)**.

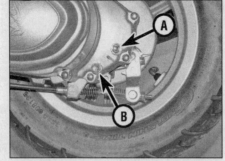

17.4 Gearbox oil filler plug (A) and drain plug (B)

⚠ *Warning: If the oil level is very low, or oil is leaking from the gearbox, refer to Chapter 3 and inspect the condition of the seals and gaskets and replace them with new ones as necessary.*

5 Position a clean drain tray below the drain plug. Unscrew the filler plug to vent the case and to act as a reminder that there is no oil in it.

6 Unscrew the drain plug and allow the oil to drain into the tray. Discard the plug sealing washers as new ones should be used.

7 When the oil has completely drained, fit the drain plug using a new sealing washer, and tighten it to the torque setting specified at the beginning of the Chapter. Avoid over-tightening as you could damage the casing.

8 Refill the gearbox using the quantity, grade and type of oil specified at the beginning of the Chapter. Fit the filler plug with a new washer. Note that scooter transmission oils are sold in small quantities

9 After riding the scooter for a few minutes check around the drain plug for leaks.

10 The old oil drained from the gearbox cannot be re-used and should be disposed of properly. Check with your local refuse disposal company, disposal facility or environmental agency to see whether they will accept the used oil for recycling. Don't pour used oil into drains or onto the ground.

18 Headlight aim

Note: *An improperly adjusted headlight may cause problems for oncoming traffic or provide poor, unsafe illumination of the road ahead. Before adjusting the headlight aim, be sure to consult local traffic laws and regulations – for UK models refer to MOT Test Checks in the Reference section.*

1 First check that the tyre pressures are correct.

2 Position the machine on level ground, with the fuel tank half full and with an assistant sitting on the seat.

3 Follow the appropriate procedure for your model in Chapter 10.

19 Stand(s)

1 All models are fitted with a centrestand and in addition some models have a sidestand **(see illustrations)**.

2 The return springs must be capable of retracting the stands fully and holding them retracted when the machine is in use. If a spring has sagged or broken it must be replaced with a new one (see Chapter 7).

3 Since the stands are exposed to the elements, the pivot bolt should be cleaned and lubricated periodically to ensure safe and trouble-free operation.

4 In order for the lubricant to be applied where it will do the most good, the stand should be removed and the old grease cleaned off the pivot bolt (see Chapter 7). However, if an aerosol lubricant is being used,

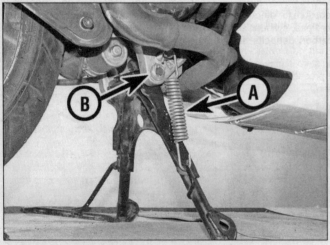

19.1a Centrestand return spring (A) and pivot bolt (B)

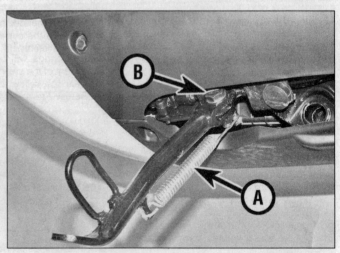

19.1b Sidestand return spring (A) and pivot bolt (B)

19.6 Location of the sidestand switch (arrowed)

21.5 Checking for freeplay in the steering head bearings

it can be applied to the pivot joint gaps and will usually work its way into the areas where friction occurs. If motor oil or light grease is being used, apply it sparingly as it will attract dirt which can cause the pivot to bind or wear at an accelerated rate.

5 Ensure the split pin securing the centrestand pivot bolt is in good condition and replace it with a new one if it is corroded.

6 Where fitted, check the operation of the sidestand switch **(see illustration)**. The switch part of a safety circuit which prevents the engine starting unless the brake is held on and the sidestand is up (see Chapter 10).

20 Nuts and bolts

1 Since vibration tends to loosen fasteners, all nuts, bolts, screws, etc. should be periodically checked for proper tightness.

2 Pay particular attention to the following:

Spark plug
Carburettor body clamps and intake duct bolts
Engine oil drain plug
Gearbox oil drain plug
Stand pivot bolts
Engine mounting bolts
Suspension bolts
Wheel bolts
Brake caliper mounting bolts
Brake hose banjo bolts
Exhaust system bolts/nuts

3 If a torque wrench is available, use it along with the torque specifications given in this manual.

21 Steering head bearings

1 The steering head bearings consist of ball bearings which run in races at the top and bottom of the steering head. The races can become dented or rough during normal use and the balls will gradually wear. In extreme cases, worn or loose steering head bearings can cause steering wobble – a condition that is potentially dangerous.

Check

2 Support the scooter on its centrestand, then have an assistant push down on the rear so the front wheel is off the ground.

3 Point the front wheel straight-ahead and slowly turn the handlebars from side-to-side. Any dents or roughness in the bearing races will be felt and the bars will not move smoothly and freely. If the bearings are damaged they must be replaced with new ones (see Chapter 7).

4 Again point the wheel straight-ahead, and tap the front of the wheel to one side. The wheel should 'fall' under its own weight to the limit of its lock, indicating that the bearings are not too tight (take into account the restriction that cables and wiring may have). Check for similar movement to the other side.

5 Next, grasp the wheel and front suspension and try to move it forwards and backwards **(see illustration)**. Any freeplay in the steering head bearings will be felt as front-to-rear movement of the steering stem. If play is felt in the bearings, follow the procedure described in Chapter 7 to adjust them.

> **HAYNES HINT** *Make sure you are not mistaking any movement between the bike and stand, or between the stand and the ground, for freeplay in the bearings. Do not pull and push the wheel too hard – a gentle movement is all that is needed.*

6 If the bearings cannot be correctly adjusted, disassemble the steering head and check the bearings and races.

7 Over a period of time the grease in the bearings will harden or may be washed out. Follow the procedure in Chapter 7 to disassemble the steering head and re-grease the bearings.

Adjustment

8 Remove the handlebar covers (see Chapter 9) and displace the handlebars (see Chapter 7).

9 Follow the procedure in Chapter 7 to adjust the bearings. Check the bearing adjustment as described in steps 2 to 5 and re-adjust if necessary.

Caution: Take great care not to apply excessive pressure because this will cause premature failure of the bearings.

10 If the bearings cannot be correctly adjusted, disassemble the steering head and check the bearings and races.

11 On completion, install the handlebars (see Chapter 7) and the handlebar covers (see Chapter 9).

22 Suspension

1 The suspension components must be in good condition to ensure rider safety. Loose, worn or damaged suspension parts decrease the scooter's stability and control.

2 Check the tightness of all suspension nuts and bolts to ensure none have worked loose. Refer to the torque settings specified at the beginning of Chapter 7.

Front suspension

3 While standing alongside the scooter, apply the front brake and push on the handlebars to compress the suspension several times **(see**

22.3 Checking the action of the front suspension

22.4a Check the front forks for fluid leaks...

illustration). See if it moves up-and-down smoothly without binding. If binding is felt, the suspension should be disassembled and inspected (see Chapter 7).

4 Inspect both front fork legs for fluid leaks and corrosion on the inner fork tubes **(see illustrations)**.

5 On Speedfight models, if the left-hand fork leg is leaking oil the inner damper cartridge has failed. Check with a Peugeot dealer as to the availability of a new cartridge and follow the procedure in Chapter 7 to fit it, otherwise a new fork assembly will have to be fitted.

6 The conventional motorcycle-type telescopic fork legs fitted to all other machines contain oil for damping and lubrication – oil leakage on these indicates a worn or damaged seal. Seal kits are available for some models – check with your Peugeot dealer.

7 Corroded and pitted inner fork tubes will have to be replaced with new ones. Refer to

Chapter 7 for details of how to disassemble and rebuild the front forks.

Rear suspension

8 With the aid of an assistant to support the scooter, compress the rear suspension several times. It should move up and down freely without binding. If any binding is felt, the worn or faulty component must be identified and renewed. The problem could be due to either the shock absorber or the engine front mounting/pivot assembly.

9 Inspect the rear shock absorber(s) for fluid leaks and corrosion on the damper rod **(see illustration)**. If a shock is faulty it should be renewed (see Chapter 7). Always renew the shocks as a pair on twin-shock models.

10 Support the scooter on its centrestand so that the rear wheel is off the ground. Grip the engine/gearbox unit at the rear and attempt to rock it from side to side – there should be no

discernible freeplay **(see illustration)**. If there is movement, refer to the relevant engine Chapter 2 for your machine, or to Chapter 7, and check the tightness of the bolts securing the front of the engine to the engine bracket and the engine bracket to the frame.

11 Re-check for movement. If freeplay is felt, disconnect the rear shock absorber lower mounting(s) and displace the shock(s), then check again – any freeplay should be more evident. If there is freeplay, inspect the bushes in the engine mounting bracket and all mounting points for wear (see Chapter 7).

12 Reconnect the rear shock absorber(s), then grasp the top of the rear wheel and pull it upwards – there should be no discernible freeplay before the shock begins to compress. Any freeplay indicates a worn shock or shock mountings. The worn components must be identified and replaced with new ones (see Chapter 7).

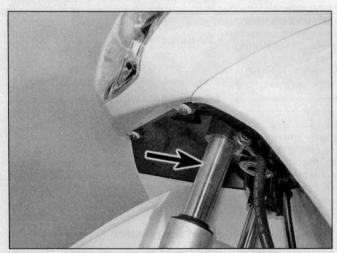

22.4b ...and for corrosion on the fork tubes

22.9 Inspect rear shock for leaks and corrosion

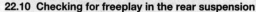

22.10 Checking for freeplay in the rear suspension

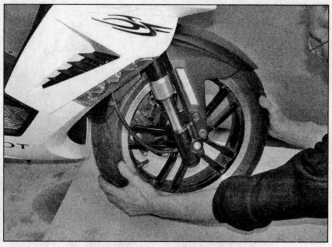

23.2 Checking the front wheel bearings

23 Wheels and tyres

Wheels

1 Cast wheels are virtually maintenance free, but they should be kept clean and checked periodically for cracks and other damage. Also check the wheel runout and alignment (see Chapter 8). Never attempt to repair damaged cast wheels; they must be replaced with new ones.

2 Support the scooter on its centrestand and check for any play in the bearings by pushing and pulling the wheel against the hub **(see illustration)**. Also rotate the wheel and check that it turns smoothly.

3 If any play is detected in the hub, or if the wheel does not rotate smoothly (and this is not due to brake drag), first check that the wheel mountings are tight (see Chapter 8). If they are the wheel bearings must be inspected for wear or damage (see Chapter 8).

4 The front wheel bearings are housed in the wheel hub – see Chapter 8.

5 There are no rear wheel bearings as such – the wheel is mounted directly onto the gearbox output shaft which turns on bearings located inside the gearbox. If any play is detected, refer to Chapter 3 to check the gearbox. On models with twin rear shock absorbers, don't forget to check the bearing in the right-hand suspension arm. Also check that play is not due to a fault or wear in the rear suspension (see Section 18). On disc brake models, check that the wheel mounting bolts as well as the hub nut are tight.

Tyres

6 Check the tyre condition and tread depth thoroughly – see *Pre-ride checks*.

7 Check that the directional arrow on the tyre sidewall is pointing in the normal direction of wheel rotation.

8 Check the valve rubber for signs of damage or deterioration and have it replaced if necessary by a tyre specialist.

9 Make sure the valve stem cap is in place and tight. On some types, the cap doubles as a tool for the valve core (these caps are available in automotive accessory shops). If a tyre loses pressure, and this is not due to damage of the tyre itself, check that the valve core is tight

10 A dab of soapy water will indicate if the valve is leaking – the leak will show as bubbles in the water. If required, use the valve cap to unscrew the old valve and install a new one.

11 If fitted, check that the wheel balance weights are firmly attached to the rim.

Type B1E40QMB – left-hand view

Type B1E40QMB – right-hand view

Chapter 2A
Air-cooled two-stroke engine – type B1E40QMB

Refer to 'Model and servicing specifications' in Chapter 1 for model identification details

Contents

Degrees of difficulty

Easy, suitable for novice with little experience	Fairly easy, suitable for beginner with some experience	Fairly difficult, suitable for competent DIY mechanic	Difficult, suitable for experienced DIY mechanic	Very difficult, suitable for expert DIY or professional

Specifications

General

Type	Single cylinder air-cooled two-stroke
Capacity	49.9 cc
Bore x stroke	39.94 x 39.8 mm
Cylinder compression	87 psi (6 Bar) @ 700rpm

Piston rings

Ring end gap (installed)	0.15 to 0.20 mm

Crankshaft and connecting rod

Big-end side clearance	
Service limit	0.70 mm
Crankshaft run-out	
Measured 50 mm from end of shaft	0.05 mm
Crankshaft seal fitment measured depth	
Left-hand side	6.0 mm
Right-hand side	17.5 mm

Torque settings

Alternator rotor nut	40 Nm
Alternator stator screws/pulse generator coil screws	10 Nm
Cooling fan bolts	7 Nm
Crankcase bolts	10 Nm
Cylinder head bolts	
Initial setting	8 Nm
Final setting	12 Nm
Engine cowling bolts	10 Nm
Engine mounting bolt/nut	60 Nm
Exhaust manifold	15 Nm
Fuel pump mounting bolts	7 Nm
Intake manifold bolts	10 Nm
Rear shock absorber lower mounting bolt	22 Nm
Rear shock absorber upper mounting bolt	45 Nm
Rear wheel nut	
Speedfight 3	100 Nm
Vivacity 3	120 Nm
Drive belt cover screws	10 Nm

1 General information

The engine is a single cylinder two-stroke with fan assisted air cooling as fitted to Speedfight 3 and Vivacity 3 50cc models. The crankshaft assembly is pressed together, incorporating the connecting rod and big-end bearing. The piston runs on a needle roller bearing fitted in the small-end of the connecting rod. The crankshaft runs in caged ball main bearings.

The crankcase divides vertically – the left-hand crankcase is an integral part of the transmission casing and gearbox.

2 Component access

A number of components, with the obvious exception of the crankshaft assembly and its bearings, can be worked on without having to remove the engine/transmission unit from the scooter. However, access to some components is severely restricted, and if several areas require attention at the same time, removal of the engine is recommended, as it is an easy task to undertake.

3 Cylinder compression test

 Warning: Be careful when working on the hot engine – the exhaust pipe, the engine and engine components can cause severe burns.

Special tools: A compression gauge with a 14 mm x 1.25 mm size threaded adapter is required for this procedure.

1 Among other things, poor starting and engine performance may be caused by a leaking head gasket or worn piston, rings and/or cylinder wall. A cylinder compression check will help pinpoint these conditions.

2 Run the engine until it reaches normal operating temperature, then turn the ignition OFF. Support the scooter securely in an upright position.

3 Follow the procedure in Chapter 1, Section 15, and remove the spark plug. Fit the plug back into the cap and position the plug with the threads contacting the engine.

4 Thread the gauge adapter into the spark plug hole then install the compression gauge.

5 Open the throttle fully and crank the engine over on the starter motor until the gauge reading stabilises – after four or five revolutions the pressure should build up to a maximum figure and then remain stable. Make a note of the pressure reading.

6 Release the pressure on the gauge, then repeat the procedure. If the reading is different this time, repeat the procedure until you obtain several readings that are the same.

7 Compare the result with the specification at the beginning of this Chapter.

8 If the compression builds up quickly and evenly, you can assume that the engine top-end is in good mechanical condition. Worn or sticking piston rings, or a worn cylinder, will produce very little initial movement of the gauge, but compression will tend to build-up as the engine turns over. A leaking head gasket is indicated by low initial compression which does not build-up.

9 To confirm your findings, use a squirt-type oil can to add a small amount of engine oil into the cylinder through the spark plug hole. The oil will tend to seal the piston rings if they are leaking. Check the compression again and if it increases significantly after the addition of the oil the rings or cylinder are definitely worn. If the compression remains low, the pressure is leaking past the head gasket.

10 When the test is complete, follow the procedure in Chapter 1, Section 15, and install the spark plug.

Note: *High compression pressure indicates excessive carbon build-up in the combustion chamber and on the top of the piston. If this is*
the case, remove the cylinder head and clean the carbon deposits off. Note that excessive carbon build-up is less likely with the use of modern fuels and two-stroke oil.

4 Engine – removal and installation

Caution: The engine/transmission unit is not heavy, however removal and installation should be carried out with the aid of an assistant; personal injury or damage could occur if the engine falls or is dropped.

Removal

1 Support the scooter securely in an upright position. Work can be made easier by raising it to a suitable height on an hydraulic ramp or a suitable platform. Make sure it is secure and will not topple over.

2 Disconnect and remove the battery (see Chapter 10).

3 Remove the storage compartment, the under body panel and the passenger footrests (see Chapter 9).

4 Remove the air filter housing (see Chapter 5).

5 Remove the rear hugger (see Chapter 9).

6 Remove the exhaust system (see Chapter 5).

7 Pull the spark plug cap off the plug and position the cap clear of the engine **(see illustration)**.

4.7 Pull off the spark plug cap

4.8 Location of the automatic choke unit

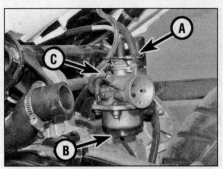

4.9 Fuel hose (A), drain screw (B) and carburettor heater terminal (C)

4.10 Disconnect the oil hose from the pump

8 Trace the wiring from the automatic choke unit and disconnect it at the connector **(see illustration)**. **Note:** *When disconnecting any wiring, it is advisable to mark or tag the wires as a reminder of where they connect.* Where fitted, disconnect the carburettor heater wiring from the terminal on the carburettor.

9 Disconnect the fuel hose from its union on the carburettor, being prepared to catch any residual fuel in a rag **(see illustration)**. Position a suitable container below the carburettor drain hose, then loosen the drain screw and drain any residual fuel from the float chamber. Tighten the drain screw.

10 Release the clip securing the oil hose to the union on the oil pump and pull the hose off, being prepared to catch any residual oil in a rag **(see illustration)**. Plug the open end of the hose to prevent any dirt getting inside.

11 Disconnect the fuel pump vacuum hose from its union on the rear, right-hand side of the crankcase **(see illustration)**.

12 Undo the screw securing the carburettor top and draw the slide assembly out from the carburettor (see Chapter 5). Secure the throttle cable and slide assembly clear of the engine to avoid damage. Stuff clean rag into the carburettor body to prevent anything falling inside.

13 Trace the wiring for the alternator and ignition pulse generator coil from the top of

4.11 Location of the vacuum hose union (arrowed)

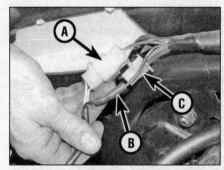

4.13 Alternator (A), ignition pulse generator (B) and starter motor (C) wiring connectors

the alternator cover on the right-hand side of the engine and disconnect it at the connector **(see illustration)**. Release the wiring on the engine side of the loom from any clips or ties.

14 The starter motor is located underneath the engine. Trace the wiring from the starter motor terminal and earth terminal and disconnect it at the connector **(see illustration 4.13)**.

15 If required, remove the rear wheel (see Chapter 8). **Note:** *On models where the centrestand is bolted to the underside of the engine unit, the rear wheel and stand provide a convenient support for the unit once it is removed from the scooter. However, it is*

useful to loosen the rear wheel nut at this point before disconnecting the rear brake.

16 Disconnect the brake cable from the brake arm (see Chapter 8). Undo any screws securing the cable to the underside of the transmission casing and detach the cable **(see illustration)**.

17 Before the engine with the centrestand can be removed, a means of supporting the scooter must be devised. A double A-frame hoist is ideally suited to most machines once the rear bodywork has been removed and where the front of the scooter can be firmly secured **(see illustration)**. Alternatively, with

4.16 Disconnect the brake cable from the casing at the points shown

4.17a Supporting the scooter with an A-frame hoist

4.17b Supporting the scooter on the left...

4.17c ...and right-hand sides...

4.17d ...leaving easy access to the engine unit

the belly panels removed, the scooter can be supported from underneath provided the weight is taken on the frame tubes and not the fuel tank. On the machine used to illustrate this procedure, a bar was passed through the frame adjacent to the engine mounting bracket, supported on both sides with axle stands **(see illustrations)**.

18 Check that all wiring, cables and hoses are clear of the engine/transmission unit.

19 Undo the upper rear shock absorber mounting bolt, then support the weight of the engine and rear wheel and withdraw the bolt. Lower the wheel to the ground. Undo the lower shock mounting bolt and remove the shock **(see illustration)**.

20 Undo the nut on the engine mounting bolt **(see illustration)**.

21 Have an assistant support the engine unit, then carefully withdraw the engine mounting bolt. Manoeuvre the engine unit back and out of the frame.

22 If the engine is dirty, particularly around its mountings, wash it thoroughly before starting any major dismantling work. This will make work much easier and rule out the possibility of dirt falling inside.

23 If required, remove the rear wheel (see Chapter 8) and the centrestand (see Chapter 7).

Installation

24 Installation is the reverse of removal, noting the following:
● Make sure no wires, cables or hoses become trapped between the engine and the frame when installing the engine.
● Tighten the engine mounting bolt, shock absorber bolts and wheel nut to the torque settings specified at the beginning of this Chapter.
● Make sure all wires, cables and hoses are correctly routed and connected, and secured by any clips or ties.
● Bleed the oil pump (see Section 13) .
● Check the operation of the rear brake before riding the machine (see Chapter 1).

5 Disassembly and reassembly – general information

Disassembly

1 Before disassembling the engine, the external surfaces of the unit should be thoroughly cleaned and degreased. This will prevent contamination of the engine

internals, and will also make working a lot easier and cleaner. A high flash-point solvent, such as paraffin can be used, or better still, a proprietary engine degreaser such as Gunk. Use an old paintbrush to work the solvent into the various recesses of the engine casings. Take care to exclude solvent or water from the electrical components and intake and exhaust ports.

⚠ *Warning: The use of petrol (gasoline) as a cleaning agent should be avoided because of the risk of fire.*

2 When clean and dry, arrange the unit on the workbench, leaving a suitable clear area for working. Gather a selection of small containers and plastic bags so that parts can be grouped together in an easily identifiable manner. Some paper and a pen should be on hand to permit notes to be made and labels attached where necessary. A supply of clean rag is also required.

3 Before commencing work, read through the appropriate section so that some idea of the necessary procedure can be gained. When removing components it should be noted that great force is seldom required, unless specified. In many cases, a component's reluctance to be removed is indicative of an

4.19 Remove the rear shock absorber

4.20 Undo the nut (arrowed) on the mounting bolt

6.1a Undo the left...

6.1b ...and right-hand bolts...

6.1c ...and lift off the engine cowling

6.2a Undo the bolt (arrowed)...

6.2b ...and remove the alternator cover

6.3 Cooling fan mounting bolts (arrowed)

incorrect approach or removal method – if in any doubt, re-check with the text.

4 When disassembling the engine, keep 'mated' parts that have been in contact with each other during engine operation together. These 'mated' parts must be reused or renewed as an assembly.

5 Complete engine disassembly should be done in the following general order with reference to the appropriate Sections (refer to Chapter 3 for details of transmission components disassembly):

● Remove the engine cowling
● Remove the cylinder head
● Remove the cylinder
● Remove the piston
● Remove the alternator
● Remove the variator (see Chapter 3)

● Remove the starter motor (see Chapter 10)
● Remove the carburettor and reed valve (see Chapter 5)
● Separate the crankcase halves
● Remove the crankshaft

Reassembly

6 Reassembly is accomplished by reversing the order of disassembly.

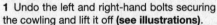

6 Engine cowling and cooling fan

1 Undo the left and right-hand bolts securing the cowling and lift it off **(see illustrations)**.
2 Undo the bolt securing the alternator cover and lift it off **(see illustrations)**.

3 Undo the three bolts securing the cooling fan to the alternator rotor and remove the fan **(see illustration)**.
4 Installation is the reverse of removal. Tighten the cooling fan bolts to the torque setting specified at the beginning of this Chapter.
5 Ensure the cowling is correctly aligned with the forward edge of the alternator cover. Tighten the cowling bolts to the specified torque.

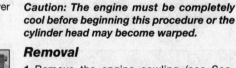

7 Cylinder head

Caution: The engine must be completely cool before beginning this procedure or the cylinder head may become warped.

Removal

1 Remove the engine cowling (see Section 6).
2 Remove the spark plug **(see illustration)**.
3 Unscrew the cylinder head bolts evenly and a little at a time in a criss-cross sequence until they are all loose and remove them **(see illustration)**. **Note:** *The cylinder head bolts pass down through the cylinder and screw into the crankcase. Once the cylinder head is loose care must be taken not to break the cylinder base gasket seal otherwise a new base gasket will have to be fitted before refitting the head (see Section 8).*
4 Lift off the cylinder head and head gasket

7.2 Remove the spark plug

7.3 Undo the head bolts in a criss-cross sequence

7.4 Lift off the head and head gasket

7.6 Check head for cracks and damaged plug threads (arrowed)

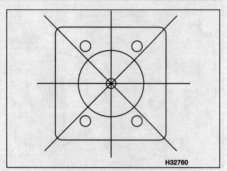

7.9 Check the cylinder head for warpage with a straight-edge

(see illustration). If the head is stuck, tap around the joint face between the head and cylinder with a soft-faced mallet to free it. Do not attempt to free the head by inserting a screwdriver between the head and cylinder – you'll damage the sealing surfaces. Note which way round the gasket is fitted (see Step 10), then discard it as a new one must be used on reassembly.

Inspection

5 Refer to Chapter 1, Section 16, and decarbonise the cylinder head.
6 Inspect the head very carefully for cracks and other damage. If cracks are found, a new head will be required (see illustration).
7 Inspect the threads in the spark plug hole. Damaged or worn threads can be reclaimed using a thread insert (see *Tools and Workshop Tips* in the *Reference* section). Most small engineering firms offer a service of this kind.
8 Check the mating surfaces on the cylinder head and cylinder for signs of leaks, which could indicate that the head is warped.
9 Using a precision straight-edge and a feeler gauge, check the head mating surface for warpage. Lay the straight-edge across the surface and measure any gap under it with feeler gauges. Check vertically, horizontally and diagonally across the head, making four checks in all (see illustration). Warpage should generally be no more than 0.05 mm. If warpage is excessive, have the cylinder head machined flat or replace it with a new one. If

there is any doubt about the condition of the head consult an automotive engineer.

Installation

10 Installation is the reverse of removal, noting the following:
● Ensure both cylinder head and cylinder mating surfaces are clean.
● Lubricate the cylinder bore with the specified type of two-stroke oil.
● Install the new head gasket. **Note:** *The gasket may be marked to identify which side should face up when it is in place, or there may be a raised section around the inner edge of the gasket. If so, fit the gasket with the raised section uppermost.*
● Tighten the cylinder head bolts evenly and a little at a time in a criss-cross pattern to the initial torque setting specified at the beginning of this Chapter, then tighten the bolts to the final setting (see illustration 7.3).
● Ensure the engine cowling is correctly secured.

8 Cylinder

Removal

1 Remove the cylinder head (see Section 7).

2 Lift the cylinder up off the crankcase, supporting the piston as it becomes accessible to prevent it hitting the crankcase opening (see illustration). If the cylinder is stuck, tap around the joint face between the cylinder and the crankcase with a soft-faced mallet to free it. Don't attempt to free the cylinder by inserting a screwdriver between it and the crankcase – you'll damage the sealing surfaces. When the cylinder is removed, stuff a clean rag into the crankcase opening around the piston to prevent anything falling inside.
3 Remove the cylinder base gasket and discard it as a new one must be fitted on reassembly (see illustration 8.11).
4 Scrape off any carbon deposits that may have formed in the exhaust port, then wash the cylinder with a suitable solvent and dry it thoroughly (see illustration). Compressed air will speed the drying process and ensure that all holes and recesses are clean.

Inspection

5 Inspect the cylinder bore carefully for scratches and score marks (see illustration).
6 If available, use a telescoping gauge and micrometer to measure the diameter of the cylinder bore to assess the amount of wear, taper and ovality (see *Tools and Workshop Tips* in the *Reference* section). Measure near the top (but below the level of the top piston ring at TDC), centre and bottom (but above the level of the bottom ring at BDC) of the bore

8.2 Support the piston as the cylinder is removed

8.4 Scrape carbon deposits out of the exhaust port (arrowed)

8.5 Inspect the bore (arrowed) for damage

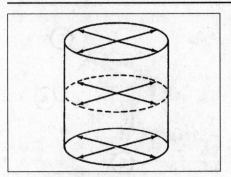

8.6 Measure the cylinder bore in the directions shown

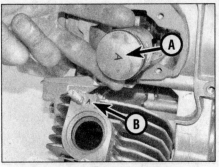

8.9 Piston crown (A) and exhaust flange (B) are stamped with the size code

8.11 Ensure the base gasket is fitted correctly

both parallel to and across the crankshaft axis **(see illustration)**.

7 Calculate any differences between the measurements to determine any wear. A cylinder bore that has worn oval will reduce the efficiency of the piston rings to achieve a seal, resulting in loss of compression.

8 Next, measure an unworn part of the cylinder bore (below the level of the bottom ring with the piston at the bottom of its stroke) and compare the result to the previous measurements to determine overall wear.

9 No service limits are available for cylinder wear, but if the bore is tapered, oval, or worn excessively, or badly scratched, scuffed or scored, the cylinder and piston will have to be renewed as a set. Note that cylinders and pistons are marked with a size code and only matching cylinders and pistons should be assembled together **(see illustration)**.

10 If there is any doubt about the serviceability of the cylinder, consult a specialist engineer.

Installation

11 Check that the mating surfaces of the cylinder and crankcase are clean and free from any traces of old gasket, then remove any rag from the crankcase opening. Lay the new base gasket in place on the crankcase making sure it is the correct way round **(see illustration)**.

12 Check that the piston rings are correctly positioned so that the ring locating pins in the piston grooves are between the ring ends (see Section 10).

13 Lubricate the cylinder bore, piston and

piston rings, and the connecting rod big and small-ends, with two-stroke oil, then locate the cylinder over the top of the piston **(see illustration 8.2)**.

14 Ensure the piston enters the bore squarely and does not get cocked sideways. Carefully compress and feed each ring into the bore as the cylinder is lowered, taking care that the rings do not rotate out of position. Do not use force if the cylinder appears to be stuck as the piston and/or rings will be damaged.

15 Once the piston is correctly installed, check that the base gasket has not been displaced and, using a cylinder head bolt as a guide, press the cylinder down onto the gasket **(see illustration)**.

16 Install the remaining components in the reverse order of removal.

9 Piston

Removal

1 Remove the cylinder and stuff a clean rag into the crankcase opening around the piston to prevent anything falling inside (see Section 8).

2 The piston top should be marked with an arrow which points towards the exhaust. If the piston was cleaned prior to disassembly, ensure that the arrow is visible or mark the piston accordingly so that it can be installed the correct way round **(see illustration)**.

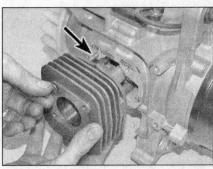

8.15 Use a head bolt (arrowed) as a guide for aligning the cylinder

3 Carefully prise the circlip out from one side of the piston using needle-nose pliers or a small flat-bladed screwdriver inserted into the notch **(see illustration)**. Check for burring around the circlip groove and remove any with a very fine file or penknife blade, then push the piston pin out from the other side and remove the piston from the connecting rod **(see illustration)**. Use a socket extension to push the piston pin out if required. Remove the other circlip and discard them both as new ones must be used on reassembly.

HAYNES HiNT *To prevent the circlip from flying away or from dropping into the crankcase, pass a rod or screwdriver with a greater diameter than the gap between the circlip ends, through the piston pin. This will trap the circlip if it springs out.*

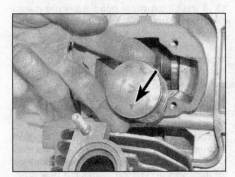

9.2 Arrow on piston should point towards the exhaust

9.3a Remove the circlip...

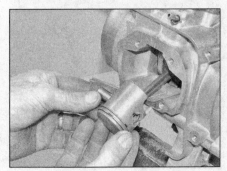

9.3b ...then push the piston pin out

9.4 Remove the small-end bearing

9.5 Remove the piston rings carefully

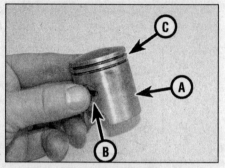

9.8 Inspect the piston skirt (A), pin bosses (B) and ring lands (C)

HAYNES HINT *If the piston pin is a tight fit in the piston bosses, heat the piston gently with a hot air gun – this will expand the alloy piston sufficiently to release its grip on the pin.*

4 The connecting rod small-end bearing is a loose fit in the rod; remove it for safekeeping, noting which way round it fits **(see illustration)**.

5 Before the inspection process can be carried out, the piston rings must be removed and the piston must be cleaned. **Note:** *If the cylinder is being renewed, piston inspection can be overlooked as a new one will be fitted.* The piston rings can be removed by hand – using your thumbs, ease the ends of each ring apart and carefully lift it off the piston, taking care not to expand it any more than is necessary **(see illustration)**. Do not nick or gouge the piston in the process.

6 Note which way up each ring fits and in which groove as they must be installed in their original positions if being re-used. The upper surface of each ring should be marked at one end and an expander is fitted behind the lower ring (see Section 10). **Note:** *It is good practice to renew the piston rings when an engine is being overhauled. Ensure that the piston and bore are serviceable before purchasing new rings.*

7 Refer to Chapter 1, Section 16, and clean all traces of carbon and gum off the piston. If the identification previously marked on the piston is cleaned off, be sure to re-mark it correctly.

Inspection

8 Inspect the piston for cracks around the skirt, at the pin bosses and at the ring lands **(see illustration)**. Check that the circlip grooves are not damaged. Normal piston wear appears as even, vertical wear on the thrust surfaces of the piston and slight looseness of the top ring in its groove. If the skirt is scored or scuffed, the engine may have been suffering from overheating and/or abnormal combustion, resulting in excessively high operating temperatures.

9 A hole in the top of the piston, in one extreme, or burned areas around the edge of the piston crown, indicate that pre-ignition or knocking under load have occurred. If you find evidence of any problems the cause must be corrected or the damage will occur again. Refer to Chapter 5 for carburation checks and Chapter 6 for ignition checks.

10 No specifications are available for measuring piston wear or for piston-to-bore clearance, but if the cylinder is in poor condition (see Section 8) or if the piston skirt is scuffed or damaged, new components will be necessary. Carbon deposits down the side of the piston are a clear indication of extreme wear.

11 If the piston is damaged but the bore is good, install a new piston and rings. Note that cylinder and piston are marked with a size code and only a matching cylinder and piston should be assembled together **(see illustration 8.9)**.

12 Use a micrometer to measure the piston pin in the middle, where it runs in the small-end bearing, and at each end where it runs in the piston **(see illustration)**. If there is any difference in the measurements the pin is worn and must be renewed.

13 If the piston pin is good, lubricate it with clean two-stroke oil, then insert it into the piston and check for any freeplay between the two **(see illustration)**. There should be no freeplay.

14 Next, check the condition of the connecting rod small-end bearing. A worn small-end bearing will produce a metallic rattle, most audible when the engine is under load, and increasing as engine speed rises. This should not be confused with big-end bearing wear, which produces a pronounced knocking noise. Inspect the bearing rollers for flat spots and pitting. Install the bearing in the connecting rod, then slide the piston pin into the bearing and check for freeplay **(see**

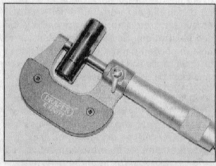

9.12 Measuring the piston pin diameter

9.13 Check for freeplay between the piston and the piston pin

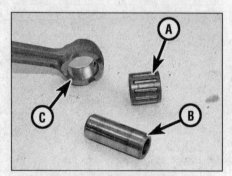

9.14a Bearing (A), piston pin (B) and rod small-end (C)

9.14b Rock the piston pin back and forth to check for freeplay

illustrations). There should only be slightly discernible freeplay between the piston pin, the bearing and the connecting rod.

15 If there is freeplay, measure the internal diameter of the connecting rod small-end **(see illustration)**. Take several measurements; if there is any difference between the measurements the small-end is worn and a new crankshaft assembly will have to be fitted (see Section 15).

16 If the small-end is good, fit a new small-end bearing.

Installation

17 Install the piston rings (see Section 10).

18 Lubricate the piston pin, the piston pin bore in the piston and the small-end bearing with two-stroke oil and install the bearing in the connecting rod.

19 Install a new circlip in one side of the piston, line up the piston on the connecting rod, making sure the arrow on the piston top faces towards the exhaust, and insert the piston pin from the other side. Secure the pin with the other new circlip. When installing the circlips, compress them only just enough to fit them in the piston, and make sure they are properly seated in their grooves with the open end away from the removal notches **(see illustration)**.

20 Install the cylinder (see Section 8).

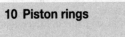

10 Piston rings

1 New piston rings should be fitted whenever an engine is being overhauled. It is important that you get new rings of the correct size for your piston so ensure that any information relating to piston size and size coding which may be stamped into the top of the piston is available when purchasing new parts **(see illustration 8.9)**.

2 Before fitting the new rings onto the piston, the ring end gaps must be checked. Insert the top ring into the bottom of the cylinder bore and square it up by pushing it in with the top of the piston. The ring should be between 15 and 20 mm from the bottom edge of the

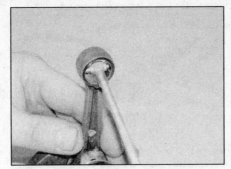

9.15 Measuring the internal diameter of the connecting rod small-end

cylinder. Measure the ring end gap using feeler gauges, slipping the gauge between the ends of the ring **(see illustration)**. Compare the result with the specification given at the beginning of this Chapter.

3 If the gap is larger or smaller than specified, check to make sure that you have the correct rings before proceeding. If the gap is larger than specified it is likely the cylinder bore is worn. If the gap is too small the ring ends may come into contact with each other during engine operation, causing serious damage.

4 Repeat the procedure for the other ring.

5 Once the ring end gaps have been checked, the rings can be installed on the piston. The upper surface of each ring should be marked at one end; make sure you fit the rings the right way up **(see illustration)**. Note that the

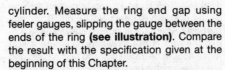

10.2 Measuring installed piston ring end gap

ends of both rings are shaped to fit around the locating pins.

6 First identify the ring locating pin in each piston ring groove – the ring must be positioned so that the pin is inbetween the ends of the ring **(see illustration 10.8)**. Fit the lower ring expander first, ensuring that the ends of the expander do not overlap the ring locating pin **(see illustration)**.

7 Next, install the lower ring, taking care not to expand the ring any more than is necessary to slide it into place **(see illustration)**. Ensure that the locating pin is between the ends of the ring.

8 Install the top ring. Always ensure that the ring end gaps are positioned each side of the locating pins before fitting the piston into the cylinder **(see illustration)**.

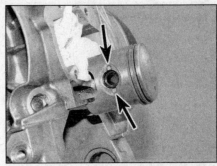

9.19 Position the open end of the circlip away from the removal notches (arrowed)

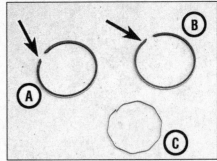

10.5 Top ring (A), lower ring (B) and expander (C). Ring markings arrowed

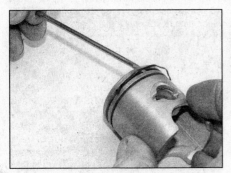

10.6 Fitting the lower ring expander

10.7 Fitting the lower ring. Note locating pin (arrowed)

10.8 Installed position of the top ring – locating pin (arrowed)

11 Alternator

Note: *This procedure can be carried out with the engine in the scooter. If the engine has been removed, ignore the steps that do not apply.*

Removal

1 The alternator is located behind the slotted cover on the right-hand side of the engine – remove the cover and the cooling fan (see Section 6).

2 To remove the rotor centre nut it is necessary to stop the rotor from turning. Peugeot produces a pin wrench (service tool Part No. 752237) for this purpose which engages in the larger holes in the rotor face – a similar home-made tool can be used or you can obtain an aftermarket version **(see illustration)**.

3 Alternatively, the rotor can be held with a strap wrench **(see illustration)**. Undo the bolts securing the ignition pulse generator coil and displace the coil to allow clearance for the strap wrench **(see illustration)**.

4 With the rotor securely held, unscrew the centre nut.

5 To remove the rotor from the taper on the crankshaft it is necessary to use a puller that threads into the internal thread in the centre of the rotor. Peugeot produces a service tool

11.2 Using the home-made tool to hold the alternator rotor

(Part No. 755985) and a cap to protect the end of the crankshaft (Part No. 068007) for this purpose. Aftermarket pullers are available.

6 If the cap is not available, position a soft metal spacer between the end of the shaft and the puller centre bolt, then screw the puller all the way in **(see illustration)**. Hold the puller with a ring spanner and tighten the centre bolt using steady pressure to draw the rotor off the taper **(see illustration)**.

7 Lift the rotor off the crankshaft **(see illustration)**.

8 Note the location of the Woodruff key on the crankshaft and remove it for safekeeping if it is loose **(see illustration)**.

9 The alternator stator coils and ignition pulse generator coil are wired together and have to be removed as an assembly. If not already done, trace the wiring back from the alternator and pulse generator and disconnect it at the

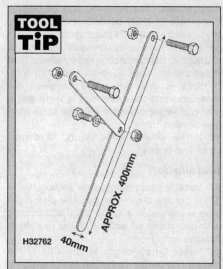

A rotor holding tool can easily be made using two strips of steel bolted together in the middle, with a bolt through each end which locates into the slots or holes in the rotor. Do not allow the bolts to extend too far through the rotor otherwise the coils could be damaged.

connectors **(see illustration 4.13)**. Free the wiring from any clips or guides and feed it through to the alternator.

10 If not already done, undo the bolts securing the pulse generator coil **(see illustration 11.3b)**, then undo the bolts securing the

11.3a Using a strap wrench to hold the rotor

11.3b Displace the ignition pulse generator coil for extra clearance

11.6a Installing the alternator rotor puller

11.6b Apply steady pressure to draw the rotor off...

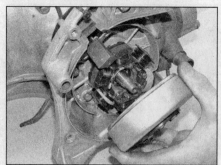

11.7 ...and remove it completely

11.8 Remove the Woodruff key for safekeeping

11.10a Alternator stator bolts (arrowed)

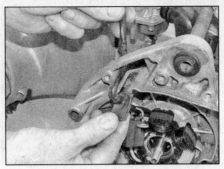

11.10b Draw out the wiring boot...

11.10c ...and remove the assembly

alternator stator **(see illustration)**. Draw the rubber wiring boot out of the engine side cover and lift the assembly off **(see illustrations)**.

Installation

11 Installation is the reverse of removal, noting the following:

● Ensure the wiring is correctly routed before installing the stator and pulse generator.

● Tighten the stator and pulse generator coil mounting screws to the torque setting specified at the beginning of this Chapter.

● Make sure that no metal objects have attached themselves to the magnets on the inside of the rotor.

● Clean the tapered end of the crankshaft and the corresponding mating surface on the inside of the rotor with a suitable solvent.

● Fit the Woodruff key into the crankshaft, align the slot in the centre of the rotor with the key, then install the rotor.

● Tighten the rotor nut to the specified torque setting.

● Secure the wiring with any clips or ties.

● Ensure that the cooling fan and cover are correctly installed (see Section 6).

12 Starter pinion and driven gear

Note: *This procedure can be carried out with the engine in the scooter.*

1 The starter motor is located on the underside of the crankcase and drives a gear on the left-hand side of the crankshaft via a spring-loaded pinion.

Removal

2 Follow the procedure in Chapter 3 to remove the variator.

3 Remove the thrust washer, then draw off the starter driven gear noting how it fits **(see illustrations)**.

4 Undo the bolt securing the starter pinion housing and lift off the housing and pinion **(see illustrations)**.

5 Lift the pinion out of the housing, noting the location of the bush inside the housing.

Inspection

6 Clean the starter pinion with a suitable solvent, then dry it with compressed air, if available. Check the assembly for any signs of damage or wear, particularly for chipped or broken teeth on either of the pinions **(see illustration)**. Check the corresponding teeth on the starter motor shaft and the starter driven gear.

7 Rotate the outer pinion and check that it moves smoothly up and down the shaft, and that it returns easily to its rest position. The starter pinion assembly is supplied as a complete unit – if any of the component parts are worn or damaged, a new unit will have to be fitted.

8 Inspect the bush in the housing for wear and fit a new one if necessary.

12.3a Remove the thrust washer...

12.3b ...and the starter driven gear

12.4a Undo the bolt (arrowed)...

12.4b ...and remove the housing and starter pinion (arrowed)

12.6 Inspect the starter pinion for damage and wear

12.9 Inspect the internal splines on the driven gear (arrowed)

9 Check the internal splines on the driven gear for wear or damage **(see illustration)**. There should be no freeplay between the gear and the crankshaft otherwise the crankshaft splines may become damaged. Fit a new driven gear if necessary.

Installation

10 Fit the starter pinion into the crankcase **(see illustration)** – the mechanism should not be lubricated as any excess oil or grease may contaminate the drive belt and cause it to slip. However, a smear of grease should be applied to both ends of the pinion shaft before installation. Ensure the larger inner pinion engages with the starter motor shaft.
11 Install the housing with its bush and secure the housing bolt securely **(see illustration 12.4a)**.
12 Slide the driven gear onto the splines on the crankshaft and fit the thrust washer **(see illustrations 12.3b and a)**.
13 Install the variator (see Chapter 3).

13 Oil pump

1 The oil pump is driven electronically and the rate of oil flow is controlled either by a dedicated pump control unit (CPH), or by a combined oil pump and engine control unit (ACPH). Details of the two control systems can be found in Chapter 10.
2 In the event of a pump failure the oil warning light in the instrument cluster flashes.

13.3 Location of the oil pump (arrowed)

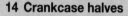

12.10 Engage larger inner pinion with the starter motor shaft

Additionally, on models with the ACPH system, the engine is stopped when engine speed drops to idle and cannot be restarted until the fault has been rectified.

Removal

3 The pump is located inside the bodywork midway between the oil tank and the carburettor **(see illustration)**. Remove the storage compartment for access (see Chapter 9).
4 Disconnect the pump wiring connector and check that the contacts are clean and undamaged.
5 Release the clip securing the oil inlet hose from the oil tank to the union on the pump and detach the hose. Clamp the hose and secure it in an upright position to minimise oil loss. Release the clip securing the oil outlet hose to the union on the carburettor and detach the hose
6 Unscrew the pump mounting bolt and remove the pump.

Installation and bleeding

7 Before installing a new pump, remove the under body panel and check the oil hoses from the tank and the oil filter. If there is any sediment inside the filter a new one should be fitted (see Chapter 1, Section 6). Check that the oil level in the tank is topped-up.
8 Tighten the pump mounting bolt securely, then push the hoses fully onto the pump unions and secure them with the clips **(see illustration 4.10)**.
9 To bleed the system, first place the lower open end of the outlet hose in a suitable container **(see illustration)**.
10 Ensure the ignition is OFF and temporarily

13.9 Position the disconnected hose over a container

connect the battery. If not already done, disconnect the pump wiring connector.
11 Turn the ignition ON then reconnect the pump wiring connector. Oil will be slowly pumped into the outlet hose – the procedure takes several minutes during which time the oil warning light should flash. Wait until oil drips regularly from the end of the hose and ensure that there are no air bubbles in the hose, then connect the hose to the union on the carburettor and turn the ignition OFF. Secure the hose to the carburettor union with its clip.

⚠ **Warning: Never run the engine without an oil supply or crank the engine on the electric starter without an oil supply.**

12 Install the remaining components in the reverse order of removal.

14 Crankcase halves

Note: *To separate the crankcase halves, the engine unit must be removed from the scooter.*

Separation

1 Follow the procedure in Section 4 and remove the engine from the frame.
2 Before the crankcase halves can be separated the following components must be removed:
● Cylinder head (see Section 7)
● Cylinder (see Section 8)
● Alternator (see Section 11)
● Variator (see Chapter 3)
● Starter motor (see Chapter 10)
● Reed valve (see Chapter 5)
● Centrestand (see Chapter 7)
3 Tape some rag around the connecting rod to prevent it knocking against the cases. Although not essential, it is advisable to remove the piston to avoid damage during this procedure.
4 Support the crankcase assembly on the work surface on its left-hand side, then loosen the crankcase bolts evenly, a little at a time and in a criss-cross sequence until they are all finger-tight, then remove them **(see illustration)**. **Note:** *Ensure that all the*

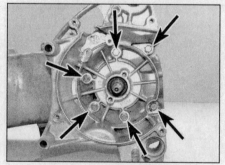

14.4 Location of the crankcase bolts

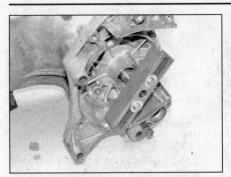

14.5 Using a puller to separate the crankcase halves

14.6a Heat the main bearing housing...

14.6b ...and apply even and steady pressure

crankcase bolts have been removed before attempting to separate the cases.

 HAYNES HINT *Make a cardboard template of the crankcase and punch a hole for each bolt location. This will ensure all bolts are installed correctly on reassembly.*

5 The cases are a tight fit on the crankshaft main bearings and Peugeot produces a puller (Part No. 755983) and a protective cap for the end of the crankshaft (Part No. 68007) to aid disassembly. Alternatively, a two-legged puller can be adapted as shown **(see illustration)**. **Note:** *If the puller is placed across the end of the crankshaft, thread the alternator centre nut on first to protect the threads.*

6 Heat the right-hand main bearing housing with a hot air gun and apply steady pressure with

the service tool centre bolt, or the two bolts as shown **(see illustrations)**. Take care to ensure that equal pressure is applied on both sides of the puller arrangement at all times. If the cases are difficult to separate, first ensure that all the crankcase bolts have been removed. Keep pressure on the puller and apply more heat to the bearing housing. **Note:** *Do not try to separate the halves by levering against the mating surfaces as they are easily scored and will not seal correctly afterwards. Do not strike the ends of the crankshaft with a hammer as damage to the end threads or the shaft itself will result.*

7 Lift the right-hand crankcase half off the left-hand half **(see illustration)**.

⚠️ *Warning: The crankcase may be very hot, grip it with some rag or wear protective gloves.*

8 The crankshaft will remain in the left-hand crankcase half. Note the location of the crankcase dowels and remove them for

safekeeping if they are loose **(see illustration)**.
9 To avoid damaging the crankshaft, the assembly should be pressed out from the left-hand crankcase. Peugeot produces a set of service tools to do this (separating tool Part No. 64706, crankshaft protective cap Part No. 69098 and baseplate Part No. 754006). Alternatively, pressure can be applied to the end of the crankshaft using the set-up shown **(see illustration)**. Thread the old variator nut onto the end of the crankshaft to protect the threads and make sure the crankshaft assembly is supported to prevent it dropping if it suddenly comes free **(see illustration)**. As before, apply heat to the bearing housing with a hot air gun.
10 Remove the crankcase gasket and discard it as a new one must be used on reassembly.
11 Clean the mating surfaces of the crankcase halves with a suitable solvent to remove any traces of old gasket or sealant. Take care not to scratch or gouge the soft aluminium.
12 The crankshaft oil seals must be renewed whenever the crankcases are separated. Note which way round they are fitted then tap them out from the inside of the cases with a hammer and suitably sized socket **(see illustration)**. Discard the old seals.
13 The main bearings should stay in place on the crankshaft assembly during disassembly. If, however, they remain in the crankcases, lay each crankcase half down on its mating surface and heat the bearing housings until the bearings drop out.

⚠️ *Warning: This procedure requires heat of between 80 to 90°C – allow the cases to cool before handling them.*

14.7 Lift off the right-hand crankcase half

14.8 Location of the crankcase dowels (arrowed)

14.9a Pressing the crankshaft out of the left-hand crankcase half

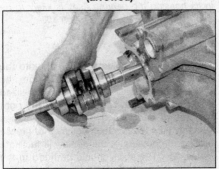

14.9b Support the crankshaft assembly to avoid damage

14.12 Tap the seals out using a suitably-sized socket

14.19 Inspect the engine mounting bushes

14.21a Position the seals closed side outermost

Note: *Peugeot advises that the main bearings should be renewed whenever the crankcases are separated (see Section 15).*

14 If required, remove the transmission assembly from the left-hand crankcase half (see Chapter 3).

Inspection

15 Wash all the components in a suitable solvent and dry them with compressed air.
Caution: Be very careful not to damage the crankcase mating surfaces which may result in loss of crankcase pressure causing poor engine performance. Check both crankcase halves very carefully for cracks and damaged threads.

16 Small cracks or holes in aluminium castings can be repaired with an epoxy resin adhesive as a temporary measure. Permanent repairs can only be effected by welding, and only a specialist in this process is in a position to advise on the economy or practical aspect of such a repair. New crankcase halves are only available together as a matching set.

17 Damaged threads can be economically reclaimed by using a thread insert. Most small engineering firms offer a service of this kind. Sheared screws can usually be removed with screw extractors (see *Tools and Workshop Tips* in the *Reference* section). If you are in any doubt about removing a sheared screw, consult an automotive engineer.

18 Always wash the crankcases thoroughly after any repair work to ensure no dirt or metal swarf is trapped inside when the engine is rebuilt.

19 Inspect the engine mounting bushes. If they show signs of deterioration replace them all at the same time (see illustration). To remove a bush, first note its position in the casing. Heat the casing with a hot air gun, then support the casing and drive the bush out with a hammer and a suitably sized socket. Alternatively, use two suitably sized sockets to press the bush out in the

14.21b Press the seals in to the specified depth

jaws of a vice. Clean the bush housing with steel wool to remove any corrosion, then reheat the casing and fit the new bush. **Note:** *Always support the casing when removing or fitting bushes to avoid breaking the casing.*

20 Inspect the bearing housings. If a bearing outer race has spun in its housing, the inside of the housing will be damaged. A bearing locking compound can be used to fix the outer race in place on reassembly if the damage is not too severe. **Note:** *If a bearing has spun in its housing the bearing itself is likely to be damaged internally – see Section 15.*

Reassembly

21 Fit the new crankshaft oil seals into the crankcase halves – press them in from the outside using a seal driver or suitably-sized socket. Ensure the seals are fitted the right way round and that they enter the cases squarely (see illustration). A smear of grease around the outside of the seals will facilitate installation. The seals should be fitted to the depths as specified at the beginning of this Chapter (see illustration).

22 Support the left-hand crankcase half on

14.25 Fit the left-hand main bearing fully into its housing

the work surface with enough space below it to provide clearance for the end of the crankshaft when it is fully installed.

23 Lubricate the left-hand crankshaft seal and main bearing with two-stroke oil and tape some rag around the connecting rod to prevent it knocking against the cases.

24 Heat the bearing housing in the crankcase with a hot air gun. **Note:** *Avoid applying heat directly onto the crankshaft oil seal.* If required, a freeze spray can be used on the main bearing to aid installation.

25 Lower the crankshaft assembly into the crankcase half carefully to avoid damaging the seal. Ensure that the main bearing is aligned with the bearing housing and that the connecting rod is aligned with the crankcase mouth, then press the crankshaft assembly in fully so that the main bearing goes all the way into its housing (see illustration). If the main bearing does not seat fully, apply more heat around the bearing housing while applying steady pressure to the crankshaft assembly.

26 Allow the case to cool, then wipe the mating surfaces of both crankcase halves with a rag soaked in a suitable solvent and fit the dowels (see illustration 14.8). Fit the crankcase gasket to the mating surface of the

14.26 Ensure the crankcase gasket is correctly installed

14.29 Heat the bearing housing and wear protective gloves during installation of the crankcase half

left-hand case making sure it locates over the dowels (see illustration).

27 Lubricate the right-hand crankshaft seal and main bearing with two-stroke oil.

28 Heat the bearing housing in the crankcase with a hot air gun. Note: *Avoid applying heat directly onto the crankshaft oil seal. If required, use a freeze spay on the main bearing.*

29 Lower the crankcase half over the crankshaft carefully to avoid damaging the seal. Ensure that the two halves of the crankcase are correctly aligned, taking special note of the position of the dowels, and that the main bearing is aligned with the bearing housing in the right-hand case (see illustration).

30 Press the crankcase on fully so that the main bearing goes all the way into its housing. If the main bearing does not seat fully, apply more heat to the area around the bearing housing while applying steady pressure to the crankcase.

31 Check that the crankcase halves are seated all the way round and that the main bearings are pressed fully into their housings (see illustration). If the casings are not correctly seated, heat the bearing housings while applying firm pressure. Note: *Do not attempt to pull the crankcase halves together using the crankcase bolts as the casing will crack and be ruined.*

32 Clean the threads of the crankcase bolts and install them finger-tight, then tighten them evenly a little at a time in a criss-cross sequence to the torque setting specified at the beginning of this Chapter (see illustration 14.4). Support the connecting rod and rotate the crankshaft by hand – if there are any signs of undue stiffness, tight or rough spots, or of

any other problem, the fault must be rectified before proceeding further.

33 Trim the crankcase gasket flush with the mating surface for the cylinder (see illustration).

34 Install the remaining components in the reverse order of removal.

15 Crankshaft assembly, big-end and main bearings

1 To access the crankshaft and the big-end bearing, the crankcase must be split into two parts (see Section 14).

2 The crankshaft assembly should give many thousands of miles of service. The most likely problems to occur will be a worn small or

14.31 Check that the crankcase halves are seated all the way round

14.33 Trim off the excess crankcase gasket

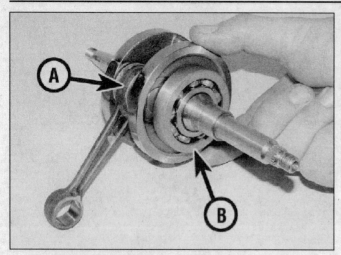

15.2 Crankshaft assembly big-end (A) and main bearings (B)

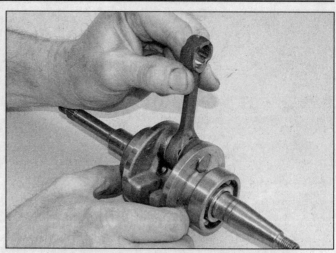

15.3a Check for up-and-down play in the big-end

big-end bearing due to poor lubrication (see illustration). A worn big-end bearing will produce a pronounced knocking noise, most audible when the engine is under load, and increasing as engine speed rises. This should not be confused with small-end bearing wear, which produces a light metallic rattle (see Section 9).

Inspection

3 To assess the condition of the big-end bearing, hold the crankshaft assembly firmly and push and pull on the connecting rod, checking for any up-and-down freeplay between the two (see illustration). If any freeplay is noted, the bearing is worn and the crankshaft assembly will have to be replaced with a new one. Using feeler gauges, measure the big-end side clearance and compare the

result with the specification at the beginning of this Chapter (see illustration).
4 If the main bearings have failed, excessive rumbling and vibration will be felt when the engine is running. Sometimes this may cause the oil seals to fail, resulting in a loss of compression and poor running. Follow the procedure in *Tools and Workshop Tips* in the *Reference* section and check the main bearings (see illustration 15.2). Evidence of extreme heat, such as discoloration or blueing, indicates that lubrication failure has occurred – be sure to check the engine lubrication system (see Chapter 1).
5 If available, place the crankshaft assembly on V-blocks and check the run-out at either end using a dial gauge (see illustration). Compare the result with the specification at the beginning of this Chapter. If the crankshaft is out-of-true it will cause excessive engine

vibration. If there is any doubt about the condition of the crankshaft have it checked by an automotive engineer.
6 Peugeot advises that the main bearings should be renewed whenever the crankcases are separated. Follow the procedure in *Tools and Workshop Tips* in the *Reference* section to remove the bearings using a two-piece puller. Note which way round the bearings are fitted. On installation, take great care to support the crankshaft securely and heat the bearing to avoid the need for excessive force. Note: *The crankshaft assembly is pressed together and is easily damaged if it is dropped.*
7 Inspect the threads on each end of the crankshaft and ensure that the retaining nuts for the alternator rotor and the variator are a good fit. Ensure that the crankshaft surface where the seals are located is not worn, scratched

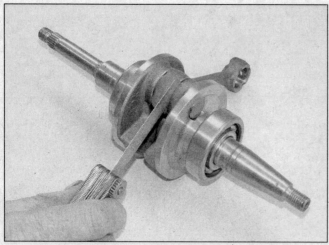

15.3b Measuring big-end side clearance

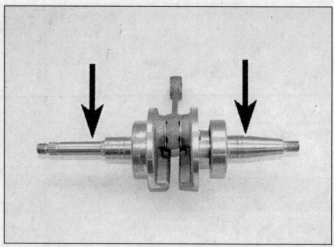

15.5 Check crankshaft run-out at the points shown

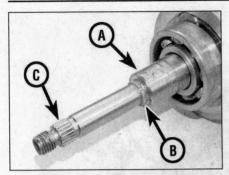

15.7 Inspect the crankshaft surface (A) for wear and pitting, inspect the splines for the starter gear (B) and for the variator (C)

or pitted **(see illustration)**. Inspect the splines for the variator pulley and for the starter driven gear on the left-hand end of the shaft.

8 Inspect the taper and the slot in the right-hand end of the shaft for the alternator Woodruff key. Damage or wear that prevents the rotor from being fitted securely will require a new crankshaft assembly.

9 Follow the procedure in Section 14 to install the crankshaft assembly.

16 Initial start-up after overhaul/running-in

Initial start-up

1 Make sure the oil tank is topped-up and the pump has been bled (see Section 13).

2 Make sure there is fuel in the tank.

3 With the ignition OFF, operate the kickstart to check that the engine turns over easily.

4 Turn the ignition ON, start the engine and allow it to run at a slow idle until it reaches operating temperature. Do not be alarmed if there is a little smoke from the exhaust – this will be due to the oil used to lubricate the engine components during assembly and should subside after a while.

5 If the engine proves reluctant to start, remove the spark plug and check that it has not become wet and oily. If it has, clean it and try again. If the engine refuses to start, go through the fault finding charts at the end of this manual to identify the problem.

6 Check carefully that there are no fuel or oil leaks and make sure the transmission and controls, especially the brakes, function properly before road testing the machine.

7 Upon completion of the road test, and after the engine has cooled down completely, check that there are no air bubbles in the engine oil outlet hose (see Section 13).

Recommended running-in procedure

8 Treat the engine gently for the first few miles to allow any new parts to bed in.

9 If a new piston, cylinder or crankshaft assembly has been fitted, the engine will have to be run-in as when new. This means a restraining hand on the throttle until at least 300 miles (500 km) have been covered. There's no point in keeping to any set speed limit – gradually increase performance up to the 600 mile (1000 km) mark. Make sure that the throttle position is varied to vary engine speed, and use full throttle only for short bursts. Experience is the best guide, since it's easy to tell when an engine is running freely.

10 Pay particular attention to the *Pre-ride checks* at the beginning of this manual. Check the tightness of all relevant nuts and bolts.

Type B1E4QMB – left-hand view

Type B1E4QMB – right-hand view

Chapter 2B
Liquid-cooled two-stroke engine – type B1E4QMB

Refer to 'Model and servicing specifications' in Chapter 1 for model identification details

Contents

Degrees of difficulty

Easy, suitable for novice with little experience	**Fairly easy,** suitable for beginner with some experience	**Fairly difficult,** suitable for competent DIY mechanic	**Difficult,** suitable for experienced DIY mechanic	**Very difficult,** suitable for expert DIY or professional

Specifications

General

Type	Single cylinder liquid-cooled two-stroke
Capacity	49.9 cc
Bore x stroke	39.94 x 39.8 mm
Cylinder compression	87 psi (6 Bar) @ 700rpm

Piston rings

Ring end gap (installed)	0.15 to 0.20 mm

Crankshaft and connecting rod

Big-end side clearance	
Service limit	0.70 mm
Crankshaft runout	
Measured 50 mm from end of shaft	0.05 mm
Crankshaft seal fitment measured depth	
Left-hand side	6.0 mm
Right-hand side	17.5 mm

Torque settings

Alternator rotor nut	40 Nm
Alternator stator screws/pulse generator coil screws	10 Nm
Crankcase bolts	10 Nm
Cylinder head bolts	
Initial setting	8 Nm
Final setting	12 Nm
Drive belt cover screws	10 Nm
Engine cowling bolts	10 Nm
Engine mounting bolt/nut	60 Nm
Exhaust manifold	15 Nm
Fuel pump mounting bolts	7 Nm
Intake manifold bolts	10 Nm
Shock absorber mounting bolt/nut	22 Nm
Temperature sensor	20 Nm
Thermostat housing bolts	10 Nm
Water pump bolts	10 Nm

1 General information

The engine is a single cylinder two-stroke with liquid cooling as fitted to Speedfight 3 scooters. The crankshaft assembly is pressed together, incorporating the connecting rod. The piston runs on a needle roller bearing fitted in the small-end of the connecting rod. The crankshaft runs in caged ball main bearings.

The crankcase divides vertically – the left-hand crankcase is an integral part of the transmission casing and gearbox.

2 Component access

A number of components, with the obvious exception of the crankshaft assembly and its bearings, can be worked on without having to remove the engine/transmission unit from the scooter. However, access to some components is severely restricted, and if several areas require attention at the same time, removal of the engine is recommended, as it is an easy task to undertake.

3 Cylinder compression test

Refer to Chapter 2A, Section 3, noting that a compression gauge with a 10 mm x 1.0 mm threaded adapter is required.

4 Engine –
removal and installation

Caution: The engine/transmission unit is not heavy, however removal and installation should be carried out with the aid of an assistant; personal injury or damage could occur if the engine falls or is dropped.

Removal

1 Support the scooter securely in an upright position. Work can be made easier by raising it to a suitable height on an hydraulic ramp or a suitable platform. Make sure it is secure and will not topple over.
2 Disconnect and remove the battery (see Chapter 10).
3 Remove the storage compartment, the under body panel and the passenger footrests (see Chapter 9).
4 Remove the air filter housing (see Chapter 5).
5 Remove the rear hugger and rear mudguard extension, if fitted (see Chapter 9).
6 Drain the cooling system (see Chapter 4). Release the clip securing the coolant hose to

4.6 Disconnect the hose (arrowed) from the thermostat housing

4.10 Disconnect the fuel hose (A). Location of drain screw (B)

4.12 Disconnect the vacuum hose (arrowed)

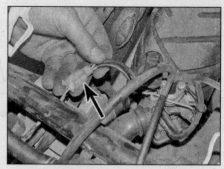

4.9 Disconnect the choke unit and carburettor heater connector (arrowed)

4.11 Disconnect the oil hose from the pump

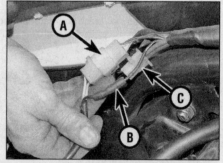

4.14 Alternator (A), ignition pulse generator (B) and starter motor (C) wiring connectors

the thermostat housing on the cylinder head and disconnect the hose **(see illustration)**.
7 Remove the exhaust system (see Chapter 5).
8 Pull the spark plug cap off the plug and position the cap clear of the engine.
9 Trace the wiring from the automatic choke unit and the carburettor heater and disconnect it at the connector **(see illustration)**. **Note:** *When disconnecting any wiring, it is advisable to mark or tag the wires as a reminder of where they connect.*
10 Disconnect the fuel hose from its union on the carburettor, being prepared to catch any residual fuel in a rag **(see illustration)**. Position a suitable container below the carburettor drain hose, then loosen the drain screw and drain any residual fuel from the float chamber. Tighten the drain screw.
11 Release the clip securing the oil hose to

the union on the oil pump and pull the hose off, being prepared to catch any residual oil in a rag **(see illustration)**. Plug the open end of the hose to prevent any dirt getting inside.
12 Disconnect the fuel pump vacuum hose from its union on the top of the crankcase **(see illustration)**.
13 Undo the screw securing the carburettor top and draw the slide assembly out from the carburettor (see Chapter 5). Secure the throttle cable and slide assembly clear of the engine to avoid damage. Stuff clean rag into the carburettor body to prevent anything falling inside.
14 Trace the wiring for the alternator and ignition pulse generator coil from the top of the alternator cover on the right-hand side of the engine and disconnect it at the connector **(see illustration)**. Release the wiring on the engine side of the loom from any clips or ties.

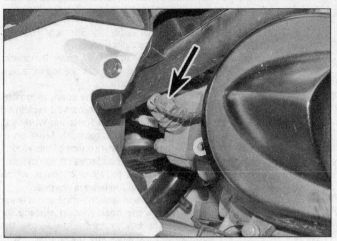

4.15 Temperature sensor wiring connector

4.18 Disconnect the brake hose from the underside of the casing

4.19a Pass a bar through the frame...

4.19b ...and support it on both sides with axle stands

15 The engine temperature sensor is located on the left-hand side of the cylinder head – disconnect the wiring connector **(see illustration)**.

16 The starter motor is located underneath the engine. Trace the wiring from the starter motor terminal and earth terminal and disconnect it at the connector **(see illustration 4.14)**.

17 If required, remove the rear wheel (see Chapter 8). **Note:** *The rear wheel and centrestand provide a convenient support for the unit once it is removed from the scooter. However, it is useful to loosen the rear wheel hub nut at this point before displacing the rear brake caliper.*

18 Displace the rear brake caliper (see Chapter 8). Undo any screws securing the brake hose to the underside of the transmission casing and detach the hose **(see illustration)**.

19 Before the engine with the centrestand can be removed, a means of supporting the scooter must be devised. A double A-frame hoist is ideally suited to most machines once the rear bodywork has been removed and

where the front of the scooter can be firmly secured **(see illustration 4.17a in Chapter 2A)**. Alternatively, with the belly panels removed, the scooter can be supported from underneath provided the weight is taken on the frame tubes and not the fuel tank. On the machine used to illustrate this procedure, a bar was passed through the frame adjacent to the engine mounting bracket, supported on both sides with axle stands **(see illustrations)**.

20 Check that all wiring, cables and hoses are clear of the engine/transmission unit.

21 Undo the upper rear shock absorber mounting bolt, then support the weight of the engine and rear wheel and withdraw the bolt. Lower the wheel to the ground. Undo the lower shock mounting bolt and remove the shock **(see illustration)**.

22 Undo the nut on the engine mounting bolt **(see illustration)**.

4.21 Remove the rear shock absorber

4.22 Undo the nut (arrowed) on the mounting bolt

23 Have an assistant support the engine unit, then carefully withdraw the engine mounting bolt. Manoeuvre the engine unit back and out of the frame.

24 If the engine is dirty, particularly around its mountings, wash it thoroughly before starting any major dismantling work. This will make work much easier and rule out the possibility of dirt falling inside.

25 If required, remove the rear wheel (see Chapter 8) and the centrestand (see Chapter 7).

Installation

26 Installation is the reverse of removal, noting the following:

- Make sure no wires, cables or hoses become trapped between the engine and the frame when installing the engine.
- Tighten the engine mounting bolt, shock absorber bolts and wheel nut to the torque settings specified at the beginning of this Chapter
- Make sure all wires, cables and hoses are correctly routed and connected, and secured by any clips or ties.
- Refill the cooling system (see Chapter 4).
- Bleed the oil pump (see Section 12) .
- Check the operation of the rear brake before riding the machine (see Chapter 1).

5 Disassembly and reassembly – general information

Refer to the general information in Chapter 2A, Section 5. The order of disassembly for this particular engine is as follows:

- Remove the cylinder head
- Remove the cylinder
- Remove the piston
- Remove the water pump (see Chapter 4)
- Remove the alternator
- Remove the variator (see Chapter 3)
- Remove the starter motor (see Chapter 10)
- Remove the carburettor and reed valve (see Chapter 5)
- Separate the crankcase halves
- Remove the crankshaft

6 Cylinder head

Caution: The engine must be completely cool before beginning this procedure or the cylinder head may become warped.

Removal

1 Remove the spark plug **(see illustration)**.

2 Remove the thermostat housing and thermostat (see Chapter 4). If required, unscrew the engine temperature sensor.

3 Unscrew the cylinder head bolts evenly and a little at a time in a criss-cross sequence until they are all loose and remove them **(see illustrations)**. **Note:** *The cylinder head bolts pass down through the cylinder and screw into the crankcase. Once the cylinder head is loose care must be taken not to break the cylinder base gasket seal otherwise a new base gasket will have to be fitted before refitting the head (see Section 7).*

4 Lift off the cylinder head and head gasket **(see illustration)**. If the head is stuck, tap around the joint face between the head and cylinder with a soft-faced mallet to free it. Do not attempt to free the head by inserting a screwdriver between the head and cylinder – you'll damage the sealing surfaces. Note which way round the gasket is fitted **(see illustration 6.10a)**, then discard it as a new one must be used on reassembly.

Inspection

5 Refer to Chapter 1, Section 16, and decarbonise the cylinder head.

6 Inspect the head very carefully for cracks and other damage. If cracks are found, a new head will be required.

7 Inspect the threads in the spark plug hole. Damaged or worn threads can be reclaimed using a thread insert (see *Tools and Workshop Tips* in the *Reference* section). Most small engineering firms offer a service of this kind.

8 Check the mating surfaces on the cylinder head and cylinder for signs of leaks, which could indicate that the head is warped.

9 Using a precision straight-edge and a feeler gauge, check the head mating surface for warpage. Lay the straight-edge across the surface and measure any gap under it with feeler gauges. Check vertically, horizontally and diagonally across the head, making four checks in all **(see illustration)**. Warpage should generally be no more than 0.05 mm. If warpage is excessive, have the cylinder head machined flat or replace it with a new one. If there is any doubt about the condition of the head consult an automotive engineer.

Installation

10 Installation is the reverse of removal, noting the following:

- Ensure both cylinder head and cylinder mating surfaces are clean.
- Lubricate the cylinder bore with two-stroke oil.

6.1 Remove the spark plug

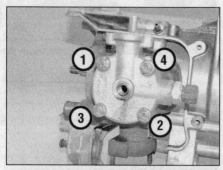

6.3a Undo the head bolts in a criss-cross sequence

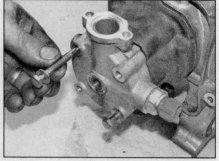

6.3b Long head bolts screw into the crankcase

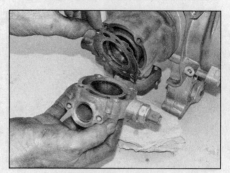

6.4 Lift off the head and head gasket

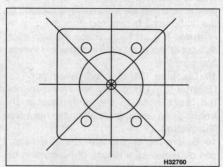

6.9 Check the cylinder head for warpage with a straight-edge

6.10a Note the tab (arrowed) on the head gasket

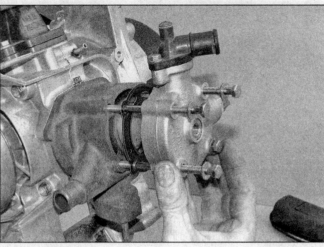

6.10b Align the head and gasket with the cylinder

● Install the new head gasket. **Note:** *The tab on the gasket must be next to the engine temperature sensor – install the head bolts and the gasket on the cylinder head, then fit the head on the engine* **(see illustrations)**.
● Tighten the cylinder head bolts evenly and a little at a time in a criss-cross pattern to the initial torque setting specified at the beginning of this Chapter, then tighten the bolts to the final setting **(see illustration 6.3a)**.
● Install the remaining components in the reverse order of removal.

7 Cylinder

Removal

1 Remove the cylinder head (see Section 6).
2 Lift the cylinder up off the crankcase, supporting the piston as it becomes accessible to prevent it hitting the crankcase opening **(see illustration)**. If the cylinder is stuck, tap around the joint face between the cylinder and the crankcase with a soft-faced mallet to free it. Don't attempt to free the cylinder by inserting a screwdriver between it and the crankcase – you'll damage the sealing surfaces. When the cylinder is removed, stuff a clean rag into the crankcase opening around the piston to prevent anything falling inside.
3 Remove the cylinder base gasket and discard it as a new one must be fitted on reassembly.
4 Scrape off any carbon deposits that may have formed in the exhaust port, then wash the cylinder with a suitable solvent and dry it thoroughly. Compressed air will speed the drying process and ensure that all holes and recesses are clean.

Inspection

5 Inspect the cylinder bore carefully for scratches and score marks **(see illustration)**.

6 If available, use a telescoping gauge and micrometer to measure the diameter of the cylinder bore to assess the amount of wear, taper and ovality (see *Tools and Workshop Tips* in the *Reference* section). Measure near the top (but below the level of the top piston ring at TDC), centre and bottom (but above the level of the bottom ring at BDC) of the bore both parallel to and across the crankshaft axis **(see illustrations)**.
7 Calculate any differences between the measurements to determine any taper or ovality in the bore. A cylinder bore that has worn oval will reduce the efficiency of the

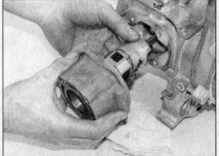

7.2 Support the piston as the cylinder is removed

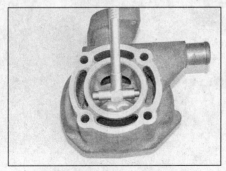

7.6a Using a telescoping gauge...

piston rings to achieve a seal, resulting in loss of compression.
8 Next, measure an unworn part of the cylinder bore (below the level of the bottom ring with the piston at the bottom of its stroke) and compare the result to the previous measurements to determine overall wear.
9 No service limits are available for cylinder wear, but if the bore is tapered, oval, or worn excessively, or badly scratched, scuffed or scored, the cylinder and piston will have to be renewed as a set. Note that cylinders and pistons are marked with a size code and only matching cylinders and pistons should be

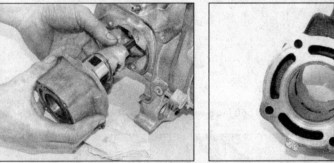

7.5 Inspect the bore for damage

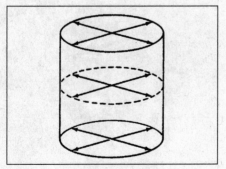

7.6b ...measure the cylinder bore in the directions shown

7.13 Ensure the base gasket is fitted correctly

7.14 Fit the cylinder over the piston carefully

assembled together. The cylinder size code is stamped into the face of the exhaust manifold, the piston size code is stamped into the top of the piston.

10 If there is any doubt about the serviceability of the cylinder, consult a specialist engineer.

Installation

11 Check that the mating surfaces of the cylinder and crankcase are clean and free from any traces of old gasket, then remove any rag from the crankcase opening.

12 Check that the piston rings are correctly positioned so that the ring locating pins in the piston grooves are between the ring ends (see Section 9). Lubricate the cylinder bore, piston and piston rings, and the connecting rod big and small-ends with two-stroke oil.

13 Lay the new base gasket in place on the base of the cylinder making sure it is the correct way round **(see illustration)**.

14 Locate the cylinder over the top of the piston, ensuring the piston enters the bore squarely and does not get cocked sideways. **(see illustration)**. Carefully compress and feed each ring into the bore as the cylinder is lowered, taking care that the rings do not rotate out of position. Do not use force if the cylinder appears to be stuck as the piston and/or rings will be damaged.

15 Once the piston is correctly installed, check that the base gasket has not been displaced and, using a cylinder head bolt as a guide, press the cylinder down onto the crankcase **(see illustrations)**.

16 Install the remaining components in the reverse order of removal.

8 Piston

1 Refer to Chapter 2A, Section 9 for piston removal, inspection and installation details **(see illustrations)**.

7.15a Using a cylinder head bolt (arrowed) as a guide...

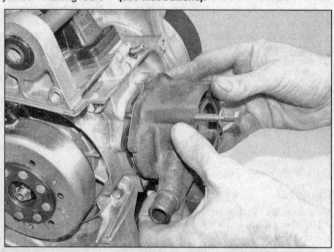

7.15b ...press the cylinder down onto the crankcase

8.1a Mark the piston before disassembly and cleaning

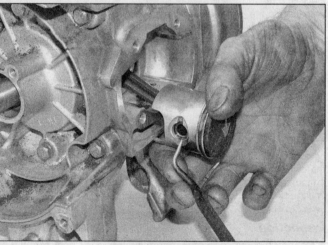

8.1b Prise out the circlip

9.1 Measuring installed piston ring end gap

9 Piston rings

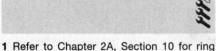

1 Refer to Chapter 2A, Section 10 for ring examination and end gap measurement details **(see illustration)**.
2 Note that the rings on liquid-cooled models should be marked on their upper surface near one end – the top ring is marked 1R and the lower ring is marked 2R.

10 Alternator

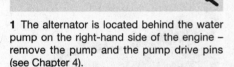

1 The alternator is located behind the water pump on the right-hand side of the engine – remove the pump and the pump drive pins (see Chapter 4).
2 Refer to Chapter 2A, Section 11 for rotor and stator removal details.

11 Starter pinion assembly and driven gear

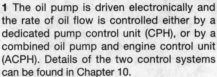

The starter motor is located on the underside of the crankcase and drives a gear on the left-hand side of the crankshaft via a spring-loaded pinion. Refer to Chapter 2A, Section 12 for full details.

12 Oil pump

1 The oil pump is driven electronically and the rate of oil flow is controlled either by a dedicated pump control unit (CPH), or by a combined oil pump and engine control unit (ACPH). Details of the two control systems can be found in Chapter 10.
2 Refer to Chapter 2A, Section 13 for removal, installation and bleeding details.

13 Crankcase halves

Note: *To separate the crankcase halves, the engine unit must be removed from the scooter.*
1 Follow the procedure in Section 4 and remove the engine from the frame.
2 Before the crankcase halves can be separated the following components must be removed:
● Cylinder head (see Section 6)
● Cylinder (see Section 7)
● Water pump (see Chapter 4)
● Alternator (see Section 10)

● Variator (see Chapter 3)
● Starter motor (see Chapter 10)
● Reed valve (see Chapter 5)
● Centrestand (Chapter 7)
3 Refer to Chapter 2A, Section 14 for the rest of the procedure.

14 Crankshaft assembly, big-end and main bearings

1 To access the crankshaft and the big-end bearing, the crankcase must be split into two parts (see Section 13).
2 The crankshaft assembly should give many thousands of miles of service. The most likely problems to occur will be a worn small or big-end bearing due to poor lubrication. A worn big-end bearing will produce a pronounced knocking noise, most audible when the engine is under load, and increasing as engine speed rises. This should not be confused with small-end bearing wear, which produces a light metallic rattle (see Section 8).
3 Refer to Chapter 2A, Section 15 for crankshaft and bearing inspection details.

15 Initial start-up after overhaul/running-in

Refer to Chapter 2A, Section 16 noting that on the liquid-cooled engine the cooling system must be refilled before attempting to start the engine. Upon completion of the road test, and after the engine has cooled down completely, check the coolant level and bleed any air out of the system (see Chapter 4). Top-up the coolant if necessary.

Type 139QMB-E – left-hand view

Type 139QMB-E – right-hand view

Chapter 2C
Four-stroke 50cc engine – type 139QMB-E

Refer to 'Model and servicing specifications' in Chapter 1 for model identification details

Contents

Degrees of difficulty

Easy, suitable for novice with little experience	**Fairly easy,** suitable for beginner with some experience	**Fairly difficult,** suitable for competent DIY mechanic	**Difficult,** suitable for experienced DIY mechanic	**Very difficult,** suitable for expert DIY or professional

Specifications

General

Type	Single cylinder air-cooled four-stroke
Capacity	49.5 cc
Bore x stroke	39.0 x 41.4 mm
Cylinder compression.	130 psi (8.95 Bar) @ 500rpm

Piston rings

Ring end gap (installed)

Top ring.	0.05 to 0.15 mm
Second ring	0.05 to 0.20 mm
Oil control ring	0.20 to 0.70 mm

Crankshaft and connecting rod

Big-end side clearance

Service limit	0.55 mm

Crankshaft runout

Measured 35 mm from left-hand end of shaft	0.10 mm
Measured 27 mm from right-hand end of shaft	0.10 mm

Torque settings

Alternator rotor centre nut	50 Nm
Alternator stator bolts	8 Nm
Cam chain tensioner bolts	10 Nm
Cam chain tensioner cap	8 Nm
Camshaft sprocket bolts	10 Nm
Camshaft stopper plate	15 Nm
Cooling fan bolts	10 Nm
Crankcase bolts	10 Nm
Cylinder head	
Nuts (internal)	18 Nm
Bolts (external)	8 Nm
Drive belt cover screws	10 Nm
Engine mounting bolt/nut	57 Nm
Exhaust manifold	18 Nm
Intake manifold nuts	10 Nm
Oil pump mounting bolts	10 Nm
Pulse air union nuts	10 Nm
Pulse generator coil bolts	6 Nm
Rear shock absorber mounting bolts	
Upper	50 Nm
Lower	22 Nm
Rear wheel nut	120 Nm
Right-hand crankcase cover bolts	10 Nm
Valve cover	10 Nm

1 General information

The Sym-manufactured engine is a single cylinder, overhead-camshaft four-stroke, with fan assisted air cooling as fitted to V-Clic and Kisbee 50 scooters. The camshaft is chain-driven off the crankshaft and operates the valves via rocker arms.

The crankshaft assembly is pressed together, incorporating the connecting rod.

The crankcase divides vertically – the left-hand crankcase is an integral part of the drive belt casing and gearbox.

2 Component access

Most components and assemblies, with the obvious exception of the crankshaft assembly and its bearings, can be worked on without having to remove the engine/transmission unit from the scooter. However, access to some components is severely restricted, and if a number of areas require attention at the same time, removal of the engine is recommended, as it is an easy task to undertake.

3 Cylinder compression test

Warning: Be careful when working on the hot engine – the exhaust pipe, the engine and engine components can cause severe burns.

Special tools: *A compression gauge with a 10mm x 1.0 mm threaded adapter (see Step 5) is required for this procedure.*

1 Among other things, poor starting and engine performance may be caused by leaking valves, a leaking head gasket or worn piston, rings and/or cylinder wall. A cylinder compression check will help pinpoint these conditions.

2 Before carrying out the test, check that the valve clearances are correct (see Chapter 1).

3 Run the engine until it reaches normal operating temperature, then turn the ignition OFF. Support the scooter securely in an upright position on its centrestand.

4 Follow the procedure in Chapter 1, Section 15, and remove the spark plug. Fit the plug back into the cap and position the plug with the threads contacting the engine.

5 Thread the gauge adapter into the spark plug hole then install the compression gauge **(see illustration).**

6 Open the throttle fully and crank the engine over on the kickstarter or starter motor until the gauge reading stabilises – after four or five revolutions the pressure should build up to a maximum figure and then remain stable. Make a note of the pressure reading.

7 Release the pressure on the gauge, then repeat the procedure. If the reading is different this time, repeat the procedure until you obtain several readings that are the same.

8 A reading of approximately 130 psi (9 Bars) indicates a cylinder in good condition.

9 If the compression builds up quickly and evenly, you can assume that the engine top-end is in good mechanical condition. Worn or sticking piston rings, or a worn cylinder, will produce very little initial movement of the gauge, but compression will tend to build-up as the engine turns over. Valve seat leakage, or head gasket leakage, is indicated by low initial compression which does not build-up.

10 To confirm your findings, use a squirt-type oil can to add a small amount of engine oil into the cylinder through the spark plug hole. The oil will tend to seal the piston rings if they are leaking. Check the compression again and if it increases significantly after the addition of the oil the rings or cylinder are definitely worn. If the compression remains low, the pressure is leaking past the valves or head gasket.

11 When the test is complete, follow the procedure in Chapter 1, Section 15, and install the spark plug.

Note: *High compression pressure indicates excessive carbon build-up in the combustion chamber and on the top of the piston. If this is the case, remove the cylinder head and clean the carbon deposits off. Note that excessive carbon build-up is less likely with the use of modern fuels.*

3.5 Install the compression gauge as described

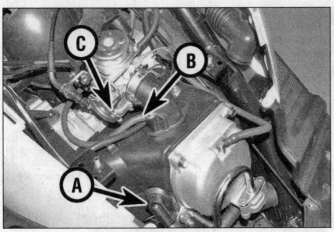

4.7 Location of the spark plug cap (A), fuel tap vacuum hose (B) and throttle cable pulley (C)

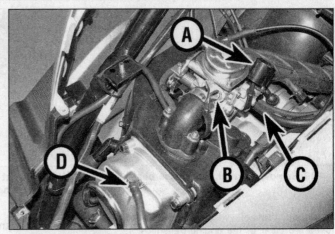

4.8 Location of the automatic choke unit (A), carburettor heater terminals (B), fuel hose (C) and engine breather union (D)

4 Engine removal and installation

Caution: The engine/transmission unit is not heavy, however removal and installation should be carried out with the aid of an assistant; personal injury or damage could occur if the engine falls or is dropped.

Removal

1 Support the scooter securely in an upright position. Work can be made easier by raising the machine to a suitable height on an hydraulic ramp or a suitable platform. Make sure it is secure and will not topple over.
2 Disconnect and remove the battery (see Chapter 10).
3 If required, drain the engine oil (see Chapter 1).
4 Remove the storage compartment, the centre cover panel and the rear mudguard (see Chapter 9). On Kisbee models, remove the seat cowling, centre cover panels, the under-body panel, the rear hugger and the left and right-hand belly panels.
5 Remove the air filter housing (see Chapter 5).
6 Remove the exhaust system (see Chapter 5).
7 Pull the spark plug cap off the plug and position the cap clear of the engine (see illustration).
8 Trace the wiring from the automatic choke

unit and disconnect it at the connector (see illustration). Note: When disconnecting any wiring, it is advisable to mark or tag the wires as a reminder of where they connect. Disconnect the carburettor heater wiring from the terminals on the carburettor.
9 Disconnect the fuel hose from its union on the carburettor, being prepared to catch any residual fuel in a rag (see illustration 4.8). Position a suitable container below the carburettor drain hose, then loosen the drain screw and drain any residual fuel from the float chamber. Tighten the drain screw.
10 Disconnect the fuel tap vacuum hose from its union on the carburettor intake manifold, then disconnect the throttle cable from the carburettor pulley (see illustration 4.7). Secure the throttle cable clear of the engine unit.
11 Release the clip securing the breather hose to the union on the valve cover and disconnect the hose (see illustration 4.8).
12 Trace the wiring for the alternator and ignition pulse generator coil from the top of the fan cover on the right-hand side of the engine and disconnect it at the connectors (see illustration). Release the wiring on the engine side of the loom from any clips or ties. The starter motor is located on the top of the engine. Trace the wiring from the starter motor terminal and earth terminal and disconnect it at the connector.

13 On Kisbee models, disconnect the speed sensor wiring connector where fitted. Trace the wiring from the drive belt cover (see Chapter 3) and disconnect it at the connector located inside the bodywork on the right-hand side. Free the wiring from any clips or ties and secure it on the engine unit free of the frame.
14 Loosen the clip securing the transmission air intake hose to the drive belt cover and disconnect the hose.
15 If required, remove the rear wheel (see Chapter 8). Note: The centrestand and rear wheel provide a convenient support for the unit once it is removed from the scooter. However, it is useful to loosen the rear wheel nut at this point before disconnecting the rear brake.
16 Disconnect the brake cable from the brake arm (see Chapter 8). Undo any screws securing the cable to the underside of the transmission casing and detach the cable (see illustration).
17 Before the engine can be removed, a means of supporting the scooter must be devised. A double A-frame hoist is ideally suited to most machines once the rear bodywork has been removed and where the front of the scooter can be firmly secured (see illustration 4.17a in Chapter 2A). Alternatively, with the belly panels removed, the scooter can be supported from underneath provided the weight is taken on the frame tubes (see illustration).

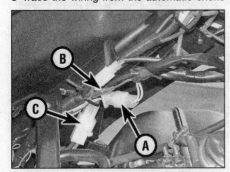

4.12 Alternator (A), ignition pulse generator (B) and starter motor wiring connectors (C)

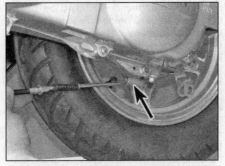

4.16 Disconnect the brake cable from the underside of the casing

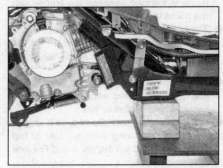

4.17 Support the weight of the scooter on wooden blocks

4.19 Remove the rear shock absorber

4.20 Undo the nut (arrowed) on the mounting bolt...

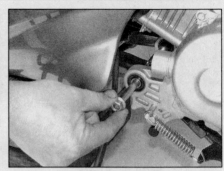

4.21 ...then withdraw the bolt carefully

18 Check that all wiring, cables and hoses are clear of the engine/transmission unit.

19 Undo the upper rear shock absorber mounting bolt, then support the weight of the engine and rear wheel and withdraw the bolt. Lower the wheel to the ground. Undo the lower shock mounting bolt and remove the shock **(see illustration)**.

20 Undo the locknut on the engine mounting bolt **(see illustration)**. **Note:** *Peugeot recommends a new nut should be used on reassembly. Alternatively, clean the threads of the engine mounting bolt and apply a suitable thread-locking compound prior to installation.*

21 Have an assistant support the engine unit, then carefully withdraw the engine mounting bolt **(see illustration)**. Manoeuvre the engine unit back and out of the frame.

22 If the engine is dirty, particularly around its mountings, wash it thoroughly before starting any major dismantling work. This will make work much easier and rule out the possibility of dirt falling inside.

23 If required, remove the rear wheel (see Chapter 8) and the centrestand (see Chapter 7).

Installation

24 Installation is the reverse of removal, noting the following:

● Make sure no wires, cables or hoses become trapped between the engine and the frame when installing the engine.
● Tighten the engine mounting bolt, shock absorber bolts and rear wheel nut to the torque settings specified at the beginning of this Chapter.
● Make sure all wires, cables and hoses are correctly routed and connected, and secured by any clips or ties.
● If the engine oil was drained, or if any oil has been lost during overhaul, refill or top up as described in Chapter 1 and *Pre-ride checks*.
● Check the operation of the rear brake before riding the machine (see Chapter 1).

5 Disassembly and reassembly – general information

Disassembly

1 Before disassembling the engine, the external surfaces of the unit should be thoroughly cleaned and degreased. This will prevent contamination of the engine internals, and will also make working a lot easier and cleaner. A high flash-point solvent, such as paraffin can be used, or better still, a proprietary engine degreaser such as Gunk. Use a degreasing brush or old paintbrushes to work the solvent into the various recesses of the engine casings. Take care to exclude solvent or water from the electrical components and intake and exhaust ports.

⚠️ *Warning: The use of petrol (gasoline) as a cleaning agent should be avoided because of the risk of fire.*

2 When clean and dry, arrange the unit on the workbench, leaving suitable clear area for working. Gather a selection of small containers and plastic bags so that parts can be grouped together in an easily identifiable manner. Some paper and a pen should be on hand to permit notes to be made and labels attached where necessary. A supply of clean rag is also required.

3 Before commencing work, read through the appropriate section so that some idea of the necessary procedure can be gained. When removing components it should be noted that great force is seldom required, unless specified. In many cases, a component's reluctance to be removed is indicative of an incorrect approach or removal method – if in any doubt, re-check with the text.

4 When disassembling the engine, keep 'mated' parts that have been in contact with each other during engine operation together. These 'mated' parts must be reused or replaced as an assembly.

5 Complete engine disassembly should be done in the following general order with reference to the appropriate Sections (refer to Chapter 3 for details of transmission components):

● Remove the engine cowling
● Remove the valve cover
● Remove the camshaft and rockers
● Remove the cylinder head
● Remove the cylinder
● Remove the piston
● Remove the alternator
● Remove the starter motor (see Chapter 10)
● Remove the variator (see Chapter 3)
● Remove the oil pump
● Separate the crankcase halves
● Remove the crankshaft

Reassembly

6 Reassembly is accomplished by reversing the order of disassembly.

6 Valve cover

Removal

1 On V-Clic models, remove the storage compartment and centre cover panel; on Kisbee models, remove the storage compartment, seat cowling and centre cover panels (see Chapter 9).

2 Release the clip securing the breather hose to the upper rear of the valve cover and detach the hose **(see illustration 4.8)**.

3 Release the clip securing the pulse air valve to the reed valve housing on the lower front of the valve cover and detach the valve.

4 Undo the nuts securing the pulse air tube flange to the cylinder head **(see illustration)**.

6.4 Undo the flange nuts (arrowed)

6.5 Remove the valve cover

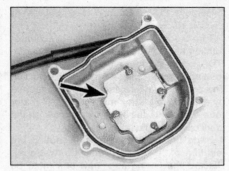

6.8 Location of the breather system baffle plate (arrowed)

6.10 Fit a new tube flange gasket

5 Undo the bolts securing the valve cover and lift it off **(see illustration)**. If the cover is stuck, tap around the joint face between the cover and the cylinder head with a soft-faced mallet to free it. Do not try to lever the cover off as this may damage the sealing surfaces.

6 Note the location of the cover gasket, then remove the gasket and discard it as a new one must be used. On Kisbee models, note the location of the half-round rubber plug in the cut-out on the left-hand side of the cylinder head. The plug is held in position by sealant – remove it carefully to avoid damage.

7 Clean the mating surfaces of the cylinder head and the valve cover with a suitable solvent to remove any traces of old gasket or sealant.

8 Note the location of the breather system baffle plate in the valve cover **(see**

illustration). If required, remove the plate and clean the inside of the cover. On installation, ensure that the screws securing the plate are tightened securely – as a precaution, clean the screw threads and apply non-permanent thread-locking compound.

9 Refer to Chapter 5 for details of the pulse air reed valve.

Installation

10 Fit a new gasket over the mounting studs for the pulse air tube flange **(see illustration)**.

11 Lay the new gasket onto the valve cover, making sure it fits correctly into the groove. On Kisbee models, secure the half-round rubber plug in the cut-out in of the cylinder head with a bead of suitable sealant.

12 Position the valve cover on the cylinder

head, making sure the gasket stays in place. Install the cover bolts, then tighten the bolts evenly and in a criss-cross sequence to the torque setting specified at the beginning of this Chapter.

13 Tighten the pulse air union nuts to the specified torque.

14 Install the breather hose and secure it with the clip.

15 Install the remaining components in the reverse order of removal.

7 Engine cowling and cooling fan

1 Undo the bolts securing the fan cover and lift it off **(see illustrations)**.

2 Remove the exhaust system (see Chapter 5). Remove the carburettor and intake manifold (see Chapter 5).

3 Undo the bolts securing the cowling on the left and right-hand sides **(see illustrations)**.

4 Ease the two halves of the cowling apart, noting how they clip together, and lift them off **(see illustration)**.

5 Note the location of the seal around the top edge of the cylinder. Remove the seal carefully, noting how it fits. If the seal is damaged or deteriorated replace it with a new one.

6 Undo the four bolts securing the cooling fan

7.1a Undo the bolts...

7.1b ...and remove the fan cover

7.3a Undo the left...

7.3b ...and right-hand bolts...

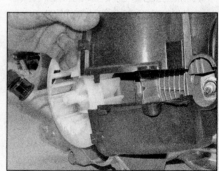

7.4 ...and separate the two halves of the cowling

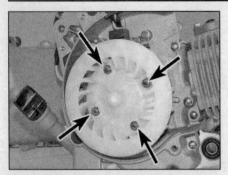

7.6 Cooling fan mounting bolts (arrowed)

to the alternator rotor and remove the fan **(see illustration)**.

7 Installation is the reverse of removal. Tighten the cooling fan bolts to the torque setting specified at the beginning of this Chapter.

8 Don't forget to install the cowling seal. Ensure both halves of the cowling and the fan cover are correctly aligned, then tighten the mounting bolts securely.

8 Camchain tensioner

Removal

1 The camchain tensioner is located on the back of the cylinder on the left-hand side. Remove the engine cowling for access (see Section 7).

2 Remove the spark plug (see Chapter 1, Section 15).

3 Turn the engine in the normal direction of rotation until the piston is at top dead centre (TDC) on its compression stroke. Do this by rotating the crankshaft via the alternator rotor. The position of the piston can be confirmed by ensuring that the T mark on the alternator rotor aligns with the static timing mark on the crankcase **(see illustration)**.

4 Undo the tensioner cap bolt, noting the location of the O-ring **(see illustrations)**. Discard the O-ring as a new one must be fitted.

5 The cap bolt retains a spring in the tensioner body – withdraw the spring.

6 Undo the tensioner mounting bolts and withdraw the tensioner from the cylinder **(see illustration)**. Remove the gasket from the base of the tensioner or from the cylinder and discard it as a new one must be used.

7 Clean all traces of old gasket material from the tensioner and cylinder with a suitable solvent. Take care not to scratch or gouge the soft aluminium. Be careful not to let any of the gasket material fall into the engine.

Inspection

8 Examine the tensioner components for signs of wear or damage.

9 Pull the plunger out from the tensioner body and examine the teeth on the ratchet **(see illustration)**. Now try to press the plunger back into the body – it should be locked in position.

10 Release the catch on the ratchet with a

small screwdriver and ensure that the plunger moves freely in and out of the tensioner body **(see illustration)**.

11 To check the operation of the tensioner spring, press the plunger into the body and temporarily install the tensioner on the back of the cylinder, then fit the spring and centre bolt. Now unscrew the centre bolt and withdraw the spring. Insert a small screwdriver into the tensioner and try to push the plunger out further against the pressure of the tensioner blade. If the plunger moves, then the spring has lost its tension.

12 If any part of the tensioner is worn or damaged, or if the plunger is seized in the body, a new tensioner must be fitted.

Installation

13 Release the ratchet mechanism and press the tensioner plunger all the way into the tensioner body **(see illustration 8.10)**. Fit a new gasket on the tensioner body and fit a new O-ring on the cap bolt.

14 Install the tensioner in the cylinder and tighten the mounting bolts.

15 Turn the engine in the normal direction of rotation – this removes all the slack in the front run of the chain between the crankshaft and the camshaft, and transfers it to the back run where it will be taken up by the tensioner. **Note:** *Take care when turning the engine with the tensioner spring removed to avoid the chain jumping over the teeth on the camshaft sprocket. If this happens, ensure that the timing marks on the alternator rotor and on the camshaft sprocket are correctly re-aligned*

8.3 T mark on the alternator rotor should align with the static timing mark (arrowed)

8.4a Undo the cap bolt...

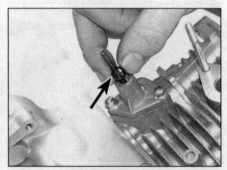

8.4b ...noting the O-ring (arrowed), then remove the spring

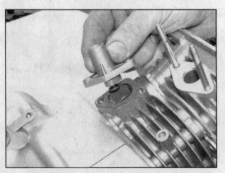

8.6 Remove the tensioner body

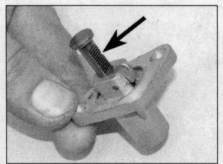

8.9 Inspect the ratchet teeth for wear

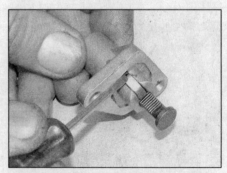

8.10 Check the operation of the plunger

9.3 Inspect the cam chain links for wear as described

9.5 The camchain should be a firm fit on the camshaft sprocket

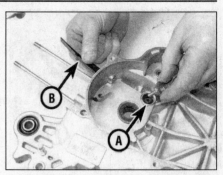

9.12 Undo the pivot bolt (A) and withdraw the tensioner blade (B)

with the piston at TDC before installing the tensioner spring (see Chapter 1, Section 14).

16 Install the spring and tighten the cap bolt securely.

17 It is advisable to remove the valve cover (see Section 6) and check that the camchain is tensioned. If it is slack, the tensioner plunger did not release. Remove the tensioner and check the operation of the plunger again.

18 Install the remaining components in the reverse order of removal.

Caution: After installing the camchain tensioner, turn the crankshaft and check that all the timing marks still align correctly. If the timing marks are not aligned exactly as described, the valve timing will be incorrect and the valves may strike the piston, causing extensive damage to the engine.

9 Camchain, blades and sprockets

Camchain

Inspection

1 The camchain runs between the drive sprocket on the crankshaft and the camshaft sprocket. To check the condition of the chain, first remove the valve cover (see Section 6) and the engine cowling (see Section 7).

2 Remove the spark plug (see Chapter 1, Section 15).

3 Using the alternator rotor, turn the engine slowly in the normal direction of rotation and inspect the inside edges of the chain links for wear **(see illustration)**.

4 Remove the camchain tensioner (see Section 8). Note the position of the plunger, then press a small screwdriver into the tensioner to see how much adjustment remains on the plunger. If there are only two or three clicks of movement left, the chain and/or tensioner blade are worn and must be renewed.

5 Hold the chain at the mid-way point around the camshaft sprocket and try to lift it off the sprocket **(see illustration)**. The chain should be a firm fit on the sprocket. Turn the engine carefully in the normal direction of rotation (see Note in Section 8, Step 15 above) and check the entire length of the chain.

6 If any of the above checks indicate that the camchain has worn, a new one must be fitted.

Removal and installation

7 If the camchain is to be removed, follow the procedure in Section 20 and separate the crankcase halves. The camchain can be removed with the crankshaft assembly.

8 On installation, before installing the chain onto the camshaft sprocket, ensure that the piston is at TDC on the compression stroke and that the timing mark T on the alternator rotor is aligned with the static timing mark on

the crankcase **(see illustration 8.3)**. Position the timing mark on the camshaft sprocket as noted on removal – the camshaft lobes should face down away from the rocker arms. Ensure any slack in the chain is in the top run where it will be taken up by the tensioner

Camchain tensioner and guide blades

9 The camchain tensioner blade is located inside the camchain tunnel and is secured by a pivot bolt on its lower end.

10 To inspect the blade, first remove the cylinder head (see Section 11). Secure the camchain to prevent it falling down into the tunnel.

11 Remove the variator (see Chapter 3).

12 Undo the pivot bolt securing the tensioner blade and lift the blade out **(see illustration)**. Note which way round the blade is fitted. Note the O-ring fitted on the pivot bolt and fit a new one on reassembly.

13 The guide blade can be removed when the cylinder head has been removed (see Section 11).

14 Check both blades for wear or damage and renew them if necessary **(see illustration)**. Check the operation of the camchain tensioner (see Section 8).

15 Installation is the reverse of removal. Ensure that the blades are fitted the correct way round **(see illustrations)**. Fit a new O-ring on the tensioner blade pivot bolt. Apply non-permanent thread-locking compound

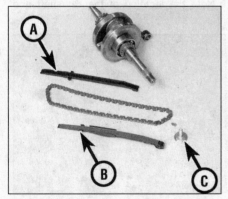

9.14 Camchain guide blade (A), tensioner blade (B) and pivot bolt (C)

9.15a Note which way round the guide blade is fitted...

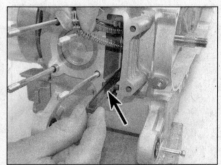

9.15b ...and locate the lugs in the top of the camchain tunnel

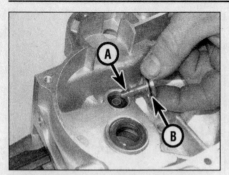

9.15c Apply locking compound to the pivot bolt threads (A). Note the O-ring (B)

10.2a Check for a small amount of clearance in the rocker arms (arrowed)

10.2b Note the alignment between the holes (arrowed) and the gasket face

to the threads of the pivot bolt and tighten it securely **(see illustration)**.

Camchain sprockets

16 On V-Clic models, the camshaft sprocket is integral with the camshaft. On Kisbee models the sprocket and camshaft are separate components. To inspect the sprocket for wear, follow the procedure in Section 10 and remove either the camshaft or sprocket as appropriate.
17 Check for wear on the sides and tips of the sprocket teeth and for chipped or hooked teeth.
18 Similar checks should be made on the crankshaft sprocket – this is integral with the crankshaft assembly and can only be inspected once the crankcase halves have

been separated and the crankshaft removed (see Section 20).
19 If the sprocket teeth are worn, the chain will also be worn. Always renew the components as an assembly – worn sprockets will soon damage a new chain.

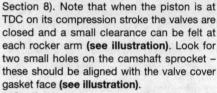

10 Camshaft and rocker arms

Removal

V-Clic

1 Remove the valve cover (see Section 6).
2 Remove the camchain tensioner (see

Section 8). Note that when the piston is at TDC on its compression stroke the valves are closed and a small clearance can be felt at each rocker arm **(see illustration)**. Look for two small holes on the camshaft sprocket – these should be aligned with the valve cover gasket face **(see illustration)**.
3 Stuff a clean rag into the camchain tunnel to prevent anything falling into the engine.
4 The camshaft and rockers are located by a holder which is retained by long studs that also secure the cylinder head and cylinder to the crankcases. Before loosening the cylinder head nuts, loosen the small bolts securing the left-hand side of the cylinder head **(see illustration)**.
5 Now unscrew the cylinder head nuts evenly and a little at a time in a criss-cross pattern, until they are all loose, then remove the nuts and washers **(see illustrations)**.
6 Note which way round the camshaft holder is fitted. On the engine used to illustrate this procedure, the holder was marked EX on the exhaust side.
7 Hold the camshaft in position in the cylinder head and lift off the camshaft holder **(see illustration)**. Note any dowels in the holder or head and remove them for safekeeping if they are loose **(see illustration 10.9a)**.
8 Lift the camchain off the sprocket and secure the chain to prevent it dropping into the engine **(see illustration)**.
9 Note the location of the camshaft and

10.4 Always loosen the small bolts (arrowed) first

10.5a Undo the cylinder head nuts evenly...

10.5b ...and remove the washers

10.7 Lift off the camshaft holder

10.8 Lift the camchain off the sprocket

10.9a Note the location of the camshaft and bearings (A). Note the dowels (B)

10.9b Lift out the camshaft

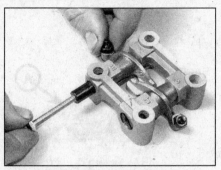

10.10 Use a suitable bolt to pull out the rocker shaft and remove the rocker arm

camshaft bearings, then lift out the camshaft **(see illustrations)**.

10 The rocker shafts are retained in the camshaft holder by the cylinder studs. Once the holder has been removed from the engine, the shafts and individual rocker arms can be disassembled. Note the position of the rocker arms and mark them so that they can be installed in their original positions, then withdraw the shafts carefully **(see illustration)**. **Note:** *If necessary, thread a suitably-sized bolt into the end of each rocker shaft to ease withdrawal.*

11 Remove the rocker arms from the holder.

12 Assemble the rockers on their shafts so that they can be installed in their original positions **(see illustration)**.

Kisbee

13 Remove the cylinder head (see Section 11).

14 On the assembled engine, the rocker shafts are held in position by the cylinder studs – note the alignment of the shafts **(see illustration)**.

15 Working on one rocker arm at a time, thread a 5 mm bolt into the end of the shaft, then support the arm and draw the shaft out **(see illustration)**. Mark the rocker arms so that they can be can be installed in their original positions and slide them back onto their shafts.

16 Undo the screw securing the camshaft stopper plate and remove the plate, noting how it fits.

17 Draw out the camshaft together with the camshaft bearings **(see illustration)**.

Inspection

All models

18 Clean all of the components with a suitable solvent and dry them.

19 Inspect the camshaft lobes for heat discoloration (blue appearance), score marks, chipped areas, flat spots and spalling **(see illustration)**. If damage is noted or wear is excessive, the camshaft must be renewed.

20 Follow the procedure in *Tools and Workshop Tips* in the *Reference* section to check the condition of the camshaft bearings **(see illustration)**. The bearings are not available individually – if a bearing is worn or damaged a new camshaft will have to be fitted.

21 Check the bearing housings for score

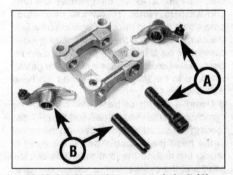

10.12 Intake rocker arm and shaft (A). Exhaust rocker arm and shaft (B)

10.14 Note the alignment of the rocker shafts (arrowed)

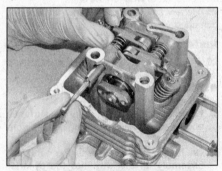

10.15 Withdraw the rocker shafts as described

10.17 Draw out the camshaft and bearings

10.19 Inspect the camshaft lobes (arrowed) for wear and damage

10.20 Camshaft assembly complete with sprocket and bearings

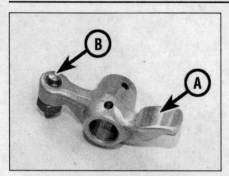

10.23 Inspect the face of the rocker arm (A) and the contact area on the adjuster screw (B)

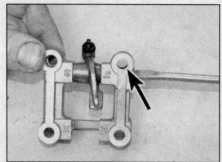

10.26 Ensure the rocker shafts are clear of the stud holes (arrowed)

11.5 Note alignment of the timing marks (arrowed) with the gasket face

marks and spalling. Any damage is an indication that the bearing has seized on the camshaft and turned inside its housing. Prior to reassembly, check that the bearing outer races are a tight fit in their housings, otherwise use some bearing locking compound to hold it in position.

22 Blow through the oil passages in the rocker arms and shafts with compressed air, if available, to ensure that they are clear.

23 Inspect the face of the rocker arm and the contact area between the adjuster screw and the valve stem for pits and spalling (see illustration).

24 Check the rocker shaft for wear. The rocker arm should be a sliding fit on the shaft without any freeplay. If available, use a micrometer to measure the diameter of the shaft in several places – any variation in the measurements is an indication of wear on the shaft.

25 Renew any components that are worn or damaged.

Installation

26 Installation is the reverse of removal, noting the following:

● Ensure the piston is at TDC on the compression stroke before you start.
● Lubricate the shafts, bearing surfaces and bearings with clean engine oil before installation.
● On Kisbee models, press the camshaft assembly all the way into the cylinder head. Apply non-permanent thread-locking compound to the threads of the camshaft

stopper plate screw and tighten it to the torque setting specified at the beginning of this Chapter.

● Position the rocker shafts so that the holes for the cylinder studs are clear (see illustration).
● Ensure any dowels are correctly installed in the camshaft holder or cylinder head.
● Tighten the cylinder head nuts a little at a time in a criss-cross sequence to the specified torque (see Section 11). Don't forget to tighten the cylinder head bolts.
● Check the valve clearances (see Chapter 1).

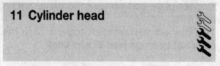

11 Cylinder head

Caution: The engine must be completely cool before beginning this procedure or the cylinder head may become warped.

Removal

1 Remove the carburettor, intake manifold and exhaust system (see Chapter 5).
2 Remove the fan cover and engine cowling (see Section 7).
3 On V-Clic models, remove the camshaft and rockers (see Section 10). Now go to Step 7.
4 On Kisbee models, remove the valve cover (see Section 6).
5 Remove the camchain tensioner (see Section 8). Note that when the piston is at TDC on its compression stroke the valves

are closed and a small clearance can be felt at each rocker arm. Look for two small lines on the camshaft sprocket – these should be parallel with the valve cover gasket face (see illustration). Stuff a clean rag into the camchain tunnel to prevent anything falling into the engine.

6 Hold the alternator rotor to prevent the engine turning, then unscrew the camshaft sprocket bolts and lift the sprocket off, noting how it fits (see illustration). If required, mark the outer face of the sprocket so that it can be installed the same way round on assembly. Secure the camchain to prevent it dropping into the engine.

7 Unscrew the two cylinder head bolts on the left-hand side of the head (see illustration). Now unscrew the cylinder head nuts evenly and a little at a time in a criss-cross pattern until they are all loose, then remove the nuts and washers. Note: The cylinder head studs pass down through the cylinder and screw into the crankcase. Once the cylinder head is loose care must be taken not to break the cylinder base gasket seal otherwise a new base gasket will have to be fitted before refitting the head (see Section 13).

8 Using a length of bent wire to hold the camchain, lift the cylinder head off the cylinder, feeding the camchain down through the tunnel in the head (see illustration). If the head is stuck, tap around the joint face between the head and the cylinder with a soft-faced mallet to free it. Do not try to lever the head off as this may damage the sealing surfaces.

11.6 Remove the camshaft sprocket

11.7 Unscrew the cylinder head bolts

11.8 Lift off the cylinder head

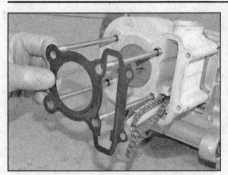

11.9a Remove the cylinder head gasket

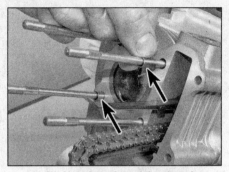

11.9b Note location of the dowels (arrowed)

11.11 Note how the lugs (arrowed) on the guide blade locate

9 Remove the old cylinder head gasket **(see illustration)**. Note the dowels in the head or cylinder and remove them for safekeeping if they are loose **(see illustration)**.
10 Secure the camchain to prevent it dropping into the engine.
11 If required, the camchain guide blade can be removed – draw the blade out, noting how the lugs locate in the recess in the top edge of the camchain tunnel **(see illustration)**.
12 Clean all traces of old gasket material from the cylinder head and cylinder with a suitable solvent. Take care not to scratch or gouge the soft aluminium. Be careful not to let any of the gasket material fall into the crankcase, the cylinder bore or the oil passages.
13 Inspect the cylinder head gasket and the mating surfaces on the cylinder head and cylinder for signs of leaks, which could indicate that the head is warped. Refer to Section 12 and check the head mating surface for warpage.
14 After inspection, discard the old gasket as a new one must be fitted on reassembly

Installation

15 Installation is the reverse of removal, noting the following:
● Lubricate the cylinder bore with clean engine oil.
● Ensure the dowels are correctly installed in the cylinder.
● If removed, install the camchain guide blade (see Step 11).

● Install a new head gasket – never re-use the old gasket.
● Ensure the camchain is correctly located around the crankshaft sprocket.
● Tighten the cylinder head nuts evenly and a little at a time in a criss-cross pattern to the torque setting specified at the beginning of this Chapter. Now tighten the cylinder head bolts to the specified torque.
● On Kisbee models, tighten the camshaft sprocket bolts to the specified torque setting.

12 Cylinder head and valves

Note: *If a valve spring compressor is available, the home mechanic can remove the valves from the cylinder head, lap the valves and renew the valve stem seals.*

Disassembly

1 Before you start, arrange to label and store the valves and their related components so that they can be returned to their original locations without getting mixed up **(see illustration)**. **Note:** *On Kisbee engines, only one spring is fitted to each valve.*
2 On Kisbee models, if not already done, remove the rocker arms and camshaft (see Section 10).
3 Compress the valve springs on the first valve with a spring compressor, making sure it

is correctly located onto each end of the valve assembly **(see illustration)**. On the underside of the head, make sure the plate on the compressor only contacts the valve and not the soft aluminium of the head – if the plate is too big for the valve, use a spacer between them. Do not compress the springs any more than is absolutely necessary to release the collets, then remove the collets, using either needle-nose pliers, a magnet or a screwdriver with a dab of grease on it **(see illustration)**.
4 Carefully release the valve spring compressor and remove the spring retainer, noting which way up it fits **(see illustration)**.
5 Remove the valve spring(s). **Note:** *The valve*

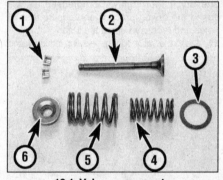

12.1 Valve components

1 Collets	4 Inner valve spring
2 Valve	5 Outer valve spring
3 Spring seat	6 Spring retainer

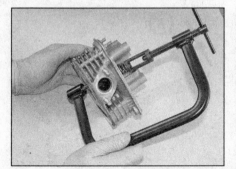

12.3a Ensure the valve spring compressor is correctly fitted

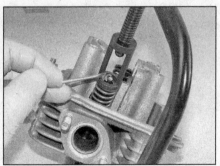

12.3b Remove the collets from the top of the valve stem

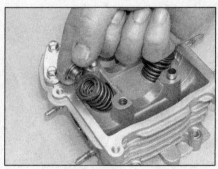

12.4 Remove the spring retainer and the valve spring(s)

12.6 Lift out the spring seat

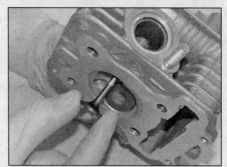

12.7a Pull out the valve

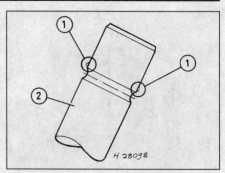

12.7b If the valve stem (2) won't pull through the guide, deburr the area (1) above the collet groove

springs have closer-wound coils that are fitted next to the cylinder head.

6 Lift out the spring seat **(see illustration)**.

7 Turn the head over and withdraw the valve – if it binds in the guide (won't pull through), push it back into the head and deburr the area around the collet groove with a very fine file **(see illustrations)**.

8 Once the valve has been removed, pull the valve stem oil seal off the top of the valve guide with pliers and discard it as a new one must be used on reassembly **(see illustration)**.

9 Repeat the procedure for the remaining valve. Remember to keep the parts for each valve together and in order so they can be reinstalled in the correct location.

10 Next, clean the cylinder head with solvent and dry it thoroughly. Compressed air will speed the drying process and ensure that all holes and recessed areas are clean.

11 Clean the valve springs, collets, retainers and

spring seats with solvent. Work on the parts from one valve at a time so as not to mix them up.

12 Scrape off any carbon deposits that may have formed on the valve, then use a motorised wire brush to remove deposits from the valve heads and stems. Again, make sure the valves do not get mixed up.

Inspection

13 Inspect the head very carefully for cracks and other damage, especially around the valve seats and the spark plug hole. If cracks are found, a new head will be required.

14 Inspect the threads in the spark plug hole. Damaged or worn threads can be reclaimed using a thread insert (see *Tools and Workshop Tips* in the Reference section). Most small engineering firms offer a service of this kind.

15 Using a precision straight-edge and a feeler gauge, check the head mating surface for warpage. Lay the straight-edge across the

surface and measure any gap under it with feeler gauges. Check vertically, horizontally and diagonally across the head, making four checks in all **(see illustration)**. Warpage should generally be no more than 0.05 mm. If warpage is excessive, have the cylinder head machined flat or replace it with a new one. If there is any doubt about the condition of the head consult an automotive engineer.

16 Examine the valve seats in the combustion chamber. If they are deeply pitted, cracked or burned, it may be possible to have them repaired and re-cut by a specialist engineer, otherwise a new head will be required. The valve seats should be a uniform width all the way round **(see illustration)**.

17 If available, use a micrometer to measure the valve stem diameter in several places along the stem length **(see illustration)**. **Note:** *Any variation in the measurements is an indication of wear on the valve stem.*

18 If no measuring equipment is available, insert a known good valve into its guide – it should be a sliding fit with no discernible freeplay. If there is freeplay, the guide is worn. Have the guides checked by a specialist engineer. If new valve guides are available, have them installed by a specialist who will also re-cut the valve seats. Otherwise a new cylinder head will have to be fitted. **Note:** *Carbon build-up inside the guide is an indication of wear.*

19 Inspect the valve face for cracks, pits and burned spots, and check the valve stem and the collet groove area for score marks and cracks **(see illustration)**. Rotate the valve

12.8 Pull off the old valve stem oil seal

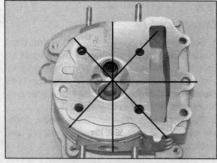

12.15 Check the cylinder head for warpage in the directions shown

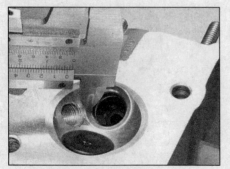

12.16 Valve seats should be the same width all the way round

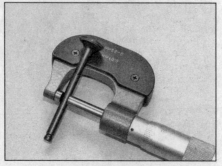

12.17 Measuring the valve stem diameter with a micrometer

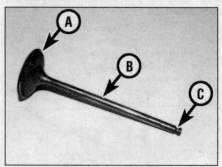

12.19 Check the valve face (A), stem (B) and collet groove (C)

12.20 Check the valve springs for bending

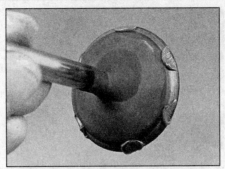

12.23 Apply the grinding paste sparingly, in small dabs, to the valve face only

12.24a Rotate the tool back-and-forth between the palms of your hands

12.24b The valve face and seat should show a uniform unbroken ring

12.27a Position the stem seal on the end of the valve guide...

12.27b ...then press it on until it clips into place

and check for any obvious indication that it is bent. Check the end of the stem for pitting and excessive wear. If any of the above conditions are found, fit a new valve. If the stem end is pitted or worn, also check the contact area of the adjuster screw in the rocker arm.

20 Check the end of each valve spring for wear. Stand the spring upright on a flat surface and check it for bend by placing a square against it **(see illustration)**. Valve springs will take a permanent set (sag) after a long period of use. If the spring is worn, or the bend is excessive, or the spring has sagged, it must be renewed. **Note:** *It is good practice to fit new springs (on both valves) when the head has been disassembled for valve servicing.*

21 Check the spring retainers and collets for obvious wear and cracks. Any questionable parts should not be reused, as extensive damage will occur in the event of failure during engine operation.

Reassembly

22 Unless the valve seats have been re-cut, before installing the valves in the head they should be lapped to ensure a positive seal between the valves and seats. This procedure requires fine valve grinding paste and a valve grinding tool. If a grinding tool is not available, a piece of rubber or plastic hose can be slipped over the valve stem (after the valve has been installed in the guide) and used to turn the valve.

23 Apply a small amount of fine grinding paste to the valve face, then slip the valve into the guide **(see illustration)**. **Note:** *Make sure each valve is installed in its correct guide and*

be careful not to get any grinding paste on the valve stem.

24 Attach the grinding tool (or hose) to the valve and rotate the tool between the palms of your hands. Use a back-and-forth motion (as though rubbing your hands together) rather than a circular motion (i.e. so that the valve rotates alternately clockwise and anti-clockwise rather than in one direction only) **(see illustration)**. Lift the valve off the seat and turn it at regular intervals to distribute the grinding paste evenly. Continue the grinding procedure until the valve face and seat contact areas are of uniform width and unbroken around the circumference **(see illustration)**.

25 Carefully remove the valve from the guide and wipe off all traces of grinding paste. Use solvent to clean the valve and wipe the seat area thoroughly with a solvent soaked cloth.

26 Repeat the procedure on the other valve.

> **HAYNES HiNT** *Check for proper sealing of each valve by pouring a small amount of solvent into the valve port while holding the valve shut. If the solvent leaks past the valve into the combustion chamber the lapping operation should be repeated.*

27 Once all the components are ready for assembly, install the valves. Place a new seal onto the end of the valve guide, then use an appropriate size deep socket to push the seal over the guide until it is felt to clip into place **(see illustrations)**. Don't twist or cock the seal sideways, or it will not seal properly

against the valve stem. Also, don't remove it again or it will be damaged.

28 Lubricate the valve stem with clean engine oil, then install it into its guide, rotating it slowly to avoid damaging the seal. Check that the valve moves up and down freely in the guide.

29 Install the spring seat, then install the valve spring(s) as noted on removal (see Step 5). Install the spring retainer, with its shouldered side facing down so that it fits into the top of the spring.

30 Apply a small amount of grease to the collets to hold them in place, then compress the spring(s) using the method employed on removal and install the collets. Compress the spring(s) only as far as is absolutely necessary to slip the collets into place. Once installed, make certain that the collets are securely locked in their retaining grooves.

31 Repeat the procedure for the other valve.

32 Support the cylinder head on blocks so the valves can't contact the workbench top, then very gently tap each of the valve stems with a soft-faced hammer. This will help seat the collets in their grooves.

13 Cylinder

Removal

1 Remove the cylinder head and the camchain guide blade (see Section 11).

2 Hold the camchain and lift the cylinder up off the crankcase, supporting the piston as it

13.2a Lift the cylinder off the crankcase

13.2b Support the piston as the cylinder is removed

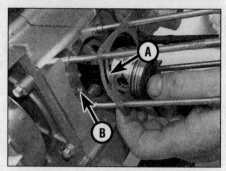

13.4a Remove the base gasket. Note how the oilway (A) aligns with the hole (B) in the crankcase

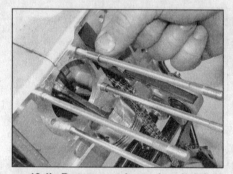

13.4b Remove any loose dowels for safekeeping

13.4c Note how the camchain locates on the crankshaft sprocket (arrowed)

becomes accessible to prevent it hitting the crankcase opening **(see illustrations)**. If the cylinder is stuck, tap around the joint face between the cylinder and the crankcase with a soft-faced mallet to free it. Don't attempt to free the cylinder by inserting a screwdriver between it and the crankcase – you'll damage the sealing surfaces.

3 Once the cylinder has been removed, stuff a clean rag into the crankcase opening around the piston to prevent anything falling inside.

4 Remove the cylinder base gasket, noting how it fits, then discard it as new one must be fitted on reassembly. Note any dowels in the cylinder or crankcase and remove them for safekeeping if they are loose **(see illustrations)**. Note how the camchain locates on the crankshaft sprocket and secure the chain to prevent it dropping into the crankcase **(see illustration)**.

5 Clean all traces of old gasket material from the cylinder and crankcase with a suitable solvent. Take care not to scratch or gouge the soft aluminium. Be careful not to let any of the gasket material fall into the crankcase.

Inspection

6 Check the cylinder bore carefully for scratches and score marks **(see illustration)**.
7 If available, use a telescoping gauge and micrometer to measure the inside diameter of the cylinder bore to assess the amount of wear, taper and ovality (see *Tools and Workshop Tips* in the *Reference* section). Measure near the top (but below the level of the top piston ring at top dead centre), centre and bottom (but above the level of the bottom ring with the piston at bottom dead centre) of the bore both parallel to and across the crankshaft axis **(see illustrations)**.

8 Calculate any differences between the measurements to determine any taper or ovality in the bore. A cylinder bore that has worn oval will reduce the efficiency of the piston rings to achieve a seal, resulting in loss of compression and increased oil consumption.

9 As no service data is available, measure an unworn part of the cylinder bore (below the level of the bottom ring with the piston at the bottom of its stroke) and compare the result to the previous measurements to determine overall wear. Alternatively, check for a lip around the (unworn) top edge of the cylinder bore as a rough indication of wear.

10 If the bore is tapered, oval, or worn excessively, badly scratched, scuffed or scored, the cylinder and piston will have to be renewed as a set. **Note:** *If there is any doubt about the condition of the cylinder, consult a specialist engineer.*

11 Check that all the cylinder studs are tight in the crankcase halves. If any are loose, remove them (see *Tools and Workshop Tips* in the *Reference* section) and clean their threads. Apply a suitable permanent thread locking compound, then screw them back into the crankcase securely.

Installation

12 Remove any rag from the crankcase opening. Ensure any dowels are correctly installed in the crankcase, then lay the new base gasket in place on the crankcase making sure it is the correct way round **(see illustrations 13.4b and a)**.

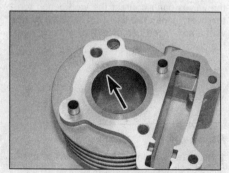

13.6 Inspect the bore (arrowed) for damage

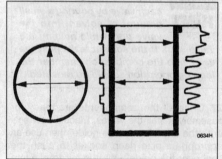

13.7a Measure the cylinder bore in the directions shown...

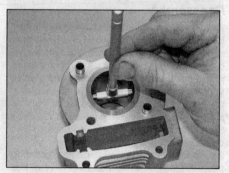

13.7b ...using a telescoping gauge

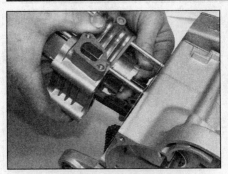

13.14 Lower the cylinder down onto the piston, carefully compressing each ring and feeding it into the bore

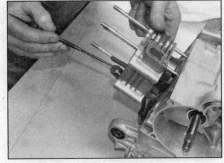

13.15 Press the cylinder down onto the base gasket

14.2 Mark the top of the piston

13 Check that the piston ring end gaps are positioned as described in Section 15.

14 Lubricate the cylinder bore, piston and piston rings, and the connecting rod big- and small-ends, with clean engine oil, then lower the cylinder down until the piston crown fits into the bore. Gently push down on the cylinder, making sure the piston enters the bore squarely and does not get cocked sideways. Carefully compress and feed each ring into the bore as the cylinder is lowered **(see illustration)**. If necessary, use a soft mallet to gently tap the cylinder down, but do not use force if it appears to be stuck as the piston and/or rings will be damaged.

15 When the piston is correctly installed in the cylinder, support the camchain and check that the base gasket has not been displaced, then press the cylinder down onto the base gasket **(see illustration)**.

16 Install the camchain guide blade, then install the cylinder head (see Section 11).

14 Piston

Removal

1 Remove the cylinder and stuff a clean rag into the crankcase opening around the piston to prevent anything falling inside (see Section 13).

2 The top of the piston should be marked with an arrow or lettering (e.g. IN on the intake side, nearest the carburettor) to show which way round it should be fitted. If no mark is visible, scratch one lightly on the top of the piston **(see illustration)**. Note that the manufacturer's mark may not be visible until the carbon deposits have been scraped off and the piston cleaned.

3 Carefully prise out the circlip on one side of the piston using needle-nose pliers or a small flat-bladed screwdriver inserted into the notch **(see illustration)**. Remove any burring around the circlip groove with a very fine file or penknife blade, then push the piston pin out from the other side and remove the piston from the connecting rod **(see illustration)**. Use a socket extension to push the piston pin out if required. Remove the other circlip and discard them both as new ones must be used on reassembly.

HAYNES HiNT *To prevent the circlip from flying away or from dropping into the crankcase, pass a rod or screwdriver with a greater diameter than the gap between the circlip ends, through the piston pin. This will trap the circlip if it springs out.*

HAYNES HiNT *If the piston pin is a tight fit in the piston bosses, heat the piston gently with a hot air gun – this will expand the alloy piston sufficiently to release its grip on the pin.*

4 Before the inspection process can be carried out, the piston rings must be removed and the piston must be cleaned. **Note:** *If the cylinder is being renewed, piston inspection can be overlooked as a new one will be fitted.*

5 If required, the piston rings can be removed by hand; using your thumbs, ease the ends of each ring apart and carefully lift it off the piston, taking care not to expand it any more than is necessary. Do not nick or gouge the piston in the process. Alternatively, use an old feeler gauge blade to ease the rings off the piston **(see illustration)**.

6 Note which way up each ring fits and in which groove they must be installed in their original positions if being re-used. The upper surface of each ring should be marked at one end. Most pistons are fitted with a three-piece third (oil control) ring; there will be an upper and lower side rail and a central rail spacer (see Section 15). **Note:** *It is good practice to renew the piston rings when an engine is being overhauled.*

7 Clean all traces of carbon from the top of the piston. A hand-held wire brush or a piece of fine emery cloth can be used once most of the deposits have been scraped away. Do not, under any circumstances, use a wire brush mounted in a drill motor; the piston material is soft and is easily damaged.

8 Use a piston ring groove cleaning tool to remove any carbon deposits from the ring grooves. If a tool is not available, a piece broken off an old ring will do the job. Be very careful to remove only the carbon deposits.

14.3a Use the notch (arrowed) to remove the circlip...

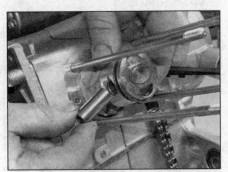

14.3b ...then push out the piston pin

14.5 Using a thin blade to remove the piston rings

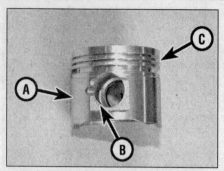

14.10 Inspect the piston skirt (A), pin bosses (B) and ring lands (C)

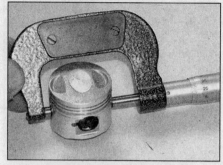

14.12 Measuring the piston diameter with a micrometer

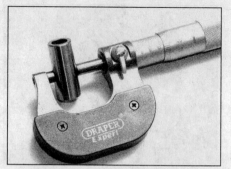

14.13 Measuring the piston pin diameter

Do not remove any metal and do not nick or gouge the sides of the ring grooves.

9 Once the carbon has been removed, clean the piston with a suitable solvent and dry it thoroughly. If the identification previously marked on the piston is cleaned off, be sure to re-mark it correctly.

Inspection

10 Inspect the piston for cracks around the skirt, at the pin bosses and at the ring lands **(see illustration)**. Check that the circlip grooves are not damaged. Normal piston wear appears as even, vertical wear on the thrust surfaces of the skirt and slight looseness of the top ring in its groove. If the skirt is scored or scuffed, the engine may have been suffering from overheating and/or abnormal

combustion, which caused excessively high operating temperatures.

11 A hole in the top of the piston, in one extreme, or burned areas around the edge of the piston crown, indicate that pre-ignition or knocking under load have occurred. If you find evidence of any problems the cause must be corrected or the damage will occur again. Refer to Chapter 5 for carburation checks and Chapter 6 for ignition checks.

12 Check the piston-to-bore clearance by measuring the cylinder bore (see Section 13) and the piston diameter. Measure the piston approximately 25 mm down from the bottom of the lower piston ring groove and at 90° to the piston pin axis **(see illustration)**. Note: *The precise point of measurement isn't critical but the aim is to measure the piston in an area where it is worn.* Subtract the piston diameter

from the bore diameter to obtain the clearance. No service data is available, but as a general guide this shouldn't exceed 0.10 mm.

13 Use a micrometer to measure the piston pin in the middle, where it runs in the small-end bearing, and at each end where it runs in the piston **(see illustration)**. If there is any difference in the measurements the pin is worn and must be renewed.

14 If the piston pin is good, lubricate it with clean engine oil, then insert it into the piston and check for any freeplay between the two **(see illustration)**. There should be no freeplay. A worn small-end will produce a metallic rattle, most audible when the engine is under load, and increasing as engine speed rises. This should not be confused with big-end bearing wear, which produces a pronounced knocking noise.

15 Lubricate the piston pin with clean engine oil, then slide it into the small-end and check for freeplay **(see illustration)**. There should only be slightly discernible freeplay between the piston pin and the connecting rod.

16 With the piston removed, the general condition of the big-end bearing can be assessed. Hold the alternator to prevent the crankshaft from turning, then push-and-pull on the connecting rod, checking for any up-and-down freeplay **(see illustration)**. If freeplay is noted, refer to Section 21 to remove and inspect the crankshaft assembly.

Installation

17 Install the piston rings (see Section 15).
18 Lubricate the piston pin, the piston pin bore in the piston and the connecting-rod small-end with clean engine oil.
19 Install a new circlip in one side of the piston, then line up the piston on the connecting rod, making sure it is the right way round (see Step 3).
20 Insert the piston pin from the other side and secure it with the other new circlip **(see illustration 14.3b)**. When installing the circlips, compress them only just enough to fit them in the piston, and make sure they are properly seated in their grooves with the open end away from the removal notch **(see illustration)**.
21 Install the cylinder (see Section 13).

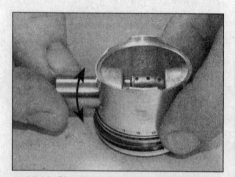

14.14 Check for freeplay between the piston and the piston pin

14.15 Rock the piston pin back-and-forth to check for freeplay

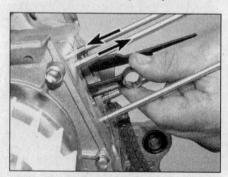

14.16 Checking for freeplay in the big-end bearing

14.20 Ensure the circlips are seated in their grooves

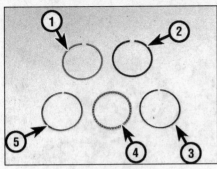

15.1 Piston ring set

1 *Top compression ring*
2 *Second compression ring*
3 *Upper side rail*
4 *Rail spacer*
5 *Lower side rail*

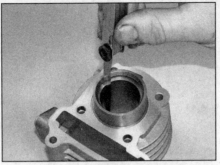

15.2 Measuring installed piston ring end gap

15 Piston rings

1 New piston rings should be fitted whenever an engine is being overhauled **(see illustration)**. It is important that you get new rings of the correct size for your piston so ensure that any information relating to piston size and size coding is available when purchasing new parts.
2 Before fitting the new rings onto the

piston, the installed ring end gaps must be checked. Insert the top ring into the bottom of the cylinder bore and square it up by pushing it in with the top of the piston. The ring should be about 15 to 20 mm from the bottom edge of the cylinder. Measure the ring end gap using feeler gauges, slipping the gauge between the ends of the ring **(see illustration)**. Ring end gaps are given in the *Specifications* at the beginning of this Chapter.
3 If the gap is larger than specified it is likely the cylinder bore is worn. If the gap is too small the ring ends may come into contact with each other during engine operation, causing serious damage.
4 Repeat the procedure for the other two rings. **Note:** *The piston is fitted with a three-piece third (oil control) ring – check the*

end gap on the upper and lower side rails only. The ends of the central rail spacer should contact each other when it is fitted on the piston.
5 Once the ring end gaps have been checked and found to be within specification, the rings can be installed on the piston. Do not expand the rings any more than is necessary to slide them into place. **Note:** *A ring installation tool can be used on the two compression rings, if desired, but not on the side rails of a three-piece oil control ring.*
6 The oil control ring (lowest on the piston) is installed first. Fit the rail spacer into the groove **(see illustration)**, then install the lower side rail as follows. Place one end of the side rail into the groove between the spacer and the lower ring land. Hold it firmly in place, then slide a thin blade around the piston while pushing the rail into the groove **(see illustration)**.
7 Install the upper side rail the same way. Ensure the ends of the spacer touch but do not overlap, then check that both side rails turn smoothly in the ring groove.
8 Next install the 2nd compression ring. The compression rings have different profiles and there should be a marking or letter A near the gap to denote the upper surface of the ring. Finally install the top ring into its groove.
9 Once the rings are correctly installed, check they move freely without snagging, then stagger their end gaps before fitting the piston into the cylinder **(see illustration)**.

16 Alternator

Note: *This procedure can be carried out with the engine in the scooter. If the engine has been removed, ignore the steps that do not apply.*

Removal

1 The alternator is located behind the slotted fan cover on the right-hand side of the engine – remove the cover and the cooling fan (see Section 7).
2 To undo the alternator rotor centre nut it is necessary to stop the rotor from turning using a pin wrench that locates in the two large holes in the face of the rotor **(see illustration)**. Peugeot produces a service tool (Part No. 752237) for this purpose. Alternatively, a similar home-made tool can be used (refer to the illustration in Chapter 2A, Section 11) or you can obtain an aftermarket version. **Note:** *Take great care not to damage the internal coils of the alternator when locating any tools through the rotor.*

15.6a Fit the rail spacer first...

15.6b ...then the lower side rail

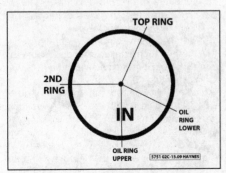

15.9 Piston ring end gap positions

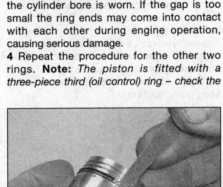

16.2 Holes (arrowed) in the face of the rotor can be used to locate the tool

16.3 Hold the rotor and undo the centre nut

16.4a Displace the ignition pulse generator coil...

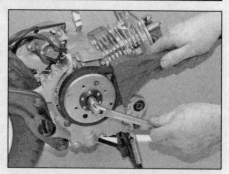

16.4b ...and use a strap wrench to hold the rotor

3 With the rotor securely held, unscrew the centre nut **(see illustration)**.

4 Alternatively, the rotor can be held with a strap wrench. If necessary, undo the bolts securing the ignition pulse generator coil and displace it to avoid damaging it when using the strap wrench **(see illustrations)**.

5 To remove the rotor from the taper on the crankshaft it is necessary to use a puller that threads into the internal thread in the centre of the rotor. Peugeot produces a service tool (Part No. 750806) for this purpose and similar aftermarket pullers are available. Alternatively, use a two-legged puller as shown **(see illustration)**. Thread the puller legs into the threaded holes in the rotor, then tighten the centre bolt exerting steady pressure to draw the rotor off the taper. **Note:** *To avoid damaging the threaded end of the crankshaft, either leave the centre nut on the shaft with just enough clearance to allow the rotor to be dislodged, or*

position a soft metal spacer between the end of the shaft and the puller centre bolt.

6 Lift the rotor off the crankshaft **(see illustration)**.

7 If it is loose, remove the Woodruff key from the shaft for safekeeping, noting how it fits **(see illustration 16.10a)**.

8 The alternator stator coils and ignition pulse generator coil are wired together and have to be removed as an assembly. If not already done, trace the wiring back from the alternator and pulse generator and disconnect it at the connectors **(see illustration 4.12)**. Free the wiring from any clips or guides and feed it through to the alternator.

9 If not already done, undo the bolts securing the pulse generator coil, then undo the bolts securing the alternator stator and lift the assembly off **(see illustrations)**. Draw the rubber wiring boot out of the engine side cover and carefully pull the wiring away, noting how it fits.

Installation

10 Installation is the reverse of removal, noting the following:

● Ensure the wiring is correctly routed before installing the alternator stator and pulse generator.

● Tighten the stator and pulse generator bolts to the torque settings specified at the beginning of this Chapter.

● Make sure that no metal objects have attached themselves to the magnets on the inside of the rotor.

● Clean the tapered end of the crankshaft and the corresponding mating surface on the inside of the rotor with a suitable solvent.

● Fit the Woodruff key into the crankshaft, align the slot in the centre of the rotor with the key, then install the rotor **(see illustrations)**.

● Tighten the rotor centre nut to the specified torque setting.

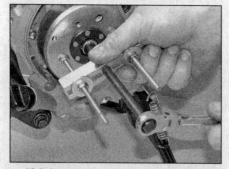

16.5 Locate the puller as shown then tighten the centre bolt

16.6 Remove the alternator rotor

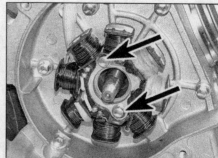

16.9a Location of the alternator stator mounting bolts

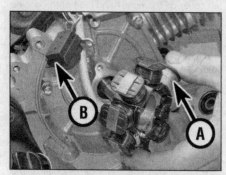

16.9b Remove the alternator stator (A) and pulse generator coil (B)

16.10a Location of the crankshaft Woodruff key

16.10b Align the slot (arrowed) in the centre of the rotor with the Woodruff key

17.4 Location of the crankshaft oil seal (arrowed)

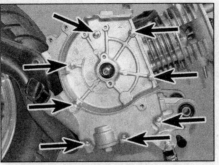

17.5 Undo the cover bolts, noting their locations

17.6 Draw the crankcase cover off

- Secure the wiring with any clips or ties.
- Ensure that the cooling fan and cover are correctly installed (see Section 7).

17 Right-hand crankcase cover

Removal

1 Remove the exhaust system (see Chapter 5).
2 Drain the engine oil (see Chapter 1, Section 6).
3 Follow the procedure in Section 16 and remove the alternator.
4 An oil seal is fitted in the cover where the crankshaft passes through it **(see illustration)**. Check around the seal for signs of oil leakage – if the seal has been leaking a new one must be fitted once the cover has been removed. **Note:** *It is good practice to renew the oil seal whenever the cover is removed.*
5 Position a drain tray underneath the engine to catch any residual oil when the cover is removed. Undo the cover bolts noting their locations **(see illustration)**.

 HAYNES HiNT *Make a cardboard template of the crankcase cover and punch a hole for each bolt location. This will ensure that they are all installed correctly on reassembly – this is important as the bolts are of different lengths.*

6 Draw the cover off **(see illustration)**. If the cover is stuck, tap around the joint face between the cover and the crankcase with a soft-faced mallet to free it. Do not try to lever the cover off as this may damage the sealing surfaces.
7 Remove the gasket and discard it as a new one must be used. Note any dowels in the cover or crankcase and remove them for safekeeping if they are loose.
8 Clean the mating surfaces of the cover and the crankcase with a suitable solvent to remove any traces of old gasket or sealant. Take care not to scratch or gouge the soft aluminium.
9 To renew the cover oil seal, support the cover on the work surface and drive the seal out from the outside with a suitably-sized socket **(see illustration)**. Note which way round the seal is fitted. Ensure that the seal

17.9 Drive the old seal out from the outside

housing is clean, then lubricate the new seal with a smear of engine oil and press it all the way into the housing from the inside.

Installation

10 If removed, fit the dowels into the crankcase, then fit a new cover gasket, making sure it locates correctly onto the dowels **(see illustration)**. If necessary, use a dab of grease to hold the gasket in position.
11 Lubricate the inside of the oil seal with engine oil, then install the cover taking care not to damage the seal on the crankshaft threads. Make sure that the gasket stays in place.
12 Install the cover bolts, making sure they are in the correct locations, then tighten the bolts evenly and in a criss-cross sequence to the torque setting specified at the beginning of this Chapter.
13 Install the remaining components in the reverse order of removal.
14 Fill the engine with the correct type and

18.2 Manoeuvre the starter pinion assembly out

17.10 Install a new cover gasket

quantity of oil (see Chapter 1 and *Pre-ride checks*)

18 Starter pinion assembly

Removal

1 Note the position of the starter motor, then remove the drive belt cover (see Chapter 3) and locate the pinion assembly adjacent to the variator pulley.
2 Withdraw the starter pinion assembly **(see illustration)**.

Inspection

3 Check the starter pinion assembly for any signs of damage or wear, particularly for chipped or broken teeth on either of the pinions **(see illustration)**. Check the corresponding

18.3 Inspect the starter pinion for damage and wear

18.4 Check the movement of the outer pinion

19.2 Using a piece of clean rag to lock the pinions together

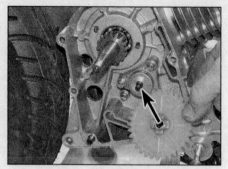

19.3 Note how the pinion locates on the pump shaft (arrowed)

19.4a Undo the retaining bolts (arrowed)...

19.4b ...and lift the pump off

19.4c Note the O-rings (A) and dowel (B)

teeth on the starter motor pinion and the ring gear around the outside of the variator pulley.
4 Rotate the outer pinion and check that it moves smoothly up and down the shaft, and that it returns easily to its rest position **(see illustration)**.
5 The starter pinion assembly is supplied as a complete unit; if any of the component parts is worn or damaged, the unit will have to be replaced with a new one. If the ring gear is worn or damaged refer to Chapter 3 and remove the outer half of the variator pulley.
6 The starter pinion mechanism should not be lubricated as any excess grease may contaminate the drive belt and cause it to slip. However, a smear of grease should be applied to both ends of the pinion shaft before reassembly.

Installation

7 Installation is the reverse of removal. Ensure

the inner pinion engages with the starter motor shaft.

19 Oil pump

Removal

1 Remove the right-hand crankcase cover (see Section 17).
2 Use a piece of clean, folded rag to lock the crankshaft and pump pinions together to prevent them turning, then undo the nut on the pump driveshaft **(see illustration)**.
3 Lift off the pump pinion, noting how it fits on the pump shaft **(see illustration)**.
4 Undo the bolts securing the pump and lift it out **(see illustrations)**. Note the location

of the O-rings in the crankcase oilways and discard them as new ones must be fitted on installation **(see illustration)**. Note the location of the dowel and remove it for safekeeping if it is loose.

Inspection

5 Check the pump body for obvious signs of damage especially around the mounting bolt holes. Turn the pump driveshaft by hand and check that the pump rotates smoothly **(see illustration)**.
6 If required, the pump can be disassembled for cleaning and inspection.
7 Undo the screws securing the cover to the pump body and remove cover, noting the location of the dowel between the cover and the body **(see illustrations)**.
8 Note any reference marks on the pump rotors; even if the rotors are not marked, it

19.5 Check that the pump rotates smoothly

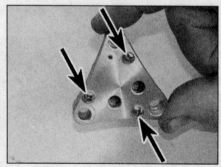

19.7a Undo the cover screws...

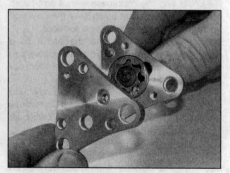

19.7b ...and lift off the cover...

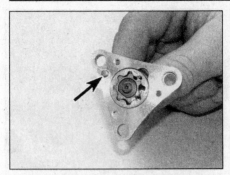

19.7c ...noting the location of the dowel

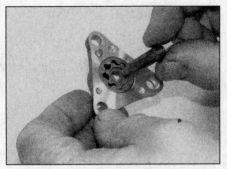

19.8a Lift out the pump shaft...

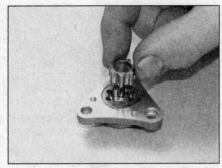

19.8b ...the inner rotor...

is essential that they are reassembled the correct way round. Lift out the pump shaft and the inner and outer rotors **(see illustrations)**.

9 Clean the pump components with a suitable solvent and dry them with compressed air, if available. Inspect the pump body, rotors and shaft for scoring and wear. If any damage, scoring, uneven or excessive wear is evident, renew the pump as an assembly.

10 If the pump is good, reassemble all the components in the reverse order of disassembly and lubricate them with clean engine oil.

11 Fit the dowel and the cover and tighten the screws securely, then rotate the pump shaft by hand to check that the rotors turn smoothly and freely.

12 Inspect the pump pinion and the crankshaft pinion or wear or damage. If necessary, fit a new pump pinion. The crankshaft pinion is part of the crankshaft assembly and is not available as a separate item **(see illustration)**.

Installation

13 Installation is the reverse of removal, noting the following:
● Fit new O-rings in the crankshaft oilways.
● Don't forget to fit the pump locating dowel.
● Tighten the pump mounting bolts to the torque setting specified at the beginning of this Chapter.

19.8c ...and the outer rotor

● Fill the engine with the correct type and quantity of oil (see Chapter 1 and *Pre-ride checks*).

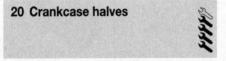

20 Crankcase halves

Separation

1 Follow the procedure in Section 4 and remove the engine from the frame.

2 Before the crankcase halves can be separated the following components must be removed:

19.12 Crankshaft pinion (arrowed) is integral with the crankshaft

● Cylinder head (Section 11)
● Cylinder (Section 13)
● Alternator (Section 16)
● Variator (Chapter 3)
● Starter motor (Chapter 10)
● Right-hand crankcase cover (Section 17)
● Oil pump (Section 19)
● Centrestand (Chapter 7)

3 Tape some rag around the connecting rod to prevent it knocking against the cases. Although not essential, it is advisable to remove the piston to avoid damage during this procedure.

4 Support the crankcase assembly on the work surface on its left-hand side. Loosen the remaining crankcase bolt **(see illustration)**.

20.4 Loosen the remaining crankcase bolt (arrowed)

20.5 Lift off the right-hand crankcase half

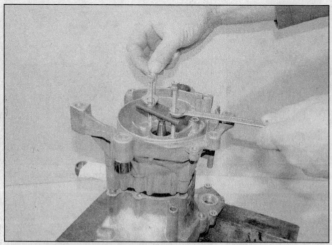

20.6 Using a puller to separate the crankcase halves

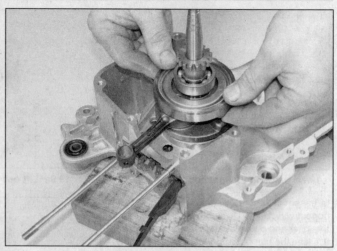

20.7 Lift the crankshaft assembly out of the left-hand crankcase half

20.8 Pressing the crankshaft out of the left-hand crankcase half

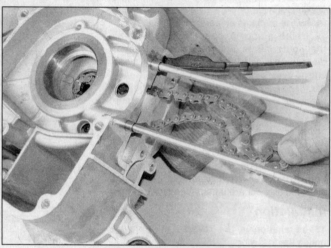

20.9 Remove the camchain

5 Lift the right-hand crankcase half off the left-hand half **(see illustration)**. If the crankcase halves do not separate easily, apply heat to the right-hand main bearing housing with a hot air gun and try lifting the right-hand half off again.
Caution: Do not try to separate the halves by levering against the mating surfaces as they are easily scored and will not seal correctly afterwards. Do not strike the ends of the crankshaft with a hammer as damage to the end threads or the shaft itself will result.
6 If the crankcase is an extremely tight fit on the crankshaft, a puller arrangement will be required to facilitate the procedure **(see illustration)**. If the puller is placed across the end of the crankshaft, thread the alternator centre nut on first to protect the threads. Take care to ensure that equal pressure is applied on both sides of the puller arrangement at all times and apply heat to the bearing housing.
7 Now lift the crankshaft assembly out of the left-hand crankcase half **(see illustration)**.

Apply heat to the main bearing housing if required. Ensure the camchain is clear of the crankshaft sprocket when the crankshaft is removed. Note that the main bearings will remain in place on the crankshaft assembly (see Section 21).
8 If the crankcase is an extremely tight fit on the crankshaft, use a similar set-up to the one in Step 6, only this time press the crankshaft out of the left-hand crankcase half **(see illustration)**. Thread the variator nut onto the end of the crankshaft to protect the threads and make sure the crankshaft assembly is supported to prevent it dropping if it suddenly comes free.
9 Remove the camchain and mark one side with a dab of paint so that it can be installed the same way round **(see illustration)**.
10 If not already done, undo the pivot bolt securing the camchain tensioner blade and lift the blade out **(see illustration 9.12)**. Note which way round the blade is fitted.
11 Remove the crankcase gasket and discard it as a new one must be used. Remove

any dowels from either crankcase half for safekeeping if they are loose.
12 Clean the mating surfaces of the crankcase halves with a suitable solvent to remove any traces of old gasket or sealant. Take care not to scratch or gouge the soft aluminium.
13 Note the position of the crankshaft oil seal in the left-hand crankcase half and note which way round it is fitted **(see illustration)**. Push

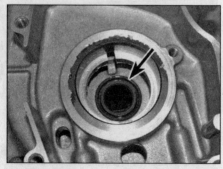

20.13 Location of the left-hand crankshaft oil seal

the seal out from the inside using a suitably sized socket and discard it as a new one must be fitted on reassembly.

14 If required, remove the transmission assembly from the left-hand crankcase half (see Chapter 3).

Inspection

15 Wash the cases in a suitable solvent and dry them with compressed air, if available.

16 Small cracks or holes in aluminium castings can be repaired with an epoxy resin adhesive as a temporary measure. Permanent repairs can only be effected by welding, and only a specialist in this process is in a position to advise on the economy or practical aspect of such a repair. On some engines, the crankcase halves can be renewed individually, on others the two halves are only available together as a matching set.

17 Damaged threads can be economically reclaimed by using a thread insert. Most small engineering firms offer a service of this kind. Sheared screws can usually be removed with screw extractors. Refer to *Tools and Workshop Tips* in the *Reference* section for further details.

18 Always wash the crankcases thoroughly after any repair work to ensure no dirt or metal swarf is trapped inside when the engine is rebuilt.

19 Inspect the engine mounting bushes **(see illustration)**. If they show signs of deterioration, renew them all at the same time. To remove a bush, first note its position in the casing. Heat the casing with a hot air gun, then support the casing and drive the bush out with a hammer and a suitably sized socket. Alternatively, use two suitably sized sockets to press the bush out in the jaws of a vice. Clean the bush housing with steel wool to remove any corrosion, then reheat the casing and fit the new bush. **Note:** *Always support the casing when removing or fitting bushes to avoid breaking the casing.*

20 Inspect the main bearing housings. If a

20.19 Inspect the engine mounting bushes

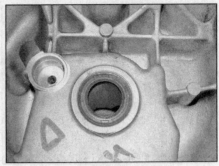

20.22 Install the crankshaft oil seal from the outside

bearing outer race has spun in its housing, the inside of the housing will be damaged. A bearing locking compound can be used to fix the outer race in place on reassembly if the damage is not too severe. **Note:** *If a bearing has spun in its housing, the bearing itself is likely to be damaged – see Section 21.*

21 Inspect the crankshaft assembly and bearings (see Section 21).

Reassembly

22 Fit the new crankshaft oil seal into the left-hand crankcase half and press it into place from the outside using a seal driver or socket **(see illustration)**. Ensure the seal is fitted the right way round and that it enters the case squarely. Lubricate the seal with clean engine oil.

23 Support the left-hand crankcase half on the work surface with enough space below it to provide clearance for the end of the crankshaft when it is fully installed. Position the camchain in the crankcase with clearance for the crankshaft sprocket **(see illustration)**.

24 Tape some rag around the connecting rod to prevent it knocking against the cases.

25 Lubricate the left-hand crankshaft main bearing with clean engine oil, then lower the crankshaft assembly into the crankcase half carefully to avoid damaging the seal. Ensure

that the main bearing is aligned with the bearing housing and that the connecting rod is aligned with the crankcase mouth. Press the crankshaft assembly in fully so that the main bearing goes all the way into its housing. If the main bearing does not seat fully, apply heat with a hot air gun around the bearing housing while keeping steady pressure to the crankshaft assembly. **Note:** *Avoid applying direct heat onto the crankshaft oil seal.* If required, a freeze spray can be used on the main bearing to aid installation.

26 Ensure that the camchain is correctly located around the crankshaft sprocket and secure it in position with wire or a cable-tie to avoid it becoming jammed inside the crankcase.

27 If necessary, allow the case to cool, then wipe the mating surfaces of both crankcase halves with a rag soaked in suitable solvent . Fit the dowels and install the new crankcase gasket on the mating surface of the left-hand case.

28 Lubricate the right-hand main bearing with clean engine oil, then lower the crankcase half over the crankshaft. Ensure that the two halves of the crankcase are correctly aligned, taking special note of the position of the dowels, and that the main bearing is aligned with the bearing housing in the right-hand case **(see illustration)**.

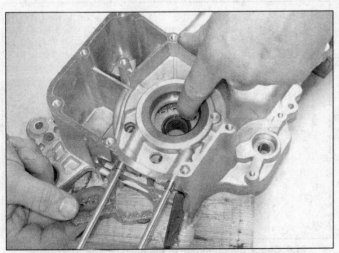

20.23 Position the camchain in the left-hand crankcase half

20.28 Lower the crankcase half into position carefully

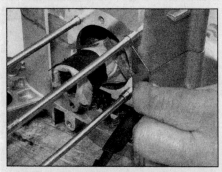

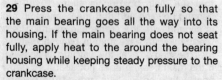

20.32 Trim off the excess gasket with a sharp blade

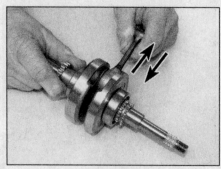

21.4 Check for up-and-down play in the big-end bearing

29 Press the crankcase on fully so that the main bearing goes all the way into its housing. If the main bearing does not seat fully, apply heat to the around the bearing housing while keeping steady pressure to the crankcase.

30 Check that the crankcase halves are seated all the way round. If the cases are not correctly seated, heat the bearing housings while applying firm pressure. **Note:** *Do not attempt to pull the crankcase halves together using the crankcase bolts as the casing will crack and be ruined.*

31 Clean the threads of the crankcase bolt and install it finger-tight, then tighten it to the torque setting specified at the beginning of this Chapter.

32 Trim off any excess gasket across the crankcase mouth **(see illustration)**.

33 Support the connecting rod and rotate the crankshaft by hand – if there are any signs of undue stiffness, tight or rough spots, or of any other problem, the fault must be rectified before proceeding further. Don't forget to support the camchain while rotating the crankshaft.

34 If required, install the camchain tensioner blade **(see illustration 9.12)**.

35 Install the remaining components in the reverse order of removal.

21 Crankshaft assembly, big-end and main bearings

Note: *The crankshaft assembly is pressed together and is easily damaged if it is dropped.*

1 To access the crankshaft assembly, the big-end bearing and the main bearings, the crankcase must be split into two parts (see Section 20).

2 The crankshaft assembly should give many thousands of miles of service. The most likely problems to occur will be a worn small or big-end bearing due to poor lubrication. A worn big-end bearing will produce a pronounced knocking noise, most audible when the engine is under load, and increasing as engine speed rises. This should not be confused with small-end bearing wear, which produces a lighter, metallic rattle (see Section 14).

3 When the crankcase halves are separated, the main bearings will remain in place on the crankshaft assembly – they are not normally available as separate items. If the main bearings have failed, excessive rumbling and vibration will be felt when the engine is running.

4 To assess the condition of the big-end bearing, hold the crankshaft assembly firmly and push and pull on the connecting rod, checking for any up-and-down freeplay between the two **(see illustration)**. If any freeplay is noted, the bearing is worn.

5 A small amount of big-end side clearance (side-to-side movement) is acceptable on the connecting rod. Measure the clearance with a feeler gauge **(see illustration)**, then compare the result with the service limit specified at the beginning of this Chapter.

6 Follow the procedure in *Tools and Workshop Tips* in the *Reference* section to check the condition of the main bearings **(see illustration)**.

7 If wear or damage is noted in any of the crankshaft assembly bearings, a new crankshaft assembly will have to be fitted. **Note:** *Evidence of extreme heat, such as discoloration or blueing, indicates that lubrication failure has occurred. Be sure to check the oil pump and bearing oil ways in the crankcases before reassembling the engine.*

8 If available, place the crankshaft assembly on V-blocks and check the runout at either end using a dial gauge – see *Specifications* at the beginning of this Chapter. If the crankshaft is out-of-true it will cause excessive engine vibration. If there is any doubt about the condition of the crankshaft have it checked by an automotive engineer.

9 Inspect the threads on each end of the crankshaft and ensure that the retaining nuts for the alternator rotor and the variator are a good fit. Inspect the splines for the variator pulley on the left-hand end of the shaft **(see**

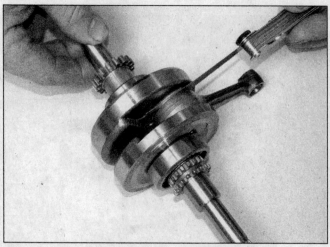

21.5 Measuring big-end side clearance

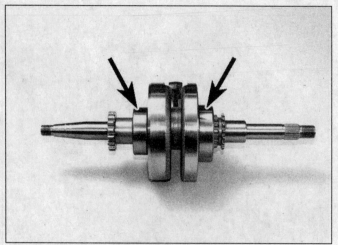

21.6 Check the condition of the main bearings (arrowed)

21.9a Inspect the camshaft drive sprocket (A) and variator splines (B)

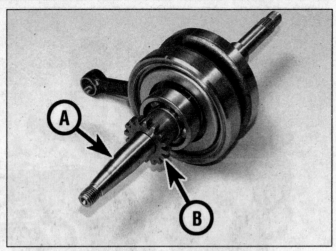

21.9b Inspect the alternator taper (A) and oil pump drive pinion (B)

illustration). Inspect the taper and the slot in the right-hand end of the shaft for the alternator Woodruff key **(see illustration)**. Damage or wear that prevents the rotor from being fitted securely will require a new crankshaft assembly.

10 Inspect the camshaft drive sprocket teeth and the oil pump pinion for damage or wear **(see illustrations 21.9a and b)**. The sprocket and pinion are installed as an integral part of the crankshaft assembly – if they are worn or damaged a new assembly will have to be fitted.

22 Initial start-up after overhaul/running-in

Initial start-up after overhaul

1 Make sure the engine oil level is correct (see *Pre-ride checks*).

2 Make sure there is fuel in the tank.

3 With the ignition OFF, operate the kickstart a couple of times to check that the engine turns over easily.

4 Turn the ignition ON, start the engine and allow it to run at a slow idle until it reaches operating temperature. Do not be alarmed if there is a little smoke from the exhaust – this will be due to the oil used to lubricate the piston and bore during assembly and should subside after a while.

5 If the engine proves reluctant to start, remove the spark plug and check that it has not become wet and oily. If it has, clean it and try again. If the engine refuses to start, go through the fault finding charts at the end of this manual to identify the problem.

6 Check carefully for fuel and oil leaks and make sure the transmission and controls, especially the brakes, function properly before road testing the machine.

7 Upon completion of the road test, and after the engine has cooled down completely, recheck the valve clearances (see Chapter 1).

Recheck the engine oil level (see *Pre-ride checks*).

Recommended running-in procedure

8 Treat the engine gently for the first few miles to allow any new parts to bed in.

9 If a new piston, cylinder or crankshaft assembly has been fitted, the engine will have to be run-in as when new. This means a restraining hand on the throttle until at least 300 miles (500 km) have been covered. There's no point in keeping to any set speed limit – the main idea is to gradually increase performance up to the 600 mile (1000 km) mark. Make sure that the throttle position is varied to vary engine speed, and use full throttle only for short bursts. Experience is the best guide, since it's easy to tell when an engine is running freely.

10 Pay particular attention to the *Pre-ride checks* at the beginning of this manual and investigate the cause of any oil loss immediately. Check the tightness of all relevant nuts and bolts (see Chapter 1).

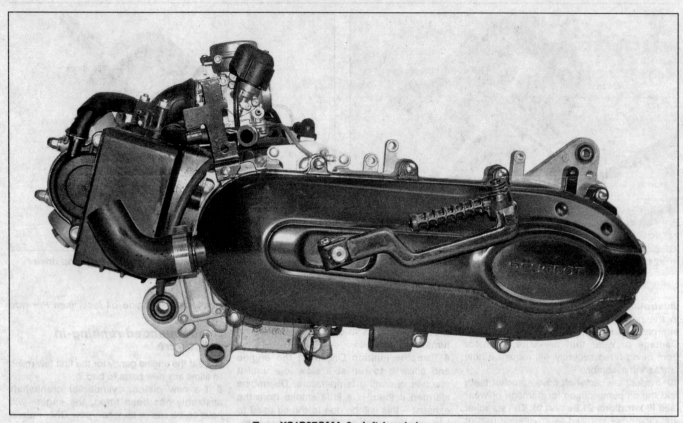

Type XS1P37QMA-2 – left-hand view

Type XS1P37QMA-2 – right-hand view

Chapter 2D
Four-stroke 50cc engine – type XS1P37QMA-2

Refer to 'Model and servicing specifications' in Chapter 1 for model identification details

Contents

Degrees of difficulty

Easy, suitable for novice with little experience 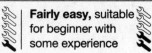	**Fairly easy,** suitable for beginner with some experience	**Fairly difficult,** suitable for competent DIY mechanic	**Difficult,** suitable for experienced DIY mechanic	**Very difficult,** suitable for expert DIY or professional

Specifications

General

Type	Single cylinder 2-valve air-cooled four-stroke
Capacity	.49.5 cc
Bore x stroke	37 x 46 mm
Cylinder compression.	138 psi (8.95 Bar) @ 550rpm

Cylinder head

Warpage (max)	0.05 mm

Valves

Valve clearances.	See Chapter 1

Cylinder bore

Standard	36.995 to 37.015 mm
Service limit	37.5 mm

Piston

Diameter (measured 9 mm up from the bottom of the skirt)

Standard	36.985 to 37.005 mm
Service limit	36.9 mm

Piston rings

Ring end gap (installed)

Top and second ring.	0.015 to 0.050 mm
Oil control ring	0.20 to 0.70 mm

Crankshaft and connecting rod

Big-end side clearance (service limit).	0.55 mm
Crankshaft runout	
Measured 90 mm from left-hand flywheel face	0.10 mm
Measured 60 mm from right-hand flywheel face	0.10 mm

Torque settings

Alternator rotor nut	55 Nm
Alternator stator/pulse generator coil screws	10 Nm
Cam chain tensioner blade bolt	10 Nm
Cam chain tensioner bolts	10 Nm
Cam chain tensioner cap bolt	8 Nm
Camshaft sprocket bolt	20 Nm
Camshaft sprocket cover screws	10 Nm
Camshaft stopper plate screw	15 Nm
Cooling fan bolts	10 Nm
Crankcase bolts	12 Nm
Cylinder head	
Nuts	20 Nm
Bolts	12 Nm
Drive belt cover screws	10 Nm
Engine mounting bolt/nut	60 Nm
Exhaust manifold	15 Nm
Intake manifold nuts	10 Nm
Oil pump mounting screws	10 Nm
Rear shock absorber mounting bolts	
Vivacity	
Upper	45 Nm
Lower	25 Nm
Tweet	
Upper	40 Nm
Lower	28 Nm
Rear wheel nut	
Vivacity	120 Nm
Tweet	110 Nm
Starter clutch housing bolts	12 Nm
Starter clutch nut (LH)	90 Nm
Valve covers	15 Nm

1 General information

The engine is a single cylinder, overhead-camshaft four-stroke, with fan assisted air cooling as fitted to Vivacity 50 4T and Tweet 50 scooters. The camshaft is chain-driven off the crankshaft and operates the valves via rocker arms.

The crankshaft assembly is pressed together, incorporating the connecting rod and big-end bearing.

The crankcase divides vertically – the left-hand crankcase is an integral part of the drive belt casing and gearbox.

2 Component access

A number of components, with the obvious exception of the crankshaft assembly and its bearings, can be worked on without having to remove the engine/transmission unit from the scooter. However, access to some components is severely restricted, and if several of areas require attention at the same time, removal of the engine is recommended, as it is an easy task to undertake.

3 Cylinder compression test

Refer to Chapter 2C, Section 3, noting the compression figure given at the beginning of this chapter.

4 Engine removal and installation

Caution: The engine/transmission unit is not heavy, however removal and installation should be carried out with the aid of an assistant; personal injury or damage could occur if the engine falls or is dropped.

Removal

1 Support the scooter securely in an upright position. Work can be made easier by raising the machine to a suitable height on a hydraulic ramp or a suitable platform. Make sure it is secure and will not topple over.

2 Disconnect and remove the battery (see Chapter 10).

3 If required, drain the engine oil (see Chapter 1).

4 Remove the storage compartment, the under-seat panel (Vivacity models) and the seat cowling (see Chapter 9).

5 Remove the air filter housing (see Chapter 5). Release the clip securing the large bore hose from the pulse-air reed valve to the exhaust system **(see illustration)** then remove the exhaust system (see Chapter 5).

6 Pull the spark plug cap off the plug and

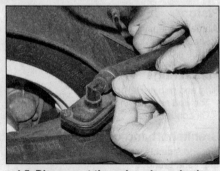

4.5 Disconnect the pulse-air reed valve hose

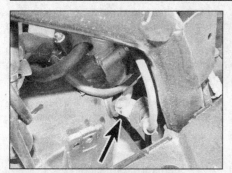

4.6 Pull off the spark plug cap (arrowed)

4.7 Disconnect the carburettor heater wiring terminals

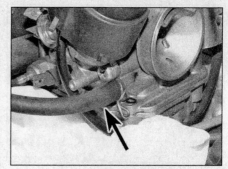

4.8 Disconnect the fuel hose

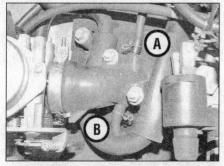

4.9 Pulse-air vacuum hose (A), fuel pump vacuum hose (B) – Vivacity models

4.10 Disconnect the throttle cable (arrowed)

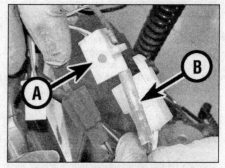

4.11 Alternator (A) and ignition pulse generator (B) wiring connectors

position the cap clear of the engine (see illustration).

7 Trace the wiring from the automatic choke unit on the carburettor and disconnect it at the connector. Note: When disconnecting any wiring, it is advisable to mark or tag the wires as a reminder of where they connect. Where fitted, disconnect the carburettor heater wiring from the terminals on the carburettor (see illustration).

8 Disconnect the fuel hose from its union on the carburettor, being prepared to catch any residual fuel in a rag (see illustration). Position a suitable container below the carburettor drain hose, then loosen the drain screw and drain any residual fuel from the float chamber. Tighten the drain screw.

9 On Vivacity models, disconnect the pulse-air vacuum hose from its union on the carburettor intake manifold, then disconnect the fuel

pump vacuum hose from the manifold (see illustration). On Tweet models, disconnect the fuel tap vacuum hose from the T-piece union alongside the carburettor.

10 Disconnect the throttle cable from the carburettor pulley (see illustration). Secure the throttle cable clear of the engine unit.

11 Trace the wiring for the alternator and ignition pulse generator coil from the top of the alternator cover on the right-hand side of the engine and disconnect it at the connectors (see illustration). Release the wiring on the engine side of the loom from any clips or ties.

12 The starter motor is located on the top of the engine. Trace the wiring from the starter motor terminal and earth terminal and disconnect it at the connector (see illustration).

13 If required, remove the rear wheel (see Chapter 8). Note: The rear wheel and stand

provide a convenient support for the unit once it is removed from the scooter. However, it is useful to loosen the rear wheel nut at this point before disconnecting the rear brake.

14 Disconnect the brake cable from the brake arm (see Chapter 8). Release the cable from the clip securing the cable to the underside of the transmission casing and detach the cable (see illustration).

15 Before the engine with the centrestand can be removed, a means of supporting the scooter must be devised. A double A-frame hoist is ideally suited to most machines once the rear bodywork has been removed and where the front of the scooter can be firmly secured (see illustration 4.17a in Chapter 2A). Alternatively, the scooter can be supported from underneath provided the weight is taken on the frame tubes and not on any bodywork or the fuel tank (see illustration).

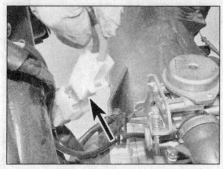

4.12 Disconnect the starter motor wiring connector (arrowed)

4.14 Release the brake cable from the underside of the casing

4.15 Support the weight of the scooter on wooden blocks

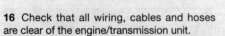

4.18 Undo the nut (arrowed) on the mounting bolt...

4.19 ...then withdraw the bolt carefully

16 Check that all wiring, cables and hoses are clear of the engine/transmission unit.
17 Undo the upper rear shock absorber mounting bolt, then support the weight of the engine and rear wheel and withdraw the bolt. Lower the wheel to the ground. Undo the lower shock mounting bolt and remove the shock (see Chapter 7).
18 Undo the locknut and washer on the engine mounting bolt **(see illustration)**. Note: *Peugeot recommends a new nut should be used on reassembly. Alternatively, clean the threads of the engine mounting bolt and apply a suitable thread-locking compound prior to installation.*
19 Have an assistant support the engine unit, then carefully withdraw the engine mounting bolt **(see illustration)**. Manoeuvre the engine unit back and out of the frame.

20 If the engine is dirty, particularly around its mountings, wash it thoroughly before starting any major dismantling work. This will make work much easier and rule out the possibility of dirt falling inside.
21 If required, remove the rear wheel (see Chapter 8) and the centrestand (see Chapter 7).

Installation

22 Installation is the reverse of removal, noting the following:
● Make sure no wires, cables or hoses become trapped between the engine and the frame when installing the engine.
● Tighten the engine mounting bolt, shock absorber bolts and wheel nut to the torque settings specified at the beginning of this Chapter.

● Make sure all wires, cables and hoses are correctly routed and connected, and secured by any clips or ties.
● If the engine oil was drained, or if any oil has been lost during overhaul, refill or top up as described in Chapter 1 and *Pre-ride checks*.
● Check the operation of the rear brake before riding the machine (see Chapter 1).

5 Disassembly and reassembly – general information

1 Refer to the general notes in Chapter 2C, Section 5.
2 For this engine, disassembly should be done in the following general order with reference to the appropriate Sections (refer to Chapter 3 for details of transmission components):
● Remove the engine cowling
● Remove the cylinder head
● Remove the camshaft and rockers
● Remove the cylinder
● Remove the piston
● Remove the alternator
● Remove the variator (see Chapter 3)
● Remove the starter clutch
● Remove the starter motor (see Chapter 10)
● Remove the oil pump
● Separate the crankcase halves
● Remove the crankshaft

6 Engine cowling and cooling fan

1 Undo the bolts securing the fan cover and lift it off **(see illustrations)**.
2 Undo the bolts securing the right-hand half of the engine cowling **(see illustration)**. Release the clip holding the two halves of the cowling together and lift off the right-hand half **(see illustrations)**.
3 Remove the carburettor and the intake manifold (see Chapter 5).
4 Undo the bolt securing the left-hand half of

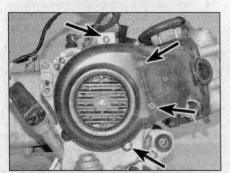

6.1a Undo the bolts...

6.1b ...and remove the fan cover

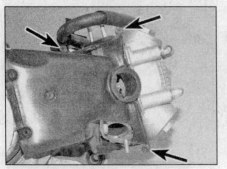

6.2a Undo the bolts (arrowed)

6.2b Release the clip (arrowed)...

6.2c ...and remove the right-hand half

6.4a Undo the bolt (arrowed)...

6.4b ...and remove the left-hand half

6.5a Undo the cooling fan mounting bolts (arrowed)...

the engine cowling and lift it off over the cam chain tensioner **(see illustrations)**.

5 Undo the four bolts securing the cooling fan to the alternator rotor and remove the fan **(see illustrations)**.

6 Installation is the reverse of removal. Tighten the cooling fan bolts to the torque setting specified at the beginning of this Chapter.

7 Ensure both halves of the cowling and the fan cover are correctly aligned, then tighten the mounting bolts securely.

7 Camchain tensioner

Removal

1 The camchain tensioner is located on the back of the cylinder on the left-hand side. Remove the engine cowling for access (see Section 6).

2 Remove the spark plug (see Chapter 1, Section 15). Remove both valve inspection caps **(see illustration)**.

3 Undo the two screws securing the camshaft sprocket cover and lift the cover off **(see illustration)**. Note the location of the O-ring seal and discard it if it is damaged or distorted. Fit a new O-ring on installation **(see illustration)**.

4 Turn the engine in the normal direction of rotation until the piston is at top dead centre (TDC) on its compression stroke. You can

6.5b ...and lift off the fan

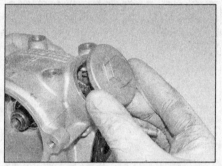

7.2 Unscrew the valve inspection caps

7.3a Remove the camshaft sprocket cover

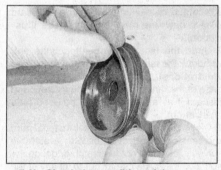

7.3b Check the condition of the cover O-ring

do this by rotating the crankshaft via the alternator rotor. The position of the piston can be confirmed by ensuring that the timing mark on the camshaft sprocket aligns with the mark on the outside edge of the inspection aperture

(see illustration). The T mark on the alternator rotor should align with the static timing mark on the crankcase **(see illustration)**.

5 Undo the tensioner cap bolt and remove the spring **(see illustration)**.

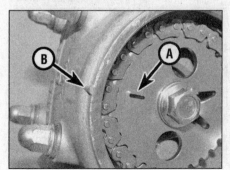

7.4a Mark on camshaft sprocket (A) should align with mark on casing (B)

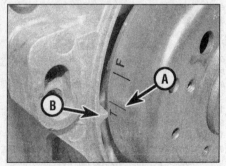

7.4b T mark (A) on the alternator rotor should align with the static timing mark (B)

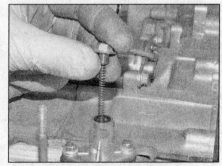

7.5 Undo the cap bolt and remove the spring

7.6 Discard the cap bolt O-ring

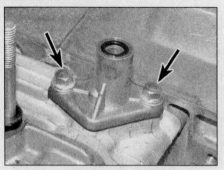

7.7a Undo the mounting bolts...

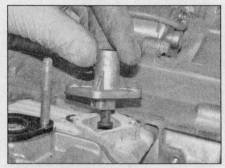

7.7b ...and withdraw the tensioner body

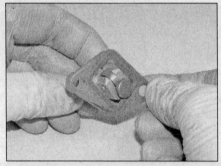

7.7c Remove the old tensioner gasket

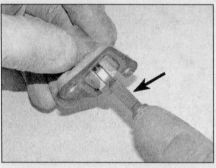

7.10 Inspect the ratchet teeth for wear

6 Note the location of the O-ring and discard it as a new one must be fitted (see illustration).

7 Undo the tensioner mounting bolts and withdraw the tensioner from the cylinder (see illustrations). Remove the gasket from the base of the tensioner or from the cylinder and discard it as a new one must be used (see illustration).

8 Clean all traces of old gasket material from the tensioner and cylinder with a suitable solvent. Take care not to scratch or gouge the soft aluminium. Be careful not to let any of the gasket material fall into the engine.

Inspection

9 Examine the tensioner components for signs of wear or damage.

10 Release the catch on the ratchet with a small screwdriver and pull the plunger out from the tensioner body, then examine the teeth on the ratchet (see illustration). Now try to press the plunger back into the body – it should be locked in position.

11 Release the catch on the ratchet and ensure that the plunger moves freely in and out of the tensioner body.

12 To test the operation of the tensioner, press the plunger into the body and temporarily install the tensioner on the back of the cylinder, then fit the spring and cap bolt. Now unscrew the cap bolt and withdraw the spring. Insert a small screwdriver into the tensioner and try to push the plunger out further against the pressure of the tensioner blade. If the

plunger moves, then the spring has lost its tension.

13 If any part of the tensioner is worn or damaged, or if the plunger is seized in the body, a new tensioner must be fitted.

Installation

14 Release the ratchet mechanism and press the tensioner plunger all the way into the tensioner body. Fit a new gasket on the tensioner body (see illustration 7.7c).

15 Install the tensioner in the cylinder and tighten the mounting bolts. Fit a new cap bolt O-ring (see illustration 7.6).

16 Turn the engine in the normal direction of rotation – this removes all the slack in the front run of the chain between the crankshaft and the camshaft, and transfers it to the back run where it will be taken up by the tensioner. Note: *Take care when turning the engine with the tensioner spring removed to avoid the chain jumping over the teeth on the camshaft sprocket. If this happens, ensure that the timing marks on the alternator rotor and on the camshaft sprocket are correctly re-aligned with the piston at TDC before installing the tensioner spring (see Chapter 1, Section 14).*

17 Install the spring and tighten the cap bolt securely (see illustration 7.5).

18 Check that the camchain is tensioned around the camshaft sprocket. If it is slack, the tensioner plunger did not release. Remove the tensioner and check the operation of the plunger again.

19 Install the remaining components in the reverse order of removal.

Caution: After installing the camchain tensioner, turn the crankshaft and check that all the timing marks still align correctly. If the timing marks are not aligned exactly as described, the valve timing will be incorrect and the valves may strike the piston, causing extensive damage to the engine.

8 Camchain, blades and sprockets

Camchain

Inspection

1 The camchain runs between the drive sprocket on the crankshaft and the camshaft sprocket. To check the condition of the chain, first remove the camchain sprocket cover (see Section 7).

2 Remove the fan cover (see Section 6) and the spark plug (see Chapter 1, Section 15).

3 Using the alternator rotor, turn the engine slowly in the normal direction of rotation and inspect the inside edges of the chain links for wear (see illustration).

4 Remove the camchain tensioner (see Section 7). Note the position of the plunger, then press a small screwdriver into the tensioner to see how much adjustment

8.3 Inspect the cam chain links for wear as described

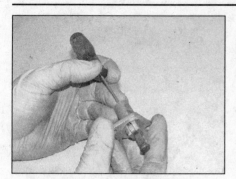

8.4 Checking the movement on the camchain tensioner plunger

8.12a Undo the pivot bolt, noting O-ring (arrowed)...

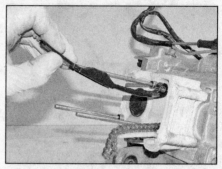

8.12b ...and withdraw the tensioner blade

remains on the plunger (see illustration). If there are only two or three clicks of movement left, the chain and/or tensioner blade are worn and must be renewed.

5 Hold the chain at the mid-way point around the camshaft sprocket and try to lift it off the sprocket. The chain should be a firm fit on the sprocket. Turn the engine carefully in the normal direction of rotation (see **Note** in Section 7, Step 16 above) and check the entire length of the chain.

6 If any of the above checks indicate that the camchain has worn, a new one must be fitted.

Removal and installation

7 If the camchain is to be removed, follow the procedure in Section 19 and separate the crankcase halves. The camchain can be removed with the crankshaft assembly.

8 On installation, before installing the chain onto the camshaft sprocket, ensure that the piston is at TDC on the compression stroke and that the timing mark T on the alternator rotor is aligned with the static timing mark on the crankcase (see illustration 7.4b). Position the timing mark on the camshaft sprocket as noted on removal – the camshaft lobes should face down away from the rocker arms. Ensure any slack in the chain is in the top run where it will be taken up by the tensioner

Camchain tensioner and guide blades

9 The camchain tensioner blade is located

inside the camchain tunnel and is secured by a pivot bolt on its lower end.

10 To inspect the blade, first remove the cylinder head (see Section 9). Secure the camchain to prevent it falling down into the tunnel.

11 Remove the variator (see Chapter 3).

12 Undo the pivot bolt securing the tensioner blade and lift the blade out (see illustrations). Note which way round the blade is fitted.

13 The guide blade can be lifted out once the cylinder head has been removed (see Section 9). Note how the guide blade is fitted (see illustration).

14 Check both blades for wear or damage and renew them if necessary. Check the operation of the camchain tensioner (see Section 7).

15 Installation is the reverse of removal. Ensure that the blades are fitted the correct way round (see illustrations 8.12b and 13). Inspect the O-ring seal fitted to the tensioner blade pivot (see illustration 8.12a) – if it is damaged or distorted fit a new one prior to installation. Apply non-permanent thread-locking compound to the threads of the pivot bolt and tighten it securely.

Camchain sprockets

16 Follow the procedure in Section 9 to remove the camshaft sprocket.

17 Check for wear on the sides and tips of the sprocket teeth and for chipped or hooked teeth.

18 Similar checks should be made on the crankshaft sprocket – this is integral with the crankshaft assembly and can only be inspected once the crankcase halves have been separated (see Section 19).

19 If the sprocket teeth are worn, the chain will also be worn. Always renew the components as an assembly – worn sprockets will soon damage a new chain.

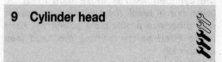

9 Cylinder head

Caution: The engine must be completely cool before beginning this procedure or the cylinder head may become warped.

Removal

1 Remove the carburettor, intake manifold and exhaust system (see Chapter 5).

2 Remove the fan cover and engine cowling (see Section 6).

3 Remove the camchain tensioner (see Section 7).

4 Using a suitable pin wrench to hold the camshaft sprocket and prevent it turning, undo the camshaft sprocket bolt and washer (see illustrations).

5 Note how the tab at the centre of the sprocket locates on the end of the camshaft

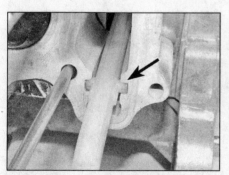

8.13 Location of the guide blade in the top of the cylinder

9.4a Hold the camshaft sprocket with a pin wrench...

9.4b ...and undo the bolt and washer

9.5a Note location of the tab (arrowed)

9.5b Lift the chain off the sprocket...

9.5c ...and remove the sprocket

(see illustration). Disengage the camchain from the sprocket and lift the sprocket out (see illustrations). Secure the chain to prevent it falling into the engine.

6 Undo the two bolts securing the left-hand side of the cylinder head (see illustration).

7 Unscrew the cylinder head nuts evenly and a little at a time in a criss-cross sequence until they are loose and remove them with the washers (see illustration). **Note:** *The cylinder head studs pass down through the cylinder and screw into the crankcase. Once the cylinder head is loose care must be taken not to break the cylinder base gasket seal otherwise a new base gasket will have to be fitted before refitting the head (see Section 12).*

8 Lift the cylinder head off the cylinder, feeding the camchain down through the tunnel in the head (see illustration). If the head is stuck, tap around the joint face between the head and the cylinder with a soft-faced mallet to free it. Do not try to lever the head off as this may damage the sealing surfaces.

9 Remove the old cylinder head gasket, noting how it fits (see illustration). Note the two dowels and remove them for safekeeping if they are loose – the dowels may be in the underside of the head or the cylinder (see illustration).

10 Secure the camchain to prevent it dropping into the engine.

11 If required, the camchain guide blade can be removed – draw the blade out, noting how the lugs locate in the recess in the top edge of the camchain tunnel (see illustration).

12 Stuff a clean rag into the camchain tunnel in the cylinder to prevent anything falling into the engine.

13 Clean all traces of old gasket material from the cylinder head and cylinder with a suitable solvent. Take care not to scratch or gouge the soft aluminium. Be careful not to let any of the gasket material fall into the crankcase, the cylinder bore or the oil passages.

14 Inspect the cylinder head gasket and the mating surfaces on the cylinder head and cylinder for signs of leaks, which could indicate that the head is warped. Refer to Chapter 2A, Section 12 and check the head mating surface for warpage.

15 After inspection, discard the old gasket as a new one must be fitted on reassembly

Installation

16 Installation is the reverse of removal, noting the following:

● Lubricate the cylinder bore with clean engine oil.

● Ensure the dowels are correctly installed in the cylinder.

● If removed, install the camchain guide blade (see Step 11).

9.6 Undo the cylinder head bolts

9.7 Undo the cylinder head nuts evenly

9.8 Lift off the cylinder head

9.9a Remove the old head gasket

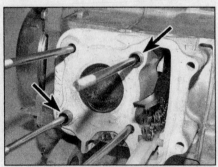

9.9b Location of the cylinder head dowels

9.11 Lift out the camchain guide blade

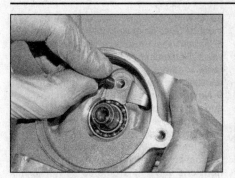

10.3 Undo the screw and remove the stopper plate

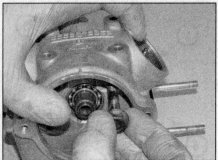

10.4a Thread a bolt into the end of the rocker shaft...

10.4b ...then draw the shaft (arrowed) out

- Install a new head gasket – never re-use the old gasket.
- Ensure the camchain is correctly located around the crankshaft sprocket.
- Tighten the cylinder head nuts evenly and a little at a time in a criss-cross pattern to the torque setting specified at the beginning of this Chapter, then tighten the bolts to the specified torque.
- Check the valve clearances (see Chapter 1).

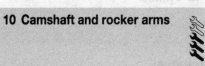

10 Camshaft and rocker arms

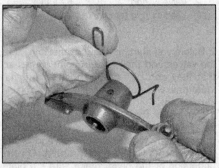

10.4c Note how the springs fit on the rocker arms

10.5 Draw out the camshaft assembly

Removal

1 Remove the camchain tensioner (see Section 7).
2 Remove the cylinder head (see Section 9).
3 Undo the screw securing the camshaft stopper plate and remove the plate, noting how it fits **(see illustration)**.
4 Working on one rocker arm at a time, thread an 8 mm bolt into the end of the shaft, then support the arm and draw the shaft out **(see illustrations)**. Note the location of the springs on the rocker arms **(see illustration)**. Mark the rocker arms so that they can be can be installed in their original positions and slide them back onto their shafts.
5 Draw out the camshaft together with the camshaft bearings **(see illustration)**.
6 If required, go to Section 11 to remove the valve assemblies.

Inspection

7 Clean all of the components with a suitable solvent and dry them.
8 Inspect the camshaft lobes for heat discoloration (blue appearance), score marks, chipped areas, flat spots and spalling **(see illustration)**. If damage is noted or wear is excessive, the camshaft must be renewed.
9 Check the condition of the camshaft bearings (see *Tools and Workshop Tips* in the Reference section). If the bearings are worn a new camshaft and bearing assembly will have to be fitted. **Note:** *If the camshaft is good, check with a bearing specialist or automotive engineer as to whether the bearings can be renewed separately.*
10 Check the bearing housings in the cylinder head for score marks and spalling **(see illustration)**. Any damage is an indication that the bearing has seized on the camshaft and

turned inside its housing. Prior to reassembly, check that the outer race is a tight fit in its housing, otherwise use some bearing locking compound to hold it in position.
11 Inspect the face of the rocker arm and the contact area between the adjuster screw and the valve stem for pits and spalling. If required, the adjuster screws are available as separate items.
12 Check the rocker shaft for wear. If available, use a micrometer to measure the diameter of the shaft in several places. **Note:** *Any variation in the measurements is an indication of wear on the shaft.*
13 If the rocker shaft is good, check for freeplay between the rocker arm and its shaft **(see illustration)**. The arm should be a sliding fit on the shaft with no discernible freeplay – if it has worn internally a new one will have to be fitted.

10.8 Inspect the camshaft lobes (arrowed) for wear and damage

10.10 Inspect the camshaft bearing housings (arrowed)

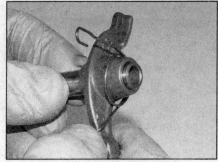

10.13 Check for freeplay between the rocker arm and its shaft

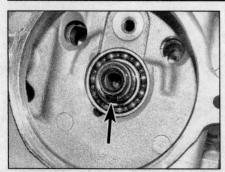

10.14 Note position of the slot (arrowed)

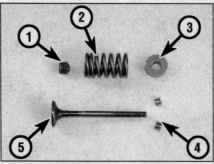

11.2 Valve components

1 *Valve stem seal*   4 *Collets*
2 *Valve spring*   5 *Valve*
3 *Valve spring retainer*

Installation

14 Installation is the reverse of removal, noting the following:

● Lubricate the shafts, bearing surfaces and bearings with clean engine oil before installation.
● Press the camshaft assembly all the way into the cylinder head. Position the slot in the left-hand end of the camshaft in the 6 o'clock position to allow for the fitting of the rocker arms **(see illustration)**.
● Don't forget to install the springs on the rocker arms before installing the rocker shafts.
● Position the rocker shafts so that the holes for the cylinder studs are clear.
● Apply non-permanent thread-locking compound to the threads of the camshaft stopper plate screw and tighten it to the torque setting specified at the beginning of this Chapter.
● Fit new O-ring seals to the rocker arm covers if required.

11 Cylinder head and valves

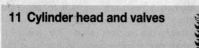

Note: *If a valve spring compressor is available, the home mechanic can remove the valves from the cylinder head, lap in the valves and renew the valve stem seals.*

Disassembly

1 If not already done, remove the camshaft and rocker arms (see Section 10).

2 Before you start, arrange to label and store the valves and their related components so that they can be returned to their original locations without getting mixed up **(see illustration)**.
3 Compress the valve spring on the first valve with a spring compressor, making sure it is correctly located onto each end of the valve assembly **(see illustrations)**. On the underside of the head, make sure the plate on the compressor only contacts the valve and not the soft aluminium of the head – if the plate is too big for the valve, use a spacer between them. Do not compress the spring any more than is absolutely necessary to release the collets; remove the collets using either needle-nose pliers, a magnet or a screwdriver with a dab of grease on it.
4 Carefully release the valve spring compressor and remove the spring retainer, noting which way up it fits.
5 Remove the valve spring. **Note:** *On some engines the valve springs have closer wound coils that are fitted next to the cylinder head. On the engine photographed, the upper ends of the springs were marked with a dab of paint.*
6 Turn the head over and withdraw the valve – if it binds in the guide (won't pull through), push it back into the head and deburr the area around the collet groove with a very fine file.
7 Once the valve has been removed, pull the valve stem oil seal off the top of the valve

guide with pliers and discard it as a new one must be used on reassembly.
8 Repeat the procedure for the remaining valve. Remember to keep the parts for each valve together and in order so they can be reinstalled in the correct location.
9 Next, clean the cylinder head with solvent and dry it thoroughly. Compressed air will speed the drying process and ensure that all holes and recessed areas are clean.
10 Clean the valve springs, collets and retainers with solvent. Work on the parts from one valve at a time so as not to mix them up.
11 Scrape off any carbon deposits that may have formed on the valves, then use a motorised wire brush to remove deposits from the valve heads and stems. Again, make sure the valves do not get mixed up.

Inspection and reassembly

12 Refer to Chapter 2C, Section 12 for details of valve inspection, lapping and reassembly.

12 Cylinder

Removal

1 Remove the cylinder head and the camchain guide blade (see Section 9).
2 Hold the camchain and lift the cylinder up off the crankcase, supporting the piston as it becomes accessible to prevent it hitting the crankcase opening **(see illustration)**. If the cylinder is stuck, tap around the joint face between the cylinder and the crankcase with a soft-faced mallet to free it. Don't attempt to free the cylinder by inserting a screwdriver between it and the crankcase – you'll damage the sealing surfaces.
3 Once the cylinder has been removed, stuff a clean rag into the crankcase opening around the piston to prevent anything falling inside.
4 Remove the cylinder base gasket, noting how it fits, then discard it as new one must be fitted on reassembly. Note the location of the dowels in the cylinder or crankcase and remove them for safekeeping if they are loose

11.3a Ensure the valve spring compressor is correctly fitted...

11.3b ...allowing access to the collets (arrowed)

12.2 Lift the cylinder off the crankcase

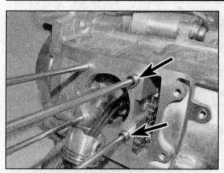

12.4 Note the location of the dowels (arrowed)

12.6 Inspect the bore (arrowed) for damage

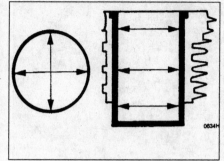

12.7a Measure the cylinder bore in the directions shown...

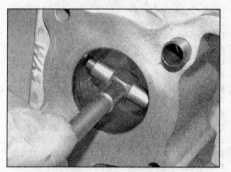

12.7b ...using a telescoping gauge

12.11 Install a new cylinder base gasket

12.13 Fit the piston into the cylinder bore

(see illustration). Note how the camchain locates on the crankshaft sprocket and secure the chain to prevent it dropping into the crankcase.

5 Clean all traces of old gasket material from the cylinder and crankcase with a suitable solvent. Take care not to scratch or gouge the soft aluminium. Be careful not to let any of the gasket material fall into the crankcase.

Inspection

6 Check the cylinder bore carefully for scratches and score marks **(see illustration)**.

7 If available, use a telescoping gauge and micrometer to measure the inside diameter of the cylinder bore to assess the amount of wear, taper and ovality (see *Tools and Workshop Tips* in the *Reference* section). Measure near the top (but below the level of the top piston ring at top dead centre), centre and bottom (but above the level of the bottom ring with the piston at bottom dead centre) of the bore both parallel to and across the crankshaft axis **(see illustrations)**.

8 Calculate any differences between the measurements to determine any taper or ovality in the bore. A cylinder bore that has worn oval will reduce the efficiency of the piston rings to achieve a seal, resulting in loss of compression and increased oil consumption.

9 Compare the results with the specifications given at the beginning of this Chapter. If the cylinder bore is worn beyond its service limit, is badly scratched, scuffed or scored, a new cylinder and piston should be fitted.

10 Check that all the cylinder studs are tight

in the crankcase halves. If any are loose, remove them (see *Tools and Workshop Tips* in the *Reference* section) and clean their threads. Apply a suitable permanent thread locking compound, then screw them back into the crankcase securely.

Installation

11 Remove any rag from the crankcase opening. Ensure the dowels are correctly installed in the crankcase **(see illustration 12.4)**, then lay the new base gasket in place on the crankcase making sure it is the correct way round **(see illustration)**.

12 Position the piston ring end gaps correctly **(see illustration 15.9 in Chapter 2C)**.

13 Lubricate the cylinder bore, piston and piston rings, and the connecting rod big and small-ends, with the clean engine oil, then lower the cylinder down until the piston crown fits into the bore **(see illustration)**.

14 Gently push down on the cylinder, making sure the piston enters the bore squarely and does not get cocked sideways. Carefully compress and feed each ring into the bore as the cylinder is lowered. If necessary, use a soft mallet to gently tap the cylinder down, but do not use force if it appears to be stuck as the piston and/or rings will be damaged.

15 When the piston is correctly installed in the cylinder, support the camchain and check that the base gasket has not been displaced, then press the cylinder down onto the base gasket.

16 Install the camchain guide blade, then install the cylinder head (see Section 9).

13 Piston

Refer to Chapter 2C, Section 14, noting the specification for piston diameter in the Specifications at the beginning of this Chapter.

14 Piston rings

Refer to Chapter 2C, Section 15, noting that on this engine the compression rings are marked near the gap to denote the upper surface of the ring – 2R for second compression ring, 1R or no marking for the top ring **(see illustration)**.

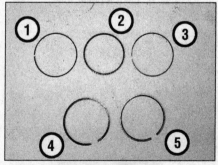

14.1 Piston ring set

1 Upper side rail
2 Rail spacer
3 Lower side rail
4 Second compression ring
5 Top compression ring

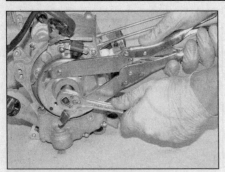

15.2a Using an aftermarkert pin wrench to hold the rotor

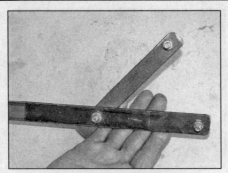

15.2b Home made pin wrench

15.3 Unscrew the alternator rotor centre nut

15 Alternator

Removal

1 The alternator is located behind the slotted fan cover on the right-hand side of the engine – remove the cover and the cooling fan (see Section 6).

2 To undo the rotor centre nut it is necessary to stop the rotor from turning using a pin wrench that locates in the two large holes in the face of the rotor. Peugeot produces a service tool (Part No. 752237) for this purpose. Alternatively, a similar home-made tool can be used (see Tool Tip in Chapter 2A, Section 11) or you can obtain an aftermarket version

(see illustrations). **Note:** *Take great care not to damage the internal coils of the alternator when locating any tools through the rotor.*

3 With the rotor securely held, loosen the centre nut and unscrew it from the crankshaft **(see illustration)**.

4 To remove the rotor from the taper on the crankshaft it is necessary to use a puller that threads into the internal thread in the centre of the rotor. Peugeot produces a service tool (Part No. 752237) and a cap to protect the end of the crankshaft (Part No. 068007) for this purpose. Aftermarket pullers are available. .

5 If the cap is not available, position a soft metal spacer between the end of the shaft and the puller centre bolt, then screw the puller all the way in **(see illustration)**. Hold the puller with a ring spanner and tighten the centre bolt

using steady pressure to draw the rotor off the taper **(see illustration)**.

6 Lift the rotor off the crankshaft. If it is loose, remove the Woodruff key from the shaft for safekeeping, noting how it fits **(see illustrations)**.

7 The alternator stator coils and ignition pulse generator coil are wired together and have to be removed as an assembly. If not already done, trace the wiring back from the alternator and pulse generator and disconnect it at the connectors **(see illustration 4.11)**. Free the wiring from any clips or guides and feed it through to the alternator.

9 If not already done, undo the bolts securing the pulse generator coil, then undo the bolts securing the alternator stator and lift the assembly off **(see illustrations)**. Draw the rubber wiring boot out of the engine side cover

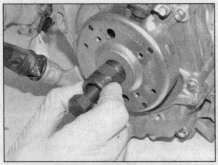

15.5a Install the puller fully...

15.5b ...then tighten the centre bolt

15.6a Remove the alternator rotor...

15.6b ...noting the location of the Woodruff key (arrowed)

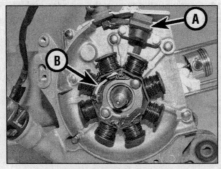

15.9a Pulse generator coil (A) and alternator stator (B)

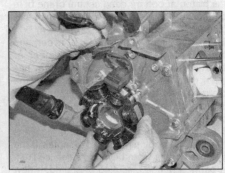

15.9b Lift the assembly off...

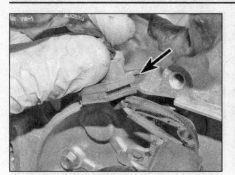

15.9c ...noting how the rubber boot fits

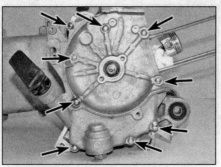

16.5 Undo the cover bolts, noting their locations

16.6 Draw the crankcase cover off

and carefully pull the wiring away, noting how it fits (see illustration).

Installation

10 Installation is the reverse of removal, noting the following:

- Ensure the wiring is correctly routed before installing the stator and pulse generator.
- Tighten the stator and pulse generator coil mounting screws to the torque setting specified at the beginning of this Chapter.
- Make sure that no metal objects have attached themselves to the magnets on the inside of the rotor.
- Clean the tapered end of the crankshaft and the corresponding mating surface on the inside of the rotor with a suitable solvent.
- Fit the Woodruff key into the crankshaft, align the slot in the centre of the rotor with the key, then install the rotor.
- Tighten the rotor centre nut to the specified torque setting.
- Secure the wiring with any clips or ties.
- Ensure that the cooling fan and cover are correctly installed (see Section 6).

16 Right-hand crankcase cover

Removal

1 Remove the exhaust system (see Chapter 5).
2 Drain the engine oil (see Chapter 1, Section 6).
3 Follow the procedure in Section 15 and remove the alternator.
4 An oil seal is fitted in the cover where the crankshaft passes through it. Check around the seal for signs of oil leakage – if the seal has been leaking a new one must be fitted once the cover has been removed. Note: *It is good practice to renew the oil seal whenever the cover is removed.*
5 Position a drain tray underneath the engine to catch any residual oil when the cover is removed, then undo the cover screws noting their locations (see illustration).

HAYNES HINT *Make a cardboard template of the crankcase cover and punch a hole for each screw location. This will ensure that they are all installed correctly on reassembly – this is important as some bolts are of different lengths.*

6 Draw the cover off (see illustration). If the cover is stuck, tap around the joint face between the cover and the crankcase with a soft-faced mallet to free it. Do not try to lever the cover off as this may damage the sealing surfaces.
7 Remove the gasket and discard it as a new one must be used. Note the dowels in the cover or crankcase and remove them for safekeeping if they are loose (see illustration).

16.7 Location of the cover dowels (arrowed)

16.9b Note which way round the seal is fitted...

8 Clean the mating surfaces of the cover and the crankcase with a suitable solvent to remove any traces of old gasket or sealant. Take care not to scratch or gouge the soft aluminium.
9 To renew the cover oil seal, support the cover on the work surface and drive the seal out from the outside with a suitably-sized socket (see illustration). Note which way round the seal is fitted. Ensure that the seal housing is clean, then lubricate the new seal with a smear of engine oil and press it all the way into the housing from the inside (see illustrations).

Installation

10 If removed, fit the dowels into the crankcase, then fit a new cover gasket, making sure it locates correctly onto the dowels (see

16.9a Drive the old seal out from the outside

16.9c ...then press it in from the inside

16.10 Fit a new cover gasket

17.2 Driven gear should rotate freely anti-clockwise

17.5 Apply steady clockwise pressure to undo the retaining nut

illustration). If necessary, use a dab of grease to hold the gasket in position.

11 Lubricate the inside of the oil seal with engine oil, then install the cover taking care not to damage the seal on the crankshaft threads. Make sure that the gasket stays in place.

12 Install the cover bolts, making sure they are in the correct locations, then tighten the bolts evenly and in a criss-cross sequence.

13 Install the remaining components in the reverse order of removal.

14 Fill the engine with the correct type and quantity of oil (see Chapter 1 and *Pre-ride checks*)

17 Starter (one-way) clutch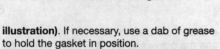

Check

1 Note the position of the starter motor, then remove the right-hand crankcase cover (see Section 16).

TOOL TiP

A peg spanner can be made by cutting castellations into one end of a length of thick-walled steel tube – measure the width and depth of the slots in the retaining nut to determine the size of the castellations. The tube should be 75 mm long to fit over the crankshaft and 31 mm diameter. Weld a heavy washer and large nut onto the opposite end of the tube so that the retaining nut can be tightened to the correct torque on installation.

2 If required, the operation of the starter clutch can be checked while it is in place. First withdraw the starter idler gear shaft and disengage the idler gear from the starter driven gear – the driven gear should now rotate freely in the *opposite* direction to crankshaft rotation (anti-clockwise), but lock when rotated clockwise (see illustration). If not, the starter clutch is faulty and should be removed for inspection.

Removal

3 If required, remove the starter motor (see Chapter 10).

4 A peg spanner (Peugeot service tool Part No. 800673) is required to undo the starter clutch retaining nut. If the correct tool is not available, one can be made from a suitable length of steel tube (see Tool Tip).

5 Use a pin wrench (see Section 15, Step 2) to prevent the crankshaft from turning while the retaining nut is being loosened. Align two

holes in the starter driven gear with two holes in the body of the starter clutch and install the pin wrench so that it locates securely in the body of the starter clutch, then use the peg spanner to undo the clutch retaining nut applying steady pressure (see illustration). Note: *This is a left hand thread – turn the peg spanner clockwise to undo the nut.*

6 Unscrew the retaining nut, noting how it fits with the flat face innermost, and remove the washer, then draw the starter clutch and driven gear assembly off the crankshaft (see illustrations). If the assembly is a tight fit, use a puller to draw it off. Note: *To avoid damaging the threaded end of the crankshaft, temporarily install the alternator centre nut.* Note the location of the Woodruff key in the shaft (see illustration) – the key retains the centre of the starter clutch and the oil pump drive gear and can be removed once the drive gear has been displaced (see Section 18).

17.6a Unscrew the retaining nut...

17.6b ...and remove the washer

17.6c Draw the assembly off the crankshaft

17.6d Note the location of the Woodruff key (arrowed)

17.7a Remove the starter idler gear...

17.7b ...and withdraw the shaft

17.9a Separate the driven gear from the starter clutch...

17.9b ...to inspect the bearing and bearing surfaces

17.10 Check the operation of the starter clutch

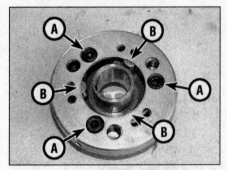

17.11 Clutch housing bolts (A) and sprags (B)

7 Slide the starter idler gear off its shaft, noting how it fits, and remove the shaft **(see illustrations)**.

Inspection

8 Inspect both sets of teeth on the idler gear and renew it if any are chipped or worn **(see illustration 17.7a)**. **Note:** *If the teeth on the larger pinion are worn or damaged, inspect the teeth on the starter motor pinion also (see Chapter 10)*. Check the idler shaft and bearing surfaces for signs of wear or damage, and renew it if necessary.

9 Inspect the teeth of the starter driven gear, the internal bearing surface and the needle roller bearing that fits between the hub of the driven gear and the starter clutch **(see illustrations)**. If any parts are worn, pitted or damaged, new components must be fitted.

10 Assemble the driven gear, bearing and starter clutch. Hold the starter clutch and check that the driven gear rotates freely anti-clockwise and locks against the starter clutch when rotated clockwise **(see illustration)**. If it doesn't, the sprags in the one-way mechanism may be worn or jammed.

11 Remove the driven gear and bearing and wash the clutch with a suitable solvent, then dry it with compressed air, if available. Lubricate the mechanism with clean engine oil and check it again. If the starter clutch still does not operate correctly, it can be disassembled and the springs and sprags renewed **(see illustration)**. On reassembly, clean the threads of the housing bolts and apply a suitable non-permanent thread-locking compound, then tighten the bolts to

the torque setting specified at the beginning of this Chapter.

12 Alternatively, a new starter clutch assembly, including the driven gear, can be fitted.

Installation

13 Installation is the reverse of removal, noting the following:

● Ensure the larger idler gear engages with the pinion on the starter motor shaft.
● Lubricate the starter clutch mechanism with clean engine oil.
● Align the slot in the centre of the starter clutch with the Woodruff key in the crankshaft, then press the assembly all the way onto the crankshaft **(see illustration 17.6c)**.
● The clutch retaining nut fits flat face innermost.
● Tighten (turn anti-clockwise) the starter clutch retaining nut to the torque setting specified at the beginning of this Chapter.

18.3a Draw off the oil pump drive gear

● Check the operation of the starter clutch (see Step 2). Ensure the driven gear engages with the smaller pinion on the idler gear.

18 Oil pump

Removal

1 Remove the right-hand crankcase cover (see Section 16).

2 Remove the starter (one-way) clutch (see Section 17).

3 If required, draw the pump drive gear off the crankshaft, noting how it fits **(see illustration)**. If it is loose, remove the Woodruff key from the shaft for safekeeping **(see illustration)**. **Note:** *If the crankcases are to be separated the drive gear and Woodruff key must be removed.*

18.3b Remove the Woodruff key

18.4a Gear is secured by E-clip (arrowed)

18.4b Remove the pump drive pin

18.5a Undo the screws (arrowed)...

18.5b ...and remove the pump

4 Remove the E-clip securing the oil pump driven gear and draw the gear off the pump shaft **(see illustration)**. Note the location of the drive pin in the pump shaft and remove it for safekeeping **(see illustration)**.
5 Undo the screws securing the oil pump, then lift off the pump, noting how it fits **(see illustrations)**.

Inspection

6 Check the pump body for obvious signs of damage. Turn the pump driveshaft by hand and check that the pump rotates smoothly.
7 If required, the pump can be disassembled for cleaning and inspection.
8 Remove the screw securing the cover to the pump body, then remove cover **(see illustrations)**. Note the location of the dowels between the cover and the body

9 Note the reference marks on the outer faces of the pump rotors **(see illustration)**. It is essential that they are reassembled the correct way round. Lift out the pump shaft, noting the location of the drive pin for the inner rotor, then lift out the inner and outer rotors.
10 Clean the pump components with a suitable solvent and dry them with compressed air, if available. Inspect the pump body, rotors and shaft for scoring and wear. If any damage, scoring, uneven or excessive wear is evident, renew the pump.
11 If the pump is good, reassemble all the components in the reverse order of disassembly and lubricate them with clean engine oil.
12 Fit the cover and tighten the screw securely, then rotate the pump shaft by hand to check that the rotors turn smoothly and

freely. If not, loosen the cover screw and adjust the position of the cover.
13 Inspect the pump driven gear and drive gear for wear or damage and renew any components as necessary. **Note:** *The driven gear is supplied as part of the pump assembly.*

Installation

14 Installation is the reverse of removal, noting the following:
● Align the pump with the crankcase and tighten the mounting screws to the torque setting specifies at the beginning of this Chapter.
● Fit the drive pin through the pump shaft, then fit the driven gear and secure it with a new E-clip.
● If removed, install the Woodruff key on the crankshaft, then press the drive gear all the way on **(see illustrations 18.3b, a and 17.6d)**.

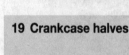
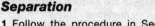

19 Crankcase halves

Separation

1 Follow the procedure in Section 4 and remove the engine from the frame.
2 Before the crankcase halves can be separated the following components must be removed:
● Cylinder head (Section 9)
● Cylinder (Section 12)
● Alternator (Section 15)
● Variator (Chapter 3)
● Starter motor (Chapter 10)
● Right-hand crankcase cover (see Section 16)
● Starter (one-way) clutch (Chapter 17)
● Oil pump (Section 18)
● Centrestand (Chapter 7)
3 Tape some rag around the connecting rod to prevent it knocking against the cases. Although not essential, it is advisable to remove the piston to avoid damage during this procedure.
4 Support the crankcase assembly on the work surface on its left-hand side. Loosen the

18.8a Undo the screw...

18.8b ...and remove the pump cover

18.9 Reference marks on pump rotors (arrowed)

19.4 Loosen the remaining crankcase bolts (arrowed)

19.5 Lift off the right-hand crankcase half

remaining crankcase bolts evenly, a little at a time until they are finger-tight, then remove them **(see illustration)**.

5 Lift the right-hand crankcase half off the left-hand half **(see illustration)**. If the crankcase halves do not separate easily, first ensure all fasteners have been removed. Next, apply heat to the right-hand main bearing housing with a hot air gun and try lifting the right-hand half off again.

Caution: Do not try to separate the halves by levering against the mating surfaces as they are easily scored and will not seal correctly afterwards. Do not strike the ends of the crankshaft with a hammer as damage to the end threads or the shaft itself will result.

6 Now lift the crankshaft assembly out of the left-hand crankcase half – apply heat to the main bearing housing if required **(see illustration)**. Ensure the camchain is clear of the crankshaft sprocket when the crankshaft is removed. Note that the main bearings will remain in place on the crankshaft assembly (see Section 20).

7 Remove the camchain and mark one side with a dab of paint so that it can be installed the same way round **(see illustration)**. If not already done, undo the pivot bolt securing the camchain tensioner blade and lift the blade out **(see illustrations 8.12a and b)**. Note which way round the blade is fitted.

8 Remove the crankcase gasket and discard it as a new one must be used. Remove the dowels from either crankcase half for safekeeping if they are loose **(see illustration 19.24)**.

9 Clean the mating surfaces of the crankcase halves with a suitable solvent to remove any traces of old gasket or sealant. Take care not to scratch or gouge the soft aluminium.

10 Note the position of the crankshaft oil seal in the left-hand crankcase half and note which way round it is fitted **(see illustration)**. Push the seal out from the inside using a suitably sized socket and discard it as a new one must be fitted on reassembly.

11 If required, remove the transmission

assembly from the left-hand crankcase half (see Chapter 3).

Inspection

12 Wash the cases in a suitable solvent and dry them with compressed air, if available.

13 Small cracks or holes in aluminium castings can be repaired with an epoxy resin adhesive as a temporary measure. Permanent repairs can only be effected by welding, and only a specialist in this process is in a position to advise on the economy or practical aspect of such a repair. On some engines, the crankcase halves can be renewed individually, on others the two halves are only available together as a matching set.

19.6 Lift the crankshaft assembly out of the left-hand crankcase half

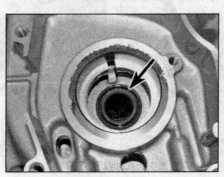

19.10 Location of the left-hand crankshaft oil seal (arrowed)

14 Damaged threads can be economically reclaimed by using a thread insert. Most small engineering firms offer a service of this kind. Sheared screws can usually be removed with screw extractors. Refer to *Tools and Workshop Tips* in the *Reference* section for further details.

15 Always wash the crankcases thoroughly after any repair work to ensure no dirt or metal swarf is trapped inside when the engine is rebuilt.

16 Inspect the engine mounting bushes **(see illustration)**. If they show signs of deterioration, renew them all at the same time. To remove a bush, first note its position in the casing. Heat the casing with a hot air gun, then support the casing and drive the

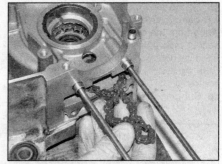

19.7 Remove the camchain

19.16 Inspect the engine mounting bushes

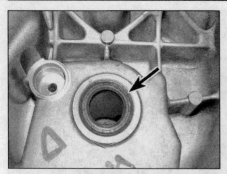

19.19 Installed position of the left-hand crankshaft oil seal

19.20 Position the camchain (arrowed) in the left-hand crankcase half

bush out with a hammer and a suitably sized socket. Alternatively, use two suitably sized sockets to press the bush out in the jaws of a vice. Clean the bush housing with steel wool to remove any corrosion, then reheat the casing and fit the new bush. **Note:** *Always support the casing when removing or fitting bushes to avoid breaking the casing.*

17 Inspect the main bearing housings. If a bearing outer race has spun in its housing, the inside of the housing will be damaged. A bearing locking compound can be used to fix the outer race in place on reassembly if the damage is not too severe. **Note:** *If a bearing has spun in its housing, the bearing itself is likely to be damaged – see Section 20.*

18 Inspect the crankshaft assembly and bearings (see Section 20).

Reassembly

19 Fit the new crankshaft oil seal into the left-hand crankcase half and press it into place from the outside using a seal driver or socket **(see illustration)**. Ensure the seal is fitted the right way round and that it enters the case squarely. Lubricate the seal with clean engine oil.

20 Support the left-hand crankcase half

on the work surface with enough space below it to provide clearance for the end of the crankshaft when it is fully installed. Position the camchain in the crankcase with clearance for the crankshaft sprocket **(see illustration)**.

21 Tape some rag around the connecting rod to prevent it knocking against the cases.

22 Lubricate the left-hand crankshaft main bearing with clean engine oil, then lower the crankshaft assembly into the crankcase half carefully to avoid damaging the seal. Ensure that the main bearing is aligned with the bearing housing and that the connecting rod is aligned with the crankcase mouth. Press the crankshaft assembly in fully so that the main bearing goes all the way into its housing. If the main bearing does not seat fully, apply heat with a hot air gun around the bearing housing while keeping steady pressure to the crankshaft assembly. **Note:** *Avoid applying direct heat onto the crankshaft oil seal.* If required, a freeze spray can be used on the main bearing to aid installation.

23 Ensure that the camchain is correctly located around the crankshaft sprocket and secure it in position with wire or a cable-tie to avoid it becoming jammed inside the crankcase.

24 If necessary, allow the case to cool, then wipe the mating surfaces of both crankcase halves with a rag soaked in suitable solvent . Fit the dowels and install the new crankcase gasket on the mating surface of the left-hand case **(see illustration)**.

25 Lubricate the right-hand main bearing with clean engine oil, then lower the crankcase half over the crankshaft. Ensure that the two halves of the crankcase are correctly aligned, taking special note of the position of the dowels, and that the main bearing is aligned with the bearing housing in the right-hand case **(see illustration 19.5)**.

26 Press the crankcase on fully so that the main bearing goes all the way into its housing. If the main bearing does not seat fully, apply heat to the around the bearing housing while keeping steady pressure to the crankcase.

27 Check that the crankcase halves are seated all the way round. If the cases are not correctly seated, heat the bearing housings while applying firm pressure. **Note:** *Do not attempt to pull the crankcase halves together using the crankcase bolts as the casing will crack and be ruined.*

28 Clean the threads of the crankcase bolts and install them finger-tight, then tighten them evenly, a little at a time to the torque setting specified at the beginning of this Chapter **(see illustration 19.4)**.

29 Trim off any excess gasket across the crankcase mouth **(see illustration)**.

30 Support the connecting rod and rotate the crankshaft by hand – if there are any signs of undue stiffness, tight or rough spots, or of any other problem, the fault must be rectified before proceeding further. Don't forget to support the camchain while rotating the crankshaft.

31 If required, install the camchain tensioner blade **(see illustrations 8.12b and a)**.

32 Install the remaining components in the reverse order of removal.

19.24 Fit the crankcase dowels (arrowed) and install the new gasket

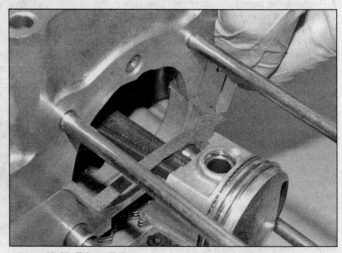

19.29 Trim off the excess gasket with a sharp blade

20 Crankshaft assembly, big-end and main bearings

Note: *The crankshaft assembly is pressed together and is easily damaged if it is dropped.*

1 To access the crankshaft assembly, the big-end bearing and the main bearings, the crankcase must be split into two parts (see Section 19).

2 The crankshaft assembly should give many thousands of miles of service. The most likely problems to occur will be a worn small or big-end bearing due to poor lubrication. A worn big-end bearing will produce a pronounced knocking noise, most audible when the engine is under load, and increasing as engine speed rises. This should not be confused with small-end bearing wear, which produces a lighter, metallic rattle (see Section 13).

3 When the crankcase halves are separated, the main bearings will remain in place on the crankshaft assembly – they are not normally available as separate items. If the main bearings have failed, excessive rumbling and vibration will be felt when the engine is running.

4 To assess the condition of the big-end bearing, hold the crankshaft assembly firmly and push and pull on the connecting rod, checking for any up-and-down freeplay between the two **(see illustration)**. If any freeplay is noted, the bearing is worn.

5 A small amount of big-end side clearance (side-to-side movement) is acceptable on the connecting rod. Measure the clearance with a feeler gauge **(see illustration)**, then compare

20.4 Check for up-and-down play in the big-end bearing

the result with the service limit specified at the beginning of this Chapter.

6 If available, place the crankshaft assembly on V-blocks and check the runout at either end using a dial gauge. Compare the result with the specification at the beginning of this Chapter. If the crankshaft is out-of-true it will cause excessive engine vibration. If there is any doubt about the condition of the crankshaft have it checked by an automotive engineer.

7 Follow the procedure in *Tools and Workshop Tips* in the *Reference* section to check the condition of the main bearings.

8 If wear or damage is noted in any of the crankshaft assembly bearings, a new crankshaft assembly will have to be fitted.
Note: *Evidence of extreme heat, such as discoloration or blueing, indicates that lubrication failure has occurred. Be sure to check the oil pump and bearing oil ways in the crankcases before reassembling the engine.*

9 Inspect the threads on each end of the crankshaft and ensure that the retaining nuts

20.5 Measuring big-end side clearance

for the alternator rotor and the variator are a good fit. Inspect the splines for the variator pulley on the left-hand end of the shaft **(see illustration)**. Inspect the alternator taper and the slots in the right-hand side of the shaft for the alternator and starter clutch Woodruff keys **(see illustration)**. Damage or wear that prevents the rotor from being fitted securely will require a new crankshaft assembly.

10 Inspect the teeth of the camshaft drive sprocket on the crankshaft for damage or wear **(see illustration 20.9a)**. The sprocket is an integral part of the crankshaft assembly – if it is worn or damaged a new assembly will have to be fitted.

21 Initial start-up after overhaul/running-in

Refer to Chapter 2C, Section 22.

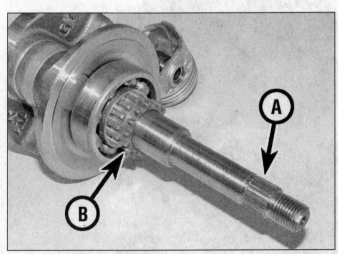

20.9a Inspect the variator splines (A) and the camshaft drive sprocket (B)

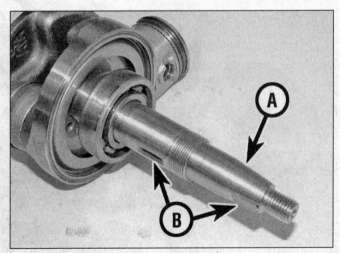

20.9b Inspect the alternator taper (A) and Woodruff key slots (B)

Type 150QMG-A – left-hand view

Type 150QMG-A – right-hand view

Chapter 2E
Four-stroke 100cc engine – type 150QMG-A

Refer to 'Model and servicing specifications' in Chapter 1 for model identification details

Contents

Degrees of difficulty

| Easy, suitable for novice with little experience | Fairly easy, suitable for beginner with some experience | Fairly difficult, suitable for competent DIY mechanic | Difficult, suitable for experienced DIY mechanic | Very difficult, suitable for expert DIY or professional |

Specifications

General
Type . . . . Single cylinder air-cooled 2-valve four-stroke
Capacity . . . . 102 cc
Bore x stroke . . . . 50 x 52 mm
Cylinder compression. . . 130 psi (8.95 Bar) @ 500rpm

Valves
Valve clearances. . . . . . See Chapter 1

Cylinder bore
Diameter
  Standard. . . . . 50.0 to 50.01 mm
  Service limit . . . . . . 50.1 mm

Piston
Diameter (measured 9 mm up from the bottom of the skirt)
  Standard. . . . . 49.97 to 49.98 mm
  Service limit . . . . . . 49.9 mm

Piston rings
Ring end gap (installed)
  Top ring and second ring . . . . . 0.10 to 0.25 mm
  Oil control ring . . . . 0.20 to 0.70 mm

Crankshaft and connecting rod
Big-end side clearance
  Service limit . . . . . . 0.55 mm
Crankshaft runout
  Measured on the left and right-hand sides of the shaft (see text) . . . 0.15 mm

Torque settings

Alternator rotor nut	50 Nm
Alternator stator bolts	10 Nm
Alternator wiring guide bolt	10 Nm
Cam chain tensioner blade bolt	10 Nm
Cam chain tensioner cap bolt	8 Nm
Cam chain tensioner mounting bolts	8 Nm
Camshaft sprocket bolts	10 Nm
Cooling fan bolts	10 Nm
Crankcase bolts	10 Nm
Crankshaft left-hand oil seal holder bolts	10 Nm
Cylinder head	
Nuts	20 Nm
Bolts	10 Nm
Drive belt cover screws	10 Nm
Engine mounting bolt/nut	57 Nm
Exhaust manifold	18 Nm
Ignition pulse generator coil bolts	10 Nm
Intake manifold bolts	10 Nm
Oil pump cover bolts	10 Nm
Oil pump mounting bolts	10 Nm
Rear shock absorber lower mounting bolt/nut	28 Nm
Rear shock absorber upper mounting bolt/nut	50 Nm
Rear wheel nut	130 Nm
Valve cover	10 Nm

1 General information

The engine is a single cylinder, overhead-camshaft four-stroke, with fan assisted air cooling as fitted to Kisbee 100 cc scooters. The camshaft is chain-driven off the crankshaft and operates the valves via rocker arms.

The crankshaft assembly is pressed together, incorporating the connecting rod.

The crankcase divides vertically – the left-hand crankcase is an integral part of the drive belt casing and gearbox.

2 Component access

Most components and assemblies, with the obvious exception of the crankshaft assembly and its bearings, can be worked on without having to remove the engine/transmission unit from the scooter. However, access to some components is severely restricted, and if a number of areas require attention at the same time, removal of the engine is recommended, as it is an easy task to undertake.

3 Cylinder compression test

Refer to Chapter 2C, Section 3 for this procedure.

4 Engine removal and installation

Caution: The engine/transmission unit is not heavy, however removal and installation should be carried out with the aid of an assistant; personal injury or damage could occur if the engine falls or is dropped.

Removal

1 Support the scooter securely in an upright position. Work can be made easier by raising the machine to a suitable height on an hydraulic ramp or a suitable platform. Make sure it is secure and will not topple over.

2 Disconnect and remove the battery (see Chapter 10).

3 If required, drain the engine oil (see Chapter 1).

4 Remove the storage compartment, the under-body panel and mudguard, the rear hugger and the centre belly panel (see Chapter 9).

5 Remove the air filter housing (see Chapter 5).

6 If required, remove the exhaust system (see Chapter 5).

7 Pull the spark plug cap off the plug and position the cap clear of the engine (see illustration).

8 Cut the cable-ties securing the wiring loom on the right-hand side of the engine compartment (see illustration). Trace the wiring for the alternator and ignition pulse generator coil from the top of the alternator cover on the right-hand side of the engine and disconnect it at the connectors (see

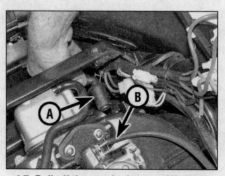

4.7 Pull off the spark plug cap (A). Note vacuum hose (B)

4.8a Cut the cable-ties on the right-hand side

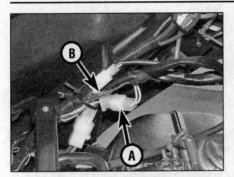

4.8b Alternator (A) and ignition pulse generator (B) wiring connectors

4.10 Location of the automatic choke unit (arrowed)

4.11 Disconnect the fuel hose from the fuel tap

illustration). Release the wiring on the engine side of the loom from any clips or ties. **Note:** *When disconnecting any wiring, it is advisable to mark or tag the wires as a reminder of where they connect.*

9 Disconnect the starter motor wiring connector.

10 Trace the wiring from the automatic choke unit and disconnect it at the connector **(see illustration)**.

11 Disconnect the fuel hose from its union on the fuel tap, being prepared to catch any residual fuel in a rag **(see illustration)**. Position a suitable container below the carburettor drain hose, then loosen the drain screw and drain any residual fuel from the float chamber. Tighten the drain screw.

12 Disconnect the fuel tap vacuum hose from its union on the inlet manifold **(see illustration 4.7)**.

13 Either displace or remove the carburettor completely, leaving the throttle cable attached if required, or just disconnect the throttle cable from the carburettor pulley (see Chapter 5). If the carburettor is displaced, ensure it is secured to a convenient part of the frame to avoid damage. Ensure that the throttle cable is unclipped from the left-hand side of the engine unit **(see illustration)**. Stuff clean rag into the intake manifold to prevent anything falling inside.

14 If required, remove the rear wheel (see Chapter 8). **Note:** *The rear wheel and stand provide a convenient support for the unit once*

4.13 Release the throttle cable from the clip (arrowed)

it is removed from the scooter. However, it is useful to loosen the rear wheel nut at this point before disconnecting the rear brake.

15 Disconnect the brake cable from the brake arm (see Chapter 8). Release the cable from the clips on the underside of the transmission casing and detach the cable.

16 Before the engine with the centrestand can be removed, a means of supporting the scooter must be devised. A double A-frame hoist is ideally suited to most machines once the rear bodywork has been removed and where the front of the scooter can be firmly secured **(see illustration 4.17a in Chapter 2A)**. Alternatively, the scooter can be supported from underneath provided the weight is taken on the frame tubes and not on any bodywork **(see illustration)**.

4.16 Supporting the weight of the scooter on a trolley jack

17 Check that all wiring, cables and hoses are clear of the engine/transmission unit.

18 Undo the upper rear shock absorber mounting bolt, then support the weight of the engine and rear wheel and withdraw the bolt (see Chapter 7). Lower the wheel to the ground. Undo the lower shock mounting bolt and remove the shock **(see illustration)**.

19 Undo the locknut on the engine mounting bolt **(see illustration)**. **Note:** *Peugeot recommends a new nut should be used on reassembly. Alternatively, clean the threads of the engine mounting bolt and apply a suitable thread-locking compound prior to installation.*

20 Have an assistant support the engine unit, then carefully withdraw the engine mounting bolt **(see illustration)**. Manoeuvre

4.18 Remove the rear shock absorber

4.19 Undo the nut (arrowed) on the mounting bolt

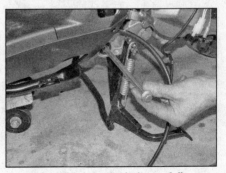

4.20a Withdraw the bolt carefully...

the engine unit back and out of the frame **(see illustration)**.

21 If the engine is dirty, particularly around its mountings, wash it thoroughly before starting any major dismantling work. This will make work much easier and rule out the possibility of dirt falling inside.

22 If required, remove the rear wheel (see Chapter 8) and the centrestand (see Chapter 7).

Installation

23 Installation is the reverse of removal, noting the following:

● Make sure no wires, cables or hoses become trapped between the engine and the frame when installing the engine.

● Tighten the engine mounting bolt, shock absorber bolts and wheel nut to the torque settings specified at the beginning of this Chapter.

● Make sure all wires, cables and hoses are correctly routed and connected, and secured by any clips or ties.

● If the engine oil was drained, or if any oil has been lost during overhaul, refill or top up as described in Chapter 1 and *Pre-ride checks*.

● Check the operation of the rear brake before riding the machine (see Chapter 1).

5 Disassembly and reassembly – general information

1 Refer to Chapter 2C, Section 5.

4.20b ...and manoeuvre the engine unit out

6 Valve cover

Removal

1 Remove the storage compartment, the under-body panel and mudguard, the seat cowling and centre cover panels (see Chapter 9).

2 Release the clip securing the breather hose to the valve cover and detach the hose **(see illustration)**.

3 Undo the bolts securing the valve cover, noting the location of the sealing washers **(see illustration)**. Check the condition of the washers and renew them prior to installation if they are damaged or distorted.

4 Lift the cover off **(see illustration)**. If the cover is stuck, tap around the joint face

6.2 Detach the breather hose (arrowed)

between the cover and the cylinder head with a soft-faced mallet to free it. Do not try to lever the cover off as this may damage the sealing surfaces.

5 Remove the gasket, noting how it locates **(see illustration)**. Note the location of the oil passage hole in the gasket, the oil channel in the cover between the oil jet and the supply hole in the mating surface of the cylinder head **(see illustrations)**.

6 Clean the mating surfaces of the cylinder head and the valve cover with a suitable solvent to remove any traces of old gasket or sealant. Blow through the oilway in the cover with compressed air to ensure it is clear. Discard the old gasket as a new one must be used

7 Note the location of the breather system baffle plate in the valve cover **(see illustration)**. If required, remove the plate and clean the inside of the cover. On installation,

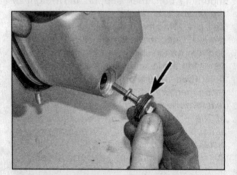
6.3 Note location of sealing washers and fit new ones if necessary

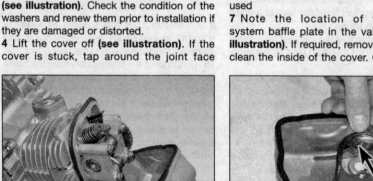
6.4 Lift off the valve cover

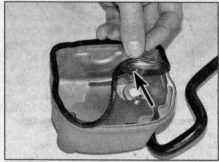
6.5a Note oil passage hole (arrowed) in gasket...

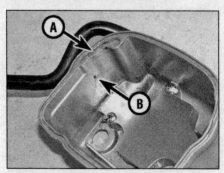
6.5b ...the oil channel (A) and oil jet (B)...

6.5c ...and the supply hole (arrowed) in the cylinder head

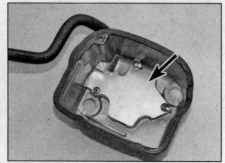
6.7 Location of the breather baffle plate

7.2a Undo the bolts...

7.2b ...and remove the fan cover

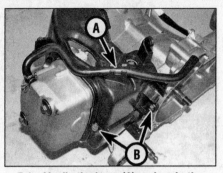

7.4a Unclip the hose (A) and undo the bolts (B)

7.4b Undo the right-hand bolt

7.5a Remove the upper...

7.5b ...and lower halves of the cowling

ensure that the screws securing the plate are tightened securely – as a precaution, clean the screw threads and apply non-permanent thread-locking compound.

Installation

8 Lay the new gasket onto the valve cover, making sure it fits correctly into the groove **(see illustration 6.5a)**.
9 Position the valve cover on the cylinder head, making sure the gasket stays in place. Install the cover bolts and washers, then tighten the bolts evenly to the torque setting specified at the beginning of this Chapter.
10 Install the breather hose and secure it with the clip.
11 Install the remaining components in the reverse order of removal.

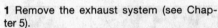

7 Engine cowling and cooling fan

1 Remove the exhaust system (see Chapter 5).
2 Undo the bolts securing the fan cover and lift it off **(see illustrations)**.
3 Remove the carburettor and intake manifold (see Chapter 5).
4 Unclip the breather hose from the upper half of the cowling, then undo the screws securing the cowling on the left and right-hand sides **(see illustrations)**.
5 Ease the two halves of the cowling apart, noting how they clip together, and lift them off **(see illustrations)**.
6 Note the location of the seal around the top

edge of the cylinder. Remove the seal carefully, noting how it fits. If the seal is damaged or deteriorated replace it with a new one.
7 Undo the four bolts securing the cooling fan to the alternator rotor and remove the fan **(see illustration)**.
8 Installation is the reverse of removal. Tighten the cooling fan bolts to the torque setting specified at the beginning of this Chapter.
9 Don't forget to install the cowling seal. Ensure both halves of the cowling and the fan cover are correctly aligned, then tighten the mounting bolts securely.

8 Camchain tensioner

Removal

1 The camchain tensioner is located on the back of the cylinder on the left-hand side. Remove the upper half of the engine cowling for access (see Section 7).
2 Remove the spark plug (see Chapter 1, Section 15).
3 Turn the engine in the normal direction of rotation until the piston is at top dead centre (TDC) on its compression stroke. You can do this by rotating the crankshaft via the alternator rotor. The position of the piston can be confirmed by ensuring that the T mark on the alternator rotor aligns with the static timing mark on the crankcase **(see illustration)**.

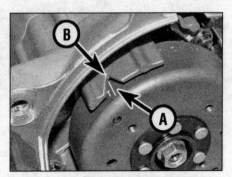

8.3 T mark (A) on the alternator rotor should align with the static timing mark (B)

7.7 Undo the cooling fan mounting bolts (arrowed)

8.4a Undo the cap bolt...

8.4b ...and remove the O-ring

8.5 Turn the tensioner clockwise

4 Undo the tensioner cap bolt, noting the location of the O-ring **(see illustrations)**. Discard the O-ring as a new one must be fitted.

5 Insert a flat-bladed screwdriver into the tensioner and turn it clockwise until it goes tight – this will retract the tensioner plunger into the tensioner body **(see illustration)**. The plunger should remain in this position.

6 Undo the tensioner mounting bolts and withdraw the tensioner from the cylinder **(see illustration)**. Remove the gasket from the base of the tensioner or from the cylinder and discard it as a new one must be used **(see illustration)**.

7 Clean all traces of old gasket material from the tensioner and cylinder with a suitable solvent. Take care not to scratch or gouge the soft aluminium. Be careful not to let any of the gasket material fall into the engine.

Inspection

8 Examine the tensioner components for signs of wear or damage.

9 Using a flat-bladed screwdriver, turn the tensioner anti-clockwise to release the plunger – the plunger should spring out to the fully extended position **(see illustration)**. Now try to press the plunger back into the body – it should be locked in position.

10 Using the screwdriver, ensure that the plunger moves freely in and out of the tensioner body **(see illustration)**.

11 If any part of the tensioner is worn or damaged, or if the plunger is seized in the body, a new tensioner must be fitted.

Installation

12 Using the screwdriver, turn the tensioner clockwise to withdraw the plunger into the tensioner body.

13 Fit a new gasket on the tensioner body, install the tensioner in the cylinder and tighten the mounting bolts to the torque setting specified at the beginning of this Chapter.

14 Turn the engine in the normal direction of rotation – this removes all the slack in the front run of the chain between the crankshaft and the camshaft, and transfers it to the back run where it will be taken up by the tensioner. **Note:** *Take care when turning the engine with the tensioner plunger withdrawn to avoid the chain jumping over the teeth on the camshaft sprocket. If this happens, ensure that the timing marks on the alternator rotor and on the camshaft sprocket are correctly re-aligned with the piston at TDC before proceeding (see Chapter 1, Section 14).*

15 Using the screwdriver, turn the tensioner anti-clockwise to release the plunger. It is advisable to remove the valve cover (see Section 6) and check that the camchain is tensioned. If it is slack, the tensioner plunger did not release. Remove the tensioner and check the operation of the plunger again.

16 Fit a new cap bolt O-ring and tighten the bolt to the specified torque.

17 Install the remaining components in the reverse order of removal.

Caution: After installing the camchain tensioner, turn the crankshaft and check that all the timing marks still align correctly. If the timing marks are not aligned exactly as described, the valve timing will be incorrect and the valves may strike the piston, causing extensive damage to the engine.

8.6a Undo the tensioner mounting bolts

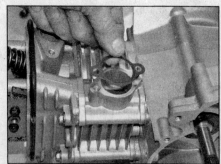

8.6b Discard the old tensioner gasket

8.9 Tensioner plunger should extend fully and lock

8.10 Check that the plunger moves freely

9 Camchain, blades and sprockets

Camchain

Inspection

1 The camchain runs between the drive sprocket on the crankshaft and the camshaft sprocket. To check the condition of the chain, first remove the valve cover (see Section 6) and the fan cover (see Section 7).

2 Remove the spark plug (see Chapter 1, Section 15).

9.3 Inspect the cam chain links for wear as described

9.7a Undo the bolts (arrowed)...

9.7b ...and remove the oil seal holder

9.7c Prise out the old oil seal...

9.7d ...noting location of the inner sealing lip (arrowed)

3 Using the alternator rotor, turn the engine slowly in the normal direction of rotation and inspect the inside edges of the chain links for wear **(see illustration)**.

4 Hold the chain at the mid-way point around the camshaft sprocket and try to lift it off the sprocket. The chain should be a firm fit on the sprocket. Turn the engine carefully in the normal direction of rotation and check the entire length of the chain.

5 If any of the above checks indicate that the camchain has worn, a new one must be fitted.

Removal

6 If the camchain is being removed, access will be required to the crankcase and the crankshaft. Since the camchain is on the left-hand side of the engine, refer to the procedure in Chapter 3 and remove the variator.

7 The left-hand crankshaft oil seal is secured by a holder – undo the mounting bolts and remove the holder **(see illustrations)**. Prise out the seal, noting how it fits **(see illustrations)**. Discard the seal as a new one must be fitted.

8 Note the location of the camchain around the sprocket on the crankshaft **(see illustration)**.

9 Before the camchain can be removed it must be disengaged from the camshaft sprocket. Follow the procedure in Section 10 to displace the camshaft sprocket, then lower the chain down the tunnel in the cylinder and withdraw it from the engine **(see illustration)**.

Installation

10 Installation is the reverse of removal, noting the following:

● Before installing the chain, ensure that the piston is at TDC on the compression stroke and that the timing mark 'T' on the alternator rotor is aligned with the register mark on the crankcase **(see illustration 8.3)**.

● Ensure the chain is fitted correctly around the crankshaft sprocket.

● Position the timing marks on the camshaft sprocket as noted on removal – the camshaft lobes should face down away from the rocker arms **(see Section 10)**.

● Ensure any slack in the chain is in the back run where it will be taken up by the tensioner

● Fit a new crankshaft oil seal (see Section 19) then tighten the oil seal holder bolts to the torque setting specified at the beginning of this Chapter.

Camchain tensioner and guide blades

11 The camchain tensioner blade is located inside the camchain tunnel and is secured by a pivot bolt on its lower end.

12 To inspect the blade, first remove the camshaft sprocket (see Section 10). Note the location of the top end of the blade **(see illustration)**. Secure the camchain to prevent it falling down into the tunnel.

13 Remove the variator (see Chapter 3).

14 Remove the crankcase oil seal holder **(see illustrations 9.7a and b)**, then undo the pivot

9.8 Note location of the camchain

9.9 Removing the camchain from the engine

9.12 Top end of camchain tensioner blade (arrowed)

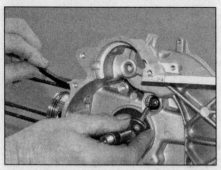

9.14a Removing the camchain tensioner blade

9.14b Fit a new pivot bolt O-ring

9.15 Removing the camchain guide blade

bolt and lift the blade out **(see illustration)**. Note which way round the blade is fitted. Note the location of the O-ring on the pivot bolt and discard it as a new one must be fitted in installation **(see illustration)**.

15 The guide blade can be removed when the cylinder head has been removed (see Section 11) **(see illustration)**.

16 Check both blades for wear or damage and renew them if necessary. Check the operation of the camchain tensioner (see Section 8).

17 Installation is the reverse of removal. Ensure that the blades are fitted the correct way round. Apply non-permanent thread-locking compound to the threads of the tensioner blade pivot bolt and tighten it to the torque setting specified at the beginning of this Chapter .

Camchain sprockets

18 To inspect the camshaft sprocket for wear, follow the procedure in Section 10 and remove the sprocket **(see illustration 10.5b)**.

19 Check for wear on the sides and tips of the sprocket teeth and for chipped or hooked teeth.

20 Similar checks should be made on the crankshaft sprocket after removing the camchain (see Steps 6 to 9). The sprocket is integral with the crankshaft assembly – if it is worn a new crankshaft will have to be fitted (see Section 20).

21 If the sprocket teeth are worn, the chain will also be worn. Always renew the components as an assembly – worn sprockets will soon damage a new chain.

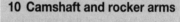

10 Camshaft and rocker arms

Removal

1 Remove the valve cover (see Section 6).

2 Remove the camchain tensioner (see Section 8). Note that when the piston is at TDC on its compression stroke the valves are closed and a small clearance can be felt at each rocker arm **(see illustration)**. Look for the timing marks on the camshaft sprocket – these should be aligned with the valve cover gasket face **(see illustration)**.

3 Stuff a clean rag into the camchain tunnel to prevent anything falling into the engine.

4 Use a pin wrench to prevent the camshaft sprocket turning and undo the camshaft sprocket bolt **(see illustration)**. Peugeot produces a service tool (Part No. 752237) for this purpose. Alternatively, a similar home-made tool can be used (see the illustration in Chapter 2A, Section 11) or you can obtain an aftermarket version.

5 Lift the camshaft sprocket off the end of the camshaft and disengage the sprocket from the chain **(see illustrations)**. Note any markings on the outside face of the sprocket to aid installation. Secure the chain to prevent it dropping into the engine.

6 The camshaft and rockers are located in a holder which is retained by long studs that also secure the cylinder head and cylinder to the

10.2a Check the rocker arms for clearance

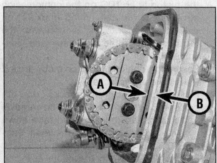

10.2b Timing mark (A) should be aligned with gasket face (B)

10.4 Hold the camshaft sprocket with a pin wrench and undo the bolt

10.5a Displace the camshaft sprocket...

10.5b ...and disengage it from the chain

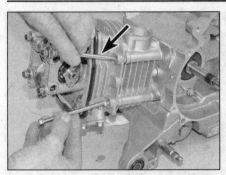

10.6 Upper bolt (arrowed) is shorter than the lower one

10.7 Remove the cylinder head nuts and washers

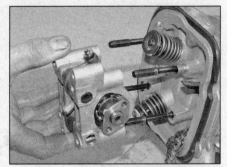

10.8a Lift off the camshaft holder

10.8b Note location of the dowels (arrowed)

10.9a Pull out the rocker shaft and remove the rocker arm

10.9b Note cut-out (arrowed) in the intake rocker shaft

crankcases. Before loosening the cylinder head nuts, remove the small bolts securing the left-hand side of the cylinder head **(see illustration)**. Note how the bolts fit, they are different lengths.

7 Now unscrew the cylinder head nuts evenly and a little at a time in a criss-cross pattern, until they are all loose, then remove the nuts and washers **(see illustration)**. **Note:** *Once the cylinder head nuts are loose care must be taken not to break the cylinder base gasket seal otherwise a new base gasket will have to be fitted (see Section 13).*

8 Lift off the camshaft holder assembly **(see illustration)**. Note the dowels in the holder or head and remove them for safekeeping if they are loose **(see illustration)**.

9 The rocker shafts are retained in the camshaft holder by the cylinder studs. Once the holder has been removed from the engine, the shafts and individual rocker arms can be disassembled. Note the position of the rocker arms and mark

them so that they can be installed in their original positions. Thread a 5 mm bolt into the end of each rocker shaft, support the rocker arm and withdraw the shafts carefully **(see illustration)**. Note the cut-out in the left-hand end of the intake valve rocker shaft which aligns with the adjacent cylinder stud **(see illustration)**. Assemble the rockers on their shafts so that they can be installed in their original positions.

10 Note the point on the camshaft sprocket flange which is uppermost when the camshaft is positioned at TDC compression **(see illustration)**.

11 Note the location of the circlip retaining the camshaft and remove it using circlip pliers to avoid damage, then draw out the camshaft **(see illustrations)**.

Inspection

12 Clean all of the components with a suitable solvent and dry them.

13 Inspect the camshaft lobes for heat discoloration (blue appearance), score marks, chipped areas, flat spots and spalling **(see illustration)**. If damage is noted or wear is excessive, the camshaft must be renewed.

10.10 Point (arrowed) should be uppermost at TDC compression

10.11a Remove the circlip...

10.11b ...and draw out the camshaft

10.13 Inspect the camshaft lobes (arrowed) for wear and damage

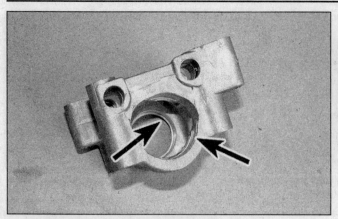

10.15 Inspect the camshaft bearing housings (arrowed)

10.20a Ensure rocker shafts do not obstruct the holes for the cylinder studs

14 Follow the procedure in *Tools and Workshop Tips* in the *Reference* section to check the condition of the camshaft bearings. The bearings are not available individually – if a bearing is worn or damaged a new camshaft will have to be fitted.

15 Check the bearing housings for score marks and spalling **(see illustration)**. Any damage is an indication that the bearing has seized on the camshaft and turned inside its housing. Prior to reassembly, check that the bearing outer races are a tight fit in their housings, otherwise use some bearing locking compound to hold it in position.

16 Blow through the oil passages in the rocker arms and shafts with compressed air, if available, to ensure that they are clear.

17 Inspect the face of the rocker arm and the contact area between the adjuster screw and the valve stem for pits and spalling.

18 Check the rocker shaft for wear. The rocker arm should be a sliding fit on the shaft without any freeplay. If available, use a micrometer to measure the diameter of the shaft in several places – any variation in the measurements is an indication of wear on the shaft.

19 Renew any components that are worn or damaged.

Installation

20 Installation is the reverse of removal, noting the following:
● Ensure the piston is at TDC on the compression stroke before you start.
● Lubricate the shafts, bearing surfaces and bearings with clean engine oil before installation.
● Position the rocker shafts so that the holes for the cylinder studs are clear **(see illustration 10.20a)**.
● Ensure any dowels are correctly installed in the camshaft holder or cylinder head.
● Tighten the cylinder head nuts a little at a time in a criss-cross sequence **(see illustration 10.20b)** to the torque setting specified at the beginning of this Chapter.
● Install the cylinder head bolts as noted on removal (see Step 6) and tighten them to the specified torque.
● Check the valve clearances (see Chapter 1).

11 Cylinder head

Caution: The engine must be completely cool before beginning this procedure or the cylinder head may become warped.

Removal

1 Remove the carburettor, intake manifold and exhaust system (see Chapter 5).
2 Remove the fan cover and engine cowling (see Section 7).
3 Remove the camshaft and rockers (see Section 10).
4 Using a length of bent wire to hold the camchain, lift the cylinder head off the cylinder, feeding the camchain down through the tunnel in the head **(see illustration)**. If the head is stuck, tap around the joint face between the head and the cylinder with a soft-faced mallet to free it. Do not try to lever the head off as this may damage the sealing surfaces. **Note:** *The cylinder head studs pass down through the cylinder and screw into the crankcase. Once*

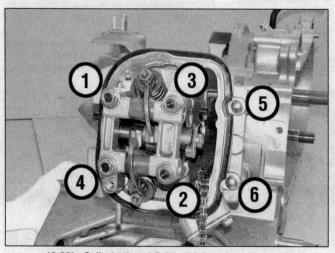

10.20b Cylinder head fixings *tightening* sequence

11.4 Lift off the cylinder head

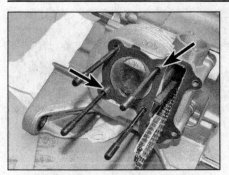

11.5a Location of the cylinder head dowels

11.5b Remove the old head gasket

11.7 Note how the lugs on the camchain guide blade locate

the cylinder head is loose care must be taken not to break the cylinder base gasket seal otherwise a new base gasket will have to be fitted before refitting the head (see Section 13).

5 Note the location of the cylinder head dowels and remove them for safekeeping if they are loose, then remove the old cylinder head gasket **(see illustrations)**.

6 Secure the camchain to prevent it dropping into the engine.

7 If required, the camchain guide blade can be removed – draw the blade out, noting how the lugs locate in the recess in the top edge of the camchain tunnel **(see illustration)**.

8 Clean all traces of old gasket material from the cylinder head and cylinder with a suitable solvent. Take care not to scratch or gouge the soft aluminium. Be careful not to let any of the gasket material fall into the crankcase, the cylinder bore or the oil passages.

9 Inspect the cylinder head gasket and the mating surfaces on the cylinder head and cylinder for signs of leaks, which could indicate that the head is warped. Refer to Chapter 2C, Section 12 and check the head mating surface for warpage.

10 After inspection, discard the old gasket as a new one must be fitted on reassembly

Installation

11 Installation is the reverse of removal, noting the following:
- Lubricate the cylinder bore with clean engine oil.
- Ensure any dowels are correctly installed in the cylinder.
- If removed, install the camchain guide blade (see Step 7).
- Install a new head gasket – never re-use the old gasket.
- Ensure the camchain is correctly located around the crankshaft sprocket.
- Install the camshaft and rockers (see Section 10).

12 Cylinder head and valves

Note: *If a valve spring compressor is available, the home mechanic can remove the valves*

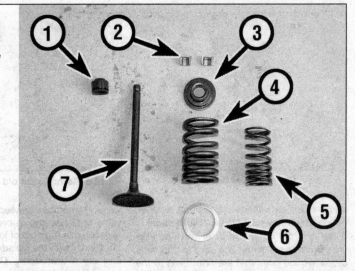

12.1 Valve components

1 Valve stem seal
2 Collets
3 Valve spring retainer
4 Outer valve spring
5 Inner valve spring
6 Valve seat
7 Valve

from the cylinder head, lap them and renew the valve stem seals.

Disassembly

1 Before you start, arrange to label and store the valves and their related components so that they can be returned to their original locations without getting mixed up **(see illustration)**.

2 If not already done, clean all traces of old gasket material from the cylinder head with a suitable solvent. Take care not to scratch or gouge the soft aluminium.

3 Compress the valve springs on the first

valve with a spring compressor, making sure it is correctly located onto each end of the valve assembly **(see illustration)**. On the underside of the head, make sure the plate on the compressor only contacts the valve and not the soft aluminium of the head – if the plate is too big for the valve, use a spacer between them. Do not compress the springs any more than is absolutely necessary to release the collets, then remove the collets, using either needle-nose pliers, a magnet or a screwdriver with a dab of grease on it **(see illustration)**.

4 Carefully release the valve spring

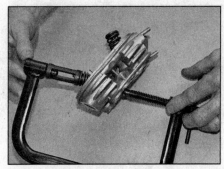

12.3a Ensure the valve spring compressor is correctly fitted...

12.3b ...allowing access to the collets (arrowed)

12.4 Remove the spring retainer

12.5 Remove the valve springs

12.6 Lift out the spring seat

12.7 Remove the valve

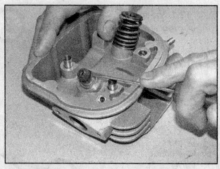

12.8 Remove the old valve stem seal

13 Cylinder

compressor and remove the spring retainer, noting which way up it fits **(see illustration)**.

5 Remove the outer and inner valve springs **(see illustration)**. Note: *The valve springs have closer wound coils that are fitted next to the cylinder head. On the engine photographed, the upper ends of the springs were marked with a dab of paint.*

6 Lift out the spring seat **(see illustration)**.

7 Turn the head over and withdraw the valve **(see illustration)**. If the valve binds in the guide (won't pull through), push it back into the head and deburr the area around the collet groove with a very fine file.

8 Once the valve has been removed, pull the valve stem oil seal off the top of the valve guide and discard it as a new one must be used on reassembly **(see illustration)**.

9 Repeat the procedure for the remaining

valve. Remember to keep the parts for each valve together and in order so they can be reinstalled in the correct location.

10 Next, clean the cylinder head with solvent and dry it thoroughly. Compressed air will speed the drying process and ensure that all holes and recessed areas are clean.

11 Clean the valve springs, collets, retainers and spring seats with solvent. Work on the parts from one valve at a time so as not to mix them up.

12 Scrape off any carbon deposits that may have formed on the valve, then use a motorised wire brush to remove deposits from the valve heads and stems. Again, make sure the valves do not get mixed up.

Inspection and reassembly

13 Refer to Chapter 2C, Section 12 for details of valve inspection, lapping and reassembly.

Removal

1 Remove the cylinder head and the camchain guide blade (see Section 11).

2 Hold the camchain and lift the cylinder up off the crankcase, supporting the piston as it becomes accessible to prevent it hitting the crankcase opening **(see illustration)**. If the cylinder is stuck, tap around the joint face between the cylinder and the crankcase with a soft-faced mallet to free it. Don't attempt to free the cylinder by inserting a screwdriver between it and the crankcase – you'll damage the sealing surfaces.

3 Once the cylinder has been removed, stuff a clean rag into the crankcase opening around the piston to prevent anything falling inside.

4 Remove the cylinder base gasket, noting how it fits, then discard it as new one must be fitted on reassembly **(see illustration)**. Note any dowels in the cylinder or crankcase and remove them for safekeeping if they are loose **(see illustration)**. Note how the camchain locates on the crankshaft sprocket and secure the chain to prevent it dropping into the crankcase.

5 Clean all traces of old gasket material from the cylinder and crankcase with a suitable solvent. Take care not to scratch or gouge the soft aluminium. Be careful not to let any of the gasket material fall into the crankcase.

13.2 Lift the cylinder off the crankcase

13.4a Remove the cylinder base gasket

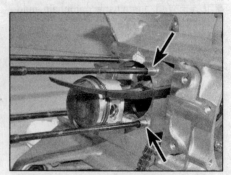

13.4b Note the location of the dowels (arrowed)

13.6 Inspect the bore (arrowed) for damage

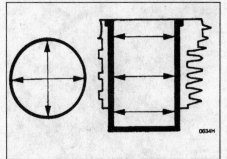

13.7a Measure the cylinder bore in the directions shown...

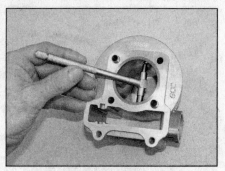

13.7b ...using a telescoping gauge

Inspection

6 Check the cylinder bore carefully for scratches and score marks **(see illustration)**.
7 If available, use a telescoping gauge and micrometer to measure the inside diameter of the cylinder bore to assess the amount of wear, taper and ovality (see *Tools and Workshop Tips* in the *Reference* section). Measure near the top (but below the level of the top piston ring at top dead centre), centre and bottom (but above the level of the bottom ring with the piston at bottom dead centre) of the bore both parallel to and across the crankshaft axis **(see illustrations)**.
8 Compare the results with the specifications at the beginning of this Chapter. If the cylinder bore is worn beyond its service limit, a new one should be fitted.
9 Calculate any differences between the measurements to determine any taper or ovality in the bore. A cylinder bore that has worn oval will reduce the efficiency of the piston rings to achieve a seal, resulting in loss of compression and increased oil consumption.
10 If no measuring tools are available, check for a lip around the (unworn) top edge of the cylinder bore as a rough indication of wear.
11 If the bore is tapered, oval, or worn excessively, badly scratched, scuffed or scored, the cylinder and piston will have to be renewed as a set.
12 Check that all the cylinder studs are tight in the crankcase halves. If any are loose, remove them (see *Tools and Workshop Tips*

in the *Reference* section) and clean their threads. Apply a suitable permanent thread locking compound, then screw them back into the crankcase securely.

Installation

13 Remove any rag from the crankcase opening. Ensure any dowels are correctly installed in the crankcase, then lay the new base gasket in place on the crankcase making sure it is the correct way round **(see illustrations 13.4b and a)**.
14 Position the piston ring end gaps correctly **(see illustration 15.9 in Chapter 2C)**.
15 Lubricate the cylinder bore, piston and piston rings, and the connecting rod big- and small-ends, with the clean engine oil, then lower the cylinder down until the piston crown fits into the bore.
16 Gently push down on the cylinder, making sure the piston enters the bore squarely and does not get cocked sideways. Carefully compress and feed each ring into the bore as the cylinder is lowered **(see illustration)**. If necessary, use a soft mallet to gently tap the cylinder down, but do not use force if it appears to be stuck as the piston and/or rings will be damaged.
17 When the piston is correctly installed in the cylinder, support the camchain and check that the base gasket has not been displaced, then press the cylinder down onto the base gasket **(see illustration)**.
18 Install the camchain guide blade, then install the cylinder head (see Section 11).

14 Piston

Refer to Chapter 2C, Section 14, noting the piston diameter figure given in the Specifications at the beginning of this Chapter.

15 Piston rings

Refer to Chapter 2C, Section 15, noting that on this engine the compression rings usually have a marking or letter near the gap to denote the upper surface of the ring **(see illustration)**.

16 Alternator

Note: *This procedure can be carried out with the engine in the scooter. If the engine has been removed, ignore the steps that do not apply.*

Removal

1 The alternator is located behind the slotted fan cover on the right-hand side of the engine

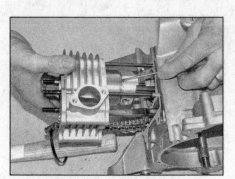

13.16 Carefully compress the rings into the cylinder bore

13.17 Press the cylinder down onto the base gasket

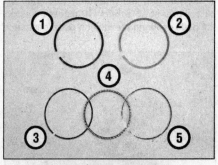

15.1 Piston ring set

1 *Top compression ring*
2 *Second compression ring*
3 *Upper side rail*
4 *Rail spacer*
5 *Lower side rail*

16.3 Using a home made pin wrench to hold the rotor

16.5a Install the puller fully...

16.5b ...then screw in the centre bolt

16.5c Hold the puller and tighten the centre bolt

16.6 Locate the puller as shown and tighten the centre bolt

– remove the cover and the cooling fan (see Section 7).

2 To undo the alternator rotor centre nut it is necessary to stop the rotor from turning using a pin wrench that locates in the two large holes in the face of the rotor. Peugeot produces a service tool (Part No. 752237) for this purpose. Alternatively, a similar home-made tool can be used (refer to the illustration in Chapter 2A, Section 11) or you can obtain an aftermarket version. **Note:** *Take great care not to damage the internal coils of the alternator when locating any tools through the rotor.*

3 With the rotor securely held, undo the centre nut and remove the washer **(see illustration)**.

4 Alternatively, the alternator rotor can be held with a strap wrench. If necessary, undo the bolts securing the ignition pulse generator

coil and displace it to avoid damaging it when using the strap wrench.

5 To remove the rotor from the taper on the crankshaft it is necessary to use a puller that threads into the internal thread in the centre of the rotor. Peugeot produces service tools (puller Part No. 750806, protective spacer Part No. 068007) for this purpose and similar aftermarket pullers are available. Ensure the puller is threaded all the way into the centre of the rotor, then screw in the centre bolt. Hold the puller and tighten the centre bolt steadily to draw the rotor off the crankshaft taper **(see illustrations)**.

6 Alternatively, use a two-legged puller as shown **(see illustration)**. Thread the puller legs into the threaded holes in the rotor, then tighten the centre bolt exerting steady pressure to draw the rotor off the taper. **Note:**

To avoid damaging the threaded end of the crankshaft, either leave the centre nut on the shaft with just enough clearance to allow the rotor to be dislodged, or position a soft metal spacer between the end of the shaft and the puller centre bolt.

7 Lift the rotor off the crankshaft **(see illustration)**.

8 If it is loose, remove the Woodruff key from the shaft for safekeeping, noting how it fits **(see illustration)**.

9 The alternator stator coils and ignition pulse generator coil are wired together and have to be removed as an assembly. If not already done, trace the wiring back from the alternator and pulse generator and disconnect it at the connectors **(see illustration 4.8b)**. Free the wiring from any clips or guides and feed it through to the alternator. Draw the rubber boot out of the crankcase **(see illustration)**.

10 If not already done, undo the bolts securing the pulse generator coil and the lower wiring guide. Undo the bolt securing the upper wiring guide inside the casing, noting how it fits, then undo the bolts securing the alternator stator and lift the assembly off **(see illustrations)**.

Installation

11 Installation is the reverse of removal, noting the following:

● Ensure the wiring is correctly routed before installing the stator and pulse generator.

● Don't forget to install the wiring guides.

● Tighten the stator, pulse generator and

16.7 Remove the alternator rotor

16.8 Location of the Woodruff key (arrowed)

16.9 Ease out the rubber boot

wiring guide bolts to the torque setting specified at the beginning of this Chapter.
● Make sure that no metal objects have attached themselves to the magnets on the inside of the rotor.
● Clean the tapered end of the crankshaft and the corresponding mating surface on the inside of the rotor with a suitable solvent.
● Fit the Woodruff key into the crankshaft, align the slot in the centre of the rotor with the key, then install the rotor.
● Tighten the rotor centre nut to the specified torque setting.
● Secure the wiring with any clips or ties.
● Ensure that the cooling fan and fan cover are correctly installed (see Section 7).

16.10a Upper wiring guide (A), pulse generator coil (B) and alternator stator (C)

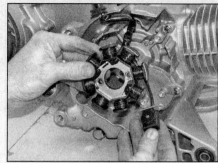

16.10b Removing the alternator/pulse generator assembly

17 Oil pump

Removal

1 The oil pump is located in a housing on the right-hand side of the crankcase. Remove the alternator for access (see Section 16).
2 Drain the engine oil (see Chapter 1).
3 Undo the bolts securing the pump outer cover and draw the cover off (see illustrations). Do not try to lever the cover off if it is stuck as this may damage the sealing surface. Thread the pulse generator coil bolts into their locations and pull on them with pliers. Note that the long cover bolt is one of the bolts that hold the crankcase halves together. Note the location of the cover O-ring and discard it as a new one must be fitted on installation.
4 Note how the pump gear pinion engages with the drive gear on the crankshaft, then pull the gear out (see illustrations). Note how the flat edge of the pump shaft engages with the inner pump rotor.
5 Undo the bolts securing the pump and draw it out, noting the location of the dowels (see illustrations). Remove the dowels for safekeeping if they are loose.

17.3a Oil pump outer cover bolts (arrowed)

17.3b Long bolt is also a crankcase bolt

17.3c Location of the cover O-ring

17.4a Note how the gears (arrowed) engage

17.4b Flat edge (arrowed) engages with inner pump rotor

17.5a Undo the pump mounting bolts

17.5b Note location of the dowels

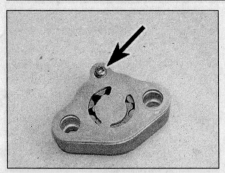

17.8a Pump cover is retained by screw (arrowed)

17.8b Reference marks on pump rotors

17.10 Dowels (arrowed) ensure alignment of the pump cover

Inspection

6 Examine the pump body for obvious signs of damage especially around the mounting bolt holes. Fit the driveshaft into the pump and turn it by hand to check that the pump rotates smoothly.

7 If required, the pump can be disassembled for cleaning and inspection.

8 Note how the pump cover fits, then undo the screw securing the cover and remove it **(see illustrations)**. Note the reference marks on the pump rotors; even if the rotors are not marked, it is essential that they are reassembled the same way around. Lift out the inner and outer rotors.

9 Clean the pump components with a suitable solvent and dry them with compressed air, if available. Inspect the pump body, rotors and shaft for scoring and wear. If any damage, scoring, uneven or excessive wear is evident, renew the pump. Ensure that the pump pinion

is a secure fit on the shaft. Inspect the teeth of the pump pinion and the crankshaft drive gear for wear or damage. If necessary, fit a new pump pinion. The drive gear is integral with the crankshaft – if it is damaged, a new crankshaft assembly will have to be fitted (see Section 20).

10 If the pump is good, reassemble the rotors in the reverse order of disassembly and lubricate them with clean engine oil **(see illustration 17.8b)**. Fit the dowels into the pump body **(see illustration)** to ensure correct alignment of the cover, then fit the cover as noted on removal and tighten the cover screw securely. Temporarily install the driveshaft and check that the rotors turn smoothly and freely. If not, readjust the position of the cover.

11 Ensure the inside of the pump housing and the pump mating surface in the crankcase are clean.

Installation

12 Installation is the reverse of removal, noting the following:

● Fill the pump with clean engine oil before installation.

● Press the pump body squarely into its housing then tighten the mounting bolts evenly to the torque setting specified at the beginning of this Chapter **(see illustration 17.5a)**.

● Ensure the pump shaft engages correctly with the inner rotor and that the pump pinion engages with the crankshaft gear.

● Fit the outer cover with a new O-ring and tighten the cover bolts to the specified torque setting.

● Fill the engine with the correct type and quantity of oil (see Chapter 1 and *Pre-ride checks*)

18 Starter pinion

Removal

1 Note the position of the starter motor. The starter pinion is located inside the transmission casing on the left-hand side. Remove the drive belt cover for access (see Chapter 3).

2 The starter pinion is located above the variator **(see illustration)**.

3 Remove the cover, noting how it fits, then withdraw the starter pinion assembly **(see illustrations)**.

Inspection

4 Check the starter pinion assembly for any signs of damage or wear, particularly for chipped or broken teeth on either of the pinions **(see illustration)**. Check the corresponding teeth on the starter motor pinion (see Chapter 10) and the variator ring gear (see Chapter 3).

5 Rotate the outer (smaller) pinion and check that it moves smoothly up and down the shaft, and that it returns easily to its rest position. The starter pinion is supplied as a complete unit; if any of the component parts are worn or damaged, the unit will have to be replaced with a new one.

6 Examine the bush inside the pinion cover and renew it if it is worn **(see illustration 18.4)**.

18.2 Location of the starter pinion cover (arrowed)

18.3a Pull out the cover...

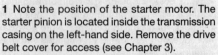

18.3b ...and withdraw the starter pinion

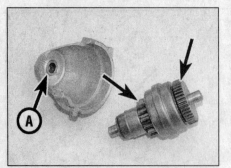

18.4 Examine the pinions (arrowed) for wear and damage. Note location of the bush (A)

7 The manufacturer recommends that the starter pinion mechanism should not be lubricated as any excess grease may contaminate the drive belt and cause it to slip. However, a smear of grease should be applied to both ends of the pinion shaft before reassembly.

Installation

8 Installation is the reverse of removal. Ensure the inner pinion engages with the starter motor shaft.

19 Crankcase halves

Separation

1 Follow the procedure in Section 4 and remove the engine from the frame.
2 Before the crankcase halves can be separated the following components must be removed:
● Camchain (Section 9)
● Cylinder head (Section 11)
● Cylinder (Section 13)
● Alternator (Section 16)
● Variator (Chapter 3)
● Starter motor (Chapter 10)
● Oil pump (Section 17)
● Centrestand (Chapter 7)
3 Tape some rag around the connecting rod to prevent it knocking against the cases. Although not essential, it is advisable to remove the piston to avoid damage during this procedure.
4 The left-hand crankshaft oil seal is secured by a holder – follow the procedure in Section 9 to remove the holder and seal and withdraw the camchain from the engine. Remove the camchain tensioner blade.
5 Support the crankcase assembly on the work surface on its left-hand side. Loosen the remaining crankcase bolts evenly, a little at a time and in a criss-cross sequence until they are all finger-tight, then remove them noting their locations **(see illustrations)**. Note: *Ensure that all the crankcase bolts have been removed before attempting to separate the cases.*

 Make a cardboard template of the crankcase and punch a hole for each bolt location. This will ensure that they are all installed correctly on reassembly – this is important as the bolts are of different lengths.

6 Lift the right-hand crankcase half off the left-hand half **(see illustration)**. If the crankcase halves do not separate easily, first ensure all fasteners have been removed. Next, apply heat to the right-hand main bearing housing with a hot air gun and try lifting the right-hand half off again.

19.5a Location of the remaining crankcase bolts

Caution: Do not try to separate the halves by levering against the mating surfaces as they are easily scored and will not seal correctly afterwards. Do not strike the ends of the crankshaft with a hammer as damage to the end threads or the shaft itself will result.

7 If the crankcase is an extremely tight fit on the crankshaft, a puller arrangement will be required to facilitate the procedure **(see illustration 20.6 in Chapter 2C)**. If the puller is placed across the end of the crankshaft, thread the alternator centre nut on first to protect the threads. Take care to ensure that equal pressure is applied on both sides of the puller arrangement at all times and apply heat to the bearing housing.
8 Now lift the crankshaft assembly out of the left-hand crankcase half – apply heat to the main bearing housing if required **(see**

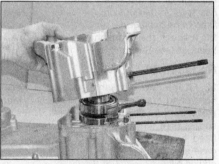

19.6 Lift off the right-hand crankcase half

19.10 Discard the old gasket. Note dowels (arrowed)

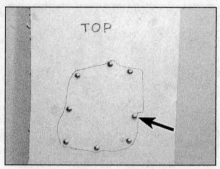

19.5b Keep bolts in a template. Note oil pump outer cover bolt (arrowed)

illustration). Note that the main bearings will remain in place on the crankshaft assembly (see Section 20).
9 If the crankcase is an extremely tight fit on the crankshaft, use a similar set-up to the one in Step 7, only this time press the crankshaft out of the left-hand crankcase half. Thread the variator nut onto the end of the crankshaft to protect the threads and make sure the crankshaft assembly is supported to prevent it dropping if it suddenly comes free.
10 Remove the gasket and discard it as a new one must be used. Remove any dowels from either crankcase half for safekeeping if they are loose **(see illustration)**.
11 If not already done, unscrew the oil strainer plug and remove the spring and strainer **(see illustration)**. Note which way round the spring and strainer are fitted. Note the location of the

19.8 Lift the crankshaft assembly out of the left-hand crankcase half

19.11 Remove the oil strainer assembly

19.13 Drive the old seal out from the outside

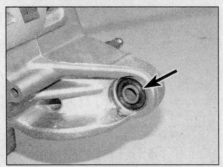

19.19 Inspect the engine mounting bushes

O-ring on the strainer plug and discard it as a new one must be fitted on reassembly.

12 Clean the mating surfaces of the crankcase halves with a suitable solvent to remove any traces of old gasket or sealant. Take care not to scratch or gouge the soft aluminium.

13 Note the position of the right-hand crankshaft oil seal and note which way round the seal is fitted. Drive the seal out from the outside using a suitably sized socket and discard it as a new one must be fitted on reassembly **(see illustration)**.

14 If required, remove the transmission assembly from the left-hand crankcase half (see Chapter 3).

Inspection

15 Wash the cases in a suitable solvent and dry them with compressed air, if available.

16 Small cracks or holes in aluminium castings can be repaired with an epoxy resin adhesive as a temporary measure. Permanent repairs can only be effected by welding, and only a specialist in this process is in a position to advise on the economy or practical aspect of such a repair. On some engines, the crankcase halves can be renewed individually, on others the two halves are only available together as a matching set.

17 Damaged threads can be economically reclaimed by using a thread insert. Most small engineering firms offer a service of this kind. Sheared screws can usually be removed with screw extractors. Refer to *Tools and Workshop Tips* in the *Reference* section for further details.

18 Always wash the crankcases thoroughly after

any repair work to ensure no dirt or metal swarf is trapped inside when the engine is rebuilt.

19 Inspect the engine mounting bushes **(see illustration)**. If they show signs of deterioration, renew them all at the same time. To remove a bush, first note its position in the casing. Heat the casing with a hot air gun, then support the casing and drive the bush out with a hammer and a suitably sized socket. Alternatively, use two suitably sized sockets to press the bush out in the jaws of a vice. Clean the bush housing with steel wool to remove any corrosion, then reheat the casing and fit the new bush. **Note:** *Always support the casing when removing or fitting bushes to avoid breaking the casing.*

20 Inspect the main bearing housings. If a bearing outer race has spun in its housing, the inside of the housing will be damaged. A bearing locking compound can be used to fix the outer race in place on reassembly if the damage is not too severe. **Note:** *If a bearing has spun in its housing, the bearing itself is likely to be damaged – see Section 20.*

21 Inspect the crankshaft assembly and bearings (see Section 20).

Reassembly

22 Fit the new crankshaft oil seal into the right-hand crankcase half and press it into place from the inside using a seal driver or socket **(see illustration)**. Ensure the seal is fitted the right way round and that it enters the case squarely. Lubricate the seal with clean engine oil.

23 Support the left-hand crankcase half on

the work surface with enough space below it to provide clearance for the end of the crankshaft when it is fully installed.

24 Lubricate the left-hand crankshaft main bearing with clean engine oil and tape some rag around the connecting rod to prevent it knocking against the cases.

25 If required, heat the bearing housing in the crankcase with a hot air gun. In addition, if the bearing is an extremely tight fit, a freeze spray can be used on the main bearing to aid installation.

26 Lower the crankshaft assembly into the crankcase half carefully. Ensure that the main bearing is aligned with the bearing housing and that the connecting rod is aligned with the crankcase mouth, then press the crankshaft assembly in fully so that the main bearing goes all the way into its housing. If the main bearing does not seat fully, apply more heat around the bearing housing while applying steady pressure to the crankshaft assembly.

27 If necessary, allow the case to cool, then wipe the mating surfaces of both crankcase halves with a rag soaked in suitable solvent and fit the dowels. Install the new crankcase gasket on the mating surface of the left-hand case.

28 Lubricate the right-hand crankshaft seal and main bearing with clean engine oil.

29 Heat the bearing housing with a hot air gun. **Note:** *Avoid applying direct heat onto the crankshaft oil seal.* If required, use a freeze spay on the main bearing.

30 Lower the crankcase half over the crankshaft carefully to avoid damaging the seal. Ensure that the two halves of the crankcase are correctly aligned, taking special note of the position of the dowels, and that the main bearing is aligned with the bearing housing in the right-hand case **(see illustration 19.6)**.

31 Press the crankcase on fully so that the main bearing goes all the way into its housing. If the main bearing does not seat fully, apply more heat to the around the bearing housing while apply steady pressure to the crankcase.

32 Check that the crankcase halves are seated all the way round. If the cases are not correctly seated, heat the bearing housings while applying firm pressure. **Note:** *Do not attempt to pull the crankcase halves together using the crankcase bolts as the casing will crack and be ruined.*

33 Clean the threads of the crankcase bolts and install them finger-tight, then tighten them evenly a little at a time in a criss-cross sequence to the torque setting specified at the beginning of this Chapter **(see illustration 19.5a)**. At this stage do not install the long bolt that retains the oil pump outer cover **(see illustration 19.5b)**.

34 Trim off any excess gasket across the crankcase mouth **(see illustration)**.

35 Support the connecting rod and rotate the crankshaft by hand – if there are any signs of undue stiffness, tight or rough spots, or of any other problem, the fault must be rectified before proceeding further.

19.22 Fit the new right-hand crankcase oil seal from the inside

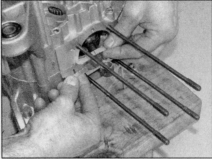

19.34 Trim off the excess gasket with a sharp blade

19.36 Level the seal with the crankcase

20.4 Check for up-and-down play in the big-end bearing

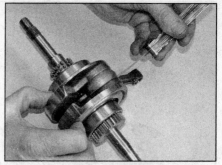

20.5 Measuring big-end side clearance

36 Install the camchain and ensure that it is correctly fitted around the crankshaft sprocket **(see illustrations 9.9 and 9.8)**. Lubricate a new left-hand crankshaft oil seal with clean engine oil than press it into place in the crankcase. Ensure the seal is fitted the right way round and that it enters the case squarely **(see illustration 9.7d)**. Level the outside edge of the seal with the crankcase using a hammer and a block of wood **(see illustration)**. Install the camchain tensioner blade (see Section 9).
37 Install the remaining components in the reverse order of removal.

20 Crankshaft assembly, big-end and main bearings

Note: *The crankshaft assembly is pressed together and is easily damaged if it is dropped.*
1 To access the crankshaft assembly, the big-end bearing and the main bearings, the crankcase must be split into two parts (see Section 19).
2 The crankshaft assembly should give many thousands of miles of service. The most likely problems to occur will be a worn small or big-end bearing due to poor lubrication. A worn big-end bearing will produce a pronounced knocking noise, most audible when the engine is under load, and increasing as engine speed rises. This should

not be confused with small-end bearing wear, which produces a lighter, metallic rattle (see Section 14).
3 When the crankcase halves are separated, the main bearings will remain in place on the crankshaft assembly – they are not available as separate items. If the main bearings have failed, excessive rumbling and vibration will be felt when the engine is running.
4 To assess the condition of the big-end bearing, hold the crankshaft assembly firmly and push and pull on the connecting rod, checking for any up-and-down freeplay between the two **(see illustration)**. If any freeplay is noted, the bearing is worn.
5 A small amount of big-end side clearance (side-to-side movement) is acceptable on the connecting rod – this can be measured with a feeler gauge **(see illustration)**. Compare the result with the specification at the beginning of this Chapter. If the clearance is greater than the service limit a new crankshaft assembly will have to be fitted.
6 Follow the procedure in *Tools and Workshop Tips* in the *Reference* section to check the condition of the main bearings.
7 If wear or damage is noted in any of the crankshaft assembly bearings, a new crankshaft assembly will have to be fitted.
Note: *Evidence of extreme heat, such as discoloration or blueing, indicates that lubrication failure has occurred. Be sure to check the oil pump and bearing oil ways in the crankcases before reassembling the engine.*

8 If available, place the crankshaft assembly on V-blocks and check the runout on either side using a dial gauge – see *Specifications* at the beginning of this Chapter **(see illustration)**. If the crankshaft is out-of-true it will cause excessive engine vibration. If there is any doubt about the condition of the crankshaft have it checked by an automotive engineer.
9 Inspect the threads on each end of the crankshaft and ensure that the retaining nuts for the alternator rotor and the variator are a good fit. Inspect the splines for the variator pulley on the left-hand end of the shaft **(see illustration)**. Inspect the taper and the slot in the right-hand end of the shaft for the alternator Woodruff key **(see illustration)**. Damage or wear that prevents the rotor from being fitted securely will require a new crankshaft assembly.
10 Inspect the camshaft sprocket teeth and the oil pump drive gear on the crankshaft for damage or wear **(see illustrations 20.9a and b)**. The sprocket and gear are an integral part of the crankshaft assembly – if they are worn or damaged a new assembly will have to be fitted.

21 Initial start-up after overhaul/running-in

Refer to Chapter 2C, Section 22.

20.8 Check the crankshaft runout at the points shown

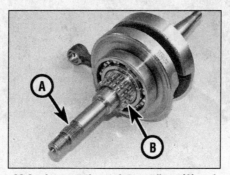

20.9a Inspect the variator splines (A) and the camshaft drive sprocket (B)

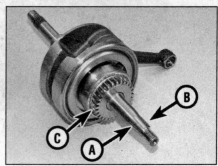

20.9b Inspect the alternator taper (A), Woodruff key slots (B) and oil pump drive gear (C)

Type P152QMI-A – left-hand view

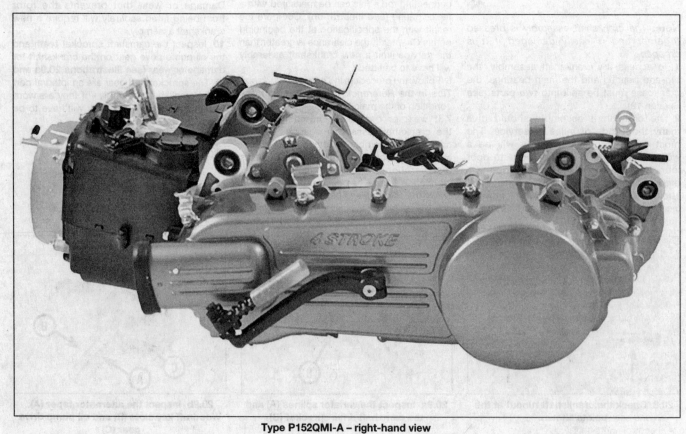

Type P152QMI-A – right-hand view

Chapter 2F
Four-stroke 125cc engine – type P152QMI-A

Refer to 'Model and servicing specifications' in Chapter 1 for model identification details

Contents

Degrees of difficulty

Easy, suitable for novice with little experience 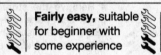	**Fairly easy,** suitable for beginner with some experience	**Fairly difficult,** suitable for competent DIY mechanic	**Difficult,** suitable for experienced DIY mechanic	**Very difficult,** suitable for expert DIY or professional

Specifications

General

Type	Single cylinder air-cooled 2-valve four-stroke
Capacity	124.6 cc
Bore x stroke	52.4 x 57.8 mm
Cylinder compression pressure	213 psi (15 Bars)

Valves

Valve clearances	See Chapter 1

Camshaft and rocker arms

Camshaft lobe height service limit	
Intake	25.68 mm
Exhaust	25.45 mm
Rocker shaft outside diameter service limit	9.91 mm

Cylinder bore

Cylinder bore diameter service limit	52.5 mm

Piston

Piston diameter service limit	52.3 mm
Piston-to-bore clearance service limit	0.10 mm
Piston pin outside diameter service limit	14.96 mm

Piston rings

Ring end gap (installed)	
Top ring	0.05 to 0.15 mm
Second ring	0.05 to 0.20 mm
Oil control ring	0.20 to 0.70 mm
Piston ring end gap service limit	
Top and second ring	0.5 mm
Oil control ring side rail	0.7 mm

Crankshaft and connecting rod

Connecting rod big-end side clearance service limit..............	0.55 mm
Connecting rod small-end internal diameter service limit	15.05 mm

Torque wrench settings

Alternator nut	60 Nm
Alternator stator bolts..	10 Nm
Cam chain tensioner bolts	10 Nm
Cam chain tensioner cap	8 Nm
Cam chain tensioner blade pivot bolt	10 Nm
Cooling fan bolts	10 Nm
Cylinder head nuts...	25 Nm
Cylinder head bolts	10 Nm
Crankcase bolts..	10 Nm
Crankcase cover bolts..	10 Nm
Clutch centre nut	55 Nm
Engine mounting bolt..	47 Nm
Intake manifold nuts...	10 Nm
Oil pump mounting bolts	10 Nm
Oil pump sprocket nut	10 Nm
Pulsair union nuts..	10 Nm
Pulse generator coil bolts..	8 Nm
Rear shock absorber bolts	
Lower	23 Nm
Upper	46 Nm
Starter clutch housing bolts..	12 Nm
Starter clutch nut	60 Nm
Valve cover bolts	10 Nm

1 General information

The engine is a single cylinder, 2-valve overhead-camshaft four-stroke, with fan assisted air cooling as fitted to the Vivacity 125. The camshaft is chain-driven off the crankshaft and operates the valves via rocker arms.

The crankshaft assembly is pressed together, incorporating the connecting rod.

The crankcase divides vertically – the left-hand crankcase is an integral part of the drive belt casing and gearbox.

2 Component access

Most components and assemblies, with the obvious exception of the crankshaft assembly and its bearings, can be worked on without having to remove the engine/transmission unit from the scooter. However, access to some components is severely restricted, and if a number of areas require attention at the same time, removal of the engine is recommended, as it is an easy task to undertake.

3 Cylinder compression test

Refer to Chapter 2C, Section 3, noting the compression figure given at the beginning of this chapter.

4 Engine removal and installation

Caution: The engine/transmission unit is not heavy, however removal and installation should be carried out with the aid of an assistant; personal injury or damage could occur if the engine falls or is dropped.

Removal

1 Support the scooter securely in an upright position on its centrestand. Work can be made easier by raising the machine to a suitable height on an hydraulic ramp or a suitable platform. Make sure it is secure and will not topple over.

2 Disconnect and remove the battery (see Chapter 10).

3 If required, drain the engine oil (see Chapter 1).

4 Remove the storage compartment, the under-seat panel, the seat cowling and the rear mudguard (see Chapter 9).

5 Remove the air filter housing and the air intake duct (see Chapter 5).

6 Remove the exhaust system (see Chapter 5).

7 Pull the spark plug cap off the plug and position the cap clear of the engine **(see illustration 4.14)**.

8 Disconnect the fuel hose from its union on the carburettor, being prepared to catch any residual fuel in a rag **(see illustration)**. Position a suitable container below the carburettor drain hose, then loosen the drain screw and drain any residual fuel from the float chamber **(see illustration)**. Tighten the drain screw. The carburettor can remain attached to the engine, but if removing it undo the drive belt casing bolt to free the drain hose guide.

9 Trace the wiring from the automatic choke unit and disconnect it at the connector (see

4.8a Disconnect the fuel hose from the union on the carburettor (arrowed)

4.8b Carburettor drain screw (arrowed)

4.11 Disconnect the fuel tap vacuum hose

4.12 Disconnect the lead from the starter motor terminal

4.13 Engine earth lead (arrowed)

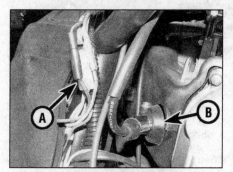

4.14 Alternator and ignition pulse generator wiring connectors (A), spark plug cap (B)

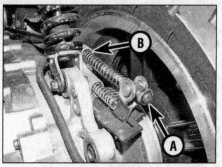

4.16a Disconnect the brake cable (A). Release the cable from the stop (B)...

4.16b ...and the clips on the top of the transmission casing

Chapter 5). **Note:** *When disconnecting any wiring, it is advisable to mark or tag the wires as a reminder of where they connect.* Disconnect the carburettor heater wiring connector.

10 Either displace or remove the carburettor completely, leaving the throttle cable attached if required, or just disconnect the throttle cable (see Chapter 5). If the carburettor is displaced, ensure it is secured to a convenient part of the frame to avoid damage. Ensure that the throttle cable and automatic choke wiring is clear of the engine unit. Stuff clean rag into the intake manifold to prevent anything falling inside.

11 Disconnect the fuel tap vacuum hose from its union on the inlet manifold **(see illustration).**

12 Pull back the boot, then undo the screw securing the lead to the starter motor terminal **(see illustration).**

13 Undo the bolt securing the earth (ground) lead to the crankcase and disconnect the lead **(see illustration).** Replace the bolt for safekeeping.

14 Trace the wiring from the alternator and ignition pulse generator coil on the right-hand side of the engine and disconnect it at the connectors **(see illustration).** Secure the wiring clear of the engine.

15 Release the clip securing the breather hose to the union on the valve cover and disconnect the hose. Detach the pipe from the pulsair on the valve cover.

16 Disconnect the rear brake cable from the brake arm **(see illustration).** Release the cable from the clips on the top of the transmission casing and pull it through the cable stop **(see illustration).**

17 Check that all wiring, cables and hoses are clear of the engine/transmission unit.

18 Working on one side at a time, undo the upper rear shock absorber mounting bolts and lower the wheel to the ground. Undo the lower shock mounting bolts and remove the shocks.

19 Remove the right-hand rear suspension arm (see Chapter 7).

20 Remove the rear wheel (see Chapter 8).

21 Undo the locknut on the engine mounting

bolt **(see illustration). Note:** *Peugeot recommends a new nut should be used on reassembly. Alternatively, clean the threads of the engine mounting bolt and apply a suitable thread-locking compound prior to installation.*

22 Have an assistant support the scooter, then carefully withdraw the engine mounting bolt **(see illustration).** Manoeuvre the engine unit back and out of the frame.

23 If the engine is dirty, particularly around its mountings, wash it thoroughly before starting any major dismantling work. This will make work much easier and rule out the possibility of dirt falling inside.

24 Check the condition of the rubber bushes

4.21 Undo the engine mounting bolt nut

4.22 Withdraw the mounting bolt carefully

4.24 Check the engine mounting bushes

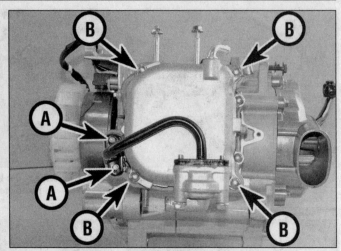

6.4 Pulsair flange nuts (A), valve cover bolts (B)

set in the engine mounting points (see illustration).

Installation

25 Installation is the reverse of removal, noting the following:

● Make sure no wires, cables or hoses become trapped between the engine and the frame when installing the engine
● Tighten the engine mounting bolt and shock absorber bolts to the torque settings in the *Specifications* at the beginning of this chapter.
● Make sure all wires, cables and hoses are correctly routed and connected, and secured by any clips or ties.
● If the engine oil was drained, or if any oil has been lost during overhaul, refill or top up as described in Chapter 1 and *Pre-ride checks*.
● Check the operation of the rear brake before riding the machine (see Chapter 1).

5 Disassembly and reassembly – general information

1 Refer to the general notes in Chapter 2C, Section 5.

6.5 Remove the valve cover

2 For this engine, disassembly should be done in the following general order with reference to the appropriate Sections (refer to Chapter 3 for details of transmission components):

● Remove the valve cover
● Remove the camshaft and rockers
● Remove the cylinder head
● Remove the cylinder
● Remove the piston
● Remove the starter motor (see Chapter 10)
● Remove the alternator
● Remove the starter clutch
● Remove the oil pump
● Separate the crankcase halves
● Remove the crankshaft

6 Valve cover

Removal

1 Remove the storage compartment and the under-seat panel (see Chapter 9).
2 If required, loosen the clip securing the breather hose to the valve cover and detach the hose.
3 Release the clip securing the pulsair valve

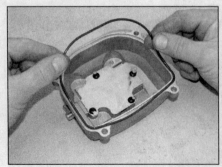

6.6 Note how gasket locates in the groove

to the reed valve housing on the lower front of the valve cover and detach the filter.
4 Undo the nuts securing the pulsair pipe flange to the cylinder head (see illustration).
5 Undo the bolts securing the valve cover, noting the location of any cable guides (see illustration 6.4), then lift the cover off (see illustration). If the cover is stuck, tap around the joint face between the cover and the cylinder head with a soft-faced mallet to free it. Do not try to lever the cover off as this may damage the sealing surfaces.
6 Remove the gasket and discard it as a new one must be used (see illustration). Clean the mating surfaces of the cylinder head and the valve cover with a suitable solvent to remove any traces of old gasket or sealant.
7 Note the location of the breather system baffle plate in the valve cover. If required, remove the plate and clean the inside of the cover. Bend back the tabs securing the plate screws carefully to avoid damaging them. On installation, ensure that the screws securing the plate are tightened securely – as a precaution, clean the screw threads and apply non-permanent thread-locking compound.

Installation

8 Fit a new gasket over the mounting studs for the pulsair pipe flange.
9 Lay the new gasket onto the valve cover, making sure it fits correctly into the groove (see illustration 6.6).
10 Position the valve cover on the cylinder head, making sure the gasket stays in place. Install the cover bolts with any cable guides as noted on removal, then tighten the bolts evenly and in a criss-cross sequence to the torque setting specified at the beginning of this Chapter.
11 Tighten the pulsair union nuts to the specified torque.
12 Install the breather hose and secure it with the clip.
13 Install the remaining components in the reverse order of removal.

7.1a Undo the bolts (arrowed)...

7.1b ...and lift off the fan cover

7.3 Pull off the spark plug cap

7   Engine cowling and cooling fan

1 Unclip any wiring or hoses from the fan cover, then undo the bolts securing the cover and remove it (see illustrations).

2 Remove any spacers for the cowling bolts for safekeeping if they are loose.

3 If not already done, pull the cap off the spark plug (see illustration).

4 Remove the exhaust system (see Chapter 5). Remove the carburettor and intake manifold (see Chapter 5).

5 Note the location of the screws securing the two halves of the cowling together, then undo the screws (see illustrations).

6 Ease the two halves of the cowling apart carefully to avoid straining the tabs securing the halves together, then lift the cowling off (see illustration).

7 Note the location of the seal around the top edge of the cylinder. Remove the seal carefully, noting how it fits. If the seal is damaged or deteriorated replace it with a new one.

8 Undo the bolts securing the cooling fan to the alternator rotor and remove the fan (see illustration).

9 Installation is the reverse of removal. Tighten the cooling fan bolts to the torque setting specified at the beginning of this Chapter.

10 Don't forget to install the cowling seal. Ensure that the two halves of the cowling fit together correctly – do not force them. Take care not to over-tighten the joining screws.

8   Camchain tensioner

Removal

1 The camchain tensioner is located on the back of the cylinder on the left-hand side. Remove the engine cowling for access (see Section 7).

2 Remove the spark plug (see Chapter 1, Section 15).

3 Turn the engine in the normal direction of rotation until the piston is at top dead centre

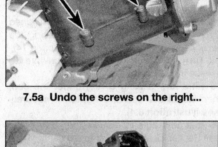

7.5a Undo the screws on the right...

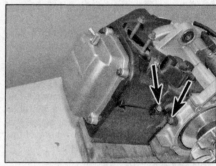

7.5b ...and left-hand sides

7.6 Ease the cowling apart carefully

7.8 Undo the bolts securing the fan

(TDC) on its compression stroke. You can do this by rotating the crankshaft via the alternator rotor. The position of the piston can be confirmed by ensuring that the timing mark 'T' on the alternator rotor is aligned with the register mark on the crankcase (see illustration).

4 Undo the tensioner cap, noting the location of the sealing O-ring (see illustration). Discard the O-ring as a new one must be fitted.

5 Using a small flat-bladed screwdriver, turn the tensioner clockwise until it goes tight – this will retract the tensioner plunger into the

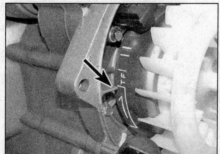

8.3 T mark should align with register mark (arrowed)

8.4 Note location of the O-ring

8.5 Turn tensioner screw clockwise

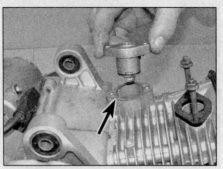

8.6 Remove the tensioner and gasket (arrowed)

8.9 Check action of the tensioner plunger

tensioner body **(see illustration)**. The plunger should remain in this position.

6 Undo the tensioner mounting bolts and withdraw the tensioner from the cylinder **(see illustration)**. Remove the gasket from the base of the tensioner or from the cylinder and discard it as a new one must be used.

7 Clean all traces of old gasket material from the tensioner and cylinder with a suitable solvent. Take care not to scratch or gouge the soft aluminium. Be careful not to let any of the gasket material fall into the engine.

Inspection

8 Examine the tensioner components for signs of wear or damage.

9 Turn the tensioner anti-clockwise to release the plunger. Now try to press the plunger back into the body – it should be locked in position **(see illustration)**.

10 By turning the screwdriver, ensure that the plunger moves freely in and out of the tensioner body. Examine the foot of the plunger for wear **(see illustration)**.

11 If any part of the tensioner is worn or damaged, or if the plunger is seized in the body, a new tensioner must be fitted.

Installation

12 Turn the tensioner clockwise to retract the plunger. Fit a new gasket on the tensioner body, install the tensioner in the cylinder and tighten the mounting bolts to the torque setting specified at the beginning of this Chapter.

13 Turn the engine in the normal direction of rotation – this removes all the slack in the front run of the chain between the crankshaft

and the camshaft, and transfers it to the back run where it will be taken up by the tensioner.

Note: *Take care when turning the engine with the tensioner spring removed to avoid the chain jumping over the teeth on the camshaft sprocket. If this happens, ensure that the timing marks on the alternator rotor and on the camshaft sprocket are correctly re-aligned with the piston at TDC before releasing the tensioner plunger (see Chapter 1, Section 14).*

14 Turn the tensioner anti-clockwise to release the plunger.

15 Fit a new sealing O-ring under the cap, then install the cap and tighten it securely **(see illustration 8.4)**.

16 It is advisable to remove the valve cover (see Section 6) and check that the camchain is tensioned. If it is slack, the tensioner plunger did not release. Remove the tensioner and check the operation of the plunger again.

17 Install the remaining components in the reverse order of removal.

9 Camchain, blades and sprockets

Camchain

Inspection

1 The camchain runs between the drive sprocket on the crankshaft and the camshaft sprocket. To check the condition of the chain, first remove the valve cover (see Section 6).

2 Remove the spark plug (see Chapter 1,

Section 15). If not already done, remove the fan cover (see Section 7).

3 Turn the engine slowly in the normal direction of rotation and inspect the inside edges of the chain links for wear. Next, hold the chain at the mid-way point around the camshaft sprocket and try to lift it off the sprocket. The chain should be a firm fit on the sprocket. Turn the engine in the normal direction of rotation and check the entire length of the chain.

4 If any of the above checks indicate that the camchain has worn, a new one must be fitted.

Removal and installation

5 The camchain cannot be removed until the crankcase halves have been separated and the crankshaft has been removed (see Section 20).

6 Installation is the reverse of removal, noting the following:

● Ensure the chain is correctly installed on the crankshaft sprocket before assembling the crankcase halves. Secure the chain to one of the cylinder studs to prevent it being displaced during engine assembly.

● Pay particular attention to the alignment of the TDC timing mark 'T' on the alternator rotor and the timing marks on the camshaft sprocket before installing the chain onto the sprocket.

● Ensure any slack in the chain is in the back run where it will be taken up by the tensioner.

Camchain guide and tensioner blades

Removal

7 The guide blade can be removed after the cylinder head has been removed (see Section 11).

8 The tensioner blade is secured by a pivot bolt on its lower end. To remove the blade, first remove the camshaft (see Section 10). Secure the camchain to prevent it falling down into the tunnel in the side of the cylinder.

9 Remove the variator (see Chapter 3).

10 Undo the pivot bolt and lift the blade out **(see illustration)**. Note which way round the blade is fitted. Note the location of the sealing O-ring on the pivot bolt and discard it as a new one must be fitted.

8.10 Examine plunger foot for wear

9.10 Removing the camchain tensioner blade

11 Check both blades for wear or damage and renew them if necessary. Check the operation of the camchain tensioner (see Section 8).

Installation

12 Installation is the reverse of removal. Ensure that the blades are fitted the correct way round **(see illustrations 9.10 and 11.8)**. Clean the threads of the tensioner blade pivot bolt and apply non-permanent thread-locking compound. Fit a new O-ring and tighten the bolt to the torque setting in the Specifications at the beginning of this Chapter.

Camchain sprockets

13 The camshaft sprocket is integral with the camshaft. To inspect the sprocket for wear, follow the procedure in Section 10 and remove the camshaft.
14 Check for wear on the sides and tips of the sprocket teeth and for chipped or hooked teeth.
15 Similar checks should be made on the crankshaft sprocket – this is integral with the crankshaft assembly (see Section 21).
16 If the sprocket teeth are worn, the chain will also be worn. Always renew the components as an assembly – worn sprockets will soon damage a new chain.
Caution: After installing the camchain tensioner, turn the crankshaft and check that all the timing marks still align correctly. If the timing marks are not aligned exactly as described, the valve timing will be incorrect and the valves may strike the piston, causing extensive damage to the engine.

10 Camshaft and rocker arms

Removal

1 Remove the valve cover (see Section 6) and engine cowlings (see Section 7). Remove the cowling seal **(see illustration)**.
2 Remove the camchain tensioner (see Section 8). Note that when the piston is at TDC on its compression stroke the valves are closed

10.1 Remove the cowling seal

10.2a Check for a small clearance in both rocker arms

10.2b Note alignment of the timing marks

10.5 Undo the cylinder head nuts

and a small clearance can be felt at each rocker arm **(see illustration)**. Look for timing marks or two small holes on the camshaft sprocket – these should be aligned with the valve cover gasket face **(see illustration)**.
3 Stuff a clean rag into the camchain tunnel to prevent anything falling into the engine.
4 The camshaft and rockers are located in a holder which is retained by long studs that also secure the cylinder head and cylinder to the crankcases. Before loosening the cylinder head nuts, loosen the small bolts securing the left-hand side of the cylinder head **(see illustration 11.4a)**.
5 Now unscrew the cylinder head nuts evenly and a little at a time in a criss-cross pattern, until they are all loose, then remove the nuts and washers **(see illustration)**.
6 Note which way round the camshaft holder is fitted. On the engine used to illustrate this

procedure, the holder was marked EX on the exhaust side. Hold the camshaft in position in the cylinder head and lift off the camshaft holder **(see illustration)**.
7 Note any dowels in the holder or head and remove them for safekeeping if they are loose **(see illustration 11.4b)**.
8 Lift the camchain off the sprocket and secure the chain to prevent it dropping into the engine **(see illustration)**.
9 Note the location of the camshaft and camshaft bearings, then lift out the camshaft **(see illustration)**.
10 The rocker shafts are retained in the camshaft holder by the cylinder studs. Once the holder has been removed from the engine, the shafts and individual rocker arms can be disassembled. Note the position of the rocker arms and mark them so that they can be installed in their original positions **(see**

10.6 Lift off the camshaft holder

10.8 Lift off the camchain and secure it

10.9 Lift out the camshaft and bearings

10.10a Mark the rocker arms (arrowed) to aid reassembly

10.10b Pull out the rocker shaft noting cut-out for cylinder stud

10.11a Location of the decompressor cam mechanism

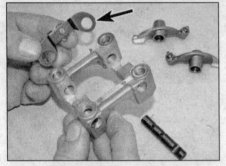

10.11b Decompressor stopper arm plate (arrowed)

10.12 Components of the camshaft holder assembly

15 Check the condition of the camshaft bearings (see *Tools and Workshop Tips* in the Reference section). The camshaft, camchain sprocket and bearings are supplied as an assembly, so if any component is worn a new assembly will have to be fitted.

16 Check the bearing housings in the camshaft holder and the cylinder head for score marks and spalling. Any damage is an indication that the bearing has seized on the camshaft and turned inside its housing. Prior to reassembly, check that the outer race is a tight fit in its housing, otherwise use some bearing locking compound to hold it in position.

17 Check the operation of the decompressor cam on the camshaft and the stopper arm (see Step 11). If any of the components are worn or do not move smoothly replace them with new ones.

18 Blow through the oil passages in the rocker arms and shafts with compressed air, if available, to ensure that they are clear.

19 Inspect the face of the rocker arm (see illustration 10.14a) and the contact area between the adjuster screw and the valve stem for pits and spalling.

20 Check the rocker shaft for wear. If available, use a micrometer to measure the diameter of the shaft in several places and compare the results with the *Specifications*. **Note:** *Any variation in the measurements is an indication of wear on the shaft.*

21 The rocker arm should be a sliding fit on the shaft without any freeplay. If the shaft is good but there is freeplay, the rocker arm is worn and should be renewed.

illustration). Working on one shaft at a time, thread a suitably-sized bolt into the end of the shaft and withdraw it carefully, removing the rocker arm when it becomes free **(see illustration)**.

11 The engine used to illustrate this procedure was fitted with a reverse decompressor cam. A one-way bearing inside the cam allows it to free-wheel when the engine is turning in the normal direction of rotation. However, if the engine kicks-back when being started and turns in the opposite direction to normal, the bearing locks and raises the lobe of the decompressor cam which opens the exhaust valve, stopping the engine. The main components of the decompressor cam mechanism are located on the right-hand end of the camshaft **(see illustration)**. A plate with a spring loaded stopper arm is located on the right-hand side

of the camshaft holder **(see illustration)**. Note which way round the plate is fitted.

12 Keep the components in order so that they can be reinstalled in their correct locations **(see illustration)**.

Inspection

13 Clean all of the components with a suitable solvent and dry them.

14 Inspect the camshaft lobes for heat discoloration (blue appearance), score marks, chipped areas, flat spots and spalling **(see illustration)**. If available, use a micrometer to measure the height of each camshaft lobe and compare the results with the specifications at the beginning of this Chapter **(see illustration)**. If damage is noted or the camshaft has worn more than the service limit it must be renewed.

Installation

22 Installation is the reverse of removal, noting the following:

● Ensure the piston is at TDC **(see illustration 8.3)** on the compression stroke before you start.

● Lubricate the shafts, bearing surfaces and bearings with clean engine oil before installation.

● Ensure the stopper arm plate for the decompressor cam is correctly installed **(see illustration 10.11b)**.

● Position the rocker shafts so that the holes for the cylinder studs are clear **(see illustration 10.10b)**.

10.14a Inspect the camshaft lobes and corresponding face of the rocker arm (arrowed)

10.14b Measuring the camshaft lobe height

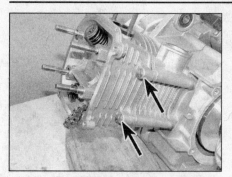

11.4a Small bolts (arrowed) secure the cylinder head

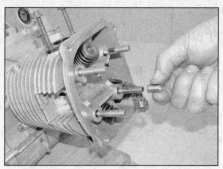

11.4b Remove the camshaft holder dowels

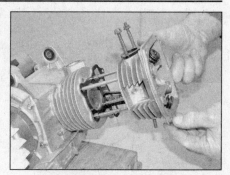

11.5 Lift off the cylinder head...

● Ensure any dowels are correctly installed in the camshaft holder or cylinder head.
● Tighten the cylinder head nuts a little at a time in a criss-cross sequence to the torque setting specified at the beginning of this Chapter.
● Tighten the smaller cylinder head bolts to the specified torque.
● Check the valve clearances (see Chapter 1).

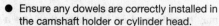

11 Cylinder head

Caution: The engine must be completely cool before beginning this procedure or the cylinder head may become warped.

Removal

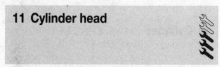

1 Remove the carburettor, intake manifold and exhaust system (see Chapter 5).
2 Remove the fan cover and engine cowling (see Section 7).
3 Remove the camshaft and rockers (see Section 10). **Note:** *The cylinder head studs pass down through the cylinder and screw into the crankcase. Once the cylinder head is loose care must be taken not to break the cylinder base gasket seal otherwise a new base gasket will have to be fitted before refitting the head (see Section 13).*
4 If not already done, remove the small bolts securing the cylinder head **(see illustration)**. Remove the camshaft holder dowels **(see illustration)**.

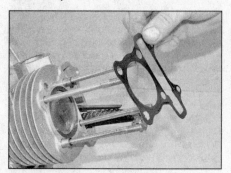

11.6 ...and remove the head gasket

5 Using a length of bent wire to hold the camchain, lift the cylinder head off the cylinder, feeding the camchain down through the tunnel in the head **(see illustration)**. If the head is stuck, tap around the joint face between the head and the cylinder with a soft-faced mallet to free it. Do not try to lever the head off as this may damage the sealing surfaces.
6 Remove the old cylinder head gasket **(see illustration)**. Note any dowels in the head or cylinder and remove them for safekeeping if they are loose.
7 Secure the camchain to prevent it dropping into the engine.
8 If required, the camchain guide blade can be removed – draw the blade out, noting how the lugs locate in the recess in the top edge of the camchain tunnel **(see illustration)**.
9 Clean all traces of old gasket material from the cylinder head and cylinder with a suitable solvent. Take care not to scratch or gouge the soft aluminium. Be careful not to let any of the gasket material fall into the crankcase, the cylinder bore or the oil passages.
10 Inspect the cylinder head gasket and the mating surfaces on the cylinder head and cylinder for signs of leaks, which could indicate that the head is warped. Refer to Chapter 2C, Section 12 and check the head mating surface for warpage.
11 After inspection, discard the old gasket as a new one must be fitted on reassembly

Installation

12 Installation is the reverse of removal, noting the following:

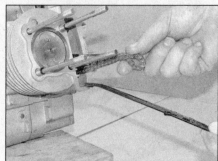

11.8 Draw out the camchain guide blade

● Lubricate the cylinder bore with clean engine oil.
● Ensure any dowels are correctly installed in the cylinder.
● If removed, install the camchain guide blade (see Step 8).
● Install a new head gasket – never re-use the old gasket.
● Ensure the camchain is correctly located around the crankshaft sprocket.
● Tighten the cylinder head nuts evenly and a little at a time in a criss-cross sequence to the torque setting specified at the beginning of this chapter. Tighten the cylinder head bolts to the specified torque.

12 Cylinder head and valves

Note: *If a valve spring compressor is available, the home mechanic can remove the valves from the cylinder head, lap the valves and renew the valve stem seals.*

Disassembly

1 Before you start, arrange to label and store the valves and their related components so that they can be returned to their original locations without getting mixed up **(see illustration)**.
2 Compress the valve springs on the first valve with a spring compressor, making sure it

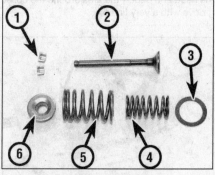

12.1 Valve components

1 Collets	4 Inner valve spring
2 Valve	5 Outer valve spring
3 Spring seat	6 Spring retainer

12.2a Ensure the valve spring compressor is correctly located on the valve head...

12.2b ...and on the spring retainer

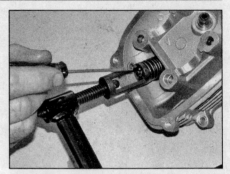

12.2c Remove the collets from the top end of the valve

12.3 Remove the spring retainer

12.4 Remove the outer and inner valve springs

may have formed on the valve, then use a motorised wire brush to remove deposits from the valve heads and stems. Again, make sure the valves do not get mixed up.

Inspection and reassembly

12 Refer to Chapter 2C, Section 12 for details of valve inspection, lapping and reassembly.

13 Cylinder

Removal

1 Remove the cylinder head and the camchain guide blade (see Section 11).
2 Hold the camchain and lift the cylinder up off the crankcase, supporting the piston as it becomes accessible to prevent it hitting the crankcase opening (see illustration). If the cylinder is stuck, tap around the joint face between the cylinder and the crankcase with a soft-faced mallet to free it. Don't attempt to free the cylinder by inserting a screwdriver between it and the crankcase – you'll damage the sealing surfaces.
3 Once the cylinder has been removed, stuff a clean rag into the crankcase opening around the piston to prevent anything falling inside.
4 Remove the cylinder base gasket, noting

is correctly located onto each end of the valve assembly (see illustrations). Do not compress the springs any more than is absolutely necessary to release the collets, then remove the collets, using either needle-nose pliers, a magnet or a screwdriver with a dab of grease on it (see illustration).
3 Carefully release the valve spring compressor and remove the spring retainer, noting which way up it fits (see illustration).
4 Remove the valve springs (see illustration). **Note:** The valve springs have closer wound coils that are fitted next to the cylinder head.
5 Lift out the spring seat (see illustration).
6 Turn the head over and withdraw the valve (see illustration). If the valve binds in the guide (won't pull through), push it back into the head and deburr the area around the collet groove with a very fine file.

7 Once the valve has been removed, pull the valve stem oil seal off the top of the valve guide with pliers and discard it as a new one must be used on reassembly (see illustration 12.5).
8 Repeat the procedure for the remaining valve. Remember to keep the parts for each valve together and in order so they can be reinstalled in the correct location.
9 Next, clean the cylinder head with solvent and dry it thoroughly. Compressed air will speed the drying process and ensure that all holes and recessed areas are clean.
10 Clean the valve springs, collets, retainers and spring seats with solvent. Work on the parts from one valve at a time so as not to mix them up.
11 Scrape off any carbon deposits that

12.5 Remove the spring seat. Note the valve stem oil seals (arrowed)

12.6 Pull out the valve

13.2 Lift the cylinder and support the piston

13.4 Discard the old cylinder base gasket

13.7 Inspect the cylinder bore for scratches and score marks

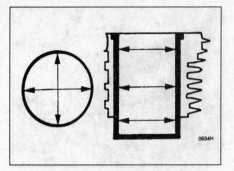

13.8a Measure the cylinder bore in the directions shown...

13.8b ...using a telescoping gauge

13.16 Feed each ring into the bore carefully as the cylinder is lowered

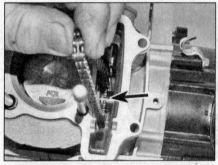

13.17 Check position of the camchain around the crankshaft sprocket (arrowed)

how it fits, then discard it as new one must be fitted on reassembly **(see illustration)**.

5 Note any dowels in the cylinder or crankcase and remove them for safekeeping if they are loose. Note how the camchain locates on the crankshaft sprocket and secure the chain to prevent it dropping into the crankcase **(see illustration 13.17)**.

6 Clean all traces of old gasket material from the cylinder and crankcase with a suitable solvent. Take care not to scratch or gouge the soft aluminium. Be careful not to let any of the gasket material fall into the crankcase.

Inspection

7 Check the cylinder bore carefully for scratches and score marks **(see illustration)**.

8 If available, use a telescoping gauge and micrometer to measure the inside diameter of the cylinder bore to assess the amount of wear, taper and ovality (see *Tools and Workshop Tips* in the *Reference* section). Measure near the top (but below the level of the top piston ring at top dead centre), centre and bottom (but above the level of the bottom ring with the piston at bottom dead centre) of the bore both parallel to and across the crankshaft axis **(see illustrations)**.

9 Calculate any differences between the measurements to determine any taper or ovality in the bore. A cylinder bore that has worn oval will reduce the efficiency of the piston rings to achieve a seal, resulting in loss of compression and increased oil consumption.

10 To determine overall wear, measure an

unworn part of the cylinder bore (below the level of the bottom ring with the piston at the bottom of its stroke) and compare the result to the previous measurements. Alternatively, check for a lip around the (unworn) top edge of the cylinder bore as a rough indication of wear.

11 If the bore is tapered, oval, or worn beyond the service limit, badly scratched, scuffed or scored, the cylinder and piston will have to be renewed as a set. **Note:** *If there is any doubt about the condition of the cylinder, consult a specialist engineer.*

12 Check that all the cylinder studs are tight in the crankcase halves. If any are loose, remove them (see *Tools and Workshop Tips* in the *Reference* section) and clean their threads. Apply a suitable permanent thread locking compound, then screw them back into the crankcase securely.

Installation

13 Remove any rag from the crankcase opening. Ensure any dowels are correctly installed in the crankcase, then lay the new base gasket in place on the crankcase making sure it is the correct way round.

14 Position the piston ring end gaps correctly **(see illustration 15.9 in Chapter 2C)**.

15 Lubricate the cylinder bore, piston and piston rings, and the connecting rod big- and small-ends, with the clean engine oil, then lower the cylinder down until the piston crown fits into the bore **(see illustration 13.2b)**.

16 Gently push down on the cylinder, making sure the piston enters the bore squarely and does

not get cocked sideways. Carefully compress and feed each ring into the bore as the cylinder is lowered **(see illustration)**. If necessary, use a soft mallet to gently tap the cylinder down, but do not use force if it appears to be stuck as the piston and/or rings will be damaged.

17 Once the piston is correctly installed in the cylinder, press the cylinder down onto the base gasket. Check that the camchain is still located around the crankshaft sprocket **(see illustration)**.

18 Install the camchain guide blade, then install the cylinder head (see Section 11).

14 Piston

Refer to Chapter 2C, Section 14, referring to the piston and piston pin diameter specifications at the beginning of this Chapter.

15 Piston rings

Refer to Chapter 2C, Section 15, noting that on this engine the compression rings usually have a marking or letter near the gap to denote the upper surface of the ring **(see illustration 15.1 in Chapter 2C)**.

16.3 Locate the holding tool in the rotor holes and loosen the centre nut

16.5 Install the puller legs and centre bolt as shown

16.6 Note location of washer (arrowed) behind centre nut

16 Alternator

Removal

1 The alternator is located behind the slotted fan cover on the right-hand side of the engine – remove the cover and the cooling fan (see Section 7).

2 To undo the alternator rotor centre nut it is necessary to stop the rotor from turning using a pin wrench that locates in the two large holes in the face of the rotor. Peugeot produces a service tool (Part No. 752237) for this purpose. Alternatively, a similar home-made tool can be used (see Tool Tip in Chapter 2A, Section 11) or you can obtain an aftermarket version. **Note:** *Take great care not to damage the*

internal coils of the alternator when locating any tools through the rotor.

3 With the rotor securely held, unscrew the centre nut and washer **(see illustration).**

4 Alternatively, the alternator rotor can be held with a strap wrench. If necessary, undo the bolts securing the ignition pulse generator coil and displace it to avoid damaging it when using the strap wrench.

5 To remove the rotor from the taper on the crankshaft it is necessary to use a puller that threads into the internal thread in the centre of the rotor. Peugeot produces a service tool (Part No. 750016) for this purpose and similar aftermarket pullers are available. Alternatively, use a two-legged puller as shown **(see illustration).** Thread the puller legs into the threaded holes in the rotor, then tighten the centre bolt exerting steady pressure to draw the rotor off the taper. **Note:** *To avoid*

damaging the threaded end of the crankshaft, either leave the centre nut on the shaft with just enough clearance to allow the rotor to be dislodged, or position a soft metal spacer between the end of the shaft and the puller centre bolt.

6 Lift the rotor off the crankshaft **(see illustration).**

7 If it is loose, remove the Woodruff key from the shaft for safekeeping, noting how it fits **(see illustration).**

8 The alternator stator coils and ignition pulse generator coil are wired together and have to be removed as an assembly. If not already done, trace the wiring back from the alternator and pulse generator and disconnect it at the connectors. Free the wiring from any clips or guides and feed it through to the alternator.

9 Undo the two long crankcase bolts securing the alternator wiring guide and remove the guide **(see illustration).** Undo the bolts securing the pulse generator coil, then undo the bolts securing the alternator stator and lift the assembly off **(see illustrations).** Note how the wiring seal fits in the cut-out in the top of the engine casing.

Installation

10 Installation is the reverse of removal, noting the following:

● Ensure the wiring is correctly routed before installing the stator and pulse generator.

● Tighten the stator and pulse generator bolts to the torque settings specified at the beginning of this Chapter.

● Make sure that no metal objects have attached themselves to the magnets on the inside of the rotor.

● Clean the tapered end of the crankshaft and the corresponding mating surface on the inside of the rotor with a suitable solvent.

● Fit the Woodruff key into the crankshaft, align the slot in the centre of the rotor with the key, then install the rotor.

● Tighten the alternator centre nut to the specified torque setting.

● Secure the wiring with any clips or ties.

● Ensure that the cooling fan and fan cover are correctly installed (see Section 7).

16.7 Note location of Woodruff key

16.9a Long bolts secure wiring guide

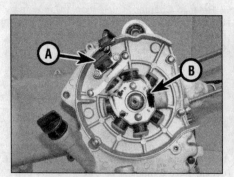

16.9b Pulse generator coil (A) and alternator stator (B)

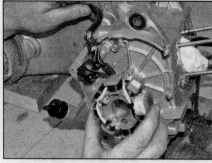

16.9c Lift off the alternator assembly

17 Right-hand crankcase cover

Removal

1 Remove the exhaust system (see Chapter 5).
2 Drain the engine oil (see Chapter 1, Section 6).
3 Follow the procedure in Section 16 and remove the alternator.
4 An oil seal is fitted in the crankcase cover where the crankshaft passes through it **(see illustration 17.6c)**. Check around the seal for signs of oil leakage – if the seal has been leaking a new one must be fitted once the cover has been removed. **Note:** *It is good practice to renew the oil seal whenever the cover is removed.*
5 Position a drain tray underneath the engine to catch any residual oil when the cover is removed, then undo the cover screws – noting their locations **(see illustration)**.
6 Draw the cover off. If it is stuck, tap around the joint face and the pry-points between the cover and the crankcase with a soft-faced mallet to free it **(see illustrations)**. Do not try to lever the cover off as this may damage the sealing surfaces. Note the location of the right-hand crankshaft oil seal **(see illustration)**.
7 Remove the gasket and discard it as a new one must be used. Note any dowels in

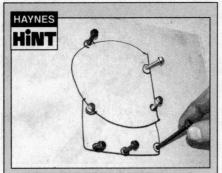

Make a cardboard template of the crankcase and punch a hole for each screw location. This will ensure that they are all installed correctly on reassembly – this is important as some bolts may be of different lengths.

the cover or crankcase and remove them for safekeeping if they are loose.
8 Clean the mating surfaces of the cover and the crankcase with a suitable solvent to remove any traces of old gasket or sealant. Take care not to scratch or gouge the soft aluminium.
9 To renew the oil seal, support the cover on the work surface and drive the seal out from the alternator side with a suitably-sized socket **(see illustration)**. Note which way round the seal is fitted. Ensure that the seal housing is clean, then lubricate the new seal with a smear of engine oil and press it all the way into the housing **(see illustration)**.

17.5 Undo the cover screws (arrowed)

Installation

10 If removed, fit the dowels, then fit a new cover gasket, making sure it locates correctly onto the dowels **(see illustration)**. If necessary, use a dab of grease to hold the gasket in position.
11 Lubricate the inside of the oil seal with engine oil, then install the cover taking care not to damage the seal on the crankshaft threads. Make sure that the gasket stays in place.
12 Install the crankcase cover bolts, making sure they are in the correct locations, then tighten the bolts evenly and in a criss-cross sequence to the torque setting specified at the beginning of this Chapter.
13 Install the remaining components in the reverse order of removal.
14 Fill the engine with the correct type and quantity of oil (see Chapter 1 and *Pre-ride checks*)

17.6a Tap around the joint face...

17.6b ...to loosen the cover

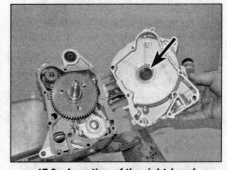
17.6c Location of the right-hand crankshaft oil seal

17.9a Drive out the oil seal with a suitable socket

17.9b Installed position of the crankshaft oil seal

17.10 Fit the gasket over the dowels (arrowed)

18.2 Check the rotation of the starter driven gear (arrowed)

18.3 Remove the starter idler gear

18.4 Use a peg spanner to undo the starter clutch nut

18 Starter idler gear and starter clutch

Note: *This procedure can be carried out with the engine in the scooter.*

Check

1 Remove the alternator (see Section 16) and the right-hand crankcase cover (see Section 17).

TOOL TiP

A peg spanner can be made by cutting castellations into one end of a length of thick-walled steel tube – measure the width and depth of the slots in the retaining nut to determine the size of the castellations. The tube should be 75 mm long to fit over the crankshaft and 31 mm diameter. Weld a heavy washer and large nut onto the opposite end of the tube so that the retaining nut can be tightened to the correct torque on installation.

2 The operation of the starter clutch can be checked while it is in place. The starter driven gear should rotate freely in the *opposite* direction to crankshaft rotation (anti-clockwise), but lock when rotated clockwise **(see illustration)**. If not, the starter clutch is faulty and should be removed for inspection.

Removal

3 Pull out the idler gear shaft and lift out the idler gear **(see illustration)**. Note how the smaller pinion engages with the starter driven gear and the larger pinion engages with the teeth on the starter motor shaft.
4 A peg spanner (Peugeot service tool Part No. 800673) is required to undo the starter clutch retaining nut **(see illustration)**. If the correct tool is not available, one can be made from a suitable length of steel tube **(see *Tool Tip*)**.
5 The crankshaft must be prevented from turning while the retaining nut is being

loosened. If the cylinder has been removed, temporarily fit the piston pin into the connecting rod small-end, then pass a rod through the centre of the pin and rest the ends of the rod on wooden blocks placed across the top of the crankcase **(see illustration)**. Alternatively, remove the drive belt cover and hold the variator with a pin wrench (Peugeot service tool Part No. 752237) located in the holes provided in the pulley **(see illustration)**. Ensure the tool is fully located on the variator before commencing the procedure. Do not try to hold the crankshaft with a spanner on the variator centre nut – the starter clutch nut is extremely tight and has a left-hand thread, attempting to loosen it will simply tighten the variator nut.
6 To undo the starter clutch retaining nut turn it clockwise **(see illustration)**.
7 Remove the nut and washer, then draw the driven gear and starter clutch assembly off the crankshaft **(see illustrations)**.

18.5a Holding the crankshaft with a rod passed through the small-end

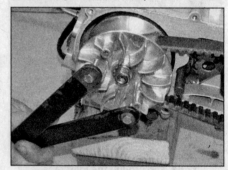

18.5b Hold the variator to prevent the crankshaft turning

18.6 Turn the nut clockwise to undo

18.7a Remove the nut and washer...

18.7b ...and the driven gear and starter clutch assembly

18.8 Location of the starter clutch Woodruff key

18.9 Inspect the idler gear and shaft for wear

18.11a Separate the driven gear from the starter clutch...

8 If it is loose, remove the Woodruff key from the shaft for safekeeping, noting how it fits **(see illustration)**.

Inspection

9 Inspect both sets of teeth on the idler gear and renew it if any are chipped or worn **(see illustration)**. **Note:** *If the teeth on the larger pinion are worn or damaged, inspect the teeth on the starter motor shaft also (see Chapter 10).* Check the idler shaft and bearing surfaces for signs of wear or damage, and renew it if necessary.

10 Hold the centre of the starter clutch assembly and check that the driven gear rotates freely in one direction and locks in the other direction. If it doesn't, the ring of sprags in the one-way mechanism may be jammed. Lift out the driven gear **(see illustration 18.11a)**, wash the assembly in suitable solvent and dry it with compressed air, if available. Lubricate the mechanism with clean engine oil, reassemble and check it again. If the starter clutch still does not operate correctly, it can be disassembled and the components inspected (see Step 13). Note that individual parts are not available and if any component is worn or damaged a complete new starter clutch assembly will have to be fitted.

11 Inspect the teeth of the starter driven gear for wear and damage. Lift the gear out from the starter clutch and remove the needle bearing **(see illustrations)**. Inspect the bearing and the bearing races in the starter clutch and the starter gear for wear and pitting.

12 Inspect the outside surface of the driven gear hub for uneven wear and scoring.

13 If required, undo the starter clutch housing bolts, then turn the assembly over and lift out the centre **(see illustration)**. Hold the spring-loaded plungers in place and lift out the clutch sprags, then remove the plungers and springs, noting how they fit **(see illustrations)**. Inspect the components carefully for wear and damage, then if everything is good, reassemble the clutch. Clean the threads of the housing bolts and apply a suitable non-permanent thread-locking compound, then tighten the bolts to the torque setting specified at the beginning of this Chapter.

Installation

14 Installation is the reverse of removal, noting the following:

18.11b ...and lift out the needle bearing

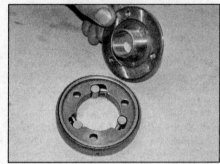

18.13a Lift out the clutch centre

18.13b Hold back the plungers to remove the sprags...

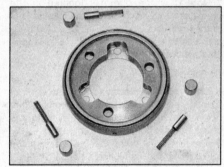

18.13c ...then remove the plungers and springs

● Lubricate the starter clutch mechanism with clean engine oil.
● Fit the Woodruff key into its slot in the shaft.
● Ensure that the starter clutch assembly is pressed all the way onto the crankshaft.
● Install the washer and tighten the retaining nut to the torque setting specified at the beginning of this Chapter. Use the same method to hold the crankshaft as on disassembly and turn the nut anti-clockwise.
● Ensure the idler gear engages with the pinion on the starter motor shaft. Lubricate the idler gear shaft.

19 Oil pump

and the right-hand crankcase cover (see Section 17).
2 Remove the starter clutch (see Section 18).
3 Undo the bolts securing the pump driven sprocket cover and remove the cover **(see illustration)**.

19.3 Undo the bolts (arrowed) and remove the sprocket cover

Removal

1 Remove the alternator (see Section 16)

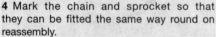

19.6 Remove the pump driven sprocket and chain

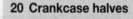

19.7a Undo the mounting bolts...

19.7b ...and lift out the oil pump

4 Mark the chain and sprocket so that they can be fitted the same way round on reassembly.

5 To prevent the oil pump from turning while the sprocket nut is being loosened, use the same method to hold the crankshaft as when undoing the starter clutch retaining nut (see Section 18).

6 Undo the nut, then lift the driven sprocket and chain off the pump driveshaft and disengage the chain from the crankshaft sprocket **(see illustration)**. Note how the hole in the centre of the driven sprocket aligns with the flat on the driveshaft.

7 Note how the pump is located in the crankcase with the arrow on the outside face of the pump body pointing UP. Undo the bolts and withdraw the pump from the engine **(see illustrations)**.

Inspection

8 Check the pump body for obvious signs of damage especially around the mounting bolt holes. Turn the pump driveshaft by hand and check that the pump rotates smoothly.

9 If required, the pump can be disassembled for cleaning and inspection.

10 Pull out the pump shaft, then undo the screw securing the cover to the pump body and remove the cover **(see illustrations)**. Note the location of the dowel between the cover and the body **(see illustration)**.

11 Note any reference marks on the pump rotors; even if the rotors are not marked, it is essential that they are reassembled the correct way round. Lift out the inner and outer

rotors, clean the components with a suitable solvent and dry them with compressed air, if available. Inspect the pump body, rotors and shaft for scoring and wear. If any damage, scoring, uneven or excessive wear is evident, renew the pump.

12 If the pump is in good condition, reassemble the inner and outer rotors and lubricate them with clean engine oil.

13 Fit the cover and tighten the screw lightly, then install the pump shaft to align the components. Tighten the cover screw fully. Lubricate the pump with clean engine oil and check that the shaft and rotors turn smoothly and freely.

14 Inspect the pump drive chain and sprockets for wear or damage, and renew them as a set if necessary. Check for wear on the sides and tips of the sprocket teeth and for chipped or hooked teeth. Lay the chain on a flat surface and check for play between the links – if there is any, renew the chain.

Installation

15 Installation is the reverse of removal, noting the following:

● Fill the pump with clean engine oil before installation.

● Ensure the pump is fitted the correct way round **(see illustration 19.7b)**.

● Tighten the mounting bolts to the torque in *Specifications* at the beginning of this Chapter.

● Ensure the chain and sprocket are fitted the correct way round.

● Tighten the pump sprocket nut to the specified torque setting.

● Fill the engine with the correct type and quantity of oil (see Chapter 1 and *Pre-ride checks*)

20 Crankcase halves

Separation

1 Follow the procedure in Section 4 and remove the engine from the frame.

2 Before the crankcase halves can be separated the following components must be removed:

● Cylinder head (Section 11)
● Cylinder (Section 13)
● Starter motor (Chapter 10)
● Alternator (Section 16)
● Variator (Chapter 3)
● Right-hand crankcase cover (Section 17)
● Starter clutch (Chapter 18)
● Oil pump (Section 19)

3 Tape some rag around the connecting rod to prevent it knocking against the cases. Although not essential, it is advisable to remove the piston to avoid damage during this procedure.

4 The kickstart mechanism driven gear is located on the left-hand side of the crankshaft behind the variator – ensure that it is removed before attempting to separate the crankcase halves (see Chapter 3).

5 The long bolts securing the alternator wiring guide and the right-hand crankcase cover also hold the crankcase halves together. Identify the remaining crankcase bolts and unscrew

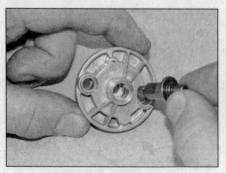

19.10a Pull out the shaft...

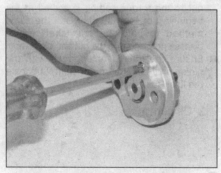

19.10b ...then undo the cover screw...

19.10c ...and lift off the cover. Note dowel (arrowed)

20.5 Unscrew the remaining crankcase bolts

20.6 Ease off the right-hand crankcase half

20.8a Remove the crankshaft assembly...

20.8b ...and disengage the camchain (arrowed) from the crankshaft

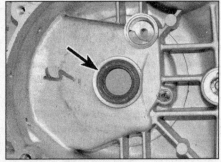

20.14 Installed position of the left-hand crankshaft oil seal

20.16 Clean the oil pump housing and oil passages carefully

them, noting where they fit **(see illustration)**. **Note:** *Ensure that all the crankcase bolts have been removed before attempting to separate the cases.*

6 Ease the right-hand crankcase half off the left-hand half being prepared to catch any residual oil **(see illustration)**. If the crankcase halves do not separate easily, first ensure all fasteners have been removed. Next, apply heat to the right-hand main bearing housing with a hot air gun and try lifting the right-hand half off again.

Caution: Do not try to separate the halves by levering against the mating surfaces as they are easily scored and will not seal correctly afterwards. Do not strike the ends of the crankshaft with a hammer as damage to the end threads or the shaft itself will result.

7 If the crankcase is an extremely tight fit on the crankshaft, a puller arrangement will be required to facilitate the procedure. If the puller is placed across the end of the crankshaft, thread the alternator centre nut on first to protect the threads. Take care to ensure that equal pressure is applied on both sides of the puller arrangement at all times and apply heat to the bearing housing.

8 Ensure the camchain is clear of the sprocket on the left-hand side of the crankshaft and pull the crankshaft assembly out of the left-hand crankcase half **(see illustrations)**. Apply heat to the main bearing housing if required.

9 If the crankshaft is an extremely tight fit in the crankcase, use a similar set-up to the one in Step 7, only this time press the crankshaft out of the left-hand crankcase half. Thread the variator nut onto the end of the crankshaft to protect the threads and make sure the

crankshaft assembly is supported to prevent it dropping if it suddenly comes free.

10 Note that the main bearings will remain in place on the crankshaft assembly (see Section 21).

11 Remove the camchain. Undo the pivot bolt securing the camchain tensioner blade and lift the blade out **(see illustration 9.10)**. Note which way round the blade is fitted.

12 Remove the gasket and discard it as a new one must be used. Remove any dowels from either crankcase half for safekeeping if they are loose.

13 Clean the mating surfaces of the crankcase halves with a suitable solvent to remove any traces of old gasket or sealant. Take care not to scratch or gouge the soft aluminium.

14 Note the position of the left-hand crankshaft oil seal and note which way round the seal is fitted **(see illustration)**. Lever the seal out carefully with a large, flat-bladed screwdriver, taking care not to damage the crankcase (see *Tools and Workshop Tips* in the *Reference* section). Discard the seal as a new one must be fitted on reassembly. **Note:** *The right-hand crankshaft oil seal is fitted in the right-hand crankshaft cover (see Section 17).*

15 If required, remove the transmission assembly from the left-hand crankcase half (see Chapter 3).

Inspection

16 Wash the cases in a suitable solvent and dry them with compressed air, if available. Pay particular attention to ensuring that the internal oil passages and the oil pump housing are clear **(see illustration)**.

17 Small cracks or holes in aluminium castings can be repaired with an epoxy resin adhesive as a temporary measure. Permanent repairs can be effected by specialist welding, or using one of the low temperature home welding kits such as Lumiweld. On some engines, the crankcase halves can be renewed individually, on others the two halves are only available together as a matching set.

18 Damaged threads can be economically reclaimed by using a thread insert. Most small engineering firms offer a service of this kind. Sheared screws can usually be removed with screw extractors. Refer to *Tools and Workshop Tips* in the *Reference* section for further details.

19 Always wash the crankcases thoroughly after any repair work to ensure no dirt or metal swarf is trapped inside when the engine is rebuilt.

20 Inspect the front and rear engine mounting bushes **(see illustrations)**. If they show

20.20a Front left-hand engine mounting bush

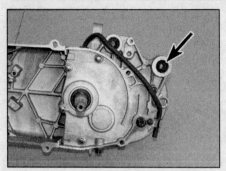

20.20b Rear left-hand engine mounting bush

20.21 Right-hand main bearing housing. Note oil passage (arrowed)

20.27 Installing the crankshaft in the left-hand casing

signs of deterioration, renew both bushes at the same time. To remove a bush, first note its position in the casing. Heat the casing with a hot air gun, then support the casing and drive the bush out with a hammer and a suitably sized socket. Alternatively, use two suitably sized sockets to press the bush out in the jaws of a vice. Clean the bush housing with steel wool to remove any corrosion, then reheat the casing and fit the new bush. **Note:** *Always support the casing when removing or fitting bushes to avoid breaking the casing.*

21 Inspect the main bearing housings **(see illustration)**. If a bearing outer race has spun in its housing, the inside of the housing will be damaged. A bearing locking compound can be used to fix the outer race in place on reassembly if the damage is not too severe. **Note:** *If a bearing has spun in its housing, the bearing itself is likely to be damaged – see Section 21.*

22 Inspect the crankshaft assembly and bearings (see Section 21).

Joining

23 Follow the procedure in Section 17 to fit a new crankshaft oil seal into the left-hand crankcase half and the right-hand crankcase cover using a seal driver or socket. Ensure the seals are fitted the right way round and that they enter the cases squarely.

24 Lubricate the left-hand crankshaft seal and main bearing with clean engine oil and tape some rag around the connecting rod to prevent it knocking against the cases.

25 Support the left-hand crankcase half securely in an upright position on the work surface. If required, have an assistant support the crankcase.

26 Heat the bearing housing in the crankcase with a hot air gun. **Note:** *Avoid applying direct heat onto the crankshaft oil seal.* If required, a freeze spray can be used on the main bearing to aid installation.

27 Support the camchain in the camchain tunnel and insert the left-hand end of the

crankshaft through the chain and the oil seal **(see illustration)**. Take care to avoid damaging the seal.

28 Ensure that the main bearing is aligned with the bearing housing and that the connecting rod is aligned with the crankcase mouth, then press the crankshaft assembly in fully so that the main bearing goes all the way into its housing. If the bearing does not seat fully, apply more heat around the bearing housing while applying steady pressure to the crankshaft assembly.

29 Check that the camchain is correctly located around the crankshaft sprocket and secure it in position with wire or a cable-tie to avoid it becoming jammed inside the crankcase. Install the camchain tensioner blade (see Section 9) **(see illustration)**.

30 If necessary, allow the case to cool, then wipe the mating surfaces of both crankcase halves with a rag soaked in suitable solvent. Fit the dowels and install the new crankcase gasket on the mating surface of the left-hand case **(see illustration)**. If necessary, use a dab of grease to hold the gasket in position.

31 Lubricate the right-hand crankshaft main bearing with clean engine oil.

32 Heat the bearing housing with a hot air gun. If required, use a freeze spay on the main bearing.

33 Fit the crankcase half over the crankshaft. Ensure that the two halves of the crankcase are correctly aligned, taking special note of the position of the dowels, and that the main bearing is aligned with the bearing housing in the right-hand case **(see illustration)**.

34 Press the crankcase on fully so that the main bearing goes all the way into its housing. If the main bearing does not seat fully, apply more heat to the bearing housing while apply steady pressure to the crankcase.

35 Check that the crankcase halves are seated all the way round. If the cases are not correctly seated, heat the bearing housings while applying firm pressure. **Note:** *Do not attempt to pull the crankcase halves together using the crankcase bolts as the casing will crack and be ruined.*

36 Clean the threads of the crankcase bolts and install them finger-tight, then tighten them evenly to the torque setting in *Specifications* at the beginning of this Chapter.

37 Trim off any excess gasket across the crankcase mouth **(see illustration)**.

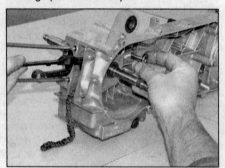

20.29 Installing the camchain tensioner blade

20.30 Fit the new gasket over the dowels (arrowed)

20.33 Align the crankcase halves carefully

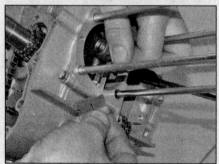

20.37 Trim off the excess crankcase gasket

38 Support the connecting rod and rotate the crankshaft by hand – if there are any signs of undue stiffness, tight or rough spots, or of any other problem, the fault must be rectified before proceeding further. Don't forget to support the camchain while rotating the crankshaft.

39 Install the remaining components in the reverse order of removal.

21 Crankshaft assembly, big-end and main bearings

Note: *The crankshaft assembly is pressed together and is easily damaged if it is dropped.*

1 To access the crankshaft assembly, the big-end bearing and the main bearings, the crankcase must be split into two parts (see Section 20).

2 The crankshaft assembly should give many thousands of miles of service. The most likely problems to occur will be a worn small or big-end bearing due to poor lubrication. A worn big-end bearing will produce a pronounced knocking noise, most audible when the engine is under load, and increasing as engine speed rises. This should not be confused with small-end bearing wear, which produces a lighter, metallic rattle (see Section 14).

3 When the crankcase halves are separated, the main bearings will remain in place on the crankshaft assembly – they are not normally available as separate items. If the main bearings have failed, excessive rumbling and vibration will be felt when the engine is running.

4 To assess the condition of the big-end bearing, hold the crankshaft assembly firmly and push and pull on the connecting rod, checking for any up-and-down freeplay between the two **(see illustration)**. If any freeplay is noted, the bearing is worn.

5 A small amount of big-end side clearance (side-to-side movement) is acceptable on the connecting rod. Measure the clearance with a feeler gauge **(see illustration)**, then compare the result with the service limit specified at the beginning of this Chapter.

6 Follow the procedure in *Tools and Workshop Tips* in the *Reference* section to check the condition of the main bearings **(see illustration)**.

7 If wear or damage is noted in any of the crankshaft assembly bearings, a new crankshaft assembly will have to be fitted. **Note:** *Evidence of extreme heat, such as discoloration or blueing, indicates that lubrication failure has occurred. Be sure to check the oil pump and bearing oilways in the crankcases before reassembling the engine.*

8 Inspect the threads on each end of the crankshaft and ensure that the retaining nuts for the alternator rotor and the variator are a good fit. Inspect the splines for the variator

21.4 Checking for play in the big-end bearing

21.5 Measuring big-end side clearance

pulley on the left-hand end of the shaft **(see illustration 21.6)**. Inspect the taper and the slot in the right-hand end of the shaft for the alternator Woodruff key. Damage or wear that prevents the rotor from being fitted securely will require a new crankshaft assembly.

9 Inspect the oil pump and the camshaft drive sprocket teeth on the crankshaft for damage or wear **(see illustration)**. The sprockets are installed as an integral part of the crankshaft assembly – if they are worn or damaged a new assembly will have to be fitted.

22 Initial start-up after overhaul/running-in

Initial start-up after overhaul

1 Make sure the engine oil level is correct (see *Pre-ride checks*).

2 Make sure there is fuel in the tank.

3 With the ignition OFF, operate the kickstart a couple of times to check that the engine turns over easily.

4 Turn the ignition ON, start the engine and allow it to run at a slow idle until it reaches operating temperature. Do not be alarmed if there is a little smoke from the exhaust – this will be due to the oil used to lubricate the piston and bore during assembly and should subside after a while.

5 If the engine proves reluctant to start, remove the spark plug and check that it has not become wet and oily. If it has, clean it and

try again. If the engine refuses to start, go through the fault finding charts at the end of this manual to identify the problem.

6 Check carefully for fuel and oil leaks and make sure the transmission and controls, especially the brakes, function properly before road testing the machine.

7 Upon completion of the road test, and after the engine has cooled down completely, recheck the valve clearances (see Chapter 1). Recheck the engine oil level (see *Pre-ride checks*).

Recommended running-in procedure

8 Treat the engine gently for the first few miles to allow any new parts to bed in.

9 If a new piston, cylinder or crankshaft assembly has been fitted, the engine will have to be run-in as when new. This means a restraining hand on the throttle until at least 300 miles (500 km) have been covered. There's no point in keeping to any set speed limit – the main idea is to gradually increase performance up to the 600 mile (1000 km) mark. Make sure that the throttle position is varied to vary engine speed, and use full throttle only for short bursts. Experience is the best guide, since it's easy to tell when an engine is running freely.

10 Pay particular attention to the *Pre-ride checks* at the beginning of this manual and investigate the cause of any oil loss immediately. Check the tightness of all relevant nuts and bolts (see Chapter 1).

21.6 Check the main bearings on both sides of the crankshaft

21.9 Inspect the crankshaft sprockets for wear

Types XS1P52QMI-4 and XS1P57QMJ-2 – left-hand view

Drive belt cover design differs on XS1P52QMI-3B type fitted to Speedfight 125

Types XS1P52QMI-4 and XS1P57QMJ-2 – right-hand view

Chapter 2G
Four-stroke 125 and 150cc engines – types XS1P52QMI-4 and XS1P57QMJ-2
(including XS1P52QMI-3B type)

Refer to 'Model and servicing specifications' in Chapter 1 for model identification details

Contents

Degrees of difficulty

Easy, suitable for novice with little experience	**Fairly easy,** suitable for beginner with some experience	**Fairly difficult,** suitable for competent DIY mechanic	**Difficult,** suitable for experienced DIY mechanic	**Very difficult,** suitable for expert DIY or professional

Specifications

General

Type	Single cylinder air-cooled 2-valve four-stroke
Capacity	
Speedfight and Tweet 125	124.6 cc
Tweet 150	150.6 cc
Bore x stroke	
Speedfight and Tweet 125	52.4 x 57.8 mm
Tweet 150	57.4 x 58.2 mm
Cylinder compression	172 psi (11.8 Bar) @ 380 rpm

Camshaft

Intake and exhaust lobe height	
Intake	27.512 mm
Exhaust	27.212 mm

Cylinder head

Warpage (max)	0.05 mm

Valves

Valve clearances	See Chapter 1

Cylinder bore
125 cc
    Standard .... 52.395 to 52.415 mm
    Service limit .... 52.5 mm
150 cc
    Standard .... 57.395 to 57.415 mm
    Service limit .... 57.5 mm

Piston
Diameter (measured 9 mm up from the bottom of the skirt)
125 cc
    Standard .... 52.385 to 52.405 mm
    Service limit .... 52.29 mm
150 cc
    Standard .... 57.385 to 57.405 mm
    Service limit .... 57.29 mm

Piston rings
Ring end gap (installed)
    Speedfight
        Top ring and second ring .... 0.10 to 0.25 mm
        Oil control ring .... 0.20 to 0.50 mm
    Tweet 125/150
        Top ring .... 0.20 to 0.40 mm
        Second ring .... 0.25 to 0.40 mm
        Oil control ring .... 0.20 to 0.70 mm

Crankshaft and connecting rod
Big-end side clearance
    Service limit .... 0.55 mm
Crankshaft runout
    Measured 80 mm from left-hand flywheel face .... 0.10 mm
    Measured 40 mm from right-hand flywheel face .... 0.10 mm

Torque settings
Alternator rotor nut
    Speedfight .... 58 Nm
    Tweet 125/150 .... 45 Nm
Alternator stator bolts .... 10 Nm
Cam chain tensioner blade bolt .... 10 Nm
Cam chain tensioner bolts .... 10 Nm
Cam chain tensioner cap bolt .... 8 Nm
Camshaft sprocket bolts .... 12 Nm
Camshaft stopper plate bolt .... 10 Nm
Cooling fan bolts .... 10 Nm
Crankcase bolts .... 12 Nm
Right-hand crankcase cover bolts .... 12 Nm
Cylinder head
    Nuts
        Speedfight .... 24 Nm
        Tweet 125/150 .... 20 Nm
    Bolts .... 12 Nm
Engine mounting bolt/nut .... 70 Nm
Exhaust manifold
    Speedfight .... 18 Nm
    Tweet 125/150 .... 15 Nm
Ignition pulse generator coil bolts .... 6 Nm
Intake manifold nuts .... 10 Nm
Oil pump mounting screws .... 10 Nm
Pulsair union nuts .... 10 Nm
Rear shock absorber upper mounting bolt/nut
    Speedfight .... 50 Nm
    Tweet 125/150 .... 40 Nm
Rear shock absorber lower mounting bolt/nut
    Speedfight .... 25 Nm
    Tweet 125/150 .... 28 Nm
Drive belt cover screws .... 10 Nm
Starter clutch assembly screws .... 12 Nm
Starter clutch nut (LH) .... 90 Nm
Valve cover .... 10 Nm

1 General information

These Sym manufactured engines are single cylinder, overhead-camshaft four-strokes, with fan assisted air cooling as fitted to the Tweet 125 and 150, and the Speedfight 125. The camshaft is chain-driven off the crankshaft and operates the valves via rocker arms.

The crankshaft assembly is pressed together, incorporating the connecting rod.

The crankcase divides vertically – the left-hand crankcase is an integral part of the drive belt casing and gearbox.

2 Component access

Most components and assemblies, with the obvious exception of the crankshaft assembly and its bearings, can be worked on without having to remove the engine/transmission unit from the scooter. However, access to some components is severely restricted, and if a number of areas require attention at the same time, removal of the engine is recommended, as it is an easy task to undertake.

3 Cylinder compression test

Refer to the procedure in Chapter 2C, Section 3, noting the compression figure given at the beginning of this Chapter.

4 Engine removal and installation

Caution: The engine/transmission unit is not heavy, however removal and installation should be carried out with the aid of an assistant; personal injury or damage could occur if the engine falls or is dropped.

Removal

1 Support the scooter securely in an upright position. Work can be made easier by raising the machine to a suitable height on an hydraulic ramp or a suitable platform. Make sure it is secure and will not topple over.
2 Disconnect and remove the battery (see Chapter 10).
3 If required, drain the engine oil (see Chapter 1).
4 Remove the storage compartment, the seat cowling with the rear mudguard, and the belly panel assembly (see Chapter 9).
5 Remove the air filter housing assembly (see Chapter 5).
6 Release the exhaust system (see Chapter 5).
7 Disconnect the fuel hose from its union on

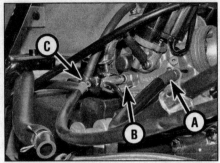

4.7 Disconnect the fuel hose (A), heater wiring connectors (B) and vacuum hose (C)

the carburettor, being prepared to catch any residual fuel in a rag **(see illustration)**. Position a suitable container below the carburettor drain hose, then loosen the drain screw and drain any residual fuel from the float chamber. Tighten the drain screw.
8 Disconnect the carburettor heater wiring connectors, then release the clip and disconnect the fuel pump vacuum hose (Speedfight models) or fuel tap vacuum hose (Tweet models) from the T-piece union alongside the carburettor **(see illustration 4.7)**. *Note: When disconnecting any wiring, it is advisable to mark or tag the wires as a reminder of where they connect.*
9 Trace the wiring from the automatic choke unit and disconnect it at the connector **(see illustration)**.
10 Either displace or remove the carburettor completely, leaving the throttle cable attached if required, or just disconnect the throttle cable

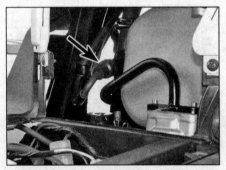

4.11 Pull off the spark plug cap (arrowed)

4.13 Bolt (arrowed) secures engine earth lead

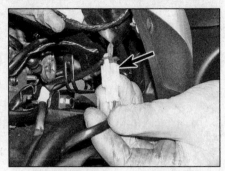

4.9 Disconnect the choke unit wiring connector (arrowed)

(see Chapter 5). If the carburettor is displaced, ensure it is secured to a convenient part of the frame to avoid damage. Ensure that the throttle cable and automatic choke wiring is clear of the engine unit. Stuff clean rag into the intake manifold to prevent anything falling inside.
11 Pull the spark plug cap off the plug and position the cap clear of the engine **(see illustration)**.
12 Pull back the boot, then undo the screw securing the lead to the starter motor terminal **(see illustration)**.
13 Undo the bolt securing the earth (ground) lead to the crankcase and disconnect the wire **(see illustration)**. Replace the bolt for safekeeping.
14 Trace the wiring from the alternator and ignition pulse generator coil on the right-hand side of the engine and disconnect it at the connectors **(see illustration)**. Secure the wiring clear of the engine.

4.12 Starter motor terminal (arrowed)

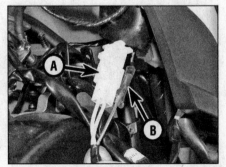

4.14 Alternator (A) and pulse generator wiring connector (B)

4.15 Clip (arrowed) secures air duct

4.16 Free the brake hose from the clips along top of transmission casing

4.18 Undo the upper shock mounting bolts (arrowed)

15 On Tweet models, release the clip securing the air duct to the front of the drive belt cover and disconnect the duct **(see illustration)**.

16 Displace the rear brake caliper (see Chapter 8). Undo any screws securing the brake hose to the top of the transmission casing and detach the hose **(see illustration)**.

17 Check that all wiring, cables and hoses are clear of the engine/transmission unit.

18 Working on one side at a time, undo the upper rear shock absorber mounting bolts and lower the wheel to the ground **(see illustration)**. Undo the lower shock mounting bolts and remove the shocks.

19 On Tweet models, remove the rear suspension sub-frame (see Chapter 7) **(see illustration)**.

20 If required, remove the rear wheel (see Chapter 8). **Note:** *The rear wheel and stand provide a convenient support for the unit once it is removed from the scooter.*

21 Before the engine can be removed, a means of supporting the scooter must be devised. A double A-frame hoist is ideally suited to most machines once the rear bodywork has been removed and where the front of the scooter can be firmly secured **(see illustration 4.17a in Chapter 2A)**. Alternatively, with the belly panels removed, the scooter can be supported from underneath provided the weight is taken on the frame tubes. On the machine used to illustrate this procedure, a 14 mm steel bar was passed through the engine bracket, supported on both sides with axle stands **(see illustration)**.

22 Undo the locknut on the engine mounting bolt **(see illustration)**. **Note:** *Peugeot recommends a new nut should be used on reassembly. Alternatively, clean the threads of the engine mounting bolt and apply a suitable thread-locking compound prior to installation.*

23 Have an assistant support the scooter, then carefully withdraw the engine mounting bolt **(see illustration)**.

24 Manoeuvre the engine unit back and out of the frame **(see illustration)**.

25 If the engine is dirty, particularly around its mountings, wash it thoroughly before starting any major dismantling work. This will make work much easier and rule out the possibility of dirt falling inside.

26 If required, remove the rear wheel (see Chapter 8) and the centrestand (see Chapter 7).

Installation

27 Installation is the reverse of removal, noting the following:
- Make sure no wires, cables or hoses become trapped between the engine and the frame when installing the engine
- Tighten the engine mounting bolt and shock absorber bolts securely to the torque settings specified at the beginning of this Chapter.
- Make sure all wires, cables and hoses are correctly routed and connected, and secured by any clips or ties.
- If the engine oil was drained, or if any oil has

4.19 Remove the rear suspension arm

4.21 Supporting the scooter with a steel bar and axle stands

4.22 Undo the engine mounting bolt nut

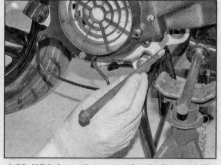

4.23 Withdraw the mounting bolt carefully

4.24 Manoeuvre the engine unit out of the frame

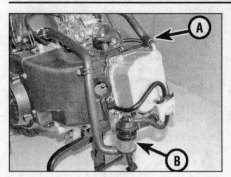

6.3 Breather hose (A), pulsair system valve (B)

6.4 Undo the pulsair flange nuts (arrowed)

6.5a Undo the bolts (arrowed)...

been lost during overhaul, refill or top up as described in Chapter 1 and *Pre-ride checks*.
● Check the operation of the rear brake before riding the machine (see Chapter 8).

5 Disassembly and reassembly – general information

1 Refer to the general notes in Chapter 2C, Section 5.
2 For this engine, disassembly should be done in the following general order with reference to the appropriate Sections (refer to Chapter 3 for details of transmission components):
● Remove the valve cover
● Remove the cylinder head
● Remove the cylinder
● Remove the piston
● Remove the starter motor (see Chapter 10)
● Remove the alternator
● Remove the starter clutch
● Remove the oil pump
● Separate the crankcase halves
● Remove the crankshaft

6 Valve cover

Removal

1 Disconnect and remove the battery (see Chapter 10).

2 Remove the storage compartment and the seat cowling with the rear mudguard (see Chapter 9).
3 Release the clip securing the breather hose to the valve cover and detach the hose **(see illustration)**. Release the clips securing the hoses to the pulsair system valve. Ease the valve off its mounting bracket.
4 Undo the nuts securing the pulsair pipe flange to the cylinder head and remove the valve mounting bracket **(see illustration)**.
5 Undo the bolts securing the valve cover, then lift the cover off **(see illustrations)**. If the cover is stuck, tap around the joint face between the cover and the cylinder head with a soft-faced mallet to free it. Do not try to lever the cover off as this may damage the sealing surfaces.
6 Remove the gasket and discard it as a new one must be used. Clean the mating surfaces of the cylinder head and the valve cover with a suitable solvent to remove any traces of old gasket or sealant.
7 Note the location of the breather system baffle plate in the valve cover. If required, remove the plate and clean the inside of the cover. Bend back the tabs securing the plate screws carefully to avoid damaging them. On installation, ensure that the screws securing the plate are tightened securely – as a precaution, clean the screw threads and apply non-permanent thread-locking compound.
8 If required, check the condition of the pulsair reed valve (see Chapter 5).

Installation

9 Fit a new gasket over the mounting studs for the pulsair pipe flange.
10 Lay the new gasket onto the valve cover, making sure it fits correctly into the groove, and apply a bead of suitable sealant around the half-round section of the gasket **(see illustration)**.
11 Position the valve cover on the cylinder head, making sure the gasket stays in place. Install the cover bolts, then tighten them evenly and in a criss-cross sequence to the torque setting specified at the beginning of this Chapter.
12 Tighten the pulsair union nuts to the specified torque – don't forget to fit the pulse air valve mounting bracket **(see illustration 6.4)**.
13 Install the pulsair system valve and secure the hoses with the clips.
14 Install the breather hose and secure it with the clip.
15 Install the remaining components in the reverse order of removal.

7 Engine cowling and cooling fan

1 Unclip any wiring or hoses from the fan cover, then undo the bolts securing the cover **(see illustration)**. Remove the wiring clip

6.5b ...and remove the valve cover

6.10 Apply sealant as shown

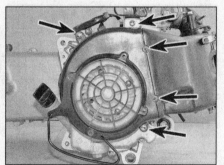

7.1a Undo the bolts (arrowed)...

7.1b ...remove the wiring clip...

7.1c ...and lift off the fan cover

7.4a Undo the lower...

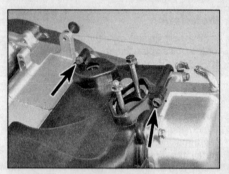

7.4b ...and upper fixing screws

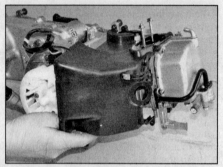

7.5 Remove the right-hand side cowling

7.6 Remove the rear brake hose guide

secured by the upper cover bolt, then lift off the cover **(see illustrations)**.

2 If not already done, pull the cap off the spark plug.

3 Remove the exhaust system (see Chapter 5). Remove the carburettor and intake manifold (see Chapter 5).

4 Note the location of the screws securing the two halves of the cowling together, then undo the screws **(see illustrations)**.

5 Ease off the right-hand side of the cowling **(see illustration)**.

6 Undo the bolt securing the rear brake hose guide on the left-hand side of the crankcase **(see illustration)**.

7 Lift off the left-hand side of the cowling **(see illustration)**.

8 Undo the bolts securing the cooling fan to the alternator rotor and remove the fan **(see illustration)**.

9 Installation is the reverse of removal. Ensure that the two halves of the cowling fit together correctly – do not force them. Take care not to over-tighten the joining screws.

8 Camchain tensioner

Removal

1 The camchain tensioner is located on the back of the cylinder on the left-hand side.

Remove the engine cowling for access (see Section 7).

2 Remove the spark plug (see Chapter 1, Section 15).

3 Turn the engine in the normal direction of rotation until the piston is at top dead centre (TDC) on its compression stroke. You can do this by rotating the crankshaft via the alternator rotor. The position of the piston can be confirmed by ensuring that the timing mark 'T' on the alternator rotor is aligned with the register mark on the crankcase **(see illustration)**.

4 Undo the tensioner cap, noting the location of the sealing O-ring **(see illustrations)**. Discard the O-ring as a new one must be fitted.

7.7 Remove the left-hand side cowling

7.8 Undo the bolts securing the fan

8.3 T mark should align with register mark (arrowed)

5 Using a small flat-bladed screwdriver, turn the tensioner clockwise until it goes tight – this will retract the tensioner plunger into the tensioner body (see illustration). The plunger should remain in this position.

6 Undo the tensioner mounting bolts and withdraw the tensioner from the cylinder (see illustration). Remove the gasket from the base of the tensioner or from the cylinder and discard it as a new one must be used .

7 Clean all traces of old gasket material from the tensioner and cylinder with a suitable solvent. Take care not to scratch or gouge the soft aluminium. Be careful not to let any of the gasket material fall into the engine.

8.4a Unscrew the tensioner cap...

8.4b ...noting location of the O-ring

Inspection

8 Examine the tensioner components for signs of wear or damage.

9 Turn the tensioner anti-clockwise to release the plunger. Now try to press the plunger back into the body – it should be locked in position (see illustrations).

10 By turning the screwdriver, ensure that the plunger moves freely in and out of the tensioner body. Examine the foot of the plunger for wear (see illustration).

11 If any part of the tensioner is worn or damaged, or if the plunger is seized in the body, a new tensioner must be fitted.

8.5 Turn tensioner screw clockwise

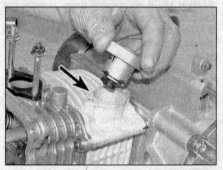

8.6 Remove the tensioner and gasket (arrowed)

Installation

12 Turn the tensioner clockwise to retract the plunger. Fit a new gasket on the tensioner body, install the tensioner in the cylinder and tighten the mounting bolts to the torque setting specified at the beginning of this Chapter.

13 Turn the engine in the normal direction of rotation – this removes all the slack in the front run of the chain between the crankshaft and the camshaft, and transfers it to the back run where it will be taken up by the tensioner. **Note:** *Take care when turning the engine with the tensioner spring removed to avoid the chain jumping over the teeth on the camshaft sprocket. If this happens, ensure that the timing marks on the alternator rotor and on the camshaft sprocket are correctly re-aligned with the piston at TDC before releasing the*

tensioner plunger (see Chapter 1, Section 14).

14 Turn the tensioner anti-clockwise to release the plunger.

15 Fit a new sealing O-ring under the cap, then install the cap and tighten it securely (see illustration 8.4b).

16 It is advisable to remove the valve cover (see Section 6) and check that the camchain is tensioned. If it is slack, the tensioner plunger did not release. Remove the tensioner and check the operation of the plunger again.

17 Install the remaining components in the reverse order of removal.

Caution: After installing the camchain tensioner, turn the crankshaft and check that all the timing marks still align correctly. If the timing marks are not aligned exactly as described, the valve timing will be

incorrect and the valves may strike the piston, causing extensive damage to the engine.

9   Camchain, blades and sprockets

Camchain
Inspection

1 The camchain runs between the drive sprocket on the crankshaft and the camshaft sprocket. To check the condition of the chain, first remove the valve cover (see Section 6).

2 Remove the spark plug (see Chapter 1,

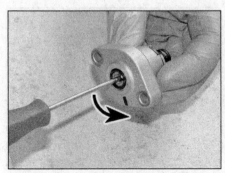

8.9a Release the tensioner plunger...

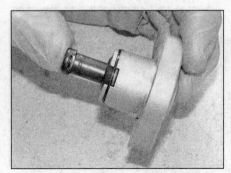

8.9b ...it should be locked in position

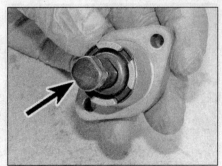

8.10 Examine plunger foot for wear

9.3 Examine the inside edges of the chain

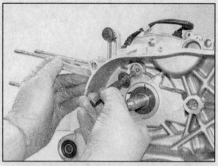

9.10 Removing the camchain tensioner blade

Section 15). If not already done, remove the fan cowling (see Section 7).

3 Using the alternator rotor, turn the engine slowly in the normal direction of rotation and inspect the inside edges of the chain links for wear **(see illustration)**. Next, hold the chain at the mid-way point around the camshaft sprocket and try to lift it off the sprocket. The chain should be a firm fit on the sprocket. Turn the engine in the normal direction of rotation and check the entire length of the chain.

4 If any of the above checks indicate that the camchain has worn, a new one must be fitted.

Removal

5 The camchain cannot be removed until the crankcase halves have been separated and the crankshaft has been removed (see Sections 20 and 21).

Installation

6 Installation is the reverse of removal, noting the following:
● Ensure the chain is correctly installed on the crankshaft sprocket before assembling the crankcase halves. Secure the chain to one of the cylinder studs to prevent it being displaced during engine assembly.
● Pay particular attention to the alignment of the TDC timing mark 'T' on the alternator rotor and the timing marks on the camshaft sprocket before installing the chain onto the sprocket.
● Ensure any slack in the chain is in the back run where it will be taken up by the tensioner.

Camchain tensioner and guide blades

Removal

7 The guide blade can be removed after the cylinder head has been removed (see Section 10).

8 The tensioner blade is secured by a pivot bolt on its lower end. To remove the blade, first remove the camshaft (see Section 11). Secure the camchain to prevent it falling down into the tunnel in the side of the cylinder.

9 Remove the variator (see Chapter 3).

10 Undo the pivot bolt and lift the blade out **(see illustration)**. Note which way round the blade is fitted. Note the location of the sealing O-ring on the pivot bolt and discard it as a new one must be fitted.

11 Check both blades for wear or damage and renew them if necessary. Check the operation of the camchain tensioner (see Section 8).

Installation

12 Installation is the reverse of removal. Ensure that the blades are fitted the correct way round **(see illustrations 9.10 and 10.16)**. Clean the threads of the tensioner blade pivot bolt and apply non-permanent thread-locking compound. Fit a new O-ring and tighten the bolt to the torque setting in the Specifications at the beginning of this Chapter.

Camchain sprockets

13 To inspect the camshaft sprocket for wear, follow the procedure in Section 10 and remove the sprocket **(see illustration 10.9)**.

14 Check for wear on the sides and tips of the sprocket teeth and for chipped or hooked teeth.

15 Similar checks should be made on the crankshaft sprocket after removing the crankshaft (see Section 21). The sprocket is integral with the crankshaft assembly – if it is worn a new crankshaft will have to be fitted.

16 If the sprocket teeth are worn, the chain will also be worn. Always renew the components as an assembly – worn sprockets will soon damage a new chain.

10 Cylinder head

Caution: The engine must be completely cool before beginning this procedure or the cylinder head may become warped.

Removal

1 Remove the carburettor, intake manifold and exhaust system (see Chapter 5).

2 Remove the valve cover (see Section 6) and the engine cowling (see Section 7).

3 Remove the spark plug (see Chapter 1).

4 Turn the engine in the normal direction of rotation until the piston is at top dead centre (TDC) on its compression stroke. You can do this by rotating the crankshaft via the alternator rotor. The position of the piston can be confirmed by ensuring that the timing mark 'T' on the alternator rotor is aligned with the register mark on the crankcase **(see illustration 8.3)**. With the piston in this position both valves should be closed and there should be a small amount of clearance in each rocker arm **(see illustration)**.

5 Look for timing marks or two small holes in the camshaft sprocket – these should be aligned with the valve cover gasket face **(see illustration)**.

6 Stuff a clean rag into the camchain tunnel to prevent anything falling into the engine.

7 Hold the alternator rotor to prevent it turning (see Section 16) and loosen the camshaft sprocket bolts **(see illustration)**. Do not remove the bolts at this stage.

8 Remove the camchain tensioner (see Section 8).

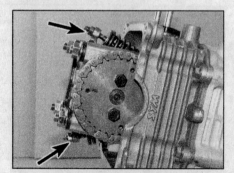

10.4 Check for a small clearance in both rocker arms

10.5 Note alignment of the timing marks (arrowed)

10.7 Loosen the sprocket bolts

10.9 Remove the camshaft sprocket

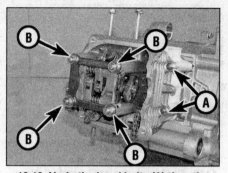
10.10 Undo the head bolts (A) then the head nuts (B)

10.12 Lift off the plate

9 Unscrew the camshaft sprocket bolts. Lift the camshaft sprocket off the end of the camshaft and disengage the sprocket from the chain **(see illustration)**. Note any markings on the outside face of the sprocket to aid installation. Secure the chain to prevent it dropping into the engine.

10 Undo the two bolts securing the left-hand side of the cylinder head **(see illustration)**.

11 Unscrew the cylinder head nuts evenly and a little at a time in a criss-cross sequence until they are loose and remove them **(see illustration 10.10)**. Note: *The cylinder head studs pass down through the cylinder and screw into the crankcase. Once the cylinder head is loose care must be taken not to break the cylinder base gasket seal otherwise a new base gasket will have to be fitted before refitting the head (see Section 13).*

12 Lift off the plate, noting how it fits **(see illustration)**.

13 Lift the cylinder head off the cylinder, feeding the camchain down through the tunnel in the head **(see illustration)**. If the head is stuck, tap around the joint face between the head and the cylinder with a soft-faced mallet to free it. Do not try to lever the head off as this may damage the sealing surfaces.

14 Remove the old cylinder head gasket, noting how it fits **(see illustration)**. Note the two dowels and remove them for safekeeping if they are loose – the dowels may be in the underside of the head or the cylinder **(see illustration)**.

15 Secure the camchain to prevent it dropping into the engine.

16 If required, the camchain guide blade can be removed – draw the blade out, noting how the lugs locate in the recess in the top edge of the camchain tunnel **(see illustration)**.

17 Stuff a clean rag into the camchain tunnel in the cylinder to prevent anything falling into the engine.

18 Clean all traces of old gasket material from the cylinder head and cylinder with a suitable solvent. Take care not to scratch or gouge the soft aluminium. Be careful not to let any of the gasket material fall into the crankcase, the cylinder bore or the oil passages.

19 Inspect the cylinder head gasket and the mating surfaces on the cylinder head and cylinder for signs of leaks, which could

indicate that the head is warped. Refer to Chapter 2C, Section 12 and check the head mating surface for warpage.

20 After inspection, discard the old gasket as a new one must be fitted on reassembly

Installation

21 Installation is the reverse of removal, noting the following:
● Lubricate the cylinder bore with clean engine oil.
● Ensure the dowels are correctly installed in the cylinder.
● If removed, install the camchain guide blade (see Step 16).
● Install a new head gasket – never re-use the old gasket.
● Ensure the camchain is correctly located around the crankshaft sprocket.

● Install the plate **(see illustration 10.12)** then tighten the cylinder head nuts first before the smaller, external bolts.
● Tighten the cylinder head nuts evenly and a little at a time in a criss-cross pattern to the torque setting specified at the beginning of this Chapter. Tighten the bolts to the specified torque.
● Ensure the piston is at TDC on the compression stroke.
● Ensure the camshaft is positioned with the punch mark on the sprocket backplate at the top **(see illustration 11.2b)**.
● Ensure the sprocket is correctly aligned before and after installing the camchain tensioner (see Step 5). Tighten the sprocket bolts to the specified torque.
● Check the valve clearances (see Chapter 1).

10.13 Lift off the cylinder head

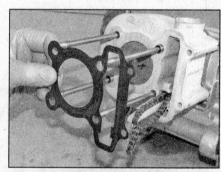
10.14a Remove the head gasket

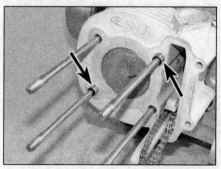
10.14b Location of the cylinder head dowels

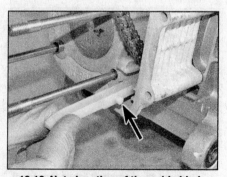
10.16 Note location of the guide blade lugs (arrowed)

11.2a Location of the stopper plate

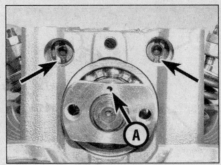

11.2b Rocker shaft slots (arrowed). Note punch mark (A)

11.3 Mark the rocker arms to aid installation

11 Camshaft and rocker arms

Removal

1 Remove the cylinder head (see Section 10).
2 The camshaft assembly and rockers are retained by a stopper plate (see illustration). Undo the bolt securing the plate and remove it, noting how both ends of the plate locate in the slots in the ends of the rocker shafts (see illustration). Note the camshaft position punch mark on the sprocket backplate.
3 Note the position of the rocker arms and mark them so that they can be installed in their original positions. (see illustration). Note how the ends of the springs on the rocker shafts locate over the rocker arms.

4 Working on one rocker assembly at a time, thread a 5 mm bolt into the end of the rocker shaft, support the rocker arm and withdraw the shaft carefully (see illustration). Assemble the rockers and springs on their shafts so that they can be installed in their original positions (see illustration).
5 Draw out the camshaft, rotating it so that the cam lobes clear the housing (see illustration).

Inspection

6 Clean all of the components with a suitable solvent and dry them.
7 Inspect the camshaft lobes for heat discoloration (blue appearance), score marks, chipped areas, flat spots and spalling (see illustration). If available, use a micrometer to measure the height of each camshaft lobe and compare the results with the specifications at the beginning of this Chapter. If damage is

noted or the camshaft has worn excessively it must be renewed.
8 Check the condition of the camshaft bearings (see Tools and Workshop Tips in the Reference section). The camshaft and bearings are supplied as an assembly, so if any component is worn a new assembly will have to be fitted.
9 Check the bearing housings in the cylinder head for score marks and spalling (see illustration). Any damage is an indication that the bearing has seized on the camshaft and turned inside its housing. Prior to reassembly, check that the outer race is a tight fit in its housing, otherwise use some bearing locking compound to hold it in position.
10 Blow through the oil passages in the rocker arms and shafts with compressed air, if available, to ensure that they are clear.
11 Inspect the roller face of the rocker arm and ensure that it turns freely (see illustration).

11.4a Withdraw the shaft and lift out the rocker arm

11.4b Keep matched components together

11.5 Manoeuvre out the camshaft

11.7 Inspect the camshaft lobes (arrowed)

11.9 Inspect the bearing housings (arrowed)

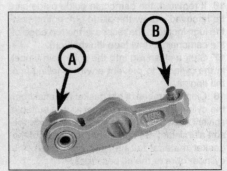

11.11 Inspect the roller (A) and adjuster screw face (B)

Inspect the contact area between the adjuster screw and the valve stem for pits and spalling.
12 Check the rocker shaft for wear. If available, use a micrometer to measure the diameter of the shaft in several places. **Note:** *Any variation in the measurements is an indication of wear on the shaft.*
13 The rocker arm should be a sliding fit on the shaft without any freeplay. If the shaft is good but there is freeplay, the rocker arm is worn and should be renewed.

Installation

14 Installation is the reverse of removal, noting the following:
● Lubricate the shafts, bearing surfaces and bearings with clean engine oil before installation.

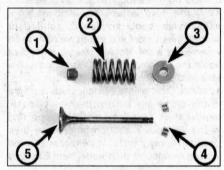

12.1 Valve components

1 *Valve stem seal*   4 *Collets*
2 *Valve spring*   5 *Valve*
3 *Spring retainer*

● Ensure the camshaft assembly is pressed all the way into its housing.
● Don't forget to fit the springs onto the rocker shafts **(see illustration 11.4b)**.
● Press the rocker shafts all the way into their locations.
● Position the rocker shafts so that the slots for the ends of the stopper plate are vertical **(see illustration 11.2b)**.
● Tighten the stopper plate bolt to the torque setting specified at the beginning of this Chapter.

12 Cylinder head and valves

Note: *If a valve spring compressor is available, the home mechanic can remove the valves from the cylinder head, lap the valves and renew the valve stem seals.*

Disassembly

1 Before you start, arrange to label and store the valves and their related components so that they can be returned to their original locations without getting mixed up **(see illustration)**.
2 Compress the valve spring on the first valve with a spring compressor, making sure it is correctly located onto each end of the valve assembly **(see illustration)**. On the underside of the head, make sure the plate on the compressor only contacts the valve and not the soft aluminium of the head – if the plate is too big for the valve, use a spacer between

them. Do not compress the springs any more than is absolutely necessary to release the collets, then remove the collets, using either needle-nose pliers, a magnet or a screwdriver with a dab of grease on it **(see illustration)**.
3 Carefully release the valve spring compressor and remove the spring retainer, noting which way up it fits **(see illustration)**.
4 Remove the valve spring. **Note:** *The valve springs have closer wound coils that are fitted next to the cylinder head. On the engine photographed, the upper ends of the springs were marked with a dab of paint.*
5 Turn the head over and withdraw the valve **(see illustration)**. If the valve binds in the guide (won't pull through), push it back into the head and deburr the area around the collet groove with a very fine file.
6 Once the valve has been removed, pull the valve stem oil seal off the top of the valve guide with pliers or lever it off with a flat-bladed screwdriver **(see illustration)**. Discard the seal as a new one must be used on reassembly.
7 The spring seat is retained by the valve guide and cannot be removed **(see illustration)**.
8 Repeat the procedure for the remaining valve. Remember to keep the parts for each valve together and in order so they can be reinstalled in the correct location.
9 Next, clean the cylinder head with solvent and dry it thoroughly. Compressed air will speed the drying process and ensure that all holes and recessed areas are clean.
10 Clean the valve springs, collets, retainers and spring seats with solvent. Work on the

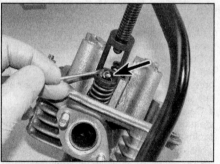

12.2b Remove the collets from the top end of the valve

12.3 Remove the spring retainer and lift out the valve spring

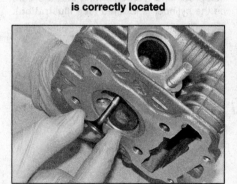

12.5 Pull out the valve

12.6 Removing the valve stem seal

12.7 Spring seat (arrowed) is fixed in position

12.2a Ensure the valve spring compressor is correctly located

13.2a Lift the cylinder...

13.2b ...and support the piston

13.4 Discard the old cylinder base gasket (arrowed)

parts from one valve at a time so as not to mix them up.

11 Scrape off any carbon deposits that may have formed on the valve, then use a motorised wire brush to remove deposits from the valve heads and stems. Again, make sure the valves do not get mixed up.

Inspection and reassembly

12 Refer to Chapter 2C, Section 12 for details of valve inspection, lapping and reassembly.

13 Cylinder

Removal

1 Remove the cylinder head and the camchain guide blade (see Section 10).
2 Hold the camchain and lift the cylinder up off the crankcase, supporting the piston as it becomes accessible to prevent it hitting the crankcase opening (see illustrations). If the cylinder is stuck, tap around the joint face between the cylinder and the crankcase with a soft-faced mallet to free it. Don't attempt to free the cylinder by inserting a screwdriver between it and the crankcase – you'll damage the sealing surfaces.
3 Once the cylinder has been removed, stuff a clean rag into the crankcase opening around the piston to prevent anything falling inside.
4 Remove the cylinder base gasket, noting how it fits (see illustration), then discard it as new one must be fitted on reassembly. Note

the dowels on the left-hand cylinder studs and remove them for safekeeping if they are loose. Note how the camchain locates on the crankshaft sprocket and secure the chain to prevent it dropping into the crankcase.
5 Clean all traces of old gasket material from the cylinder and crankcase with a suitable solvent. Take care not to scratch or gouge the soft aluminium. Be careful not to let any of the gasket material fall into the crankcase.

Inspection

6 Check the cylinder bore carefully for scratches and score marks (see illustration).
7 If available, use a telescoping gauge and micrometer to measure the inside diameter of the cylinder bore to assess the amount of wear, taper and ovality (see Tools and Workshop Tips in the Reference section). Measure near the top (but below the level of the top piston ring at top dead centre), centre and bottom (but above the level of the bottom ring with the piston at bottom dead centre) of the bore both parallel to and across the crankshaft axis (see illustration 13.7a in Chapter 2C).
8 Compare the results with the specifications at the beginning of this Chapter. If the cylinder bore is worn beyond its service limit, a new one should be fitted.
9 Calculate any differences between the measurements to determine any taper or ovality in the bore. A cylinder bore that has worn oval will reduce the efficiency of the piston rings to achieve a seal, resulting in loss of compression and increased oil consumption.

10 If no measuring tools are available, check for a lip around the (unworn) top edge of the cylinder bore as a rough indication of wear.
11 If the bore is tapered, oval, or worn excessively, badly scratched, scuffed or scored, the cylinder and piston will have to be renewed as a set. Note: If there is any doubt about the condition of the cylinder, consult a specialist engineer.
12 Check that all the cylinder studs are tight in the crankcase halves. If any are loose, remove them (see Tools and Workshop Tips in the Reference section) and clean their threads. Apply a suitable permanent thread locking compound, then screw them back into the crankcase securely.

Installation

13 Remove any rag from the crankcase opening. Ensure any dowels are correctly installed in the crankcase, then lay the new base gasket in place on the crankcase making sure it is the correct way round (see illustration).
14 Position the piston ring end gaps correctly (see illustration 15.9 in Chapter 2C).
15 Lubricate the cylinder bore, piston and piston rings, and the connecting rod big- and small-ends, with the clean engine oil, then lower the cylinder down until the piston crown fits into the bore.
16 Gently push down on the cylinder, making sure the piston enters the bore squarely and does not get cocked sideways. Carefully compress and feed each ring into the bore as the cylinder is lowered (see illustration).

13.6 Inspect the cylinder bore for scratches and score marks

13.13 Base gasket must not obstruct oilway (arrowed)

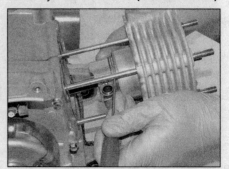

13.16 Feed each ring into the bore carefully as the cylinder is lowered

If necessary, use a soft mallet to gently tap the cylinder down, but do not use force if it appears to be stuck as the piston and/or rings will be damaged.

17 When the piston is correctly installed in the cylinder, support the camchain and check that the base gasket has not been displaced, then press the cylinder down onto the base gasket.

18 Install the camchain guide blade **(see illustration 10.16)**, then install the cylinder head (see Section 10).

14 Piston

Refer to Chapter 2C, Section 14, noting the piston diameter specification at the beginning of this Chapter.

15 Piston rings

Refer to Chapter 2C, Section 15, noting that on this engine the compression rings are marked near the gap to denote the upper surface of the ring – 2R for second compression ring, 1R for top ring **(see illustration)**.

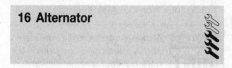

16 Alternator

Removal

1 The alternator is located behind the slotted fan cover on the right-hand side of the engine

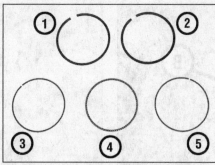

15.1 Piston ring set

1 Top (compression) ring
2 Second (compression) ring
3 Upper side rail
4 Rail spacer
5 Lower side rail

– remove the cover and the cooling fan (see Section 7).

2 To undo the alternator rotor centre nut it is necessary to stop the rotor from turning using a pin wrench that locates in the two large holes in the face of the rotor. Peugeot produces a service tool (Part No. 752237) for this purpose. Alternatively, a similar home-made tool can be used (see Tool Tip in Chapter 2A,

Section 11) or you can obtain an aftermarket version. **Note:** *Take great care not to damage the internal coils of the alternator when locating any tools through the rotor.*

3 With the rotor securely held, undo the centre nut **(see illustration)**.

4 Alternatively, the alternator rotor can be held with a strap wrench. If necessary, undo the bolts securing the ignition pulse generator coil and displace it to avoid damaging it when using the strap wrench.

5 To remove the rotor from the taper on the crankshaft it is necessary to use a puller that threads into the internal thread in the centre of the rotor. Peugeot produces a service tool (puller Part No. 750016) for this purpose and similar aftermarket pullers are available. Note that the puller has a left-hand thread – to screw it into the rotor turn it anti-clockwise. Ensure the puller is threaded all the way into the centre of the rotor, then screw in the centre bolt. Hold the puller and tighten the centre bolt steadily to draw the rotor off the crankshaft taper **(see illustration)**.

6 Lift the washer and rotor off the crankshaft **(see illustration)**.

7 If it is loose, remove the Woodruff key from the shaft for safekeeping, noting how it fits **(see illustration)**.

8 The alternator stator coils and ignition pulse

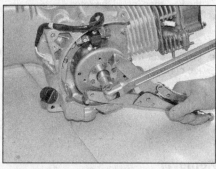

16.3 Using an aftermarkert pin wrench to hold the rotor

16.5 Apply steady pressure with the puller centre bolt

16.6 Remove the washer and alternator rotor

16.7 Note location of Woodruff key (arrowed)

16.9a Pulse generator coil (A), wiring guide (B) and alternator stator (C)

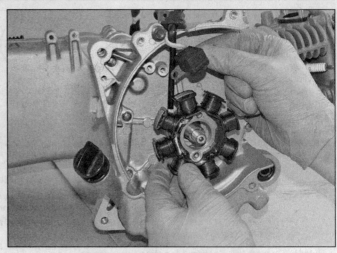

16.9b Lift off the alternator assembly

generator coil are wired together and have to be removed as an assembly. If not already done, trace the wiring back from the alternator and pulse generator and disconnect it at the connectors (see illustration 4.14). Free the wiring from any clips or guides and feed it through to the alternator.

9 If not already done, undo the bolts securing the pulse generator coil, then undo the bolts securing the wiring guide and the alternator stator and lift the assembly off (see illustrations). Note how the wiring seal fits in the cut-out in the top of the engine casing.

Installation

10 Installation is the reverse of removal, noting the following:
● Ensure the wiring is correctly routed before installing the stator and pulse generator.
● Tighten the stator and pulse generator bolts to the torque settings specified at the beginning of this Chapter.
● Make sure that no metal objects have

attached themselves to the magnets on the inside of the rotor.
● Clean the tapered end of the crankshaft and the corresponding mating surface on the inside of the rotor with a suitable solvent.
● Fit the Woodruff key into the crankshaft, align the slot in the centre of the rotor with the key, then install the rotor.
● Tighten the alternator centre nut to the specified torque setting.
● Secure the wiring with any clips or ties.
● Ensure that the cooling fan and fan cover are correctly installed (see Section 7).

17 Right-hand crankcase cover

Removal

1 Remove the exhaust system (see Chapter 5).

2 Drain the engine oil (see Chapter 1, Section 6).

3 Follow the procedure in Section 16 and remove the alternator.

4 An oil seal is fitted in the crankcase cover where the crankshaft passes through it (see Step 9). Check around the seal for signs of oil leakage – if the seal has been leaking a new one must be fitted once the cover has been removed. **Note:** *It is good practice to renew the oil seal whenever the cover is removed.*

5 Position a drain tray underneath the engine to catch any residual oil when the cover is removed, then undo the cover screws – noting their locations (see illustrations).

HAYNES HINT *Make a cardboard template of the crankcase and punch a hole for each screw location. This will ensure that they are all installed correctly on reassembly – this is important as the bolts are of different lengths.*

17.5a Undo the cover screws (arrowed)...

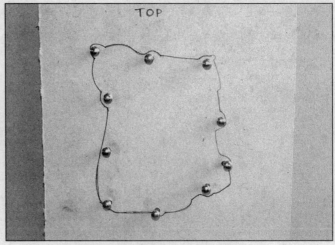

17.5b ...and store them in a template

17.6 Remove the crankcase cover

17.7 Remove the gasket noting the dowels (arrowed)

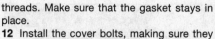

17.9a Drive out the oil seal with a suitable socket

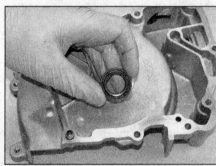

17.9b Install the new crankshaft oil seal from the inside of the cover

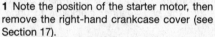

6 Draw the cover off **(see illustration)**. If the cover is stuck, tap around the joint face between the cover and the crankcase with a soft-faced mallet to free it. Do not try to lever the cover off as this may damage the sealing surfaces.

7 Remove the gasket and discard it as a new one must be used. Note any dowels in the cover or crankcase and remove them for safekeeping if they are loose **(see illustration)**.

8 Clean the mating surfaces of the cover and the crankcase with a suitable solvent to remove any traces of old gasket or sealant. Take care not to scratch or gouge the soft aluminium.

9 To renew the cover oil seal, support the cover on the work surface and drive the seal

out from the outside with a suitably-sized socket **(see illustration)**. Note which way round the seal is fitted **(see illustration)**. Ensure that the seal housing is clean, then lubricate the new seal with a smear of engine oil and press it all the way into the housing from the inside.

Installation

10 If removed, fit the dowels into the crankcase, then fit a new cover gasket, making sure it locates correctly onto the dowels **(see illustration 17.7)**. If necessary, use a dab of grease to hold the gasket in position.

11 Lubricate the inside of the oil seal with engine oil, then install the cover taking care not to damage the seal on the crankshaft

threads. Make sure that the gasket stays in place.

12 Install the cover bolts, making sure they are in the correct locations, then tighten the bolts evenly and in a criss-cross sequence. to the torque setting specified at the beginning of this Chapter.

13 Install the remaining components in the reverse order of removal.

14 Fill the engine with the correct type and quantity of oil (see Chapter 1 and *Pre-ride checks*)

18 Starter (one way) clutch

Check

1 Note the position of the starter motor, then remove the right-hand crankcase cover (see Section 17).

2 If required, the operation of the starter clutch can be checked while it is in place. First withdraw the starter idler gear shaft and disengage the idler gear from the starter driven gear (see Step 4) – the driven gear should now rotate freely in the *opposite* direction to crankshaft rotation (anti-clockwise), but lock when rotated clockwise **(see illustration)**. If not, the starter clutch is faulty and should be removed for inspection.

Removal

3 If required, remove the starter motor (see Chapter 10).

4 Withdraw the starter idler gear shaft and lift out the idler gear **(see illustration)**.

5 A peg spanner (Peugeot service tool Part No. 800673) is required to undo the starter clutch retaining nut **(see illustration)**. If the correct tool is not available, one can be made from a suitable length of steel tube **(see Tool Tip in Chapter 2F, Section 18)**.

6 Use a pin wrench (see Section 16) to prevent the crankshaft from turning while the retaining nut is being loosened. Align two holes in the starter driven gear with two holes in the body of the starter clutch

18.2 Starter driven gear should rotate freely anti-clockwise

18.4 Remove the shaft and starter idler gear

18.5 Castellations on peg spanner must fit the retaining nut

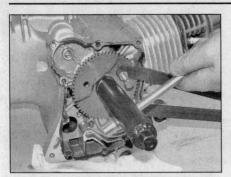

18.6 Turn the nut clockwise to undo

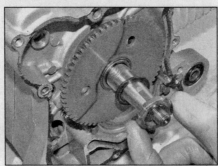

18.7a Remove the nut and washer...

18.7b ...and the driven gear and starter clutch assembly

and install the pin wrench so that it locates securely in the body of the starter clutch, then use the peg spanner to undo the clutch retaining nut applying steady pressure **(see illustration)**. **Note:** *This is a left-hand thread – turn the peg spanner clockwise to undo the nut.*

7 Unscrew the retaining nut, noting how it fits, and remove the washer, then draw the starter clutch and driven gear assembly off the crankshaft **(see illustrations)**. If the assembly is a tight fit, use a puller to draw it off. **Note:** *To avoid damaging the threaded end of the crankshaft, temporarily install the alternator centre nut.*

8 If it is loose, remove the Woodruff key from the shaft for safekeeping, noting how it fits **(see illustration)**. **Note:** *On the machine used to illustrate this procedure the oil pump drive*

gear came off the crankshaft with the starter clutch.

Inspection

9 Inspect both sets of teeth on the idler gear and renew it if any are chipped or worn **(see illustration 18.4)**. **Note:** *If the teeth on the larger pinion are worn or damaged, inspect the teeth on the starter motor shaft also (see Chapter 10). Check the idler shaft and bearing surfaces for signs of wear or damage, and renew it if necessary.*

10 Hold the starter clutch and check that the driven gear rotates freely anti-clockwise and locks when turned clockwise **(see illustration)**. If it doesn't, the sprags in the one-way mechanism may be jammed. Lift out the driven gear **(see illustration 18.11a)**,

wash the assembly in suitable solvent and dry it with compressed air, if available. Lubricate the mechanism with clean engine oil, reassemble and check it again. If the starter clutch still does not operate correctly, it can be disassembled and the components inspected (see Step 13).

11 Inspect the teeth of the starter driven gear for wear and damage. Lift the gear out from the starter clutch and remove the needle bearing **(see illustrations)**. Inspect the bearing and the bearing races in the starter clutch and the starter gear for wear and pitting.

12 Inspect the outside surface of the driven gear hub for uneven wear and scoring.

13 If required, undo the starter clutch assembly screws, then turn the assembly over and lift out the centre **(see illustration)**. Hold the spring-loaded plungers in place and lift out the clutch sprags, then remove the plungers and springs, noting how they fit **(see illustrations 18.13a, b and c in Chapter 2F)**. Inspect the components carefully for wear and damage and renew any components as necessary. Reassemble the starter clutch in the reverse order of disassembly. Clean the threads of the assembly screws and apply a suitable non-permanent thread-locking compound, then tighten the screws to the torque setting specified at the beginning of this Chapter.

14 Note the location of the oil pump drive gear on the back of the starter clutch **(see**

18.8 Location of the starter clutch Woodruff key

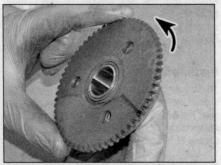

18.10 Checking starter clutch operation

18.11a Separate the driven gear from the starter clutch...

18.11b ...and lift out the needle bearing

18.13 Undo the assembly screws (arrowed)

illustration). The gear is an integral part of the clutch assembly.

Installation

15 Installation is the reverse of removal, noting the following:

● Lubricate the starter clutch mechanism with clean engine oil.
● Fit the Woodruff key into its slot in the shaft.
● Ensure that the starter clutch assembly is pressed all the way onto the crankshaft.
● Install the washer and tighten the retaining nut to the torque setting specified at the beginning of this Chapter. Use the same method to hold the crankshaft as on disassembly and turn the nut anti-clockwise.
● Ensure the idler gear engages with the pinion on the starter motor shaft. Lubricate the idler gear shaft.

19 Oil pump

Removal

1 Remove the alternator (see Section 16) and the right-hand crankcase cover (see Section 17).
2 Remove the starter clutch (see Section 18).
3 Undo the bolts securing the pump driven gear cover and remove the cover **(see illustration)**.
4 The pump driven gear is retained by an E-clip – ease the clip off and remove the gear, noting the location of the drive pin in the gear shaft **(see illustrations)**. Remove the drive pin for safekeeping. A new E-clip should be fitted on reassembly.
5 Note how the pump is located in the crankcase – undo the mounting screws and withdraw the pump **(see illustrations)**.

Inspection

6 Check the pump body for obvious signs of damage especially around the mounting bolt holes. Turn the pump driveshaft by hand and check that the pump rotates smoothly **(see illustration)**.

18.14 Note location of the oil pump drive gear (arrowed)

19.4a E-clip (arrowed) retains pump gear

19.3 Undo the bolts (arrowed) and remove the sprocket cover

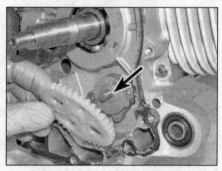

19.4b Note location of drive pin

7 If required, the pump can be disassembled for cleaning and inspection.
8 Undo the screw securing the cover to the back of the pump body and remove cover, noting how it fits.
9 Note any reference marks on the pump rotors; even if the rotors are not marked, it is essential that they are reassembled the correct way round. Lift out the pump shaft and the inner and outer rotors.
10 Clean the pump components with a suitable solvent and dry them with compressed air, if available. Inspect the pump body, rotors and shaft for scoring and wear. If any damage, scoring, uneven or excessive wear is evident, renew the pump.
11 If the pump is good, reassemble all the components in the reverse order of disassembly and lubricate them with clean engine oil.

12 Fit the cover and tighten the screw securely, then rotate the pump shaft by hand to check that the rotors turn smoothly and freely.

Installation

13 Installation is the reverse of removal, noting the following:

● Fill the pump with clean engine oil before installation.
● Press the pump body squarely into its housing then tighten the mounting screws evenly to the torque setting specified at the beginning of this Chapter.
● Fit the drive pin and driven gear and secure them with a new E-clip.
● Tighten the bolts securing the gear cover securely.
● Fill the engine with the correct type and quantity of oil (see Chapter 1 and *Pre-ride checks*).

19.5a Undo the mounting screws (arrowed)...

19.5b ...and lift out the oil pump

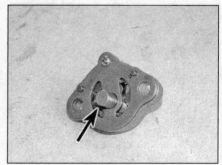

19.6 Check that the driveshaft (arrowed) rotates smoothly

20.4 Unscrew the remaining crankcase bolts

20.5 Ease off the right-hand crankcase half

20.6 Lift out the crankshaft assembly

20 Crankcase halves

Separation

1 Follow the procedure in Section 4 and remove the engine from the frame.
2 Before the crankcase halves can be separated the following components must be removed:
● Cylinder head (Section 10)
● Cylinder (Section 13)
● Starter motor (Chapter 10)
● Alternator (Section 16)
● Variator (Chapter 3)
● Right-hand crankcase cover (Section 17)
● Oil pump (Section 19)
● Centrestand (Chapter 7)
3 Tape some rag around the connecting rod to prevent it knocking against the cases. Although not essential, it is advisable to remove the piston to avoid damage during this procedure.
4 Support the crankcase assembly on the work surface on its left-hand side. Loosen the remaining crankcase bolts evenly, a little at a time until they are finger-tight, then remove them **(see illustration)**.
5 Lift the right-hand crankcase half off the left-hand half **(see illustration)**. If the crankcase halves do not separate easily, first ensure all fasteners have been removed. Next, apply heat to the right-hand main bearing

housing with a hot air gun and try lifting the right-hand half off again.
Caution: Do not try to separate the halves by levering against the mating surfaces as they are easily scored and will not seal correctly afterwards. Do not strike the ends of the crankshaft with a hammer as damage to the end threads or the shaft itself will result.
6 Now lift the crankshaft assembly out of the left-hand crankcase half – apply heat to the main bearing housing if required **(see illustration)**. Ensure the camchain is clear of the crankshaft sprocket when the crankshaft is removed. Note that the main bearings will remain in place on the crankshaft assembly (see Section 21).
7 Remove the camchain and mark one side with a dab of paint so that it can be installed the same way round **(see illustration 20.22)**. If not already done, undo the pivot bolt securing the camchain tensioner blade and lift the blade out **(see illustration 9.10)**. Note which way round the blade is fitted.
8 Remove the crankcase gasket and discard it as a new one must be used. Remove the dowels from either crankcase half for safekeeping if they are loose **(see illustration 20.25)**.
9 Clean the mating surfaces of the crankcase halves with a suitable solvent to remove any traces of old gasket or sealant. Take care not to scratch or gouge the soft aluminium.
10 Note the position of the crankshaft oil seal in the left-hand crankcase half and note which

way round it is fitted **(see illustration)**. Push the seal out from the inside using a suitably sized socket and discard it as a new one must be fitted on reassembly **(see illustration)**.
11 If required, remove the transmission assembly from the left-hand crankcase half (see Chapter 3).

Inspection

12 Wash the cases in a suitable solvent and dry them with compressed air, if available.
13 Small cracks or holes in aluminium castings can be repaired with an epoxy resin adhesive as a temporary measure. Permanent repairs can only be effected by welding, and only a specialist in this process is in a position to advise on the economy or practical aspect of such a repair. On some engines, the crankcase halves can be renewed individually, on others the two halves are only available together as a matching set.
14 Damaged threads can be economically reclaimed by using a thread insert. Most small engineering firms offer a service of this kind. Sheared screws can usually be removed with screw extractors. Refer to *Tools and Workshop Tips* in the *Reference* section for further details.
15 Always wash the crankcases thoroughly after any repair work to ensure no dirt or metal swarf is trapped inside when the engine is rebuilt.
16 Check that the oil passages are clean and clear – blow them through with compressed air, if available **(see illustration)**.

20.10a Location of the crankshaft oil seal

20.10b Using a socket to drive out the old seal

20.16 Clean the oil pump housing and oil passages (arrowed) carefully

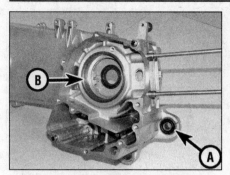

20.17 Front left-hand engine mounting bush (A), bearing housing (B)

20.20 Level the seal with a block of wood

20.22 Allow clearance for the crankshaft sprocket

17 Inspect the engine mounting bushes **(see illustration)**. If they show signs of deterioration, renew them all at the same time. To remove a bush, first note its position in the casing. Heat the casing with a hot air gun, then support the casing and drive the bush out with a hammer and a suitably sized socket. Alternatively, use two suitably sized sockets to press the bush out in the jaws of a vice. Clean the bush housing with steel wool to remove any corrosion, then reheat the casing and fit the new bush. **Note:** *Always support the casing when removing or fitting bushes to avoid breaking the casing.*

18 Inspect the main bearing housings **(see illustration 20.17)**. If a bearing outer race has spun in its housing, the inside of the housing will be damaged. A bearing locking compound can be used to fix the outer race in place on reassembly if the damage is not too severe. **Note:** *If a bearing has spun in its housing, the bearing itself is likely to be damaged – see Section 21.*

19 Inspect the crankshaft assembly and bearings (see Section 21).

Reassembly

20 Fit the new crankshaft oil seal into the left-hand crankcase half and press it into place from the outside using a seal driver or socket. Ensure the seal is fitted the right way round and that it enters the case squarely. Level the seal with the edge of the housing with a small block of wood **(see illustration)**. Lubricate the seal with clean engine oil.

21 Tape some rag around the connecting rod to prevent it knocking against the cases.
22 Support the left-hand crankcase half on the work surface with enough space below it to provide clearance for the end of the crankshaft when it is fully installed. Position the camchain in the crankcase with clearance for the crankshaft sprocket **(see illustration)**.
23 Lubricate the left-hand crankshaft main bearing with clean engine oil, then lower the crankshaft assembly into the crankcase half carefully to avoid damaging the seal. Ensure that the main bearing is aligned with the bearing housing and that the connecting rod is aligned with the crankcase mouth. Press the crankshaft assembly in fully so that the main bearing goes all the way into its housing. If the main bearing does not seat fully, apply heat with a hot air gun around the bearing housing while keeping steady pressure to the crankshaft assembly. **Note:** *Avoid applying direct heat onto the crankshaft oil seal. If required, a freeze spray can be used on the main bearing to aid installation.*
24 Ensure that the camchain is correctly located around the crankshaft sprocket and secure it in position with wire or a cable-tie to avoid it becoming jammed inside the crankcase.
25 If necessary, allow the case to cool, then wipe the mating surfaces of both crankcase halves with a rag soaked in suitable solvent. Fit the dowels and install the new crankcase gasket on the mating surface of the left-hand case **(see illustration)**.

26 Lubricate the right-hand main bearing with clean engine oil, then lower the crankcase half over the crankshaft. Ensure that the two halves of the crankcase are correctly aligned, taking special note of the position of the dowels, and that the main bearing is aligned with the bearing housing in the right-hand case **(see illustration 20.5)**.
27 Press the crankcase on fully so that the main bearing goes all the way into its housing. If the main bearing does not seat fully, apply heat to the around the bearing housing while keeping steady pressure to the crankcase.
28 Check that the crankcase halves are seated all the way round. If the cases are not correctly seated, heat the bearing housings while applying firm pressure. **Note:** *Do not attempt to pull the crankcase halves together using the crankcase bolts as the casing will crack and be ruined.*
29 Clean the threads of the crankcase bolts and install them finger-tight, then tighten them evenly a little at a time to the torque setting specified at the beginning of this Chapter **(see illustration 20.4)**.
30 Trim off any excess gasket across the crankcase mouth **(see illustration)**.
31 Support the connecting rod and rotate the crankshaft by hand – if there are any signs of undue stiffness, tight or rough spots, or of any other problem, the fault must be rectified before proceeding further. Don't forget to support the camchain while rotating the crankshaft.
32 If required, install the camchain tensioner blade (see Section 9).
33 Install the remaining components in the reverse order of removal.

21 Crankshaft assembly, big-end and main bearings

Note: *The crankshaft assembly is pressed together and is easily damaged if it is dropped.*
1 To access the crankshaft assembly, the big-end bearing and the main bearings, the crankcase must be split into two parts (see Section 20).
2 The crankshaft assembly should give

20.25 Fit the dowels (arrowed) and the crankcase gasket

20.30 Trim off the excess crankcase gasket

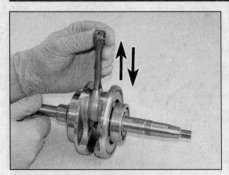

21.4 Checking for play in the big-end bearing

21.5 Measuring big-end side clearance

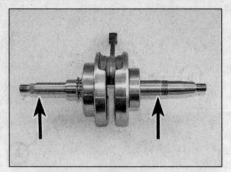

21.6 Check runout at the positions indicated

many thousands of miles of service. The most likely problems to occur will be a worn small or big-end bearing due to poor lubrication. A worn big-end bearing will produce a pronounced knocking noise, most audible when the engine is under load, and increasing as engine speed rises. This should not be confused with small-end bearing wear, which produces a lighter, metallic rattle (see wSection 14).

3 When the crankcase halves are separated, the main bearings will remain in place on the crankshaft assembly – they are not normally available as separate items. If the main bearings have failed, excessive rumbling and vibration will be felt when the engine is running.

4 To assess the condition of the big-end bearing, hold the crankshaft assembly firmly and push and pull on the connecting rod, checking for any up-and-down freeplay between the two **(see illustration)**. If any freeplay is noted, the bearing is worn.

5 A small amount of big-end side clearance (side-to-side movement) is acceptable on the connecting rod. Measure the clearance with a feeler gauge **(see illustration)**, then compare the result with the service limit specified at the beginning of this Chapter.

6 If available, place the crankshaft assembly on V-blocks and check the runout at either end using a dial gauge **(see illustration)**. Compare the result with the specification at the beginning of this Chapter. If the crankshaft is out-of-true it will cause excessive engine vibration. If there is any doubt about the condition of the crankshaft have it checked by an automotive engineer

7 Follow the procedure in *Tools and Workshop Tips* in the *Reference* section to check the condition of the main bearings.

8 If wear or damage is noted in any of the crankshaft assembly bearings, a new crankshaft assembly will have to be fitted. **Note:** *Evidence of extreme heat, such as discoloration or blueing, indicates that lubrication failure has occurred. Be sure to check the oil pump and bearing oil ways in the crankcases before reassembling the engine.*

9 Inspect the threads on each end of the crankshaft and ensure that the retaining nuts for the alternator rotor and the variator are a

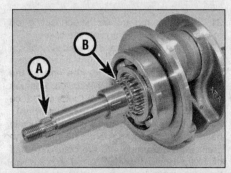

21.9a Variator splines (A) and camshaft drive sprocket (B)

good fit. Inspect the splines for the variator pulley on the left-hand end of the shaft **(see illustration)**. Inspect the taper and the slot in the right-hand end of the shaft for the alternator Woodruff key **(see illustration)**. Damage or wear that prevents the rotor from being fitted securely will require a new crankshaft assembly.

10 Inspect the teeth of the camshaft drive sprocket on the crankshaft for damage or wear **(see illustration 21.9a)**. The sprocket is an integral part of the crankshaft assembly – if it is worn or damaged a new assembly will have to be fitted.

22 Initial start-up after overhaul/running-in

Initial start-up after overhaul

1 Make sure the engine oil level is correct (see *Pre-ride checks*).

2 Make sure there is fuel in the tank.

3 With the ignition OFF, operate the kickstart a couple of times to check that the engine turns over easily.

4 Turn the ignition ON, start the engine and allow it to run at a slow idle until it reaches operating temperature. Do not be alarmed if there is a little smoke from the exhaust – this will be due to the oil used to lubricate the piston and bore during assembly and should subside after a while.

5 If the engine proves reluctant to start, remove the spark plug and check that it has

21.9b Taper and key for alternator (A), key for starter clutch (B)

not become wet and oily. If it has, clean it and try again. If the engine refuses to start, go through the fault finding charts at the end of this manual to identify the problem.

6 Check carefully for fuel and oil leaks and make sure the transmission and controls, especially the brakes, function properly before road testing the machine.

7 Upon completion of the road test, and after the engine has cooled down completely, recheck the valve clearances (see Chapter 1). Recheck the engine oil level (see *Pre-ride checks*).

Recommended running-in procedure

8 Treat the engine gently for the first few miles to allow any new parts to bed in.

9 If a new piston, cylinder or crankshaft assembly has been fitted, the engine will have to be run-in as when new. This means a restraining hand on the throttle until at least 300 miles (500 km) have been covered. There's no point in keeping to any set speed limit – the main idea is to gradually increase performance up to the 600 mile (1000 km) mark. Make sure that the throttle position is varied to vary engine speed, and use full throttle only for short bursts. Experience is the best guide, since it's easy to tell when an engine is running freely.

10 Pay particular attention to the *Pre-ride checks* at the beginning of this manual and investigate the cause of any oil loss immediately. Check the tightness of all relevant nuts and bolts (see Chapter 1).

Chapter 3
Transmission: Belt drive components and gearbox

Contents

Clutch and clutch pulley 6
Drive belt 5
Drive belt cover 2
Drive pulley and variator 4
Gearbox 7
General information 1
Kickstart mechanism 3

Degrees of difficulty

Easy, suitable for novice with little experience	Fairly easy, suitable for beginner with some experience	Fairly difficult, suitable for competent DIY mechanic	Difficult, suitable for experienced DIY mechanic	Very difficult, suitable for expert DIY or professional

Specifications

Clutch

Clutch lining material thickness (min)
Speedfight (all models) .... 1 mm
Vivacity, V-Clic, Kisbee and Tweet models .... 2 mm

Drive belt

Minimum width of outer run .... see Chapter 1

Torque settings

Clutch assembly nut
V-Clic, Kisbee 50, Vivacity 125 .... 50 Nm
Speedfight 50 .... 40 Nm
Vivacity 50, Tweet 50 .... 55 Nm
Kisbee 100, Tweet 125/150, Speedfight 125 .... 55 Nm
Clutch pulley nut
V-Clic and Kisbee 50 .... 50 Nm
Vivacity 50, Tweet 50 .... 55 Nm
Speedfight 50 .... 45 Nm
Kisbee 100, Tweet 125/150 .... 55 Nm
Speedfight 125 .... 58 Nm
Vivacity 125 .... 70 Nm
Gearbox bolts
V-Clic, Kisbee 50 and Vivacity 125 .... 12 Nm
Vivacity 50 4T, Tweet 50 .... 22 Nm
Kisbee 100, Vivacity 50 2T, Speedfight 50 .... 10 Nm
Tweet 125/150, Speedfight 125 .... 22 Nm
Vivacity 125 .... not available
Variator pulley nut
V-Clic and Kisbee 50 .... 50 Nm
Vivacity 50, Tweet 50 .... 55 Nm
Speedfight 50 .... 40 Nm
Kisbee 100 .... 55 Nm
Speedfight 125 .... 58 Nm
Tweet 125/150 .... 55 Nm
Vivacity 125 .... 70 Nm

1 General information

The transmission on all models is fully automatic in operation. Power is transmitted from the engine to the rear wheel by belt, via a variator on the drive pulley, which automatically varies the gearing with engine speed, an automatic clutch on the driven pulley, and a reduction gearbox. Both the variator and the automatic clutch work on the principal of centrifugal force.

2 Drive belt cover

Removal

See also page 1.16

Speedfight 50, V-Clic 50 and Vivacity 50 2T

1 Remove the air filter housing cover (see Chapter 1) to access the screws on the top edge of the drive belt cover. Undo the screw securing the air filter housing to the drive belt housing **(see illustration)**.
2 On V-Clic models, loosen the clip securing the air cooling duct to the front of the drive belt cover and detach the duct **(see illustration)**.
3 Displace the air filter housing and unscrew the drive belt cover screws **(see illustration)**.
4 Ease the cover off. If the cover is stuck, tap around the joint face between the cover

2.1 Screw (arrowed) secures air filter housing – Speedfight shown

and the drive belt housing with a soft-faced mallet to free it. Do not try to lever the cover off as this may damage the sealing surfaces. Note any dowels in the cover or the drive belt housing and remove them for safekeeping if they are loose.

Vivacity 50 4T

5 Undo the drive belt cover screws **(see illustration)**.
6 Follow the procedure in Step 4 to remove the cover. Note the location of the cover gasket. If the gasket is damaged a new one must be fitted on reassembly. Clean the mating surfaces of the cover and drive belt housing with a suitable solvent to remove any traces of old gasket.

Tweet 50/125/150, and Speedfight 125

7 Undo the screws securing the air filter housing to the drive belt housing **(see illustration)**.

2.2 Release the clip (arrowed) and detach the air cooling duct

8 Loosen the clip securing the air cooling duct to the front of the drive belt cover and detach the duct **(see illustration)**.
9 Unscrew the drive belt cover screws **(see illustration)**.
10 Follow the procedure in Step 4 to remove the cover. Note the location of the cover gasket. If the gasket is damaged a new one must be fitted on reassembly.
11 On Tweet 125/150 and Speedfight 125 models, note where the inner end of the kickstart shaft locates in the drive belt housing **(see illustration)**.
12 Clean the mating surfaces of the cover and drive belt housing with a suitable solvent to remove any traces of old gasket.

Kisbee 50 and 100

13 On 50 cc models, undo the screw securing the air filter housing to the drive belt housing. Disconnect the speed sensor wiring connector

2.3 Location of the drive belt cover screws

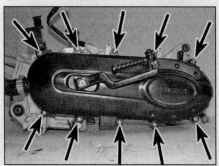

2.5 Location of the drive belt cover screws – Vivacity 50 4T shown

2.7 Screws (arrowed) secure air filter housing – Tweet shown

2.8 Loosen the clip (arrowed)

2.9 Location of the drive belt cover screws

2.11 Kickstart shaft location (arrowed)

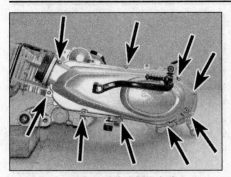

2.15a Location of the drive belt cover screws – Kisbee 100 shown

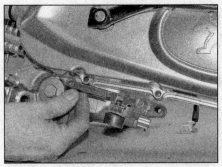

2.15b Remove the centrestand stop plate

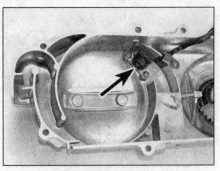

2.17 Location of the speed restrictor sensor (arrowed)

where fitted. Trace the wiring from the drive belt cover and disconnect it at the connector located inside the bodywork.

14 On 100 cc models, undo the two screws securing the air filter housing to the drive belt housing.

15 Displace the air filter housing and unscrew the drive belt cover screws (see illustration). Note the location of the centrestand stop plate secured by two of the cover screws (see illustration).

16 Follow the procedure in Step 4 to remove the cover. Note the location of the cover gasket. If the gasket is damaged a new one must be fitted on reassembly. Clean the mating surfaces of the cover and drive belt housing with a suitable solvent to remove any traces of old gasket.

17 Where fitted on 50 cc models, note the location of the speed restrictor sensor inside the cover (see illustration).

Vivacity 125

18 Remove the kickstart lever (see Section 3).

19 Undo the screws securing the air filter housing to the drive belt housing. Displace the air filter housing and unscrew the drive belt cover screws.

20 Follow the procedure in Step 4 to remove the cover. Note the location of the cover gasket. If the gasket is damaged a new one must be fitted on reassembly. Clean the mating surfaces of the cover and drive belt housing with a suitable solvent to remove any traces of old gasket.

Inspection

21 If the kickstart mechanism is located inside the cover, note the position of the kickstart quadrant and the engaging pinion (see Section 3). On some models the kickstart mechanism is located behind a cover.

22 On V-Clic and Kisbee 50 models, note how the outer end of the starter pinion is retained by the drive belt cover (see Chapter 2C).

Installation

23 Installation is the reverse of removal, noting the following:

● If removed, fit the dowels in the case. Where applicable, apply a smear of grease to the cover gasket to hold it in place and fit the gasket over the dowels (see illustration).

● On V-Clic and Kisbee 50 models, apply a smear of grease to the end of the starter motor pinion.

● On Tweet 125 and Speedfight 125 models, apply a smear of grease to the inner end of the kickstart shaft.

● Apply a smear of grease to the threads of the cover bolts.

● Don't forget to fit any clips and the centrestand stop plate to the cover bolts (see illustration 2.15b).

● Tighten the cover bolts evenly in a criss-cross pattern.

● On Vivacity 125 models, install the kickstart lever, then operate the lever to ensure the mechanism engages correctly with the kickstart driven gear and that the lever returns to its proper rest position afterwards.

3 Kickstart mechanism

Kickstart lever

1 Before removing the kickstart lever, note the rest position – if necessary, mark the end of the shaft next to the slot in the lever with a dab of paint.

2 Undo the lever pinch bolt and pull the lever off (see illustration).

3 Inspect the splines on the end of the kickstart shaft and the splines on the kickstart lever for damage (see illustration 3.13). If necessary, remove the drive belt cover (see Section 2) and renew any damaged components.

4 Installation is the reverse of removal. Fit the lever in the rest position (see Step 1) and tighten the pinch bolt securely. Operate the lever to check that it turns smoothly and returns to its rest position under spring pressure.

Kickstart mechanism – cover-mounted

Note: The kickstart mechanism is mounted inside the drive belt cover on all models except the Vivacity 125.

5 Remove the drive belt cover (see Section 2). On Tweet 50, Vivacity 50 4T and Kisbee 100 models, ease back the tabs locking the cover plate fixing screws, then undo the screws and lift the cover off (see illustration).

2.23 Locate the cover gasket over the dowels

3.2 Mark the kickstart shaft with a dab of paint (arrowed) and undo the lever pinch bolt

3.5 Cover plate fixing screws (arrowed)

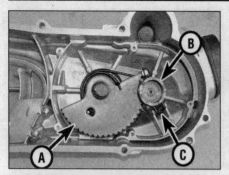

3.6 Kickstart quadrant (A), engaging pinion (B) and location of pinion spring (C)

3.7a Hold the kickstart lever and withdraw the pinion

3.7b Note the washer on the pinion shaft

6 On all models except Tweet 125/150 and Speedfight 125 models (see Steps 25 to 36), note the position of the kickstart quadrant and how it engages with the engaging pinion, and note how the spring on the engaging pinion locates in the cover **(see illustration)**.

7 If the kickstart lever has been removed, fit it onto its shaft temporarily. Apply light hand pressure on the kickstart lever, then pull the engaging pinion out of its recess in the cover, noting the washer on the pinion shaft **(see illustrations)**. Release the kickstart lever

slowly and allow the quadrant to rest against the stop inside the cover. Remove the kickstart lever (see Steps 1 and 2).

8 Remove the circlip and washer from the kickstart shaft on the outside of the cover **(see illustrations)**. Ease the kickstart shaft out of the cover and release the tension on the kickstart return spring. Unhook the spring from the kickstart quadrant and withdraw the shaft, **(see illustration)**.

9 Note how the return spring locates inside the cover and how one end is hooked around the post, then remove the spring **(see illustration)**.

10 Remove the kickstart shaft sleeve **(see illustration)**.

11 Clean all the components with a suitable solvent.

12 Inspect the teeth on the kickstart quadrant and the teeth on the engaging pinion for wear and damage **(see illustration)**. Check the shafts of the engaging pinion, the kickstart shaft and the shaft sleeve, for signs of wear.

13 Inspect the splines on the end of the kickstart shaft and the splines in the kickstart lever for damage **(see illustration)**.

14 Check the dogs on the end of the engaging pinion and the corresponding dogs on the kickstart driven gear (see Section 4, Step 5).

15 If any components are worn or damaged they should be renewed. **Note:** *To renew the kickstart driven gear, follow the procedure in Section 4.*

16 Ensure the spring on the engaging pinion

3.8a Remove the kickstart shaft circlip...

3.8b ...and the washer

3.8c Withdraw the kickstart shaft

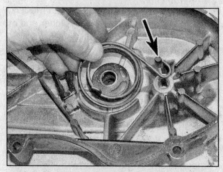

3.9 Unhook the spring from the post (arrowed)

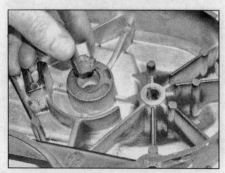

3.10 Lift out the sleeve

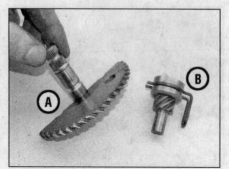

3.12 Inspect the kickstart quadrant (A) and engaging pinion (B) as described

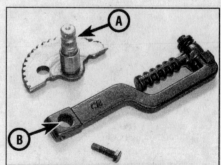

3.13 Inspect the splines on the shaft (A) and in the kickstart lever (B)

3.19 Allow the quadrant to rest against the stop (arrowed)

3.23 Install the engaging pinion as described

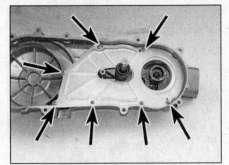

3.25a Undo the screws...

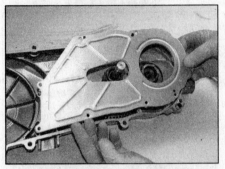

3.25b ...and remove the cover plate

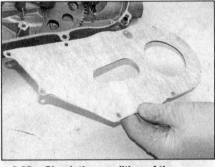

3.25c Check the condition of the cover plate gasket

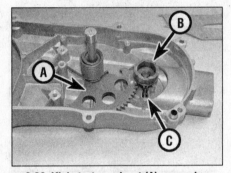

3.26 Kickstart quadrant (A), engaging pinion (B) and location of pinion spring (C)

is a firm fit and inspect the kickstart return spring for cracks and wear at each end. When fitted, the return spring should return the kickstart lever to the rest position and hold it there; if not, it has sagged and should be replaced with a new one.

17 Install the return spring with its long end innermost. Hook the long end around the post on the inside of the cover **(see illustration 3.9)**.

18 Lubricate the kickstart shaft sleeve with a smear of multi-purpose grease and fit it into the cover **(see illustration 3.10)**.

19 Lubricate the kickstart shaft with a smear of grease and insert it into the sleeve **(see illustration 3.8c)**. Hook the outer end of the return spring onto the quadrant. Rotate the shaft anti-clockwise against the spring tension until the quadrant can be butted against the stop on the inside of the cover **(see illustration)**.

20 Ensure the shaft is pressed all the way

into the cover, then secure it on the outside with the washer and circlip **(see illustrations 3.8b and a)**.

21 Fit the kickstart lever (see Step 4).

22 Lubricate the shaft of the engaging pinion with a smear of grease and install the washer **(see illustration 3.7b)**.

23 To fit the pinion into the cover, align the spring with the detent in the cover, then turn the kickstart quadrant against spring pressure and engage it with the engaging pinion – movement of the quadrant will draw the pinion into the cover **(see illustration)**. Check the operation of the mechanism.

24 Refit the drive belt cover (see Section 2).

25 On Tweet 125/150 and Speedfight 125 models, undo the screws securing the cover plate and lift the plate off **(see illustrations)**. Note the location of the gasket and fit a new one on reassembly if it is damaged **(see illustration)**.

26 Note the position of the kickstart quadrant and how it engages with the engaging pinion, and note how the spring on the engaging pinion locates in the cover **(see illustration)**.

27 If the kickstart lever has been removed, fit it onto its shaft temporarily. Apply light hand pressure on the kickstart lever, then pull the engaging pinion off its shaft in the cover, noting the washer on the shaft **(see illustrations)**. Release the kickstart lever slowly and allow the quadrant to rest against the stop inside the cover. Remove the kickstart lever (see Steps 1 and 2).

28 Remove the circlip and washer from the kickstart shaft on the outside of the cover. Note the location of the kickstart return spring **(see illustration)**. Ease the kickstart shaft out of the cover and release the tension on the return spring carefully. Lift out the kickstart shaft and spring.

29 Remove the kickstart shaft sleeve.

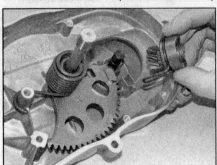

3.27a Hold the kickstart lever and withdraw the pinion

3.27b Note the washer on the pinion shaft

3.28 Note where the ends of the return spring (arrowed) locate

3.35 Installed position of the kickstart pinion

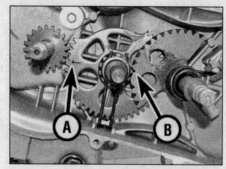

3.39 Register mark on the engaging pinion (A) and kickstart quadrant (B)

3.40a Undo the bolt (arrowed) and remove the plate

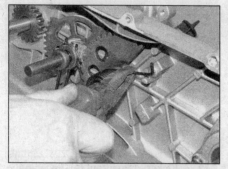

3.40b Use pliers to ease out the spring

3.41a Remove the kickstart shaft assembly

3.41b Return spring locates on peg (arrowed)

30 Clean all the components with a suitable solvent, then follow Steps 12 to 16 to check the kickstart components for wear and damage.
31 Lubricate the kickstart shaft sleeve with a smear of multi-purpose grease and fit it into the cover. Lubricate the kickstart shaft with a smear of grease and insert it into the sleeve.
32 Hook the shorter end of the return spring onto the quadrant and the longer end over the post inside the cover, then carefully rotate the shaft anti-clockwise against the spring tension until the quadrant can be butted against the stop on the inside of the cover, then press the kickstart shaft all the way into the cover (see illustration 3.28). Secure the shaft on the outside with the washer and circlip.
33 Fit the kickstart lever (see Step 4).
34 Lubricate the shaft of the engaging pinion with a smear of grease and install the washer (see illustration 3.27b).
35 To fit the pinion into the cover, align the

spring with the detent in the cover, then turn the kickstart quadrant against spring pressure and mesh it with the engaging pinion – movement of the quadrant will draw the pinion into the cover (see illustration). Check the operation of the mechanism.
36 Refit the drive belt cover (see Section 2).

Kickstart mechanism – casing mounted

Note: The kickstart mechanism is located in the back of the drive belt casing.
37 Follow the procedure in Section 2 and remove the drive belt cover. Note the location of the washer on the outer end of the kickstart shaft.
38 Remove the variator (see Section 4).
39 Note the position of the kickstart quadrant and how it engages with the engaging pinion, which in turn engages with the driven gear on the crankshaft (see illustration). There should

be register marks on the teeth of the kickstart quadrant, the helical gear of the engaging pinion and the teeth of the engaging pinion gear to aid installation – if not, make your own with a dab of paint.
40 Undo the kickstart return spring plate bolt and remove the plate (see illustration). Ease the long end of the spring out from the stop in the casing with care – the spring is under tension (see illustration).
41 Withdraw the kickstart shaft assembly (see illustration). Slide off the washer and the return spring, noting how the short end of the spring locates around the peg on the shaft (see illustration).
42 Withdraw the engaging pinion noting how the pin behind the pinion locates in the recess in the casing (see illustration). Compress the spring on the pinion shaft, withdraw the pin and remove the washer, then slide the pinion off the shaft noting the location of the spring (see illustrations).

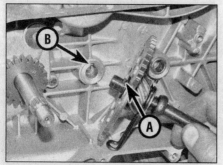

3.42a Pin (A) locates in recess (B)

3.42b Remove the pin and washer (arrowed)

3.42c Slide off the pinion, noting the spring (arrowed)

3.43 Kickstart shaft bush is located in the casing

3.49a Draw the driven gear off with a puller

3.49b Ensure both tapers (arrowed) are clean

43 Note the location of the kickstart shaft bush in the casing **(see illustration)**.
44 Clean all the components with a suitable solvent.
45 Inspect the teeth on the kickstart quadrant, the engaging pinion and the driven gear on the crankshaft for wear and damage. Check the shafts of the engaging pinion and the kickstart quadrant for signs of wear. Check the kickstart shaft bush.
46 Ensure the spring on the engaging pinion is a firm fit and inspect the kickstart return spring for cracks and wear at each end. When fitted, the return spring should return the kickstart lever to the rest position and hold it there; if not, it has sagged and should be replaced with a new one.
47 Inspect the splines on the end of the kickstart shaft and the splines in the kickstart lever for damage.
48 If any components are worn or damaged they should be renewed. **Note:** *Only the engaging pinion spring clip is available as a separate item. Both the kickstart shaft and engaging pinion shaft/pinion are supplied as assemblies.*
49 To remove the kickstart driven gear, use a suitable puller to draw it off the taper on the crankshaft **(see illustration)**. Temporarily install the variator centre nut to avoid damaging the threads on the end of the crankshaft. If the gear is a tight fit, heat it with a hot air gun. Once the gear has been removed, note the location of any Woodruff key on the crankshaft and ensure it is a tight fit in its slot before installing the gear on reassembly. To install the driven gear, clean

the taper on the crankshaft and inside the gear with a suitable solvent **(see illustration)**. Fit the gear onto the crankshaft, then temporarily assemble the variator centre sleeve and outer pulley half and tighten the centre nut to press the driven gear firmly onto its taper. The gear should remain in position once the variator components have been removed.
50 Assemble the spring and engaging pinion on the pinion shaft, then compress the spring and install the washer and pin **(see illustrations 3.42c and b)**. Lubricate the ends of the engaging pinion shaft with a smear of multi-purpose grease and install the engaging pinion. Align the pin behind the pinion with the recess in the casing **(see illustration 3.42a)**. Ensure the register mark on the pinion teeth aligns with the driven gear on the crankshaft **(see illustration 3.39)**. Align the closed end of the spring clip with the detent in the case.
51 Install the bush for the kickstart shaft **(see illustration 3.43)**. Fit the return spring and washer onto the shaft **(see illustration 3.41b)**. Lubricate the shaft with a smear of grease, then install the shaft, ensuring that the register marks on the kickstart quadrant and the engaging pinion helical gear align (see Step 39).
52 Turn the long end of the return spring clockwise to tension the spring and locate the cranked end against the stop in the casing **(see illustration 3.40c)**. Secure the spring with the plate and tighten the bolt securely.
53 Install the variator (see Section 4).
54 Install the drive belt cover (see Section 2).
55 Follow the procedure in Step 4 and install the kickstart lever.

4 Drive pulley and variator

Removal

1 Remove the drive belt cover (see Section 2).
2 To loosen the variator centre nut, the crankshaft must be locked to stop it turning. On Kisbee and V-Clic models, first remove the starter pinion (see Chapter 2C or 2E). The outer half of the variator pulley acts as the starter motor ring gear and a Peugeot service tool (Part No. 759467 for Kisbee 50 and V-Clic, Part No. 803322 for Kisbee 100) which locks onto the ring gear is required to hold the crankshaft. Alternatively, a home-made tool with a forked extension to fit into the gear teeth can be fabricated **(see illustration)**. It is essential that the holding tool aligns precisely with the ring gear. Secure the tool to the drive belt housing with two drive belt cover screws. Ensure that the tool is held firmly in place to prevent damage to the gear teeth and apply steady pressure to the centre nut to loosen it.
3 On all other engines, a pin wrench that locates into sockets on the outer face of the variator pulley is required. Peugeot produces a service tool for this purpose (Part No. 752237). Alternatively, an proprietary holding tool can be used **(see illustration)**.
4 Remove the variator centre nut and washer (if fitted) **(see illustration)**.

4.2 Home-made tool for holding the ring gear

4.3 Holding the variator with a proprietary tool

4.4 Remove the variator centre nut

4.5a Remove the kickstart driven gear – Speedfight shown

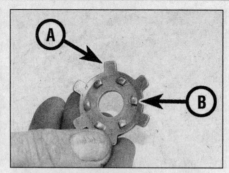

4.5b Kickstart driven gear tabs (A) and gear teeth (B)

4.5c Kickstart driven gear – Kisbee 100 shown

4.5d Note location of the plain washer

4.6 Remove the outer half of the variator pulley

4.7 Displace the drive belt from the crankshaft

4.8 Pull off the variator assembly

4.9a Withdraw the centre sleeve...

4.9b ...and lift out the ramp plate

5 On all models except the Vivacity 125, remove the kickstart driven gear. Note that on some machines, tabs around the edge of the gear locate against the face of the variator pulley **(see illustrations)**. On others, the gear locates over splines on the end of the crankshaft **(see illustration)**. Check the condition of the splines. Where fitted, remove the plain washer from behind the driven gear **(see illustration)**.

6 Remove the outer half of the variator pulley **(see illustration)**. Note the splines in the centre of the pulley half.

7 Move the drive belt aside – unless you are removing the clutch assembly, leave the belt on the clutch pulley **(see illustration)**. Mark the belt with a directional arrow if it is removed so that it can be refitted the correct way round.

8 The variator assembly comprises a centre

sleeve, ramp plate and variator body – grip the assembly so that the ramp plate at the back is held into the variator body, then draw the complete assembly off the shaft **(see illustration)**.

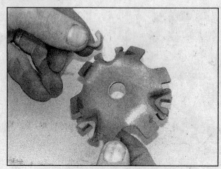

4.10a Remove the ramp guides

9 Withdraw the centre sleeve and lift out the ramp plate, noting how it fits **(see illustrations)**.

10 Remove the ramp guides **(see illustrations)**. Lift out the rollers, noting which

4.10b Ramp guides on Tweet 125 variator

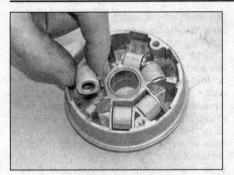

4.10c Lift out the rollers

4.12 Measure the diameter of each roller

4.13 Inspect the variator ramps (arrowed)
for wear

way round they fit **(see illustration)**. Each end of the roller is different, with the covered end facing the direction of thrust.

11 Clean all the components using a suitable solvent.

Inspection

Note: *The variator and rollers should be checked at the specified service interval (see Chapter 1).*

12 Measure the diameter of each roller; they should all be the same size **(see illustration)**. Inspect the surface of each roller for flat spots. Renew all the rollers as a set. **Note:** *Variator rollers are not interchangeable between different models. Always specify the year and model of your scooter when buying new rollers.*

13 Inspect the surface of the ramps in the variator body and the ramp plate for wear or damage **(see illustration)**. Check the slots in the ramp guides where they fit in the variator body and fit new components as necessary.

14 Inspect the surface of the variator sleeve for wear and fit a new one if necessary.

15 Check the condition of the splines in the centre of the outer half of the variator pulley **(see illustration 4.6)**. Inspect the inner face of the pulley for signs of overheating or blueing, caused by the pulley running out of alignment. Renew the pulley half if it is damaged.

Installation

16 Make sure the inner surfaces of both pulley halves, the sleeve, the rollers and the ramps are clean and oil-free.

17 Fit the rollers into the housing, making sure they are in their original positions (unless new ones are used), and that the covered side faces the direction of thrust **(see illustration 4.10c)**. Check that the guides are correctly fitted on the ramp plate, then fit the plate **(see illustrations 4.10a and b)**.

18 Grip the variator so that the ramp plate is held into the body and install the assembly and the centre sleeve onto the crankshaft (see Step 9). **Note:** *If the ramp plate moves and the rollers are dislodged, disassemble the variator and reposition the rollers correctly.*

19 Compress the clutch pulley centre spring and press the drive belt into the clutch pulley to facilitate fitting it over the variator pulley **(see illustration)**. If necessary, hold the belt in place on the clutch pulley temporarily using a cable-tie **(see illustration)**. If the belt has been removed, or if you are fitting a new belt, make sure any directional arrows point in the direction of normal rotation. Ensure there is sufficient slack in the belt to avoid it being trapped when the outer half of the variator pulley is installed.

20 Install the outer half of the variator pulley. Ensure that the splines align with the crankshaft.

21 Install the kickstart driven gear (see Step 5), then fit the washer and centre nut finger-tight. Make sure the outer pulley half butts against the centre sleeve and is not skewed by the belt.

22 Install the locking tool used on removal (see Step 2 or 3) and tighten the nut to the torque setting specified at the beginning of this Chapter.

23 Ease the drive belt out of the clutch pulley to reduce the slack in the belt, then fit the cover (see Section 2).

5 Drive belt

Inspection

1 The drive belt should be renewed at the specified service interval (see Chapter 1), but it is good practice to check the condition of the belt whenever the cover is removed. Follow the procedure in Chapter 1 to check the belt for wear and damage.

2 The belt will wear during the normal course of use and dust will accumulate inside the cover. However, a large amount of dust or debris inside the cover is an indication of abnormal wear and the cause, such as high spots on the pulleys or pulley misalignment, should be investigated.

4.19a Press the belt into the clutch pulley and fit it onto the
crankshaft

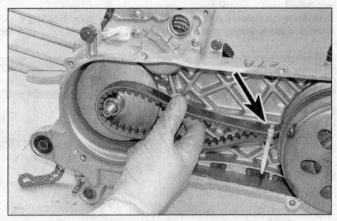

4.19b Hold belt in place with a cable-tie (arrowed)

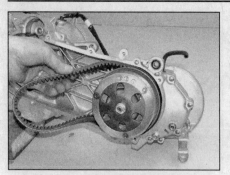

5.4 Ease the belt out of the clutch pulley

Removal and installation

Note: *Drive belts are not interchangeable between different models. Always specify the year and model of your scooter when buying a new belt. If in doubt, check the part number marked on the belt.*

3 Follow the procedure in Section 4 and remove the outer half of the variator pulley – hold the variator in position on the crankshaft as you remove it to avoid dislodging the rollers (if the ramp plate moves and the rollers are dislodged, disassemble the variator and reposition the rollers correctly).

4 Lift the belt off the crankshaft and ease it out of the clutch pulley **(see illustration)**. If necessary, pull the outer clutch pulley half back against the spring tension and manoeuvre the belt out. **Note:** *On some models, such as the*

Kisbee 100, Tweet 125/150 and Speedfight 125, there may be insufficient clearance inside the casing to remove the drive belt. Follow the procedure in Section 6 to remove the clutch with the drive belt in situ.

5 Installation is the reverse of removal. Ensure the directional arrows on the belt point in the direction of normal rotation.

6 Clutch and clutch pulley

Removal

1 Remove the drive belt cover (see Section 2).

2 Before removing the clutch pulley, grip the assembly firmly and try to rock it backwards and forwards. If there is any freeplay between the clutch and the gearbox input shaft it is likely the pulley hub bearings are worn. Individual components for the clutch hub are not available – a new assembly will have to be fitted.

3 Follow the procedure in Section 4 and remove the outer half of the variator pulley. If possible, remove the drive belt, otherwise leave the belt around the clutch pulley until it has been removed.

4 To loosen the clutch centre nut it is necessary to hold the clutch drum to prevent it turning. A proprietary tool that locates in

the holes in the clutch drum can be used **(see illustration)** or a holding tool can be made from two strips of steel (see **Tool Tip** in Chapter 2A, Section 11). Alternatively you can use a strap wrench **(see illustration)**.

5 Unscrew the centre nut and remove the clutch drum, then draw the clutch and pulley assembly off the gearbox input shaft **(see illustrations)**. If applicable, remove the drive belt. **Note:** *The clutch centre nut is a locknut and a new one should be fitted on reassembly.*

6 To disassemble the clutch and pulley assembly, it is necessary first to hold it securely while the large nut is loosened, then to compress and hold the clutch spring while the nut is undone fully.

7 Lay the clutch on a flat surface, fit a holding tool and loosen the nut **(see illustrations)**. Now have an assistant press down on the clutch to compress the clutch spring while the nut is unscrewed by hand and removed.

⚠️ *Warning: The clutch assembly is under pressure from the centre spring – take care to maintain downwards pressure to avoid damage or injury.*

8 On machines with an engine size greater than 50 cc it is advisable to clamp the assembly to take the spring pressure off the nut. Peugeot produces a range of service tools to suit different models. Alternatively, an automotive puller can be used, taking care not to damage the two halves of the

6.4a Lock the holding tool onto the clutch drum and apply steady pressure on the nut

6.4b Holding the clutch with a strap wrench

6.5a Remove the clutch drum...

6.5b ...then pull the clutch and pulley off the shaft

6.7a Hold the clutch with a rotor clamp...

6.7b ...or with the home-made tool

6.8a Apply light pressure with a puller...

6.8b ...before unscrewing the nut

6.9a Remove the clutch shoes and backplate (arrowed)

6.9b Lift off the spring seat (A) and spring (B)

6.10a Examine the inner surface of the clutch drum (arrowed)

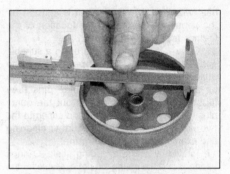

6.10b Measure the internal diameter of the drum as described

clutch pulley (see illustration). Only apply sufficient pressure with the puller to retain the clutch backplate while the nut is undone (see illustration). Once the nut has been removed, release the spring pressure gradually by loosening the puller.

9 Remove the clutch shoes and backplate, then remove the spring seat and spring (see illustrations).

Inspection

10 Check the inner surface of the clutch drum for damage and scoring. Measure the internal diameter of the drum at several points to determine if it is worn or out-of-round. If the drum is out-of-round or badly scored, replace it with a new one (see illustrations). Inspect

the splines in the centre of the drum and those on the gearbox shaft. The clutch drum should be a firm fit on the shaft, with no backlash between the drum and the shaft.

11 Check the amount of friction material remaining on the clutch shoes (see illustration). If the friction material has worn to the service limit specified in the *Specifications* at the beginning of this Chapter, or the shoes are worn unevenly, fit a new shoe assembly.

12 Inspect the shoe springs for wear, cracks and stretching (see illustration). Ensure that the shoes are not seized on their pivot pins and that the retaining circlips, where fitted, are secure on the ends of the pins. If any parts are worn or damaged, fit a new shoe backplate assembly.

13 Inspect the inner faces of the clutch pulley for signs of overheating or bluing, caused by the pulley running out of alignment (see illustration). If the pulley has run out of alignment, first check the condition of the bearings in the hub of the inner half (see illustration 6.16b), then check for play in the gearbox input shaft bearings (see Section 7).

14 Examine the clutch pulley. If grease has leaked out from inside, either the bearing seals or pulley O-rings have failed and a new pulley assembly will have to be fitted.

15 Check the operation of the pulley. Hold the inner face of the pulley and twist the outer face – the outer face should move up-and-down the hub smoothly. If the pulley

6.11 Measure the thickness of the clutch friction material

6.12 Check the components on the clutch backplate

6.13 Inspect the inner faces of the clutch pulley (arrowed)

6.15 Location of the clutch pulley O-rings

6.16a Pulley should move smoothly on the guide pins

6.16b Separate the pulley halves

has seized, or the movement is stiff, lift off the centre sleeve, noting the location of the O-rings **(see illustration)**.

16 Clean off any old grease using a suitable solvent and check the operation of the pulley again – the outer face should slide up-and-down around the guide pins **(see illustration)**. If required, pull out the guide pins using long nosed pliers and separate the two halves of the pulley for further cleaning and examination **(see illustration)**.

17 Individual parts, including seals, O-rings bearings and the spring are not available for the clutch pulley. If there is any evidence of wear or damage, a new pulley will have to be fitted.

18 If applicable, reassemble the clutch pulley, lubricating the components with molybdenum disulphide grease. Take care not to damage the O-rings when installing the centre sleeve

Installation

19 Ensure the inner surfaces of both pulley halves and the inside surface of the clutch drum are clean and grease-free.

20 Install the spring and spring seat **(see illustration 6.9b)**.

21 Position the shoe assembly on the spring seat, ensuring the flats on the shoe backplate are aligned with the pulley hub. Compress the spring using the same method as for disassembly and install the large assembly nut finger-tight **(see illustrations 6.8a and b)**. Hold the clutch to prevent it turning and tighten the nut to the torque setting specified at the

beginning of this Chapter **(see illustration 6.7b or a)**. If applicable, release the clamp.

22 Lubricate the needle bearing in the hub of the pulley with molybdenum disulphide grease.

23 If the drive belt was removed with the pulley, fit the belt around the pulley, forcing it between the pulley halves. Ensure the directional arrows on the belt point in the direction of normal rotation.

24 Install the clutch and pulley assembly on the gearbox input shaft **(see illustration 6.5b)**.

25 Install the clutch drum, ensuring the splines align with the shaft. Hold the clutch to prevent it turning and tighten the nut (see Step 4).

26 Install the remaining components in the reverse order of removal.

7 Gearbox

Speedfight 50 and Vivacity 50 2T
Removal

1 Remove the clutch and clutch pulley (see Section 6).

2 Remove the rear wheel (see Chapter 8). On drum brake models, remove the brake shoes. On disc brake models remove the rear hub and brake disc.

3 Before removing the gearbox cover, grip the input shaft and try to move it from side-to-side **(see illustration)**. If there is any freeplay in the shaft it is likely the shaft bearings are worn. Check for freeplay in the output shaft on the right-hand side. Further inspection of the bearings can be made when the gearbox is disassembled.

4 Position a drain tray underneath the drive belt casing to catch the gearbox oil when the cover is removed.

5 Undo the gearbox cover bolts and carefully ease the cover together with the input shaft away from the casing **(see illustrations)**. If the cover is stuck, tap around the joint face between the cover and the casing with a soft-faced mallet to free it. Do not try to lever the cover off as this may damage the sealing surfaces.

HAYNES HiNT *Make a cardboard template of the gearbox cover and punch a hole for each bolt location. This will ensure all bolts are installed correctly on reassembly – this is important as some bolts are of different lengths.*

6 Discard the gasket as a new one must be fitted on reassembly. Note the position of the dowels in the casing and remove them for safekeeping if they are loose.

7 Note how the gear pinions on the output shaft and intermediate shaft mesh together

7.3 Checking the gearbox input shaft for side-to-side freeplay

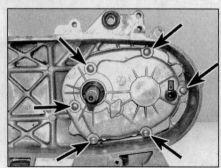
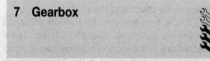

7.5a Undo the gearbox cover bolts (arrowed)...

7.5b ...and ease the cover off

7.7a Location of the output shaft (A) and intermediate shaft (B)

7.7b Remove the washer from the intermediate shaft

7.8a Withdraw the output shaft and pinion

(see illustration). As they are removed, check the shafts for any thrust washers and remove them, noting where they fit. Check carefully – sometimes the washers will stick to the shaft bearings. Remove the washer from the intermediate shaft **(see illustration).**

8 Withdraw the output shaft and pinion, then lift out the intermediate shaft noting the location of the thrust washer **(see illustrations).**

9 To remove the input shaft drive it out from the cover using a soft-faced mallet **(see illustration).** If necessary, heat the casing with a hot air gun to aid removal. The bearing will come out with the shaft.

Inspection

10 Clean all traces of old gasket material from the gearbox mating surfaces, taking care not to scratch or gouge the soft aluminium. Wash all the components in a suitable solvent and dry them with compressed air **(see illustration).**

11 Check the pinion teeth for cracking, chipping, pitting and other obvious wear or damage. Check for signs of scoring or bluing on the pinions and shafts caused by overheating due to inadequate lubrication.

12 Inspect the splines and threads on the input and output shafts.

13 Renew any damaged or worn components. **Note:** *The pinions on the gearbox shafts are integral with the shafts.*

14 Check the condition of the input and output shaft oil seals **(see illustrations).**

7.8b Remove the intermediate shaft and washer

Any loss of gearbox oil must be remedied immediately to avoid expensive damage or seizure. If the input shaft oil seal fails, oil will run into the drive belt case behind the clutch. If either of the shafts has been removed, it is good practice to fit a new seal prior to installation (see *Tools and Workshop Tips* in the *Reference* section). Lever the input shaft seal out from the clutch side of the casing; lever the output shaft seal out from the inside of the gearbox housing.

15 Inspect the bearings in the casing and the gearbox cover (see *Tools and Workshop Tips* in the *Reference* section). If the bearings need renewing, the output shaft bearing can be driven out from the outside using a bearing driver or suitably-sized socket. Bearings that are fitted into blind holes require an

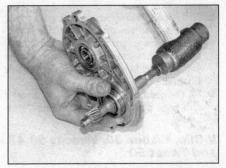

7.9 Drive out the input shaft together with its bearing

internal bearing puller and slide-hammer to extract them without damaging the case **(see illustrations 7.14a and b).** Always heat the bearing housing first to aid removal and fitting. Don't forget to check the bearing on the input shaft **(see illustration 7.9).** If specialist tools are not available consult an automotive engineer.

Installation

16 Installation is the reverse of removal, noting the following:

● Smear the inside of the oil seals with grease before installing the shafts.

● Ensure the thrust washers are fitted to the shafts before assembly.

● Lubricate both ends of the intermediate shaft with molybdenum disulphide grease before installation.

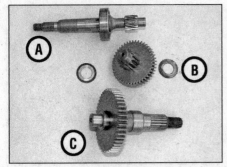

7.10 Input shaft (A), intermediate shaft (B) and output shaft (C)

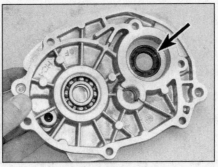

7.14a Input shaft oil seal

7.14b Output shaft oil seal

7.16a Fit the gasket onto the dowels (arrowed)

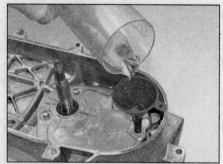

7.16b Measure the precise amount of oil and pour it into the gearbox carefully

7.16c Ensure the filler plug fits securely

- Fit the dowels into the cover and use a new cover gasket (see illustration 7.16a).
- Tighten the gearbox cover bolts evenly and in a criss-cross pattern to the torque setting specified at the beginning of this Chapter.
- Fill the gearbox with the specified amount and type of oil (see illustrations 7.16b and c).

V-Clic, Kisbee 50, Vivacity 50 4T and Tweet 50

Removal

17 Remove the clutch and clutch pulley (see Section 6).
18 Remove the rear wheel and brake shoes (see Chapter 8). Drain the gearbox oil (see Chapter 1).

19 Before removing the gearbox cover, grip the input shaft and try to move it from side-to-side (see illustration 7.3). If there is any freeplay in the shaft it is likely the shaft bearings are worn. Check for freeplay in the output shaft on the right-hand side. Further inspection of the bearings can be made when the gearbox is disassembled.
20 Unscrew the bolts securing the gearbox to the drive belt casing (see illustration). See Haynes Hint on page 3•12.
21 Support the casing on a block of wood, then carefully ease the gearbox away from the casing and remove it (see illustrations). If the gearbox is stuck, tap around the joint face between the cover and the box with a soft-faced mallet to free it. Do not try to

lever the gearbox off as this may damage the sealing surfaces.
22 Discard the gasket as a new one must be fitted on reassembly. Note the position of the dowels on the casing or gearbox housing and remove them for safekeeping if they are loose.
23 Note how the gear pinions on the output shaft and intermediate shaft mesh together. As they are removed, check the shafts for any thrust washers and remove them, noting where they fit. Check carefully – sometimes the washers will stick to the shaft bearings.
24 Lift out the output shaft pinion, then lift out the intermediate shaft noting the location of the thrust washer fitted between the shaft pinion and the bearing in the gearbox housing (see illustrations).

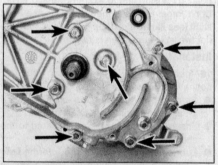

7.20 Undo the gearbox bolts (arrowed)

7.21a Support the casing...

7.21b ...then lift away the gearbox

7.24a Lift out the output shaft pinion...

7.24b ...and the intermediate shaft

7.24c Note the location of the thrust washer

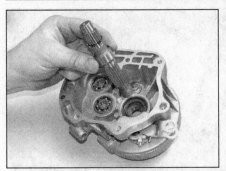

7.25 Lift out the output shaft

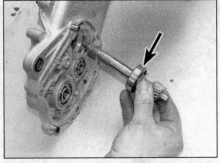

7.26 Note the location of the input shaft bearing (arrowed)

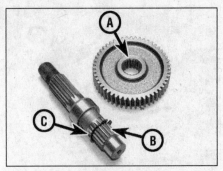

7.28 Check for wear on the pinion splines (A) and on the shaft (B). Note the circlip (C) – output shaft shown

25 Lift out the output shaft, noting the location of the circlip behind the shaft pinion **(see illustration)**.

26 The input shaft is a press fit in its bearing and should not be removed unless the shaft, the bearing or the oil seal is to be renewed. To remove the shaft, first fit the clutch centre nut to protect the threads, then drive the shaft out using a soft-faced mallet. If necessary, heat the casing with a hot air gun to aid removal. The bearing will come out with the shaft **(see illustration)**.

Inspection

27 Clean all traces of old gasket material from the gearbox mating surfaces, taking care not to scratch or gouge the soft aluminium. Wash all the components in a suitable solvent and dry them with compressed air.

28 Check the pinion teeth for cracking, chipping, pitting and other obvious wear or damage. Check for signs of scoring or bluing on the pinions and shafts caused by overheating due to inadequate lubrication **(see illustration)**.

29 Inspect the splines and threads on the input and output shafts.

30 Renew any damaged or worn components.

31 Check the condition of the input and output shaft oil seals. Any loss of gearbox oil must be remedied immediately to avoid

expensive damage or seizure. If the input shaft oil seal fails, oil will run into the drive belt case behind the clutch. If either of the shafts has been removed, it is good practice to fit a new seal prior to installation (see *Tools and Workshop Tips* in the *Reference* section). Lever the input shaft seal out from the clutch side of the casing; lever the output shaft seal out from the inside of the gearbox housing **(see illustrations)**.

32 Inspect the bearings (see *Tools and Workshop Tips* in the *Reference* section). If the bearings need renewing, the output shaft bearing can be driven out from the outside using a bearing driver or suitably-sized socket. Bearings that are fitted into blind holes require an internal bearing puller and slide-hammer

to extract them without damaging the case **(see illustration)**. Always heat the bearing housing first to aid removal and fitting. Don't forget to check the bearing on the input shaft **(see illustration 7.26)**. If specialist tools are not available consult an automotive engineer.

Installation

33 Installation is the reverse of removal, noting the following:

● Smear the inside of the oil seals with grease before installing the shafts.
● Lubricate both ends of the intermediate shaft with molybdenum disulphide grease before installation.
● Fit the dowels into the cover and use a new cover gasket **(see illustration)**.

7.31a Levering out the input shaft oil seal

7.31b Levering out the output shaft oil seal

7.32 Using an internal bearing puller with slide-hammer attachment

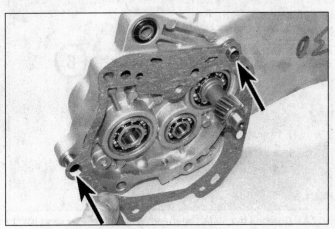

7.33 Fit the cover gasket onto the dowels (arrowed)

7.38 Undo the gearbox bolts (arrowed)

7.39 Lift off the gearbox casing

- Tighten the gearbox bolts evenly and in a criss-cross pattern to the torque setting specified at the beginning of this Chapter.
- Fit a new sealing washer to the gearbox drain plug.
- Fill the gearbox with the specified amount and type of oil (see Chapter 1).

7.40 Discard the old gearbox gasket

Kisbee 100, Tweet 125/150 and Speedfight 125

Removal

34 Remove the clutch and clutch pulley (see Section 6).

35 Remove the rear wheel (see Chapter 8). On drum brake models, remove the brake shoes. On disc brake models remove the rear hub and brake disc.

36 Before removing the gearbox cover, grip the input shaft and try to move it from side-to-side **(see illustration 7.3)**. If there is any freeplay in the shaft it is likely the shaft bearings are worn. Check for freeplay in the output shaft on the right-hand side. Further inspection of the bearings can be made when the gearbox is disassembled.

37 Drain the gearbox oil (see Chapter 1).

38 Support the engine unit on blocks of wood on the work surface, then unscrew the bolts securing the gearbox to the drive belt casing **(see illustration)**. See *Haynes Hint on page 3•12*.

39 Lift off the gearbox casing **(see illustration)**. If the casing is stuck, tap around the joint face with a soft-faced mallet to free it. Do not try to lever the gearbox off as this may damage the sealing surfaces.

40 Discard the gasket as a new one must be fitted on reassembly **(see illustration)**. Note the position of the dowels on the casing or drive belt housing and remove them for safekeeping if they are loose. On Kisbee and Speedfight models, note the location of the breather hose in the top of the casing. If the hose is damaged or deteriorated a new one must be fitted on reassembly. Note how the hose sealing grommet fits in the casing.

41 Note how the gear pinions on the output, intermediate and input shafts mesh together **(see illustration)**. As they are removed, check the shafts for any thrust washers and remove them, noting where they fit. Check carefully – sometimes the washers will stick to the shaft bearings.

42 Where fitted, remove the washer from the end of the intermediate shaft **(see illustration)**.

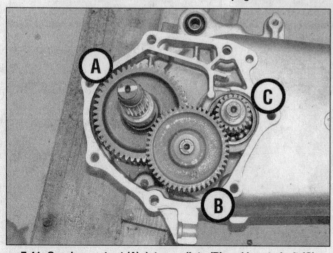

7.41 Gearbox output (A), intermediate (B) and input shaft (C)

7.42 Remove the washer from the end of the intermediate shaft

7.43a Lift out the intermediate pinion...

7.43b ...and intermediate shaft

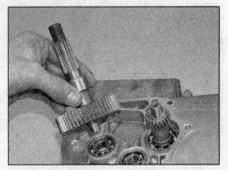

7.44 Lift out the output shaft and pinion

7.45a Location of the input shaft (arrowed)

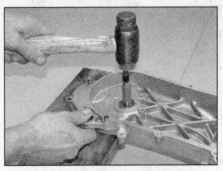

7.45b Drive out the input shaft...

7.45c ...together with the bearing

43 Lift out the intermediate pinion and intermediate shaft **(see illustrations)**.

44 Lift out the output shaft and pinion **(see illustration)**.

45 The input shaft is a press fit in its bearing and should not be removed unless the shaft, the bearing or the oil seal is to be renewed **(see illustration)**. To remove the shaft, turn the engine unit over and fit the clutch centre nut to protect the shaft threads. Drive the shaft out using a soft-faced mallet sufficiently to free the bearing from its housing **(see illustration)**. If necessary, heat the casing with a hot air gun to aid removal. Turn the engine unit over and remove the shaft – the bearing will come out with the shaft **(see illustration)**.

Inspection

46 Follow Steps 27 to 30 to clean the components and inspect the pinions and shafts.

47 Check the condition of the input and output shaft oil seals. Any loss of gearbox oil must be remedied immediately to avoid expensive damage or seizure. If the input shaft oil seal fails, oil will run into the drive belt case behind the clutch. If either of the shafts has been removed, it is good practice to fit a new seal prior to installation (see *Tools and Workshop Tips* in the *Reference* section). Lever the input shaft seal out from the clutch side of the casing; lever the output shaft seal out from the inside of the gearbox housing **(see illustrations)**.

48 Inspect the bearings (see *Tools and Workshop Tips* in the *Reference* section). If the bearings need renewing, the output shaft bearing can be driven out from the outside

using a bearing driver or suitably-sized socket. Bearings that are fitted into blind holes require an internal bearing puller and slide-hammer to extract them without damaging the case **(see illustration)**. Always heat the bearing housing first to aid removal and fitting. Don't forget to check the bearing on the input shaft **(see illustration 7.45c)**. If specialist tools are not available consult an automotive engineer.

Installation

49 Installation is the reverse of removal, noting the following:

● Smear the inside of the oil seals with grease before installing the shafts.

● To install the input shaft use a suitable deep socket that bears on the outer race of the shaft bearing **(see illustration 7.49a)**.

● Lubricate both ends of the intermediate

7.47a Fitted location of the input shaft seal (arrowed)...

7.47b ...and the output shaft seal

7.48 Location of the output (A) and input shaft (B) bearings

7.49a Installing the gearbox input shaft

7.49b Ensure the shafts and dowels are aligned

7.49c Tap the casing down onto the gasket

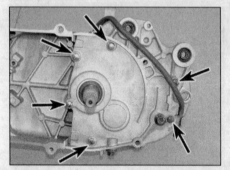

7.53 Undo the gearbox bolts (arrowed)

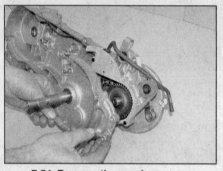

7.54 Remove the gearbox cover

7.55 Remove the breather hose. Note location of seal (arrowed)

shaft with molybdenum disulphide grease before installation.
● Fit the dowels into the cover and use a new cover gasket (see illustration 7.40).
● Lower the gearbox casing over the output shaft carefully to avoid damaging the seal. Ensure that the casing is correctly aligned, taking special note of the position of the dowels (see illustration 7.49b). Tap the casing gently to ensure it fits down onto the gasket (see illustration 7.49c).
● Tighten the gearbox bolts evenly and in a criss-cross pattern to the torque setting specified at the beginning of this Chapter.
● Fit a new sealing washer to the gearbox drain plug.
● Fill the gearbox with the specified amount and type of oil (see Chapter 1).

Vivacity 125
Removal

50 Remove the clutch and clutch pulley (see Section 6).
51 Remove the rear wheel and brake shoes (see Chapter 8).
52 Drain the gearbox oil (see Chapter 1).
53 Unscrew the bolts securing the gearbox cover to the drive belt casing (see illustration). See Haynes Hint on page 3•12.
54 Carefully ease the cover together with the input shaft away from the casing (see illustration). If the cover is stuck, tap around the joint face between the cover and the casing with a soft-faced mallet to free it. Do not try to lever the cover off as this may damage the sealing surfaces.

55 Discard the gasket as a new one must be fitted on reassembly. Note the position of the dowels on the casing and remove them for safekeeping if they are loose. Note the location of the gearbox breather hose and remove it (see illustration).
56 Note how the gear pinions on the output shaft and intermediate shaft mesh together.
57 Lift out the output shaft pinion, then lift out the intermediate shaft (see illustrations).
58 Withdraw the output shaft noting the location of the circlip on the shaft (see illustration).
59 The input shaft is a press fit in its bearing and should not be removed unless the shaft, the bearing or the oil seal is to be renewed

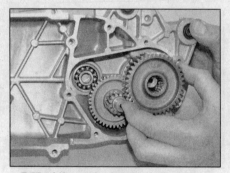

7.57a Lift out the output shaft pinion...

7.57b ...and the intermediate shaft

7.58 Location of the output shaft circlip

7.59 Location of the input shaft (A). Note bearing for the intermediate shaft (B) and output shaft (C)

7.60 Check the pinions and shafts for damage

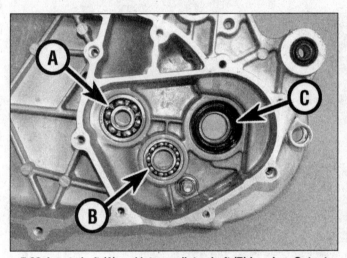

7.62 Input shaft (A) and intermediate shaft (B) bearing. Output shaft oil seal and bearing (C)

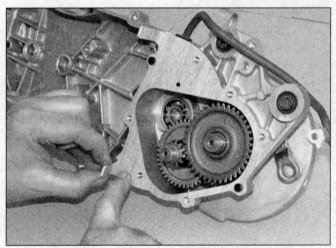

7.63a Fold the tabs on the gasket over...

(see illustration). To remove the shaft, first fit the clutch centre nut to protect the threads, then drive the shaft out using a soft-faced mallet on the clutch end – if necessary, heat the casing with a hot air gun to aid removal. The bearing will come out with the shaft.

Inspection

60 Follow Steps 27 to 30 to clean the components and inspect the pinions and shafts (see illustration).
61 Check the condition of the input and output shaft oil seals. Any loss of gearbox oil must be remedied immediately to avoid expensive damage or seizure. If the input shaft oil seal fails, oil will run into the drive belt case behind the clutch. If either of the shafts has been removed, it is good practice to fit a new seal prior to installation (see Tools and Workshop Tips in the Reference section). Lever the input shaft seal out from the clutch side of the casing; lever the output shaft seal out from the inside of the gearbox housing.
62 Inspect the bearings in the casing and the

gearbox cover (see Tools and Workshop Tips in the Reference section). If the bearings need renewing, the output shaft bearing can be driven out using a bearing driver or suitably-sized socket (see illustration). Bearings that are fitted into blind holes require an internal bearing puller and slide-hammer to extract them without damaging the case (see illustration 7.59). Always heat the bearing housing first to aid removal and fitting. Don't forget to check the bearing on the input shaft. If specialist tools are not available consult an automotive engineer.

Installation

63 Installation is the reverse of removal, noting the following:
● Smear the inside of the oil seals with grease before installing the shafts.
● Lubricate both ends of the intermediate shaft with molybdenum disulphide grease before installation.
● Fit any dowels into the cover and use a new cover gasket (see illustrations).

● Tighten the gearbox bolts evenly and in a criss-cross pattern to the torque setting specified at the beginning of this Chapter.
● Fit a new sealing washer on the gearbox drain plug.
● Fill the gearbox with the specified amount and type of oil (see Chapter 1).

7.63b ...to seal against the ends of the belt casing (arrowed)

Chapter 4
Cooling system – liquid-cooled engine

Contents

Degrees of difficulty

Easy, suitable for novice with little experience	**Fairly easy,** suitable for beginner with some experience	**Fairly difficult,** suitable for competent DIY mechanic	**Difficult,** suitable for experienced DIY mechanic	**Very difficult,** suitable for expert DIY or professional

Specifications

Coolant

Mixture type	Pre-mix coolant or 50% distilled water / 50% corrosion inhibited ethylene glycol anti-freeze
Coolant capacity	see Chapter 1

Torque settings

Engine temperature sensor	20 Nm
Thermostat housing bolts	10 Nm
Water pump mounting bolts	10 Nm

1 General information

This Chapter covers the cooling system components fitted to the Speedfight 50 with engine type B1E4QMB.

The cooling system uses a water and anti-freeze coolant mixture to carry away excess heat from the engine and maintain as constant a temperature as possible. The cylinder and combustion chamber are surrounded by a water jacket through which coolant is circulated by thermo-syphonic action in conjunction with a water pump. Hot coolant from the engine passes via the thermostat on the cylinder head to the radiator at the front of the machine. The coolant flows across the core of the radiator, down to the water pump and back into the engine where the cycle is repeated.

The water pump is located on the right-hand side of the crankcase. The pump is mechanical, driven off the crankshaft via drive pins on the alternator rotor.

A thermostat is fitted in a housing on the cylinder head to prevent the coolant flowing through the radiator when the engine is cold, therefore accelerating the speed at which the engine reaches normal operating temperature. A temperature sensor mounted in the cylinder head transmits engine temperature information to the temperature gauge on the instrument panel.

The complete cooling system is partially sealed and pressurised, the pressure being controlled by a valve contained in the reservoir cap. By pressurising the coolant the boiling point is raised, preventing premature boiling in adverse conditions. The overflow pipe from the system is connected to a reservoir into which excess coolant is expelled under pressure. The discharged coolant automatically returns to the radiator by the vacuum created when the engine cools.

⚠ **Warning: Do not remove the cap from the reservoir when the engine is hot. Scalding hot coolant and steam may be blown out under pressure, which could cause serious injury. When the engine has cooled slowly remove the cap allowing any residual pressure to escape.**
Caution: Do not allow anti-freeze to come in contact with your skin or painted surfaces of the motorcycle. Rinse off any spills immediately with plenty of water. Anti-freeze is highly toxic if ingested. Never leave anti-freeze lying around in an open container or in puddles on the floor; children and pets are attracted by its sweet smell and may drink it. Check with the local authorities about disposing of used anti-freeze. Many communities will have collection centres which will see that anti-freeze is disposed of safely.
Caution: At all times use the specified type of anti-freeze, and always mix it with distilled water in the correct proportion, or purchase pre-mix coolant. The anti-freeze contains corrosion inhibitors which are essential to avoid damage to the cooling system. A lack of these inhibitors could lead to a build-up of corrosion which would block the coolant passages, resulting in overheating and severe engine damage. Distilled water must be used as opposed to tap water to avoid a build-up of scale which would also block the passages.

2 Coolant change

⚠ **Warning: Allow the engine to cool completely before performing this maintenance operation. Also, don't allow anti-freeze to come into contact with your skin or the painted surfaces of the motorcycle. Rinse off spills immediately with plenty of water. Anti-freeze is highly toxic if ingested. Never leave anti-freeze lying around in an open container or in puddles on the floor; children and pets are attracted by its sweet smell and may drink it. Check with local authorities (councils) about disposing of anti-freeze. Many communities have collection centres which will see that anti-freeze is disposed of safely. Anti-freeze is also combustible, so don't store it near open flames.**

Draining

1 Support the scooter on its centrestand on a level surface. Follow the procedure in Chapter 9 to remove the coolant reservoir cover and the storage compartment.
2 Slowly unscrew the reservoir cap (see illustration). If you hear a hissing sound (indicating there is still pressure in the system), wait until it stops before fully removing the cap.
3 Position a suitable container beneath the engine on the right-hand side. Release the clip securing the hose to the lower union on the water pump, detach the hose and allow the coolant to completely drain from the system (see illustration). Hold the hose low down to ensure complete draining. Check the condition of the clip – if it is sprained or corroded it must be replaced with a new one.

Flushing

4 Flush the cooling system with clean tap water by inserting a hose in the reservoir filler neck. Allow the water to run through the system until it is clear. If there is a large amount of rust or sediment in the water, remove the radiator (see Section 6) and have it cleaned by a specialist.
5 Reconnect the coolant hose to the water pump and secure it with the clip (see illustration 2.3).
6 Fill the system via the reservoir filler with clean water mixed with a flushing compound. Make sure the flushing compound is compatible with aluminium components, and follow the manufacturer's instructions carefully. Fit the reservoir cap.
7 Start the engine and allow it to reach normal operating temperature. Let it run for about ten minutes (or as specified by the flushing compound manufacturer).

⚠ **Warning: Make sure that the rear wheel is off the ground before starting the engine. If necessary, place a support under the centrestand to prevent the wheel touching the ground.**
8 Stop the engine. Let it cool for a while, then cover the reservoir cap with a heavy rag and slowly unscrew it – if you hear a hissing sound (indicating there is still pressure in the system), wait until it stops before fully removing the cap.
9 Drain the system once again.
10 Fill the system with clean water, then fit the reservoir cap and repeat the procedure.

Refilling

11 Connect the coolant hose to the water pump and secure it with the clip.
12 Fill the system up to the MAX level line on the reservoir with the proper coolant mixture (see this Chapter's Specifications). **Note:** *Pour the coolant in slowly to minimise the amount of air entering the system.* Carefully shake the scooter to dislodge any trapped air.

2.2 Unscrew the reservoir cap (arrowed)

2.3 Detach the hose from the lower pump union

2.13 Loosen the bleed screw (arrowed)

3.7 Location of the temperature sensor

13 Loosen the bleed screw on the thermostat housing to release any trapped air **(see illustration)**. Once the air has escaped, tighten the bleed screw securely.

14 Start the engine and allow it to idle for two to three minutes. Flick the throttle twistgrip part open three or four times to increase engine speed, then stop the engine.

15 Loosen the bleed screw to release any trapped air then tighten it securely.

16 Let the engine cool then check that the coolant level is still up to the MAX level line. Top-up if necessary.

17 Check the system for leaks.

18 Install the coolant reservoir cover and the storage compartment (see Chapter 9).

19 Do not dispose of the old coolant by pouring it down the drain. Instead pour it into a heavy plastic container, cap it tightly and take it into an authorised disposal site or service station – see *Warning* at the beginning of this Section.

3 Temperature gauge and temperature sensor

Temperature gauge

1 The circuit consists of the gauge in the instrument cluster and the sensor mounted in the cylinder head.

2 The gauge should appear on the multi-function display when the ignition is turned ON. There are five segments in the display from C (one – cold) to H (five – hot). As the engine warms up the segments should illuminate progressively. If the engine becomes over-heated, the first four segments will illuminate and the H segment and the temperature symbol will flash.

3 If the gauge malfunctions, first check that the battery is fully charged.

4 Refer to the appropriate wiring diagram at the end of Chapter 10 and check for continuity in the wiring between the instrument cluster wiring connector and the temperature sensor connector. Check that the terminals in the connectors are not dirty or damaged.

5 Check the installation of the temperature sensor **(see illustration 3.10)**.

6 If no fault can be found, and only the temperature gauge on the multi-function display is not working, have the instrument cluster checked by a Peugeot dealer. **Note:** *The temperature gauge is an integral part of the instrument cluster. If the gauge is faulty a new instrument cluster will have to be fitted.* Refer to the procedure in Chapter 10 to remove and install the instrument cluster.

Temperature sensor

7 The temperature sensor is located on the left-hand side of the cylinder head **(see illustration)**. Remove the storage compartment for access (see Chapter 9).

8 There are no specifications for testing the sensor. The only way to confirm that it is faulty is by substitution with a known good sensor.

9 To remove the sensor, first drain the cooling system (see Section 2).

10 Disconnect the sensor wiring connector, then unscrew and remove the sensor **(see illustration)**. Discard the old sealing washer as a new one must be used.

11 Apply a suitable sealant to the threads of the sensor, making sure none gets on the sensor head. Fit a new sealing washer, then install the sensor and tighten it to the torque setting specified at the beginning of this Chapter. Connect the wiring.

12 Refill the cooling system (see Section 2).

3.10 Unscrew the temperature sensor

4 Thermostat

1 The thermostat is automatic in operation and should give many years service without requiring attention. In the event of a failure, the valve will probably jam open, in which case the engine will take much longer than normal to warm up. Conversely, if the valve jams shut, the coolant will be unable to circulate and the engine will overheat. Neither condition is acceptable, and the fault must be investigated promptly.

Removal

 Warning: The engine must be completely cool before carrying out this procedure.

2 The thermostat housing is located on the rear of the cylinder head. Remove the storage compartment for access (see Chapter 9).

3 Drain the cooling system (see Section 2).

4 Release the clip securing the hose to the thermostat housing and disconnect the hose, being prepared to catch any residual coolant in a suitable container.

5 Undo the bolts securing the housing and lift

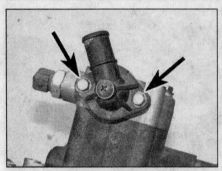

4.5a Undo the housing bolts (arrowed)

4.5b Note location of the thermostat bypass hole

4.6 Thermostat in the closed position

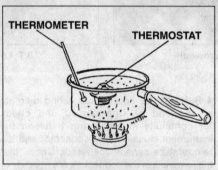

4.7 Set-up for testing the thermostat

it off **(see illustration)**. Lift out the thermostat, noting how it fits **(see illustration)**.

Check

6 Examine the thermostat visually before carrying out the test. If it remains in the open position at room temperature, it should be replaced with a new one **(see illustration)**. Check the condition of the rubber seal around the thermostat – if it is damaged, deformed or deteriorated a new thermostat will have to be fitted.
7 Suspend the thermostat by a piece of wire in a container of cold water. Place a thermometer

capable of reading temperatures up to 100°C in the water so that the bulb is close to the thermostat **(see illustration)**. Heat the water, noting the temperature when the thermostat opens. No specifications are available for testing the thermostat, but it should open at approximately 70°C and be fully open after it has been heated for a few minutes at 80°C. If the thermostat does not behave as described replace it with a new one.
8 In the event of thermostat failure, as an emergency measure only, it can be removed and the machine used without it (this is better than leaving a permanently closed thermostat

in, but if it is permanently open, you might as well leave it in). **Note:** *Take care when starting the engine from cold as it will take much longer than usual to warm up.* Ensure that a new unit is installed as soon as possible.

Installation

9 Smear some fresh coolant over the thermostat seal, then install the thermostat, making sure it locates correctly with the bypass hole towards the front **(see illustration 4.5b)**.
10 Fit the housing and tighten the bolts to the torque setting specified at the beginning of this Chapter.
11 Refill the cooling system (see Section 2).

5 Coolant reservoir

Removal

1 Remove the headlight panel and the kick panel (see Chapter 9).
2 Drain the cooling system (see Section 2).
3 Release the clips securing the large-bore hose on the left-hand side between the reservoir and the radiator and detach the hose **(see illustration)**.
4 Release the clips securing the small-bore hose on the right-hand side between the reservoir and the radiator and detach the hose **(see illustration)**.
5 Undo the bolt securing the reservoir and lift it off.

Installation

6 Installation is the reverse of removal. Make sure the coolant hoses are in good condition (see Chapter 1), and are securely retained with the clips. If any clips are sprained or corroded they should be renewed.
7 Refill the cooling system with the specified coolant mixture (see Section 2).

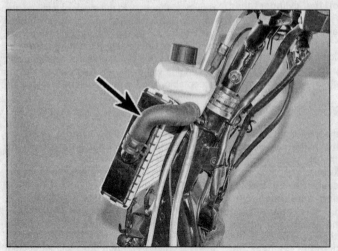

5.3 Detach the large-bore hose (arrowed)

5.4 Detach the small-bore hose (A). Note mounting bolt (B)

6 Radiator

Removal

1 Remove the headlight panel and the kick panel (see Chapter 9).
2 Drain the cooling system (see Section 2).
3 Remove the coolant reservoir (see Section 5).
4 Release the clips securing the coolant hoses to the right-hand side of the radiator and detach the hoses **(see illustration)**.
5 Undo the bolts securing the radiator and lift it off **(see illustration)**.
6 Check the radiator for signs of damage and clear any dirt or debris that might obstruct airflow and inhibit cooling. If the radiator fins are badly damaged or broken the radiator must be replaced with a new one.

Installation

7 Installation is the reverse of removal, noting the following.
● Tighten the mounting bolts securely.
● Ensure the coolant hoses are in good condition (see Chapter 1), and are securely retained by their clips. If any clips are sprained or corroded they should be renewed.
● Install the coolant reservoir and refill the cooling system with the specified coolant mixture.

7 Water pump

Check

1 The water pump is located on the outside the alternator on the right-hand side of the engine. Check the around the pump for signs of leakage. Ensure the coolant hoses are

6.4 Detach the coolant hoses

6.5 Location of the radiator mounting bolts

7.7a Undo the bolts (arrowed)...

7.7b ...and remove the pump assembly

pushed fully onto the unions on the outside of the pump and held securely by the hose clips.
2 Check the underside of the pump for evidence of leakage. If coolant is leaking from the pump the internal seals will have failed and a new pump will have to be fitted – individual components are not available.
3 If the pump is noisy either the internal bearing has failed and a new pump will have to be fitted, or the drive pins are worn – remove the pump to check.

Removal

4 Drain the cooling system (see Section 2).
5 Release the clip securing the hose to the

upper union on the water pump and detach the hose.
6 Remove the exhaust system (see Chapter 5).
7 Undo the bolts securing the water pump and alternator cover assembly and lift it off **(see illustrations)**.
8 Note how the drive pins on the alternator rotor locate in the slots in the back of the pump impeller **(see illustration)**. The impeller should turn freely without any freeplay in its bearing.
9 Inspect the rubber drive pins for wear and renew them as a set if necessary **(see illustration)**. Tighten the drive pins securely on installation

7.8 Alternator rotor (A), pump impeller (B)

7.9 Inspect the drive pins (arrowed) for wear

8.6 Jubilee or hose clips should not be over-tightened

Installation

10 Installation is the reverse of removal, noting the following.
● Align the slots in the pump impeller with the drive pins.
● Tighten the pump mounting bolts to the torque setting specified at the beginning of this Chapter.

● Ensure the coolant hoses are in good condition (see Chapter 1), and are securely retained by their clips.
● Refill the cooling system with the specified coolant mixture (see Section 2).

8 Coolant hoses

Removal

1 Remove the body panels as necessary to access the coolant hose (see Chapter 9).
2 Drain the coolant (see Section 2).
3 Using pliers, release the hose clips at both ends of the hose **(see illustration 2.3)**. Slide the clips back along the hose and clear of the union. If any clips are sprained or corroded they should be renewed prior to installation.
Caution: The radiator unions are fragile. Do not use excessive force when attempting to remove the hoses.
4 If a hose proves stubborn, release it by

rotating it on its union before working it off. If all else fails, cut the hose with a sharp knife. Whilst this means replacing the hose with a new one, it is preferable to buying a new radiator.

Installation

5 Slide the clips onto the hose and then work the hose on to its union as far as possible.

 HAYNES HiNT *If the hose is difficult to push on its union, soften it by soaking it in very hot water, or alternatively a little soapy water on the union can be used as a lubricant.*

6 Rotate the hose on its unions to settle it in position before sliding the clips into place and releasing them. If using a Jubilee clip as a replacement **(see illustration)** take care not to over-tighten it and damage the hose union.
7 Refill the cooling system with specified coolant mixture (see Section 2).

Chapter 5
Fuel and exhaust systems

Contents

Degrees of difficulty

Easy, suitable for novice with little experience 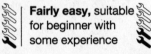	Fairly easy, suitable for beginner with some experience 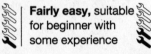	Fairly difficult, suitable for competent DIY mechanic 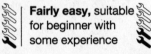	Difficult, suitable for experienced DIY mechanic 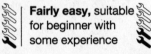	Very difficult, suitable for expert DIY or professional

Specifications

Fuel
Fuel type and tank capacity................................. see Chapter 1

Carburettor – Speedfight 50
Type/ID no.
  Air-cooled model .... TK PZ12
  Liquid-cooled model.................................. TK PZ15
TK PZ12 (unrestricted) settings
  Type 502
  Idle speed... 1800 rpm
  Mixture screw.. 1 3/8 turns out
  Main jet... 54
  Idle jet.. 44
TK PZ12 (restricted) settings
  Type 503
  Idle speed... 1200 rpm
  Mixture screw.. 1 3/8 turns out
  Main jet... 42
  Idle jet.. 32
TK PZ15 settings
  Type 504
  Idle speed... 1800 rpm
  Mixture screw.. 1 3/4 turns out
  Main jet... 52
  Idle jet.. 48

Carburettor – Vivacity 50 2T

Type/ID no.	TK PZ12, 502
Idle speed	1600 rpm
Mixture screw	1 3/8 turns out
Main jet	54
Idle jet	44

Carburettor – V-Clic

Type/ID no.	DENI PD18J
Idle speed	1600 rpm
Mixture screw	2 to 3 turns out
Main jet	82
Idle jet	30
Needle	DA8M

Carburettor – Kisbee 50

Type/ID no.	DENI PD18J
Idle speed	1800 rpm
Mixture screw	2 turns out
Main jet	78
Idle jet	30
Needle	DA8M

Carburettor – Vivacity 50 4T and Tweet 50

Type/ID no.	Keihin NCV18
Idle speed	2100 rpm
Mixture screw	2 1/2 turns out
Main jet	88
Idle jet	35
Needle	DA8M

Carburettor – Kisbee 100

Type/ID no.	DENI PD20J
Settings	not available

Carburettor – Speedfight 125

Type/ID no.	DENI DPD24J
Idle speed	1800 rpm
Mixture screw	2 1/4 turns out
Main jet	115
Idle jet	38

Carburettor – Tweet 125/150

Type/ID no.	DENI DPD24J
Idle speed	1600 rpm
Mixture screw	2 1/4 turns out
Main jet	98
Idle jet	35

Carburettor – Vivacity 125

Type/ID no.	ZHONGCHENG PD24J-9
Idle speed	1600 rpm
Mixture screw	2 1/4 turns out
Main jet	108
Idle jet	33

Fuel level sensor

Resistance

Fuel tank full	6.4 to 12 ohms
Fuel tank empty	76 to 114 ohms

Reed valve

Valve stopper plate, fixed distance	6.2 mm

Torque setting

Intake manifold bolts	10 Nm

1 General information and precautions

The fuel system consists of the fuel tank, fuel filter, carburettor, fuel hoses and throttle cable. On scooters with a two-stroke engine, and on Vivacity four-stroke engined machines due to the position of the fuel tank, a fuel pump is fitted. The pump acts as a fuel tap, cutting the supply to the carburettor when the engine isn't running.

A fuel tap is fitted to the underside of the tank on Kisbee and Tweet models. The tap is automatic in operation and is opened by engine vacuum. A filter is incorporated in the tap and, as on all other scooters, a filter is fitted in the fuel line. V-Clic models have an in-line, vacuum-operated tap.

For cold starting, an electrically-operated automatic choke is fitted in the carburettor. Some models, such as the Kisbee, also have an electrically-operated carburettor heater.

Air is drawn into the carburettor via an air filter which is housed above the drive belt cover.

All models have a fuel gauge incorporated in the instrument cluster, actuated by a level sensor inside the fuel tank.

A catalytic converter is incorporated in the exhaust system to minimise the level of exhaust pollutants released into the atmosphere. In addition, the Peugeot Pulsair system allows oxygen to be drawn into the exhaust system to further reduce carbon monoxide and unburned hydrocarbon levels.

Several fuel system service procedures are considered routine maintenance items and for that reason are included in Chapter 1.
Note: *On two-stroke engines, lubricating oil is mixed with the fuel in the carburettor venturi. Refer to the relevant engine chapter for details of the oil pump.*

Precautions

⚠ *Warning: Petrol (gasoline) is extremely flammable, so take extra pre-cautions when you work on any part of the fuel system. Don't smoke or allow open flames or bare light bulbs near the work area, and don't work in a garage where*

2.1a Fuel tap location – Kisbee

a natural gas-type appliance is present. If you spill any fuel on your skin, rinse it off immediately with soap and water. When you perform any kind of work on the fuel system, wear safety glasses and have a fire extinguisher suitable for a class B type fire (flammable liquids) on hand.

Always perform service procedures in a well-ventilated area to prevent a build-up of fumes.

Never work in a building containing a gas appliance with a pilot light, or any other form of naked flame. Ensure that there are no naked light bulbs or any sources of flame or sparks nearby.

Do not smoke (or allow anyone else to smoke) while in the vicinity of petrol or of components containing it. Remember the possible presence of vapour from these sources and move well clear before smoking.

Check all electrical equipment belonging to the house, garage or workshop where work is being undertaken (see the Safety first! section of this manual). Remember that certain electrical appliances such as drills, cutters etc. create sparks in the normal course of operation and must not be used near petrol or any component containing it. Again, remember the possible presence of fumes before using electrical equipment.

Always mop up any spilt fuel and safely dispose of the rag used.

Any stored fuel that is drained off during servicing work must be kept in sealed containers that are suitable for holding petrol, and clearly marked as such; the containers themselves should be kept in a safe place.

2.1b Fuel tap location – V-Clic

Read the Safety first! section of this manual carefully before starting work.

2 Fuel tap and filter

⚠ *Warning: Refer to the precautions given in Section 1 before starting work.*

Fuel tap

Check

Note: *Some scooters do not have a separate fuel tap – instead the tap function is controlled by the fuel pump, which will only allow fuel to flow when the engine is turning over. See Section 12 for fuel pump check and renewal.*
1 The fuel tap is located either on the underside of the fuel tank, or in the fuel line between the tank and the carburettor **(see illustrations)**. Remove the storage compartment, side panels and seat cowling as required for access (see Chapter 9).
2 The tap is automatic, operated by a vacuum created when the engine is running which opens a diaphragm inside the tap. If the tap is faulty, it must be renewed – it is a sealed unit for which no individual components are available. The most likely problem is a hole or split in the tap diaphragm.
3 To check the tap, release the clip securing the fuel hose and detach it from the carburettor, being prepared to catch any residual fuel in a rag. Place the open end of the hose in a small container **(see illustration)**. Detach the vacuum hose from the intake manifold **(see illustration)**

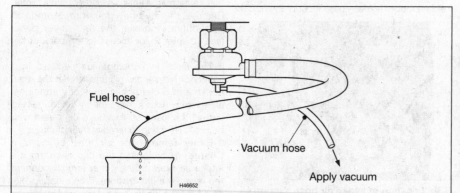

Fuel hose

Vacuum hose

Apply vacuum

2.3a Set-up for checking vacuum tap operation

2.3b Detach the fuel tap vacuum hose

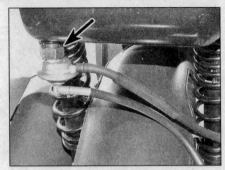

2.7 Fuel tap union nut (arrowed)

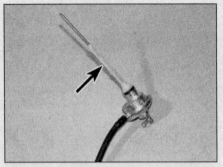

2.8 Clean the filter (arrowed) and check it for holes

2.12a Check the filter for blockages

2.12b Remove the filter from its holder

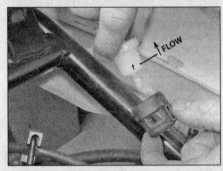

2.13 Arrow indicates direction of fuel flow

and apply a vacuum to it (suck on the hose end). If you are not sure which hose is which on your model, trace the hoses from the tap. Fuel should flow from the tap and into the container – if it doesn't, the tap diaphragm is probably split.

4 Before renewing the tap, check that the vacuum hose is securely attached, and that there are no splits or cracks in the hose. If in doubt, attach a spare hose to the vacuum union on the tap and again apply a vacuum. If fuel still does not flow, remove the tap and fit a new one.

Removal

Note: *The tap should not be removed unnecessarily from the tank otherwise the seal or filter may be damaged.*

5 Before removing the tap, connect a drain hose to the fuel hose union and insert its end in a container suitable and large enough for storing the petrol. Apply a vacuum to the vacuum hose (see Step 3) and allow the tank to drain.

6 Release the clips and detach the hoses from the tap, noting where they fit.

7 To remove the tap from the fuel tank, either unscrew the union nut or loosen the clamp securing the tap and withdraw the tap assembly **(see illustration)**. Be prepared to catch any residual fuel in a rag. Check the condition of the O-ring seal. If it is in good condition it can be re-used, though it is better to use a new one. If deteriorated or damaged it must be renewed.

8 Allow the gauze filter to dry, then remove all traces of dirt and fuel sediment with a soft brush **(see illustration)**. Check the gauze for holes. If any are found, a new tap should be fitted as the filter is not available separately.

9 To remove an in-line tap, undo the mounting

bolt and lift the tap off, noting which way round it fits.

Installation

10 Installation is the reverse of removal. If the tap is located on the tank, ensure that the union nut or clamp is tightened securely. Fit the fuel and vacuum hoses onto their respective unions and secure them with their clips.

In-line filter

Note 1: *A new fuel filter should be fitted at the specified service interval (see Chapter 1).*

Note 2: *On two-stroke engines, a small filter element is fitted inside the fuel hose union on the carburettor (see Section 8).*

11 Remove any body panels as required for access (see Chapter 9).

12 The filter has a clear plastic body – check for signs of sediment or a clogged element **(see illustration)**. On some models the filter is located inside a rubber holder – ease it out of the holder

for inspection **(see illustration)**. The filter is a sealed unit. If it is dirty or clogged, fit a new one.

13 To remove the filter, release the clips securing the fuel hoses to each end and detach the hoses, being prepared to catch any residual fuel in a rag. Note which way round the filter is fitted – an arrow on the filter body indicates the direction of fuel flow **(see illustration)**.

14 Installation is the reverse of removal. Ensure the filter is the correct way round. Renew the clips on the fuel hoses if the old ones are sprained or corroded.

3 Air filter housing

Removal

1 The filter housing is located above the drive belt cover on the left-hand side of the scooter. Remove the storage compartment and, on Speedfight models, the rear cover panel (see Chapter 9) for access to the back of the housing.

2 The air filter housings are secured in a variety of ways – always ensure that the main intake and outlet hoses, plus any additional air system hoses, have been disconnected and all the fixing screws have been removed before attempting to remove the housing.

3 Either remove the air filter cover (see Chapter 1) or loosen the clip securing the intake air hose to the cover and disconnect the hose **(see illustration)**. Where applicable, note how the intake hose is secured inside the frame and release the hose **(see illustration)**.

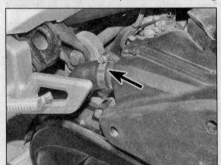

3.3a Intake air hose clip (arrowed)

3.3b Location of intake air hose supports – Tweet shown

3.4 Clip (arrowed) secures hose to carburettor

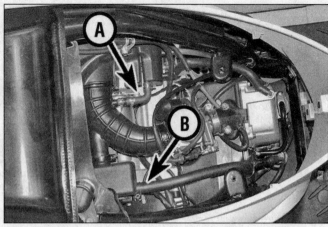

3.5 Engine breather hose (A), Pulsair system hose (B)

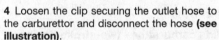

3.6 Undo the housing mounting bolts (arrowed)

3.7 Detach the housing from the rear hugger

3.8a Remove the housing – Speedfight

4 Loosen the clip securing the outlet hose to the carburettor and disconnect the hose **(see illustration)**.

5 Where applicable, disconnect the engine breather hose and the Pulsair system hose from the air filter housing assembly **(see illustration)**.

6 Remove the bolts securing the air filter housing to the engine unit **(see illustration)**.

7 Check for any screws securing the housing to the rear hugger and remove the screws **(see illustration)**.

8 Lift the filter housing off **(see illustrations)**.

Installation

9 Installation is the reverse of removal. Install the housing loosely and ensure that the hoses are correctly routed before tightening the hose clips and mounting bolts and screws.

3.8b Air filter housing assembly – Kisbee

3.8c Air filter housing assembly – Tweet

at idle speed is set using the mixture screw **(see illustrations)**. Adjustment of the screw is not normally necessary and should only

be performed if the engine is running roughly, stalls continually, or if a new mixture screw has been fitted.

| 4 | Fuel/air mixture adjustment |

⚠️ *Warning: Adjustment of the mixture screw is made with the engine running. To prevent accidents caused by the rear wheel contacting the ground, ensure that the scooter is on its main stand and if necessary place a support under the scooter to prevent the rear wheel contacting the ground.*

1 The fuel/air mixture with the engine running

4.1a Location of the mixture screw – slide carburettor

4.1b Location of the mixture screw – CV carburettor

5.3a Automatic choke unit location – slide carburettor

5.3b Automatic choke unit location – CV carburettor

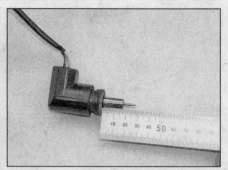

5.6 Measure the protrusion of the choke plunger

2 If the mixture screw is removed during a carburettor overhaul, record its current setting by turning the screw it in until it seats lightly, counting the number of turns necessary to achieve this, then unscrew it fully. On installation, turn the screw in until it seats lightly, then back it out the number of turns you've recorded. When fitting a new mixture screw, turn it in until it seats, then back it out the number of turns shown in the carburettor specifications at the beginning of this Chapter. This is known as the base adjustment setting.

3 Mixture screw adjustment must be made with the engine running and at normal working temperature. Stop the engine and turn the screw in until it seats lightly, then back it out to the base setting described in Step 2. Start the engine and set the idle speed to the specified amount (see Chapter 1).

4 Now try turning the mixture screw inwards by no more than a ¼ turn, noting its effect on the idle speed, then repeat the process, this time turning the screw outwards.

5 The mixture screw should be set in the position which gives the most consistent, even idle speed without the automatic transmission engaging, and so that the engine does not stall when the twistgrip is opened. **Note:** *It will not be possible to achieve an even idle speed if the spark plug needs adjustment or if the air filter element is dirty. On four stroke engines ensure the valve clearances are correctly set.*

6 Once a satisfactory mixture screw setting has been achieved, further adjustments to the

idle speed can be made with the idle speed adjuster screw (see Chapter 1).

5 Automatic choke unit

1 Poor starting or poor engine performance and an increase in fuel consumption are possible signs that the automatic choke is not working properly.

2 Turn the ignition on with the engine cold – after 3 to 5 minutes it should be possible feel the choke unit getting warm.

3 The resistance of the choke should be checked with a multimeter after the engine has been warmed to normal operating temperature and then allowed to cool for ten minutes. Remove the storage compartment (see Chapter 9) then trace the wiring from the automatic choke unit on the carburettor **(see illustrations)** and disconnect it at the connector.

4 Measure the resistance between the terminals on the choke unit side of the connector with the multimeter set to the ohms scale. Specific figures are not available, but you should get a reading of 20 to 40 ohms if the unit is in good condition.

5 To check that the plunger is not seized in the choke body, first remove the choke unit cover. Remove the retaining plate and withdraw the choke unit from the carburettor (see Section 8 or 10).

6 Measure the protrusion of the plunger from the body **(see illustration)**. Next, use jumper wires to connect a good 12V battery to the choke unit terminals and measure the protrusion again after 5 minutes. If the measurement has not increased by approximately 3 to 6 mm (depending on the type of carburettor) the unit is faulty and should be renewed.

6 Carburettor –
removal and installation

⚠ **Warning: Refer to the precautions given in Section 1 before starting work.**

Removal

Slide carburettor – two-stroke engine

1 Remove the storage compartment and, on Speedfight models, the rear cover panel (see Chapter 9).

2 Remove the air filter housing (see Section 3).

3 Trace the wiring from the automatic choke unit and disconnect it at the connector **(see illustration)**.

4 Where fitted, disconnect the carburettor heater wiring connectors.

5 Disconnect the fuel hose from its union on the carburettor, being prepared to catch any residual fuel in a rag **(see illustration 6.3)**. Position a suitable container below the carburettor drain hose, then loosen the drain screw and drain any residual fuel from the float chamber. Tighten the drain screw.

6 Release the clip securing the oil hose to the union on the oil pump and pull the hose off, being prepared to catch any residual oil in a rag **(see illustration 6.3)**. Plug the open end of the hose to prevent any dirt getting inside.

7 Undo the screw securing the carburettor top cover **(see illustration)** and draw the slide assembly out from the carburettor. Note the location of the O-ring inside the cover. Secure the throttle cable and slide assembly clear of the engine to avoid damage. To detach the slide assembly from the cable, see Section 8.

8 Note how the lug on the carburettor locates

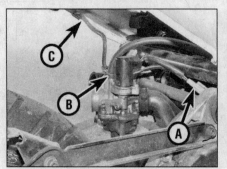

6.3 Choke wiring connector (A), fuel hose union (B) and oil hose union (C)

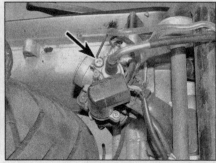

6.7 Screw (arrowed) secures carburettor top

6.8 Note location of lug (arrowed)

6.13 Location of the carburettor heater

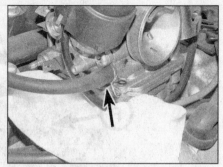

6.14 Disconnect the fuel hose

against the intake manifold, then release the clamp securing the carburettor and ease the carburettor off **(see illustration)**.
Caution: Stuff clean rag into the intake after removing the carburettor to prevent anything from falling inside.
9 If required, remove the intake manifold. The manifold is fixed to the upper surface of the crankcase and secures the reed valve assembly (see Section 9).

CV carburettor – four-stroke engine

10 Remove the storage compartment and any body panels as required on your scooter to access the carburettor (see Chapter 9).
11 Remove the air filter housing (see Section 3).
12 Trace the wiring from the automatic choke unit and disconnect it at the connector **(see illustration 5.3b)**.
13 Where fitted, disconnect the carburettor heater wiring connector(s) **(see illustration)**.
14 Disconnect the fuel hose from its union on the carburettor, being prepared to catch any residual fuel in a rag **(see illustration)**. Position a suitable container below the carburettor drain hose, then loosen the drain screw and drain any residual fuel from the float chamber. Tighten the drain screw.
15 Undo the locknut securing the lower end of the throttle cable to the bracket on the carburettor and release the cable from the bracket, then detach the inner cable end from the pulley **(see illustrations)**.
16 Note how the lug on the carburettor locates against the intake manifold, then loosen the clamp securing the carburettor and ease the carburettor off **(see illustration)**.

6.15a Undo the locknut (arrowed)

Caution: Stuff clean rag into the intake after removing the carburettor to prevent anything from falling inside.
17 If required, remove the intake manifold. First disconnect the vacuum hose(s) from the manifold, then undo the bolts securing the manifold and lift it off **(see illustration)**. Note the location of the manifold gasket and discard it as a new one must be fitted on installation **(see illustration)**.

Installation

18 Installation is the reverse of removal, noting the following:
● Ensure that the seals and gaskets on the intake manifold are in good condition.
● Make sure the lug on the carburettor is fully engaged with the intake manifold.
● Tighten the clamp securely.
● Make sure all hoses are correctly routed and secured and not trapped or kinked.

6.15b Detach the inner cable end from the pulley

● Ensure the wiring connectors are secure.
● Follow the procedure in Section 8 to install the throttle slide assembly (two-stroke engine).
● Reverse the procedure in Step 15 to install the throttle cable (four-stroke engine).
● Check the throttle cable adjustment (see Chapter 1).
● Check the idle speed and adjust as necessary (see Chapter 1).

7 Carburettor overhaul – general information

1 Poor engine performance, difficult starting, stalling, flooding and backfiring are all signs that carburettor maintenance may be required.
2 Keep in mind that many so-called

6.16 Note location of lug (arrowed)

6.17a Unbolt the intake manifold

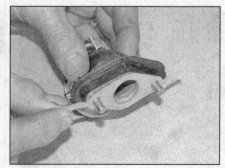

6.17b Note location of the manifold gasket

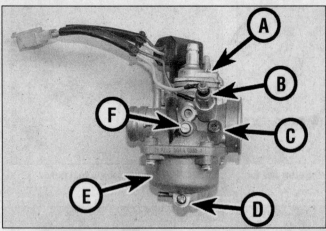

8.1 Top cover (A), heater (B), mixture screw (C), drain screw (D), float chamber (E), idle speed screw (F)

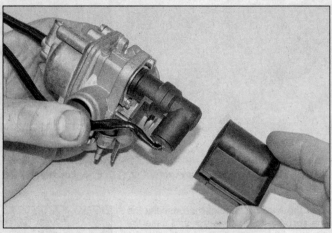

8.2a Remove the choke unit cover...

8.2b ...undo the retaining plate screws...

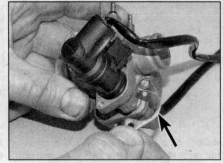

8.2c ...and slide off the retaining plate

type carburettor, whereas four-stroke engines use a CV (constant vacuum) type – ensure that you follow the correct procedure according to your machine (see Section 8 or 10).

8 Carburettor overhaul – slide type

⚠ **Warning: Refer to the precautions given in Section 1 before starting work.**

Note: *Slide-type carburettors are fitted to two-stroke engines – Speedfight 50 and Vivacity 50 2T.*

Disassembly

1 Remove the carburettor (see Section 6). Take care when removing components to note their exact locations and any springs or O-rings that may be fitted **(see illustration)**.
2 Remove the cover on the automatic choke unit and remove the retaining plate **(see illustrations)**. Withdraw the choke unit from the carburettor body, noting how it fits.
3 To detach the throttle slide assembly from the cable, first compress the slide spring then slot the cable end out of its recess inside the slide **(see illustrations)**. Remove the spring and top cover **(see illustration)**.
4 Note the location of the spring clip securing

carburettor problems can often be traced to mechanical faults within the engine or ignition system malfunctions. Try to establish for certain that the carburettor is in need of maintenance before beginning a major overhaul.
3 Check the fuel tap and filter, the fuel and vacuum hoses, the fuel pump (where fitted), the intake manifold joints, the air filter, the ignition system and the spark plug before assuming that a carburettor overhaul is required.
4 Most carburettor problems are caused by dirt particles, varnish and other deposits which build up in and eventually block the fuel jets and air passages inside the carburettor. Also, in time, gaskets and O-rings deteriorate

and cause fuel and air leaks which lead to poor performance.
5 When overhauling the carburettor, disassemble it completely and clean the parts thoroughly with a carburettor cleaning solvent. If available, blow through the fuel jets and air passages with compressed air to ensure they are clear. Once the cleaning process is complete, reassemble the carburettor using new gaskets and O-rings.
6 Before disassembling the carburettor, make sure you have the correct carburettor gasket set, some carburettor cleaner, a supply of clean rags, some means of blowing out the carburettor passages and a clean place to work.
Note: *Carburettor design differs for 2-stroke and 4-stroke engines. Two-stroke engines use a slide*

8.3a Compress the slide spring...

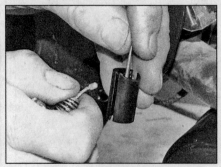

8.3b ...then slot the cable end out of the slide

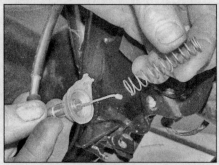

8.3c Remove the spring and top cover

8.4 Spring clip (arrowed) secures carburettor needle

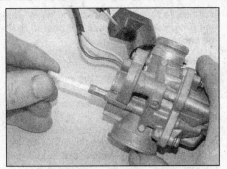

8.5 Pull out the fuel filter element

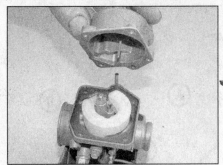

8.6a Lift off the float chamber...

8.6b ...and remove the gasket

8.7 Undo the screw and lift out the float assembly

the needle inside the slide and remove the clip and needle **(see illustration)**.
5 Withdraw the filter element from the fuel hose union **(see illustration)**.
6 Undo the screws securing the float chamber to the base of the carburettor and remove it noting the location of the gasket **(see illustrations)**.
7 Undo the screw securing the float pin and lift out the float assembly **(see illustration)**.
8 Unhook the float needle valve, noting how it fits onto the tab on the float **(see illustration)**.
9 Note the location of the carburettor jets **(see illustration)**. The jets will be marked with an identification number which should correspond with the specifications at the beginning of this Chapter. Unscrew the idle jet carefully to avoid damage. Unscrew the main jet then press the atomiser out from inside the carburettor body **(see illustration)**.
10 Unscrew the carburettor heater, then unscrew the idle speed adjuster screw noting its setting **(see illustration 8.1)**. Note the location of the spring on the adjuster screw.
11 The mixture screw can be removed if required, but note that its setting will be disturbed (see *Haynes Hint*). Unscrew and

 HAYNES HiNT *To record the mixture screw's current setting, turn the screw in until it seats lightly, counting the number of turns necessary to achieve this, then unscrew it fully. On installation, turn the screw in until it seats, then back it out the number of turns you've recorded.*

remove the screw along with its spring and O-ring **(see illustrations 8.1 and 8.9b)**.

Cleaning

Caution: Use only a petroleum-based solvent for carburettor cleaning. Don't use caustic cleaners.

12 Use carburettor cleaning solvent to loosen and dissolve the varnish and other deposits on the carburettor body and float chamber; use a nylon-bristled brush to remove the stubborn deposits. Dry the components with compressed air. **Note:** *Avoid soaking the carburettor body in solvent if any O-ring seals remain inside and remove the gasket and drain screw O-ring from the float chamber.*
13 If available, use compressed air to blow out the jets and the air passages in the carburettor body, not forgetting the passages in the carburettor intake.

Caution: Never clean the jets or passages with a piece of wire or a drill bit, as they will be enlarged, causing the fuel and air metering rates to be upset.

Inspection

14 If removed, check the tapered portion of the mixture screw and the spring for wear or damage. If necessary, renew the screw, spring and O-ring.
15 Check the carburettor body, float chamber and top cover for cracks, distorted sealing surfaces and other damage. If any defects are found, renew the faulty component, although a new carburettor will probably be necessary.
16 Insert the throttle slide in the carburettor body and check that it moves up-and-down smoothly. Check the surface of the slide for wear. If it's worn or scored excessively

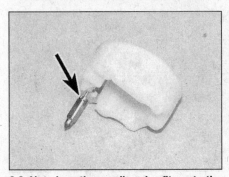

8.8 Note how the needle valve fits onto the float tab

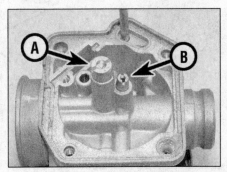

8.9a Main jet (A) and idle jet (B)

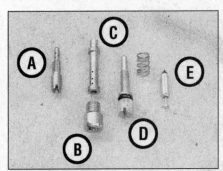

8.9b Idle jet (A), main jet (B), atomiser (C), mixture screw (D) and float needle valve (E)

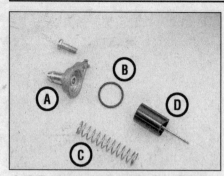

8.16 Top cover (A), cover O-ring (B), slide spring (C) and slide with needle

or doesn't move smoothly, renew the components as necessary **(see illustration)**.

17 Check the needle for straightness by rolling it on a flat surface such as a piece of glass. Fit a new needle if it's bent or if the tip is worn.

18 Inspect the tip of the float needle valve. If it has grooves or scratches in it, or is in any way worn, it must be renewed. If the valve seat in the carburettor body is damaged a new carburettor body will have to be fitted. **Note:** *On scooters with a pumped fuel system, a worn valve seat will not be able to shut off the fuel supply sufficiently to prevent carburettor flooding and excessive use of fuel.*

19 Check the float for damage. This will usually be apparent by the presence of fuel inside the float. If the float is damaged, it must be renewed.

20 Inspect the automatic choke unit plunger

9.2a Undo the bolts securing the intake manifold

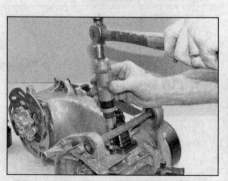

9.2c ...and undo it with an impact driver

and needle for signs of wear and renew the unit if necessary. To check the operation of the choke unit see Section 5.

Reassembly

Note: *When reassembling the carburettor, be sure to use new O-rings and gaskets. Do not overtighten the carburettor jets and screws as they are easily damaged.*

21 If removed, install the mixture screw, spring and O-ring; adjust the screw to the setting as noted on removal (see Step 11). If fitting a new screw refer to Section 4.

22 Install the idle speed adjuster screw and spring, set the screw to the setting as noted on removal.

23 If removed, install the carburettor heater.

24 Install the atomiser, then install the main jet **(see illustrations 8.9b and a)**. Install the pilot jet.

25 Hook the float needle valve onto the float tab, then position the float assembly in the carburettor, making sure the needle valve enters its seat **(see illustration 8.8)**. Secure the float pin with its screw.

26 Fit a new float chamber gasket, making sure it is seated properly, then install the float chamber and tighten the screws securely. Ensure that the O-ring is fitted on the drain screw and tighten the screw securely.

27 Install the choke unit and secure it with the retaining plate and screws. Install the choke unit cover.

28 Install the carburettor (see Section 6).

29 Install the needle in the throttle slide **(see illustration 8.4)**.

9.2b Cut a slot in the shear-head bolt...

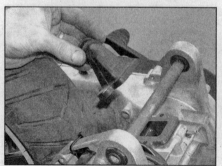

9.3 Remove the intake manifold

30 Install the top cover, O-ring and spring on the cable **(see illustration 8.3c)**. Compress the spring, then insert the inner cable end into the slide **(see illustration 8.3a)**.

31 Install the throttle slide assembly into the carburettor body carefully. Ensure that the needle is aligned with the top of the atomiser and that the slot in the slide is aligned with the lug inside the carburettor body. Hold the top cover in position and secure it with the screw.

32 Check the throttle cable freeplay and idle speed adjustment (see Chapter 1).

9 Reed valve (two-stroke engines)

Removal

1 Remove the carburettor (see Section 6).

2 Undo the bolts securing the intake manifold **(see illustration)**. To undo the anti-tamper shear-head bolt, first cut a slot in the bolt head with a hacksaw, then unscrew it with an impact driver **(see illustrations)**. Note that a new bolt will be required on installation.

3 Lift the manifold off, noting the seal on the underside **(see illustration)**.

4 Lift out the reed valve noting the location of the gasket **(see illustration)**. Discard the gasket as a new one must be fitted on installation.

Inspection

Note: *Do not disassemble the reed valve as individual components are not available.*

5 Inspect the reed valve body closely for cracks, distortion and any other damage, particularly around the mating surfaces between the crankcase and the intake manifold – a good seal must be maintained between the components, otherwise crankcase pressure and therefore engine performance will be affected.

6 Check the reeds for cracks, distortion and any other damage. Check also that there are no dirt particles trapped between the reeds and their seats. The reeds should sit flat against the valve body so that a good seal is obtained when the crankcase is under

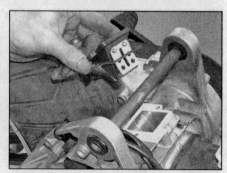

9.4 Remove the reed valve and gasket

pressure **(see illustration)**. If required, clean the reeds carefully with a suitable solvent to remove any gum.

7 After prolonged use, the reeds tend to become bent and will not therefore seal properly, in which case the assembly should be renewed. A good way to check is to hold the valve up to the light – if light is visible between the reeds and the body they are not sealing properly. If the engine is difficult to start or idles erratically, this could be the problem.

8 Check that the stopper plate retaining screws are tight. Measure the fixed distance between the tip of the reeds and the stopper plates **(see illustration)** and compare the result with the specification at the beginning of this Chapter. If the distance varies a new reed valve will have to be fitted.

Installation

9 Installation is the reverse of removal, noting the following:
● Ensure all mating surfaces are clean and perfectly smooth.
● Use new gaskets where applicable
● Tighten the manifold bolts to the specified torque.

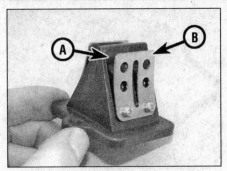

9.6 Reed (A) and stopper plate (B)

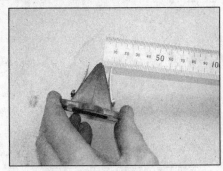

9.8 Measuring the stopper plate fixed distance

10 Carburettor overhaul – CV type

⚠ **Warning: Refer to the precautions given in Section 1 before proceeding.**

Note: *CV-type carburettors are fitted to four-stroke engines – V-Clic, Vivacity 50 4T, Kisbee 50, Tweet 50 and all 125/150cc models.*

Disassembly

1 Remove the carburettor (see Section 6). Take care when removing components to note their exact locations and any springs or O-rings that may be fitted **(see illustration)**.

2 Remove the cover on the automatic choke unit **(see illustration)**. Undo the screw(s) securing the retaining plate and slide the plate off, then withdraw the choke unit from the choke holder **(see illustrations)**.

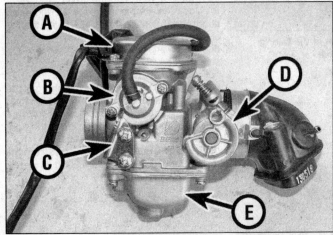

10.1 Top cover (A), richening diaphragm cover (B), throttle cable bracket (C), throttle pulley (D) and float chamber (E)

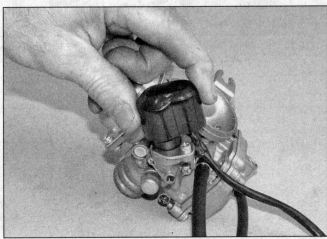

10.2a Remove the choke unit cover

10.2b Remove the retaining plate...

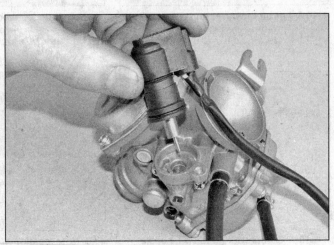

10.2c ...and lift out the choke unit

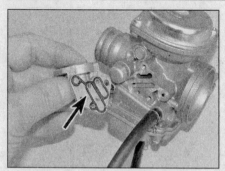

10.3 Note choke holder gasket (arrowed)

10.4a Undo the screws...

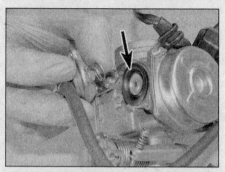

10.4b ...and remove the cover, spring and diaphragm (arrowed)

10.4c Richening diaphragm cover – Vivacity 50 4T

10.4d Note location of the O-ring (arrowed)

3 Undo the screws securing the choke holder and lift it off, noting the location of the gasket (see illustration).

4 Where fitted, undo the screws securing the richening diaphragm cover, then remove the cover, spring and diaphragm (see illustrations). Note which way round the diaphragm fits – the pin in the centre of the diaphragm locates in the valve in the carburettor body. On Vivacity 50 and Tweet 50 models, remove the cover and note the location of the passage O-ring (see illustration). The O-ring is fitted with the flat side towards the carburettor body.

5 Unscrew and remove the top cover retaining screws, then lift off the cover and remove the spring (see illustration).

6 Note how the tab on the diaphragm fits in the recess in the carburettor body, then carefully peel the diaphragm away from its sealing groove and withdraw the diaphragm and piston assembly (see illustration).

Caution: Do not use a sharp instrument to displace the diaphragm as it is easily damaged.

7 Remove the needle retainer, noting the spring fitted underneath, then push the needle up from the bottom of the piston and withdraw it from the top (see illustration).

8 Undo the screws securing the float chamber to the base of the carburettor and remove it – note the location of the gasket on the float chamber (see illustration).

9 Withdraw the float pin (see illustration).

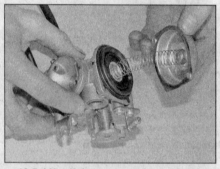

10.5 Lift off the cover and remove the spring

10.6 Note location of diaphragm tab (arrowed)

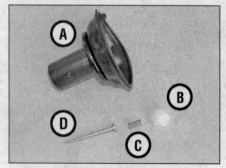

10.7 Carburettor piston (A), needle retainer (B), spring (C) and needle (D)

10.8 Note location of float chamber gasket

10.9a Withdraw the float pin

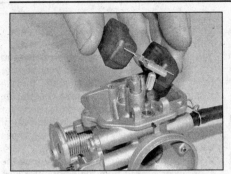

10.9b Lift out the float and needle valve

10.10 Cam (arrowed) on the cable pulley actuates accelerator pump arm

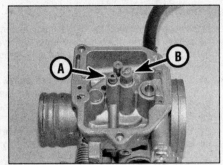

10.11a Idle jet (A), main jet and atomiser (B)

Remove the float and unhook the float needle valve, noting how it fits onto the tab on the float **(see illustration)**.

10 Vivacity 50 and Tweet 50 Keihin carburettors are fitted with an accelerator pump. Undo the screws securing the throttle cable bracket and remove the bracket, noting how the top of the accelerator pump piston locates in the arm on the back of the bracket **(see illustration)**. Remove the bush from the top of the piston and remove the rubber boot, then withdraw the piston and spring from the underside of the carburettor body. The accelerator pump valve is located in the float chamber immediately below the piston. Unscrew the valve and remove the spring and ball.

11 Note the location of the carburettor jets **(see illustration)**. The jets will be marked with an identification number which should correspond with the specifications at the beginning of this Chapter. Unscrew the idle jet carefully to avoid damage. Unscrew the main jet then unscrew the atomiser **(see illustration)**.

12 Where fitted, unscrew the carburettor heater.

13 The mixture screw can be removed if required, but note that its setting will be disturbed (see **Haynes Hint**). Unscrew and remove the screw along with its spring and O-ring, where fitted.

> **HAYNES HINT** *To record the mixture screw's current setting, turn the screw in until it seats lightly, counting the number of turns necessary to achieve this, then unscrew it fully. On installation, turn the screw in until it seats, then back it out the number of turns you've recorded.*

Cleaning

Caution: Use only a petroleum-based solvent for carburettor cleaning. Don't use caustic cleaners.

14 Follow Steps 12 and 13 in Section 8 to clean the carburettor body and jets. If the carburettor has an accelerator pump, pay

particular attention to the fuel passage in the float chamber. **Note:** *Avoid soaking the carburettor body in solvent if any O-ring seals remain inside and remove the gasket and drain screw O-ring from the float chamber.*

Caution: Never clean the jets or passages with a piece of wire or a drill bit, as they will be enlarged, causing the fuel and air metering rates to be upset.

Inspection

15 If removed, check the tapered portion of the mixture screw and the spring for wear or damage. If necessary, renew the screw or spring. If applicable, fit a new O-ring to the pilot screw.

16 Check the carburettor body, float chamber and top cover for cracks, distorted sealing surfaces and other damage. If any defects are found, replace the faulty component, although replacement of the entire carburettor will probably be necessary.

17 Inspect the piston diaphragm for splits, holes and general deterioration. Holding it up to a light will help to reveal problems of this nature. Insert the piston in the carburettor body and check that the piston moves up-and-down smoothly. Check the surface of the piston for wear. If it's worn or scored excessively or doesn't move smoothly, replace the components as necessary.

18 Check the needle for straightness by rolling it on a flat surface such as a piece of glass. Fit a new needle if it's bent or if the tip is worn.

19 Inspect the tip of the float needle valve. If it has grooves or scratches in it, or is in any way worn, it must be renewed. If the valve seat is damaged, check the availability of new parts, otherwise a new carburettor body will have to be fitted. **Note:** *On scooters with a pumped fuel system, a worn valve seat will not be able to shut off the fuel supply sufficiently to prevent carburettor flooding and excessive use of fuel.*

20 Operate the throttle shaft to make sure the throttle butterfly valve opens and closes smoothly. If it doesn't, cleaning the throttle linkage may help. Otherwise, renew the carburettor. **Note:** *Do not remove the screws securing the throttle butterfly to the throttle shaft.*

21 Check the float for damage. This will usually be apparent by the presence of fuel inside the float. If the float is damaged, it must be renewed.

22 Inspect the automatic choke unit plunger and needle for signs of wear and renew the unit if necessary. To check the operation of the choke unit see Section 5.

23 Inspect the accelerator pump components for wear and general deterioration. Ensure that the springs and the rubber boot are not damaged or deformed and renew them if necessary. Check the operation of the accelerator pump lever **(see illustration)**.

24 Inspect the richening diaphragm for splits, holes and general deterioration. Ensure that the spring and the O-ring are not damaged or deformed and renew them if necessary.

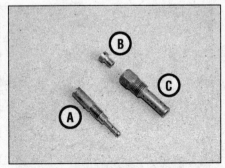

10.11b Idle jet (A), main jet (B) and atomiser (C)

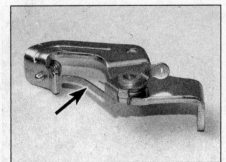

10.23 Check the operation of the accelerator pump lever (arrowed)

Reassembly

Note: *When reassembling the carburettor, be sure to use new O-rings and seals. Do not overtighten the carburettor jets and screws as they are easily damaged*.

25 If removed, install the mixture screw, spring and O-ring; adjust the screw to the setting as noted on removal (see Step 13).

26 If removed, install the carburettor heater.

27 Install the atomiser, then install the main jet **(see illustration 10.11a)**. Install the pilot jet.

28 On Vivacity 50 and Tweet 50 models, install the accelerator pump mechanism in the reverse order of removal. Ensure that the rubber boot and bush are correctly installed on the piston, then fit the throttle cable bracket. Ensure that the arm on the back of the bracket engages with the top of the piston. Ensure that the piston operates smoothly. Fit the ball and spring into the float chamber and install the pump valve.

29 Hook the float needle valve onto the float tab, then position the float assembly in the carburettor, making sure the needle valve enters its seat **(see illustration 10.9b)**. Install the pin, making sure it is located centrally between the supports.

30 Fit the gasket onto the float chamber, making sure it is seated properly in its groove. Install the float chamber onto the carburettor and tighten the screws securely **(see illustrations 10.8)**. Ensure that the O-ring is fitted on the drain screw and tighten the screw securely.

31 Insert the needle, spring and needle retainer into the piston **(see illustration 10.7)**.

32 Insert the piston assembly into the carburettor body and push it down lightly, ensuring the needle is correctly aligned with the atomiser **(see illustration 10.6)**. Align the tab on the diaphragm with the recess in the carburettor body, then press the diaphragm outer edge into its groove, making sure it is correctly seated. Check the diaphragm is not creased, and that the piston moves smoothly up and down in its bore.

33 Install the spring into the piston and fit the top cover to the carburettor, making sure the spring locates over the raised section on the inside of the cover, then tighten the cover screws securely **(see illustration 10.5)**.

34 On carburettors with a richening diaphragm, install the diaphragm and spring, then fit the cover and tighten the screws securely **(see illustrations 10.4b and a)**. On Vivacity 50 and Tweet 50 models, don't forget to fit the passage O-ring **(see illustration 10.4d)**.

35 Fit the gasket onto the choke holder and install the holder **(see illustration 10.3)**.

36 Install the automatic choke unit and secure it with its retaining plate (see Step 2). Install the choke unit cover.

37 Install the carburettor (see Section 6).

11 Throttle cable and twistgrip

 Warning: Refer to the precautions given in Section 1 before proceeding.

Two-stroke engine

Removal

1 Remove the storage compartment and any body panels as required on your scooter to access the carburettor and the throttle twistgrip on the handlebar (see Chapter 9). Note that the cable run between the handlebar and the carburettor may require removal of the front panel or belly panel for access to ties securing the cable (see **Haynes Hint**).

2 Remove the carburettor top and draw the slide assembly out from the carburettor (see Section 6).

3 Detach the throttle slide assembly from the cable (see Section 8).

4 Ensure the cable is free from any clips or ties.

5 Pull back the rubber boot on the cable adjuster at the twistgrip end. Loosen the adjuster locknut and thread the adjuster fully in to slacken the cable **(see illustration)**.

6 Undo the twistgrip housing screws and separate the two halves of the housing **(see illustration)**. Lift off the rear half of the housing, noting the location of the switch gear.

7 Detach the inner cable end from the twistgrip pulley **(see illustration)**.

8 Note how the peg on the outside edge of the front half of the twistgrip housing locates in the hole in the handlebar **(see illustration)**.

9 Note how the cable elbow locates inside the twistgrip housing, then draw the cable out of the housing **(see illustration)**.

10 If required, undo the screw securing the bar end, then slide the twistgrip off the handlebar **(see illustration)**.

11.5 Cable adjuster locknut (arrowed)

11.6 Undo the twistgrip housing screws

11.7 Detach the inner cable end from the twistgrip pulley

11.8 Note how the peg (A) locates in the hole (B)

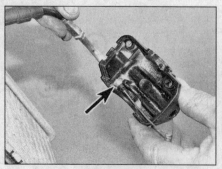

11.9 Note how the inner end of the cable elbow locates

11.10 Screw (arrowed) secures bar end

11.14 Note routing of the throttle cable (arrowed)

11.15 Release the cable from the bracket and the throttle pulley (arrowed)

11 Withdraw the throttle cable from the machine, noting the correct routing.

Installation

12 Installation is the reverse of removal, noting the following:
- Lubricate the upper end of the cable with grease before fitting it into the twistgrip.
- Locate the peg on the twistgrip housing with the hole in the handlebar.
- Ensure the cable is correctly routed and clipped into place – it must not interfere with any other component and should not be kinked or bent sharply.
- Adjust the cable freeplay (see Chapter 1).

11.16 Free the cable from any guides

- Check the cable operation before riding the scooter.

Four-stroke engine
Removal

13 Remove the storage compartment and any body panels as required on your scooter to access the carburettor and the throttle twistgrip on the handlebar (see Chapter 9). Note that the cable run between the handlebar and the carburettor may require removal of the front panel or belly panel for access to ties securing the cable (see *Haynes Hint*).
14 Note the routing of the cable inside the engine compartment **(see illustration)**.
15 Undo the locknut securing the lower end of the throttle cable to the bracket on the carburettor and release the cable from the bracket, then detach the inner cable end from the pulley **(see illustration)**.
16 Ensure the cable is free from any clips or ties **(see illustration)**.
17 Follow the procedure in Steps 5 to 9 to disconnect the cable from the twistgrip.
18 Withdraw the throttle cable from the machine, noting the correct routing.

Installation

19 Installation is the reverse of removal (see Step 12).

12.2 Location of the fuel pump. Note vacuum hose (arrowed)

12 Fuel pump

> **Warning: Refer to the precautions given in Section 1 before proceeding.**

1 On all Speedfight models and Vivacity 50 models, the fuel tank is located underneath the floor panel and fuel has to be pumped up to the carburettor.
2 The fuel pump is mounted on the frame adjacent to the fuel tank **(see illustration)**. Remove the body panels as required on your scooter to access the pump (see Chapter 9).
3 A vacuum hose connects the engine to the pump – when the engine is running, the alternating vacuum and pressure in the crankcase opens and closes the diaphragm in the pump, sucking fuel from the tank, via an in-line filter, and pumping it to the carburettor.
4 The most likely cause of pump failure will be a split in the pump diaphragm.

Check

5 To check whether the pump is operating, release the clip securing the fuel supply hose to the carburettor and detach the hose **(see illustration 6.3 or 6.14)**. Place the open end of the hose in a container suitable for storing petrol. Turn the engine over on the starter motor and check whether fuel flows from the hose into the container. If fuel flows, the pump is working correctly.
6 If no fuel flows from the pump, first check that this is not due to a blocked filter or fuel hose, or due to a split in the vacuum hose. Check all the hoses for splits, cracks and kinks, and check that they are securely connected on each end and that the hose clips are not sprained or corroded. Check that any air vent for the fuel tank is not blocked. If the filter and hoses are good, renew the pump.

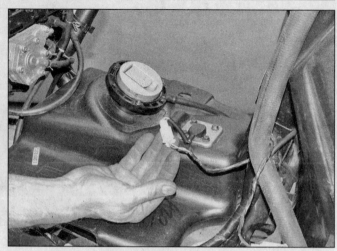

12.7 Fuel hose from tank (A). Hose to carburettor (B)

13.2 Disconnect the fuel level sensor wiring connector

Renewal

7 Release the clips securing the fuel and vacuum hoses and detach them from the pump, noting which fits where **(see illustration)**. Be prepared to catch any residual fuel in a suitable container. The fuel hoses should be clamped to prevent fuel leaks using any of the methods shown in *Tools and Workshop Tips* in the *Reference* section.

8 Undo the pump mounting bracket bolt and remove the pump.

9 Install the new pump, making sure the hoses are correctly attached and secured with the clips. Follow the procedure in Step 5 to ensure the fuel system is primed ready for use.

13 Fuel gauge and level sensor

 Warning: Petrol (gasoline) is extremely flammable, so take extra precautions when you work on any part of the fuel system. Don't smoke or allow open flames or bare light bulbs near the work area, and don't work in a garage where a natural gas-type appliance is present. If you spill any fuel on your skin, rinse it off immediately with soap and water. When you perform any kind of work on the fuel system, wear safety glasses and have a fire extinguisher suitable for a class B type fire (flammable liquids) on hand.

Fuel gauge

1 Remove any body panels as required for access to the top of the fuel tank (see Chapter 9).

2 Trace the wiring from the top of the fuel level sensor to the connector and disconnect it **(see illustration)**.

3 Connect a jumper wire between the terminals on the wiring loom side of the connector. With the ignition switched ON, the fuel gauge should read FULL. If it doesn't, check the wiring between the connector and the gauge. If the wiring is good, then the gauge is confirmed faulty and a new instrument cluster will have to be fitted (see Chapter 10).

Fuel level sensor

4 Disconnect the wiring connector from the fuel level sensor (see Steps 1 and 2). Remove the sensor from the tank – on some machines the sensor backing plate is retained by four bolts, on others it is retained by a locking ring **(see illustrations)**. Manoeuvre the unit out, noting how it fits **(see illustration)**. Note the location of the seal and fit a new one on reassembly if it is damaged or deformed

 Warning: Block the opening in the tank to prevent the escape of petrol fumes and accidental fuel spillage.

5 Check the operation of the sensor – the arm should move freely without binding **(see illustration)**. Also check that the float is held securely on the arm and that it is not damaged. This will usually be apparent by the presence of fuel inside the float. If any of the component parts are faulty or damaged, fit a new sensor.

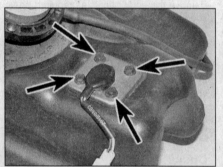

13.4a Backing plate retained by bolts

13.4b Backing plate retained by locking ring

13.4c Remove the sensor carefully to avoid damage

13.5 Check the operation of the sensor arm

6 Check the operation of the sensor using a multimeter set to the ohms scale. Connect the probes to the terminals in the wiring connector with the float UP (tank full), and note the reading, then take a second reading with the float DOWN (tank empty).

7 Compare the results with the specifications at the beginning of this Chapter. If the results are not within the specifications the sensor is faulty and must be renewed.

8 If the sensor is good, check the wiring between the sensor and the gauge.

9 Check the condition of the sensor seal and fit a new one if it is deformed or perished. Insert the sensor carefully into the tank, then secure it in position.

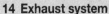

14 Exhaust system

⚠️ *Warning: If the engine has been running the exhaust system will be very hot. Allow the system to cool before carrying out any work.*

Removal

1 Where necessary, remove the storage compartment and any body panels to gain

14.2a Disconnecting a remotely mounted Pulsair valve

full access to the exhaust system and cylinder head (see Chapter 9).

2 On most models the Pulsair system (see Section 15) is connected to the exhaust system via a hose. Loosen the clip securing the hose and disconnect it **(see illustrations)**.

3 Undo the nuts securing the downpipe to the

HAYNES HINT *Exhaust system fixings tend to become corroded and seized. It is advisable to spray them with penetrating oil before attempting to loosen them.*

14.2b Disconnecting the hose from an exhaust mounted Pulsair valve

exhaust port and displace the pipe flange **(see illustrations)**.

4 Where a rear hugger is fitted, it may be supported by the exhaust silencer **(see illustration)**. Undo the mounting bolt noting the location of any insulating washers. On others, the hugger partially covers the mounting bracket **(see illustration)**. Remove the hugger for access (see Chapter 9).

5 Loosen the bolts securing the silencer bracket, then support the exhaust system and remove the bolts **(see illustration)**. Lower the downpipe clear of the frame and bodywork, then lift the complete exhaust system off the

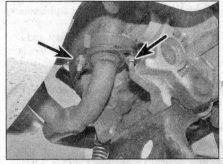

14.3a Undo the nuts (arrowed)...

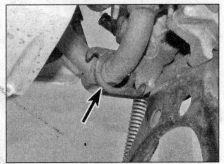

14.3b ...and displace the flange

14.4a Rear hugger mounting bolt (arrowed)

14.4b Hugger covers upper exhaust mounting bracket – Speedfight shown

14.5a Remove the mounting bolts (arrowed)

14.5b Manoeuvre the exhaust system off

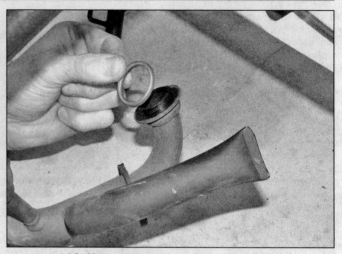

14.6 Always use a new gasket on installation

scooter **(see illustration)**. Note: *Handle the exhaust system with care. If it is dropped the internal catalytic converter could be damaged.*
6 Remove the exhaust port-to-pipe gasket and discard it as a new one must be used **(see illustration)**.
7 Examine the exhaust system and mounting bracket for splits and cracks, especially around welds and mounting holes.

Installation

8 Installation is the reverse of removal, noting the following:
● Clean the exhaust port studs and lubricate them with a suitable copper-based grease before reassembly.
● Clean the jointing surfaces of the exhaust port and the pipe.
● Use a new port-to-pipe gasket.
● Smear the port gasket with grease to hold it in place while fitting the exhaust system.
● Leave all fixings finger-tight until the system

has been installed and correctly aligned, then tighten the exhaust port nuts first.
● Run the engine and check that there are no exhaust gas leaks.

15 Pulsair system

⚠ **Warning: If the engine has been running the exhaust system will be very hot. Allow the system to cool before carrying out any work.**
1 The Pulsair system sucks fresh air into the exhaust pipe via a reed valve to promote the burning of unburnt gases. This reduces the emission of hydrocarbons and raises the temperature inside the exhaust so that the catalytic converter works at optimum efficiency.
2 On most models the Pulsair system is

sealed and requires no maintenance other than inspection of the air filters and hoses for damage or deterioration. Note that on some models the system draws air from the engine air filter housing.
3 On Speedfight 125 and Tweet 125/150 models the system differs in that the reed valve is located in the engine valve cover and can be removed for inspection and cleaning (see Steps 11 to 15).
4 Remove the storage compartment and any body panels to access the Pulsair system (see Chapter 9).
5 On some scooters the reed valve is mounted directly onto the exhaust system **(see illustration)**. On others the valve is connected to the exhaust via a hose – release the clip and disconnect the hose **(see illustrations 14.2)**, then unclip the valve from its mounting and remove the valve and filter assembly **(see illustration)**.

15.5a Location of the Pulsair reed valve – Kisbee 100

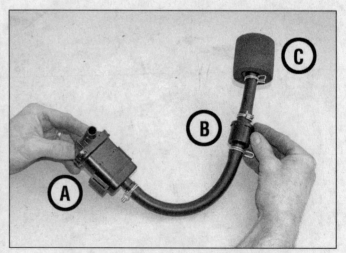

15.5b Pulsair valve (A), filter (B) and pre-filter (C)

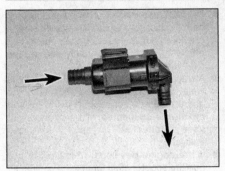

15.6 Valve operation check

15.7 Pulsair hose connection to junction box (arrowed)

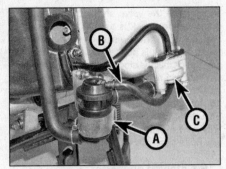

15.8 Pulsair valve (A), vacuum hose (B) and reed valve housing (C)

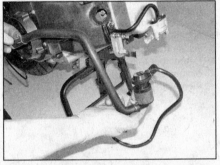

15.9 Remove the Pulsair valve assembly

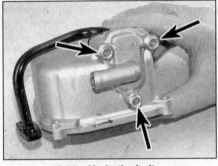

15.11a Undo the bolts...

15.11b ...and remove the reed valve cover

6 Operation of the sealed valve can be checked by blowing air into the inlet (air filter) side – the valve should open and the air should come out the outlet side **(see illustration)**. Air blown into the outlet side of the valve should close the valve.

7 On Speedfight 125 and Tweet 125/150 models, note how the Pulsair system is connected to the junction box at the back of the engine air filter housing **(see illustration)**. Disconnect the long hose from the junction box and release the hose from the guide on the engine cowling.

8 Note the location of the hoses connected

to the Pulsair valve **(see illustration)**. Disconnect the vacuum hose from the engine intake manifold and disconnect the short hose between the Pulsair valve and the reed valve housing on the engine valve cover.

9 Ease the Pulsair valve off its mounting bracket **(see illustration)**.

10 The Pulsair valve is a non-service item – if it appears to be damaged or any of the hoses are deteriorated they should be renewed.

11 To inspect the reed valve, first undo the bolts securing the cover and lift it off **(see illustrations)**.

12 Lift out the reed valve noting which way round it fits **(see illustration)**.

13 Check the reed for cracks, distortion and any other damage. Check also that there are no dirt particles trapped between the reed and its seat. The reed should sit flat against the valve body so that a good seal is obtained against back pressure in the exhaust manifold **(see illustration)**. If required, clean the reed carefully with a suitable solvent to remove any gum.

14 After prolonged use, the reed may become bent and will not therefore seal properly, in

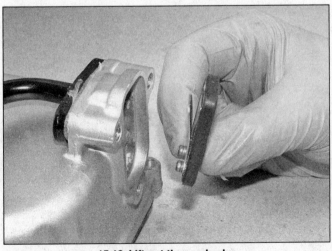

15.12 Lift out the reed valve

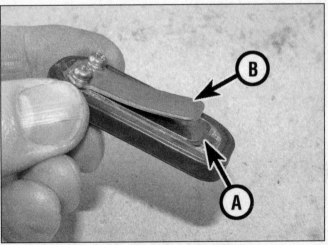

15.13 Reed (A) and stopper plate (B)

which case the valve should be renewed. A good way to check is to hold the valve up to the light – if light is visible between the reed and the body it is not sealing properly.

15 Check that the stopper plate retaining screws are tight; do not disassemble the reed valve as individual components are not available.

16 Installation is the reverse of removal. Ensure that the reed valve is fitted the correct way round **(see illustration 15.12)**. Renew any hose clips that are sprained or corroded.

16 Catalytic converter

General information

1 A catalytic converter is incorporated in the exhaust system to minimise the level of exhaust pollutants released into the atmosphere.

2 The catalytic converter consists of a canister containing a fine mesh impregnated with a catalyst material, over which the hot exhaust gases pass. The catalyst speeds up the oxidation of harmful carbon monoxide, unburned hydrocarbons and soot, effectively reducing the quantity of harmful products released into the atmosphere via the exhaust gases.

Precautions

3 To prolong the lift of the catalytic converter and to minimise carbon build-up inside the exhaust system, owners are advised to avoid running the engine continuously at low rpm over long periods. Equally important is warming the engine up to operating temperature quickly after a cold start.

4 The catalytic converter is a reliable and simple device which requires no maintenance. However, the following points should be noted:

- DO NOT use leaded or lead replacement petrol (gasoline) – the additives will coat the precious metals, reducing their converting efficiency and will eventually destroy the catalytic converter.
- Always keep the ignition and fuel systems well-maintained in accordance with the manufacturer's schedule – if the fuel/air mixture is suspected of being incorrect have it checked on an exhaust gas analyser.
- If the engine develops a misfire, do not ride the scooter at all (or at least as little as possible) until the fault is cured.
- DO NOT use fuel or engine oil additives – these may contain substances harmful to the catalytic converter.
- DO NOT continue to use the scooter if the engine burns oil to the extent of leaving a visible trail of smoke.
- Remember that the catalytic converter and oxygen sensor are FRAGILE – do not strike them with tools during servicing work.

Chapter 6
Ignition system

Contents

Degrees of difficulty

Easy, suitable for novice with little experience	**Fairly easy,** suitable for beginner with some experience	**Fairly difficult,** suitable for competent DIY mechanic	**Difficult,** suitable for experienced DIY mechanic	**Very difficult,** suitable for expert DIY or professional

Specifications

Spark plug
Plug type . . . .   see Chapter 1
Cap resistance . . . .   approx. 5 K-ohms

Pulse generator coil resistance
Speedfight 125. . . . .   130 to 160 ohms
Vivacity 50 4T and Tweet 50. . . . .   92 to 138 ohms
Vivacity 125, Kisbee and Tweet 125/150 . . . .   116 to 174 ohms

Alternator ignition source coil resistance
Vivacity 125 . . . .   400 to 600 ohms
Kisbee . . . .   517 ohms
Tweet 125/150 . . . .   480 to 720 ohms

Ignition coil
Speedfight 125
  Primary winding resistance . . . .   0.60 to 0.66 ohm
  Secondary winding resistance . . . .   2.4 to 3.6 K-ohms
Vivacity 50 4T, Tweet models
  Primary winding resistance . . . .   0.16 to 0.24 ohm
  Secondary winding resistance . . . .   4.0 to 6.0 K-ohms
Vivacity 125 and Kisbee models
  Primary winding resistance . . . .   0.4 to 0.6 ohm
  Secondary winding resistance . . . .   2.96 to 4.44 K-ohms

1 General information

All scooters covered by this manual are fitted with a fully transistorised electronic capacitor discharge ignition system known commonly as CDI. The system comprises the alternator ignition source coil, ignition trigger, pulse generator coil, CDI unit, ignition coil and spark plug. Due to its lack of mechanical parts, the system is totally maintenance-free.

On two-stroke models, the system differs slightly in that the CDI unit incorporates the oil pump control unit. Refer to Chapter 10 and to *Wiring diagrams* for further details.

The ignition trigger, which is on the outside surface of the alternator rotor, activates the pulse generator coil as the crankshaft rotates, sending a signal to the CDI unit which in turn supplies the ignition coil with the power necessary to produce a spark at the plug. The ignition source coil produces the power for the ignition system when the engine is running, and on most machines the battery provides the power for initial starting.

The CDI unit incorporates an electronic advance system controlled by signals from the pulse generator coil. This varies the timing of the ignition spark depending on engine speed. There is no provision for adjusting the ignition timing.

Depending upon the model specification, most ignition systems incorporate a safety circuit which prevents the engine from being started unless one of the brake levers is pulled in and/or the sidestand is up (refer to your scooter handbook or wiring diagram for details). On Tweet models, a circuit breaker switch inside the storage compartment enables the ignition system to be isolated.

Due to their lack of mechanical parts, the components of the ignition system are totally maintenance-free. If ignition system troubles occur, and the faulty component can be isolated by a series of checks, the only cure is to replace it with a new one. Keep in mind that most electrical parts, once purchased, cannot be returned. To avoid unnecessary expense, make sure the faulty component has been positively identified before buying a replacement.

2 Ignition system – check

⚠ Warning: The energy levels in electronic systems can be very high. On no account should the ignition be switched on whilst the plug or plug cap is being held – shocks from the HT circuit can be most unpleasant. Secondly, it is vital that the engine is not turned over with the plug cap removed, and that the plug is soundly earthed when the system is checked for sparking. The ignition system components can be seriously damaged if the HT circuit becomes isolated.

1 As no means of adjustment is available, any failure of the system can be traced to failure of a system component or a simple wiring fault. Of the two possibilities, the latter is by far the most likely. In the event of failure, check the system in a logical fashion, as described below.

2 Disconnect the HT lead from the spark plug. Connect the lead to a new plug of the correct specification and lay the plug on the engine with the thread earthed **(see illustration)**. If necessary, hold the spark plug with an insulated tool.

⚠ Warning: Do not remove the spark plug from the engine to perform this check – atomised fuel being pumped out of the open spark plug hole could ignite, causing severe injury!

3 Having observed the above precautions, turn the ignition switch ON and turn the engine over on the starter motor. If the system is in good condition a regular, fat blue spark should be evident between the plug electrodes. If the spark appears thin or yellowish, or is non-existent, further investigation will be necessary. Before proceeding further, turn the ignition OFF.

Caution: Some ignition systems are designed for the combined resistance of the spark plug and spark plug cap. To avoid the risk of damaging the CDI unit, a spark testing tool should not be used.

4 Ignition faults can be divided into two categories, namely those where the ignition system has failed completely and those which are due to a partial failure. The likely faults are listed below, starting with the most probable source of failure. Work through the list systematically, referring to the subsequent sections for full details of the necessary checks and tests. **Note:** *Before checking the following items ensure that the battery is fully charged and that the fuse is in good condition.*

● Loose, corroded or damaged wiring connections, broken or shorted wiring between any of the component parts of the ignition system (see the appropriate wiring diagram at the end of Chapter 10).
● Faulty spark plug with dirty, worn or corroded plug electrodes, or incorrect gap between electrodes (see Chapter 1)
● Faulty HT lead or spark plug cap
● Faulty ignition coil
● Faulty ignition switch (see Chapter 10)
● Faulty ignition source coil
● Faulty pulse generator coil
● Faulty CDI unit

5 If the above checks don't reveal the cause of the problem, have the ignition system tested by a Peugeot dealer.

3 Ignition coil and spark plug cap

Check

1 Disconnect the battery negative (-ve) lead (see Chapter 10).
2 Follow the procedure in Chapter 1 and remove the storage compartment and any associated body panels to access the spark plug. Trace the HT lead back from the plug cap to the ignition coil **(see illustration)**.

2.2 Earth the spark plug thread on the engine

3.2 Location of the ignition coil – Kisbee 100

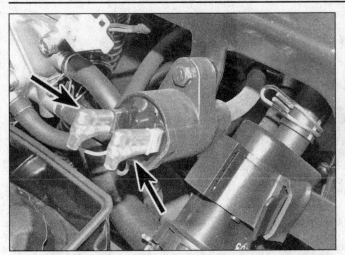

3.5a Disconnect the primary circuit wiring connectors (arrowed)

3.5b Ignition coil primary winding check

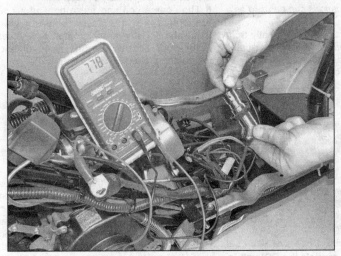

3.6 Ignition coil secondary winding check

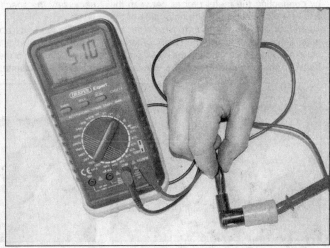

3.8 Measuring the resistance of the spark plug cap

3 Pull the spark plug cap off the plug and inspect the cap, HT lead and coil for cracks and other damage.

4 The condition of the coil primary and secondary windings can be checked with a multimeter. **Note:** *Test data is not available for all models but where necessary the specifications at the beginning of this Chapter can be used as a guide. If the results are outside the specified range, the only way to determine conclusively that the ignition coil is defective is to substitute it with a known good one. If the fault is rectified, the original unit is faulty.*

5 Note the position of the primary circuit wiring connectors, then disconnect them noting where they fit **(see illustration)**. Set the multimeter to the appropriate ohms scale and connect the meter probes to the primary circuit wiring terminals **(see illustration)**. This will give a resistance reading for the coil primary windings which should be consistent with the *Specifications*. If the reading is outside the specified range, it is likely the coil is defective.

6 Next set the multimeter to the K-ohms scale. Refer to the appropriate wiring diagram at the end of Chapter 10 and connect the meter probes to the earth primary circuit wiring terminal and the spark plug terminal inside the plug cap **(see illustration)**. This will give a resistance reading for the coil secondary windings. If the reading is not within the specified range, unscrew the plug cap from the HT lead and connect the probes to the earth primary circuit wiring terminal and the core of the lead. If the reading is now as specified, the plug cap is suspect. If the reading is still outside the specified range, it is likely that the coil is defective.

7 Should any of the above checks not produce the expected result, have your findings confirmed by a Peugeot dealer wherever possible. If the coil is confirmed to be faulty, it must be renewed – the coil is a sealed unit and cannot be repaired.

8 To check the condition of the spark plug cap, set the multimeter to the appropriate ohms scale and connect the meter probes to the HT lead and plug terminals inside the

cap **(see illustration)**. If the reading is outside the specified range, the cap is defective and a new one must be fitted. **Note:** *In many cases, the resistance rating of the cap, such as 5 K-ohms, will be marked on the outside. If the reading is as specified, the cap connection may have been faulty. Remake the connection between the cap and the HT lead and check the resistance reading for the coil secondary windings again (see Step 6).*

Removal and installation

9 Disconnect the battery negative (-ve) lead (see Chapter 10).

10 Remove any body panels as required for access (see Step 2).

11 Note the position of the primary circuit wiring connectors and then disconnect them **(see illustration 3.5a)**. Disconnect the HT lead from the spark plug.

12 Undo the bolt securing the coil to the frame and remove it.

13 Installation is the reverse of removal. Make sure the wiring connectors and HT lead are securely connected.

4 Source coil and pulse generator coil

1 To check the condition of the ignition source coil and the pulse generator coil it is first necessary to identify the wiring for the individual components. Remove the storage compartment (see Chapter 9) for access and disconnect the battery negative (-ve) lead (see Chapter 10).

2 Trace the source coil (part of the alternator stator) and pulse generator coil wiring from the back of the engine cowling or water pump according to your scooter and disconnect it at the connectors **(see illustration)**. Use your scooter's wiring diagram (at the back of Chapter 10) to identify the appropriate wires.

3 Using a multimeter set to the appropriate ohms scale, measure the source coil resistance by connecting the meter probes between the coil wire terminal on the alternator side of the connector and earth (ground). Now reset the multimeter and measure the pulse generator coil resistance by connecting the meter probes between the pulse generator wire terminal on

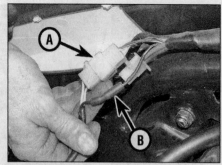

4.2 Ignition source coil (A) and pulse generator coil (B) connectors

the alternator side of the connector and earth (ground).

4 Compare the results with the specifications at the beginning of this Chapter. **Note:** *Test data is not available for all models but where necessary the specifications can be used as a guide.*

5 If the readings obtained differ greatly from those given, particularly if the meter indicates a short circuit (no measurable resistance) or an open circuit (infinite, or very high resistance),

4.6 Pulse generator coil (arrowed) and alternator stator assembly

the alternator stator and pulse generator coil assembly must be renewed. However, first check that the fault is not due to a damaged or broken wire from the coil to the connector; pinched or broken wires can usually be repaired.

6 The source coil and pulse generator coil are integral with the alternator stator **(see illustration)**. Refer to the appropriate Chapter 2 for your scooter for the removal and installation procedure.

5 CDI unit

Check

1 If the tests shown in the preceding sections have failed to isolate the cause of an ignition fault, it is possible that the CDI unit itself is faulty. In order to determine conclusively that the unit is defective, it should be substituted with a known good one. If the fault is rectified, the original unit is faulty. **Note:** *The CDI unit will be damaged if a non-resistor type spark plug or spark plug cap are fitted. When fitting a new CDI unit, always ensure the spark plug and cap are of the correct specification before starting the engine.*

Removal and installation

2 Disconnect the battery negative (-ve) lead (see Chapter 10).

3 The location of the CDI unit varies from model to model **(see illustrations)**. Refer to Chapter 9 and remove any body panels as necessary to access the unit.

4 If applicable, unclip the CDI unit from its holder, then release the catch on the wiring connector and disconnect it.

5 Installation is the reverse of removal. Make sure the wiring connector is correctly and securely connected.

5.3a On V-Clic and Tweet models, lift the ignition unit out from the battery compartment

5.3b On Speedfight models the CDI unit is underneath the oil tank at the rear

5.3c On Vivacity models the CDI unit is behind the seat cowling on the right-hand side

5.3d On Kisbee models the CDI unit is inside the seat cowling on the right-hand side

Chapter 7
Frame and suspension

Contents

Degrees of difficulty

Easy, suitable for novice with little experience	**Fairly easy,** suitable for beginner with some experience	**Fairly difficult,** suitable for competent DIY mechanic	**Difficult,** suitable for experienced DIY mechanic	**Very difficult,** suitable for expert DIY or professional

Specifications

Front forks

Fork oil type	SAE 10W fork oil
Fork oil capacity	
V-Clic	87 cc each leg
Vivacity 50	85 cc each leg
Vivacity 125	85 cc each leg
Kisbee 50	35 cc each leg
Kisbee 100	43 cc each leg
Tweet 50 and 125	100 cc each leg

Torque settings

V-Clic	
Engine mounting bracket	
Bracket-to-engine bolt	80 Nm
Bracket-to-frame bolt	98 Nm
Rear shock absorber mounting bolts	29 Nm
Steering stem adjustment	Hand tighten
Steering stem locknut	30 Nm
Kisbee	
Engine mounting bracket	
Bracket-to-engine bolt	52 to 62 Nm
Bracket-to-frame bolt	52 to 62 Nm
Rear shock absorber mounting bolts	
Upper	43 to 50 Nm
Lower	20 to 25 Nm
Front fork clamp bolt	30 to 40 Nm
Front fork damper bolt	25 to 30 Nm
Fork leg top bolt	18 to 20 Nm
Handlebar stem bolt	35 to 45 Nm
Steering stem adjuster nut	
Initial torque	38 to 42 Nm
Final torque	15 to 19 Nm
Steering stem middle nut	Hand tighten
Steering stem locknut	70 to 80 Nm

Torque settings (continued)

Speedfight 50

Engine mounting bracket
- Bracket-to-engine bolt .... 60 Nm
- Bracket-to-frame bolt .... 60 Nm

Rear shock absorber mounting bolts
- Upper .... 45 Nm
- Lower .... 22 Nm

Front fork stanchion bolt .... 25 Nm

Handlebar stem bolt .... 40 Nm

Steering stem adjuster nut
- Initial torque .... 40 Nm
- Final torque .... 17 Nm

Steering stem middle nut .... Hand tighten

Steering stem locknut .... 70 Nm

Vivacity 50

Engine mounting bracket
- Bracket-to-engine bolt .... 60 Nm
- Bracket-to-frame bolt .... 60 Nm

Rear shock absorber mounting bolts
- Upper .... 45 Nm
- Lower .... 22 Nm

Handlebar stem bolt .... 25 Nm

Steering stem adjuster nut
- Initial torque .... 40 Nm
- Final torque .... 23 Nm

Steering stem middle nut .... Hand tighten

Steering stem locknut .... 70 Nm

Tweet models

Engine mounting bracket
- Bracket-to-engine bolt – 50 cc .... 60 Nm
- Bracket-to-engine bolt – 125/150 cc .... 70 Nm
- Bracket-to-frame bolt .... 50 Nm

Rear shock absorber mounting bolts
- Upper .... 40 Nm
- Lower .... 28 Nm

Front fork clamp bolt .... 28 Nm

Front fork damper bolt .... 25 Nm

Handlebar stem bolt .... 45 Nm

Steering stem adjustment .... 2/8 to 3/8 turn

Steering stem locknut .... 20 Nm

Vivacity 125

Engine mounting bracket
- Bracket-to-engine bolt .... 64 Nm
- Bracket-to-frame bolt .... 47 Nm

Rear shock absorber mounting bolts
- Upper .... 46 Nm
- Lower .... 23 Nm

Front fork clamp bolt .... 20 to 25 Nm

Front fork damper bolt .... 25 Nm

Fork leg top bolt .... 18 to 20 Nm

Handlebar stem bolt .... 40 Nm

Steering stem adjuster nut
- Initial torque .... 40 Nm
- Final torque .... 23 Nm

Steering stem middle nut .... 17 Nm

Steering stem locknut .... 75 Nm

Speedfight 125

Engine mounting bracket-to-engine bolt .... 48 to 52 Nm

Rear shock absorber mounting bolts
- Upper .... 43 to 50 Nm
- Lower .... 20 to 25 Nm

Steering stem locknut .... 70 to 80 Nm

1 General information

All scooters covered by this manual are fitted with a tubular and pressed steel one-piece frame.

The engine/transmission unit is linked to the frame by a bracket that acts as a pivoting suspension arm at the front, and by the shock absorber(s) at the rear, making the unit an integral part of the rear suspension.

Front suspension is by conventional telescopic forks or 'upside-down' telescopic forks.

Ancillary items such as stands and handlebars are covered in this Chapter.

2 Frame

1 The frame should not require attention unless accident damage has occurred. In most cases, frame renewal is the only satisfactory remedy for such damage. A few frame specialists have the jigs and other equipment necessary for straightening the frame to the required standard of accuracy, but even then there is no simple way of assessing to what extent the frame may have been over-stressed.

2 After a high mileage, the frame should be examined closely for signs of cracking or splitting at the welded joints. Loose engine mount and suspension bolts can cause ovaling or fracturing of the mounting points. Minor damage can often be repaired by specialist welding, depending on the extent and nature of the damage.

3 Remember that a frame which is out of alignment will cause handling problems. If misalignment is suspected as the result of an accident, it will be necessary to strip the machine completely so the frame can be thoroughly checked.

3 Stands

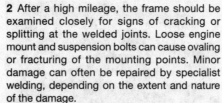

Centrestand

1 Support the scooter securely in an upright position using an auxiliary stand. **Note:** *Do not rest the weight of the machine on the bodywork – if necessary, remove the belly panel to expose the frame (see Chapter 9).*

2 The centrestand is fixed directly to the underside of the engine cases.

3 The stand is held in position by one or two springs – take great care when removing the springs as they are under considerable tension **(see illustrations). Note:** *On some scooters,*

the single spring can be left in position and removed with the stand (see Step 5).

4 Remove the split pin and washer securing the pivot pin, then withdraw the pivot pin **(see illustrations).**

5 Ease the stand off – if the spring is still attached, unhook it from the lug on the crankcase. Note that on some models, pivot bushes are fitted inside the mounting lugs **(see illustration).**

6 Thoroughly clean the stand and remove all road dirt and old grease. Inspect the pivot pin, pivot bushes and the pivot holes in the bracket for wear and renew them if necessary **(see illustration).** Inspect the spring; if it is sagged or is cracked a new spring must be fitted. If fitted, inspect the rubber stop on the stand and renew it if it is worn or perished.

7 Installation is the reverse of removal, noting the following:
● Apply grease to the pivot pin and all pivot points.
● Secure the pivot pin with a new split pin.
● Ensure that the spring holds the stand up securely when it is not in use – an accident is almost certain to occur if the stand extends while the machine is in motion. If necessary, fit a new spring.

Sidestand

8 Support the scooter on its main stand.

9 If necessary, remove the belly panel to access the stand pivot bolt (see Chapter 9).

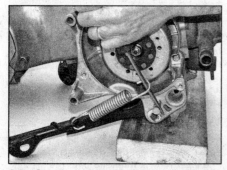

3.3a Stand springs are under considerable tension

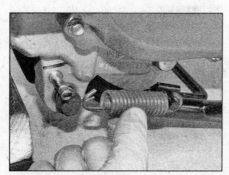

3.3b Note secondary spring inside main spring – Tweet shown

3.4a Remove the split pin and washer (arrowed)

3.4b Support the stand and withdraw the pivot pin

3.5 Centrestand pivot bushes – Tweet 125 shown

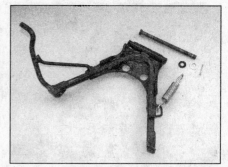

3.6 Inspect the centrestand components for wear and damage

3.10 Location of the sidestand spring

3.11 Location of the sidestand switch

4.4 Disconnect the brake light switch wiring

10 Unhook the stand spring, noting how it fits **(see illustration)**.
11 Unscrew the stand pivot bolt and remove the bolt, washer and stand. Note the location of the stand switch **(see illustration)**.
12 Installation is the reverse of removal, noting the following:
● Apply grease to the pivot bolt.
● Check the spring tension – it must hold the stand up when it is not in use. If necessary, fit a new spring.
● Check the operation of the sidestand switch (see Chapter 10).

4 Handlebars

Removal

1 Remove the mirrors, handlebar covers and any body panels as necessary to access the steering stem (see Chapter 9).
2 In most cases, the handlebars can be displaced from the steering stem for access to the steering head bearings without having to detach any cables, hoses or wiring. If so, ignore the Steps which do not apply. **Note:** *Take great care not to strain any wiring or wiring connectors and make provision to support the handlebars securely once they have been displaced.*
3 On some models, the instrument cluster is mounted directly onto the handlebars. Follow

the procedure in Chapter 10 to disconnect the speedometer cable and wiring connector and remove the instrument cluster.
4 Disconnect the wiring from each brake light switch **(see illustration)**.
5 Remove the throttle twistgrip (see Chapter 5).
6 If the left-hand handlebar switch housing is clamped around the handlebar, undo the screws and displace the housing (see Chapter 10). **Note:** *On some scooters, the switch housing incorporates the rear brake lever bracket (see Chapter 8).*
7 If the rear brake lever bracket is clamped around the handlebar, undo the bolts and displace the lever.
8 Unscrew the front brake (and rear brake where appropriate) master cylinder assembly clamp bolts and position the assembly clear of the handlebar, making sure no strain is placed on the brake hose (see Chapter 8). Keep the master cylinder reservoir upright to prevent air entering the system.
9 Remove the left-hand grip; peel the grip off the end of the bar, or if necessary cut it off.
10 The handlebars are secured by a stem bolt **(see illustration)**. Undo the nut and withdraw the bolt, noting the location of the shaped spacer where fitted **(see illustration)**.
11 Lift the handlebars off the steering stem **(see illustration)**.

Installation

12 Installation is the reverse of removal, noting the following:

● Tighten the handlebar stem bolt securely. Torque settings where available are given in the Specifications at the beginning of this Chapter.
● Use a suitable adhesive to secure the left-hand grip on the handlebar.
● Don't forget to reconnect the brake light switch wiring connectors.
● Check the operation of the brakes and lights before riding the scooter.

5 Steering head bearings – adjustment

1 The steering head bearings should be adjusted whenever freeplay is noted (see Chapter 1).
2 Support the machine on the centrestand with the front wheel raised off the ground. **Note:** *Do not rest the weight of the machine on the bodywork – if necessary, remove the belly panel to expose the frame (see Chapter 9).*
3 Remove the mirrors, handlebar covers and any body panels as necessary to access the steering stem (see Chapter 9).

V-Clic and Tweet

4 The bearings are adjusted by turning the upper bearing inner race on the steering stem. The inner race is threaded onto the steering stem and is held in place by a lock washer and locknut. Hold the inner race and loosen

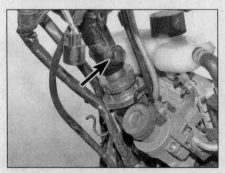

4.10a Handlebar stem bolt (arrowed)

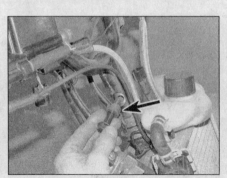

4.10b Note location of the shaped spacer

4.11 Lift off the handlebars

5.4 Loosen the locknut as described

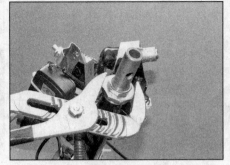

5.5 Adjusting the bearings with slip-joint pliers

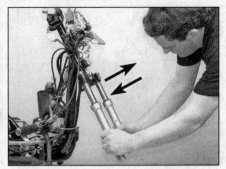

5.6 Checking for front-to-rear movement in the bearings

the locknut using suitable spanners or grips **(see illustration)**.

5 Loosen the inner race slightly to take pressure off the bearing then tighten it until all freeplay is removed **(see illustration)**. On Tweet models, now tighten the inner race a further 2/8 to 3/8 of a turn.

Caution: Take great care not to apply excessive pressure because this will cause premature failure of the bearings.

6 Check that the steering still turns freely from side-to-side with no front-to-rear movement (see Chapter 1, Section 21). The object is to set the adjustment so that the bearings are under a very light loading, just enough to remove any freeplay **(see illustration)**.

7 With the bearings correctly adjusted, hold the inner race to prevent it from moving, then tighten the locknut. A torque setting is specified for the steering stem locknut (see *Specifications* at the beginning of this Chapter), however to apply this a special torque wrench adapter is required. Alternatively a suitable deep socket can be used although this requires the handlebars to be removed (see Section 4).

8 Check the bearing adjustment and re-adjust if necessary, then install the remaining components in the reverse order of removal.

All other models

9 Remove the handlebars (see Section 4).

10 Undo the steering stem locknut – use either a C-spanner or a special tool fabricated

5.11a Remove the locknut...

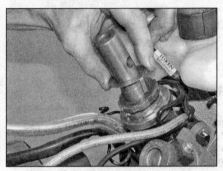

5.11b ...and the lock washer

to fit into the castellations of the nut **(see illustration 5.16)**. Peugeot produces a service tool (Part No. 757860) to do this.

11 Remove the locknut then lift off the lock washer, noting how the tabs fit into the notches in the middle nut and the bearing adjuster nut **(see illustrations)**.

12 Unscrew the middle nut and lift off the rubber washer **(see illustrations)**.

13 Loosen the adjuster nut slightly to take pressure off the bearing then tighten it to the initial torque setting specified at the beginning of this Chapter. Now loosen the adjuster nut and then tighten it to the final specified torque setting. Use the fabricated tool of the service tool to apply the correct torque.

14 Check that the steering still turns freely from side-to-side with no front-to-rear movement (see Chapter 1, Section 21). The object is to set the adjustment so that the

bearings are under a very light loading, just enough to remove any freeplay.

Caution: Take great care not to apply excessive pressure because this will cause premature failure of the bearings.

15 Fit the rubber washer and tighten the middle nut so that the notches in the adjuster nut and middle nut align. On Vivacity 125 models the steering stem middle nut should be tightened to the specified torque. On all other models the middle nut should be hand tightened. Fit the lock washer **(see illustration 5.11b)**.

16 Install the steering stem locknut. Hold the adjuster nut to prevent it turning, then tighten the steering stem locknut to the specified torque setting **(see illustration)**.

17 Check the bearing adjustment and re-adjust if necessary, then install the remaining components in the reverse order of removal.

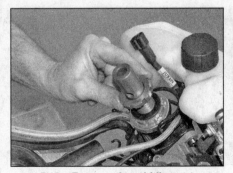

5.12a Remove the middle nut...

5.12b ...and the rubber washer

5.16 Hold the adjuster nut and tighten the locknut with the special tool

6.2 Release the speedometer cable and brake hose

6.5a Unscrew the upper bearing inner race...

6.5b ...and lower the stem out of the steering head

6 Steering stem

Removal

1 Displace the brake caliper and remove the front wheel (see Chapter 8).

2 If the front mudguard or inner mudguard are mounted on the front suspension, remove them (see Chapter 9). Release the front brake hose and speedometer cable from any clips on the front fork yoke (see illustration).

3 Remove the handlebars (see Section 4).

4 Remove the steering stem locknut and bearing adjuster locknut as applicable (see Section 5).

5 On V-Clic and Tweet models, support the steering stem and unscrew the upper bearing inner race (see illustration). Once the race is free, lift it off and carefully lower the stem out of the steering head (see illustration).

6 On all other models, support the steering stem, then unscrew the bearing adjuster nut and remove the dust cover (see illustrations). Carefully lower the stem out of the steering head.

Note: On all models, the ball bearings in the steering head are held in cages. If they are badly worn or damaged the bearings may fall out. Place a rag on the floor beneath the steering head to catch them. These old bearings should not be re-used.

7 The ball bearings in the lower race will remain on the steering stem with the lower inner race (see illustration). The upper bearing will remain in the top of the steering head.

8 If not already done, lift out the upper inner race and bearing (see illustration).

9 Clean the bearings and races with a suitable solvent to remove all traces of old grease and inspect them for wear or damage (see Section 7). Note: Do not attempt to remove the outer races from the steering head or the lower bearing inner race from the steering stem unless they are to be renewed.

Installation

10 Apply a liberal quantity of grease to the bearing inner and outer races and install the upper bearing (see illustration).

11 Assemble the lower race ball bearings on the lower inner race on the steering stem and lubricate them with grease (see illustration).

12 Carefully lift the steering stem up through

6.6a Unscrew the bearing adjuster nut...

6.6b ...and remove the dust cover

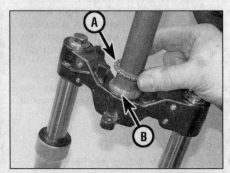

6.7 Lower bearing (A) and lower inner race (B)

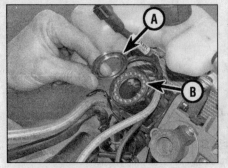

6.8 Upper inner race (A) and upper bearing (B)

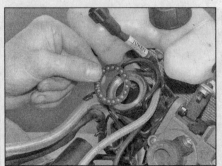

6.10 Install the upper bearing

6.11 Lubricate the lower race bearing

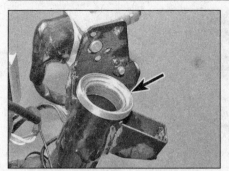

7.3a Inspect the races in the top...

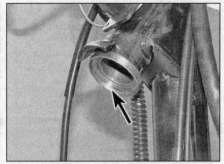

7.3b ...and the bottom of the steering head

7.4 Location of the upper inner race –
V-Clic and Tweet

7.6 Location of the lower inner race

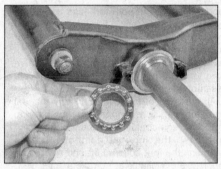

7.7 Examine the ball bearings and the
bearing cage

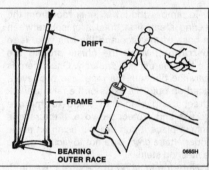

7.9 Drive the outer races out with a brass
drift

the steering head, ensuring the upper race ball bearings remain in place.

13 On V-Clic and Tweet models, thread the upper inner race onto the steering stem until it makes firm contact with the ball bearings.

14 On all other models, slide the upper inner race down the steering stem and press it firmly into the ball bearings. Install the dust cover and the bearing adjuster nut.

15 Follow the procedure in Section 5 to adjust the steering head bearings, then install the remaining components in the reverse order of removal.

7 Steering head bearings – inspection and renewal

Inspection

1 Remove the steering stem (see Section 6).
2 Clean all traces of old grease from the bearings and races and check them for wear or damage.
3 The races should be polished and free from indentations. The outer races are in the steering head (see illustrations).
4 On V-Clic and Tweet models, the upper inner race threads onto the steering stem (see illustration).
5 On all other models, the upper inner race rests on top of the top bearing (see illustration 6.8).
6 The lower inner race is on the steering stem (see illustration).

7 Inspect the ball bearings for signs of wear, pitting or corrosion and examine the bearing cages for cracks or splits (see illustration).
8 If there are any signs of wear or damage on any of the above components both upper and lower bearing assemblies must be replaced as a set. Only remove the races from the steering head and the stem if new ones are to be fitted – do not re-use them once they have been removed.

Renewal

9 The outer races are an interference fit in the steering head and can be tapped from position with a suitable drift (see illustration). Tap firmly and evenly around each race to ensure that it is driven out squarely. It may prove advantageous to curve the end of the drift slightly to improve access.

10 Alternatively, the races can be pulled out using a slide-hammer with internal expanding extractor (see *Tools and Workshop Tips* in the *Reference* section).

11 The new outer races can be pressed into the steering head using a drawbolt arrangement (see illustration). Ensure that the drawbolt washers bear only on the outer edges of the races and do not contact the bearing surface.

> **HAYNES HINT** *Installation of new bearing outer races is made much easier if the races are left overnight in the freezer. This causes them to contract slightly making them a looser fit.*

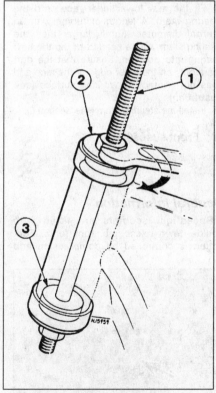

7.11 Use a drawbolt to install the outer
races

1 Long bolt or threaded bar
2 Thick washer
3 Guide for lower race

7.12 Use a chisel to displace the lower inner race

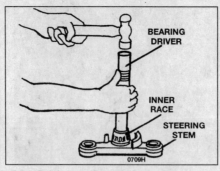

7.14 Driving on the new lower inner race

8.6 Location of the fork top bolt

12 To remove the lower inner race from the steering stem, first drive a chisel between the base of the race and the fork yoke (see illustration). Work the chisel around the race to ensure it lifts squarely. Once there is clearance beneath the race, use two levers placed on opposite sides of the race to work it free, using blocks of wood to improve leverage and protect the yoke. If the race is firmly in place it can be split using an angle grinder – take great care not to nick or gouge the steering stem.

13 Note the location of the dust cover and, on some models, washer fitted below the lower inner race and renew them if they have been damaged when the race was removed.

14 Fit the new lower inner race onto the steering stem. A length of tubing with an internal diameter slightly larger than the steering stem will be needed to tap the new bearing into position. Ensure that the drift bears only on the inner edge of the race and does not contact its working surface (see illustration).

15 Install the steering stem (see Section 6).

8 Front suspension

General information

1 Speedfight scooters are fitted with upside-down telescopic front forks. Fork action is controlled by compression and rebound springs in both fork legs and by an hydraulic damper inside the left-hand leg. If the left-hand fork leg is leaking oil the inner damper cartridge has failed. The internal fork bushes are grease lubricated. Upside-down front forks are normally supplied as complete assemblies.

2 All other scooters covered in this manual are fitted with conventional telescopic forks. Both fork legs contain a quantity of oil which lubricates the internal components and dampens the fork action. Left and right-hand fork legs are available as complete units.

3 Before commencing work always check with a Peugeot dealer as to the availability of new parts. On some scooters, individual parts are not available – if the fork legs are damaged or worn, new leg assemblies will have to be fitted.

Conventional telescopic forks

Removal

4 Displace the brake caliper and remove the front wheel (see Chapter 8).

5 Follow the procedure in Chapter 9 to remove the front mudguard and any body panels as required to access the fork top bolts and clamp bolts (see illustrations 8.6 and 8.7a).

6 Note the position of the fork top bolt (see illustration). On some machines the top bolt is accessible through holes in the inner front mudguard when the forks are turned to full left or right-hand lock. If the fork leg is going to be disassembled or the fork oil is going to be changed, loosen the fork top bolt while the leg is still clamped in the fork yoke. Note that on Tweet models, a plug secured by a circlip is fitted in the top of each fork tube. The plug can be removed once the fork leg is off the machine (see Step 15).

7 Undo and remove the fork clamp bolts (see illustration). Remove the fork leg by twisting it and pulling it downwards (see illustrations).

> **HAYNES HiNT** *If the fork legs are seized in the yokes, spray the area with penetrating oil and allow time for it to soak in before trying again.*

Installation

8 Remove all traces of corrosion from the fork tubes and the yoke. Install each fork leg individually. Slide the leg up through the yoke until the top edge of the fork tube is level with the top edge of the yoke and ensure the location groove for the clamp bolt is correctly aligned (see illustration 8.7c).

9 Install the clamp bolts and tighten them to the torque setting specified at the beginning of this Chapter.

10 If not already done, tighten the top bolt (see Step 6).

11 Install the remaining components in the reverse order of removal. Check the operation of the front forks and brake before riding the scooter.

Disassembly

12 Remove the fork leg (see Steps 4 to 7).

8.7a Remove the fork clamp bolts...

8.7b ...and withdraw the fork leg

8.7c Note the groove for the clamp bolt

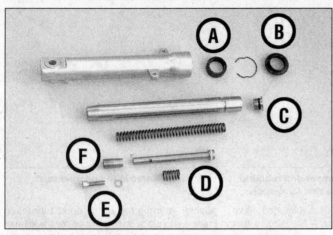

8.12 Conventional telescopic fork components

A Oil seal
B Dust seal
C Top bolt and O-ring
D Damper and rebound spring
E Damper bolt
F Damper seat

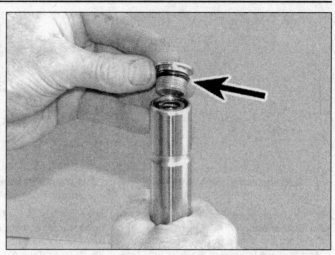

8.14 Note location of the O-ring

Always dismantle the fork legs separately to avoid interchanging parts **(see illustration)**. Store all components in separate, clearly marked containers.

13 The damper bolt should be loosened at this stage. Invert the fork leg and compress the fork inner tube into the outer tube so that the spring exerts maximum pressure on the damper, then loosen the bolt in the base of the outer tube **(see illustration 8.19)**.

14 If the fork top bolt was not loosened with the fork on the scooter, carefully clamp the inner tube in a vice equipped with soft jaws, taking care not to overtighten or score the tube's surface, and loosen the top bolt. Unscrew the bolt noting the location of the O-ring **(see illustration)**. If the O-ring is damaged, fit a new one on reassembly.

⚠ *Warning: The fork spring is pressing on the fork top bolt with considerable pressure. Unscrew the bolt very carefully, keeping a downward pressure on it and release it slowly as it is likely to spring clear. It is advisable to wear some form of eye and face protection when carrying out this operation.*

15 On Tweet models, to remove the fork top plug, press the plug down against the pressure of the fork spring and remove the retaining circlip **(see illustration)**. Ease the plug out noting the location of the O-ring **(see illustration)**. If the O-ring is damaged, fit a new one on reassembly.

16 Slide the inner tube down into the outer tube and withdraw the spring **(see illustration)**. Note which way up the spring is fitted.

17 Invert the fork leg over a suitable container and pump the fork vigorously to expel as much fork oil as possible.

18 Carefully prise out the dust seal from the top of the outer tube **(see illustration)**.

19 Remove the previously loosened damper bolt and its sealing washer from the bottom of the outer tube **(see illustration)**. Discard the sealing washer as a new one must be used on reassembly. If the damper bolt was not loosened before dismantling the fork, temporarily install the spring and press down on it to prevent the damper from turning.

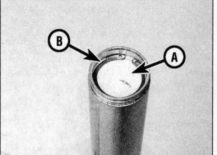

8.15a Press down on plug (A) to remove circlip (B)

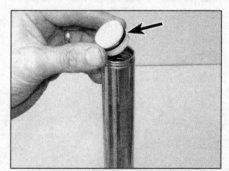

8.15b Note location of the O-ring

8.16 Withdraw the fork spring

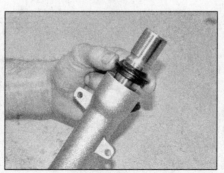

8.18 Remove the dust seal

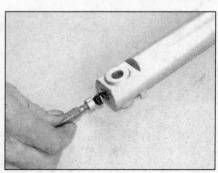

8.19 Unscrew the damper bolt and washer

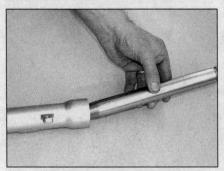

8.20 Pull out the fork inner tube

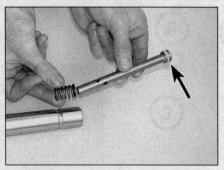

8.21 Withdraw the damper and rebound spring. Note sealing ring (arrowed)

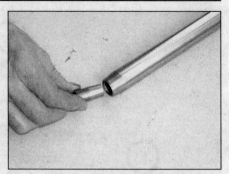

8.22 Remove the damper seat

20 Pull the inner tube out of the outer tube **(see illustration)**.

21 Withdraw the damper and rebound spring from the top end of the inner tube **(see illustration)**.

22 Withdraw the damper seat from the bottom of the inner tube **(see illustration)**.

23 Prise the retaining clip out of its groove in the top of the fork outer tube, then prise out the oil seal **(see illustrations)**. Note which way round the seal is fitted. Discard the oil and dust seals as new ones must be used on reassembly.

Inspection

24 Clean all parts in a suitable solvent and dry them with compressed air, if available.

25 Inspect the fork inner tubes for score marks, pitting or flaking of the chrome finish and excessive or abnormal wear. Check the straightness of the tubes with a straight-

edge. If either of the tubes is damaged, worn or bent, renew them both – never have fork tubes straightened.

26 If the surface of the inner tubes is worn or pitted, it is likely that the inside bearing surface of the outer tubes will be damaged also. If the surface is scored or pitted, renew the outer tubes **(see illustration)**.

27 Inspect the springs for cracks, sagging and other damage. Measure the spring free length – the spring in both forks must be the same length. If one spring is defective, renew the springs as a pair.

28 Where fitted, check the condition of the rebound spring as well as the main spring, and inspect the sealing ring on the damper for wear and damage **(see illustration 8.21)**. **Note:** *Do not remove the sealing ring from the damper.*

Reassembly

29 Lubricate the new oil seal with fork oil and

position it in the top of the outer tube, then press it into place so that it is below the level of the groove for the retaining clip. If necessary, use a suitably sized socket to tap the seal carefully into position **(see illustration)**.

30 Fit the retaining clip, making sure it is correctly located in its groove **(see illustration)**.

31 Slide the rebound spring onto the damper, ensuring it is the correct way round **(see illustration 8.21)**. Insert the damper into the top of the fork inner tube and slide it down so that it protrudes out from the bottom of the tube, then fit the damper seat **(see illustration 8.22)**.

32 Lubricate the inside of the oil seal with fork oil then slide the inner tube all the way into the outer tube **(see illustration 8.20)**.

33 Hold the damper firmly against the bottom of the outer tube with a long screwdriver or dowel. Fit a new sealing washer on the damper bolt and screw the bolt into the damper seat **(see illustration)**. Tighten the bolt to the

8.23a Prise out the retaining clip...

8.23b ...then lever out the oil seal

8.26 Inspect the inside surface of the outer tubes for wear

8.29 Installing the new oil seal

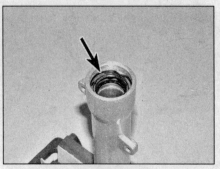

8.30 Ensure the retaining clip is correctly installed

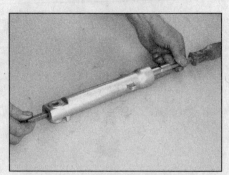

8.33 Screw the damper bolt into the damper seat

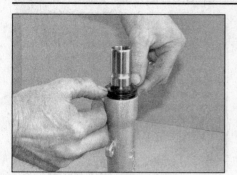

8.34 Install the new dust seal

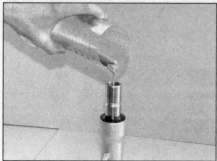

8.35 Pour in the specified quantity of fork oil

8.41 Remove the front fork assembly

torque setting specified at the beginning of this Chapter.

34 Lubricate the inside of the new dust seal then slide it down the inner tube and press it into position **(see illustration)**.

35 Slowly pour in the specified quantity of fork oil **(see illustration)**. Carefully pump the fork to distribute the oil evenly.

36 Extend the fork leg and insert the spring, ensuring it is the correct way round (see Step 16).

37 If necessary, fit a new O-ring to the fork top bolt or fork plug. Lubricate the O-ring with clean fork oil. Keep the fork leg fully extended and press down on the spring whilst threading the bolt into the top of the inner tube. Turn the bolt carefully to ensure it is not cross-threaded. Where listed, tighten the top bolt to the specified torque setting. **Note:** *The top bolt can be tightened fully when the fork leg has been installed and is securely held in the yoke.* On Tweet models, press the plug down onto the spring until the circlip groove is visible and install the circlip **(see illustrations 8.15b and a)**. Ensure the circlip is correctly located in its groove.

> ⚠ *Warning: It will be necessary to compress the spring by pressing it down with the top bolt in order to engage the threads of the top bolt with the fork tube. This is a potentially dangerous operation and should be performed with care, using an assistant if necessary. Wipe off any excess oil before starting to prevent the possibility of slipping.*

38 Install the fork leg (see Steps 8 to 11).

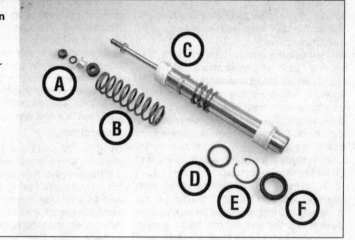

8.43 Upside-down telescopic fork components

A *Locknut, spacer and grommet*
B *Compression spring*
C *Fork inner tube with damper assembly*
D *Rubber washer*
E *Circlip*
F *Dust seal*

Upside-down telescopic forks

Removal and installation

39 Displace the brake caliper and remove the front wheel (see Chapter 8).

40 Remove the front mudguard and inner mudguard (see Chapter 9).

41 Remove the handlebars (see Section 4) then follow the procedure in Section 6 and remove the steering stem and front fork assembly **(see illustration)**.

42 Installation is the reverse of removal. Note that the fork assembly should be supported once the stem has been located in the steering head. The adjuster nut can then be installed without danger of damaging the threads on the nut or steering stem. Check the operation of the front forks and brake before riding the scooter.

Disassembly

43 Remove the fork assembly (see Steps 39 to 41). Always dismantle the fork legs separately to avoid interchanging parts **(see illustration)**. Store all components in separate, clearly marked containers.

44 Temporarily clamp the front wheel axle between the fork stanchions and unscrew the stanchion bolts **(see illustrations)**. Remove the axle and draw the stanchions off the fork inner tubes, noting how they fit **(see illustration)**.

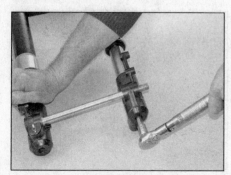

8.44a Use the axle to prevent the fork legs turning...

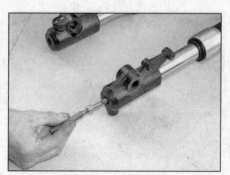

8.44b ...unscrew the stanchion bolts

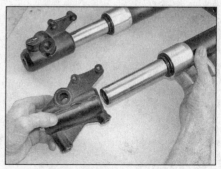

8.44c Pull off the stanchions

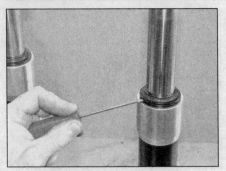

8.45 Prise out the dust seal

8.46a Remove the circlip...

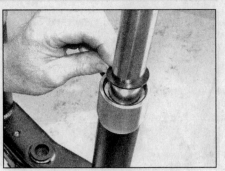

8.46b ...and the rubber washer

45 Carefully prise out the dust seal from the bottom of the outer tube **(see illustration)**. Discard the dust seals as new ones must be used on reassembly.

46 Remove the circlip from the bottom of the outer tube **(see illustration)**. Lift out the rubber washer **(see illustration)**.

47 Now withdraw the right-hand inner tube assembly from the outer tube **(see illustration)**. The upper and lower bushes and rebound spring will come out on the inner tube. Note which way round the bushes are fitted. Withdraw the compression spring and the rubber suspension stop.

48 To remove the left-hand inner tube assembly, first hold the top of the damper rod to prevent it turning and undo the locknut **(see illustration)**. Remove the nut, spring washer and top hat spacer **(see illustration)**. **Note:** *A new locknut should be fitted on reassembly.*

49 Withdraw the left-hand inner tube and damper assembly from the outer tube **(see illustration)**. The upper and lower bushes and rebound spring will come out on the inner tube. Note which way round the bushes are fitted. Withdraw the compression spring **(see illustration)**.

50 Remove the grommet from the top of the outer tube **(see illustration)**. If the grommet is damaged fit a new one on reassembly.

Inspection

51 Clean all parts in a suitable solvent and dry them with compressed air, if available.

52 Inspect the fork inner tubes for score marks, pitting or flaking of the chrome finish and excessive or abnormal wear. Check the straightness of the tubes with a straight-edge. If either of the tubes is damaged, worn or bent, renew them both – never have fork tubes straightened.

53 Examine the working surface of each bush. If they are worn or scuffed the bushes should be renewed as a set.

54 Look for dents in the outer tubes and fit a new fork assembly if any damage is found.

55 Check the action of the damper. If the rod slides freely in and out of the cartridge, or if it binds in the cartridge, fit a new fork inner tube – the damper is integral with the left-hand inner tube.

56 Inspect the springs for cracks, sagging and other damage. Measure the spring free length – the spring in both forks must be the same length. If one spring is defective, renew the springs as a pair.

Reassembly

57 Fit the grommet into the top of the left-hand outer tube. Lubricate the fork bushes with a smear of lithium-based grease. Install the compression spring and

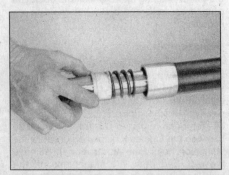

8.47 Withdraw the right-hand inner tube assembly from the outer tube

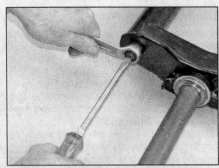

8.48a Undo the damper rod locknut

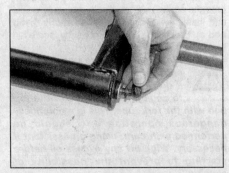

8.48b Remove the nut, washer and spacer

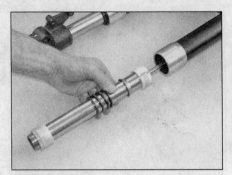

8.49a Withdraw the left-hand inner tube and damper assembly from the outer tube

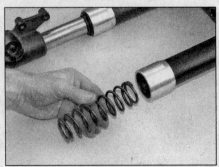

8.49b Withdraw the compression spring

8.50 Prise out the grommet

8.58 Ensure the circlip is correctly installed

the inner tube assembly with the upper and lower bushes and rebound spring **(see illustrations 8.49b and a)**. Locate the damper rod through the grommet and fit the top hat spacer, washer and locknut, then hold the rod and tighten the locknut securely **(see illustration 8.48a)**.

58 Press the inner tube into the outer tube and fit the rubber washer, then secure the inner tube with the circlip **(see illustrations 8.46b and a)**. Ensure the circlip is correctly located in its groove **(see illustration)**.

59 Lubricate the new dust seal with a smear of grease and press it firmly into the bottom of the outer tube.

60 Install the suspension stop and compression spring in the right-hand outer tube. Lubricate the fork bushes with a smear of lithium-based grease. Install the inner tube assembly with the upper and lower bushes

and rebound spring. Follow the procedure in Step 58 to secure the inner tube.

61 Press the left and right-hand stanchions onto the fork inner tubes. Ensure they are fitted correctly – the brake caliper brackets should be on the left, the axle pinchbolt on the right **(see illustration 8.44c)**.

62 Temporarily clamp the front wheel axle between the fork stanchions and tighten the stanchion bolts securely **(see illustration 8.44a)**.

63 Install the fork assembly (see Step 42).

9 Rear suspension

1 V-Clic, Vivacity 50, Speedfight, Kisbee and Tweet 50 models have a single rear shock absorber. Vivacity 125 and Tweet 125/150 models have twin rear shocks; they also have a rear subframe located on the right-hand side of the engine/transmission unit.

Shock absorber

Removal

2 Support the machine on its centrestand and position a support under the rear wheel so that the engine does not drop when the shock absorber is removed, but also making sure that the weight of the machine is off the rear suspension so that the shock is not compressed.

3 The shock absorber is secured to the frame at the top and the transmission casing at the

bottom. To access the upper mounting bolt, remove the luggage compartment or body panels as necessary according to model (see Chapter 9). If necessary, remove the air filter housing to access the lower mounting bolt (see Chapter 5). On scooters with twin rear shocks, remove the exhaust system (see Chapter 5).

4 Undo and remove the bolt, or the nut and bolt, securing the top of the shock absorber to the frame **(see illustrations)**.

5 Undo the nut and bolt securing the bottom of the shock absorber to the transmission casing; support the shock and remove the bolt, then manoeuvre the shock away from the machine **(see illustrations)**.

Inspection

6 Inspect the shock absorber for obvious physical damage and the shock spring for looseness, cracks or signs of fatigue. If the shock absorber has a spring preload adjuster ensure it is clean and that the spring seat rotates freely around the adjustment ramp **(see illustration)**.

7 Inspect the damper rod for signs of bending, pitting and oil leaks **(see illustration)**. Check the mountings at the top and bottom of the shock, and the mounting bolts, for wear or damage

Installation

8 Installation is the reverse of removal. Tighten the shock absorber mounting bolts to the torque settings given at the beginning of this Chapter.

9.4a Upper shock mounting bolt – Speedfight 50

9.4b Upper shock mounting bolt – Kisbee 100

9.5a Undo the lower mounting bolt...

9.5b ...and lift the shock off

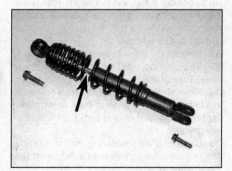

9.6 Spring seat (arrowed) must rotate freely

9.7 Inspect the damper rod (arrowed)

9.13 Remove the right-hand shock
absorber

9.14 Undo the rear axle locknut

9.15a Undo the subframe bolts (arrowed)...

9.15b ...and lift the subframe off

9.16 Note the location of the axle spacers

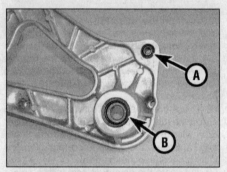

9.18 Shock mounting bush (A), note axle
bearing (B)

Adjustment

9 On some scooters, the rear shock absorber
is adjustable for spring pre-load. Adjustment
is made using a suitable C-spanner to turn
the spring seat on the bottom of the shock
absorber **(see illustration 9.6)**.

10 Support the scooter on the centrestand
with no load on the rear suspension. To
increase the pre-load (stiffen the suspension),
turn the spring seat to a higher position on the
adjustment ramp. To decrease the pre-load
(soften the suspension), turn the spring seat
to a lower position on the ramp. **Note:** *Always
use the correct tool to adjust the spring
pre-load to avoid damaging the spring seat.*

Rear subframe

Removal

11 Support the machine on its centrestand
and position a support under the rear wheel.
Ensure that the weight of the machine is off the
rear suspension so that the shock absorbers
are not compressed.
12 Remove the exhaust system (see Chapter 5).
13 Remove the right-hand shock absorber
(see illustration).
14 Have an assistant apply the rear brake and
undo the rear axle locknut **(see illustration)**.
Note: *A new locknut should be fitted on
reassembly.*
15 Undo the bolts securing the subframe to
the engine case and lift the subframe off **(see
illustrations)**.
16 Note the location of the axle spacers fitted
in the subframe bearing **(see illustration)**.

Inspection

17 Inspect the subframe for obvious physical
damage and stripped threads. Damaged
threads can be economically reclaimed by
using a thread insert. Most small engineering
firms offer a service of this kind. Refer to *Tools
and Workshop Tips* in the *Reference* section
for further details.
18 Inspect the rear shock mounting bush **(see
illustration)**. If it show signs of deterioration
it should be renewed. Use the same method
as described in the appropriate Chapter 2
to remove and install the engine mounting
bushes.
19 Inspect the axle bearing in the subframe
(see *Tools and Workshop Tips* in the *Reference*
section). If the bearing needs renewing, it can
be driven out from the inside **(see illustration
9.18)** using a bearing driver or suitably-sized
socket. Ensure the subframe is supported on
the work surface and heat the bearing housing
to aid removal and fitting.

Installation

20 Installation is the reverse of removal.
Don't forget to fit the axle spacer between
the rear wheel and the subframe and the
second spacer on the outside of the subframe
bearing.
21 Tighten the subframe mounting bolts
securely. Tighten the shock absorber mounting
bolts to the torque settings specified at the
beginning of this Chapter. Tighten the new
axle locknut to the torque setting specified at
the beginning of Chapter 8.

10 Rear suspension arm/engine mounting bracket

1 The front engine mounting bracket acts as
part of the rear suspension. It is also the main
link between the engine/transmission unit and
the frame **(see illustration)**. In all cases, the
mounting bracket employs rubber-in-torsion
'silentbloc' bushes and damping rubbers to
restrict movement.
2 If a check of the rear suspension highlights
wear in the bushes the engine will have to be
removed for further inspection (refer to the
appropriate Chapter 2). Don't forget to inspect
the mounting bushes in the engine crankcase
mounting lugs at the same time.

10.1 Location of the engine front mounting
bracket (arrowed)

10.5a Undo the locknut...

10.5b ...then withdraw the bolt...

10.5c ...and lift the mounting bracket off –
Kisbee 50 shown

Removal

3 Remove the engine/transmission unit (see the appropriate Chapter 2 for your scooter).

4 If any part of the engine mounting bracket is used to support the machine for this procedure an alternative method of support will have to be found before the bracket can be removed. A double A-frame hoist is ideally suited to most machines once the rear bodywork has been removed and where the front of the scooter can be firmly secured (see Chapter 2). Alternatively, with the belly panels removed, the scooter can be supported from underneath provided the weight is taken on the frame tubes and not the fuel tank.

5 On some scooters the bracket is secured by a single bolt, on others by two bolts, one on each side. Counterhold the bolt and undo the locknut, then withdraw the bolt and remove the mounting bracket **(see illustrations)**.

6 Note the location of the rubber damper(s) **(see illustrations)**.

Inspection

7 Thoroughly clean the bracket and bolts, removing all traces of dirt, corrosion and grease.

8 Inspect the bushes closely, looking for obvious signs of deterioration such as

10.5d Undo the nuts and withdraw the
bolts

10.5e Lift the mounting bracket off –
Speedfight 50 shown

compression, cracks or distortion **(see illustration)**. The bushes are generally a very tight fit and an internal puller or drawbolt tool will be required to remove the old ones and to press the new ones in (see *Tools and Workshop Tips* in the *Reference* section at the end of this manual). **Note:** *For some models, bushes are available separately, for others the mounting bracket is supplied as an assembly.*

9 Check the bracket and mounting bolts for wear. If the bolts are not a precise fit in the bracket the components must be replaced with new ones.

10 Inspect the rubber dampers and renew them if necessary **(see illustrations 10.6a and b)**.

Installation

11 Installation is the reverse of removal. Smear some grease on the bracket and engine mounting bolts before installation. Always use new locknuts on the bracket and engine mounting bolts. Tighten all mounting bolts to the torque setting specified at the beginning of this Chapter.

10.6a Note location of the single damper

10.6b Note location of the twin dampers

10.8 Bushes are fitted in both ends of the
mounting bracket

Chapter 8
Brakes, wheels and tyres

Contents

Degrees of difficulty

Easy, suitable for novice with little experience 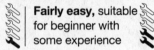	Fairly easy, suitable for beginner with some experience	Fairly difficult, suitable for competent DIY mechanic	Difficult, suitable for experienced DIY mechanic	Very difficult, suitable for expert DIY or professional

Specifications

Brakes

V-Clic, Kisbee 50/100 and Tweet 50

Disc thickness

Standard	4.0 mm
Service limit	3.5 mm
Pad minimum thickness	1.5 mm
Brake drum diameter	110 mm (V-Clic, Kisbee), 130 mm (Tweet)
Brake lining thickness	4 mm

Speedfight 50 and Vivacity 50

Disc thickness (front and rear)

Standard	3.5 mm
Service limit	3.0 mm
Pad minimum thickness	1.5 mm
Brake drum diameter	110 mm
Brake lining thickness	4 mm

Vivacity 125

Disc thickness

Standard	3.5 mm
Service limit	3.0 mm
Pad minimum thickness	1.5 mm
Brake drum diameter	130 mm
Brake lining thickness	3.5 mm

Tweet 125/150

Disc thickness (front and rear)

Standard	4.0 mm
Service limit	3.5 mm
Pad minimum thickness	1.5 mm
Fluid type (all models)	DOT 4

Tyres

Tyre pressure	see *Pre-ride checks*
Tyre sizes	see Model Specification pages in Chapter 1

Torque settings

Front axle nut

V-Clic	53 Nm
Kisbee models	50 to 60 Nm
Speedfight 50	60 to 70 Nm
Speedfight 125	70 Nm
Vivacity 50	60 to 70 Nm
Vivacity 125	53 Nm
Tweet models	50 to 70 Nm

Front axle pinch bolt (Speedfight) ... 10 Nm

Front brake caliper mounting bolts

V-Clic	26 Nm
Kisbee models	27 to 32 Nm
Speedfight 50	43 to 50 Nm
Speedfight 125	50 Nm
Vivacity 50	25 to 35 Nm
Vivacity 125	25 Nm
Tweet models	30 Nm

Front brake disc mounting bolts

V-Clic	23 Nm
Kisbee models	27 to 23 Nm
Speedfight 50	27 to 32 Nm
Speedfight 125	32 Nm
Vivacity 50	27 to 32 Nm
Vivacity 125	23 Nm
Tweet models	40 Nm

Rear brake arm bolt (drum brake)

V-Clic and Kisbee models	8 to 11 Nm
Speedfight	8 Nm
Vivacity 50	6 Nm
Vivacity 125	10 Nm
Tweet 50	6 Nm

Rear brake caliper mounting bolts

Speedfight	30 Nm
Tweet 50 RS and 125	30 Nm

Rear brake disc mounting bolts

Speedfight	30 Nm
Tweet 50 RS and 125/150	34 to 40 Nm

Rear wheel bolts – Speedfight ... 30 Nm

Rear wheel hub nut

V-Clic	120 Nm
Kisbee models	110 to 130 Nm
Speedfight 50	100 to 120 Nm
Speedfight 125	120 Nm
Vivacity 50	100 to 120 Nm
Vivacity 125	120 Nm
Tweet models	100 to 110 Nm

1 General information

An hydraulic front disc brake is fitted to all models. A disc brake is fitted at the rear of the liquid-cooled Speedfight 50, Speedfight 125, Tweet 50 RS and Tweet 125/150 models; all other models have a cable-operated drum rear brake.

The master cylinder for the disc brakes is integral with the brake lever, although it is necessary to remove one of the handlebar covers to access the brake fluid reservoir.

The rear wheel is mounted directly onto the gearbox output shaft – there is no separate rear wheel axle. Consequently the rear wheel turns on the bearings located inside the gearbox. On Vivacity 125 and Tweet 125/150 models, which have twin rear shock absorbers, an additional shaft bearing is located in the rear subframe.

The cast wheels are fitted with tubeless tyres. A tyre information label on the scooter will give appropriate tyre size and recommended pressures, otherwise refer to the *Model identification* data at the beginning of Chapter 1 and the *Pre-ride checks* at the beginning of this manual.

Caution: Disc brake components rarely require disassembly. Do not disassemble components unless absolutely necessary. If an hydraulic brake hose is loosened, the entire system must be, drained, cleaned and then properly filled and bled upon reassembly (see Section 7). Do not use solvents on internal brake components. Solvents will cause the seals to swell and distort. Use only clean brake fluid, a dedicated brake cleaner or denatured alcohol for cleaning. Use care when working with brake fluid as it can injure your eyes; it will also damage painted surfaces and plastic parts.

2.1 Loosen the slider pin (arrowed)

2.4 Rotate the caliper clear of the bracket and draw it off the fixed pin

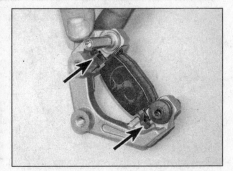

2.5 Springs (arrowed) retain the pads

2 Front brake pads

⚠️ *Warning: The dust created by the brake system may contain asbestos, which is harmful to your health. Never blow it out with compressed air and don't inhale any of it. An approved filtering mask should be worn when working on the brakes.*

Removal and installation

Note: *Do not operate the brake lever while the brake caliper is off the disc.*

V-Clic

1 First loosen the brake caliper slider pin **(see illustration)**.

2 Undo the bolts that secure the caliper bracket to the front fork and draw the caliper assembly off the disc.

3 Unscrew the slider pin.

4 Rotate the caliper around the fixed slider pin until it is clear of the caliper bracket, then draw the caliper off the pin **(see illustration)**.

5 The pads are retained in the bracket by springs at both ends **(see illustration)**. Note how the springs are located in the bracket, then lift the pads out carefully noting how they fit.

6 Follow the procedure in Steps 52 to 59 to inspect the brake pads.

7 Note the location of the rubber boots on the slider pins. Ensure the components are in good condition and lubricate the slider pins before installing the pads (see Section 3).

2.9 Leave space between the pads for the brake disc

8 Install the inner and outer pads as noted on removal with the friction material facing the disc. Rotate the caliper around the fixed slider pin until the holes for the removable slider pin align, then install the pin. The pin can be fully tightened once the caliper assembly has been installed on the front fork.

9 Ensure there is sufficient space between the pads to slide the caliper assembly onto the disc **(see illustration)**.

10 Fit the caliper onto the disc and align the bracket with the front fork mounting. Tighten the caliper bracket bolts to the torque setting specified at the beginning of this Chapter. Don't forget to tighten the pad pin.

11 On completion, operate the brake lever several times to bring the pads into contact with the disc. Check the brake fluid level and top-up if necessary (see *Pre-ride checks*).

2.12 Undo the mounting bolts and draw the caliper off the disc

Check the operation of the brake before riding the scooter.

Kisbee

12 Undo the bolts that secure the caliper bracket to the front fork and draw the caliper assembly off the disc **(see illustration)**.

13 Lift out the outer brake pad noting how the tabs on the backing plate locate in the caliper bracket **(see illustration)**.

14 Press the slider pins on the backing plate into the caliper body to free the inner brake pad **(see illustration)**.

15 Follow the procedure in Steps 52 to 59 to inspect the brake pads.

16 If required, separate the caliper from the caliper bracket **(see illustration)**. Note the location of the rubber boots on the slider pins and the pad spring. Ensure the components are in good condition and lubricate the slider pins before installing the pads (see Section 3).

2.13 Note location of tabs on both sides of the pad

2.14 Compress the caliper assembly to free the inner brake pad

2.16 Pull the caliper off the bracket slider pins

2.17 Allow clearance (arrowed) for installing the inner pad

2.18 Leave space between the pads for the brake disc

2.21 Location of the pad pins (arrowed)

17 Prior to installing the inner pad, position the caliper bracket to allow sufficient clearance for installing the pad (see illustration).
18 Install the inner and outer pads as noted on removal with the friction material facing the disc. Ensure there is sufficient space between the pads to slide the caliper assembly onto the disc (see illustration).
19 Fit the caliper onto the disc and align the bracket with the front fork mounting. Tighten the caliper bracket bolts to the torque setting specified at the beginning of this Chapter.
20 On completion, carry out the checks in Step 11 before riding the scooter.

Speedfight

21 First identify the recessed pad pins on the right-hand side of the brake caliper and loosen them (see illustration).
22 Undo the bolts that secure the caliper to

the front fork and draw the caliper off the disc (see illustration).
23 Note the location of the pad spring inside the caliper, then unscrew the pad pins (see illustrations).
24 Withdraw the brake pads from the caliper, noting how they fit (see illustration). Remove the pad spring if it is loose (see illustration).
25 Follow the procedure in Steps 52 to 59 to inspect the brake pads.
26 Before installing the pads, ensure that the raised centre section of the pad spring is facing the open side of the caliper so that it presses on the pads when they are installed.
27 Fit the pads as noted on removal with the friction material facing the disc. Press the pads against the spring and insert the pad pins so that they pass underneath the spring

(see illustration 2.23b). The pins can be fully tightened once the caliper assembly has been installed on the front fork.
28 Ensure there is sufficient space between the pads to slide the caliper onto the disc.
29 Fit the caliper onto the disc and align it with the front fork mounting. Tighten the caliper mounting bolts to the torque setting specified at the beginning of this Chapter. Don't forget to tighten the pad pins.
30 On completion, carry out the checks in Step 11 before riding the scooter.

Vivacity 50

31 Straighten the tab washer securing the pad pins on the right-hand side of the caliper and loosen the pins.
32 Undo the bolts that secure the caliper bracket to the front fork and draw the caliper assembly off the disc (see illustration).

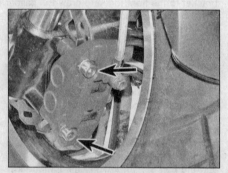

2.22 Caliper mounting bolts

2.23a Location of the pad spring

2.23b Unscrew the pad pins

2.24a Lift out the brake pads

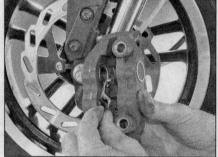

2.24b Note how the pad spring fits

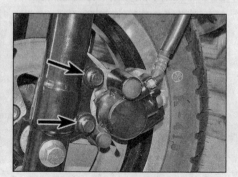

2.32 Caliper mounting bolts

2.33 Unscrew the pins...

2.34a ...and lift out the pads

2.34b Note location of the pad spring

33 Unscrew the pins **(see illustration)**. Discard the tab washer as a new one should be fitted on reassembly.

34 Lift the pads out, noting how they fit **(see illustration)**. Note the location of the anti-chatter shim on the back of the left-hand pad between the pad and the caliper piston. Note the location of the pad spring inside the caliper and remove it if it is loose **(see illustration)**.

35 Follow the procedure in Steps 52 to 59 to inspect the brake pads.

36 Check that the caliper moves freely along the slider pins on the mounting bracket – if the caliper has seized refer to Section 3 to clean and lubricate the slider pins.

37 Before installing the pads, ensure that the raised centre section of the pad spring is facing the open side of the caliper so that it presses on the pads when they are installed.

38 Fit the pads as noted on removal with the friction material facing the disc. Ensure the anti-chatter shim is installed on the back of the left-hand pad. Press the pads against the spring and install the pad pins with a new tab washer. The pins can be fully tightened once the caliper assembly has been installed on the front fork.

39 Ensure there is sufficient space between the pads to slide the caliper onto the disc.

40 Fit the caliper onto the disc and align the bracket with the front fork mounting. Tighten

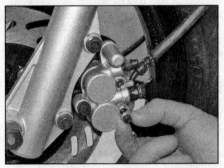

2.42 Unscrew the pad pin plugs

2.43 Undo the mounting bolts and draw the caliper off the disc

the caliper mounting bolts to the torque setting specified at the beginning of this Chapter. Don't forget to tighten the pad pins and bend the tab washer over the heads of the pins.

41 On completion, carry out the checks in Step 11 before riding the scooter.

Tweet (all models) and Vivacity 125

42 Unscrew the plugs from the pad pin locations on the brake caliper, then loosen the pad pins **(see illustration)**.

43 Undo the bolts that secure the caliper bracket to the front fork and draw the caliper assembly off the disc **(see illustration)**.

44 Unscrew the pad pins and lift out the brake pads, noting how they fit **(see illustration)**.

45 Follow the procedure in Steps 52 to 59 to inspect the brake pads.

46 If required, separate the caliper from the caliper bracket – pull the bracket and caliper apart, then rotate the bracket around the upper slider pin until it is free of the caliper **(see illustration)**. Note the location of the rubber boots on the slider pins and the position of the pad spring **(see illustration)**. Ensure the components are in good condition and lubricate the slider pins before installing the pads (see Section 3). Remove the pad spring if it is loose.

47 Prior to installation, ensure that the pad spring is located securely in the caliper and press the slider pins into their locations in the caliper. Install the outer brake pad with the

2.44 Unscrew the pad pins

2.46a Rotate the bracket around the upper slider pin (arrowed)

2.46b Location of the pad spring

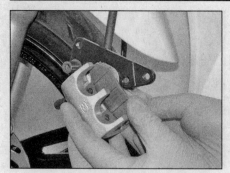

2.47a Hold the outer pad in place...

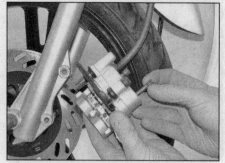

2.47b ...and insert the pad pins

2.48 Hook the inner pad around the post on the bracket

friction material facing the disc, hold it down against the spring and secure it with the pad pins **(see illustrations)**.

48 Hook the inner pad around the post on the caliper bracket **(see illustration)** then press it down against the pad spring and screw the pad pins all the way in **(see illustration 2.44)**. The pins can be fully tightened once the caliper assembly has been installed on the front fork.

49 Ensure there is sufficient space between the pads to slide the caliper onto the disc.

50 Fit the caliper onto the disc and align the bracket with the front fork mounting. Tighten the caliper mounting bolts to the torque setting specified at the beginning of this Chapter. Don't forget to tighten the pad pins.

51 On completion, carry out the checks in Step 11 before riding the scooter.

Inspection

52 Inspect the surface of each pad for contamination and check if the pads are worn **(see illustration)**. If either pad is worn down to, or beyond, the specified minimum thickness (see Chapter 1, Section 3), is fouled with oil or grease, or heavily scored or damaged, both pads must be renewed. *Note: It is not possible to degrease the friction material. If the pads are contaminated in any way they must be renewed.*

53 If the pads are in good condition, clean them carefully using a fine wire brush which is completely free of oil and grease to remove all traces of road dirt and corrosion. Spray

the caliper with a dedicated brake cleaner to remove any dust and remove any traces of corrosion which might cause sticking of the caliper/pad operation.

54 Remove all traces of corrosion from the pad pins **(see illustration 2.33)**. Inspect the pins for wear and damage. Prior to reassembly, smear the pins with copper-based grease.

55 Clean the caliper slider pins and inspect them for wear (see Section 3).

56 Remove all traces of corrosion from the pad spring **(see illustration 2.34b)**.

57 Check the condition of the brake disc (see Section 4).

58 To make it easier to fit the caliper onto the disc, especially if new pads are being installed, slowly push the piston as far back into the caliper as possible using hand pressure or a piece of wood for leverage. This will displace brake fluid back into the hydraulic reservoir, so it may be necessary to remove the reservoir cap, plate and diaphragm and siphon out some fluid (depending on how much fluid was in there in the first place and how far the piston has to be pushed in). If the piston is difficult to push back, attach a length of clear hose to the bleed valve and place the open end in a suitable container, then open the valve and try again. Take great care not to draw any air into the system and don't forget to tighten the valve once the piston has been sufficiently displaced. If in doubt, bleed the brakes afterwards (see Section 7).
Caution: Never lever the caliper against the brake disc to push a piston back into the caliper as damage to the disc will result.

59 Prior to installation, smear the backs of the pads with copper-based grease, making sure that none gets on the front or sides of the pads.

3 Front brake caliper

> **Warning: If a caliper indicates the need for renewal (usually due to leaking fluid or sticky operation), all old brake fluid should be flushed from the system at the same time. Also, the dust created by the brake system may contain asbestos, which is harmful to your health. Never blow it out with compressed air and don't inhale any of it. An approved filtering mask should be worn when working on the brakes. Do not, under any circumstances, use petroleum-based solvents to clean brake parts. Use a dedicated brake cleaner or denatured alcohol only, as described. To prevent damage from spilled brake fluid, always cover paintwork when working on the braking system.**

Removal

Note 1: *Do not operate the brake lever while the caliper is off the disc.*
Note 2: *It is not necessary to remove the caliper completely for cleaning and inspection.*

1 If the caliper is just being displaced, the brake pads can be left in place. Follow the procedure in Section 2 to undo the caliper mounting bolts and draw the caliper assembly off the disc. Support the caliper with a cable-tie to ensure no strain is placed on the brake hose.

2 If the caliper is being removed completely from the scooter, first note the alignment of the banjo fitting on the caliper, then loosen and lightly tighten the brake hose banjo bolt **(see illustration)**.

3 Follow the procedure in Section 2 to undo the caliper mounting bolts and draw the caliper assembly off the disc. Remove the brake pads.

4 Unscrew the banjo bolt and separate the

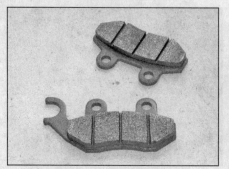

2.52 Inspect the pads for wear and contamination

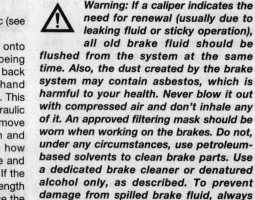

3.2 Brake hose banjo bolt

hose from the caliper **(see illustration)**. Discard the sealing washers as new ones must be used on installation. Wrap a plastic bag tightly around the end of the hose to prevent dirt entering the system and secure the hose in an upright position to minimise fluid loss.

Inspection

5 If the caliper is being cleaned and inspected, remove the brake pads and note the location of the pad spring (see Section 2). Where applicable, separate the caliper from the caliper bracket. On Vivacity 50 models, ease out the plug and unscrew the slider pin to separate the caliper and bracket **(see illustrations)**.
6 Clean the caliper with denatured alcohol or brake system cleaner. Inspect the caliper for signs of damage, especially around the mounting lugs and the bleed screw and renew it if necessary.
7 If brake fluid is leaking from around the edge of the piston(s) **(see illustration)** the internal piston seal has failed and a new caliper will have to be fitted. Overhaul kits are not available.
8 Clean all old grease off the caliper slider pins and inspect them for wear. If the pins are corroded, check the rubber boots on the caliper and bracket for damage and renew then if new components are available. Prior to reassembly, smear the pins with red rubber brake system grease.
9 Follow the procedure in Section 2 to install the brake pads.

Installation

10 If the caliper has just been displaced, install the caliper on the brake disc (see Section 2).
11 If the caliper was removed from the machine, or a new caliper is being fitted, first install the brake pads, then fit the caliper onto the front fork mounting (see Section 2).
12 Connect the brake hose to the caliper, using new sealing washers on both sides of the banjo fitting. Align the banjo fitting as noted on removal and tighten the banjo bolt securely.
13 Top-up the brake fluid reservoir (see *Pre-ride checks*). Bleed the brake system (see Section 7).

3.4 Unscrew the banjo bolt and detach the brake hose

3.5b ...and separate the caliper from the bracket. Note fixed pin (arrowed)

14 Check for fluid leaks and check the operation of the brake before riding the scooter.

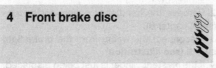
4 Front brake disc

Inspection

1 Inspect the surface of the disc for score marks and other damage **(see illustration)**. Light scratches are normal after use and won't affect brake operation, but deep grooves and heavy score marks will reduce braking efficiency and accelerate pad wear. If a disc is badly grooved it must be machined or renewed.
2 The disc must not be machined or allowed to wear down to a thickness less than the minimum stamped on the disc **(see illustration 4.1)**. Check the thickness of the disc

3.5a Unscrew the slider pin...

3.7 Check for brake fluid leaks

with a micrometer and renew it if necessary **(see illustration)**. If no measuring equipment is available, check for a ridge between the rim of the disc and the pad contact area and renew the disc as necessary.
3 If the disc is running out-of-true, the lever will pulse when the brake is applied. To check disc warpage, support the scooter on its centrestand with the front wheel raised off the ground. Attach a dial gauge to the fork leg with the tip of the gauge touching the surface of the disc about 10 mm from the outer edge **(see illustration)**. **Note:** *On models fitted with wavy Shuricane discs this test is not practicable.* Rotate the wheel and watch the gauge needle; a small amount of movement is acceptable. If excessive movement is indicated, first check the wheel bearings for play (see Chapter 1, Section 23). If the bearings are good, the disc is warped and should be replaced with a new one.

4.1 Inspect the surface of the disc. Note minimum thickness (arrowed)

4.2 Measuring the thickness of the brake disc

4.3 Set-up for checking brake disc runout

4.5 Disc mounting bolts (arrowed). Note directional arrow (A)

5.3 Brake light switch wiring connectors (arrowed)

Removal

4 Remove the front wheel (see Section 14).
Caution: Do not lay the wheel down and allow it to rest on the disc – the disc could become warped.
5 If you are not replacing the disc with a new one, mark the relationship of the disc to the wheel so that it can be installed in the same position. Unscrew the disc retaining bolts, loosening them a little at a time to avoid distorting the disc, then remove the disc **(see illustration)**.

Installation

6 Before installing the disc, make sure there is no dirt or corrosion where the disc seats on the hub. If the disc does not sit flat when it is bolted down, it will appear to be warped when checked or when the front brake is used.
7 Install the disc, making sure that the minimum thickness information is facing up and that the directional arrow points in the direction of normal wheel rotation. Align the previously applied register marks, if you are reinstalling the original disc. Install the bolts and tighten them evenly and a little at a time in a criss-cross sequence to the torque setting specified at the beginning of this Chapter.
8 Clean the disc using acetone or brake system cleaner. If a new brake disc has been installed, remove any protective coating from its working surfaces.
9 Install the front wheel (see Section 14).
10 Operate the brake lever several times to bring the pads into contact with the disc. Check the operation of the brake before riding the scooter.

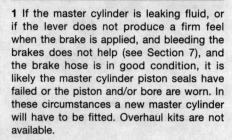

5 Disc brake master cylinder

1 If the master cylinder is leaking fluid, or if the lever does not produce a firm feel when the brake is applied, and bleeding the brakes does not help (see Section 7), and the brake hose is in good condition, it is likely the master cylinder piston seals have failed or the piston and/or bore are worn. In these circumstances a new master cylinder will have to be fitted. Overhaul kits are not available.

Removal

2 Remove the handlebar covers for access (see Chapter 9).
3 Disconnect the wiring from the brake light switch **(see illustration)**.
4 If the master cylinder is just being displaced, ensure the fluid reservoir cover is secure. Note the UP mark on the back of the handlebar clamp, then unscrew the clamp bolts and lift the master cylinder and lever assembly off **(see illustrations)**.
5 Position the assembly clear of the handlebar, making sure no strain is placed on the brake hose. Keep the fluid reservoir upright to prevent air entering the hydraulic system.
6 If the master cylinder is being removed, follow the procedure in *Pre-ride checks* to

remove the reservoir cover, diaphragm plate (if fitted) and diaphragm. Siphon the brake fluid out of the reservoir, then temporarily fit the diaphragm, plate and cover.
Caution: To prevent damage from spilled brake fluid, always cover painted components and bodywork.
7 Unscrew the brake hose banjo bolt and detach the banjo fitting, noting its alignment with the master cylinder **(see illustration)**. Once disconnected, secure the hose in an upright position to minimise fluid loss. Wrap a clean plastic bag tightly around the end to prevent dirt entering the system. Discard the sealing washers as new ones must be fitted on reassembly.
8 Undo the master cylinder clamp bolts and remove the master cylinder and lever assembly **(see illustrations 5.4a and b)**.
9 If required, remove the brake light switch(see Chapter 10).
10 If required, remove the brake light switch (see Chapter 10).
11 Inspect the fluid reservoir cover, diaphragm plate and diaphragm. If any parts are damaged or deteriorated a new master cylinder will have to be fitted.

Installation

12 Installation is the reverse of removal, noting the following:
● Ensure the back of the master cylinder clamp is correctly fitted **(see illustration 5.4a)**.
● Tighten the upper clamp bolt first.
● Ensure the brake light wiring is connected securely.
● Align the banjo fitting as noted on removal.
● Connect the brake hose to the master cylinder, using new sealing washers on both sides of the banjo fitting.
● Fill the fluid reservoir with new brake fluid (see *Pre-ride checks*).
● Bleed the air from the system (see Section 7).
● Ensure the reservoir diaphragm is correctly seated and that the cover screws are tightened securely.
13 Check the operation of the brake and the brake light before riding the scooter.

5.4a Note UP mark on back of the clamp

5.4b Remove the lever and master cylinder assembly

5.7 Note alignment of the banjo fitting (arrowed)

6.3 Check where the brake hose joins the banjo union

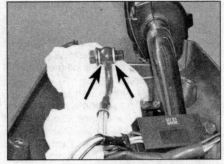

6.8 Use new sealing washers on both sides of banjo fittings

6 Brake hoses and fittings

Inspection

1 Brake hose condition should be checked regularly and the hose replaced every three years (see Chapter 1).
2 Remove the body panels as necessary to inspect the full length of the hose (see Chapter 9).
3 Twist and flex the hose while looking for cracks, bulges and seeping fluid. Check extra carefully where the hose connects to the banjo fittings, as this is a common area for hose failure **(see illustration)**.
4 Inspect the banjo fittings – if they are rusted, cracked or damaged, fit new hoses.

Renewal

Caution: To prevent damage from spilled brake fluid while renewing the brake hose, always cover painted components and bodywork.
5 The brake hoses have banjo fittings on both ends. Unscrew the banjo bolts carefully, noting the alignment of the fittings with the master cylinder or brake caliper **(see illustrations 5.7 and 6.3)**.
6 Free the hose from any clips or guides and remove it, noting its routing. Discard the sealing washers. **Note:** *Do not operate the brake lever while a brake hose is disconnected.*
7 Position the new hose, making sure it is not twisted or otherwise strained, and ensure

that it is correctly routed through any clips or guides and is clear of all moving components.
8 Check that the fittings align correctly, then install the banjo bolts, using new sealing washers on both sides of the fittings **(see illustration)**. Tighten the banjo bolts securely.
9 Flush the old brake fluid from the system, refill with new brake fluid and bleed the air from the system (see Section 7).
10 Check the operation of the brake before riding the scooter.

7 Brake bleeding and fluid change

Brake bleeding

Caution: Support the scooter in a upright position and ensure that the brake fluid reservoir is level while carrying-out these procedures.
1 Bleeding the brake is simply the process of removing air from the brake fluid reservoir, master cylinder, the hose and the brake caliper. Bleeding is necessary whenever a brake system connection is loosened, or when a component is replaced or renewed. Leaks in the system may also allow air to enter, but leaking brake fluid will reveal their presence and warn you of the need for repair.
2 To bleed the brake, you will need some new DOT 4 brake fluid, a small container partially filled with new brake fluid, a length of clear vinyl or plastic hose, some rags and a spanner to fit the brake caliper bleed valve.

3 Remove the handlebar covers for access to the fluid reservoir (see Chapter 9).
Caution: To prevent damage from spilled brake fluid while bleeding the brake, always cover painted components and bodywork.
4 Remove the reservoir cover, diaphragm plate (if fitted) and diaphragm and slowly pump the brake lever a few times, until no air bubbles can be seen floating up from the holes in the bottom of the reservoir. This bleeds air from the master cylinder end of the system. Temporarily refit the reservoir cover.
5 Pull the dust cap off the caliper bleed valve **(see illustration)**. Attach one end of the clear hose to the bleed valve and submerge the other end in the brake fluid in the container **(see illustrations)**. **Note:** *To avoid damaging the bleed valve during the procedure, loosen it and then tighten it temporarily with a ring spanner before attaching the hose. With the hose attached, the valve can then be opened and closed with an open-ended spanner.*
6 Check the fluid level in the reservoir. Do not allow the fluid level to drop below the half-way mark during the procedure.
7 Carefully pump the brake lever three or four times and hold it in while opening the caliper bleed valve. When the valve is opened, brake fluid will flow out of the caliper into the clear hose and the lever will move toward the handlebar.
8 Tighten the bleed valve, then release the brake lever gradually. Repeat the process until no air bubbles are visible in the brake fluid leaving the caliper and the lever is firm when applied. On completion, disconnect the hose, ensure the bleed valve is tightened securely and fit the dust cap.
9 Top-up the reservoir, install the diaphragm, diaphragm plate and cover, and wipe up any spilled brake fluid. Check the entire system for fluid leaks.

> **HAYNES HINT** *If it's not possible to produce a firm feel to the lever the fluid may be aerated. Let the brake fluid in the system stabilise for a few hours and then repeat the procedure when the tiny bubbles in the system have settled out. To speed this process up, tie the brake lever to the handlebar so that the system is pressurised.*

7.5a Pull the dust cap off the bleed valve

7.5b Set-up for bleeding the front brake system

7.5c Set-up for bleeding the rear brake system

Fluid change

Note: *Some manufacturers recommend back-filling the brake system with a syringe to avoid troublesome air locks (see Steps 16 to 22).*

10 Changing the brake fluid is a similar process to bleeding the brakes and requires the same materials plus a suitable tool for siphoning the fluid out of the hydraulic reservoir. Also ensure that the container is large enough to take all the old fluid when it is flushed out of the system.

11 Follow the procedure in Step 5, then remove the reservoir cover, diaphragm plate and diaphragm and siphon the old fluid out of the reservoir. Wipe any remaining fluid out of the reservoir with a clean rag. Fill the reservoir with new brake fluid, then follow the procedure in Step 7.

12 Tighten the bleed valve, then release the brake lever gradually. Keep the reservoir topped-up with new fluid at all times or air may enter the system and greatly increase the length of the task. Repeat the process until new fluid can be seen emerging from the bleed valve.

 HAYNES HINT *Old brake fluid is invariably much darker in colour than new fluid, making it easy to see when all old fluid has been expelled from the system.*

13 Disconnect the hose, ensure the bleed valve is tightened securely and install the dust cap.

14 Top-up the reservoir, install the diaphragm, diaphragm plate and cover, and wipe up any spilled brake fluid. Check the entire system for fluid leaks.

15 Check the operation of the brake before riding the scooter.

16 If, after changing the brake fluid, it proves impossible to obtain a firm feel at the brake lever, it may be necessary to back-fill the brake system. To back-fill the system, remove the reservoir cover, diaphragm plate and diaphragm and siphon the fluid out of the reservoir. Temporarily refit the reservoir cover but do not tighten the fixing screws.

17 Remove the brake caliper (see Section 3 or 9). Slowly push the piston(s) as far back into the caliper as possible using hand pressure or a piece of wood between the brake pads for leverage, then siphon any residual fluid from the reservoir. Leave the cover off the reservoir. Refit the brake caliper.

18 Fill a suitable syringe with approximately 40 ml of new brake fluid and connect a short length of hose to the syringe. Bleed any air from the syringe and hose, then connect the hose to the caliper bleed valve. **Note:** *To avoid damaging the bleed valve during the procedure, loosen it and then tighten it temporarily with a ring spanner before attaching the hose. With the hose attached, the valve can then be opened and closed with an open-ended spanner.*

19 Open the bleed valve and carefully inject fluid into the system until the level in the reservoir is up to the half-way mark. Tighten the bleed valve, disconnect the hose and refit the dust cap.

20 Operate the brake lever carefully several times to bring the pads into contact with the disc, then check the fluid level in the reservoir and top-up if necessary (see *Pre-ride checks*).

21 Install the diaphragm, diaphragm plate and cover, and wipe up any spilled brake fluid. Check the system for fluid leaks.

22 Check the operation of the brake before riding the scooter.

8 Rear drum brake

Warning: The dust created by the brake system may contain asbestos, which is harmful to your health. Never blow it out with compressed air and don't inhale any of it. An approved filtering mask should be worn when working on the brake.

Inspection

1 The brake is fitted with a brake wear indicator – if the wear indicator aligns with the index mark when the brake is applied, the shoes should be renewed **(see illustration)**.

2 Alternatively, remove the wheel (see Section 15) and check the amount of friction material on the brake shoes **(see illustration)**. If the friction material has worn to less than half the original thickness (see *Specifications* at the beginning of this Chapter) new brake shoes should be fitted.

3 Inspect the friction material for contamination. If it is fouled with oil or grease, or heavily scored or damaged, both shoes must be renewed as a set. Note that it is not possible to degrease the friction material; if the shoes are contaminated in any way they must be renewed. **Note:** *Any evidence of oil inside the rear brake suggests a worn seal on the gearbox output shaft which must be rectified (see Chapter 3).*

4 If the shoes are in good condition, clean them carefully using a fine wire brush which is completely free of oil and grease to remove all traces of dust and corrosion.

5 Check the condition of the brake shoe springs; they should hold the shoes tightly in place against the operating cam and pivot post **(see illustration 8.2)**. Remove the shoes (see Steps 13 and 14) and renew the springs if they appear weak or are obviously deformed or damaged.

6 Clean the surface of the brake drum using brake system cleaner. Examine the surface for scoring and excessive wear **(see illustration)**. While light scratches are to be expected, any heavy scoring will impair braking and there is no satisfactory way of removing it. In this event the wheel should be renewed, although you could consult a specialist engineer who might be able to skim the surface.

7 If available, measure the internal diameter of the brake drum with a Vernier caliper – take several measurements to ensure the drum has not worn out-of-round. If the drum is out-of-round, fit a new wheel. **Note:** *A brake drum that is out-of-round will cause the brake lever to pulse when the brake is applied.*

8 To check and lubricate the brake cam, first remove the brake shoes (see Steps 13 and 14).

9 Disconnect the brake cable from the brake arm (see Section 10). Where fitted, remove the

8.1 Rear brake wear indicator – Kisbee 100 shown

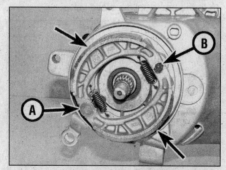

8.2 Inspect the friction material on the brake shoes (arrowed). Operating cam (A) and pivot post (B)

8.6 Check the surface of the brake drum

8.9 Location of the brake arm return spring

8.10 Location of the brake arm pinch bolt

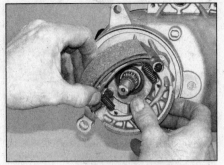

8.14 Fold the shoes inwards to release the spring tension

brake arm return spring, noting how it fits (see illustration).

10 Note the position of the brake arm, then loosen the brake arm pinch bolt (see illustration) and pull the cam out of the brake backplate.

11 Clean all traces of old grease off the cam and shaft. If the bearing surfaces of the cam or shaft are worn the cam should be renewed. Lubricate the shaft of the cam with a smear of copper-based grease. Position the brake arm as noted on removal, then install the cam in the backplate or casing, ensuring it locates fully into the brake arm. Tighten the pinch bolt securely. Lubricate the cam and the pivot post with a smear of copper grease and install the brake shoes.

Shoe removal and installation

12 Remove the wheel (see Section 15).

13 Slacken the adjustment in the brake cable to reduce the tension in the brake shoe springs. If the shoes are not going to be renewed they must be installed in their original positions – mark them to aid reassembly. Note how the springs are fitted.

14 Grasp the outer edge of each shoe and fold them inwards towards each other to release the spring tension and remove the shoes (see illustration). Remove the springs from the shoes.

15 Where fitted, note the location of the rubber brake shoe supports pressed into the brake backplate (see illustration).

16 To install the shoes, first lubricate the cam and the pivot post with a smear of copper

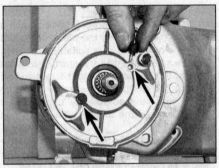

8.15 Location of the brake shoe supports (arrowed)

grease. Align the shoes with the cam and pivot post ends together and hook the springs onto the shoes (see illustration). Position the shoes in a V on the cam and pivot post, then fold them down into position (see illustration 8.14). Operate the brake arm to check that the cam and shoes work correctly.

17 Install the wheel.

18 Adjust the brake cable (see Chapter 1) and test the operation of the brake before riding the scooter.

9 Rear disc brake

⚠ Warning: The dust created by the brake system may contain asbestos, which is harmful to your

8.16 Align the brake shoes and attach the springs

health. Never blow it out with compressed air and don't inhale any of it. An approved filtering mask should be worn when working on the brakes.

Brake pads

Note: Do not operate the brake lever while the caliper is off the disc.

Speedfight

1 To allow clearance for removing the brake caliper, first undo the rear wheel bolts and displace the wheel (see Section 15).

2 Loosen the brake pad pin, then undo the caliper mounting bolts and draw the caliper off the disc (see illustration).

3 Unscrew the pad pin and remove the pad spring, noting how it fits (see illustration).

4 Withdraw the brake pads, noting how they fit (see illustration).

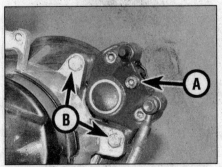

9.2 Pad pin (A) and caliper mounting bolts (B)

9.3 Unscrew the pad pin and remove the pad spring (arrowed)

9.4 Note how the brake pads fit

9.10 Fit the pad pin to secure the outermost pad

9.11 Hold the pin against the tension of the spring during installation

9.12 Install the caliper on the disc

5 Follow the procedure in Section 2, Steps 52 and 53, to inspect the brake pads.

6 Remove any traces of corrosion from the pad pin and inspect the pin for wear and damage. Remove all traces of corrosion from the pad spring.

7 Check the condition of the brake disc (see Step 38).

8 To make it easier to fit the caliper onto the disc, especially If new pads are being installed, slowly push the pistons as far back into the caliper as possible using hand pressure or a piece of wood for leverage. This will displace brake fluid back into the hydraulic reservoir, so it may be necessary to remove the reservoir cap, plate and diaphragm and siphon out some fluid (depending on how much fluid was in there in the first place and how far the piston has to be pushed in). If

the piston is difficult to push back, attach a length of clear hose to the bleed valve and place the open end in a suitable container, then open the valve and try again. Take great care not to draw any air into the system and don't forget to tighten the valve once the piston has been sufficiently displaced. If in doubt, bleed the brakes afterwards (see Section 7).

Caution: Never lever the caliper against the brake disc to push a piston back into the caliper as damage to the disc will result.

9 Prior to installation, smear the backs of the pads with copper-based grease, making sure that none gets on the front or sides of the pads.

10 Install the brake pads with the friction material facing the disc. Support the pads and fit the pad pin through from the left-hand side

so that it just passes through the top of the left-hand pad **(see illustration)**.

11 Install the pad spring with the wire end hooked over the top edge of the caliper **(see illustration 9.3)**. Press the pin into the caliper, over the top of the spring and through the top of the right-hand pad – it will be necessary to hold the end of the pin down to guide it through the pad and into the hole in the right-hand side of the caliper **(see illustration)**. Screw the pin into the caliper – it can be tightened fully once the caliper has been installed on the scooter.

12 Fit the caliper onto the disc **(see illustration)** then tighten the caliper mounting bolts to the torque setting specified at the beginning of this Chapter. Don't forget to tighten the pad pin securely.

13 Install the rear wheel.

14 On completion, operate the rear brake lever several times to bring the pads into contact with the disc. Check the brake fluid level and top-up if necessary (see *Pre-ride checks*). Check the operation of the brake before riding the scooter.

Tweet

15 Undo the caliper mounting bolts and draw the caliper off the disc **(see illustration)**.

16 Unclip the plastic cover from the caliper **(see illustration)**.

17 Pull out the R-clip from the end of the pad pin and pull out the pin, noting how it locates over the pad spring **(see illustrations)**. Remove the spring **(see illustration)**.

9.15 Undo the mounting bolts and lift the caliper off

9.16 Unclip the plastic cover

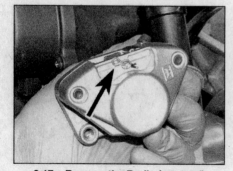

9.17a Remove the R-clip (arrowed)

9.17b Note how the pad pin fits above the pad spring

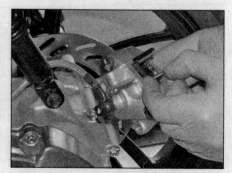

9.17c Lift out the pad spring

9.18 Lift the pads out of the caliper

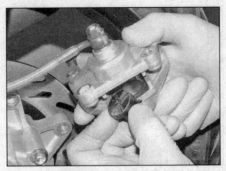

9.19 Note location of the piston inserts

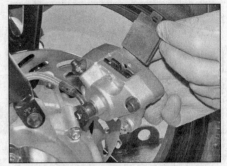

9.22 Install the pads and hold them in position from underneath

18 Push the pads up from the underside of the caliper and lift them out (see illustration).
19 Note the location of the caliper piston inserts inside the caliper and remove them if they are loose (see illustration).
20 Follow the procedure in Section 2, Steps 52 and 53, to inspect the brake pads.
21 Remove any traces of corrosion from the pad pin and inspect the pin for wear and damage. Remove all traces of corrosion from the pad spring. Check the condition of the brake disc (see Step 38).
22 Prior to installing the brake pads, push the pistons back into the caliper and ensure the piston inserts are in place. Fit the pads with the friction material facing the disc (see illustration). Support the pads from underneath.
23 Install the pad spring with the wide end resting on the top edge of the caliper (see illustration 9.17c). Press the pin into the caliper, through the top of the left-hand pad, over the top of the spring and through the top of the right-hand pad (see illustration 9.17b). Secure the pin with the R-clip (see illustration 9.17a).
24 Fit the plastic cover then fit the caliper onto the disc. Tighten the caliper mounting bolts to the torque setting specified at the beginning of this Chapter.
25 On completion, operate the rear brake lever several times to bring the pads into contact with the disc. Check the brake fluid level and top-up if necessary (see Pre-ride checks). Check the operation of the brake before riding the scooter.

Brake caliper

⚠️ Warning: If the caliper indicates the need for renewal (usually due to leaking fluid or sticky operation), all old brake fluid should be flushed from the system at the same time. Also, the dust created by the brake system may contain asbestos, which is harmful to your health. Never blow it out with compressed air and don't inhale any of it. An approved filtering mask should be worn when working on the brake. Do not, under any circumstances, use petroleum-based solvents to clean brake parts. Use a dedicated brake cleaner or denatured alcohol only, as described. To

prevent damage from spilled brake fluid, always cover paintwork when working on the braking system.
Note: It is not necessary to remove the caliper completely for cleaning and inspection.
26 If the caliper is just being displaced, the brake pads can be left in place. Follow the procedure in Steps 1 and 2 (for Speedfight) or 15 (for Tweet) to remove the caliper. Support the caliper with a cable-tie to ensure no strain is placed on the brake hose. To install the caliper follow the procedure in Steps 12 and 14 (for Speedfight) or 24 and 25 (for Tweet).
27 If the caliper is being removed completely from the scooter, first note the alignment of the banjo fitting on the caliper, then loosen and lightly tighten the brake hose banjo bolt (see illustrations 9.2 or 9.15).
28 Undo the caliper mounting bolts and draw the caliper assembly off the disc. Remove the brake pads.
29 Unscrew the banjo bolt and separate the hose from the caliper. Discard the sealing washers as new ones must be used on installation. Wrap a plastic bag tightly around the end of the hose to prevent dirt entering the system and secure the hose in an upright position to minimise fluid loss.
30 If the caliper is being cleaned and inspected, remove the brake pads. On Tweet models, ease out the caliper piston inserts (see illustration 9.19).
31 Clean the caliper with denatured alcohol or brake system cleaner. Inspect the caliper for signs of damage, especially around the mounting lugs and the bleed screw and renew it if necessary.
32 If brake fluid is leaking from around the edge of either piston the internal piston seal has failed and a new caliper will have to be fitted. Overhaul kits are not available.
33 To install the caliper if it has just been displaced, follow the procedure in Steps 12 and 14 (for Speedfight) or 24 and 25 (for Tweet).
34 If the caliper was removed from the machine, or a new caliper is being fitted, first install the brake pads, then fit the caliper onto the disc.
35 Connect the brake hose to the caliper, using new sealing washers on both sides

of the banjo fitting. Align the banjo fitting as noted on removal and tighten the banjo bolt securely.
36 Top-up the brake fluid reservoir (see Pre-ride checks). Bleed the brake system (see Section 7).
37 Check for fluid leaks and check the operation of the brake before riding the scooter.

Brake disc

38 Refer to Section 4 and use the same procedures for checking the rear brake disc. If checking the disc for warpage, support the scooter on its centrestand with the rear wheel raised off the ground. Attach a dial gauge to the suspension or the rear of the transmission casing. Note: This test is not feasible on the Shuricane wavy pattern disc. If excessive movement is indicated, first check the gearbox output shaft for play (see Chapter 1, Section 23). If the bearings are good, the disc is warped and should be replaced with a new one.
39 Remove the rear wheel (see Section 15).
40 On Tweet models, the disc is attached directly to the wheel (see illustration).
Caution: Do not lay the wheel down and allow it to rest on the disc – the disc could become warped.
41 If you are not replacing the disc with a new one, mark the relationship of the disc to the wheel so that it can be installed in the same position. Unscrew the disc retaining bolts, loosening them a little at a time to avoid distorting the disc, then remove the disc.

9.40 Disc is bolted directly to the wheel – Tweet models

9.42a Hold the hub to prevent it turning

9.42b Holding the hub with a bar between two wheel bolts

9.42c Remove the large flat washer...

9.42d ...then draw the hub off the shaft

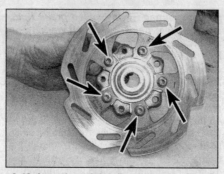

9.43 Location of the disc mounting bolts

system cleaner. If a new brake disc has been installed, remove any protective coating from its working surfaces.

47 On Speedfight models, install the hub and the flat washer, then tighten the hub locknut to the specified torque.

48 Install the rear wheel (see Section 15).

49 Operate the rear brake lever several times to bring the pads into contact with the disc. Check the operation of the brake before riding the scooter.

10 Brake cable

42 On Speedfight models, the disc is bolted to the rear hub. Using a proprietary holding tool to prevent to hub turning, undo the hub locknut (see illustration). Alternatively, use two rear wheel bolts and a strong bar to hold the hub (see illustration). Note: *A new locknut should be fitted on reassembly.* Remove the large flat washer then draw the hub off the gearbox output shaft (see illustrations).

43 Turn the hub over to access the disc mounting bolts (see illustration). Note the direction of rotation arrow and minimum thickness specification are stamped on this (left-hand) side of the disc. If required, unscrew the disc retaining bolts, loosening them a little at a time to avoid distorting the disc, then remove the disc. If you are not replacing the disc with a new one, mark the relationship of

the disc to the hub so that it can be installed in the same position.

44 Before installing the disc, make sure there is no dirt or corrosion where the disc seats on the wheel or hub. If the disc does not sit flat when it is bolted down, it will appear to be warped when checked or when the rear brake is used.

45 Install the disc, making sure that the minimum thickness information and direction of rotation arrow will be facing the left-hand side when the wheel or hub are installed. Align the previously applied register marks, if you are reinstalling the original disc. Install the bolts and tighten them evenly and a little at a time in a criss-cross sequence to the torque setting specified at the beginning of this Chapter.

46 Clean the disc using acetone or brake

1 Remove the body panels as necessary (although see *Haynes Hint*) to access the full length of the cable from the handlebar lever to the rear brake (see Chapter 9).

2 Fully unscrew the adjuster on the lower end of the cable and release the cable from the brake arm (see illustration). Note the location of the return spring on the cable, if fitted.

3 Release the cable from the stop on the underside of the transmission casing (see illustration 10.2) and any clips retained by the belt cover screws.

4 Pull the outer cable out of the handlebar lever bracket and free the inner cable end from its socket in the underside of the lever (see illustrations).

5 Withdraw the cable from the scooter, noting its routing.

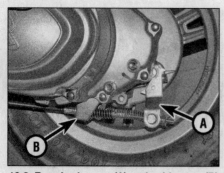

10.2 Rear brake arm (A) and cable stop (B)

10.4a Pull the cable out of the handlebar bracket

10.4b Release the inner cable end from the lever

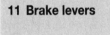

HAYNES HiNT *When fitting a new cable, tape the lower end of the new cable to the upper end of the old cable before removing it from the machine. Slowly pull the lower end of the old cable out, guiding the new cable down into position. Using this method will ensure the cable is routed correctly and will avoid having to remove any of the body panels.*

6 Installation is the reverse of removal. Make sure the cable is correctly routed and clipped into place. Lubricate the cable trunnion at the handlebar end with grease before fitting it into the lever and adjust the cable freeplay (see Chapter 1).

7 Check the operation of the brake before riding the scooter.

11 Brake levers

Removal

1 Remove the handlebar covers (see Chapter 9).

2 To remove the front and rear brake levers for disc brakes, first unscrew the lever pivot bolt locknut on the underside of the lever (see illustration), then withdraw the pivot bolt and remove the lever from its bracket. Note how the lever locates against the master cylinder pushrod and the brake light switch (see Section 5). The lever bracket is integral with the front brake master cylinder (see Section 5).

3 When removing the rear drum brake lever, first unscrew the adjuster on the lower end of the cable to slacken the cable, then disconnect the inner cable from the lever (see Section 10).

4 Unscrew the lever pivot bolt locknut on the underside of the lever (see illustration), then withdraw the pivot bolt and remove the lever from its bracket. Note how the lever locates against the brake light switch.

5 The rear brake lever bracket is integral with the handlebar switch unit. To remove the lever

11.2 Brake lever pivot bolt locknut (arrowed) – disc brake

bracket, undo the switch unit screws (see illustration). Displace the switch unit, then lift the lever bracket off the handlebar noting how the peg on the inside of the bracket locates in the hole in the handlebar (see illustration).

Installation

6 Installation is the reverse of removal. Apply grease to the pivot bolt shank and the contact areas between the lever and its bracket.

7 When installing the rear brake lever, lubricate the cable trunnion at the handlebar end with grease before fitting it into the lever and adjust the cable freeplay (see Chapter 1).

8 Check the operation of the brakes and the brake light before riding the scooter.

12 Wheels – inspection and repair

1 In order to carry out a proper inspection of the wheels, it is necessary to support the scooter upright so that the wheel being inspected is raised off the ground. Clean the wheels thoroughly to remove mud and dirt that may interfere with the inspection procedure or mask defects. Make a general check of the wheels (see Chapter 1) and tyres (see *Pre-ride checks*).

2 If available, attach a dial gauge to the fork leg (front) or the transmission casing (rear) with the tip of the gauge touching the side of the rim. Spin the wheel slowly and check the axial (side-to-side) runout of the rim (see illustration).

3 In order to accurately check radial (out-of-

11.4 Brake lever pivot bolt locknut (arrowed) – drum brake

round) runout with the dial gauge, the wheel should be removed from the machine, and the tyre from the wheel. With the axle clamped in a vice or jig and the dial gauge positioned on the top of the rim, the wheel can be rotated to check the runout.

4 An easier, though slightly less accurate, method is to attach a stiff wire pointer to the front suspension or transmission casing with the end of the pointer a fraction of an inch from the edge of the wheel rim where the wheel and tyre join. If the wheel is true, the distance from the pointer to the rim will be constant as the wheel is rotated. **Note:** *If front wheel runout is excessive, check the wheel bearings very carefully before renewing the wheel (see Section 16).*

5 The wheels should also be visually inspected for cracks, flat spots on the rim and other damage. Look very closely for dents in the area where the tyre bead contacts the rim. Dents in this area may prevent complete sealing of the tyre against the rim, which leads to deflation of the tyre over a period of time. If damage is evident, or if runout is excessive, the wheel will have to be replaced with a new one. Never attempt to repair a damaged cast alloy wheel.

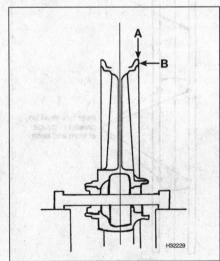

12.2 Check the wheel for radial (out-of-round) runout (A) and axial (side-to-side) runout (B)

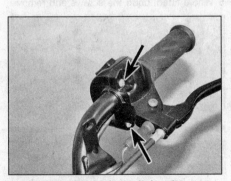

11.5a Location of the switch unit screws

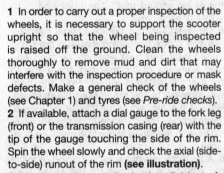

11.5b Peg on bracket locates in hole (arrowed)

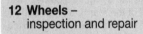

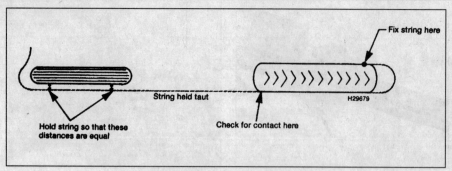

Fix string here

String held taut

Hold string so that these distances are equal

Check for contact here

H29679

13.5 Wheel alignment check using string

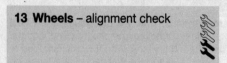

13 Wheels – alignment check

1 Misalignment of the wheels can cause strange and potentially serious handling problems and will most likely be due to bent frame or suspension components as the result

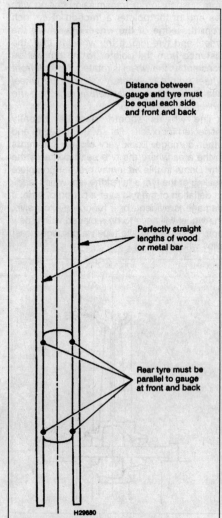

Distance between gauge and tyre must be equal each side and front and back

Perfectly straight lengths of wood or metal bar

Rear tyre must be parallel to gauge at front and back

H29680

13.6 Wheel alignment check using a straight-edge

of an accident. If the frame or suspension are at fault, repair by a frame specialist or replacement with new parts are the only options.

2 To check wheel alignment you will need an assistant, a length of string or a perfectly straight piece of wood and a ruler. A plumb bob or spirit level for checking that the wheels are vertical will also be required. Support the scooter in an upright position on its main stand.

3 If a string is used, have your assistant hold one end of it about halfway between the floor and the centre of the rear wheel, with the string touching the back edge of the rear tyre sidewall.

4 Run the other end of the string forward and pull it tight so that it is roughly parallel to the floor. Slowly bring the string into contact with the front sidewall of the rear tyre, then turn the front wheel until it is parallel with the string. Most models covered use the same size tyre front and rear, meaning that if correctly aligned the string should touch the front and back edges of each tyre.

5 On Tweet 125/150 models a larger diameter rear tyre is fitted, meaning that with the string pulled tight and held against the front and rear sidewalls of the rear tyre there should be a small distance (offset) from the front tyre sidewall to the string (see illustration). Repeat the procedure on the other side of the machine. The distance from the front tyre sidewall to the string should be equal on both sides.

6 A perfectly straight length of wood or metal bar may be substituted for the string (see illustration).

14.3 Unscrew the knurled ring (arrowed)

7 If the distance between the string and tyre is greater on one side, or if the rear wheel appears to be out of alignment, have your machine checked by a specialist.

8 If the front-to-back alignment is correct, the wheels still may be out of alignment vertically.

9 Using a plumb bob or spirit level, check the rear wheel to make sure it is vertical. To do this, hold the string of the plumb bob against the tyre upper sidewall and allow the weight to settle just off the floor. If the string touches both the upper and lower tyre sidewalls and is perfectly straight, the wheel is vertical. If it is not, adjust the main stand until it is.

10 Once the rear wheel is vertical, check the front wheel in the same manner. If both wheels are not perfectly vertical, the frame and/or major suspension components are bent.

14 Front wheel

Removal

Caution: Don't lay the wheel down and allow it to rest on the brake disc – it could become warped. Set the wheel on wood blocks so the disc doesn't support the weight of the wheel.

1 Support the scooter in an upright position on its main stand. Place a support under the frame at the front so that the scooter is tipped back to rest on the rear wheel.

2 Unscrew the brake caliper mounting bolts and displace the caliper (see Section 2). **Note:** *Do not operate the front brake lever while the caliper is off the disc.*

3 On models with a cable-driven speedometer (V-Clic, Kisbee (except Street Zone), Tweet) unscrew the knurled ring and disconnect the speedometer cable from the speedometer drive housing (see illustration). All other models have an electronic speedometer; do not attempt to disconnect the speedometer wire from the drive housing.

4 On Speedfight models, loosen the axle pinch bolt on the right-hand fork leg (see illustration).

5 Where fitted, undo the screws and remove

14.4 Location of the axle pinch bolt – Speedfight models

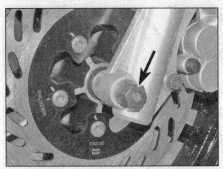

14.5 Remove the plastic covers

14.6 Remove the axle nut and washer

14.7 Support the wheel and withdraw the axle

14.8 Speedometer drive housing locates against fork lug (arrowed)

15 Lift the wheel into place. Check that the speedometer drive housing is located correctly against the inside of the fork **(see illustration 14.8)**.

16 Slide the axle in carefully ensuring all the components remain in alignment.

17 Install the washer and axle nut, then tighten the nut to the torque setting specified at the beginning of this Chapter. Where fitted, install the plastic covers on the ends of the axle **(see illustration 14.5)**.

18 On Speedfight models, tighten the axle pinch bolt to the specified torque **(see illustration 14.4)**.

19 Re-connect the speedometer cable (where applicable).

20 Install the brake caliper, making sure the pads sit squarely on each side of the disc (see Section 2).

21 Move the scooter off its stand, apply the front brake and pump the suspension a few times to settle all components in position.

22 Check the operation of the front brake before riding the scooter.

15 Rear wheel

Removal

1 Support the scooter in an upright position on its centrestand with the rear wheel off the ground.

2 Remove the exhaust system (see Chapter 5).

3 On machines with twin rear shock absorbers, remove the rear subframe (see Chapter 7, Section 9), then on Tweet 125/150 models, displace the rear brake caliper (see Section 9). The rear wheel can now be drawn off the gearbox output shaft.

4 On Speedfight models, have an assistant apply the rear brake and undo the rear wheel bolts **(see illustration)**. The rear wheel can now be drawn off the gearbox output shaft leaving the brake disc in position on the hub.

the plastic covers from the ends of the axle **(see illustration)**.

6 Counterhold the axle, undo the axle nut and remove the washer **(see illustration)**. **Note:** *If a locknut is used on the axle a new one should be fitted on reassembly.*

7 Support the wheel and withdraw the axle from the wheel and front suspension **(see illustration)**.

8 Lower the wheel out of the forks and lift off the speedometer drive housing **(see illustration)**. Note how the drive housing locates against the inside of the fork.

9 Note the position of any axle spacers and remove them from the wheel for safekeeping.

10 Clean the axle and remove any corrosion using steel wool. Check the axle for straightness by rolling it on a flat surface such as a piece of plate glass. If the axle is bent, renew it.

11 Check the condition of the wheel bearings (see Section 16).

Installation

12 Lubricate the axle with a smear of grease.

13 Install any axle spacers in the hub seals.

14 Manoeuvre the wheel into position. Apply some grease to the inside of the speedometer drive housing, then install the housing, ensuring it locates correctly on the wheel hub **(see illustration)**.

14.14 Drive housing locates on tabs (arrowed)

15.4 Rear wheel bolts – Speedfight models

15.5a Unscrew the locknut...

15.5b ...and remove the washer

15.6a Inspect the splines on the shaft...

15.6b ...and in the centre of the wheel hub

**15.6c Splines in the centre of the hub –
Speedfight models**

16.2 Remove any axle spacers

5 On all other models, lever off the centre cover, where fitted, with a small flat-bladed screwdriver. Have an assistant apply the rear brake, then unscrew the hub locknut and remove the washer **(see illustrations)**. **Note:** *A new locknut should be fitted on reassembly.* Draw the wheel off the gearbox shaft and manoeuvre it out of the back of the machine.
6 Inspect the splines on the shaft and on the inside of the hub for wear and damage **(see illustrations)**. On Speedfight models, follow the procedure in Section 9 to remove the brake disc/hub assembly in order to check the splines **(see illustration)**.
7 If the splines are worn, both the wheel/hub and the shaft should be replaced with new ones. Refer to the procedure in Chapter 3 to renew the gearbox shaft.

Installation

8 Installation is the reverse of removal, noting the following:
● On drum braked models, slide the wheel onto the shaft carefully to avoid disturbing the alignment of the brake shoes. Tighten the hub nut to the torque setting specified at the beginning of this Chapter.
● On disc braked models, install the brake caliper, then have an assistant apply the rear brake and tighten the rear wheel nut.
● On Speedfight models, tighten the rear wheel bolts to the specified torque setting.
● Check the operation of the rear brake before riding the scooter.

16 Front wheel bearings

Note: *The front wheel bearings are located inside the wheel hub. There are no rear wheel bearings as such, the rear axle/gearbox output shaft bearings are located inside the gearbox (see Chapter 3).*

Check

1 Remove the front wheel (see Section 14).
Caution: Don't lay the wheel down and allow it to rest on the brake disc – it could become warped. Set the wheel on wood blocks so the wheel rim supports the weight of the wheel.

2 Remove any spacers from the wheel hub **(see illustration)**.
3 On some models, such as Speedfight and Kisbee, the left-hand spacer is secured by a metal retainer **(see illustration)**. Refer to *Tools and Workshop Tips* in the *Reference* and use an expanding bearing puller and slide hammer to remove the spacer and retainer **(see illustration)**.
4 Lever out the hub seal with a flat-bladed screwdriver to gain access to the bearings **(see illustration)**. A new seal must be fitted on reassembly.
5 Inspect the bearings (see *Tools and Workshop Tips* in the *Reference* section at the end of the manual).
6 If there is any doubt about the condition of a bearing, replace both wheel bearings with

**16.3a Metal retainer (arrowed) secures
axle spacer**

16.3b Removing the spacer and retainer

16.4 Lever out the hub seal

16.9a Driving a bearing out of the hub

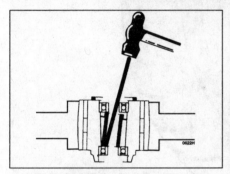

16.9b Locate the rod as shown to drive out the bearing

16.12a Driving in a new bearing

16.12b Installed wheel bearing, sealed side (arrowed) outermost

new ones. **Note:** *Always renew the wheel bearings in sets, never individually.*

Renewal

7 If not already done, lever out the bearing seal or fixed spacer. Check for any retaining circlips and remove them.

8 To remove the bearings from the hub, support the wheel on wooden blocks. Note the position of the bearings before removing them.

Caution: Don't support the wheel on the brake disc when driving out the bearings.

9 Use a metal rod (preferably a brass punch) inserted through the centre of the bearing on one side of the wheel hub to tap evenly around the outer race of the bearing on the other side

(see illustrations). The bearing spacer (if fitted) will come out with the bearing.

10 Turn the wheel over and remove the remaining bearing using the same procedure.

11 Thoroughly clean the bearing housings with a suitable solvent and inspect them for scoring and wear. If a housing is damaged, indicating that the bearing has seized and spun in use, it may be possible to secure the new bearing in place with a suitable bearing locking solution.

12 Fit a new bearing into one side of the hub, with the marked or sealed side facing outwards (see *Tools and Workshop Tips* in the *Reference* section). Using a bearing driver or a socket large enough to contact the outer race of the bearing, drive it in until it is completely seated **(see illustrations)**.

13 Turn the wheel over, fit the bearing spacer and install the other new bearing.

14 If applicable, secure the bearing with the circlip and ensure the circlip is properly located in its groove.

15 Install new hub seals – lubricate the seals with a smear of grease, then press or drive them in using a suitably-sized socket that bears on the outer edge of the seal.

16 On models with a fixed spacer, fit the spacer then tap the retainer into place so that it is level with the hub using a hammer and block of wood **(see illustrations)**.

17 As noted on removal, install the axle spacer **(see illustration 16.2)**, then install the wheel (see Section 14).

16.16a Install the fixed spacer...

16.16b ...and the retainer

16.16c Level the top edge of the retainer with the hub

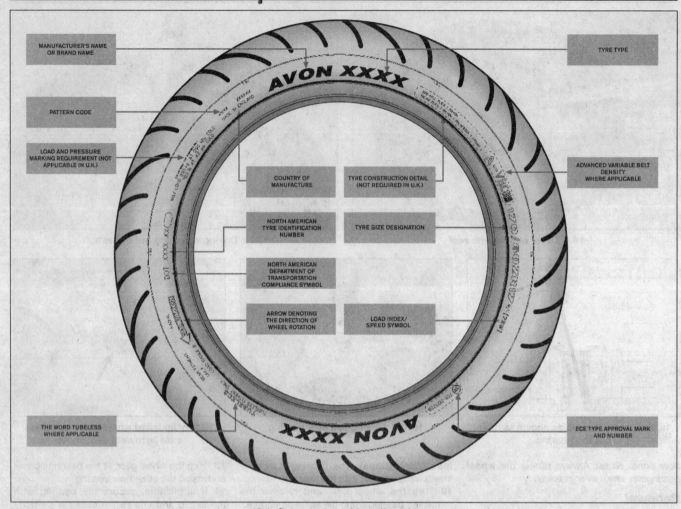

MANUFACTURER'S NAME OR BRAND NAME

PATTERN CODE

LOAD AND PRESSURE MARKING REQUIREMENT (NOT APPLICABLE IN U.K.)

TYRE TYPE

ADVANCED VARIABLE BELT DENSITY WHERE APPLICABLE

COUNTRY OF MANUFACTURE

TYRE CONSTRUCTION DETAIL (NOT REQUIRED IN U.K.)

NORTH AMERICAN TYRE IDENTIFICATION NUMBER

TYRE SIZE DESIGNATION

NORTH AMERICAN DEPARTMENT OF TRANSPORTATION COMPLIANCE SYMBOL

ARROW DENOTING THE DIRECTION OF WHEEL ROTATION

LOAD INDEX/ SPEED SYMBOL

THE WORD TUBELESS WHERE APPLICABLE

ECE TYPE APPROVAL MARK AND NUMBER

17.1 Common tyre sidewall markings

17 Tyre fitting

1 When selecting new tyres, refer to the tyre information label on the scooter or the information given in the owners handbook. Ensure that front and rear tyre types are compatible, the correct size and correct speed rating **(see illustration)**. If necessary seek advice from a motorcycle tyre fitting specialist.
2 It is recommended that tyres are fitted by a tyre specialist rather than attempted in the home workshop. This is particularly relevant in the case of tubeless tyres because the force required to break the seal between the wheel rim and tyre bead is substantial, and is usually beyond the capabilities of an individual working with normal tyre levers. Additionally, the specialist will be able to balance the wheel after tyre fitting.
3 Punctured tubeless tyres can in some cases be repaired depending on the location of the hole and its size – refer to a tyre fitting specialist for advice. Never fit an inner tube in a tubeless tyre.

Chapter 9
Bodywork

Contents

Degrees of difficulty

Easy, suitable for novice with little experience	Fairly easy, suitable for beginner with some experience	Fairly difficult, suitable for competent DIY mechanic	Difficult, suitable for experienced DIY mechanic	Very difficult, suitable for expert DIY or professional

Specifications

Torque settings

Grab handle bolts – all models	25 Nm
Storage compartment bolts	
Speedfight	8 Nm
V-Clic, Kisbee, Vivacity and Tweet	10 Nm
Seat cowling screws – Vivacity	8 Nm
Floor panel bolts	
Speedfight, Kisbee and Vivacity	8 Nm
V-Clic and Tweet	10 Nm
Belly panel bolts	
V-Clic	10 Nm
Tweet	8 Nm
Front mudguard screws/bolts	
Speedfight, Kisbee, Vivacity and Tweet	10 Nm
V-Clic	12 Nm
Kick panel bolts – Speedfight	8 Nm

1 General information

Almost all the functional components are enclosed by body panels, making removal of relevant panels a necessary part of most servicing and maintenance procedures. Panel removal is straightforward, and as well as facilitating access to mechanical components, it avoids the risk of accidental damage to the panels.

Most panels are retained by screws and inter-locking tabs. Once the evident fasteners have been removed, try to withdraw the panel as described but DO NOT FORCE IT. If it will not release, check that all the fasteners have been removed and try again.

Where a panel engages another by means of tabs, be careful not to break the tab or its mating slot. Remember that a few moments of patience at this stage will save you a lot of money in replacing broken panels.

When installing a body panel, check the fasteners and associated fittings removed with it to be sure of returning everything to its correct place. Check that all the mounting brackets are straight and repair or renew them if necessary before attempting to install the panel.

Tighten the fasteners securely but be careful not to overtighten any of them or the panel may break (not always immediately) due to the uneven stress.

In the case of damaged body parts, it is usually necessary to replace the broken component with a new (or used) one. There are, however, some shops that specialise in 'plastic welding', so it may be worthwhile seeking the advice of one of these specialists before consigning an expensive component to the bin. Additionally, proprietary repair kits can be obtained for repair of small components (see illustration).

Typical repair kit for plastic panels

2 Speedfight models

Seat and storage compartment

1 Unlock the seat and swing it upright. Remove the battery (see Chapter 10).
2 Undo the bolts securing the storage compartment **(see illustration)**.
3 On 50cc two-stroke engined models, temporarily remove the oil tank filler cap **(see illustration)**.
4 Lift the seat and storage compartment assembly out and disconnect the electrical accessory socket wiring connector **(see illustrations)**.
5 Install the oil tank filler cap.
6 If required, undo the seat hinge pivot bolt and remove the seat **(see illustration)**.
7 Installation is the reverse of removal. Note the location of the fuse holders and take care not to dislodge them on installation **(see illustration)**. Ensure that the wiring for the accessory socket is routed in front of the mounting bracket on the frame. Tighten the mounting bolts to the torque setting specified at the beginning of this Chapter.

Underbody panel, rear wheel hugger, mudflap and mudguard

8 Undo the single screw securing the underbody panel, then draw the panel backwards to release the support hooks that

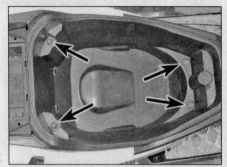

2.2 Location of the storage compartment bolts

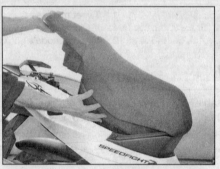

2.4a Lift out the storage compartment...

locate in the lower edge of the seat cowling **(see illustrations)**.
9 Undo the screw securing the hugger to the exhaust mounting bracket **(see illustration)**.

2.3 Unscrew the oil filler cap

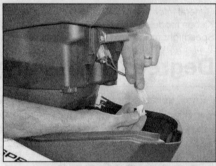

2.4b ...and disconnect the accessory socket connector

Note the location of the insulating washers.
10 Undo the bolt securing the hugger to the transmission case behind the air filter housing **(see illustration)**.

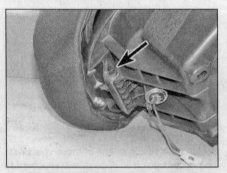

2.6 Seat hinge pivot bolt (arrowed)

2.7 Location of the fuse holders

2.8a Undo the screw...

2.8b ...and draw the panel backwards

2.9 Hugger-to-exhaust bracket screw

2.10 Undo the left-hand mounting bolt...

2.11 ...and right-hand screw

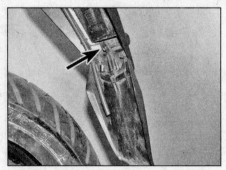

2.12 Undo the screw (arrowed)...

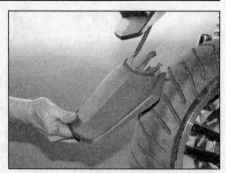

2.13 ...and draw the mudflap off

11 Undo the screw securing the hugger on the right-hand side, then lift the hugger off **(see illustration)**.
12 Undo the screw securing the mudflap on the inside of the mudguard **(see illustration)**.
13 Release the tabs securing the mudflap and draw it off **(see illustration)**.
14 Note the location of the battery breather hose **(see illustration)**. Disconnect the hose from the battery vent union (see Chapter 10) and feed it through to the underside of the machine.
15 Undo the bolts securing the mudguard on both sides and remove it with the breather hose **(see illustration)**.
16 If required, the mudguard support bracket can be removed once the storage

compartment has been removed (see Steps 1 to 4). Undo the bolts securing the mudguard support bracket and lift the bracket out from inside the bodywork, noting how it fits **(see illustrations)**. The bracket also provides the location for the underbody panel screw. On installation, ensure the bracket aligns with the holes for the mudguard mounting bolts.
17 Install the components in the reverse order of removal.

Seat cowling

Note: *The seat cowling is a two-piece assembly – the front and rear sections must be removed separately.*

18 Remove the storage compartment, underbody panel and rear mudguard (see above). Remove the mudguard support bracket (see Step 16).
19 Undo the left and right-hand screws securing the top edge of the cowling **(see illustration)**.
20 Undo the left and right-hand screws inside the bodywork securing the sides of the cowling **(see illustration)**.
21 Undo the screws on the left and right-hand sides securing the rear section of the cowling to the front section **(see illustration 2.20)**. Note the location of the screw U-clips and ensure that they are secure. Renew the U-clips if they are damaged.
22 Ease the rear section backwards and

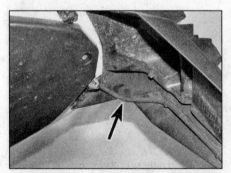

2.14 Location of the battery breather hose

2.15 Remove the mudguard and breather hose

2.16a Undo the bolts (arrowed)...

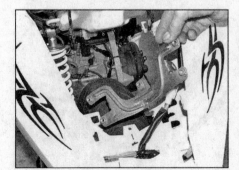

2.16b ...and remove the mudguard support bracket

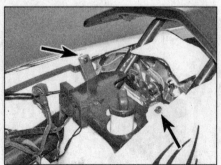

2.19 Undo the screws (arrowed) on the top edge

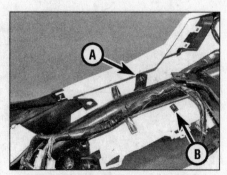

2.20 Screw (A) secures side of cowling. Screw (B) holds sections together

2.22 Ease the rear section backwards

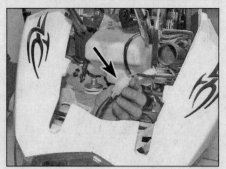

2.23 Tail light wiring connector (arrowed)

2.25 Release the oil hose clip

release the tabs securing the two parts together **(see illustration)**.

23 Disconnect the tail light wiring connector and lift the rear section of the cowling off **(see illustration)**.

24 The rear section is a two-piece assembly incorporating the tail light assembly. If required, refer to Chapter 10 to separate the components.

25 Release the oil hose clip from the left-hand side of the front section **(see illustration)**.

26 Undo the screws securing the front section of the cowling to the top edge of the floor panel **(see illustration)**.

27 Ease the front section forwards and lift it off **(see illustration)**.

28 Installation is the reverse of removal. Check the operation of the tail light and turn signals before riding the scooter.

Grab handle and seat lock

29 The grab handle and seat lock can be removed once the rear section of the seat cowling has been removed (see Steps 18 to 23).

30 To remove the grab handle, undo the mounting bolts on both sides, noting how the mounting brackets for the seat cowling locate **(see illustration)**.

31 If the seat lock is just being displaced, the cable can be left connected. Otherwise, loosen the adjuster locknut and thread the adjuster fully in to slacken the cable **(see illustration)**.

Disconnect the end of the inner cable from the lock mechanism **(see illustration)**. If required, the cable can be disconnected from the ignition switch assembly **(see illustration)** once the kick panel has been removed (see Steps 49 to 54).

32 Installation is the reverse of removal. Ensure that the seat lock cable is correctly adjusted and check the operation of the lock before installing the storage compartment. Tighten the grab handle mounting bolts to the torque setting specified at the beginning of this Chapter.

Coolant reservoir cover/front top cover

33 Undo the screws securing the cover

2.26 Undo screws (arrowed)...

2.27 ...and remove the front section

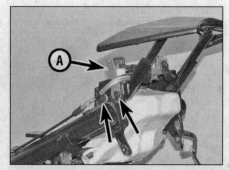

2.30 Grab handle bolts (arrowed). Cowling bracket (A)

2.31a Seat lock cable adjuster locknut

2.31b Disconnect the cable from the lock mechanism

2.31c Disconnect the cable from the ignition switch assembly

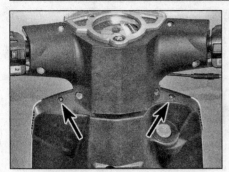

2.33 Undo the top screws (arrowed)...

2.34 ...and the screw at the front

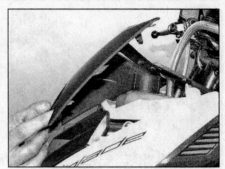

2.35 Note how the tabs on the back locate

through the top of the kick panel **(see illustration)**.

34 Undo the screw under the front edge of the cover **(see illustration)**.

35 Draw the cover off, noting how the tabs locate in the top edge of the headlight panel **(see illustration)**.

36 Installation is the reverse of removal.

Headlight panel

37 Remove the coolant reservoir cover/front top cover according to model (see Steps 33 to 35).

38 Undo the screws securing the lower front edge of the panel **(see illustration)**.

39 Undo the screws securing the panel through the kick panel on both sides **(see illustration)**.

40 Draw the panel forwards and disconnect the headlight wiring connector **(see illustration)**.

41 If required, undo the screws securing the grille and remove it **(see illustration)**.

42 Installation is the reverse of removal. Check the operation of the headlights before riding the scooter.

Handlebar covers

43 To remove the front cover, first undo the screws from the rear cover **(see illustration)**.

44 Ease the front cover forwards, unclipping it from the rear cover at the top and at each side **(see illustration)**.

45 To remove the rear cover, first remove the front cover.

2.38 Screws on the front lower edge

46 Undo the screws securing the rear cover to the handlebar **(see illustration)**.

47 Ease the cover backwards and disconnect

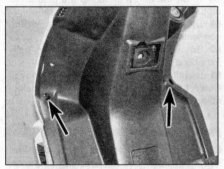

2.39 Undo the screws through the kick panel

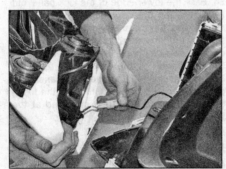

2.40 Disconnect the headlight wiring connector

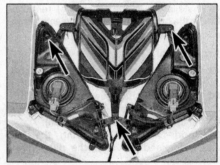

2.41 Screws (arrowed) secure grille

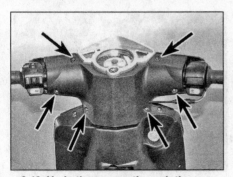

2.43 Undo the screws through the rear cover

2.44 Unclip the front cover

2.46 Undo the screws (arrowed)

2.47 Disconnect the instrument cluster connector

2.50 Remove the switch bezel and the bag hook screw (arrowed)

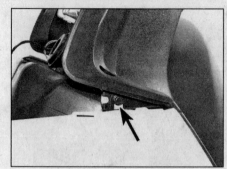

2.51 Undo the bolts on both sides

2.52 Undo the bolts on the lower edge

2.53 Free the top edge from the steering head

2.54 Free the lower edge of the kick panel

the instrument cluster wiring connector (see illustration). If required, separate the instrument cluster from the cover (see Chapter 10).
48 Installation is the reverse of removal. Check the operation of the instruments before riding the scooter.

Kick panel

49 Remove the headlight panel and handlebar covers (see above).
50 Turn the ignition switch bezel anti-clockwise to remove it and undo the screw behind the bag hook (see illustration).
51 Undo the bolts securing the left and right-hand sides of the panel (see illustration).
52 Undo the bolts securing the lower edge of the panel (see illustration).

53 Ease the top edge of the panel from around the steering head (see illustration).
54 Ease the lower edge of the kick panel out from between the floor panel and the front side panels, then lift the panel noting how the sides of the kick panel locate over the upper edge of the side panels (see illustration).
55 Installation is the reverse of removal. Ensure that the tabs on the side panels are correctly located before tightening the fixing bolts to the torque setting specified at the beginning of this Chapter.

Front side panels

56 Remove the headlight panel, handlebar covers and kick panel (see above).
57 Working on one side at a time, undo the

screws securing the side panels to the front inner panel (see illustration).
58 Undo the screw securing the side panel on the inside of the panel (see illustration).
59 Disconnect the turn signals wiring connector (see illustration).
60 Separate the side panel from the belly panel and lift it off.
61 Installation is the reverse of removal. Check the operation of the turn signals before riding the scooter.

Floor panel

62 Remove the storage compartment, seat cowling panels, headlight panel, handlebar covers and kick panel (see above).
63 Where fitted, remove the floor plates (see

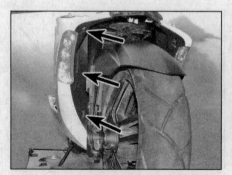

2.57 Location of the screws in the inner panel

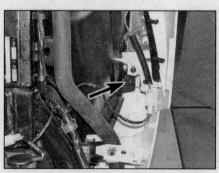

2.58 Location of the inside panel screw

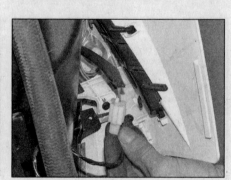

2.59 Turn signals wiring connector

2.63a Remove the floor plates...

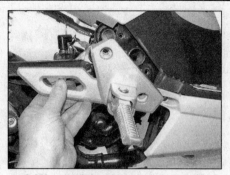

2.63b ...and the passenger footrests

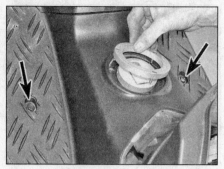

2.64 Remove the filler cap trim. Note floor panel bolts (arrowed)

2.66 Bolts secure the lower edges of the floor panel

2.67a Release the hooked tabs

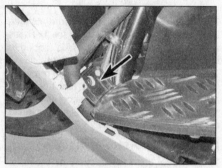

2.67b Note how the front of the panel locates

illustration). Undo the bolts and remove the passenger footrests (see illustration).

64 Undo the screws securing the fuel tank filler cap trim and lift it off (see illustration).

65 Undo the central floor panel bolts (see illustration 2.64).

66 Undo the bolts on both sides securing the lower edges of the panel (see illustration).

67 Ease the panel backwards and release the hooked tabs on both sides from the slots in the top edges of the belly panels (see illustration). Note how the front of the panel is located over the mounting bracket for the belly panel (see illustration).

68 Installation is the reverse of removal. Tighten the mounting bolts to the torque setting specified at the beginning of this Chapter.

Belly panel

69 Follow the procedure to remove the floor panel (see above). Note that on 50cc models with a liquid-cooled engine the left and right-hand radiator hoses pass underneath the belly panel mounting brackets. The rear brake cable (drum braked 50cc models) is secured by a clip secured between the two halves of the belly panel.

70 The belly panel is a two-piece assembly. For ease of removal, undo the screws along its lower edge, separate the two halves and lift them off (see illustration).

71 Installation is the reverse of removal. Ensure the fuel tank breather hose is correctly located through the panel.

Fuel tank

⚠ **Warning: Refer to the precautions given in Chapter 5, Section 1 before proceeding.**

Note: *Before removing the fuel tank ensure that any residual fuel is drained into a suitable container. Refer to the procedure in Chapter 5, Section 2. Alternatively, use a commercially available fuel siphon pump to empty the tank.*

72 Remove the floor panel and the belly panel (see above).

73 Release the clip securing the fuel hose from the tank to the union on the fuel pump and disconnect the hose (see illustration). Plug the open end of the hose to avoid spillage.

74 Disconnect the fuel level sensor wiring connector (see illustration).

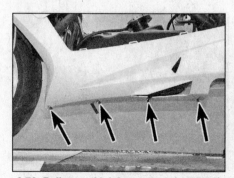

2.70 Belly panel joining screws (arrowed)

2.73 Disconnect the fuel hose from the pump

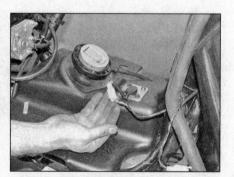

2.74 Fuel level sensor wiring connector

2.75a Lift off the fuel tank

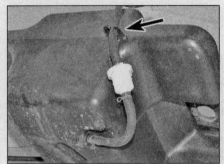

2.75b Location of the fuel filter and hose clip (arrowed)

2.78 Location of the oil level sensor

75 Lift the tank off its mounting brackets (see illustration). Note the position of the fuel hose and filter, and note how the hose is clipped to the back of the tank (see illustration).
76 Installation is the reverse of removal. Check the condition of the fuel hose and hose clips and renew them if necessary. Don't forget to reconnect the fuel level sensor wiring connector.

Oil tank – two-stroke models

77 Remove the rear section of the seat cowling (see Steps 18 to 22).
78 Trace the wiring from the oil level sensor and disconnect it at the connector (see illustration).
79 Release the clip securing the oil hose to

the oil tank union and detach the hose (see illustration). Plug the oil tank union. Clamp the hose and secure it in an upright position to minimise oil loss.
80 Undo the oil tank mounting bolts (see illustration 2.79) and lower the tank off.
81 Installation is the reverse of removal. Follow the procedure in Chapter 2A to bleed the oil pump and lubrication system.

Front mudguard

82 Release the speedometer cable clip from the right-hand side of the mudguard (see illustration).
83 Remove the front wheel (see Chapter 8).
84 Release the front brake hose from the guide on the left-hand side of the mudguard.

85 Undo the screws securing the mudguard on both sides of the front fork and lift the mudguard off (see illustrations).
86 If required, undo the bolts securing the guide plate to the underside of the front fork yoke (see illustrations).
87 Installation is the reverse of removal. Ensure the brake hose and speedometer cable are correctly secured. Tighten the mounting screws to the torque setting specified at the beginning of this Chapter.

Front inner panel

88 Remove the headlight panel, handlebar covers, kick panel and front side panels (see above).

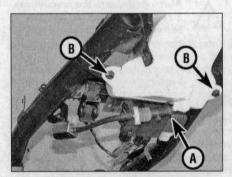

2.79 Detach the oil hose (A). Tank mounting bolts (B)

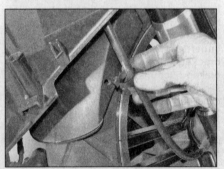

2.82 Release the speedometer cable clip

2.85a Undo the screws on both sides

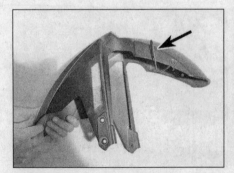

2.85b Note location of brake hose guide

2.86a Undo the bolts...

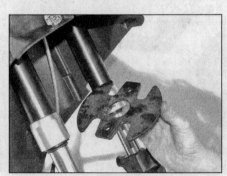

2.86b ...and remove the guide plate

2.89 Horn mounting bolt (arrowed)

2.90 Location of the front inner panel mounts

2.91 Remove the mounting bracket

2.92 Inner panel rests on frame tabs

2.93 Ease the panel off the steering stem

2.95 Prise out the plug

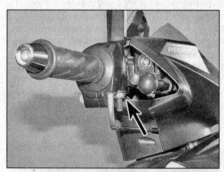

2.96a Counter-hold the nut (arrowed)...

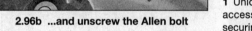

2.96b ...and unscrew the Allen bolt

89 Undo the horn mounting bolt and displace the horn (see illustration).
90 Draw the inner panel off the top mounting bracket tabs (see illustration).
91 Undo the mounting bracket bolts and remove the bracket, noting how it fits (see illustration).
92 Note how the lower rear edge of the inner panel is supported on the frame tabs (see illustration).
93 Using the split in the panel, ease it apart and off the steering stem (see illustration).
94 Installation is the reverse of removal. Position the inner panel as shown before securing it to the frame tabs and mounting bracket. Check the operation of the horn before riding the scooter.

Mirrors

95 Remove the plug from the lower end of the mirror stem (see illustration).

96 Counter-hold the nut on the lower end of the mounting Allen bolt and unscrew the bolt (see illustrations).

97 On installation, position the mirror as required, then tighten the mounting bolt securely

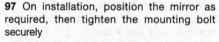

3 V-Clic models

Seat and storage compartment – carburettor access

1 Unlock the seat and swing it upright. For access to the carburettor, undo the screw securing the central panel and lift it up (see illustration).
2 To remove the storage compartment, first undo the bolt on the front top edge of the compartment (see illustration).

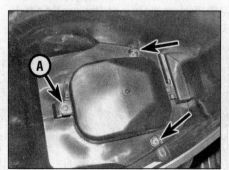

3.1 Undo the screw (A). Note fixing nuts (arrowed)

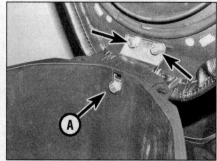

3.2 Bolt on the front top edge of the compartment (A). Note hinge bolts (arrowed)

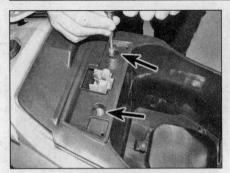

3.3a Fixing nuts at the rear of the compartment

3.3b Lift out the seat and storage compartment

3.7a Lift up the floor mat...

3 Undo the two nuts in the bottom of the compartment (**see illustration 3.1a**) and the two next to the seat catch (**see illustration**). Remove the washers, then lift the seat and storage compartment off (**see illustration**).
4 If required, undo the bolts securing the seat to the seat hinge and remove the seat (**see illustration 3.2**).
5 Installation is the reverse of removal. Tighten the mounting bolts to the torque setting specified at the beginning of this Chapter.

Underseat panel

6 Remove the storage compartment (see Steps 1 to 3).
7 Lift up the floor mat, noting how it fits (**see illustration**). Undo the left and right-hand screws in the floor panel (**see illustration**).
8 Undo the screws on the inside of the underseat panel (**see illustration**).
9 Note the location of the tabs securing both sides of the underseat panel to the slots in the forward edge of the seat cowling (**see**

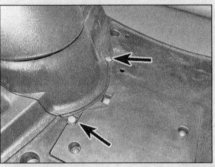

3.7b ...and undo the screws (arrowed)

3.8 Screws on the inside of the panel

illustration). Release the tabs and lift the panel off (**see illustration**).
10 Installation is the reverse of removal. Ensure the floor mat is fixed securely.

Lower side panels

11 Undo the screws securing the trim panel

underneath the tail light and remove the panel, noting how it fits (**see illustrations**).
12 Working on one side at a time, undo the screws securing the lower side panel (**see illustrations**).
13 Release the tabs securing the front edge of the side panel (**see illustration**), then draw

3.9a Location of the tabs

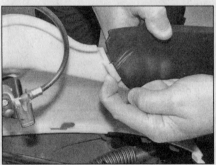

3.9b Release the tabs and remove the panel

3.11a Undo the screws...

3.11b ...and remove the trim panel

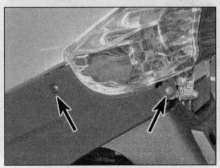

3.12a Screws at the back...

3.12b ...and on upper edge

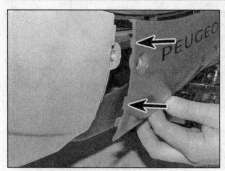

3.13a Release tabs on the front edge

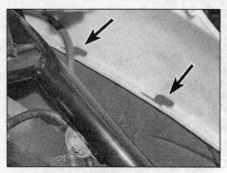

3.13b Hooked tabs locate in seat cowling...

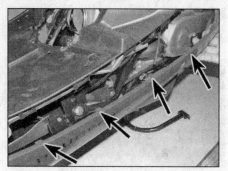

3.13c ...and along edge of floor panel

3.14 Check the screw U-clips

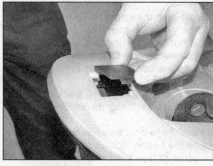

3.17a Remove the plastic cover

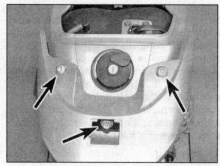

3.17b Undo the bolts...

the panel backwards to release the hooked tabs along its top edge from the seat cowling and the floor panel **(see illustrations)**.

14 Note the location of the screw U-clips and ensure that they are secure **(see illustration)**. Renew the U-clips if they are damaged.

15 Installation is the reverse of removal. Ensure that all the hooked tabs are engaged before tightening the fixing screws.

Seat cowling

16 Remove the storage compartment, front underseat panel and both lower side panels (see above).

17 Prise out the plastic cover in the top of the grab handle **(see illustration)**. Undo the bolts securing the grab handle and lift it off **(see illustrations)**.

18 Undo the screws on the lower edge of the cowling on both sides **(see illustration)**.

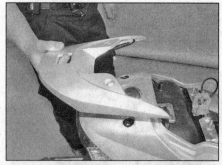

3.17c ...and lift the grab handle off

19 Disconnect the cable from the seat lock **(see illustration)**.

20 Temporarily remove the fuel tank filler cap.

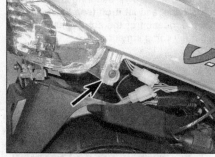

3.18 Undo the screws on both sides

21 Draw the cowling backwards to release the hooked tabs along its lower front edge **(see illustrations)**.

22 Install the fuel tank filler cap.

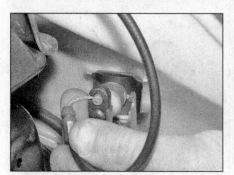

3.19 Disconnect the cable from the seat lock

3.21a Draw the cowling backwards...

3.21b ...to release the hooked tabs

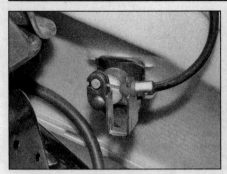

3.24 Cable correctly fitted to seat lock

3.26 Screws secure battery access panel

3.29 Location of the floor panel bolts

23 The seat cowling is a three-piece assembly. If required, undo the screws and separate the components.

24 Installation is the reverse of removal. Ensure that the seat lock cable is correctly fitted **(see illustration)** and check the operation of the lock before installing the storage compartment. Tighten the grab handle mounting bolts to the torque setting specified at the beginning of this Chapter.

Floor panel

25 Remove the storage compartment, front underseat panel, both lower side panels and the seat cowling (see above).

26 Undo the screws securing the battery access panel and lift it off **(see illustration)**. Note the location of the components inside the battery compartment

27 Make sure the ignition is OFF and remove the battery (see Chapter 10).

28 Lift out the CDI unit and disconnect the wiring connector (see Chapter 6)

29 Undo the bolts securing the floor panel **(see illustration)**.

30 Draw the floor panel backwards to release the tabs along its front edge **(see illustration)**.

31 Pass the wiring through the slot in the back of the battery compartment and lift the floor panel off **(see illustration)**.

32 Installation is the reverse of removal. Ensure the wiring is not strained. Locate the tabs along the front edge with the rear edge of the kick panel before tightening the fixing bolts. Tighten the mounting bolts to the torque setting specified at the beginning of this Chapter.

Rear mudguard

33 Remove the storage compartment, underseat panel, both lower side panels and the seat cowling (see above).

34 Remove the tail light assembly (see Chapter 10).

35 The mudguard is supported by the lower tail light mounting studs and a tab on the frame underneath the fuel tank **(see illustrations)**. Draw the mudguard backwards to remove it.

36 Installation is the reverse of removal. Check the operation of the tail light and turn signals before riding the scooter.

Fuel tank

⚠️ **Warning: Refer to the precautions given in Chapter 5, Section 1 before proceeding.**

Note: Before removing the fuel tank ensure that any residual fuel is drained into a suitable container. Refer to the procedure in Chapter 5, Section 2. Alternatively, use a commercially available fuel siphon pump to empty the tank.

37 Remove the storage compartment, underseat panel, both lower side panels and the seat cowling (see above).

38 Remove the tail light assembly (see Chapter 10).

39 Trace the wiring from the fuel level sensor and disconnect it at the connector **(see illustration)**.

40 Release the clip securing the fuel hose to

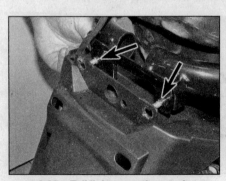

3.30 Release the tabs along the front edge

3.31 Pass the wiring through the slot

3.35a Tail light mounting studs

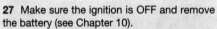

3.35b Mudguard support tab

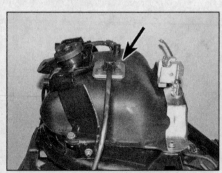

3.39 Location of the fuel level sensor

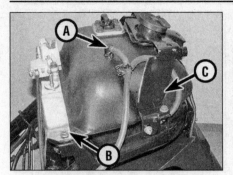

3.40 Disconnect the fuel hose (A). Note seat lock bracket (B) and grab handle bracket (C)

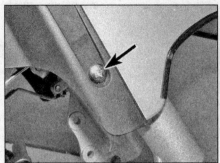

3.46a Mudguard mounting screw

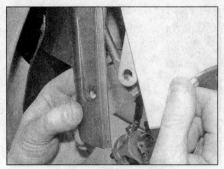

3.46b Separate the mounting tabs from the mounting bracket

the union on the tank and disconnect the hose **(see illustration)**.

41 Undo the nuts securing the seat lock bracket on both sides and remove the bracket **(see illustration 3.40)**.

42 Undo the nuts and bolts securing the grab handle bracket on both sides **(see illustration 3.40)**. Temporarily remove the fuel tank filler cap and remove the grab handle bracket, then fit the filler cap.

43 Lift off the fuel tank.

44 Installation is the reverse of removal. Check the condition of the fuel hose and hose clips and renew them if necessary. Tighten the seat lock and grab handle bracket fixings securely. Don't forget to reconnect the fuel level sensor wiring connector.

Front mudguard

45 Remove the front wheel (see Chapter 8).

46 Undo the screws on both sides of the front fork and separate the mounting tabs for the front and rear sections of the mudguard from the arms of the mounting bracket **(see illustrations)**.

47 Unclip the front section of the mudguard from the top of the mounting bracket and lift it off **(see illustration)**.

48 Unclip the front brake hose from the clip on the left-hand mounting bracket arm **(see illustration)**.

49 Undo the screws securing the top of the mounting bracket **(see illustration)**. Lower the bracket/mudguard assembly and pass the speedometer cable through the hole in the mudguard **(see illustration)**.

50 Separate the mudguard from the mounting bracket, noting how it fits **(see illustration)**.

51 Installation is the reverse of removal. Ensure the rear section of the mudguard, the bracket, speedometer cable and brake hose are all correctly assembled and installed before fitting the front section of the mudguard. Tighten the mounting screws to the torque setting specified at the beginning of this Chapter.

Upper front panel

52 Remove the front wheel (see Chapter 8) and the front section of the front mudguard (see Steps 46 and 47).

53 Undo the screws securing the upper front panel through the kick panel on both sides **(see illustration)**.

3.47 Unclip the mudguard and lift it off

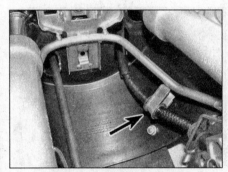

3.48 Release the brake hose

3.49a Screws secure the top of the mounting bracket

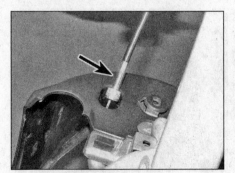

3.49b Release the speedometer cable

3.50 Separate the mudguard from the mounting bracket

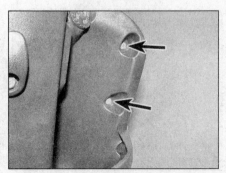

3.53 Undo the screws on both sides

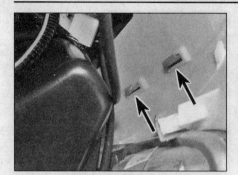

3.54a Release tabs on the underside of the lower front panel...

3.54b ...and lift upper front panel

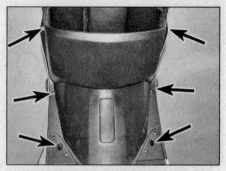

3.58 Undo the screws through the kick panel

54 Release the tabs securing the front edge of the upper front panel to the lower front panel – the tabs are accessible from the underside of the lower front panel **(see illustrations)**. Lift the panel off.
55 Installation is the reverse of removal. Ensure the panel is correctly aligned and the tabs secure before installing the mounting screws.

Lower front panel

56 Remove both lower side panels (see Steps 11 to 13).
57 Remove the upper front panel.
58 Undo the screws securing the lower front panel through the kick panel on both sides **(see illustration)**.
59 Refer to the wiring diagram at the end

of Chapter 10 and disconnect the front turn signal wiring connectors **(see illustration)**.
60 Undo the left and right-hand screws securing the panel at the front **(see illustration)**.
61 Draw the panel forwards to release it from the support bracket **(see illustration)**. Pull the sidelight bulbholder out of its socket, then lower the panel down and off the front forks **(see illustration)**.
62 Installation is the reverse of removal. Don't forget to install the sidelight bulbholder before securing the panel. Check the operation of the turn signals before riding the scooter.

Kick panel

63 Remove both lower side panels (see Steps 11 to 13).

64 Remove the front wheel (see Chapter 8).
65 Remove the front section of the front mudguard and the upper front panel (see above).
66 Undo the screws securing the panel at the front **(see illustration 3.60)**.
67 Undo the screws securing the kick panel on both sides **(see illustration 3.58)**.
68 Lift up the floor mat, noting how it fits **(see illustration 3.7a)**.
69 Undo the two bolts securing the front edge of the floor panel **(see illustration 3.29)**.
70 Remove the ignition switch bezel **(see illustration)**.
71 Undo the bolt securing the bag hook and remove it noting how it fits **(see illustration)**.

3.59 Disconnect the front turn signal connectors

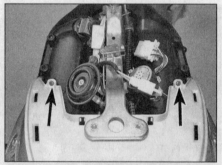

3.60 Undo the front fixing screws

3.61a Lower front panel support bracket

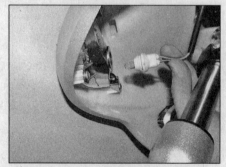

3.61b Pull out the sidelight bulbholder and lower the panel off the front forks

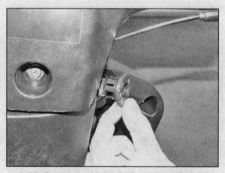

3.70 Remove the ignition switch bezel

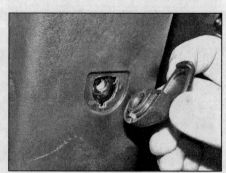

3.71 Remove the bag hook

3.72 Ease the panel off the steering head

3.74 Kick panel joining screws

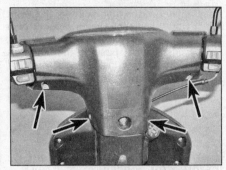

3.79a Undo screws through the rear cover...

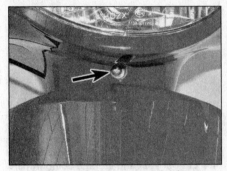

3.79b ...and the screw at the front

3.80a Release the tabs along the top edge

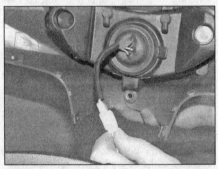

3.80b Disconnect the headlight connector

72 Ease the top edge of the panel from around the steering head **(see illustration)**.

73 Carefully release the tabs along the front edge of the floor panel from the lower edge of the kick panel **(see illustration 3.30)**, then lift the kick panel off.

74 The kick panel is a two-piece assembly. If required, undo the screws and separate the components **(see illustration)**.

75 Installation is the reverse of removal. Ensure that the tabs on the edge of the floor panel are correctly located before tightening the fixing bolts.

Belly panel

76 Remove both lower side panels, upper front panel and lower front panel (see above).

77 Undo the two bolts on both sides securing the belly panel and lower it off.

78 Installation is the reverse of removal. Tighten the mounting bolts to the torque setting specified at the beginning of this Chapter.

Handlebar covers

79 To remove the front cover (and headlight) undo the screws from the rear cover and the single screw below the headlight **(see illustrations)**. Place a rag under the headlight when undoing the front screw as it is easy to drop it down inside the kick panel

80 Ease the front cover away, unclipping it from the rear cover along the top edge, then

disconnect the headlight wiring connector **(see illustrations)**.

81 To remove the rear cover, first remove the front cover.

82 Undo the screws securing the instrument cluster to the rear cover **(see illustration)**.

83 Undo the screws securing the rear cover to the handlebar **(see illustration 3.82)**.

84 Undo the screw securing the back of the cover and lift the cover off **(see illustrations)**.

85 Installation is the reverse of removal. Check the operation of the headlight before riding the scooter.

Mirrors

86 Loosen the locknut on the mirror stem,

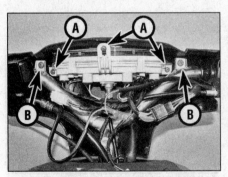

3.82 Screws (A) secure the instrument cluster. Screws (B) secure the rear cover

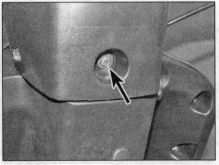

3.84a Undo the screw (arrowed)...

3.84b ...and remove the rear cover

then unscrew the mirror from the front half of the handlebar switch housing (see illustration).

87 On installation, position the mirror as required, then tighten the locknut securely

4 Kisbee models

Seat and storage compartment – carburettor access

1 Unlock the seat and swing it upright. For access to the carburettor, undo the screw securing the central panel and lift it up (see illustration).

2 To remove the storage compartment, first undo the bolts securing it to the frame (see illustration).

3 Temporarily remove the fuel filler cap.

4 Lift the seat and storage compartment assembly out (see illustration).

5 Install the fuel filler cap.

6 If required, undo the bolts securing the seat to the seat hinge and remove the seat.

7 Installation is the reverse of removal. Tighten the mounting bolts to the torque setting specified at the beginning of this Chapter.

Rear hugger, underbody panel and mudguard

8 Undo the bolts securing the hugger to the top of the air filter housing (see illustration).

9 Undo the bolts securing the hugger to the exhaust system bracket (see illustration).

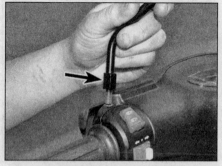
3.86 Mirror stem locknut

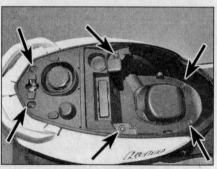
4.2 Bolts (arrowed) secure storage compartment

10 Lift the hugger out (see illustration).

11 Undo the fixings on both sides securing the underbody panel (see illustration).

12 Draw the panel backwards to release the

4.1 Lift central panel for carburettor access

4.4 Lift out seat and storage compartment

hooks at the front and disconnect the licence plate light wiring (see illustration).

13 Lift the underbody panel and mudguard off (see illustration).

4.8 Bolts secure hugger to the air filter housing

4.9 Bolts secure hugger to the exhaust bracket

4.10 Lift out the hugger

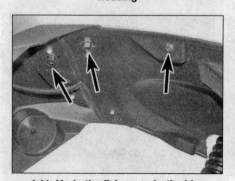
4.11 Undo the fixings on both sides

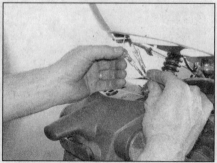
4.12 Disconnect the licence plate light wiring

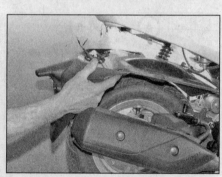
4.13 Remove the under body panel and mudguard

4.16 Undo the bolts (arrowed) and remove the grab handle

4.17 Undo the screws on both sides

4.18 Tail light assembly wiring connector

14 Install the components in the reverse order of removal. Check the operation of the licence plate light before riding the scooter.

Seat cowling

15 Remove the storage compartment and underbody panel (see above).
16 Undo the bolts securing the grab handle and lift it off **(see illustration)**.
17 Undo the screws on the front edge of the cowling on both sides **(see illustration)**.
18 Draw the cowling backwards, disconnect the tail light assembly wiring connector, then lift the cowling off **(see illustration)**.
19 The seat cowling is a two-piece assembly incorporating the tail light assembly. If required, refer to Chapter 10 to separate the components.
20 Installation is the reverse of removal. Tighten the grab handle mounting bolts to the torque setting specified at the beginning of this Chapter. Check the operation of the tail light and turn signals before riding the scooter.

Fuel tank

 Warning: Refer to the precautions given in Chapter 5, Section 1 before proceeding.

Note: *Before removing the fuel tank ensure that any residual fuel is drained into a suitable container. Refer to the procedure in Chapter 5, Section 2. Alternatively, use a commercially available fuel siphon pump to empty the tank.*
21 Remove the storage compartment, underbody panel and the seat cowling (see above).

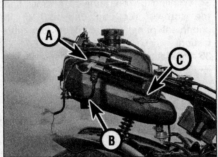

4.22 Fuel level sensor connector (A). Support bracket (B). Mounting bracket (C)

22 Trace the wiring from the fuel level sensor and disconnect it at the connector **(see illustration)**.
23 Release the clips securing the fuel and vacuum hoses to the fuel tap and disconnect the hoses (see Chapter 5).
24 Support the tank, then undo the bolts securing the tank support bracket and remove the bracket **(see illustration 4.22)**.
25 Undo the bolts securing the tank to the mounting brackets on both sides **(see illustration 4.22)**.
26 Remove the support and lift off the fuel tank.
27 Installation is the reverse of removal. Check the condition of the fuel hose and hose clips and renew them if necessary. Don't forget to reconnect the fuel level sensor wiring connector.

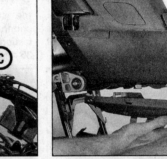

4.28 Remove the belly panel centre section

Belly panel

Note: *The belly panel is a three-piece assembly – the centre and side sections must be removed separately.*
28 Undo the four screws securing the centre section, release the tabs securing it along both sides and drop it down **(see illustration)**.
29 Undo the screws securing the left and right-hand sides of the belly panel and lift them off **(see illustrations)**.

Underseat panel

30 Remove the storage compartment, underbody panel, seat cowling and belly panels (see above).
31 Undo the bolts securing the passenger footrests and remove them both **(see illustration)**.

4.29a Undo the screws (arrowed)...

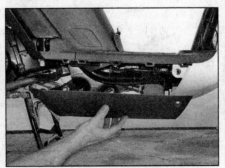

4.29b ...and remove the side sections

4.31 Bolt (arrowed) secures passenger footrest

4.32 Remove the battery cover

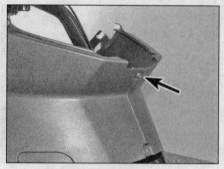

4.33 Undo the screw (arrowed)

4.34 Undo the screws and lift off half the panel

32 Undo the screw securing the battery cover and lift it off **(see illustration)**.
33 Undo the screw at the front securing the left and right-hand sides of the underseat panel together **(see illustration)**.

34 Working on one side at a time, undo the screws securing one half of the underseat panel and lift it off **(see illustration)**.
35 Installation is the reverse of removal.

Handlebar covers

36 To remove the front cover undo the screws through the rear cover **(see illustration)**. Ease the front cover away, unclipping it from the rear cover along the top edge **(see illustration)**.
37 To remove the rear cover, first remove the front cover.
38 Displace the rubber boot at the top of the speedometer cable and unscrew the knurled ring to disconnect the cable from the instrument cluster **(see illustration)**. Disconnect the instrument cluster wiring connector.
39 Undo the screws securing the rear cover to the handlebar **(see illustration)**.
40 Lift the rear cover and instrument cluster assembly off. If required, separate the instrument cluster from the cover (see Chapter 10).
41 Installation is the reverse of removal. Check the operation of the instruments before riding the scooter.

Headlight panel

42 Undo the screws securing the lower front edge of the panel **(see illustration)**.
43 Undo the screws securing the panel through the kick panel on both sides **(see illustration)**.
44 Draw the panel forwards, releasing the tabs from the front edge of the kick panel **(see illustration)**.
45 Disconnect the wiring connectors for the headlight and turn signals **(see illustration)**.

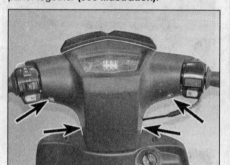

4.36a Undo the screws...

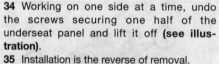

4.36b ...and release the tabs along the top edge

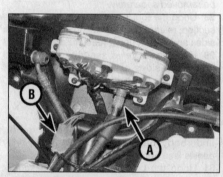

4.38 Speedometer cable (A). Instrument cluster connector (B)

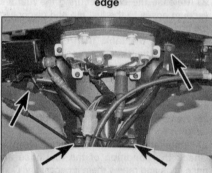

4.39 Screws secure rear cover to handlebar

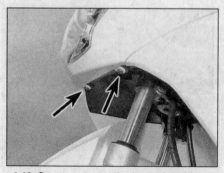

4.42 Screws secure the lower front edge

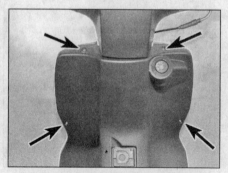

4.43 Undo the screws through the kick panel

4.44 Draw the headlight panel forwards...

4.45 ...and disconnect the wiring connectors

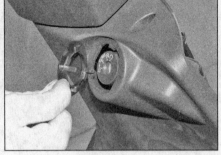

4.48 Remove the ignition switch bezel

4.49 Bolts secure lower edge of kick panel

46 Installation is the reverse of removal. Check the operation of the headlight and turn signals before riding the scooter.

Kick panel

47 Remove the handlebar covers and the headlight panel (see above).
48 Turn the ignition switch bezel anticlockwise to remove it **(see illustration)**.
49 Undo the bolts securing the lower edge of the panel **(see illustration)**.
50 Working from the front of the scooter, undo the screws securing the kick panel to the mounting bracket and to the top edges of the lower front panel **(see illustration)**.
51 Draw the panel back and up to release the tabs along the bottom edge from the front edge of the floor panel **(see illustration)**.
52 Installation is the reverse of removal. Ensure the tabs along the bottom edge are

correctly located before tightening the fixing screws.

Lower front panel

53 Remove the handlebar covers, headlight panel and kick panel (see above).
54 Undo the screws securing the lower front panel to the frame and front inner panel on both sides **(see illustration)**.
55 Ease the panel down and off the machine **(see illustration)**.
56 Note the location of the plastic inserts for the mounting screws and ensure they are in good condition.
57 Installation is the reverse of removal.

Floor panel

58 The floor panel can only be removed once all the other bodywork panels have been removed (see above).

59 Remove the battery, the starter relay and the fuse holder from the battery compartment (see Chapter 10).
60 Undo the bolts securing the rear, left and right-hand sides of the panel and the bolts in the centre of each side, then lift the floor panel off.
61 Installation is the reverse of removal. Tighten the mounting bolts to the torque setting specified at the beginning of this Chapter.

Front mudguard

62 Undo the mounting bolts on both sides of the front fork and displace the guides for the front brake hose and the speedometer cable **(see illustration)**.
63 Lift the mudguard, tip it to one side and draw it off **(see illustration)**.
64 Note the location of the threaded

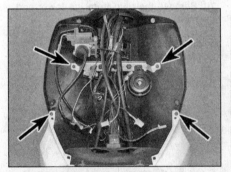

4.50 Undo the screws (arrowed)

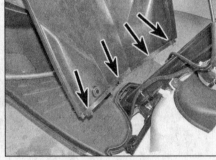

4.51 Release the tabs along the bottom edge

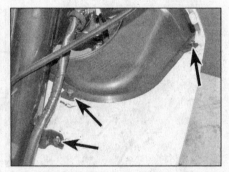

4.54 Undo the screws (arrowed)

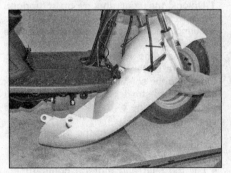

4.55 Manoeuvre the panel off

4.62 Undo the mudguard mounting bolts...

4.63 ...and draw the mudguard off

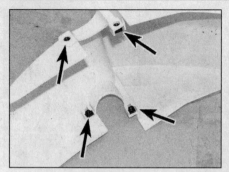

4.64 Note the threaded inserts (arrowed)

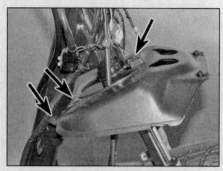

4.67 Undo the mounting screws

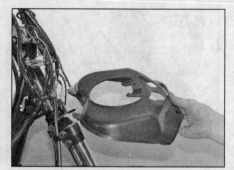

4.68 Ease the panel off the steering stem

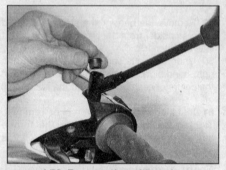

4.70 Remove the rubber plug

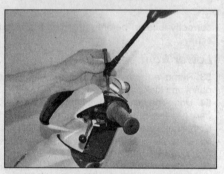

4.71a Retaining bolt is secured...

4.71b ...by locknut and washer

inserts for the mounting bolts and remove them for safekeeping if they are loose **(see illustration)**.
65 Installation is the reverse of removal. Tighten the mounting bolts to the torque setting specified at the beginning of this Chapter.

Front inner panel

66 Remove the handlebar covers, headlight panel, kick panel and lower front panel (see above).
67 Undo the two screws at the rear and the single screw at the front securing the

panel to the frame and steering head **(see illustration)**.
68 Using the split in the panel, ease it apart and off the steering stem **(see illustration)**.
69 Installation is the reverse of removal.

Mirrors

70 Remove the plug from the lower end of the mirror stem **(see illustration)**.
71 Counter-hold the locknut on the lower end of the mounting Allen bolt and unscrew the bolt **(see illustrations)**.
72 On installation, position the mirror as required, then tighten the mounting bolt securely

5 Vivacity models

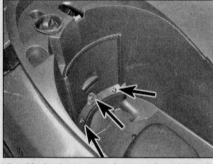

5.1 Undo the screws (arrowed) and lift off the battery cover

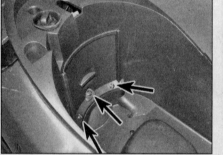

5.2 Undo the screw (A) and the bolts (B)

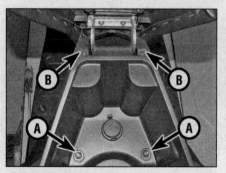

5.3 Undo the bolts (A) and the screws (B)

5.4 Disconnect the accessory socket connector

Seat and storage compartment – battery access

1 Unlock the seat and swing it upright. For access to the battery, undo the screws securing the cover panel and lift it off **(see illustration)**.
2 To remove the storage compartment, undo the centre battery cover panel screw only, then undo the screw adjacent to the oil tank filler cap (two-stroke models) and the bolts at the rear top edge of the compartment **(see illustration)**.
3 Undo the two bolts in the bottom of the compartment and the two screws next to the seat hinge **(see illustration)**.
4 Lift the seat and storage compartment out and disconnect the electrical accessory socket wiring connector **(see illustration)**.

5 If required, undo the bolts securing the seat to the seat hinge and remove the seat.

6 Installation is the reverse of removal. Don't forget to reconnect the accessory socket connector. Tighten the mounting bolts to the torque setting specified at the beginning of this Chapter.

Grab handle

7 Remove the storage compartment (see above).

8 Undo the bolts securing the handle and lift it off **(see illustration)**.

9 Installation is the reverse of removal. Tighten the mounting bolts to the torque setting specified at the beginning of this Chapter.

Underseat panel

10 Remove the storage compartment (see Steps 1 to 4).

11 Undo the left and right-hand screws securing the top and bottom rear edges of the panel to the front edges of the seat cowling **(see illustrations)**.

12 Undo the screw on the lower, centre edge of the panel **(see illustration)**.

13 Draw the underseat panel forwards to disengage the tabs along the top and bottom edges from the slots in the seat cowling and floor panel **(see illustration)**.

14 Installation is the reverse of removal. Ensure that all the tabs are engaged before tightening the fixing screws.

Seat cowling

15 Remove the storage compartment, grab handle and underseat panel (see above).

16 Remove the battery (see Chapter 10).

17 Undo the screws on the front edge of the

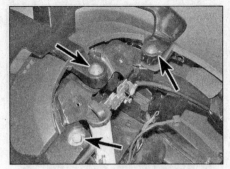

5.8 Undo the bolts (arrowed) and lift off the grab handle

5.11b ...and bottom edges on both sides

cowling on both sides **(see illustration)**. Note the location of the screw U-clips and ensure that they are secure. Renew the U-clips if they are damaged.

18 Undo the screw at the rear of the cowling, noting the location of the washer **(see illustration)**.

19 Ease the lower front edge mounting tabs

5.11a Undo the screws on the top...

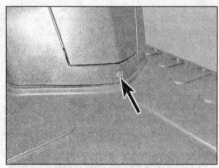

5.12 Screw on the lower centre edge

out to release the pegs on the inside of the tabs **(see illustration)**, then draw the cowling backwards and disconnect the tail light assembly wiring connectors **(see illustration)**.

20 Lift the seat cowling assembly off.

21 The rear mudguard is fixed to the underside of the seat cowling by a series of screws **(see illustration)**. If required, undo the

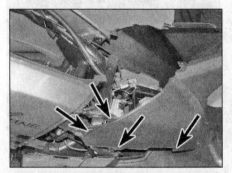

5.13 Release the tabs securing the panel

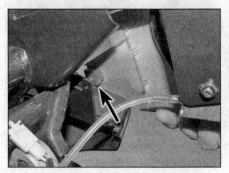

5.19a Release the pegs on both sides

5.17 Undo the screws on both sides

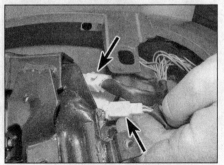

5.19b Disconnect the wiring connectors

5.18 Undo the screw (arrowed)

5.21 Screws secure the rear mudguard

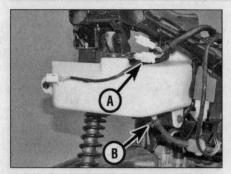

5.25 Oil level sensor connector (A). Oil
tank hose union (B)

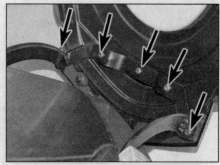

5.29 Screws secure lid to hinge

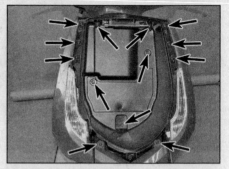

5.30 Screws secure the front storage
compartment

screws and separate the assembly. Note the location of the battery breather hose.
22 The seat cowling is a three-piece assembly. If required, undo the screws and separate the components.
23 Installation is the reverse of removal. Tighten the mounting screws to the torque setting specified at the beginning of this Chapter. Check the operation of the tail light and turn signals before riding the scooter.

Oil tank – 50cc two-stroke models

24 Remove the storage compartment, grab handle, underseat panel and seat cowling (see above).
25 Trace the wiring from the oil level sensor and disconnect it at the connector (see illustration).

26 Release the clip securing the oil hose to the oil tank union and detach the hose (see illustration 5.25). Plug the oil tank union. Clamp the hose and secure it in an upright position to minimise oil loss.
27 Undo the three oil tank fixing bolts – on the left and right-hand side and the filler neck – and lower the tank off.
28 Installation is the reverse of removal. Follow the procedure in Chapter 2A to bleed the oil pump and lubrication system.

Front storage compartment

29 Open the storage compartment and undo the screws securing the lid to the hinge (see illustration).
30 Undo the screws securing the storage compartment (see illustration).
31 Ease the top edge of the compartment

out from underneath the lip of the kick panel, then lift the compartment to access the horn attached at the bottom and disconnect the horn wiring (see illustrations).
32 Installation is the reverse of removal. Don't forget to reconnect the horn wiring and check the operation of the horn before riding the scooter.

Kick panel

33 Remove the front storage compartment (see above).
34 Undo the screws securing the panel at the front of the machine (see illustration).
35 Remove the ignition switch bezel (see illustration).
36 Undo the screws securing the panel at the back (see illustration).
37 Raise the kick panel to release the tabs on

5.31a Ease the top edge of the
compartment out

5.31b Lift the compartment...

5.31c ...to access the horn wiring
connectors

5.34 Undo the screws (arrowed)

5.35 Remove the ignition switch bezel

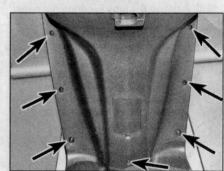

5.36 Location of the kick panel screws

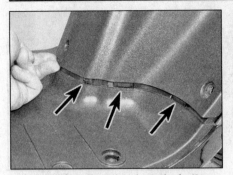

5.37 Release the tabs along the bottom edge

5.40 Undo the bolts on both sides

5.41 Draw the mudguard forwards

the bottom edge from the floor panel and lift it off **(see illustration)**.
38 Installation is the reverse of removal.

Front mudguard

39 Remove the front wheel (see Chapter 8).
40 Undo the rear mounting bolts on both sides of the front fork and displace the guides for the front brake hose and the speedometer cable **(see illustration)**.
41 Undo the front mounting bolts, then draw the mudguard forwards **(see illustration)**.
42 Note the location of the threaded inserts in the mudguard for the mounting bolts and remove them for safekeeping if they are loose.
43 Installation is the reverse of removal. Tighten the mounting bolts to the torque setting specified at the beginning of this Chapter.

Front panel

44 Remove the front storage compartment, kick panel, front wheel and front mudguard (see above).
45 Remove the belly panel (see Steps 55 to 62).
46 Disconnect the wiring connectors for the left and right-hand front turn signals and the ambient temperature sensor **(see illustration)**.
47 Undo the screws on both sides securing the front panel to the front inner panel and frame **(see illustration)**.
48 Ease the lower ends of the panel off the frame supports and release the tabs securing it to the front inner panel **(see illustrations)**.
49 Lower the panel off the machine.
50 Installation is the reverse of removal. Ensure the panel is correctly aligned with

the inner panel and the tabs secure before installing the mounting screws. Check the operation of the turn signals before riding the scooter.

Front inner panel

51 Remove the front panel (see above). Note the location of the ambient temperature sensor in the top right-hand side of the upper front panel.
52 Remove the left-hand fork leg (see Chapter 7).
53 Unclip the hinged section of the panel and ease the panel off the mounting bracket on the steering head **(see illustration)**. Fold the hinged section back, then manoeuvre the panel over the left-hand side of the fork yoke and lower it off **(see illustration)**.
54 Installation is the reverse of removal.

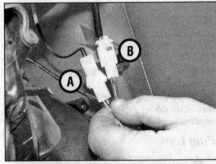

5.46 Wiring connectors for the ambient temperature sensor (A) and right-hand turn signals (B)

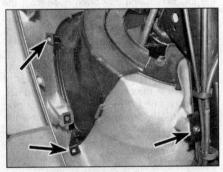

5.47 Undo the screws (arrowed)

5.48a Ease the lower ends off the frame supports

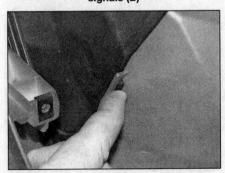

5.48b Release the tabs on the front inner panel

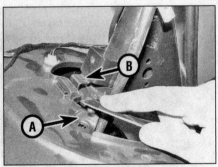

5.53a Unclip the hinged section at (A). Panel mounting bracket (B)

5.53b Manoeuvre the front inner panel over the fork yoke

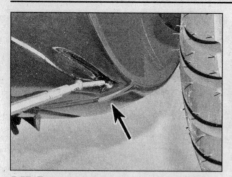

5.57 Front screw secures tab (arrowed) on lower edge of front panel

5.58 Note screw threads of different sizes

5.59a Undo floor panel bolts...

5.59b ...and passenger footrest bolt

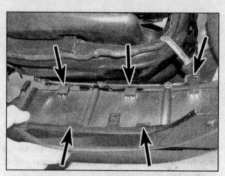

5.60 Free tabs along the centre join and outer edge

5.61 Note location of the drain hose grommet

Belly panel

55 Remove the seat and storage compartment, underseat panel, front storage compartment and kick panel (see above).

56 The belly panel is a two-piece assembly – remove the right-hand side first.

57 Undo the screws along the bottom edge of the panels, noting that the longest screw fits at the front (see illustration).

58 Undo the two screws on the upper front edge, noting how they fit (see illustration).

59 Undo the front and rear bolts in the floor panel and the bolt in the passenger footrest (see illustrations).

60 Ease the right-hand side of the belly panel away from the fixed left-hand side to release the tabs along the centre join and, if necessary, raise the outer edge of the floor

panel to free the mounting tabs along the top edge of the belly panel (see illustration).

61 Before removing the left-hand side, free the fuel filler catch tray drain hose from the slot in the rear of the panel (see illustration).

62 Follow Steps 58 to 60 to remove the left-hand belly panel, noting how it fits over the sidestand.

63 Installation is the reverse of removal. Install the screws along the bottom edge of the panels in the correct order (see Step 57). Take care not to over-tighten the screws. Tighten the floor panel bolts to the torque setting specified at the beginning of this Chapter.

Floor panel

64 Remove the seat and storage compartment, underseat panel, front storage

compartment, kick panel and belly panel (see above).

65 Undo the lower screws on the front edge of the seat cowling on both sides (see illustration 5.17).

66 Undo the bolts in the centre of the floor panel (see illustration).

67 Ease the lower ends of the front panel and the front tabs on the floor panel off the frame supports, then lift the floor panel off (see illustrations).

68 Installation is the reverse of removal. Tighten the floor panel bolts to the torque setting specified at the beginning of this Chapter.

Fuel tank

⚠️ Warning: Refer to the precautions given in Chapter 5, Section 1 before proceeding.

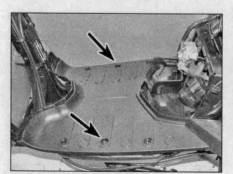

5.66 Undo the floor panel bolts (arrowed)

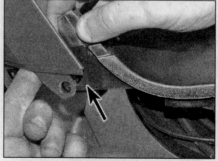

5.67a Free the front tabs (arrowed) from the frame supports...

5.67b ...and lift the floor panel off

5.70a Disconnect the fuel hose (arrowed)

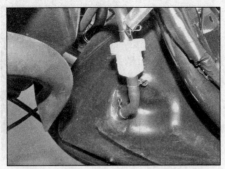

5.70b Location of the fuel tank hose union and filter

5.71 Fuel level sensor wiring connector

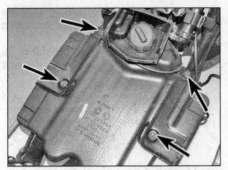

5.72 Bolts (arrowed) secure fuel tank

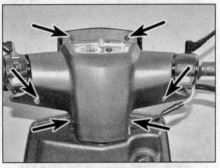

5.74 Undo the screws securing the front cover

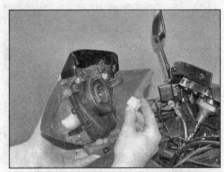

5.75 Disconnect the headlight connector

Note: *Before removing the fuel tank ensure that any residual fuel is drained into a suitable container. Refer to the procedure in Chapter 5, Section 2. Alternatively, use a commercially available fuel siphon pump to empty the tank.*
69 Remove the floor panel (see above).
70 Release the clip securing the fuel hose from the tank to the union on the fuel pump and disconnect the hose (see illustration). Plug the open end of the hose to avoid spillage. Note the position of the fuel hose connection to the tank and the fuel filter (see illustration).
71 Disconnect the fuel level sensor wiring connector (see illustration).
72 Undo the bolts securing the tank (see illustration) then lift it off its mounting brackets.
73 Installation is the reverse of removal. Check the condition of the fuel hose and hoes clips

and renew them if necessary. Don't forget to reconnect the fuel level sensor wiring connector.

Handlebar covers
74 To remove the front cover (and headlight) undo the screws from the rear cover (see illustrations).
75 Ease the front cover away, unclipping it from the rear cover along the top edge, then disconnect the headlight wiring connector (see illustration).
76 To remove the rear cover, first remove the front cover.
77 Displace the rubber boot from the instrument cluster wiring connector and disconnect the connector (see illustration).
78 If required, undo the screws securing the instrument cluster to the rear cover and remove the instrument cluster (see illustrations).

5.77 Disconnect the wiring connector

79 Undo the screws securing the rear cover to the handlebar and lift the cover off (see illustrations).
80 Installation is the reverse of removal. Note

5.78a Undo the screws (arrowed)...

5.78b ...and remove the instrument cluster

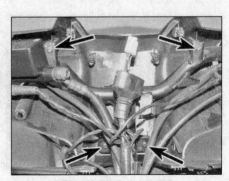

5.79a Undo the screws...

5.79b ...and remove the handlebar rear cover

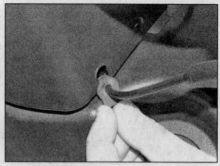

5.80 Note location of throttle cable grommet

5.81 Remove the rubber plug

5.82a Counter-hold the locknut...

5.82b ...and unscrew the Allen bolt

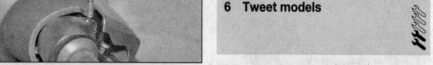

the location of the grommet on the throttle cable where it passes through the rear cover **(see illustration)**. Check the operation of the headlight before riding the scooter.

Mirrors

81 Remove the plug from the lower end of the mirror stem **(see illustration)**.
82 Counter-hold the locknut on the lower end of the mounting Allen bolt and unscrew the bolt **(see illustrations)**. Note the washer on the lower end of the bolt.
83 On installation, position the mirror as required, then tighten the mounting bolt securely

6 Tweet models

Seat and storage compartment – carburettor access

1 Unlock the seat and swing it upright. For access to the carburettor to adjust the engine idle speed, prise out the rubber blanking plug **(see illustrations)**.
2 To remove the storage compartment, first undo the bolts securing it to the frame **(see illustration)**.
3 Undo the screw below the front edge of the seat **(see illustration)**.
4 Lift the seat and storage compartment assembly out and disconnect the wiring connector for the circuit breaker switch (ignition immobiliser) **(see illustration)**.
5 If required, undo the bolts securing the seat to the seat hinge and remove the seat.
6 Installation is the reverse of removal. Don't forget to reconnect the circuit breaker wiring connector. Tighten the mounting bolts to the torque setting specified at the beginning of this Chapter.

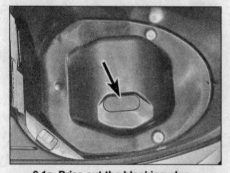

6.1a Prise out the blanking plug...

6.1b ...to adjust the engine idle speed

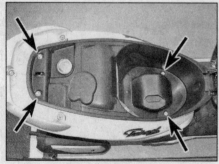

6.2 Undo the bolts...

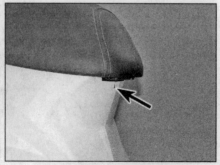

6.3 ...and the screw (arrowed)

6.4 Disconnect the circuit breaker switch connector

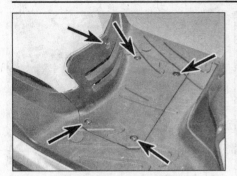

6.7a Undo the screws...

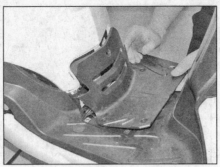

6.7b ...and remove the battery access panel

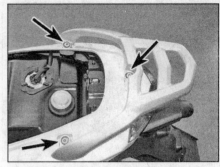

6.10 Undo the bolts and lift off the grab handle

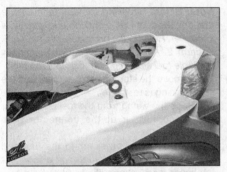

6.11 Note the location of the rubber washers

6.12 Undo the screws on both sides

6.13 Undo the screw on both sides

Battery access panel

7 Undo the screws securing the panel and lift it off **(see illustrations)**.
8 Installation is the reverse of removal.

Seat cowling and rear mudguard

9 Remove the storage compartment and battery access panel (see above).
10 Undo the bolts securing the grab handle and lift it off **(see illustration)**.
11 Note the location of the rubber washers on both side mounting points **(see illustration)**.
12 Undo the screws on the upper rear edge of the floor panel on both sides **(see illustration)**.
13 Undo the screws on the inside of the cowling securing the cowling to the floor panel **(see illustration)**.
14 Undo the bolts securing the rear mudguard to the frame on both sides **(see illustration)**.

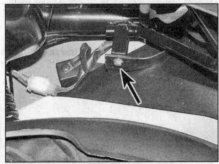

6.14 Undo the bolt on both sides

15 Undo the bolt securing the centre of the rear mudguard to the frame **(see illustration)**.
16 Disconnect the tail light assembly wiring connector, then lift the cowling off **(see illustration)**.

6.15 Undo the bolt at the rear

17 Note the location of the rubber washers on both side mounting points **(see illustration)**.
18 If required, undo the screws securing the rear mudguard to the cowling **(see illustration)**. Disconnect the licence plate

6.16 Disconnect the wiring connector

6.17 Note the location of the rubber washers

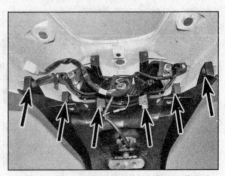

6.18a Screws secure rear mudguard to the cowling

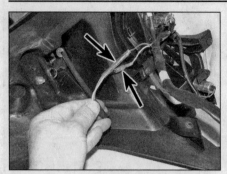

6.18b Licence plate light wiring connectors

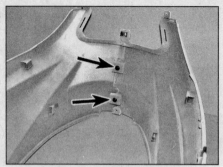

6.19 Screws (arrowed) hold the panels together at the front

6.21 Hugger mounting spacer and insulating washer

light wiring connectors **(see illustration)** and remove the mudguard.
19 The seat cowling is a two-piece assembly incorporating the tail light assembly. To separate the two halves, first remove the tail light assembly (see Chapter 10). Undo the screw at the rear and the screws at the front **(see illustration)** to separate the cowling.
20 Installation is the reverse of removal. Tighten the grab handle mounting bolts to the torque setting specified at the beginning of this Chapter. Check the operation of the tail light, turn signals and the licence plate light before riding the scooter.

Rear hugger

21 Undo the bolt securing the hugger to the exhaust system bracket, noting the location of the spacer and insulating washer **(see illustration)**.
22 Undo the mounting bolts on the right and left-hand sides and lift the hugger off **(see illustrations)**.

23 Installation is the reverse of removal.

Belly panel

Note: *The belly panel is a three-piece assembly – the side and centre sections must be removed separately.*
24 Working on one side at a time, undo the screws securing the side section of the belly panel, then draw it backwards to release the hooked tabs along the top edge from the floor panel **(see illustrations)**.
25 Undo the four bolts securing the centre section, then lower it noting how it fits over the sidestand **(see illustration)**.
26 Installation is the reverse of removal. Tighten the centre section bolts to the torque setting specified at the beginning of this Chapter.

Fuel tank

⚠️ **Warning: Refer to the precautions given in Chapter 5, Section 1 before proceeding.**

Note: *Before removing the fuel tank ensure that any residual fuel is drained into a suitable container. Refer to the procedure in Chapter 5, Section 2. Alternatively, use a commercially available fuel siphon pump to empty the tank.*
27 Remove the storage compartment and the seat cowling (see above).
28 Trace the wiring from the fuel level sensor and disconnect it at the connector **(see illustration)**.
29 Release the clips securing the fuel and vacuum hoses to the fuel tap and disconnect the hoses (see Chapter 5).
30 Undo the four bolts securing the tank to the mounting brackets and lift off the fuel tank.
31 Installation is the reverse of removal. Check the condition of the fuel hose and hoes clips and renew them if necessary. Don't forget to reconnect the fuel level sensor wiring connector.

6.22a Mounting bolt – right-hand side

6.22b Mounting bolt – left-hand side

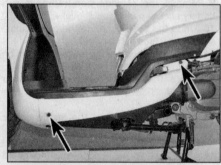

6.24a Undo the screws (arrowed)...

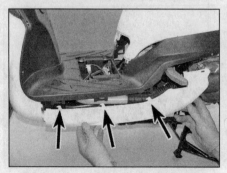

6.24b ...then release the hooked tabs

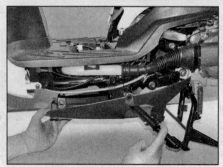

6.25 Note location of the sidestand

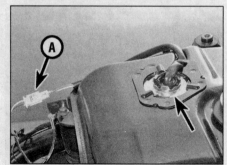

6.28 Fuel level sensor (arrowed) and wiring connector (A)

6.32 Undo the screws through the kick panel

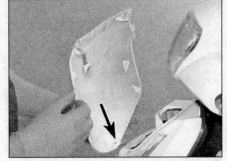

6.33 Release the tabs and hook (arrowed)

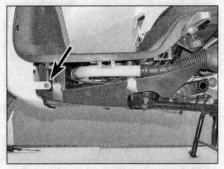

6.36 Undo the screws (arrowed) on both sides

Front top panel

32 Undo the screws securing the panel through the kick panel **(see illustration)**.
33 Ease the panel forwards to release the tabs on the inside and the hook on the lower edge from the main front panel **(see illustration)**.
34 Installation is the reverse of removal.

Front panel

35 Remove the front top panel (see above).
36 Remove the left and right-hand sections of the belly panel (see Step 24). Undo the screws on both sides securing the front panel bottom brackets **(see illustration)**.
37 Undo the screws securing the centre section of the front panel and lift it off **(see illustration)**.
38 Undo the screws securing the panel through the kick panel **(see illustration)**.

39 Undo the front centre mounting bolt **(see illustration)**.
40 Draw the panel forwards and disconnect the turn signal wiring connectors **(see illustration)**.
41 Note the location of the centre section screw U-clips and ensure that they are secure **(see illustration)**. Renew the U-clips if they are damaged.
42 Installation is the reverse of removal. Check the operation of the turn signals before riding the scooter.

Kick panel

43 Remove the front top panel and the front panel (see above).
44 Turn the ignition switch bezel anti-clockwise to remove it **(see illustration)**.
45 Undo the screws securing the lower edge of the panel and the screw securing the bag hook **(see illustration)**.
46 Draw the kick panel back and up to

release the tabs along the bottom edge from the front edge of the floor panel.
47 Installation is the reverse of removal. Ensure the tabs along the bottom edge are correctly located before tightening the fixing screws.

6.37 Remove the front panel centre section

6.38 Undo the screws through the kick panel

6.39 Undo the bolt at the front

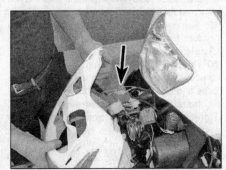

6.40 Draw the front panel forwards and disconnect the turn signal connectors

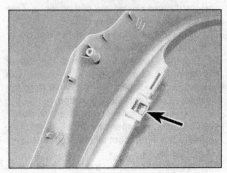

6.41 Check the screw U-clips

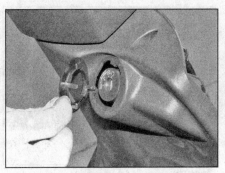

6.44 Remove the ignition switch bezel

6.45 Remove the lower screws and the bag hook screw

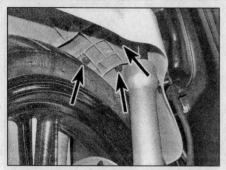

6.53 Location of the mudguard mounting bolts

6.58 Mirror stem locknut (arrowed)

6.61a Undo the screws through the rear cover...

6.61b ...and the screw located centrally below the headlight

6.62a Release the tabs on the front cover...

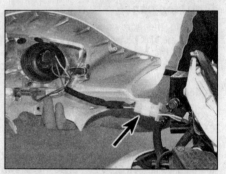

6.62b ...and disconnect the headlight connector

Floor panel

48 The floor panel can only be removed once all the other bodywork panels have been removed (see above).

49 Remove the battery, CDI unit and fuse holders from the battery compartment (see Chapter 10).

50 Prise out the plugs from the floor panel to access the mounting bolts, then undo the bolts and lift the floor panel off.

51 Installation is the reverse of removal. Tighten the mounting bolts to the torque setting specified at the beginning of this Chapter.

Front mudguard

52 Remove the front top panel and the front panel (see above).

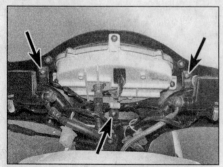

6.65 Screws (arrowed) secure rear cover to the handlebars

53 The front mudguard is secured to the front fork yoke by three bolts on the underside of the yoke **(see illustration)**.

54 Release the front brake hose and the speedometer cable from the clips on the mudguard.

55 Remove the front wheel (see Chapter 8) and both front fork legs (see Chapter 7).

56 Undo the mudguard mounting bolts and remove the mudguard.

57 Installation is the reverse of removal

Mirrors

58 Displace the rubber boot on the lower end of the mirror stem. Loosen the locknut on the mirror stem, then unscrew the mirror from the handlebar bracket **(see illustration)**.

59 On installation, position the mirror as required, then tighten the locknut securely

6.66 Disconnect the speedometer cable

Handlebar covers

60 Remove the mirrors (see Step 58).

61 To remove the front cover (and headlight) undo the screws from the rear cover and the single screw below the headlight **(see illustrations)**. Place a rag under the headlight when undoing the front screw as it is easy to drop it down inside the kick panel.

62 Ease the front cover away, unclipping it from the rear cover at the top and at each side, then disconnect the headlight wiring connector **(see illustrations)**.

63 To remove the rear cover, first remove the front cover.

64 Remove the front top panel and the front panel to access the wiring connectors for the handlebar switches and the instrument cluster (see above). Trace the wiring from the switches and instrument cluster and disconnect it. Free the wiring from any clips or ties.

65 Undo the screws securing the rear cover to the handlebars **(see illustration)**.

66 Displace the rubber boot at the top of the speedometer cable and unscrew the knurled ring to disconnect the cable from the instrument cluster **(see illustration)**.

67 Lift the rear cover with the handlebar switches and instrument cluster off. If required, separate the instrument cluster from the cover (see Chapter 10).

68 Installation is the reverse of removal. Check the operation of the instruments and handlebar switches before riding the scooter.

Chapter 10
Electrical system

Contents

Degrees of difficulty

| **Easy,** suitable for novice with little experience | 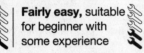 | **Fairly easy,** suitable for beginner with some experience | | **Fairly difficult,** suitable for competent DIY mechanic | | **Difficult,** suitable for experienced DIY mechanic | | **Very difficult,** suitable for expert DIY or professional | |

Specifications

Battery
Capacity
  V-Clic, Speedfight 50, Vivacity 50, Kisbee 50 . . . . 12 V, 4 Ah
  Tweet - all models. . . . . 12 V, 6 Ah
  Vivacity 125, Speedfight 125, Kisbee 100 . . . . 12 V, 7 Ah
Voltage
  Fully-charged . . . . 13.0 to 13.2 V
  Discharged . . . . below 12.65 V
Charging rate
  Normal . . . . 1.0 A for 5 hrs
  Quick . . . . 3.0 A for 1 hr

Carburettor heater
Resistance at 20°C. . . . . 6.8 to 10.2 ohms

Charging system

Current leakage	0.5 mA (max)

Alternator resistance
  V-Clic
    Yellow wire . . . . 0.9 ohms
    White wire . . . . 1.0 ohms
  Speedfight 50, Vivacity 50
    Yellow wire . . . . 0.6 ohms
    Yellow/white wire . . . . 0.5 to 0.8 ohms
  Vivacity 125
    Red/black wire . . . . 400 to 600 ohms
    Yellow/blue wire . . . . 115 to 175 ohms
    Pink to yellow wire . . . . 0.8 to 1.2 ohms
  Kisbee 50, Speedfight 125 and Tweet 125/150
    Red/black wire . . . . 480 to 720 ohms
    Yellow/blue wire . . . . 115 to 175 ohms
Regulated voltage output (all models) . . . . 14 to 15 V

Fuse

Main fuse
  V-Clic, Vivacity 125 . . . . 10 A
  Speedfight 50, Vivacity 50, Kisbee 50/100, ... 7.5 A
  Speedfight 125, Tweet 50, Tweet 125/150 . . . . 15 A
Secondary fuse
  Speedfight 50, Vivacity 50, Vivacity 125. . . . . 5 A
  Speedfight 125, Tweet 50. . . . . 10 A

Bulbs

Headlight
  Speedfight . . . . 12V, 35W x 2
  All other models 12V, 35/35W
Sidelight
  V-Clic, Tweet 50 . . . . 12V, 3W
  Speedfight 125, Vivacity 125, Kisbee 50/100, Tweet 125/150 . . . . . . 12V, 5W
Tail/brake light
  V-Clic, Speedfight, Kisbee, Tweet 12V, 5/21W
  Vivacity . . . . 12V, 2.3W x 10 (5 per side)
Licence plate light – 100/125/150 models 12V, 5W
Turn signals
  V-Clic, Kisbee, Tweet 12V, 10W
  Speedfight, Vivacity . . . . 12V, 2.3W x 14 amber (4 front, 3 rear per side)
Instrument cluster warning lights - V-Clic, Kisbee 12V, 1.2W
Instrument cluster illumination
  Kisbee 12V, 1.2W
  V-Clic 12V, 2W

Tachometer

Speed sensor gap . . . . 0.7 mm

Torque settings

Speed sensor mounting bolts . . . . 10 Nm

---

1 General information

All models have 12-volt electrical systems charged by a three-phase alternator with a separate regulator/rectifier. The regulator maintains the charging system output within a specified range to prevent overcharging, and the rectifier converts the AC (alternating current) output of the alternator to DC (direct current) to power the lights and other components and to charge the battery. The alternator is mounted on the right-hand end of the crankshaft.

The starting system comprises the starter motor, the battery, the starter relay and the various switches. A safety system, using the brake light switches and, where fitted, the sidestand switch, prevents the engine from being started unless one of the brake levers is pulled in and the sidestand is in the UP position.

The location of electrical components such as relays, resistors and sensors varies enormously. Refer to the appropriate wiring diagram at the end of this Chapter and trace the wiring to the component, removing any body panels as necessary to gain access (see Chapter 9).

A wiring diagram is useful when tracing electrical faults, if only to identify which are the power supply and earth wires leading from components. Use the diagram for your scooter in conjunction with the information in the following Sections when identifying and checking electrical components.

Note: *Keep in mind that electrical parts, once purchased, cannot be returned. To avoid unnecessary expense, make very sure the faulty component has been positively identified before buying a replacement part.*

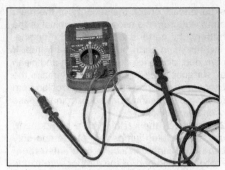

2.4a A digital multimeter can be used for all electrical tests

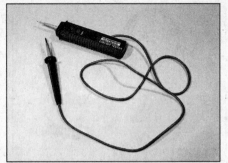

2.4b A battery-powered continuity tester

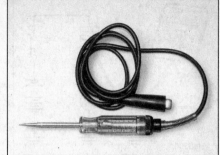

2.4c A simple test light is useful for voltage tests

2 Fault finding

⚠️ *Warning: To prevent the risk of short circuits, the ignition switch must always be OFF and the battery negative (-ve) terminal should be disconnected before any of the scooter's other electrical components are disturbed. Don't forget to reconnect the terminal securely once work is finished or if battery power is needed for circuit testing.*

1 A typical electrical circuit consists of an electrical component, the switches, relays, etc, related to that component and the wiring and connectors that link the component to the battery and the frame.

2 Before tackling any troublesome electrical circuit, first study the wiring diagram thoroughly to get a complete picture of what makes up that individual circuit. Trouble spots, for instance, can often be narrowed down by noting if other components related to that circuit are operating properly or not. If several components or circuits fail at one time, chances are the fault lies either in the fuse or in the common earth (ground) connection, as several circuits are often routed through the same fuse and earth (ground) connections.

3 Electrical problems often stem from simple causes, such as loose or corroded connections or a blown fuse. Prior to any electrical fault finding, always visually check the condition of the fuse, wires and connections in the problem circuit. Intermittent failures can be especially frustrating, since you can't always duplicate the failure when it's convenient to test. In such situations, a good practice is to clean all connections in the affected circuit, whether or not they appear to be good. All of the connections and wires should also be wiggled to check for looseness which can cause intermittent failure.

4 If you don't have a multimeter it is highly advisable to obtain one – they are not expensive and will enable a full range of electrical tests to be made. Go for a modern digital one with LCD display as they are easier to use. A continuity tester and/or test light are useful for certain electrical checks as an alternative, though

are limited in their usefulness compared to a multimeter **(see illustrations)**.

Continuity checks

5 The term continuity describes the uninterrupted flow of electricity through an electrical circuit. Continuity can be checked with a multimeter set either to its continuity function (a beep is emitted when continuity is found), or to the resistance (ohms / Ω) function, or with a dedicated continuity tester. Both instruments are powered by an internal battery, therefore the checks are made with the ignition OFF. As a safety precaution, always disconnect the battery negative (-) lead before making continuity checks, particularly if ignition system checks are being made.

6 If using a multimeter, select the continuity function if it has one, or the resistance (ohms) function. Touch the meter probes together and check that a beep is emitted or the meter reads zero, which indicates continuity. If there is no continuity there will be no beep or the meter will show infinite resistance. After using the meter, always switch it OFF to conserve its battery.

7 A continuity tester can be used in the same way – its light should come on or it should beep to indicate continuity in the switch ON position, but should be off or silent in the OFF position.

8 Note that the polarity of the test probes doesn't matter for continuity checks, although care should be taken to follow specific test procedures if a diode or solid-state component is being checked.

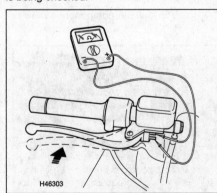

2.10 Continuity should be indicated across switch terminals when lever is operated

Switch continuity checks

9 If a switch is at fault, trace its wiring to the wiring connectors. Separate the connectors and inspect them for security and condition. A build-up of dirt or corrosion here will most likely be the cause of the problem – clean up and apply a water dispersant such as WD-40, or alternatively use a dedicated contact cleaner and protection spray.

10 If using a multimeter, select the continuity function if it has one, or the resistance (ohms) function, and connect its probes to the terminals in the connector **(see illustration)**. Simple ON/OFF type switches, such as brake light switches, only have two wires whereas combination switches, like the handlebar switches, have many wires. Study the wiring diagram to ensure that you are connecting to the correct pair of wires. Continuity should be indicated with the switch ON and no continuity with it OFF.

Wiring continuity checks

11 Many electrical faults are caused by damaged wiring, often due to incorrect routing or chaffing on frame components. Loose, wet or corroded wire connectors can also be the cause of electrical problems.

12 A continuity check can be made on a single length of wire by disconnecting it at each end and connecting the meter or continuity tester probes to each end of the wire **(see illustration)**. Continuity should be indicated if the wire is good. If no continuity is shown, suspect a broken wire.

13 To check for continuity to earth in any

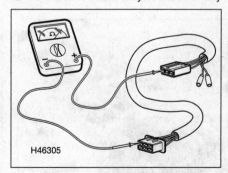

2.12 Wiring continuity check. Connect the meter probes across each end of the same wire

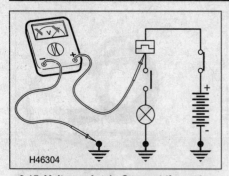

2.15 Voltage check. Connect the meter positive probe to the component and the negative probe to earth

2.23 A selection of insulated jumper wires

earth wire connect one probe of your meter or tester to the earth wire terminal in the connector and the other to the frame, engine, or battery earth (-) terminal. Continuity should be indicated if the wire is good. If no continuity is shown, suspect a broken wire or corroded or loose earth point (see below).

Voltage checks

14 A voltage check can determine whether power is reaching a component. Use a multimeter set to the dc (direct current) voltage scale to check for power from the battery or regulator/rectifier, or set to the ac (alternating current) voltage scale to check for power from the alternator. A test light can be used to check for dc voltage. The test light is the cheaper component, but the meter has the advantage of being able to give a voltage reading.

15 Connect the meter or test light in parallel, i.e. across the load **(see illustration)**.

16 First identify the relevant wiring circuit by referring to the wiring diagram at the end of this manual. If other electrical components share the same wiring circuit, take note whether they are working correctly – this is useful information in deciding where to start checking the circuit.

17 If using a meter, check first that the meter leads are plugged into the correct terminhals on the meter (red to positive (+), black to negative (-). Set the meter to the appropriate volts function (dc or ac), where necessary at

a range suitable for the battery voltage – 0 to 20 vdc. Connect the meter red probe (+) to the power supply wire and the black probe to a good metal earth (ground) on the scooter's frame or directly to the battery negative terminal. Battery voltage, or the specified voltage, should be shown on the meter with the ignition switch, and if necessary any other relevant switch, ON.

18 If using a test light **(see illustration 2.4c)**, connect its positive (+) probe to the power supply terminal and its negative (-) probe to a good earth (ground) on the scooter's frame. With the switch, and if necessary any other relevant switch, ON, the test light should illuminate.

19 If no voltage is indicated, work back towards the power source continuing to check for voltage. When you reach a point where there is voltage, you know the problem lies between that point and your last check point.

Earth (ground) checks

20 Earth connections are made either directly to the engine or frame (such as the starter motor or ignition coil which only have a positive feed) or by a separate wire into the earth circuit of the wiring harness. Alternatively a short earth wire is sometimes run from the component directly to the scooter's frame.

21 Corrosion is a common cause of a poor earth connection, as is a loose earth terminal fastener.

22 If total or multiple component failure is

experienced, check the security of the main earth lead from the negative (-) terminal of the battery, the earth lead bolted to the engine, and the main earth point(s) on the frame. If corroded, dismantle the connection and clean all surfaces back to bare metal. Remake the connection and prevent further corrosion from forming by smearing battery terminal grease over the connection.

23 To check the earthing of a component, use an insulated jumper wire to temporarily bypass its earth connection **(see illustration)** – connect one end of the jumper wire to the earth terminal or metal body of the component and the other end to the scooter's frame. If the circuit works with the jumper wire installed, the earth circuit is faulty.

24 To check an earth wire first check for corroded or loose connections, then check the wiring for continuity (Step 13) between each connector in the circuit in turn, and then to its earth point, to locate the break.

> **HAYNES HINT** *Remember that all electrical circuits are designed to conduct electricity from the battery, through the wires, switches, relays, etc. to the electrical component (light bulb, starter motor, etc). From there it is directed to the frame (earth) where it is passed back to the battery. Electrical problems are basically an interruption in the flow of electricity from the battery or back to it.*

3 Battery

⚠ *Warning: Be extremely careful when handling or working around the battery. Do not allow electrolyte to come in contact with your skin or painted or plastic surfaces of the scooter. Rinse off any spills immediately with plenty of water. Check with the local authorities about disposing of an old battery. Many communities will have collection centres which will see that batteries are disposed of safely.*

Removal and installation

1 Make sure the ignition is switched OFF.

2 On Speedfight models, unlock the seat and swing it upright (see Chapter 9). Remove the battery cover **(see illustration)**.

3 On V-Clic models, first remove the floor mat, then undo the screws securing the battery access panel and lift it off (see Chapter 9). Note the location of the battery **(see illustration)**.

4 On Kisbee models, undo the screw securing the battery cover in the centre of the floor panel and lift the cover off (see Chapter 9).

5 On Vivacity models, unlock the seat and swing it upright. Undo the screws securing the battery cover panel and lift it off (see

3.2 Remove the battery cover – Speedfight

3.3 Location of the battery – V-Clic

3.5 Release the battery strap – Vivacity

3.7 Always disconnect the negative lead first

3.8 Disconnect the battery breather hose

Chapter 9). Release the battery strap **(see illustration)**.

6 On Tweet models, undo the screws securing the battery access panel and lift it off (see Chapter 9).

7 Undo the negative (-) terminal screw first and disconnect the lead from the battery, then undo the positive (+) terminal screw and disconnect the lead **(see illustration)**.

8 Lift the battery from its holder. If a traditional 'wet' lead/acid battery is fitted, disconnect the battery breather hose **(see illustration)**.

9 Before installation, clean the battery terminals, terminal screws, nuts and lead ends with a wire brush, knife or steel wool to ensure a good electrical connection.

10 Install the battery – don't forget to connect the breather hose where fitted. Reconnect the leads, connecting the positive (+) lead first.

11 Secure the battery as noted on removal and fit the cover or access panel.

> **HAYNES HINT** *Battery corrosion can be kept to a minimum by applying a layer of petroleum jelly to the terminals after the leads have been connected.*

Inspection and maintenance

12 Either a sealed maintenance-free (MF) battery or a traditional wet lead-acid battery will be fitted. *Never attempt to open a maintenance-free battery as resulting damage will mean that it will be unfit for further use.*

13 Check the battery terminals and leads

for tightness and corrosion. If corrosion is evident, remove the battery (see above) and wash the terminals and lead ends in a solution of baking soda and hot water, then dry them thoroughly. Reconnect the leads and apply a thin coat of petroleum jelly or battery terminal grease to the connections to prevent further corrosion.

14 The battery should be kept clean to prevent current leakage, which can discharge the battery over a period of time (especially when it sits unused). Wash the outside of the battery with a solution of baking soda and water. Rinse the battery thoroughly, then dry it.

15 Look for cracks in the battery case and renew the battery if any are found. If acid has been spilled on the battery holder or surrounding bodywork, neutralise it with a baking soda and water solution, dry it thoroughly, then touch up any damaged paint.

16 The condition of the battery can be assessed by measuring the voltage present at the battery terminals with a multimeter. Connect the meter positive (+) probe to the battery positive (+) terminal, and the negative (-) probe to the battery negative (-) terminal **(see illustration)**. A fully charged battery should have a terminal voltage of between 12.8 and 13.2V. If the voltage falls below 12.65 volts the battery must be removed and recharged as described below. **Note:** *Before taking the measurement, wait at least 30 minutes after any charging has taken place (including running the engine).*

17 If battery condition is suspect, connect the

multimeter to the battery terminals as before (see Step 16), turn the ignition ON and press the starter button. If the meter reading drops below 8V a new battery is required.

18 If the machine is not used for long periods of time, disconnect the leads from the battery terminals and charge the battery once every month to six weeks or obtain a trickle charger.

Topping-up a wet lead-acid battery

19 The level of the electrolyte in a traditional battery will fall gradually in use. It is essential to maintain the level of the electrolyte above the lower level line on the side of the battery by adding distilled water.

20 Remove the battery (see Steps 1 to 8) and stand it on the workbench. Remove the cell caps – either six individual caps or a strip as shown **(see illustration)**. Place the caps on a clean paper towel so that they do not become contaminated with dirt.

21 Top-up each cell to the upper level line with distilled water **(see illustration)**. Do not use tap water (except in an emergency) and do not overfill.

22 Install the cell caps making sure they screw or press in firmly, otherwise the battery will leak when the scooter is in use.

Battery charging

Caution: Be extremely careful when handling or working around the battery. The electrolyte is very caustic and an explosive gas (hydrogen) is given off when the battery is charging.

3.16 Checking battery voltage

3.20 Remove the cell caps carefully

3.21 Top-up with distilled water

23 Ensure the charger is suitable for charging a 12V battery. When charging a maintenance free battery, make sure that you use a regulated battery charger.

24 Remove the battery (see Steps 1 to 8). Connect the charger to the battery **BEFORE** switching the charger ON. Make sure that the positive (+) lead on the charger is connected to the positive (+) terminal on the battery, and the negative (-) lead is connected to the negative (-) terminal.

25 Refer to the markings on the battery for the recommended charge rate – the Peugeot recommendation for original fitment batteries is given in the *Specifications* at the beginning of this Chapter. Exceeding this figure can cause the battery to overheat, buckling the plates and rendering it useless.

26 Ideally charge the battery using one of the dedicated motorcycle chargers as shown **(see illustration)**. If a normal domestic charger is used check that after a possible initial peak, the charge rate falls to a safe level. If the battery becomes hot during charging. **STOP**. Further charging will cause damage. **Note:** *In emergencies the battery can be charged at the quick rate specified. However, this is not recommended and the normal charging rate is by far the safer method of charging the battery.*

27 If the recharged battery discharges rapidly when left disconnected it is likely that an internal short caused by physical damage or sulphation has occurred. A new battery will be required. A sound battery will tend to lose its charge at about 1% per day.

28 Install the battery (see Steps 9 to 11).

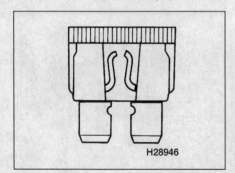
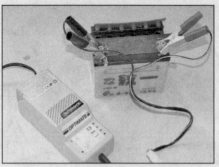

3.26 Battery connected to a charger

4 Fuses

1 The electrical system is protected by a main fuse and most models have a secondary fuse protecting individual electrical circuits. Refer to the *Wiring diagrams* at the end of this Chapter for details of your scooter. The fuses are located near or next to the battery (see Section 3). On Vivacity models the fuses are located on the underside of the battery tray **(see illustration)** – remove the storage compartment for access (see Chapter 9).

2 If one particular circuit or component fails to work, e.g. the brake lights, the turn signals or the accessory socket, check the secondary fuse for that circuit. If there are no electrical systems working at all, check the main fuse.

4.3a Glass cartridge fuse – Tweet shown

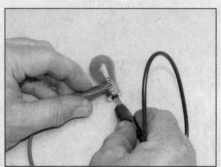

4.3b Flat-bladed fuse – Speedfight shown

4.4 A blown fuse can be identified by a break in its element

5.2 Checking a bulb filament for continuity

4.1 Location of the fuses – Vivacity

Refer to *Specifications* at the beginning of this Chapter for the rating of each fuse.

3 Unclip the fusebox lid to access the fuses. Two types of fuse are fitted – the glass cartridge type and the flat-bladed type **(see illustrations)**.

4 The fuses can be removed and checked visually. If you can't pull the fuse out with your fingertips, use a pair of suitable pliers. A blown fuse is easily identified by a break in the element **(see illustration)**. **Note:** *If the break in the element is not obvious, use a multimeter and check across the fuse ends for continuity (see Section 2).*

5 Each fuse is clearly marked with its rating and must only be replaced by a fuse of the correct rating. It is advisable to carry spare fuses on the scooter at all times.

⚠️ *Warning: Never fit a fuse of a higher rating or bridge the terminals with any other substitute, however temporary it may be. Serious damage may be done to the circuit, or a fire may start.*

6 If the fuse blows, be sure to check the wiring circuit very carefully for evidence of a short-circuit. Look for bare wires and chafed, melted or burned insulation. If a new fuse is fitted before the cause is located, it will blow immediately.

7 Occasionally the fuse will blow or cause an open-circuit for no obvious reason. Corrosion of the fuse ends and fuse holder terminals may occur and cause poor fuse contact. If this happens, remove the corrosion with a wire brush or steel wool, then spray the fuse ends and fuse holder terminals with electrical contact cleaner.

5 Lighting system checks

1 The lighting system consists of the headlight, sidelight (on most models), tail light, brake light, turn signals, instrument panel lights, handlebar switches, ignition switch and fuse(s).

2 If an individual light fails, first remove the bulb (see relevant Section below) and check it for a broken filament. It is advisable to back up a visual check with a continuity test of the filament as it is not always apparent that it is broken **(see illustration)**. When testing for

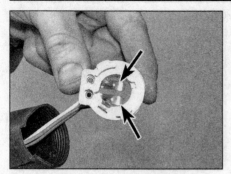

5.3 Make sure the bulb terminals (arrowed) are clean

6.1a Disconnect the connector...

6.1b ...and free the bulb – Speedfight

continuity, remember that in most cases it is the metal body of the bulb that is the earth (ground). On single filament H8 type halogen bulbs, an earth terminal is located in the bulb body.

3 Check that the terminals in the bulbholder are clean and free from corrosion **(see illustration)** and ensure that the bulb wiring connector is secure.

4 Next check for voltage on the supply side of the bulbholder or wiring connector with a test light or multimeter with the light switch ON. Don't forget that the engine may have to be running to do this check. When checking the headlight, select either high or low beam at the handlebar switch. When checking the brake light, pull either brake lever in.

5 If no voltage is indicated, check the wiring between the bulbholder and the light switch, then check the switch (see Section 17). Also, check the relevant fuse (see Section 4).

6 If voltage is indicated, check for continuity

between the earth wire terminal and an earth point on the scooter frame. If there is no continuity, check the earth circuit for a broken or poor connection.

7 If none of the lights work, always check battery voltage before proceeding. Low battery voltage indicates either a faulty battery or a defective charging system. Refer to Section 3 for battery checks and Section 27 for charging system tests. If there is more than one problem at the same time, it is likely to be a fault relating to a multi-function component, such as the main fuse, or the ignition switch.

6 Headlight and sidelight bulbs

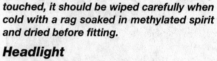

Caution: If the headlight bulb is of the quartz-halogen type, do not touch the bulb glass as skin acids will shorten the

bulb's service life. If the bulb is accidentally touched, it should be wiped carefully when cold with a rag soaked in methylated spirit and dried before fitting.

Headlight

1 On Speedfight models, remove the headlight panel (see Chapter 9). Disconnect the connector from the back of the H8 type bulb, then twist the bulb to release it from the headlight unit **(see illustrations)**.

2 On V-Clic models, remove the front handlebar cover (see Chapter 9). Remove the dust cover and disconnect the wiring connector from the bulb terminals **(see illustrations)**. Note how the bulb is located, then release the wire clip and lift out the bulb **(see illustrations)**.

3 On Kisbee models, remove the headlight panel (see Chapter 9). Remove the dust cover, then twist the bulbholder to release it from the headlight unit **(see illustrations)**. Push

6.2a Remove the dust cover...

6.2b ...and disconnect the wiring connector – V-Clic

6.2c Release the wire clip (arrowed)...

6.2d ...and lift out the bulb

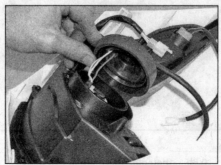

6.3a Remove the dust cover...

6.3b ...and release the bulbholder – Kisbee

6.3c Free the bulb from the bulbholder

6.4a Remove the dust cover – Vivacity

6.4b Release the wire clip...

6.4c ...and lift out the bulb

6.5a Remove the dust cover – Tweet

handlebar cover (see Chapter 9). Disconnect the wiring connector from the bulb terminals and remove the dust cover (see illustration). Note how the bulb is located, then release the wire clip and lift out the bulb (see illustrations).

6 Fit the new bulb in the reverse order.

> **HAYNES HiNT**
> *Always use a paper towel or dry cloth when handling bulbs to prevent injury if the bulb should break and to increase the life of a new bulb.*

7 Check the operation of the headlight.

Sidelight

8 On Speedfight 125 and Kisbee models, remove the headlight panel (see Chapter 9). Ease the bulbholder out from the back of the headlight unit, then pull the bulb out of the bulbholder (see illustrations).

9 On V-Clic models, the sidelight bulbholder is accessible from the underside of the lower front panel – pull the bulbholder out (see illustration) then pull the bulb out of the bulbholder. For access to the sidelight unit, refer to Chapter 9 and remove the lower front panel. The sidelight unit is mounted on the back of the panel (see illustration 12.2).

10 On Tweet models, remove the front handlebar cover (see Chapter 9). Ease the bulbholder out from the underside of the

6.5b Release the wire clip...

6.5c ...and lift out the bulb

the bulb in and twist it to release it from the bulbholder (see illustration).

4 On Vivacity models, remove the front handlebar cover (see Chapter 9). Remove the

dust cover (see illustration). Note how the bulb is located, then release the wire clip and lift out the bulb (see illustrations).

5 On Tweet models, remove the front

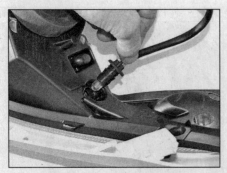

6.8a Ease out the bulbholder...

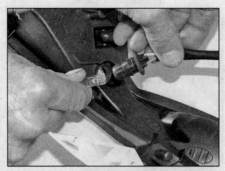

6.8b ...then pull out the capless bulb

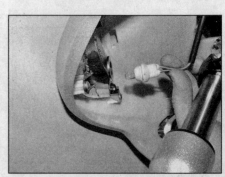

6.9 Removing the sidelight bulbholder – V-Clic

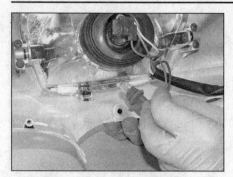

6.10 Removing the sidelight bulbholder – Tweet

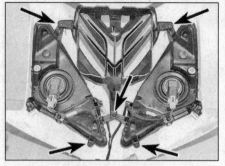

7.2 Screws (arrowed) secure the grille and headlights – Speedfight

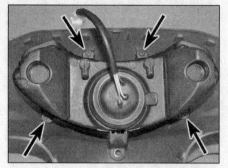

7.3 Screws (arrowed) secure the headlight – V-Clic

headlight unit **(see illustration)** then pull the bulb out of the bulbholder.

11 Fit the new bulb in the reverse order.
12 Check the operation of the sidelight.

7 Headlight unit

Removal and installation

1 On Speedfight models, remove the headlight panel (see Chapter 9). Mark the headlight wiring connectors so that they can be reconnected in the correct positions, then disconnect the connectors and remove the headlight sub loom.
2 Undo the screws securing the grille and remove it, then undo the remaining screws securing the left and right-hand headlight units and remove them **(see illustration)**.
3 On V-Clic models, remove the front handlebar cover (see Chapter 9). Undo the screws securing the headlight unit and remove it **(see illustration)**.
4 On Kisbee models, remove the headlight panel (see Chapter 9). Undo the screws securing the headlight/turn signal unit and remove it **(see illustration)**.
5 On Vivacity models, remove the front handlebar cover (see Chapter 9). Undo the screws securing the headlight unit and remove it **(see illustration)**.
6 On Tweet models, remove the front

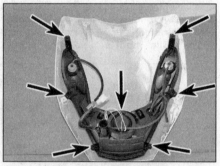

7.4 Screws (arrowed) secure the headlight unit – Kisbee

handlebar cover (see Chapter 9). Undo the screws securing the headlight unit **(see illustration)**. Release the headlight aim adjuster from the cover noting how it fits, then remove the headlight unit.
7 If required remove the headlight and sidelight bulbs (see Section 6).
8 Installation is the reverse of removal. Make sure all the wiring is correctly routed, connected and secured. Check the operation of the headlight(s) and sidelight(s). Check the headlight aim.

Headlight aim

Note: *Before adjusting the headlight aim, be sure to consult local traffic laws and regulations – for UK models refer to MOT Test Checks in the Reference section.*

7.5 Screws (arrowed) secure the headlight unit – Vivacity

9 The headlight beam can adjusted vertically.
10 First check that the tyre pressures are correct.
11 Position the machine on level ground and with an assistant sitting on the seat – the scooter should not be supported on its stand. If you usually carry a passenger, have a second assistant sit on the back.
12 On Speedfight models the adjuster screws for the left and right-hand headlights are accessed on both sides through the kick panel using a cross-head screwdriver **(see illustration)**.
13 On V-Clic and Vivacity models, the adjuster screw is located below the front of the headlight unit **(see illustration)**.
14 On Kisbee models, the cross-head

7.6 Undo the screws (arrowed). Note adjuster (A) – Tweet

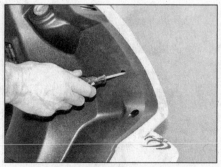

7.12 Adjusting the right-hand headlight – Speedfight

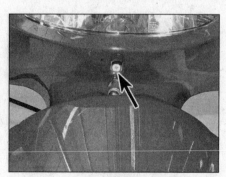

7.13 Headlight beam adjuster – V-Clic and Vivacity

adjuster screw is located through a hole in the kick panel adjacent to the bag hook **(see illustration)**.

15 On Tweet models, a hex-headed adjuster is located below the front of the headlight unit **(see illustration)**.

8	Brake/tail light and licence plate light bulbs

Note: *It is a good idea to use a paper towel or dry cloth when handling bulbs to prevent injury if the bulb should break and to increase the life of a new bulb.*

Brake/tail light bulb

1 On Speedfight models, undo the screws securing the combined tail light/turn signals

8.1a Screws secure combination lens – Speedfight

8.1c Push the bulb in and twist to release

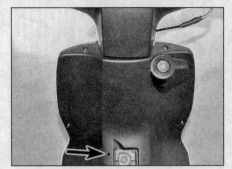

7.14 Headlight adjuster location – Kisbee

lens and lift it off **(see illustrations)**. Note the location of the thin lens seal. Push the bulb in and twist it to release it from the bulbholder **(see illustration)**.

2 On V-Clic models, undo the screws

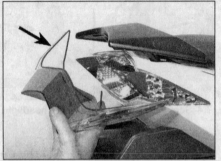

8.1b Remove the lens, noting how the seal (arrowed) fits

8.2a Undo the screws – V-Clic

8.2c Push the bulb in and twist to release

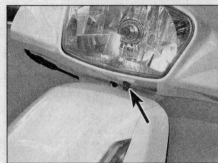

7.15 Headlight beam adjuster – Tweet

securing the trim panel underneath the tail light and remove the panel (see Chapter 9). Undo the screws securing the tail light lens and remove the lens, noting how the tab on the top edge locates under the lip of the seat cowling **(see illustrations)**. Push the bulb in and twist it to release it from the bulbholder **(see illustration)**.

3 On Kisbee and Tweet models, undo the screws securing the combined tail light/turn signals lens and lift it off **(see illustrations)**. Push the bulb in and twist it to release it from the bulbholder.

4 On Vivacity models, follow the procedure in Chapter 9 to remove the seat cowling. If necessary, refer to the wiring diagram to identify the tail light bulbholder (yellow wire on 50cc and black wire on 125cc) – there is only one tail light bulb fitted in each tail light unit. Ease the grey bulbholder out from the

8.2b Note location of tab on top edge

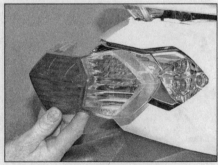

8.3b ...and lift off the lens – Kisbee shown

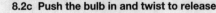

8.3a Undo the screws (arrowed)...

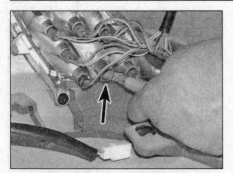

8.4 Ease out the tail light bulbholder – Vivacity

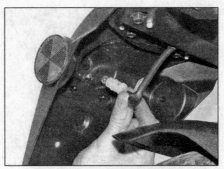

8.7a Ease out the licence plate light bulbholder...

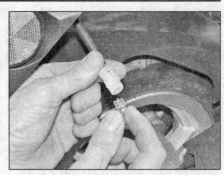

8.7b ...then pull out the capless bulb

back of the unit **(see illustration)**, then pull the bulb out of the bulbholder. Identify the (black) brake light bulbholders – there are four in each tail light unit. Ease the bulbholder out from the back of the unit, then pull the bulb out of the bulbholder. Note that the tail light and brake light bulbs are clear glass, the turn signal bulbs are coloured amber.

5 Fit the new bulb in the reverse order. Do not over-tighten the screws as it is easy to strip the threads or crack the lens. Check the operation of the tail and brake lights.

Licence plate light bulb

6 Kisbee and Tweet models are fitted with a separate licence plate light unit **(see illustration 8.9a)**.
7 To remove the bulb, ease the bulbholder out from the back of the unit, then pull out the bulb **(see illustrations)**.
8 Fit the new bulb in reverse order. Check the operation of the light.
9 To remove the licence plate light unit, undo the screw securing it to the mudguard and lift it off **(see illustrations)**.

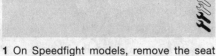

9 Tail light unit

1 On Speedfight models, remove the seat cowling (see Chapter 9). Undo the screws securing the seat cowling and tail light unit together and separate the components **(see illustration)**.
2 On V-Clic models, remove the lower side

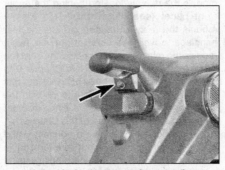

8.9a Undo the screw (arrowed)...

panels and seat cowling (see Chapter 9). Disconnect the light unit wiring connector **(see illustration)**. Undo the upper bolts and lower domed nuts securing the light unit and lift it off **(see illustrations)**.

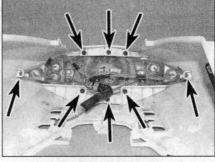

9.1 Undo the screws (arrowed) – Speedfight

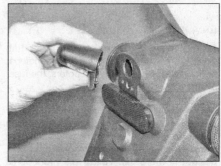

8.9b ...and lift off the licence plate light

3 On Kisbee models, remove the seat cowling (see Chapter 9). Undo the screws securing the seat cowling and tail light unit together and separate the components **(see illustration)**.
4 On Vivacity models, remove the seat cowling

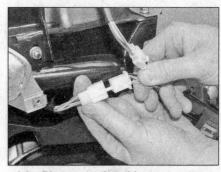

9.2a Disconnect the wiring connector – V-Clic

9.2b Undo the fixings (arrowed)...

9.2c ...and lift off the light unit

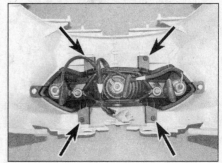

9.3 Undo the screws (arrowed) – Kisbee

(see Chapter 9). Undo the screws securing the left and right-hand light units and lift them off, noting how they fit **(see illustration)**. If required, remove the bulbholders, making careful note of their locations.

5 On Tweet models, remove the seat cowling (see Chapter 9). Disconnect the licence plate light wiring connectors, then undo the screws securing the light unit and lift it it off **(see illustration)**.

6 Installation is the reverse of removal. Make sure all the wiring is correctly routed, connected and secured. Check the operation of the tail and brake lights and turn signals.

10 Turn signal system

1 The turn signal system consists of the turn signal lights, instrument panel light, handlebar switch, relay and, on some scooters, the fuse.

Turn signal lights

2 Most turn signal problems are the result of a failed bulb or corroded socket (see Section 11). This is especially true when the turn signals function properly in one direction, but not in the other. Follow the procedures described in Section 5 to check the bulbs and the sockets, then check the operation of the turn signal switch and the turn signal warning light in the instrument cluster.

Turn signal relay

3 If the bulbs and sockets are good, test the power supply to the signal relay. On V-Clic

9.4 Undo the screws (arrowed) – Vivacity

models the relay is located behind the upper front panel **(see illustration)**. On Kisbee models the relay is located behind the rear handlebar cover **(see illustration)**. On Tweet models the relay is located behind the front top panel **(see illustration)**. Refer to Chapter 9 to remove the appropriate body panels. Note that on other models the relay is integral with the instrument cluster – refer to the wiring diagram for your machine at the end of this Chapter.

4 Disconnect the relay wiring connector and check for voltage at the input wire terminal in the connector with the engine running, using a multimeter or test light connected to a good earth. Turn the engine OFF. If there is no voltage, use the wiring diagram to check the supply circuit.

5 If there is voltage, reconnect the wiring connector to the relay and use a test light to check for voltage on the output side of the relay wiring connector with the engine running.

9.5 Undo the screws (arrowed) – Tweet

The light should flash – if it does not, fit a new relay.

11 Turn signal bulbs

Note: *It is a good idea to use a paper towel or dry cloth when handling bulbs to prevent injury if the bulb should break and to increase the life of a new bulb.*

1 On Speedfight models, access to the front turn signal bulbs is from the back of the front side panels. Follow the procedure in Chapter 9 to remove the kick panel. Ease the bulbholder out from the back of the unit then pull the bulb out of the bulbholder **(see illustration)**. The rear turn signals are integral with the tail light unit **(see illustrations 8.1a and b)**. Pull the capless bulb(s) out of the bulbholder **(see illustration)**.

10.3a Location of the turn signal relay (arrowed) – V-Clic

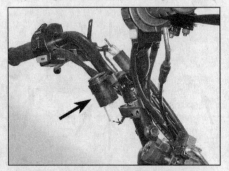
10.3b Location of the turn signal relay – Kisbee

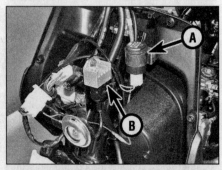
10.3c Turn signal relay (A), regulator/ rectifier (B) – Tweet

11.1a Access to front turn signal bulbs – Speedfight

11.1b Pull out the capless bulb

11.1c Access to the rear turn signal bulbs

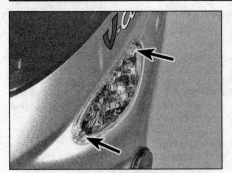

11.2a Undo the screws...

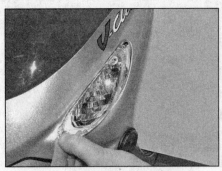

11.2b ...and draw the lens forwards – V-Clic

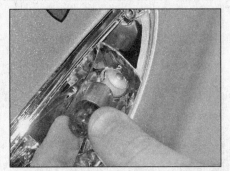

11.2c Push in and twist to release the bulb

11.2d Undo the screw (arrowed)

11.2e Ease the panel back to remove the lens

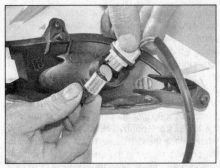

11.3 Push in and twist to release the bulb from the bulbholder – Kisbee

2 On V-Clic models, undo the screws securing the front turn signal lens and draw the lens forwards (see illustrations). Push the bulb in and twist it to release it from the bulbholder (see illustration). The rear turn signals are integral with the tail light unit – follow the procedure in Section 8 to remove the tail light lens. As appropriate, undo the screw securing the rear of the left or right-hand lower side panel, ease the rear end of the panel back and remove the turn signal lens (see illustrations). Push the bulb in and twist it to release it from the bulbholder.

3 On Kisbee models, remove the headlight panel (see Chapter 9). Twist the bulbholder to release it from the headlight unit, then push the bulb in and twist it to release it from the bulbholder (see illustration). The rear turn signals are integral with the tail light unit (see illustrations 8.3a and b). Push the bulb in and twist it to release it from the bulbholder.

4 On Vivacity models, remove the front storage compartment (see Chapter 9). Ease the bulbholder out from the back of the turn signal unit (see illustration) then pull the bulb out of the bulbholder. The rear turn signals are integral with the tail light unit – remove the seat cowling for access (see Chapter 9). Refer to the wiring diagram to identify the turn signal bulbholders – there are three in each tail light unit. Ease the bulbholder out from the back of the unit (see illustration), then pull the bulb out of the bulbholder.

5 On Tweet models, remove the front panel (see Chapter 9). Ease the bulbholder out from the back of the turn signal unit (see

illustration) then pull the bulb out of the bulbholder. The rear turn signals are integral with the tail light unit (see illustrations 8.3a and b). Push the bulb in and twist to release it from the bulbholder.

6 Fit the new bulb in the reverse order, noting that the pins on amber bulbs are slightly offset (see illustration 11.2c). Do not over-tighten the screws as it is easy to strip the threads or crack the lens. Check the operation of the turn signals and associated lights.

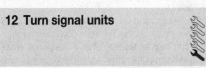

12 Turn signal units

1 On Speedfight models, the front turn signal units are mounted on the inside of the front

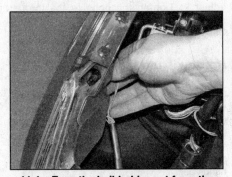

11.4a Ease the bulbholder out from the back – Vivacity

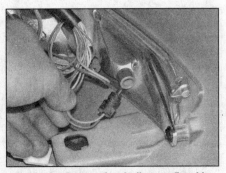

11.4b Capless amber bulbs are fitted in the turn signal bulbholders

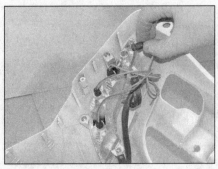

11.5 Access to the front turn signal bulbs – Tweet

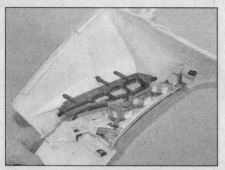

12.1 Location of the left-hand front turn signal unit – Speedfight

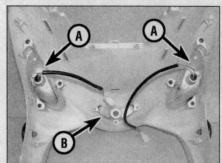

12.2 Front turn signal units (A), side light (B) – V-Clic

side panels (see illustration). Follow the procedure in Chapter 9 to remove the side panels. Undo the screws securing the units and lift them off, noting how they fit. The rear turn signals are integral with the tail light unit (see Section 9).

2 On V-Clic models, the front turn signal units are mounted on the back of the lower front panel – refer to Chapter 9 and remove the lower front panel. Remove the turn signal lenses (see illustrations 11.2a and b). Undo the screws securing the units and lift them off, noting how they fit (see illustration). The rear turn signals are integral with the tail light unit (see Section 9).

3 On Kisbee models, the front turn signals are integral with the headlight unit (see Section 7). The rear turn signals are integral with the tail light unit (see Section 9).

4 On Vivacity models, the front turn signal units are mounted on the back of the front panel – refer to Chapter 9 and remove the kick panel for access. Remove the bulbholders, making careful note of their locations. Undo the screws securing the units (see illustration) and lift them off forwards. The rear turn signals are integral with the tail light unit (see Section 9).

5 On Tweet models, the front turn signal units are mounted on the back of the front panel – refer to Chapter 9 and remove the panel. Note the location of the clips for the turn signal sub loom, then undo the screws securing the units and lift them off (see illustration). The rear

turn signals are integral with the tail light unit (see Section 9).

6 Installation is the reverse of removal. Check the operation of the turn signals and associated lights.

13 Instrument cluster

Check

1 If none of the instruments or displays are working, first check the relevant fuse(s) (see Section 4).

2 Next remove the handlebar cover(s) (see Chapter 9) according to your scooter to access the instrument cluster wiring connector. Disconnect the wiring connector.

3 Refer to the appropriate wiring diagram at the end of this Chapter and identify the power supply wire from the ignition switch. Check for battery voltage at the wire terminal(s) in the loom side of the wiring connector with the ignition ON. Turn the ignition OFF.

4 If there is no voltage, check the wire for continuity, then check the ignition switch (see Section 18).

5 Identify the earth (ground) wire in the instrument cluster connector and check for continuity to earth at the wire terminal in the loom side of the connector. There should be continuity.

6 If no fault can be found, have the instrument cluster checked by a Peugeot dealer.

7 If the speedometer does not work on V-Clic, Kisbee or Tweet models, first check the cable then check the drive gear in the front wheel hub (Section 15). Speedfight and Vivacity models have an electronically-operated speedometer; check the wiring and connector between the instruments and sensor unit on the wheel hub.

8 The engine temperature gauge and sensor are covered in Chapter 4.

9 The fuel gauge and level sensor are covered in Chapter 5.

10 The oil level warning light, as fitted to two-stroke models, has a dual function. It acts as a warning when the oil level in the tank drops to a critical level (see Section 19) and it acts as a warning when the oil pump control unit detects a malfunction see Section 20).

11 The ambient temperature gauge displays the outside air temperature. If the temperature falls below 3°C the 'risk of black ice' symbol is displayed. The gauge is connected to the temperature sensor located at the front of the scooter on the front inner panel (see Chapter 9, Section 5). No test information is available for the sensor other than to ensure that the wiring and wiring connectors are in good condition.

12 Late Speedfight models are fitted with an analog revolution counter (tachometer). When the ignition is switched ON the tachometer needle should sweep across the dial and return to zero as an instrument check. The tachometer does not register engine speeds below 1000 rpm. If, when the engine is running, the needle is not stable or if the indicated rpm value drops, check and adjust the speed sensor gap as follows. The sensor/ignition pulse generator coil, is located on the right-hand side of the engine adjacent to the alternator rotor (refer to the appropriate part of Chapter 2 for your model). Turn the alternator rotor until the trigger on the outside of the rotor is immediately in front of the sensor and measure the gap with a feeler gauge. If the gap is not as specified at the beginning of this Chapter, loosen the sensor mounting bolts and adjust it. Tighten the bolts to the torque setting specified at the beginning of this Chapter.

Removal and installation

13 Remove the handlebar cover(s) (see Chapter 9) to access the instrument cluster wiring connector. Disconnect the wiring connector. Where fitted, disconnect the speedometer cable.

14 If not already done, undo the screws securing the instrument cluster to the handlebars.

15 If the instrument cluster is located inside the handlebar top cover, undo the

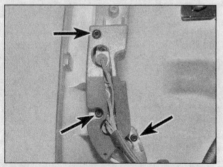

12.4 Screws (arrowed) secure front turn signal unit – Vivacity

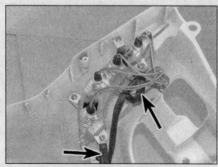

12.5 Note location of wiring clips (arrowed) – Tweet

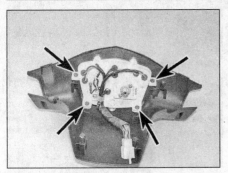

**13.15 Screws secure instrument cluster –
Kisbee shown**

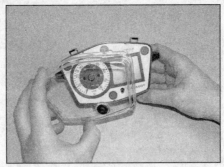

**13.16 Vivacity instrument cluster lens
unclips**

screws securing it and lift it out **(see illustration)**.
16 On some models, the instrument cluster lens can be unclipped from the body **(see illustration)**.
17 Installation is the reverse of removal. Make sure all wiring is correctly routed and all connectors are secure.

14 Instrument and warning lights

1 The instrument cluster and warning lights on V-Clic and Kisbee models are illuminated by capless bulbs. To access the bulbs, first remove the handlebar cover(s) (see Chapter 9) according to your machine. If necessary, disconnect the speedometer cable (see Section 15).
2 Refer to the wiring diagram for your scooter to identify the bulbs. Ease the bulbholder out from the instrument cluster then pull the bulb out of the holder **(see illustrations)**. Fit the new bulb in the reverse order.
3 If one light fails to work, but the bulb is good, check for voltage on the supply side of the bulbholder with the engine running and the appropriate switch ON. Turn the ignition OFF. If no voltage is indicated, check the wiring for continuity. If there is voltage, check for continuity to earth (ground) between the bulbholder and an earth point on the scooter frame. If there is no continuity, check the earth circuit for a broken or poor connection.

4 All other models have LED instrument and warning lights. Before assuming that an LED has failed, check the cause is not due to the source that supplies its signal, and that all wiring and connectors between the source and the instrument cluster are good.
5 If an LED has failed a new instrument cluster will have to be fitted – individual components are not available.

15 Speedometer drive

V-Clic, Kisbee and Tweet models
Removal

1 V-Clic, Kisbee and Tweet models have a conventional cable-driven speedometer.

2 To access the upper end of the cable remove the handlebar front cover (see Chapter 9).
3 To ensure the cable is correctly routed on installation, refer to Chapter 9 and on V-Clic models remove the upper front panel, on Kisbee models remove the headlight panel and on Tweet models remove the front top panel.
4 Displace the rubber boot on the upper end of the cable and unscrew the knurled ring securing the cable to the instrument cluster **(see illustration)**.
5 Unscrew the knurled ring securing the lower end of the speedometer cable **(see illustration)**. Pull the inner cable out of the drive housing noting how it locates.
6 Free the cable from any guides on the front mudguard and the front suspension, then withdraw it from the machine, noting its routing.
7 If the front wheel has been removed, clean the inside of the speedometer drive housing and ensure that the drive gear rotates freely **(see illustration)**. Lubricate the gear with a smear of grease and ensure that the tabs on the gear locate with the drive tabs on the wheel hub on installation.

Installation

8 Route the cable up through its guides and connect it to the back of the instrument cluster **(see illustration 15.4)**. Refit the rubber boot.
9 Locate the lower end of the inner cable in the drive housing and tighten the knurled ring **(see illustration 15.5)**.
10 Check that the cable doesn't restrict steering movement or interfere with any other components.

14.2a Ease the bulbholder out...

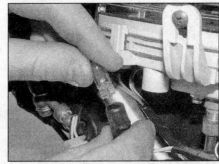

14.2b ...then pull out the bulb

**15.4 Disconnect the cable from the
instrument cluster**

**15.5 Disconnect the cable from the drive
housing**

**15.7 Ensure that the drive gear rotates
freely**

11 Install the body panels as removed (see Step 3) then install the handlebar front cover.

Speedfight and Vivacity models

Removal

12 Speedfight and Vivacity models have an electronically operated speedometer. A wire connects the sensor on the wheel hub to the speedometer head. Do not try to disconnect the wire from the sensor.
13 To access the upper end of the wire remove the handlebar front cover (see Chapter 9). In addition, on Speedfight models remove the coolant reservoir/front top cover and on Vivacity models remove the front storage compartment.
14 Trace the wire from the sensor to the three-way connector at the handlebar end and disconnect it (see illustrations). Pull the cable out carefully, releasing it from any guides and noting its correct routing.
15 Remove the front wheel (see Chapter 8) and lift off the sensor (see illustration). Clean the inside of the sensor housing and ensure that the sensor rotor turns freely (see illustration). Do not lubricate the inside of the housing.

Installation

16 Route the wire up through the guides on the front suspension and inside the bodywork to the instrument cluster and connect the upper end securely (see illustration 15.14b).
17 Position the sensor over the drive tabs on the wheel hub and install the front wheel (see Chapter 8).

15.14a Trace the wire to the connector (arrowed)...

15.15a Lift off the speedometer sensor

18 Check that the wire doesn't restrict steering movement or interfere with any other components.
19 Install the body panels as removed (see Step 13) then install the handlebar front cover.

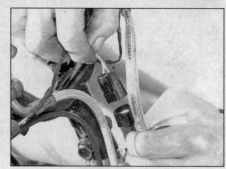
15.14b ...and disconnect it

15.15b Ensure the sensor rotor turns freely

16 Starter system

1 The starter system consists of the starter switch, starter motor, battery, starter relay and fuse (see *Wiring diagrams* at the end of this Chapter). The brake light switches and, where fitted, the sidestand switch, are part of a safety circuit which prevents the engine starting unless the brake is held on and the sidestand is UP. On two-stroke scooters, the oil level sensor is also part of the safety circuit (see Section 19).
2 If the starter circuit is faulty, first check the fuse (see Section 4). Also check that the battery is fully-charged (see Section 3). If, after testing, the starter system is good, check the starter pinion assembly or starter clutch (see Chapter 2 as applicable for your scooter).

Starter relay

3 To locate the starter relay, trace the lead from the positive terminal of the battery to the relay, or trace the lead back from the starter motor to the relay (see illustrations). Depending on your scooter, it may be necessary to remove the storage compartment and, if necessary, the seat cowling (see Chapter 9) to access the relay (see illustrations).
4 Disconnect the starter motor lead from the relay. With the ignition switch ON and the brake lever pulled in, press the starter switch. The relay should be heard to click. Switch the ignition OFF. If the relay doesn't click it can be tested on the workbench as follows.

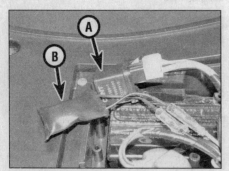
16.3a Starter relay (A), thermoswitch (B) – V-Clic

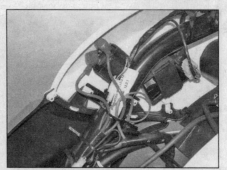
16.3b Location of the starter relay – Kisbee

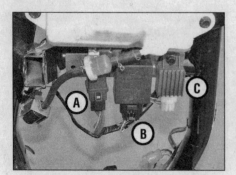
16.3c Starter relay (A), CDI unit (B) and regulator/rectifier (C) – Speedfight

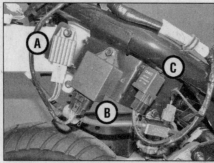
16.3d Regulator/rectifier (A), CDI unit (B) and starter relay (C) – Vivacity

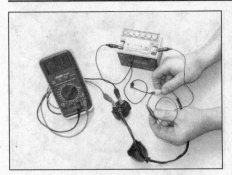

16.7 Set-up for testing the starter relay

16.10 Location of the sidestand switch – Kisbee

16.11 Sidestand switch wiring connectors (arrowed)

5 Disconnect the battery terminals, remembering to disconnect the negative (-) terminal first.
6 Disconnect both leads from the starter relay, making a careful note of which lead fits on which terminal (the terminals are usually numbered). Trace the wiring from the relay and disconnect it at the connector. Remove the relay.
7 Set a multimeter to the ohms x 1 scale and connect it across the relay's battery and starter motor terminals – there should be no continuity. Using a fully-charged 12 volt battery and two insulated jumper wires, connect across the terminals of the wiring connector **(see illustration)**. At this point the relay should be heard to click and the multimeter read 0 ohms (continuity) indicating the relay is good.
8 If the relay does not click when battery voltage is applied and the multimeter indicates infinite resistance (no continuity), the relay is faulty and must be renewed.
9 If the relay is good, check for battery voltage across the terminals of the wiring connector with the ignition ON and the brake lever pulled in when the starter switch is pressed. If there is no battery voltage, check the other components and wiring in the starter circuit as described in Step 1.

Sidestand switch

10 The sidestand switch is mounted on the stand bracket **(see illustration)**. Remove the belly panel for access (see Chapter 9).
11 To test the switch, trace the wiring back

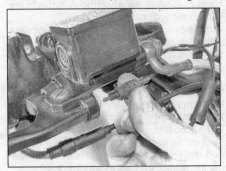

16.17 Unscrew the switch from the lever bracket

16.14a Brake light switch wiring connectors

to the connector(s) and disconnect it **(see illustration)**.
12 Connect a multimeter or continuity tester to the terminals on the switch side of the connector. With the sidestand UP there should be continuity (zero resistance) between the terminals, with the stand DOWN there should be no continuity (infinite resistance).
13 If the switch does not work as expected, check that the fault is not caused by a sticking switch plunger due to the ingress of road dirt. If required, follow the procedure in Chapter 7 and remove the stand, then spray the switch with a water dispersant aerosol. If the switch still does not work it is defective and a new one must be fitted.

Brake light switches

14 On most models, the brake light switches are accessible from the front of the machine. Remove the handlebar front cover (see

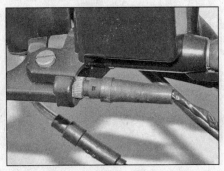

16.18 Ensure the rubber boot is correctly installed

16.14b Front brake light switch – V-Clic

Chapter 9), then pull back the rubber boot and disconnect the switch wiring connectors **(see illustration)**. On V-Clic models, a different type of switch is fitted to the front brake master cylinder. The switch is accessible from the underside of the handlebar **(see illustration)** – remove both handlebar covers.
15 Using a continuity tester, connect a probe to each terminal on the switch. With the brake lever at rest, there should be no continuity. Pull the brake lever in – there should now be continuity.
16 If the switch is good, refer the wiring diagram in your scooter handbook to check the brake light circuit using a multimeter or test light (see Section 2).
17 If the switch is faulty, disconnect the wiring connectors and unscrew the switch from the handlebar lever bracket **(see illustration)**. On V-Clic models, undo the mounting screw to remove the switch **(see illustration 16.14b)**.
18 On installation take care not to over-tighten the switches. Don't forget to fit the rubber boot **(see illustration)**.

17 Handlebar switches

1 Generally speaking, the switches are reliable and trouble-free. Most problems, when they do occur, are caused by dirty or corroded contacts, but wear and breakage of internal parts is a possibility that should not be overlooked when tracing a fault. If

17.4 Handlebar switch wiring connector – V-Clic shown

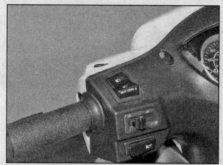

17.6a Handlebar switches on Tweet models...

17.6b ...are fitted into the handlebar rear cover

17.7a Undo the screws (arrowed)...

17.7b ...and separate the switch housing

breakage does occur, the entire switch and related wiring harness will have to be renewed as individual parts are not available.

2 The switches can be checked for continuity using a multimeter or test light and battery. Always disconnect the battery negative (-) lead, which will prevent the possibility of a short circuit, before making the checks.

3 Remove the handlebar covers and any front body panels as necessary to trace the wiring from the switch in question back to its connector (see Chapter 9). Refer to the wiring diagram for your scooter to identify the wiring connector.

4 Disconnect the wiring connector **(see illustration)**. Using the wiring diagram, check for continuity between the terminals of the switch wiring with the switch in the various positions (i.e. switch OFF – no continuity, switch ON – continuity).

5 If the checks indicate a problem exists, the switches should be examined.

6 On Tweet models, the switches are fitted into the handlebar rear cover **(see illustrations)**. The switches are sealed units with no provision for maintenance. To remove a switch, first disconnect the wiring connector, then unclip the unit from the cover.

7 On all other models, undo the screws securing the two halves of the housing and separate them **(see illustrations)**. Note the location of the housing screws – they are often different lengths. Note that on most scooters, the right-hand housing is integral with the throttle twistgrip (see Chapter 5).

8 Spray the switch contacts with electrical contact cleaner. If they are accessible, the contacts can be scraped clean carefully with a knife or polished with crocus cloth. If switch components are damaged or broken, it will be obvious when the switch is disassembled.

9 Clean the inside of the switch body thoroughly and smear the contacts with suitable grease before reassembly.

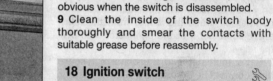

18 Ignition switch

> **Warning: To prevent the risk of short circuits, disconnect the battery negative (-) lead before making any ignition switch checks.**

Check

1 The ignition switch is integral with the steering lock and is fixed to the top of the frame steering head **(see illustration)**. On most models, the switch also incorporates the cable mechanism for releasing the seat catch **(see illustration)**.

2 Remove the kick panel and any front body panels as necessary to access the switch and the switch wiring connector (see Chapter 9).

3 Ensure the battery negative (-) lead is disconnected. Disconnect the wiring connector. Refer to the appropriate wiring diagram at the end of this Chapter and using a multimeter or continuity tester, check the continuity between the switch terminal pairs. Continuity should exist between the connected terminals when the switch is in the indicated position.

4 If the switch fails any of the tests, replace it with a new one.

5 Provision is made for adjustment of the seat catch cable should it be required.

Removal

6 Disconnect the battery negative (-) lead and the switch wiring connector.

7 If applicable, undo the screw securing the seat cable elbow to the body of the switch and disconnect the inner cable end from the catch mechanism **(see illustration)**.

8 In most cases the switch is secured to the frame by one normal bolt and one shear-head

18.1a Location of the ignition switch – V-Clic

18.1b Ignition switch and seat catch release cable – Kisbee

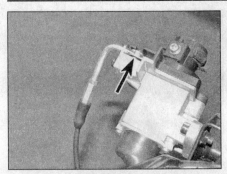

18.7 Disconnect the inner cable end (arrowed)

18.12 Location of the ignition immobiliser switch

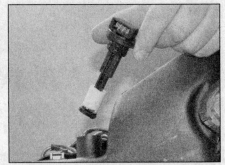

19.3 Withdraw the sensor from the oil tank

bolt. To remove a shear-head bolt, drill off the bolt head, then remove the switch. The threaded section of the shear-head bolt can then be unscrewed with pliers.

Installation

9 Installation is the reverse of removal. Tighten the bolts finger-tight, then operate the key to ensure the steering lock mechanism is correctly aligned with the frame and steering stem. Now tighten the bolts securely – when tightening a shear-head bolt, turn it until the head snaps off.

10 Where fitted, connect the inner end of the seat cable to the catch mechanism, then align the plate on the cable elbow with the body of the switch and tighten the screw securely. Check the operation of the seat catch and adjust the cable as required. Don't forget to tighten the cable adjuster locknut.

11 Reconnect the battery negative (-) lead once all electrical connections have been made to the switch.

Circuit breaker (ignition immobiliser) switch

12 On Tweet models, a switch located in the bottom of the storage compartment isolates the ignition pulse generator coil from the ignition unit when it is in the LOCK position (see illustration).

13 To check the operation of the switch, first remove the storage compartment (see Chapter 9). Check for continuity between the terminals in the switch wiring connector. In the LOCK position there should be no continuity, in the UNLOCK position there should be continuity.

14 If the switch does not operate as described it should be replaced with a new one.

19 Oil level warning circuit (two-stroke engines)

1 The oil level warning light in the instrument cluster should come on and flash whenever the oil level in the tank is low. As a check of the warning circuit, the light should come when the ignition is first turned ON and go off when the engine starts.

2 If the light fails to come on, first check the wiring between the instrument cluster and the sensor in the oil tank. Refer to the appropriate Section in Chapter 9 for access to the oil tank.

3 To test the sensor, disconnect the wiring connector and withdraw the sensor from the oil tank (see illustration).

 Warning: Cover the opening in the tank to prevent anything falling inside.

4 Connect a multimeter or continuity tester to the terminals in the sensor wiring connector and check for continuity with the sensor float UP (tank full). Now slowly lower the float to the DOWN (tank empty) position. There should be no continuity (infinite resistance) until the float nears the empty position, when continuity should be shown. If this is not the case the sensor is faulty and a new one must be fitted.

20 Oil pump control unit (two-stroke engines)

1 The engine oil pump is driven electronically and the rate of oil flow is controlled either by a dedicated pump control unit (CPH), or by a combined oil pump and CDI unit (ACPH).

2 Both systems alert the rider to loss of oil supply or a pump failure. If this happens it is essential that any air is bled from the oil pump and hoses before the engine is run again (see Chapter 2A or 2B).

3 To identify which system is fitted to your scooter make a visual check of the system components. The ACPH circuit is shown in the wiring diagrams at the end of this Chapter.

CPH system

4 The system features a separate pump control unit with a six-pin wiring connector and a separate CDI unit. The ignition switch has a two-pin wiring connector. The oil warning light in the instrument cluster also acts as a diagnostic indicator light.

5 In the event of loss of oil supply or a pump failure the oil warning light in the instrument cluster flashes. The rider must stop the engine immediately to avoid serious engine damage.

ACPH system

6 The system features a combined pump control unit and CDI unit with an eight-pin wiring connector. The ignition switch has a four-pin wiring connector. The oil warning light in the instrument cluster also acts as a diagnostic indicator light. In addition, a separate STOP warning light may be fitted in the instrument display.

7 In the event of loss of oil supply or a pump failure the oil warning light in the instrument cluster flashes. The ignition is cut as soon as the engine speed drops to idle and the engine cannot be restarted until the fault has been rectified.

21 Carburettor heater and thermoswitch

1 Poor starting with a cold engine could be caused by a faulty carburettor heater thermoswitch (also check the operation of automatic choke unit – see Chapter 5).

2 The thermoswitch is located on the frame behind the seat cowling (see illustration). Refer to the procedure in Chapter 9 to remove the storage compartment and seat cowling. Apart from wiring checks the performance of the thermoswitch cannot be checked.

3 The carburettor heater screws into the body of the carburettor (see illustration 6.13 in Chapter 5). A figure is given in the Specifications at the beginning of this Chapter for heater resistance.

21.2 Location of the thermoswitch – Tweet

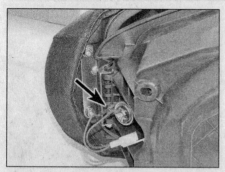

23.3a Disconnect the wire from the outer terminal...

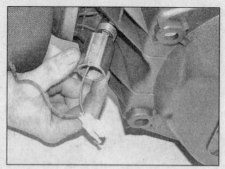

23.3b ...and unscrew the sleeve...

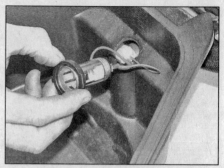

23.3c ...then withdraw the socket

22 Ambient temperature sensor

1 The ambient temperature sensor is located at the front of the scooter on the front inner panel (see Chapter 9, Section 5). No test information is available for the sensor other than to ensure that the wiring and wiring connectors are in good condition. The only way to confirm that a sensor is faulty is to substitute a known good one.

24.3 Location of the seat catch wiring connector

23 Accessory socket

1 The 12 volt accessory socket is located inside the storage compartment. The socket is connected directly to the battery and is not switched. The socket is protected by a secondary fuse in addition to the scooter's main fuse (see Section 4).
2 If the socket is thought to be faulty, first check the fuse, then remove the storage compartment (see Chapter 9) and check the wiring connector.
3 To remove the socket, first disconnect the earth (ground) wire from the outer terminal, then unscrew the metal sleeve (see illustrations). Withdraw the socket from the inside of the storage compartment (see illustration).
4 Reassemble the socket and test for continuity between the wire terminals in the connector and the centre (live) and outer (earth) terminals on the socket. Note there should be no continuity between the centre and outer terminals on the socket.
5 Installation is the reverse of removal.

24 Seat catch

1 Tweet 125/150 models are fitted with a seat catch that can be released either electronically or by cable. In both cases the operation is undertaken after inserting the key in the ignition switch.
2 If the electric catch fails to work, first test the ignition switch (see Section 18).
3 If the switch is good, remove the seat cowling (see Chapter 9). Disconnect the electric catch wiring connector (see illustration) and check for battery voltage between the terminals on the loom side of the connector with the ignition key in the 'unlock' position. If there is no voltage, refer to the wiring diagram at the end of this Chapter and check the loom between the ignition switch and the connector for continuity.
4 If there is voltage, remove the seat catch shield and examine the catch mechanism (see illustrations).
5 To remove the electric catch mechanism, first note how it engages with the catch arm, then undo the mounting bolts and lift it off.

24.4a Remove the seat catch shield...

24.4b ...and examine the catch mechanism

25.1a Location of the horn – Tweet

25.1b Location of the horn – V-Clic

25.2 Disconnect the horn wiring connectors

6 If required, clean the catch mechanism and spray it with a dry film lubricant. Prior to installation the mechanism can be tested using a fully charged 12 volt battery and two insulated jumper wires connected across the terminals in the wiring connector.

7 Check the operation of the electric catch and the cable before installing the seat cowling.

25 Horn

Check

1 The horn is located at the front of the scooter – remove any body panels as required for access (see Chapter 9) **(see illustrations)**.

2 Disconnect the wiring connectors from the horn and ensure that the contacts are clean and free from corrosion **(see illustration)**.

3 To test the horn, use insulated jumper wires to connect one of the horn terminals to the positive (+) terminal of a 12 volt battery and the other horn terminal to the battery negative (-) terminal. If the horn sounds, check the handlebar switch (see Section 17) and the wiring between the switch and the horn.

4 If the horn doesn't sound, replace it with a new one.

Renewal

5 Disconnect the wiring connectors from the horn, then unscrew the bolt securing the horn and remove it.

6 Install the horn and tighten the mounting bolt securely. Connect the wiring connectors, turn the ignition ON and test the horn.

26 Starter motor

Removal

1 If the starter motor fails to work and the fault is not due to a problem with the starter system (see Section 16), the starter pinion assembly or starter clutch, remove the starter motor as follows.

2 Disconnect the battery negative (–) lead (see Section 3).

3 On Speedfight 50 models and Vivacity 50 models with a two-stroke engine, the starter

motor is located on the underside of the engine unit – remove the exhaust system for access (see Chapter 5). Trace the wiring from the starter motor, disconnect it at the connector and feed it back to the starter motor. Undo the two bolts securing the starter motor to the crankcase, noting the earth lead **(see illustration)**. Draw the starter motor out and remove it **(see illustration)**.

4 On V-Clic models, the starter motor is located on the top of the engine unit – remove the storage compartment (see Chapter 9) and the air filter housing (see Chapter 5) for access. Pull back the boot on the starter motor terminal and disconnect the lead from the terminal **(see illustration)**. Undo the two bolts securing the starter motor to the crankcase, noting the earth lead **(see illustration)**. Draw the starter motor out and remove it.

5 On Kisbee models, the starter motor is

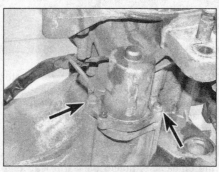

26.3a Undo the mounting bolts (arrowed)...

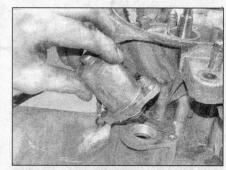

26.3b ...and draw the starter motor out – Speedfight

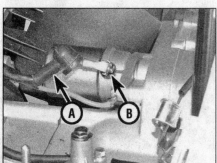

26.4a Pull back the boot (A) and disconnect the lead from the terminal (B)

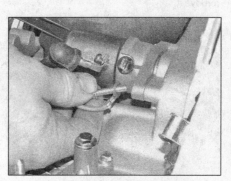

26.4b Disconnect the earth lead

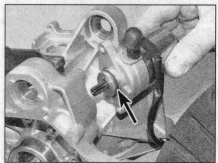

26.4c Note location of the O-ring

26.5a Location of the starter motor terminal – Kisbee

26.5b Withdraw the starter motor

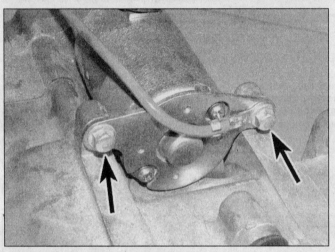

26.6a Undo the mounting bolts...

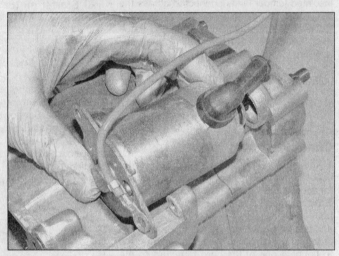

26.6b ...and remove the starter motor – Vivacity

located on the top of the engine unit – remove the storage compartment and the rear hugger (see Chapter 9) and the air filter housing (see Chapter 5) for access. Pull back the boot on the starter motor terminal and disconnect the lead from the terminal (see illustration). Undo the screw and rear mounting bolt securing the earth leads and detach the leads, then undo the front mounting bolt and draw the starter motor out (see illustration).

6 On Vivacity models, the starter motor is located on the top of the engine unit – remove the air filter housing (see Chapter 5) for access. Trace the wiring from the starter motor, disconnect it at the connector and feed it back to the starter motor. Undo the two bolts securing the starter motor to the crankcase, noting the earth lead (see illustration). Draw the starter motor out and remove it.

7 On Tweet and Speedfight 125 models, the starter motor is located on the top of the engine unit – remove the air filter housing (see Chapter 5) and the rear hugger (see Chapter 9) for access. Pull back the boot on the starter motor terminal and disconnect the lead from the terminal (see illustration). Undo the two bolts securing the starter motor to the crankcase, then draw the starter motor out and remove it (see illustrations).

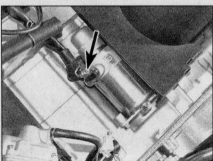

26.7a Disconnect the lead from the terminal (arrowed)

26.7b Undo the mounting bolts...

26.7c ...and remove the starter motor – Tweet

Check

8 Remove the O-ring on the end of the starter motor and discard it as a new one must be used (see illustration). Inspect the teeth on the starter motor shaft for wear and damage. If the teeth are in poor condition a new starter motor will have to be fitted – individual components are not available.

9 Wrap the starter motor body in some rag and clamp the motor in a soft-jawed vice – do not over-tighten it.

10 Using a fully-charged 12 volt battery and two insulated jumper wires, connect the negative (–) battery terminal to one of the motor's mounting lugs, then touch the positive (+) terminal to the protruding terminal on the starter motor – at this point the starter motor should spin. If this is the case the motor is proved good. If the motor does not spin, replace it with a new one.

Installation

11 Fit a new O-ring onto the end of the starter motor, making sure it is seated in its groove (see illustration 26.8). Apply a smear of engine oil to the O-ring.

12 Manoeuvre the motor into position and press it into the crankcase. Install the mounting bolts, not forgetting to secure the earth lead(s), and tighten the bolts securely.

13 Either connect the starter lead to the motor terminal then fit the rubber boot or reconnect the starter motor wiring.

14 Install the remaining components in the reverse order of removal.

15 Connect the battery negative (–) lead (see Section 3).

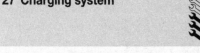

27 Charging system

1 If the performance of the charging system is suspect, the system as a whole should be checked first, followed by testing of the individual components and circuits. Note: Before beginning the checks, make sure the battery is fully charged and that all circuit connections are clean and tight.

2 Checking the output of the charging system and the performance of the various components within the charging system requires the use of a multimeter – if a multimeter is not available, have the system tested a Peugeot dealer or auto electrician.

3 When making the checks, follow the procedures carefully to prevent incorrect connections or short circuits, as irreparable damage to electrical system components may result if short circuits occur.

Leakage test

4 Disconnect the battery negative (-) terminal.

5 Set the multimeter to the Amps function and connect its negative (-) probe to the battery negative (-) terminal, and positive (+) probe to the disconnected negative (-) lead

26.8 Location of the O-ring (A). Inspect the shaft teeth (B)

(see illustration). Always set the meter to a high Amps range initially and then bring it down to the mA (milli Amps) range; if there is a high current flow in the circuit it may blow the meter's fuse.

Caution: Always connect an ammeter in series, never in parallel with the battery, otherwise it will be damaged. Do not turn the ignition ON or operate the starter motor when the meter is connected – a sudden surge in current will blow the meter's fuse.

6 Battery current leakage should not exceed the maximum limit (see *Specifications* at the beginning of this Chapter). If a higher leakage rate is shown there is a short circuit in the wiring, although if an after-market immobiliser or alarm is fitted, its current draw should be taken into account. Disconnect the meter and reconnect the battery negative (–) lead.

7 If leakage is indicated, refer to *Wiring diagrams* at the end of this Chapter to systematically disconnect individual electrical components and repeat the test until the source is identified.

Alternator

Regulated output test

8 Start the engine and warm it up to normal operating temperature, then stop the engine and turn the ignition OFF.

9 Support the scooter on its main stand with the rear wheel clear of the ground.

10 To check the regulated voltage output, set the multimeter to the 0 – 50 volts DC scale

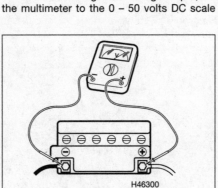

27.10 Checking the charging system regulated voltage – connect the meter as shown

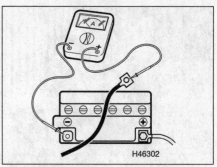

27.5 Checking the charging system leakage rate – connect the meter as shown

(voltmeter). Connect the meter positive (+) probe to the battery positive (+) terminal, and the negative (-) probe to the battery negative (-) terminal (see illustration).

11 Start the engine then slowly increase the engine speed to a fast idle and note the reading obtained. Compare the result with the specification at the beginning of this Chapter.

12 If the regulated voltage output is outside the specification there is a fault either in the regulator/rectifier or the alternator itself. If available, substitute the regulator/rectifier with a known good one and test again (see Section 28). If the voltage is still outside the specified limits, check the alternator coil resistance (see below).

> **HAYNES HINT** *Clues to a faulty regulator are constantly blowing bulbs, with brightness varying considerably with engine speed, and battery overheating.*

Coils resistance test

13 Disconnect the battery negative (-) terminal. Refer to the appropriate Chapter 2 for your scooter and trace the wiring from the alternator cover or water pump on the right-hand side of the engine and disconnect it at the connector.

14 Refer to the wiring diagram for your machine at the end of this Chapter and

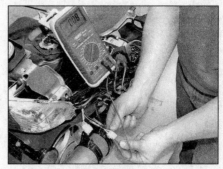

27.14 Checking the resistance in the alternator coils

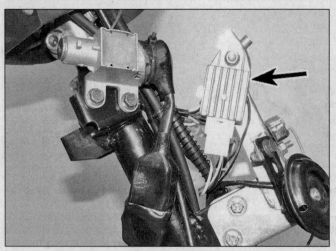

28.2 Location of the regulator/rectifier – V-Clic

28.3 Location of the regulator/rectifier – Kisbee

identify the wire terminals for the charging coil and lighting coil in the alternator side of the connector. Set the multimeter to the ohms x 1 scale and connect the meter probes to the charging coil wire terminal and to earth, and then to the lighting coil wire terminal and earth. This will give resistance readings for the coils which should be consistent with the specifications at the beginning of this Chapter **(see illustration)**.

15 If the readings obtained differ greatly from those specified, particularly if the meter indicates a short circuit (no measurable resistance) or an open circuit (infinite, or very high resistance), the alternator stator assembly must be renewed. However, first check that the

fault is not due to a damaged or broken wire from the alternator to the connector; pinched or broken wires can usually be repaired.

16 Refer to the appropriate Chapter 2 for details of alternator removal and installation.

28 Regulator/rectifier

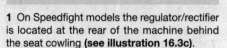

1 On Speedfight models the regulator/rectifier is located at the rear of the machine behind the seat cowling **(see illustration 16.3c)**.

2 On V-Clic models the regulator/rectifier is located at the front of the machine behind the upper front panel **(see illustration)**.

3 On Kisbee models the regulator/rectifier is located on the right-hand side behind the front under seat panel **(see illustration)**.

4 On Vivacity models the regulator/rectifier is located behind the seat cowling on the right-hand side **(see illustration 16.3d)**.

5 On Tweet models the regulator/rectifier is located behind the front top panel **(see illustration 10.3c)**.

6 Follow the procedures in Chapter 9 to remove the appropriate body panels.

7 Undo the bolt securing the unit, then disconnect the wiring connector and lift it off .

8 Installation is the reverse of removal. Ensure that the wire terminals inside the connector are clean and free from corrosion.

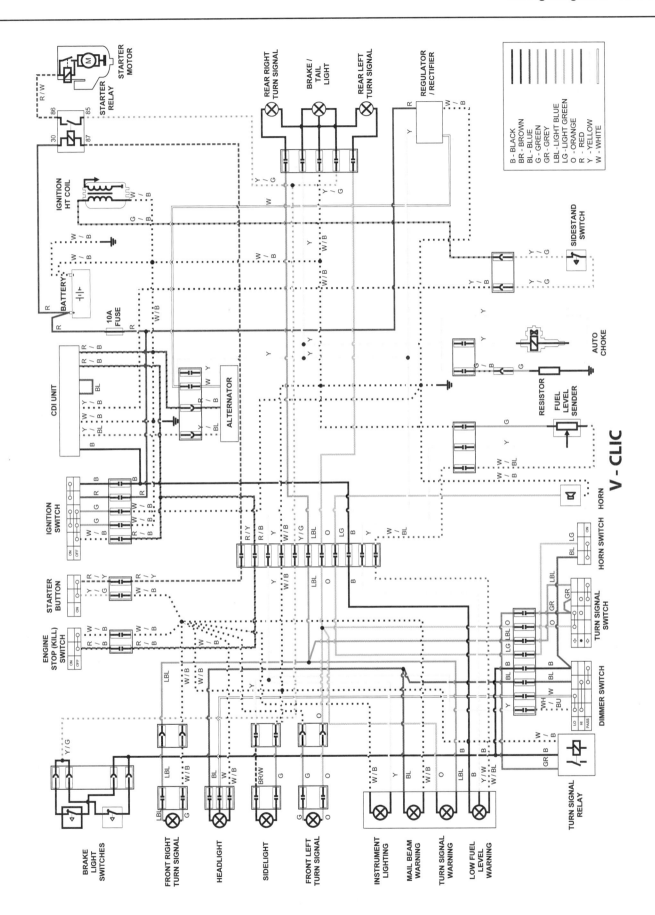

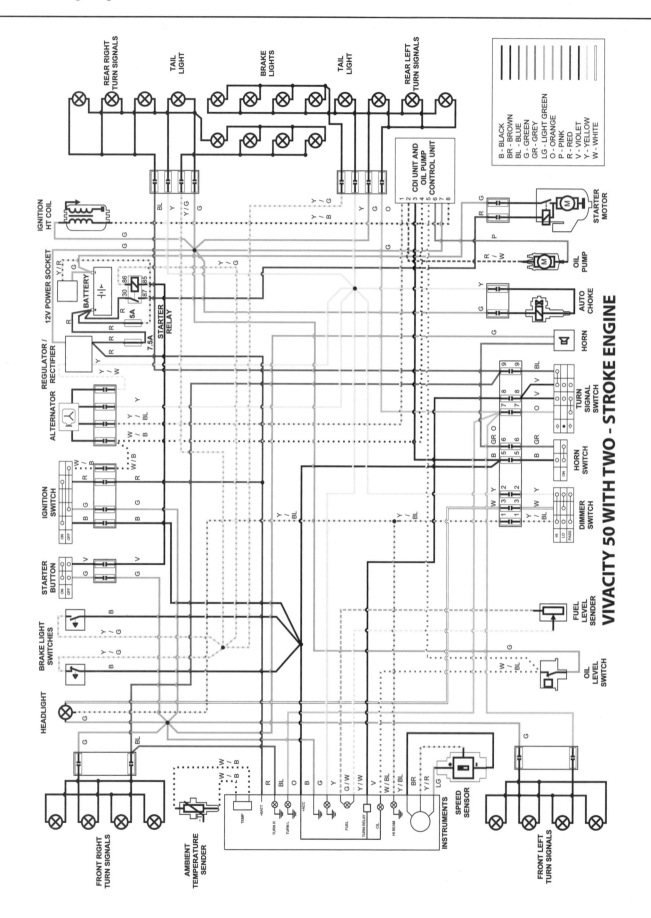

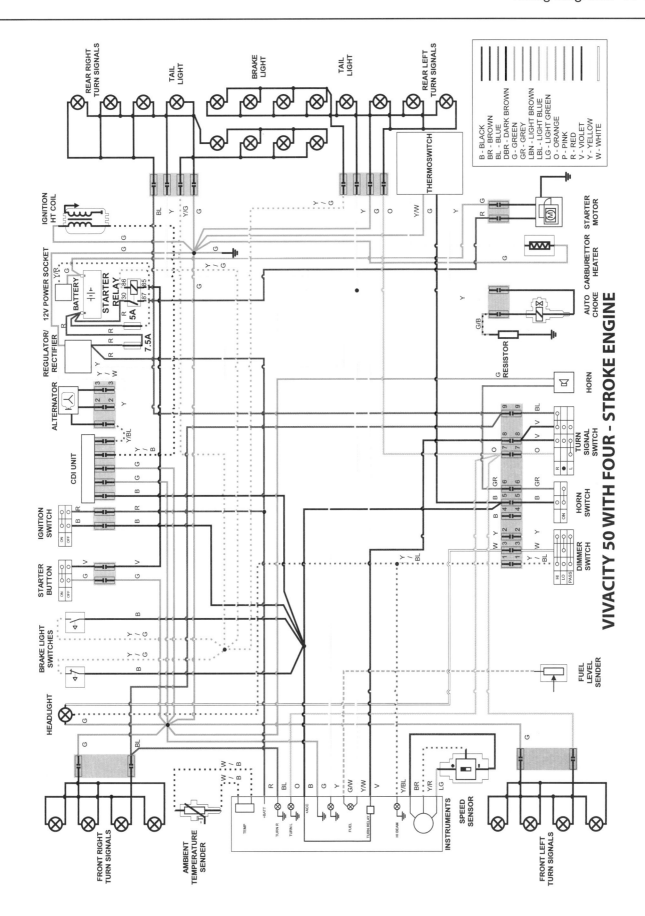

VIVACITY 50 WITH FOUR - STROKE ENGINE

B - BLACK
BR - BROWN
BL - BLUE
DBR - DARK BROWN
G - GREEN
GR - GREY
LBN - LIGHT BROWN
LBL - LIGHT BLUE
LG - LIGHT GREEN
O - ORANGE
P - PINK
R - RED
V - VIOLET
Y - YELLOW
W - WHITE

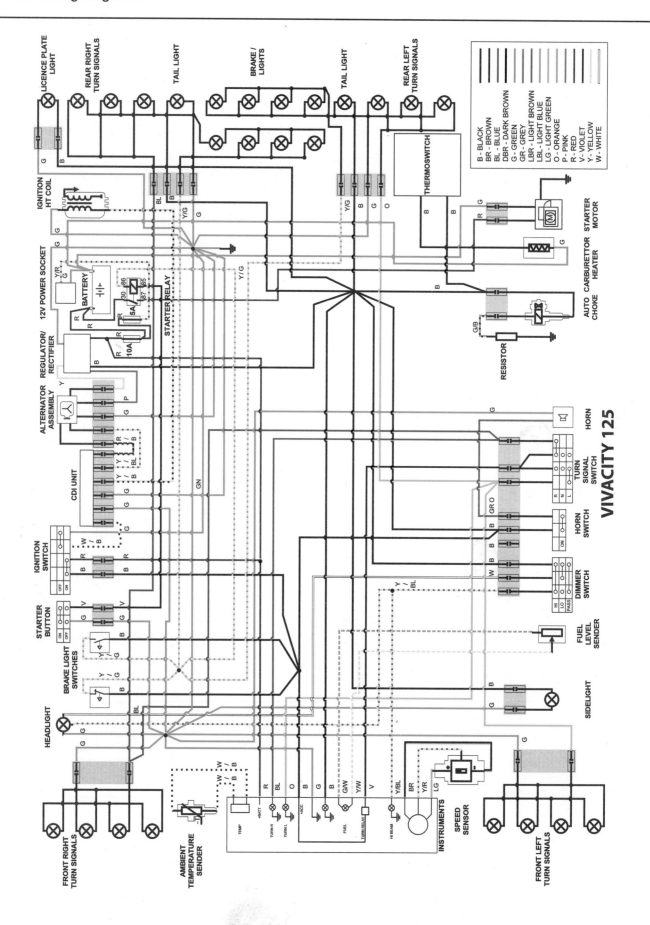

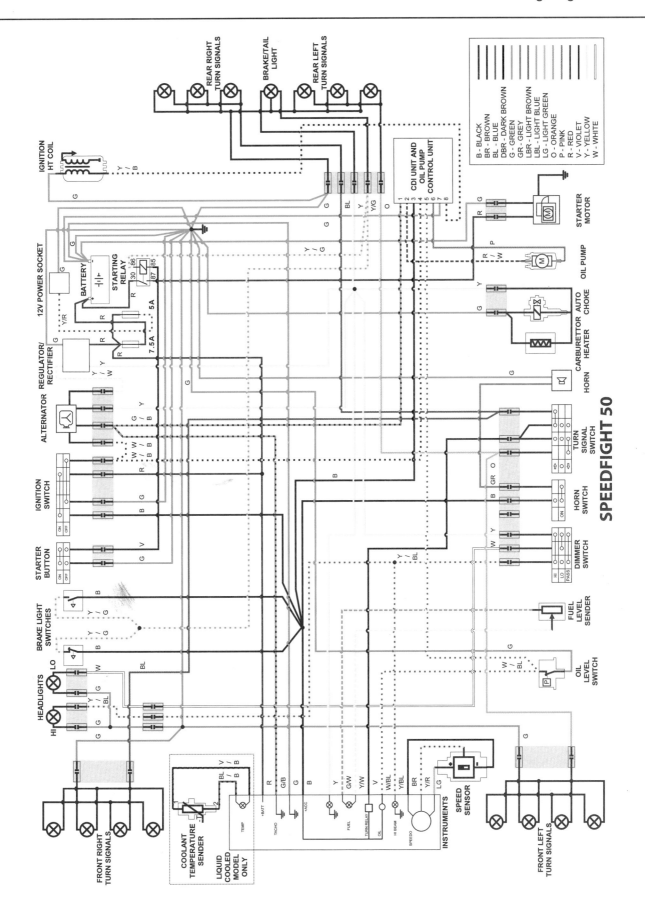

SPEEDFIGHT 50

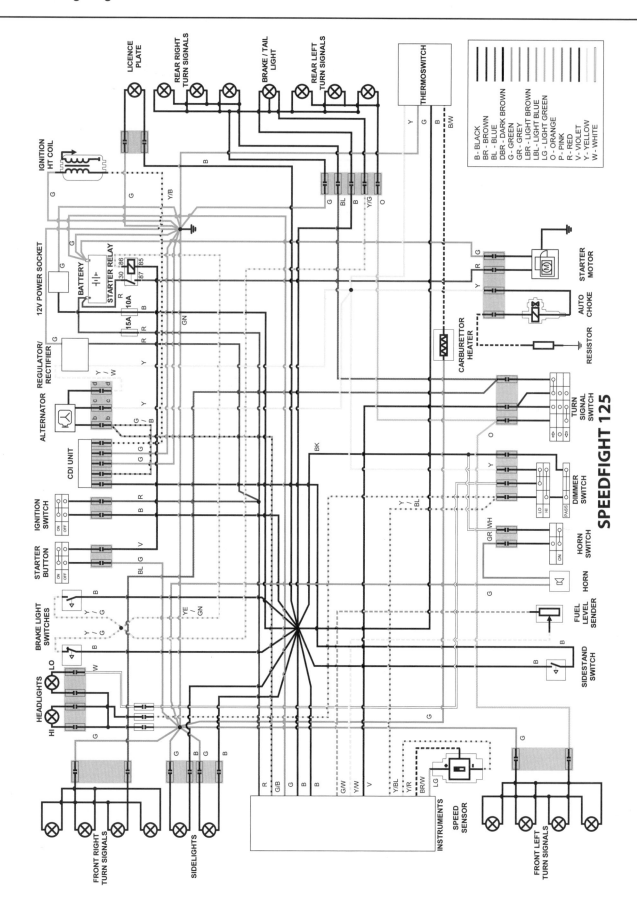

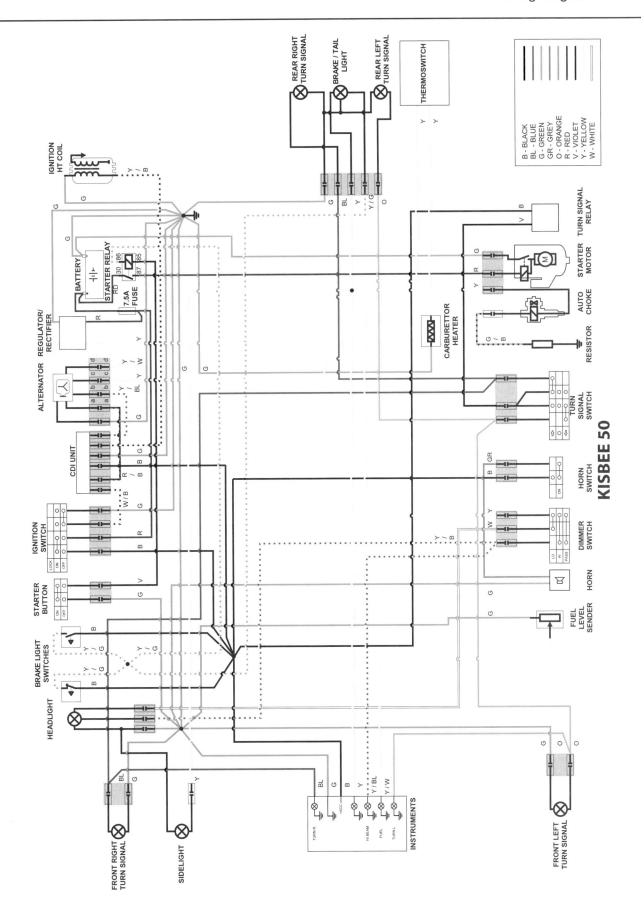

KISBEE 50

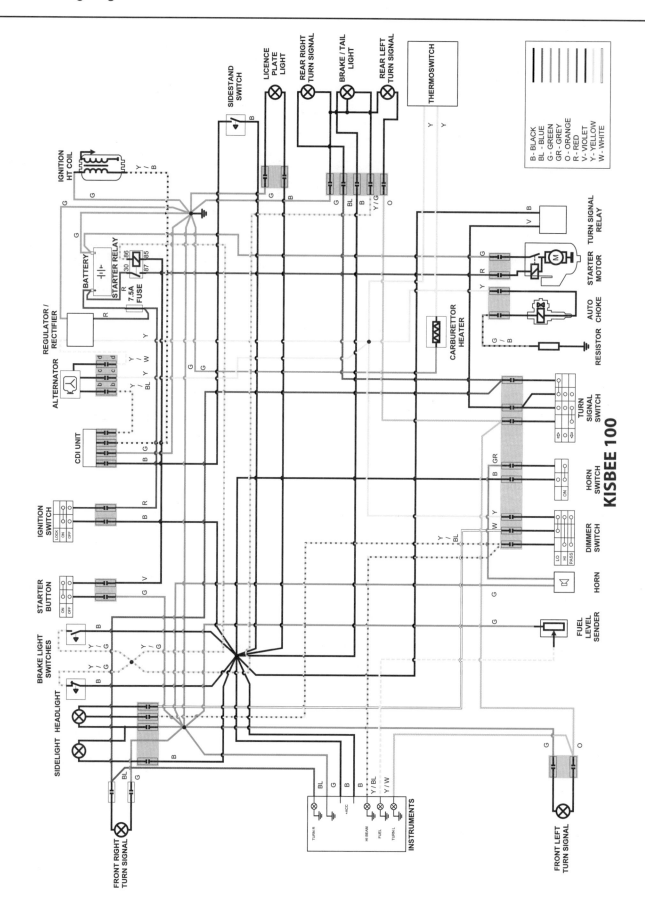

KISBEE 100

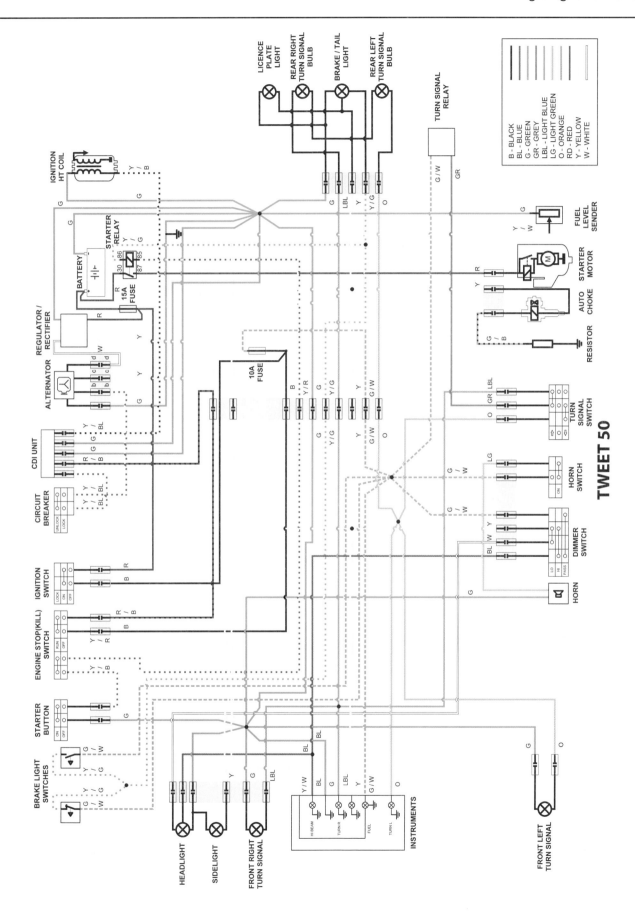

TWEET 50

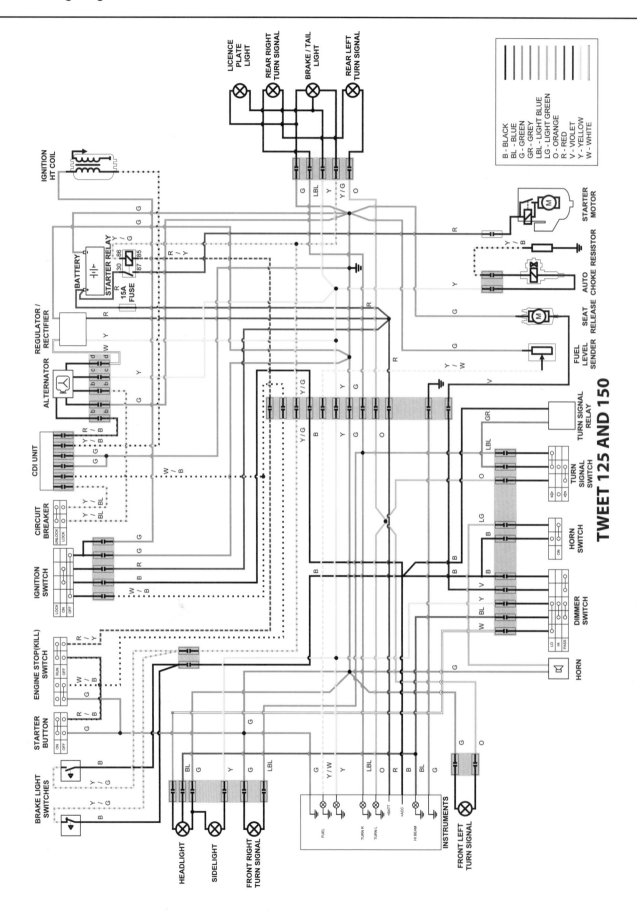

Reference

Tools and Workshop Tips

Buying tools

A toolkit is a fundamental requirement for servicing and repairing a scooter. Although there will be an initial expense in building up enough tools for servicing, this will soon be offset by the savings made by doing the job yourself. As experience and confidence grow, additional tools can be added to enable the repair and overhaul of the scooter. Many of the specialist tools are expensive and not often used so it may be preferable to hire them, or for a group of friends or scooter club to join in the purchase.

As a rule, it is better to buy more expensive, good quality tools. Cheaper tools are likely to wear out faster and need to be renewed more often, nullifying the original saving.

 Warning: To avoid the risk of a poor quality tool breaking in use, causing injury or damage to the component being worked on, always aim to purchase tools which meet the relevant national safety standards.

The following lists of tools do not represent the manufacturer's service tools, but serve as a guide to help the owner decide which tools are needed for this level of work. In addition, items such as an electric drill, hacksaw, files, soldering iron and a workbench equipped with a vice, may be needed. Although not classed as tools, a selection of bolts, screws, nuts, washers and pieces of tubing always come in useful.

For more information about tools, refer to the Haynes *Motorcycle Workshop Practice Techbook* (Bk. No. 3470).

Manufacturer's service tools

Inevitably certain tasks require the use of a service tool. Where possible an alter native tool or method of approach is recommended, but sometimes there is no option if personal injury or damage to the component is to be avoided. Where required, service tools are referred to in the relevant procedure.

Service tools can usually only be purchased from a scooter dealer and are identified by a part number. Some of the commonly-used tools, such as rotor pullers, are available in aftermarket form from mail-order motorcycle tool and accessory suppliers.

Maintenance and minor repair tools

- [ ] *Set of flat-bladed screwdrivers-*
- [ ] *Set of Phillips head screwdrivers*
- [ ] *Combination open-end and ring spanners*
- [ ] *Socket set (3/8 inch or 1/2 inch drive)*
- [ ] *Set of Allen keys or bits*
- [ ] *Set of Torx keys or bits*
- [ ] *Pliers, cutters and self-locking grips (Mole grips)*
- [ ] *Adjustable spanners*
- [ ] *C-spanners*
- [ ] *Tread depth gauge and tyre pressure gauge*
- [ ] *Cable oiler clamp*
- [ ] *Feeler gauges*
- [ ] *Spark plug gap measuring tool*
- [ ] *Spark plug spanner or deep plug sockets*
- [ ] *Wire brush and emery paper*
- [ ] *Calibrated syringe, measuring vessel and funnel*

- [ ] *Oil filter adapters (4-stroke engines)*
- [ ] *Oil drainer can or tray*
- [ ] *Pump type oil can*
- [ ] *Grease gun*
- [ ] *Straight-edge and steel rule*
- [ ] *Continuity tester*
- [ ] *Battery charger*
- [ ] *Hydrometer (for battery specific gravity check)*
- [ ] *Anti-freeze tester (for liquid-cooled engines)*

Repair and overhaul tools

- [ ] *Torque wrench (small and mid-ranges)*
- [ ] *Conventional, plastic or soft-faced hammers*
- [ ] *Impact driver set*
- [ ] *Vernier gauge*
- [ ] *Circlip pliers (internal and external, or combination)*
- [ ] *Set of cold chisels and punches*
- [ ] *Selection of pullers*
- [ ] *Breaker bars*
- [ ] *One-man brake bleeder kit*
- [ ] *Wire stripper and crimper tool*
- [ ] *Multimeter (measures amps, volts and ohms)*
- [ ] *Stroboscope (for dynamic timing checks)*
- [ ] *Hose clamp*
- [ ] *Clutch holding tool*

Specialist tools

- [ ] *Micrometers (external type)*
- [ ] *Telescoping gauges*
- [ ] *Dial gauge*
- [ ] *Stud extractor*
- [ ] *Screw extractor set*
- [ ] *Bearing driver set*
- [ ] *Valve spring compressor (4-stroke engines)*
- [ ] *Piston pin drawbolt tool*
- [ ] *Piston ring clamp*

1.1 Hydraulic motorcycle ramp

1.2 Use an approved can only for storing petrol (gasoline)

1.3 A fire extinguisher, goggles, mask and protective gloves should be at hand in the workshop

1 Workshop equipment and facilities

The workbench

● Work is made much easier by raising the scooter up on a ramp – components are much more accessible if raised to waist level. The hydraulic or pneumatic types seen in the dealer's workshop are a sound investment if you undertake a lot of repairs or overhauls **(see illustration 1.1)**.

● If raised off ground level, the scooter must be supported on the ramp to avoid it falling. Most ramps incorporate a front wheel locating clamp which can be adjusted to suit different diameter wheels. When tightening the clamp, take care not to mark the wheel rim or damage the tyre – use wood blocks on each side to prevent this.

Fumes and fire

● Refer to the Safety first! page at the beginning of the manual for full details. Make sure your workshop is equipped with a fire extinguisher suitable for fuel-related fires (Class B fire – flammable liquids) – it is not sufficient to have a water-filled extinguisher.

● Always ensure adequate ventilation is available. Unless an exhaust gas extraction system is available for use, ensure that the engine is run outside of the workshop.

● If working on the fuel system, make sure the

workshop is ventilated to avoid a build-up of fumes. This applies equally to fume build-up when charging a battery. Do not smoke or allow anyone else to smoke in the workshop.

Fluids

● If you need to drain fuel from the tank, store it in an approved container marked as suitable for the storage of petrol (gasoline) **(see illustration 1.2)**. Do not store fuel in glass jars or bottles.

● Use proprietary engine degreasers or solvents which have a high flash-point, such as paraffin (kerosene), for cleaning off oil, grease and dirt – never use petrol (gasoline) for cleaning. Wear rubber gloves when handling solvent and engine degreaser. The fumes from certain solvents can be dangerous – always work in a well-ventilated area.

Dust, eye and hand protection

● Protect your lungs from inhalation of dust particles by wearing a filtering mask over the nose and mouth. Many frictional materials still contain asbestos which is dangerous to your health. Protect your eyes from spouts of liquid and sprung components by wearing a pair of protective goggles **(see illustration 1.3)**.

● Protect your hands from contact with solvents, fuel and oils by wearing rubber gloves. Alternatively apply a barrier cream to your hands before starting work. If handling hot components or fluids, wear suitable gloves to protect your hands from scalding and burns.

What to do with old fluids

● Old cleaning solvent, fuel, coolant and oils should not be poured down domestic drains or onto the ground. Package the fluid up in old oil containers, label it accordingly, and take it to a garage or disposal facility. Contact your local authority for location of such sites.

2 Fasteners – screws, bolts and nuts

Fastener types and applications

Bolts and screws

● Fastener head types are either of hexagonal, Torx or splined design, with internal and external versions of each type **(see illustrations 2.1 and 2.2)**; splined head fasteners are not in common use on scooters. The conventional slotted or Phillips head design is used for certain screws. Bolt or screw length is always measured from the underside of the head to the end of the item **(see illustration 2.11)**.

● Certain fasteners on the scooter have a tensile marking on their heads, the higher the marking the stronger the fastener. High tensile fasteners generally carry a 10 or higher marking. Never replace a high tensile fastener with one of a lower tensile strength.

Washers (see illustration 2.3)

● Plain washers are used between a fastener

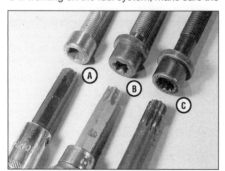

2.1 Internal hexagon/Allen (A), Torx (B) and splined (C) fasteners, with corresponding bits

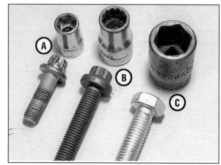

2.2 External Torx (A), splined (B) and hexagon (C) fasteners, with corresponding sockets

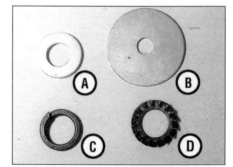

2.3 Plain washer (A), penny washer (B), spring washer (C) and serrated washer (D)

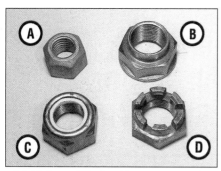

2.4 Plain nut (A), shouldered locknut (B), nylon insert nut (C) and castellated nut (D)

2.5 Bend split pin (cotter pin) arms as shown (arrows) to secure a castellated nut

2.6 Bend split pin (cotter pin) arms as shown to secure a plain nut

head and a component to prevent damage to the component or to spread the load when torque is applied. Plain washers can also be used as spacers or shims in certain assemblies. Copper or aluminium plain washers are often used as sealing washers on drain plugs.

● The split-ring spring washer works by applying axial tension between the fastener head and component. If flattened, it is fatigued and must be renewed. If a plain (flat) washer is used on the fastener, position the spring washer between the fastener and the plain washer.

● Serrated star type washers dig into the fastener and component faces, preventing loosening. They are often used on electrical earth (ground) connections to the frame.

● Cone type washers (sometimes called Belleville) are conical and when tightened apply axial tension between the fastener head and component. They must be installed with the dished side against the component and often carry an OUTSIDE marking on their outer face. If flattened, they are fatigued and must be renewed.

● Tab washers are used to lock plain nuts or bolts on a shaft. A portion of the tab washer is bent up hard against one flat of the nut or bolt to prevent it loosening. Due to the tab washer being deformed in use, a new tab washer should be used every time it is disturbed.

● Wave washers are used to take up endfloat on a shaft. They provide light springing and prevent excessive side-to-side play of a component. Can be found on rocker arm shafts.

Nuts and split pins

● Conventional plain nuts are usually six-sided (see illustration 2.4). They are sized by thread diameter and pitch. High tensile nuts carry a number on one end to denote their tensile strength.

● Self-locking nuts either have a nylon insert, or two spring metal tabs, or a shoulder which is staked into a groove in the shaft – their advantage over conventional plain nuts is a resistance to loosening due to vibration. The nylon insert type can be used a number of times, but must be renewed when the friction of the nylon insert is reduced, ie when the nut spins freely on the shaft. The spring tab type

2.7 Correct fitting of R-pin. Arrow indicates forward direction

can be reused unless the tabs are damaged. The shouldered type must be renewed every time it is disturbed.

● Split pins (cotter pins) are used to lock a castellated nut to a shaft or to prevent slackening of a plain nut. Common applications are wheel axles and brake torque arms. Because the split pin arms are deformed to lock around the nut a new split pin must always be used on installation – always fit the correct size split pin which will fit snugly in the shaft hole. Make sure the split pin arms are correctly located around the nut **(see illustrations 2.5 and 2.6)**.

● R-pins (shaped like the letter R), or slip pins as they are sometimes called, are sprung and can be reused if they are otherwise in good condition. Always install R-pins with their closed end facing forwards **(see illustration 2.7)**.

Caution: If the castellated nut slots do not align with the shaft hole after tightening to the torque setting, tighten the nut until

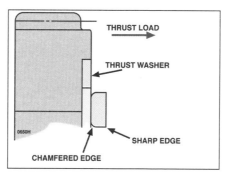

2.9 Correct fitting of a stamped circlip

THRUST LOAD

THRUST WASHER

SHARP EDGE

CHAMFERED EDGE

0650H

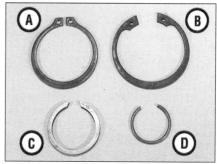

2.8 External stamped circlip (A), internal stamped circlip (B), machined circlip (C) and wire circlip (D)

the next slot aligns with the hole – never slacken the nut to align its slot.

Circlips (see illustration 2.8)

● Circlips (sometimes called snap-rings) are used to retain components on a shaft or in a housing and have corresponding external or internal ears to permit removal. Parallel-sided (machined) circlips can be installed either way round in their groove, whereas stamped circlips (which have a chamfered edge on one face) must be installed with the chamfer facing away from the direction of thrust load **(see illustration 2.9)**.

● Always use circlip pliers to remove and install circlips; expand or compress them just enough to remove them. After installation, rotate the circlip in its groove to ensure it is securely seated. If installing a circlip on a splined shaft, always align its opening with a shaft channel to ensure the circlip ends are well supported and unlikely to catch **(see illustration 2.10)**.

● Circlips can wear due to the thrust of components and become loose in their

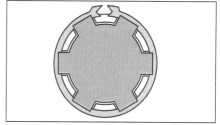

2.10 Align circlip opening with shaft channel

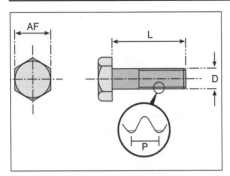

2.11 Fastener length (L), thread diameter (D), thread pitch (P) and head size (AF)

2.12 Using a thread gauge to measure pitch

2.13 A sharp tap on the head of a fastener will often break free a corroded thread

grooves, with the subsequent danger of becoming dislodged in operation. For this reason, renewal is advised every time a circlip is disturbed.

● Wire circlips are commonly used as piston pin retaining clips. If a removal tang is provided, long-nosed pliers can be used to dislodge them, otherwise careful use of a small flat-bladed screwdriver is necessary. Wire circlips should be renewed every time they are disturbed.

Thread diameter and pitch

● Diameter of a male thread (screw, bolt or stud) is the outside diameter of the threaded portion (see illustration 2.11). Most scooter manufacturers use the ISO (International Standards Organisation) metric system expressed in millimetres, eg M6 refers to a 6 mm diameter thread. Sizing is the same for nuts, except that the thread diameter is measured across the valleys of the nut.

● Pitch is the distance between the peaks of the thread (see illustration 2.11). It is expressed in millimetres, thus a common bolt size may be expressed as 6.0 x 1.0 mm (6 mm thread diameter and 1 mm pitch). Generally pitch increases in proportion to thread diameter, although there are always exceptions.

● Thread diameter and pitch are related for conventional fastener applications and the accompanying table can be used as a guide. Additionally, the AF (Across Flats), spanner or socket size dimension of the bolt or nut (see illustration 2.11) is linked to thread and pitch specification. Thread pitch can be measured with a thread gauge (see illustration 2.12).

● The threads of most fasteners are of the right-hand type, ie they are turned clockwise to tighten and anti-clockwise to loosen. The reverse situation applies to left-hand thread fasteners, which are turned anti-clockwise to tighten and clockwise to loosen. Left-hand threads are used where rotation of a component might loosen a conventional right-hand thread fastener.

AF size	Thread diameter x pitch (mm)
8 mm	M5 x 0.8
8 mm	M6 x 1.0
10 mm	M6 x 1.0
12 mm	M8 x 1.25
14 mm	M10 x 1.25
17 mm	M12 x 1.25

Seized fasteners

● Corrosion of external fasteners due to water or reaction between two dissimilar metals can occur over a period of time. It will build up sooner in wet conditions or in countries where salt is used on the roads during the winter. If a fastener is severely corroded it is likely that normal methods of removal will fail and result in its head being ruined. When you attempt removal, the fastener thread should be heard to crack free and unscrew easily – if it doesn't, stop there before damaging something.

● A smart tap on the head of the fastener will often succeed in breaking free corrosion which has occurred in the threads (see illustration 2.13).

● An aerosol penetrating fluid (such as WD-40) applied the night beforehand may work its way down into the thread and ease removal.

Depending on the location, you may be able to make up a Plasticine well around the fastener head and fill it with penetrating fluid.

● If you are working on an engine internal component, corrosion will most likely not be a problem due to the well lubricated environment. However, components can be very tight and an impact driver is a useful tool in freeing them (see illustration 2.14).

● Where corrosion has occurred between dissimilar metals (eg steel and aluminium alloy), the application of heat to the fastener head will create a disproportionate expansion rate between the two metals and break the seizure caused by the corrosion. Whether heat can be applied depends on the location of the fastener – any surrounding components likely to be damaged must first be removed (see illustration 2.15). Heat can be applied using a paint stripper heat gun or clothes iron, or by immersing the component in boiling water – wear protective gloves to prevent scalding or burns to the hands.

● As a last resort, it is possible to use a hammer and cold chisel to work the fastener head unscrewed (see illustration 2.16). This will damage the fastener, but more importantly extreme care must be taken not to damage the surrounding component.

Caution: Remember that the component being secured is generally of more value than the bolt, nut or screw – when the fastener is freed, do not unscrew it with force, instead work the fastener back and forth when resistance is felt to prevent thread damage.

2.14 Using an impact driver to free a fastener

2.15 Using heat to free a seized fastener

2.16 Using a hammer and chisel to free a seized fastener

2.17 Using a stud extractor tool to remove a broken crankcase stud

2.18 Two nuts can be locked together to unscrew a stud from a component

2.19 When using a screw extractor, first drill a hole in the fastener . . .

Broken fasteners and damaged heads

● If the shank of a broken bolt or screw is accessible you can grip it with self-locking grips. The knurled wheel type stud extractor tool or self-gripping stud puller tool is particularly useful for removing the long studs which screw into the cylinder mouth surface of the crankcase or bolts and screws from which the head has broken off **(see illustration 2.17)**. Studs can also be removed by locking two nuts together on the threaded end of the stud and using a spanner on the lower nut **(see illustration 2.18)**.

● A bolt or screw which has broken off below or level with the casing must be extracted using a screw extractor set. Centre punch the fastener to centralise the drill bit, then drill a hole in the fastener **(see illustration 2.19)**. Select a drill bit which is approximately half to three-quarters the diameter of the fastener and drill to a depth which will accommodate the extractor. Use the largest size extractor possible, but avoid leaving too small a wall thickness otherwise the extractor will merely force the fastener walls outwards wedging it in the casing thread.

● If a spiral type extractor is used, thread it anti-clockwise into the fastener. As it is screwed in, it will grip the fastener and unscrew it from the casing **(see illustration 2.20)**.

 Warning: Stud extractors are very hard and may break off in the fastener if care is not taken – ask an engineer about spark erosion if this happens.

● If a taper type extractor is used, tap it into the fastener so that it is firmly wedged in place. Unscrew the extractor (anti-clockwise) to draw the fastener out.

● Alternatively, the broken bolt/screw can be drilled out and the hole retapped for an oversize bolt/screw or a diamond-section thread insert. It is essential that the drilling is carried out squarely and to the correct depth, otherwise the casing may be ruined – if in doubt, entrust the work to an engineer.

● Bolts and nuts with rounded corners cause the correct size spanner or socket to slip when force is applied. Of the types of spanner/socket available always use a six-point type rather than an eight or twelve-point type – better grip is obtained. Surface drive spanners grip the middle of the hex flats, rather than the corners, and are thus good in cases of damaged heads **(see illustration 2.21)**.

● Slotted-head or Phillips-head screws are often damaged by the use of the wrong size screwdriver. Allen-head and Torx-head screws are much less likely to sustain damage. If enough of the screw head is exposed you can use a hacksaw to cut a slot in its head and then use a conventional flat-bladed screwdriver to remove it. Alternatively use a hammer and cold chisel to tap the head of the fastener around to slacken it. Always replace damaged fasteners with new ones, preferably Torx or Allen-head type.

2.20 . . . then thread the extractor anti-clockwise into the fastener

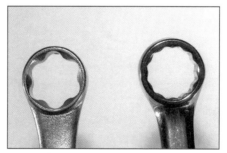

2.21 Comparison of surface drive ring spanner (left) with 12-point type (right)

A dab of valve grinding compound between the screw head and screw-driver tip will often give a good grip.

2.22 A thread repair tool being used to correct an internal thread

2.23 A thread repair tool being used to correct an external thread

Thread repair

● Threads (particularly those in aluminium alloy components) can be damaged by overtightening, being assembled with dirt in the threads, or from a component working loose and vibrating. Eventually the thread will fail completely, and it will be impossible to tighten the fastener.

● If a thread is damaged or clogged with old locking compound it can be renovated with a thread repair tool (thread chaser) **(see illustrations 2.22 and 2.23)**; special thread

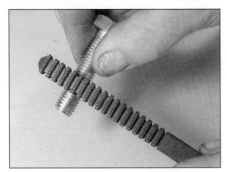

2.24 Using a thread restorer file

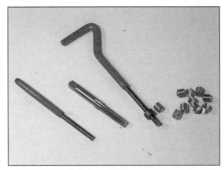

2.25 Obtain a thread insert kit to suit the thread diameter and pitch required

2.26 To install a thread insert, first drill out the original thread . . .

chasers are available for spark plug hole threads. The tool will not cut a new thread, but clean and true the original thread. Make sure that you use the correct diameter and pitch tool. Similarly, external threads can be cleaned up with a die or a thread restorer file **(see illustration 2.24)**.

● It is possible to drill out the old thread and retap the component to the next thread size. This will work where there is enough surrounding material and a new bolt or screw can be obtained. Sometimes, however, this is not possible – such as where the bolt/screw passes through another component which must also be suitably modified, also in cases where a spark plug or oil drain plug cannot be obtained in a larger diameter thread size.

● The diamond-section thread insert (often known by its popular trade name of Heli-Coil)

is a simple and effective method of renewing the thread and retaining the original size. A kit can be purchased which contains the tap, insert and installing tool **(see illustration 2.25)**. Drill out the damaged thread with the size drill specified **(see illustration 2.26)**. Carefully retap the thread **(see illustration 2.27)**. Install the insert on the installing tool and thread it slowly into place using a light downward pressure **(see illustrations 2.28 and 2.29)**. When positioned between a 1/4 and 1/2 turn below the surface withdraw the installing tool and use the break-off tool to press down on the tang, breaking it off **(see illustration 2.30)**.

● There are epoxy thread repair kits on the market which can rebuild stripped internal threads, although this repair should not be used on high load-bearing components.

Thread locking and sealing compounds

● Locking compounds are used in locations where the fastener is prone to loosening due to vibration or on important safety-related items which might cause loss of control of the scooter if they fail. It is also used where important fasteners cannot be secured by other means such as lockwashers or split pins.

● Before applying locking compound, make sure that the threads (internal and external) are clean and dry with all old compound removed. Select a compound to suit the component being secured – a non-permanent general locking and sealing type is suitable for most applications, but a high strength type is needed for permanent fixing of studs in castings. Apply a drop or two of the compound to the first few threads of the fastener, then thread it into place and tighten to the specified torque. Do not apply excessive thread locking compound otherwise the thread may be damaged on subsequent removal.

● Certain fasteners are impregnated with a dry film type coating of locking compound on their threads. Always renew this type of fastener if disturbed.

● Anti-seize compounds, such as copper-based greases, can be applied to protect threads from seizure due to extreme heat and corrosion. A common instance is spark plug threads and exhaust system fasteners.

2.27 . . . tap a new thread . . .

2.28 . . . fit insert on the installing tool . . .

3 Measuring tools and gauges

Feeler gauges

● Feeler gauges (or blades) are used for measuring small gaps and clearances **(see illustration 3.1)**. They can also be used to measure endfloat (sideplay) of a component on a shaft where access is not possible with a dial gauge.

● Feeler gauge sets should be treated with care and not bent or damaged. They are etched with their size on one face. Keep

2.29 . . . and thread into the component . . .

2.30 . . . break off the tang when complete

3.1 Feeler gauges are used for measuring small gaps and clearances – thickness is marked on one face of gauge

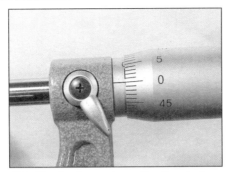

3.2 Check micrometer calibration before use

them clean and very lightly oiled to prevent corrosion build-up.

● When measuring a clearance, select a gauge which is a light sliding fit between the two components. You may need to use two gauges together to measure the clearance accurately.

Micrometers

● A micrometer is a precision tool capable of measuring to 0.01 or 0.001 of a millimetre. It should always be stored in its case and not in the general toolbox. It must be kept clean and never dropped, otherwise its frame or measuring anvils could be distorted resulting in inaccurate readings.

● External micrometers are used for measuring outside diameters of components and have many more applications than internal micrometers. Micrometers are available in different size ranges, eg 0 to 25 mm, 25 to 50 mm, and upwards in 25 mm steps; some large micrometers have interchangeable anvils to allow a range of measurements to be taken. Generally the largest precision measurement you are likely to take on a scooter is the piston diameter.

● Internal micrometers (or bore micrometers) are used for measuring inside diameters, such as valve guides and cylinder bores. Telescoping gauges and small hole gauges are used in conjunction with an external micro-meter, whereas the more expensive internal micrometers have their own measuring device.

External micrometer

Note: *The conventional analogue type instrument is described. Although much easier to read, digital micrometers are considerably more expensive.*

● Always check the calibration of the micrometer before use. With the anvils closed (0 to 25 mm type) or set over a test gauge (for the larger types) the scale should read zero **(see illustration 3.2)**; make sure that the anvils (and test piece) are clean first. Any discrepancy can be adjusted by referring to the instructions supplied with the tool. Remember that the micrometer is a precision measuring tool – don't force the anvils closed, use the ratchet (4) on the end of the micrometer to close it. In this way, a measured force is always applied.

● To use, first make sure that the item being measured is clean. Place the anvil of the micrometer (1) against the item and use the thimble (2) to bring the spindle (3) lightly into contact with the other side of the item **(see illustration 3.3)**. Don't tighten the thimble down because this will damage the micrometer – instead use the ratchet (4) on the end of the micrometer. The ratchet mechanism applies a measured force preventing damage to the instrument.

● The micrometer is read by referring to the linear scale on the sleeve and the annular scale on the thimble. Read off the sleeve first to obtain the base measurement, then add the fine measurement from the thimble to obtain the overall reading. The linear scale on the sleeve represents the measuring range of the micrometer (eg 0 to 25 mm). The annular scale on the thimble will be in graduations of 0.01 mm (or as marked on the frame) – one full revolution of the thimble will move 0.5 mm on the linear scale. Take the reading where the datum line on the sleeve intersects the thimble's scale. Always position the eye directly above the scale otherwise an inaccurate reading will result.

In the example shown the item measures 2.95 mm **(see illustration 3.4)**:

Linear scale	2.00 mm
Linear scale	0.50 mm
Annular scale	0.45 mm
Total figure	**2.95 mm**

Most micrometers have a locking lever (6) on the frame to hold the setting in place, allowing the item to be removed from the micrometer.

● Some micrometers have a vernier scale on their sleeve, providing an even finer measurement to be taken, in 0.001 increments of a millimetre. Take the sleeve and thimble measurement as described above, then check which graduation on the vernier scale aligns with that of the annular scale on the thimble **Note:** *The eye must be perpendicular to the scale when taking the vernier reading – if necessary rotate the body of the micrometer to ensure this.* Multiply the vernier scale figure by 0.001 and add it to the base and fine measurement figures.

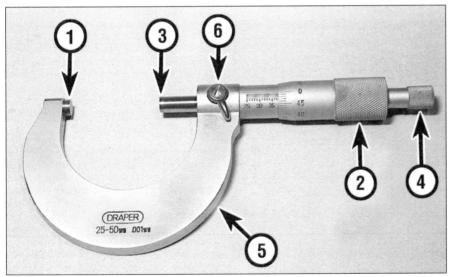

3.3 Micrometer component parts

1	Anvil	3	Spindle	5	Frame
2	Thimble	4	Ratchet	6	Locking lever

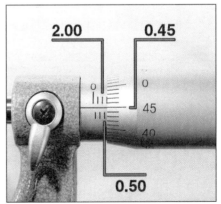

3.4 Micrometer reading of 2.95 mm

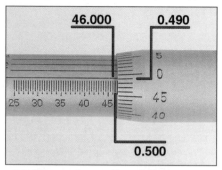

3.5 Micrometer reading of 46.99 mm on linear and annular scales . . .

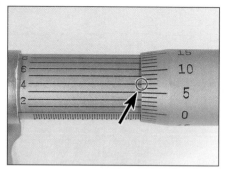

3.6 . . . and 0.004 mm on vernier scale

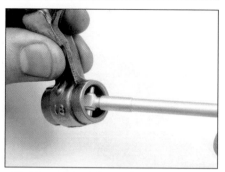

3.7 Expand the telescoping gauge in the bore, lock its position . . .

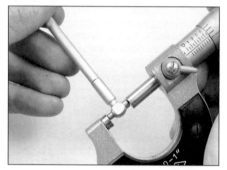

3.8 . . . then measure the gauge with a micrometer

3.9 Expand the small hole gauge in the bore, lock its position . . .

3.10 . . . then measure the gauge with a micrometer

In the example shown the item measures 46.994 mm **(see illustrations 3.5 and 3.6)**:

Linear scale (base)	46.000 mm
Linear scale (base)	00.500 mm
Annular scale (fine)	00.490 mm
Vernier scale	00.004 mm
Total figure	**46.994 mm**

Internal micrometer

● Internal micrometers are available for measuring bore diameters, but are expensive and unlikely to be available for home use. It is suggested that a set of telescoping gauges and small hole gauges, both of which must be used with an external micrometer, will suffice for taking internal measurements on a scooter.
● Telescoping gauges can be used to measure internal diameters of components. Select a gauge with the correct size range, make sure its ends are clean and insert it into the bore. Expand the gauge, then lock its position and withdraw it from the bore **(see illustration 3.7)**. Measure across the gauge ends with a micrometer **(see illustration 3.8)**.
● Very small diameter bores (such as valve guides) are measured with a small hole gauge. Once adjusted to a slip-fit inside the component, its position is locked and the gauge withdrawn for measurement with a micrometer **(see illustrations 3.9 and 3.10)**.

Vernier caliper

Note: *The conventional linear and dial gauge type instruments are described. Digital types are easier to read, but are far more expensive.*
● The vernier caliper does not provide the precision of a micrometer, but is versatile in being able to measure internal and external diameters. Some types also incorporate a depth gauge. It is ideal for measuring clutch plate friction material and spring free lengths.
● To use the conventional linear scale vernier, slacken off the vernier clamp screws (1) and set its jaws over (2), or inside (3), the item to be measured **(see illustration 3.11)**. Slide the jaw into contact, using the thumb-wheel (4) for fine movement of the sliding scale (5) then tighten the clamp screws (1). Read off the main scale (6) where the zero on the sliding scale (5) intersects it, taking the whole number to the left of the zero; this provides the base measurement. View along the sliding scale and select the division which lines up exactly with any of the divisions on the main scale, noting that the divisions usually represents 0.02 of a millimetre. Add this fine measurement to the base measurement to obtain the total reading.

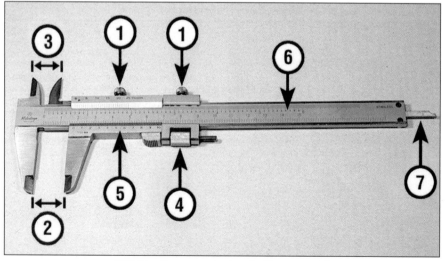

3.11 Vernier component parts (linear gauge)

1	Clamp screws	3	Internal jaws	5	Sliding scale	7 Depth gauge
2	External jaws	4	Thumbwheel	6	Main scale	

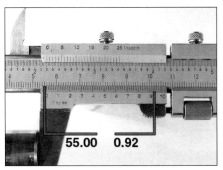

3.12 Vernier gauge reading of 55.92 mm

In the example shown the item measures 55.92 mm **(see illustration 3.12)**:

Base measurement	55.00 mm
Fine measurement	00.92 mm
Total figure	**55.92 mm**

● Some vernier calipers are equipped with a dial gauge for fine measurement. Before use, check that the jaws are clean, then close them fully and check that the dial gauge reads zero. If necessary adjust the gauge ring accordingly. Slacken the vernier clamp screw (1) and set its jaws over (2), or inside (3), the item to be measured **(see illustration 3.13)**. Slide the jaws into contact, using the thumbwheel (4) for fine movement. Read off the main scale (5) where the edge of the sliding scale (6) intersects it, taking the whole number to the left of the zero; this provides the base measurement. Read off the needle position on the dial gauge (7) scale to provide the fine measurement; each division represents 0.05 of a millimetre. Add this fine measurement to the base measurement to obtain the total reading.

In the example shown the item measures 55.95 mm **(see illustration 3.14)**:

Base measurement	55.00 mm
Fine measurement	00.95 mm
Total figure	**55.95 mm**

Dial gauge or DTI (Dial Test Indicator)

● A dial gauge can be used to accurately measure small amounts of movement. Typical uses are measuring shaft runout or shaft endfloat (sideplay) and setting piston position for ignition timing on two-strokes. A

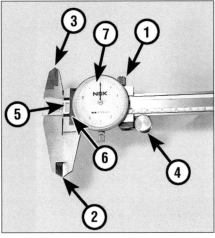

3.13 Vernier component parts (dial gauge)

1 Clamp screw	5 Main scale
2 External jaws	6 Sliding scale
3 Internal jaws	7 Dial gauge
4 Thumbwheel	

dial gauge set usually comes with a range of different probes and adapters and mounting equipment.
● The gauge needle must point to zero when at rest. Rotate the ring around its periphery to zero the gauge.
● Check that the gauge is capable of reading the extent of movement in the work. Most gauges have a small dial set in the face which records whole millimetres of movement as well as the fine scale around the face periphery which is calibrated in 0.01 mm divisions. Read off the small dial first to obtain the base measurement, then add the measurement from the fine scale to obtain the total reading.
In the example shown the gauge reads 1.48 mm **(see illustration 3.15)**:

Base measurement	1.00 mm
Fine measurement	0.48 mm
Total figure	**1.48 mm**

● If measuring shaft runout, the shaft must be supported in vee-blocks and the gauge mounted on a stand perpendicular to the shaft. Rest the tip of the gauge against the centre of the shaft and rotate the shaft slowly whilst watching the gauge reading **(see illustration 3.16)**. Take several measurements along the

3.14 Vernier gauge reading of 55.95 mm

length of the shaft and record the maximum gauge reading as the amount of runout in the shaft. **Note:** *The reading obtained will be total runout at that point – some manufacturers specify that the runout figure is halved to compare with their specified runout limit.*
● Endfloat (sideplay) measurement requires that the gauge is mounted securely to the surrounding component with its probe touching the end of the shaft. Using hand pressure, push and pull on the shaft noting the maximum endfloat recorded on the gauge **(see illustration 3.17)**.
● A dial gauge with suitable adapters can be used to determine piston position BTDC on two-stroke engines for the purposes of ignition timing. The gauge, adapter and suitable length probe are installed in the place of the spark plug and the gauge zeroed at TDC. If the piston position is specified as 1.14 mm BTDC, rotate the engine back to 2.00 mm BTDC, then slowly forwards to 1.14 mm BTDC.

4 Torque and leverage

What is torque?

● Torque describes the twisting force about a shaft. The amount of torque applied is determined by the distance from the centre of the shaft to the end of the lever and the amount of force being applied to the end of the lever; distance multiplied by force equals torque.
● The manufacturer applies a measured

3.15 Dial gauge reading of 1.48 mm

3.16 Using a dial gauge to measure shaft runout

3.17 Using a dial gauge to measure shaft endfloat

4.1 Set the torque wrench index mark to the setting required, in this case 12 Nm

4.2 Angle tightening can be accomplished with a torque-angle gauge . . .

4.3 . . . or by marking the angle on the surrounding component

torque to a bolt or nut to ensure that it will not slacken in use and to hold two components securely together without movement in the joint. The actual torque setting depends on the thread size, bolt or nut material and the composition of the components being held.
● Too little torque may cause the fastener to loosen due to vibration, whereas too much torque will distort the joint faces of the component or cause the fastener to shear off. Always stick to the specified torque setting.

Using a torque wrench

● Check the calibration of the torque wrench and make sure it has a suitable range for the job. Torque wrenches are available in Nm (Newton-metres), kgf m (kilograms-force metre), lbf ft (pounds-feet), lbf in (inch-pounds). Do not confuse lbf ft with lbf in.
● Adjust the tool to the desired torque on the scale **(see illustration 4.1)**. If your torque wrench is not calibrated in the units specified, carefully convert the figure (see *Conversion Factors*). A manufacturer sometimes gives a torque setting as a range (8 to 10 Nm) rather than a single figure – in this case set the tool midway between the two settings. The same torque may be expressed as 9 Nm ± 1 Nm. Some torque wrenches have a method of locking the setting so that it isn't inadvertently altered during use.
● Install the bolts/nuts in their correct location and secure them lightly. Their threads must be clean and free of any old locking compound. Unless specified the threads and flange should be dry – oiled threads are necessary in certain

circumstances and the manufacturer will take this into account in the specified torque figure. Similarly, the manufacturer may also specify the application of thread-locking compound.
● Tighten the fasteners in the specified sequence until the torque wrench clicks, indicating that the torque setting has been reached. Apply the torque again to double-check the setting. Where different thread diameter fasteners secure the component, as a rule tighten the larger diameter ones first.
● When the torque wrench has been finished with, release the lock (where applicable) and fully back off its setting to zero – do not leave the torque wrench tensioned. Also, do not use a torque wrench for slackening a fastener.

Angle-tightening

● Manufacturers often specify a figure in degrees for final tightening of a fastener. This usually follows tightening to a specific torque setting.
● A degree disc can be set and attached to the socket **(see illustration 4.2)** or a protractor can be used to mark the angle of movement on the bolt/nut head and the surrounding casting **(see illustration 4.3)**.

Loosening sequences

● Where more than one bolt/nut secures a component, loosen each fastener evenly a little at a time. In this way, not all the stress of the joint is held by one fastener and the components are not likely to distort.
● If a tightening sequence is provided, work

in the REVERSE of this, but if not, work from the outside in, in a criss-cross sequence **(see illustration 4.4)**.

Tightening sequences

● If a component is held by more than one fastener it is important that the retaining bolts/nuts are tightened evenly to prevent uneven stress build-up and distortion of sealing faces. This is especially important on high-compression joints such as the cylinder head.
● A sequence is usually provided by the manufacturer, either in a diagram or actually marked in the casting. If not, always start in the centre and work outwards in a criss-cross pattern **(see illustration 4.5)**. Start off by securing all bolts/nuts finger-tight, then set the torque wrench and tighten each fastener by a small amount in sequence until the final torque is reached. By following this practice, the joint will be held evenly and will not be distorted. Important joints, such as the cylinder head and big-end fasteners often have two- or three-stage torque settings.

Applying leverage

● Use tools at the correct angle. Position a socket wrench or spanner on the bolt/nut so that you pull it towards you when loosening. If this can't be done, push the spanner without curling your fingers around it **(see illustration 4.6)** – the spanner may slip or the fastener loosen suddenly, resulting in your fingers being crushed against a component.
● Additional leverage is gained by extending the length of the lever. The best way to do this is to use a breaker bar instead of the regular length tool, or to slip a length of tubing over the end of the spanner or socket wrench.
● If additional leverage will not work, the fastener head is either damaged or firmly corroded in place (see *Fasteners*).

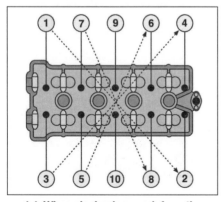

4.4 When slackening, work from the outside inwards

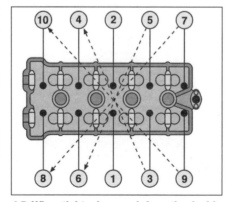

4.5 When tightening, work from the inside outwards

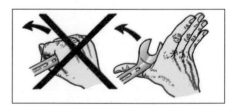

4.6 If you can't pull on the spanner to loosen a fastener, push with your hand open

5.1 Using a bearing driver against the bearing's outer race

5.2 Using a large socket against the bearing's outer race

5.3 This bearing puller clamps behind the bearing and pressure is applied to the shaft end to draw the bearing off

5 Bearings

Bearing removal and installation

Drivers and sockets

● Before removing a bearing, always inspect the casing to see which way it must be driven out – some casings will have retaining plates or a cast step. Also check for any identifying markings on the bearing and if installed to a certain depth, measure this at this stage. Some roller bearings are sealed on one side – take note of the original fitted position.

● Bearings can be driven out of a casing using a bearing driver tool (with the correct size head) or a socket of the correct diameter. Select the driver head or socket so that it contacts the outer race of the bearing, not the balls/rollers or inner race. Always support the casing around the bearing housing with wood blocks, otherwise there is a risk of fracture. The bearing is driven out with a few blows on the driver or socket from a heavy mallet. Unless access is severely restricted (as with wheel bearings), a pin-punch is not recommended unless it is moved around the bearing to keep it square in its housing.

● The same equipment can be used to install bearings. Make sure the bearing housing is supported on wood blocks and line up the bearing in its housing. Fit the bearing as noted on removal – generally they are installed with their marked side facing outwards. Tap the bearing squarely into its housing using a driver or socket which bears only on the bearing's outer race – contact with the bearing balls/rollers or inner race will destroy it **(see illustrations 5.1 and 5.2)**.

● Check that the bearing inner race and balls/rollers rotate freely.

Pullers and slide-hammers

● Where a bearing is pressed on a shaft a puller will be required to extract it **(see illustration 5.3)**. Make sure that the puller clamp or legs fit securely behind the bearing and are unlikely to slip out. If pulling a bearing off a gear shaft for example, you may have to locate the puller behind a gear pinion if there is no access to the race and draw the gear pinion off the shaft as well **(see illustration 5.4)**.

Caution: Ensure that the puller's centre bolt locates securely against the end of the shaft and will not slip when pressure is applied. Also ensure that puller does not damage the shaft end.

● Operate the puller so that its centre bolt exerts pressure on the shaft end and draws the bearing off the shaft.

● When installing the bearing on the shaft, tap only on the bearing's inner race – contact with the balls/rollers or outer race will destroy the bearing. Use a socket or length of tubing as a drift which fits over the shaft end **(see illustration 5.5)**.

5.4 Where no access is available to the rear of the bearing, it is sometimes possible to draw off the adjacent component

5.6 Expand the bearing puller so that it locks behind the bearing . . .

● Where a bearing locates in a blind hole in a casing, it cannot be driven or pulled out as described above. A slide-hammer with knife-edged bearing puller attachment will be required. The puller attachment passes through the bearing and when tightened expands to fit firmly behind the bearing **(see illustration 5.6)**. By operating the slide-hammer part of the tool the bearing is jarred out of its housing **(see illustration 5.7)**.

● It is possible, if the bearing is of reasonable weight, for it to drop out of its housing if the casing is heated as described opposite. If this method is attempted, first prepare a work surface which will enable the casing to be tapped face down to help dislodge the bearing – a wood surface is ideal since it will not damage the casing's gasket surface.

5.5 When installing a bearing on a shaft use a piece of tubing which bears only on the bearing's inner race

5.7 . . . attach the slide hammer to the bearing puller

5.8 Tapping a casing face down on wood blocks can often dislodge a bearing

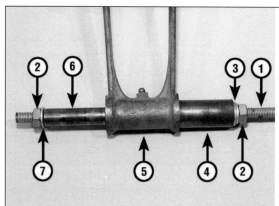

1 Bolt or length of threaded bar
2 Nuts
3 Washer (external diameter greater than tubing internal diameter)
4 Tubing (internal diameter sufficient to accommodate bearing)
5 Suspension arm with bearing
6 Tubing (external diameter slightly smaller than bearing)
7 Washer (external diameter slightly smaller than bearing)

5.10 Drawing the bearing out

5.9 Drawbolt component parts assembled on a suspension arm

Wearing protective gloves, tap the heated casing several times against the work surface to dislodge the bearing under its own weight **(see illustration 5.8)**.

● Bearings can be installed in blind holes using the driver or socket method described above.

Drawbolts

● Where a bearing or bush is set in the eye of a component, such as a suspension linkage arm or connecting rod small-end, removal by drift may damage the component. Furthermore, a rubber bushing in a shock absorber eye cannot successfully be driven out of position. If access is available to a engineering press, the task is straightforward. If not, a drawbolt can be fabricated to extract the bearing or bush.

● To extract the bearing/bush you will need a long bolt with nut (or piece of threaded bar with two nuts), a piece of tubing which has

an internal diameter larger than the bearing/ bush, another piece of tubing which has an external diameter slightly smaller than the bearing/ bush, and a selection of washers **(see illustrations 5.9 and 5.10)**. Note that the pieces of tubing must be of the same length, or longer, than the bearing/bush.

● The same kit (without the pieces of tubing) can be used to draw the new bearing/bush back into place **(see illustration 5.11)**.

Temperature change

● If the bearing's outer race is a tight fit in the casing, the aluminium casing can be heated to release its grip on the bearing. Aluminium will expand at a greater rate than the steel bearing outer race. There are several ways to do this, but avoid any localised extreme heat

(such as a blow torch) – aluminium alloy has a low melting point.

● Approved methods of heating a casing are using a domestic oven (heated to 100°C) or immersing the casing in boiling water **(see illustration 5.12)**. Low temperature range localised heat sources such as a paint stripper heat gun or clothes iron can also be used **(see illustration 5.13)**. Alternatively, soak a rag in boiling water, wring it out and wrap it around the bearing housing.

⚠️ *Warning: All of these methods require care in use to prevent scalding and burns to the hands. Wear protective gloves when handling hot components.*

● If heating the whole casing note that plastic components, such as the oil pressure switch, may suffer – remove them beforehand.

● After heating, remove the bearing as described above. You may find that the expansion is sufficient for the bearing to fall out of the casing under its own weight or with a light tap on the driver or socket.

● If necessary, the casing can be heated to aid bearing installation, and this is sometimes the recommended procedure if the scooter manufacturer has designed the housing and bearing fit with this intention.

● Installation of bearings can be eased by placing them in a freezer the night before installation. The steel bearing will contract slightly, allowing easy insertion in its housing. This is often useful when installing steering head outer races in the frame.

Bearing types and markings

● Plain bearings, ball bearings, needle roller bearings and tapered roller bearings will all be found on scooters **(see illustrations 5.14 and 5.15)**. The ball and roller types are usually caged between an inner and outer race, but uncaged variations may be found.

● Plain bearings are sometimes found at the crankshaft main and connecting rod big-end where they are good at coping with high loads. They are made of a phosphor-bronze material and are impregnated with self-lubricating properties.

of the suspension arm

5.11 Installing a new bearing (1) in the suspension arm

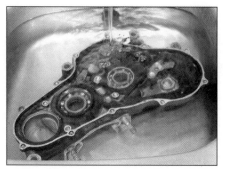

5.12 A casing can be immersed in a sink of boiling water to aid bearing removal

5.13 Using a localised heat source to aid bearing removal

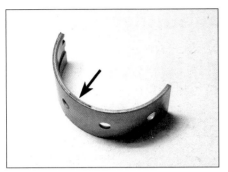

5.14 Bearings are either plain or grooved. They are usually identified by colour code (arrow)

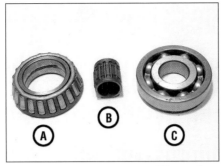

5.15 Tapered roller bearing (A), needle roller bearing (B) and ball journal bearing (C)

5.16 Typical bearing marking

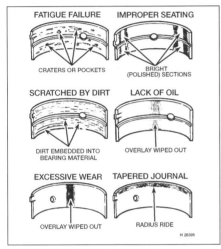

5.17 Typical bearing failures

5.18 Example of ball journal bearing with damaged balls and cages

5.19 Hold outer race and listen to inner race when spun

● Ball bearings and needle roller bearings consist of a steel inner and outer race with the balls or rollers between the races. They require constant lubrication by oil or grease and are good at coping with axial loads. Tapered roller bearings consist of rollers set in a tapered cage set on the inner race; the outer race is separate. They are good at coping with axial loads and prevent movement along the shaft – a typical application is in the steering head.

● Bearing manufacturers produce bearings to ISO size standards and stamp one face of the bearing to indicate its internal and external diameter, load capacity and type **(see illustration 5.16)**.

● Metal bushes are usually of phosphor-bronze material. Rubber bushes are used in suspension mounting eyes. Fibre bushes have also been used in suspension pivots.

Bearing fault finding

● If a bearing outer race has spun in its housing, the housing material will be damaged. You can use a bearing locking compound to bond the outer race in place if damage is not too severe.

● Plain bearings will fail due to damage of their working surface, as a result of lack of lubrication, corrosion or abrasive particles in the oil **(see illustration 5.17)**. Small particles

of dirt in the oil may embed in the bearing material whereas larger particles will score the bearing and shaft journal. If a number of short journeys are made, insufficient heat will be generated to drive off condensation which has built up on the bearings.

● Ball and roller bearings will fail due to lack of lubrication or damage to the balls or rollers. Tapered roller bearings can be damaged by overloading them. Unless the bearing is sealed on both sides, wash it in paraffin (kerosene) to remove all old grease then allow it to dry. Make a visual inspection looking to dented balls or rollers, damaged cages and worn or pitted races **(see illustration 5.18)**.

● A ball bearing can be checked for wear by listening to it when spun. Apply a film of light oil to the bearing and hold it close to the ear – hold the outer race with one hand and spin the inner race with the other hand **(see illustration 5.19)**. The bearing should be almost silent when spun; if it grates or rattles it is worn.

6 Oil seals

Oil seal removal and installation

● Oil seals should be renewed every time a component is dismantled. This is because the seal lips will become set to the sealing surface and will not necessarily reseal.

● Oil seals can be prised out of position using a large flat-bladed screwdriver **(see**

illustration 6.1). In the case of crankcase seals, check first that the seal is not lipped on the inside, preventing its removal with the crankcases joined.

● New seals are usually installed with their marked face (containing the seal reference code) outwards and the spring side towards the fluid being retained. In certain cases, such as a two-stroke engine crankshaft seal, a double lipped seal may be used due to there being fluid or gas on each side of the joint.

● Use a bearing driver or socket which bears only on the outer hard edge of the seal to install it in the casing – tapping on the inner edge will damage the sealing lip.

Oil seal types and markings

● Oil seals are usually of the single-lipped type. Double-lipped seals are found where a liquid or gas is on both sides of the joint.

6.1 Prise out oil seals with a large flat-bladed screwdriver

6.2 These oil seal markings indicate inside diameter, outside diameter and seal thickness

7.1 If a pry point is provided, apply gently pressure with a flat-bladed screwdriver

7.2 Tap around the joint with a soft-faced mallet if necessary – don't strike cooling fins

● Oil seals can harden and lose their sealing ability if the scooter has been in storage for a long period – renewal is the only solution.

● Oil seal manufacturers also conform to the ISO markings for seal size – these are moulded into the outer face of the seal **(see illustration 6.2)**.

7 Gaskets and sealants

Types of gasket and sealant

● Gaskets are used to seal the mating surfaces between components and keep lubricants, fluids, vacuum or pressure contained within the assembly. Aluminium gaskets are sometimes found at the cylinder joints, but most gaskets are paper-based. If the mating surfaces of the components being joined are undamaged the gasket can be installed dry, although a dab of sealant or grease will be useful to hold it in place during assembly.

● RTV (Room Temperature Vulcanising) silicone rubber sealants cure when exposed to moisture in the atmosphere. These sealants are good at filling pits or irregular gasket faces, but will tend to be forced out of the joint under very high torque. They can be used to replace a paper gasket, but first make sure that the width of the paper gasket is not essential to the shimming of internal components. RTV sealants should not be used on components containing petrol (gasoline).

● Non-hardening, semi-hardening and hard

setting liquid gasket compounds can be used with a gasket or between a metal-to-metal joint. Select the sealant to suit the application: universal non-hardening sealant can be used on virtually all joints; semi-hardening on joint faces which are rough or damaged; hard setting sealant on joints which require a permanent bond and are subjected to high temperature and pressure. **Note:** *Check first if the paper gasket has a bead of sealant impregnated in its surface before applying additional sealant.*

● When choosing a sealant, make sure it is suitable for the application, particularly if being applied in a high-temperature area or in the vicinity of fuel. Certain manufacturers produce sealants in either clear, silver or black colours to match the finish of the engine.

● Do not over-apply sealant. That which is squeezed out on the outside of the joint can be wiped off, whereas an excess of sealant on the inside can break off and clog oilways.

Breaking a sealed joint

● Age, heat, pressure and the use of hard setting sealant can cause two components to stick together so tightly that they are difficult to separate using finger pressure alone. Do not resort to using levers unless there is a pry point provided for this purpose **(see illustration 7.1)** or else the gasket surfaces will be damaged.

● Use a soft-faced hammer **(see illustration 7.2)** or a wood block and conventional hammer to strike the component near the mating surface. Avoid hammering against cast extremities since they may break off. If this method fails, try using a wood wedge between the two components.

Most components have one or two hollow locating dowels between the two gasket faces. If a dowel cannot be removed, do not resort to gripping it with pliers – it will almost certainly be distorted. Install a close-fitting socket or Phillips screwdriver into the dowel and then grip the outer edge of the dowel to free it.

Caution: If the joint will not separate, double-check that you have removed all the fasteners.

Removal of old gasket and sealant

● Paper gaskets will most likely come away complete, leaving only a few traces stuck on the sealing faces of the components. It is imperative that all traces are removed to ensure correct sealing of the new gasket.

● Very carefully scrape all traces of gasket away making sure that the sealing surfaces are not gouged or scored by the scraper **(see illustrations 7.3, 7.4 and 7.5)**. Stubborn

7.3 Paper gaskets can be scraped off with a gasket scraper tool . . .

7.4 . . . a knife blade . . .

7.5 . . . or a household scraper

7.6 Fine abrasive paper is wrapped around a flat file to clean up the gasket face

7.7 A kitchen scourer can be used on stubborn deposits

deposits can be removed by spraying with an aerosol gasket remover. Final preparation of the gasket surface can be made with very fine abrasive paper or a plastic kitchen scourer **(see illustrations 7.6 and 7.7)**.

● Old sealant can be scraped or peeled off components, depending on the type originally used. Note that gasket removal compounds are available to avoid scraping the components clean; make sure the gasket remover suits the type of sealant used.

8 Hoses

Clamping to prevent flow

● Small-bore flexible hoses can be clamped to prevent fluid flow whilst a component is worked on. Whichever method is used, ensure that the hose material is not permanently distorted or damaged by the clamp.

 a) *A brake hose clamp available from auto accessory shops* **(see illustration 8.1)**.
 b) *A wingnut type hose clamp* **(see illustration 8.2)**.

 c) *Two sockets placed each side of the hose and held with straight-jawed self-locking grips* **(see illustration 8.3)**.
 d) *Thick card each side of the hose held between straight-jawed self-locking grips* **(see illustration 8.4)**.

Freeing and fitting hoses

● Always make sure the hose clamp is moved well clear of the hose end. Grip the hose with your hand and rotate it whilst pulling it off the union. If the hose has hardened due to age and will not move, slit it with a sharp knife and peel its ends off the union **(see illustration 8.5)**.

● Resist the temptation to use grease or soap on the unions to aid installation; although it helps the hose slip over the union it will equally aid the escape of fluid from the joint. It is preferable to soften the hose ends in hot water and wet the inside surface of the hose with water or a fluid which will evaporate.

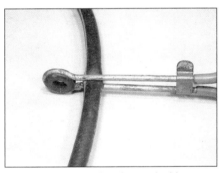

8.1 Hoses can be clamped with an automotive brake hose clamp . . .

8.2 . . . a wingnut type hose clamp . . .

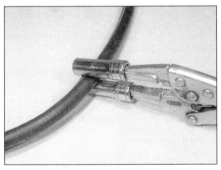

8.3 . . . two sockets and a pair of self-locking grips . . .

8.4 . . . or thick card and self-locking grips

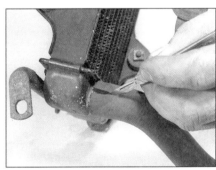

8.5 Cutting a coolant hose free with a sharp knife

About the MOT Test

In the UK, all vehicles more than three years old are subject to an annual test to ensure that they meet minimum safety requirements. A current test certificate must be issued before a machine can be used on public roads, and is required before a road fund licence can be issued. Riding without a current test certificate will also invalidate your insurance.

For most owners, the MOT test is an annual cause for anxiety, and this is largely due to owners not being sure what needs to be checked prior to submitting the scooter for testing. The simple answer is that a fully roadworthy scooter will have no difficulty in passing the test.

This is a guide to getting your scooter through the MOT test. Obviously it will not be possible to examine the scooter to the same standard as the professional MOT tester, particularly in view of the equipment required for some of the checks. However, working through the following procedures will enable you to identify any problem areas before submitting the scooter for the test.

It has only been possible to summarise the test requirements here, based on the regulations in force at the time of printing. Test standards are becoming increasingly stringent, although there are some exemptions for older vehicles. More information about the MOT test can be obtained from the TSO publications, *How Safe is your Motorcycle* and *The MOT Inspection Manual for Motorcycle Testing*.

Many of the checks require that one of the wheels is raised off the ground. Additionally, the help of an assistant may prove useful.

Check that the frame number is clearly visible.

Electrical System

Lights, turn signals, horn and reflector

● With the ignition on, check the operation of the following electrical components. **Note:** *The electrical components on certain small-capacity machines are powered by the generator, requiring that the engine is run for this check.*

a) *Headlight and tail light. Check that both illuminate in the low and high beam switch positions.*
b) *Position lights. Check that the front position (or sidelight) and tail light illuminate in this switch position.*
c) *Turn signals. Check that all flash at the correct rate, and that the warning light(s) function correctly. Check that the turn signal switch works correctly.*
d) *Hazard warning system (where fitted). Check that all four turn signals flash in this switch position.*

e) *Brake stop light. Check that the light comes on when the front and rear brakes are independently applied. Models first used on or after 1st April 1986 must have a brake light switch on each brake.*
f) *Horn. Check that the sound is continuous and of reasonable volume.*

● Check that there is a red reflector on the rear of the machine, either mounted separately or as part of the tail light lens.
● Check the condition of the headlight, tail light and turn signal lenses.

Headlight beam height

● The MOT tester will perform a headlight beam height check using specialised beam setting equipment **(see illustration 1)**. This equipment will not be available to the home mechanic, but if you suspect that the headlight is incorrectly set or may have been maladjusted in the past, you can perform a rough test as follows.

● Position the scooter in a straight line facing a brick wall. The scooter must be off its stand, upright and with a rider seated. Measure the height from the ground to the centre of the headlight and mark a horizontal line on the wall at this height. Position the scooter 3.8 metres from the wall and draw a vertical line up the wall central to the centreline of the scooter. Switch to dipped beam and check that the beam pattern falls slightly lower than the horizontal line and to the left of the vertical line **(see illustration 2)**.

Headlight beam height checking equipment

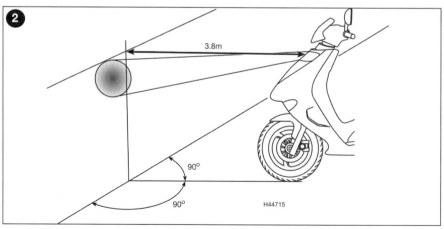

3.8m

90°

90°

H44715

Home workshop beam alignment check

Exhaust System

Exhaust

● Check that the exhaust mountings are secure and that the system does not foul any of the rear suspension components.

● Start the scooter. When the revs are increased, check that the exhaust is neither holed nor leaking from any of its joints. On a linked system, check that the collector box is not leaking due to corrosion.

● Note that the exhaust decibel level ("loudness" of the exhaust) is assessed at the discretion of the tester. If the scooter was first used on or after 1st January 1985 the silencer must carry the BSAU 193 stamp, or a marking relating to its make and model, or be of OE (original equipment) manufacture. If the silencer is marked NOT FOR ROAD USE, RACING USE ONLY or similar, it will fail the MOT.

Steering and Suspension

Steering

● With the front wheel raised off the ground, rotate the steering from lock to lock. The handlebar or switches must not contact anything. Problems can be caused by damaged lock stops on the lower yoke and frame, or by the fitting of non-standard handlebars.

● When performing the lock to lock check, also ensure that the steering moves freely without drag or notchiness. Steering movement can be impaired by poorly routed cables, or by overtight head bearings or worn bearings. The tester will perform a check of the steering head bearing lower race by mounting the front wheel on a surface plate, then performing a lock to lock check with the weight of the machine on the lower bearing (see illustration 3).

● Grasp the fork sliders (lower legs) and attempt to push and pull on the forks (see illustration 4). Any play in the steering head bearings will be felt. Note that in extreme cases, wear of the front fork bushes can be misinterpreted for head bearing play.

● Check that the handlebars are securely mounted.

● Check that the handlebar grip rubbers are secure. They should by bonded to the bar left end and to the throttle twistgrip on the right end.

Front suspension

● With the scooter off the stand, hold the front brake on and pump the front suspension up and down (see illustration 5). Check that the movement is adequately damped.

● Inspect the area above and around the front fork oil seals (see illustration 6). There should be no sign of oil on the fork tube (stanchion) nor leaking down the slider (lower leg).

● On models with leading or trailing link front suspension, check that there is no freeplay in the linkage when moved from side to side.

Front wheel mounted on a surface plate for steering head bearing lower race check

Checking the steering head bearings for freeplay

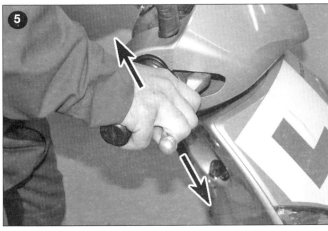

Hold the front brake on and pump the front suspension up and down to check operation

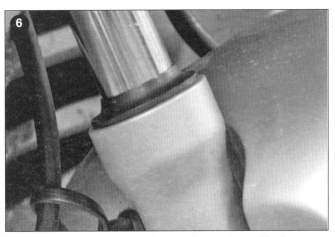

Inspect the area around the fork dust seal for oil leakage

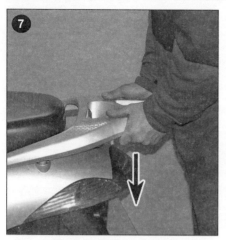

Bounce the rear of the scooter to check rear suspension operation

Grasp the rear wheel to check for play in the engine-to-frame mountings

Rear suspension

● With the scooter off the stand and an assistant supporting the scooter by its handlebars, bounce the rear suspension (see illustration 7). Check that the suspension components do not foul the bodywork and check that the shock absorber(s) provide adequate damping.

● Visually inspect the shock absorber(s) and check that there is no sign of oil leakage from its damper.

● With the rear wheel raised off the ground, grasp the wheel as shown and attempt to move it from side to side (see illustration 8). Any play in the engine-to-frame mountings will be felt as movement.

Brakes, Wheels and Tyres

Brakes

● With the wheel raised off the ground, apply the brake then free it off, and check that the wheel is about to revolve freely without brake drag.

Brake pad wear can usually be viewed without removing the caliper. Some pads have wear indicator grooves (arrow)

● On disc brakes, examine the disc itself. Check that it is securely mounted and not cracked.

● On disc brakes, view the pad material through the caliper mouth and check that the pads are not worn down beyond the limit (see illustration 9).

● On drum brakes, check that when the brake is applied the angle between the operating

On drum brakes, check the angle of the operating lever with the brake fully applied. Most drum brakes have a wear indicator pointer and scale

lever and cable or rod is not too great (see illustration 10). Check also that the operating lever doesn't foul any other components.

● On disc brakes, examine the flexible hoses from top to bottom. Have an assistant hold the brake on so that the fluid in the hose is under pressure, and check that there is no sign of fluid leakage, bulges or cracking. If there are any metal brake pipes or unions, check that these are free from corrosion and damage.

● The MOT tester will perform a test of the scooter's braking efficiency based on a calculation of rider and scooter weight. Although this cannot be carried out at home, you can at least ensure that the braking systems are properly maintained. For hydraulic disc brakes, check the fluid level, lever/pedal feel (bleed of air if its spongy) and pad material. For drum brakes, check adjustment, cable or rod operation and shoe lining thickness.

Wheels and tyres

● Check the wheel condition. Cast wheels should be free from cracks and if of the built-up design, all fasteners should be secure.

● With the wheel raised off the ground, spin the wheel and visually check that the tyre and wheel run true. Check that the tyre does not foul the suspension or mudguards.

● With the wheel raised off the ground, grasp the wheel and attempt to move it about the axle (see illustration 11). Any play felt here indicates wheel bearing failure.

● Check the tyre tread depth, tread condition and sidewall condition (see illustration 12).

● Check the tyre type. Front and rear tyre types must be compatible and be suitable for

Check for wheel bearing play by trying to move the wheel about the axle (spindle)

Checking the tyre tread depth

Tyre direction of rotation arrow can be found on tyre sidewall

Two straight-edges are used to check wheel alignment

road use. Tyres marked NOT FOR ROAD USE, COMPETITION USE ONLY or similar, will fail the MOT.

● If the tyre sidewall carries a direction of rotation arrow, this must be pointing in the direction of normal wheel rotation **(see illustration 13)**.

● Check that the wheel axle nuts (where applicable) are properly secured. A self-locking nut or castellated nut with a split-pin or R-pin can be used.

● Wheel alignment is checked with the scooter off the stand and a rider seated. With the front wheel pointing straight ahead, two perfectly straight lengths of metal or wood and placed against the sidewalls of both tyres **(see illustration 14)**. The gap each side of the front tyre must be equidistant on both sides. Incorrect wheel alignment may be due to a cocked rear wheel or in extreme cases, a bent frame.

General checks and condition

● Check the security of all major fasteners, bodypanels, seat and mudguards.

● Check that the pillion footrests, handlebar levers and stand are securely mounted.

● Check for corrosion on the frame or any load-bearing components. If severe, this may affect the structure, particularly under stress.

Introduction

In less time than it takes to read this introduction, a thief could steal your motorcycle. Returning only to find your bike has gone is one of the worst feelings in the world. Even if the motorcycle is insured against theft, once you've got over the initial shock, you will have the inconvenience of dealing with the police and your insurance company.

The motorcycle is an easy target for the professional thief and the joyrider alike and the

official figures on motorcycle theft make for depressing reading; on average a motor-cycle is stolen every 16 minutes in the UK!

Motorcycle thefts fall into two categories, those stolen 'to order' and those taken by opportunists. The thief stealing to order will be on the look out for a specific make and model and will go to extraordinary lengths to obtain that motorcycle. The opportunist thief on the other hand will look for easy targets which can be stolen with the minimum of effort and risk.

Whilst it is never going to be possible to make your machine 100% secure, it is estimated that around half of all stolen motorcycles are taken by opportunist thieves. Remember that the opportunist thief is always on the look out for the easy option: if there are two similar motorcycles parked side-by-side, they will target the one with the lowest level of security. By taking a few precautions, you can reduce the chances of your motorcycle being stolen.

Security equipment

There are many specialised motorcycle security devices available and the following text summarises their applications and their good and bad points.

Once you have decided on the type of security equipment which best suits your needs, we recommended that you read one of the many equipment tests regularly carried out by the motorcycle press. These tests

Ensure the lock and chain you buy is of good quality and long enough to shackle your bike to a solid object

compare the products from all the major manufacturers and give impartial ratings on their effectiveness, value-for-money and ease of use.

No one item of security equipment can provide complete protection. It is highly recommended that two or more of the items described below are combined to increase the security of your motorcycle (a lock and chain plus an alarm system is just about ideal). The more security measures fitted to the bike, the less likely it is to be stolen.

Lock and chain

Pros: *Very flexible to use; can be used to secure the motorcycle to almost any immovable object. On some locks and chains, the lock can be used on its own as a disc lock (see below).*

Cons: *Can be very heavy and awkward to carry on the motorcycle, although some types*

will be supplied with a carry bag which can be strapped to the pillion seat.

● Heavy-duty chains and locks are an excellent security measure **(see illustration 1).** Whenever the motorcycle is parked, use the lock and chain to secure the machine to a solid, immovable object such as a post or railings. This will prevent the machine from being ridden away or being lifted into the back of a van.

● When fitting the chain, always ensure the chain is routed around the motorcycle frame or swingarm **(see illustrations 2 and 3).** Never merely pass the chain around one of the wheel rims; a thief may unbolt the wheel and lift the rest of the machine into a van, leaving you with just the wheel! Try to avoid having excess chain free, thus making it difficult to use cutting tools, and keep the chain and lock off the ground to prevent thieves attacking it with a cold chisel. Position the lock so that its lock barrel is facing downwards; this will make it harder for the thief to attack the lock mechanism.

Pass the chain through the bike's frame, rather than just through a wheel . . .

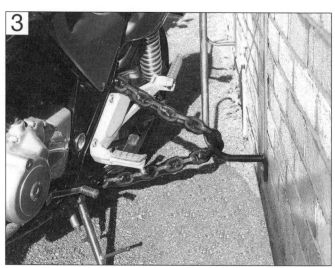

. . . and loop it around a solid object

U-locks

Pros: *Highly effective deterrent which can be used to secure the bike to a post or railings. Most U-locks come with a carrier which allows the lock to be easily carried on the bike.*

Cons: *Not as flexible to use as a lock and chain.*

● These are solid locks which are similar in use to a lock and chain. U-locks are lighter than a lock and chain but not so flexible to use. The length and shape of the lock shackle limit the objects to which the bike can be secured **(see illustration 4)**.

Disc locks

Pros: *Small, light and very easy to carry; most can be stored underneath the seat.*

Cons: *Does not prevent the motorcycle being lifted into a van. Can be very embarrassing if*

A typical disc lock attached through one of the holes in the disc

U-locks can be used to secure the bike to a solid object – ensure you purchase one which is long enough

you forget to remove the lock before attempting to ride off!

● Disc locks are designed to be attached to the front brake disc. The lock passes through one of the holes in the disc and prevents the wheel rotating by jamming against the fork/brake caliper **(see illustration 5)**. Some are equipped with an alarm siren which sounds if the disc lock is moved; this not only acts as a theft deterrent but also as a handy reminder if you try to move the bike with the lock still fitted.

● Combining the disc lock with a length of cable which can be looped around a post or railings provides an additional measure of security **(see illustration 6)**.

Alarms and immobilisers

Pros: *Once installed it is completely hassle-free to use. If the system is 'Thatcham' or 'Sold Secure-approved', insurance companies may give you a discount.*

Cons: *Can be expensive to buy and complex to install. No system will prevent the motorcycle from being lifted into a van and taken away.*

● Electronic alarms and immobilisers are available to suit a variety of budgets. There are three different types of system available: pure alarms, pure immobilisers, and the more expensive systems which are combined alarm/immobilisers **(see illustration 7)**.
● An alarm system is designed to emit an audible warning if the motorcycle is being tampered with.
● An immobiliser prevents the motorcycle being started and ridden away by disabling its electrical systems.
● When purchasing an alarm/immobiliser system, check the cost of installing the system unless you are able to do it yourself. If the motorcycle is not used regularly, another consideration is the current drain of the system. All alarm/immobiliser systems are powered by the motorcycle's battery; purchasing a system with a very low current drain could prevent the battery losing its charge whilst the motorcycle is not being used.

A disc lock combined with a security cable provides additional protection

A typical alarm/immobiliser system

Indelible markings can be applied to most areas of the bike – always apply the manufacturer's sticker to warn off thieves

Chemically-etched code numbers can be applied to main body panels . . .

. . . again, always ensure that the kit manufacturer's sticker is applied in a prominent position

Security marking kits

Pros: *Very cheap and effective deterrent. Many insurance companies will give you a discount on your insurance premium if a recognised security marking kit is used on your motorcycle.*

Cons: *Does not prevent the motorcycle being stolen by joyriders.*

● There are many different types of security marking kits available. The idea is to mark as many parts of the motorcycle as possible with a unique security number **(see illustrations 8, 9 and 10)**. A form will be included with the kit to register your personal details and those of the motorcycle with the kit manufacturer. This register is made available to the police to help them trace the rightful owner of any motorcycle or components which they recover should all other forms of identification have been removed. Always apply the warning stickers provided with the kit to deter thieves.

Ground anchors, wheel clamps and security posts

Pros: *An excellent form of security which will deter all but the most determined of thieves.*

Cons: *Awkward to install and can be expensive.*

● Whilst the motorcycle is at home, it is a good idea to attach it securely to the floor or a solid wall, even if it is kept in a securely locked garage. Various types of ground anchors, security posts and wheel clamps are available for this purpose **(see illustration 11)**. These security devices are either bolted to a solid concrete or brick structure or can be cemented into the ground.

Permanent ground anchors provide an excellent level of security when the bike is at home

Security at home

A high percentage of motorcycle thefts are from the owner's home. Here are some things to consider whenever your motorcycle is at home:

● Where possible, always keep the motorcycle in a securely locked garage. Never rely solely on the standard lock on the garage door, these are usual hopelessly inadequate. Fit an additional locking mechanism to the door and consider having the garage alarmed. A security light, activated by a movement sensor, is also a good investment.

● Always secure the motorcycle to the ground or a wall, even if it is inside a securely locked garage.
● Do not regularly leave the motorcycle outside your home, try to keep it out of sight wherever possible. If a garage is not available, fit a motorcycle cover over the bike to disguise its true identity.
● It is not uncommon for thieves to follow a motorcyclist home to find out where the bike is kept. They will then return at a later date. Be aware of this whenever you are returning

home on your motorcycle. If you suspect you are being followed, do not return home, instead ride to a garage or shop and stop as a precaution.
● When selling a motorcycle, do not provide your home address or the location where the bike is normally kept. Arrange to meet the buyer at a location away from your home. Thieves have been known to pose as potential buyers to find out where motorcycles are kept and then return later to steal them.

Security away from the home

As well as fitting security equipment to your motorcycle here are a few general rules to follow whenever you park your motorcycle.
● Park in a busy, public place.
● Use car parks which incorporate security features, such as CCTV.

● At night, park in a well-lit area, preferably directly underneath a street light.
● Engage the steering lock.
● Secure the motorcycle to a solid, immovable object such as a post or railings with an additional lock. If this is not possible,

secure the bike to a friend's motorcycle. Some public parking places provide security loops for motorcycles.
● Never leave your helmet or luggage attached to the motorcycle. Take them with you at all times.

Length (distance)

Inches (in)	x 25.4	= Millimetres (mm)	x 0.0394	= Inches (in)
Feet (ft)	x 0.305	= Metres (m)	x 3.281	= Feet (ft)
Miles	x 1.609	= Kilometres (km)	x 0.621	= Miles

Volume (capacity)

Cubic inches (cu in; in^3)	x 16.387	= Cubic centimetres (cc; cm^3)	x 0.061	= Cubic inches (cu in; in^3)
Imperial pints (Imp pt)	x 0.568	= Litres (l)	x 1.76	= Imperial pints (Imp pt)
Imperial quarts (Imp qt)	x 1.137	= Litres (l)	x 0.88	= Imperial quarts (Imp qt)
Imperial quarts (Imp qt)	x 1.201	= US quarts (US qt)	x 0.833	= Imperial quarts (Imp qt)
US quarts (US qt)	x 0.946	= Litres (l)	x 1.057	= US quarts (US qt)
Imperial gallons (Imp gal)	x 4.546	= Litres (l)	x 0.22	= Imperial gallons (Imp gal)
Imperial gallons (Imp gal)	x 1.201	= US gallons (US gal)	x 0.833	= Imperial gallons (Imp gal)
US gallons (US gal)	x 3.785	= Litres (l)	x 0.264	= US gallons (US gal)

Mass (weight)

Ounces (oz)	x 28.35	= Grams (g)	x 0.035	= Ounces (oz)
Pounds (lb)	x 0.454	= Kilograms (kg)	x 2.205	= Pounds (lb)

Force

Ounces-force (ozf; oz)	x 0.278	= Newtons (N)	x 3.6	= Ounces-force (ozf; oz)
Pounds-force (lbf; lb)	x 4.448	= Newtons (N)	x 0.225	= Pounds-force (lbf; lb)
Newtons (N)	x 0.1	= Kilograms-force (kgf; kg)	x 9.81	= Newtons (N)

Pressure

Pounds-force per square inch (psi; lbf/in^2; lb/in^2)	x 0.070	= Kilograms-force per square centimetre (kgf/cm^2; kg/cm^2)	x 14.223	= Pounds-force per square inch (psi; lbf/in^2; lb/in^2)
Pounds-force per square inch (psi; lbf/in^2; lb/in^2)	x 0.068	= Atmospheres (atm)	x 14.696	= Pounds-force per square inch (psi; lbf/in^2; lb/in^2)
Pounds-force per square inch (psi; lbf/in^2; lb/in^2)	x 0.069	= Bars	x 14.5	= Pounds-force per square inch (psi; lbf/in^2; lb/in^2)
Pounds-force per square inch (psi; lbf/in^2; lb/in^2)	x 6.895	= Kilopascals (kPa)	x 0.145	= Pounds-force per square inch (psi; lbf/in^2; lb/in^2)
Kilopascals (kPa)	x 0.01	= Kilograms-force per square centimetre (kgf/cm^2; kg/cm^2)	x 98.1	= Kilopascals (kPa)
Millibar (mbar)	x 100	= Pascals (Pa)	x 0.01	= Millibar (mbar)
Millibar (mbar)	x 0.0145	= Pounds-force per square inch (psi; lbf/in^2; lb/in^2)	x 68.947	= Millibar (mbar)
Millibar (mbar)	x 0.75	= Millimetres of mercury (mmHg)	x 1.333	= Millibar (mbar)
Millibar (mbar)	x 0.401	= Inches of water (inH_2O)	x 2.491	= Millibar (mbar)
Millimetres of mercury (mmHg)	x 0.535	= Inches of water (inH_2O)	x 1.868	= Millimetres of mercury (mmHg)
Inches of water (inH_2O)	x 0.036	= Pounds-force per square inch (psi; lbf/in^2; lb/in^2)	x 27.68	= Inches of water (inH_2O)

Torque (moment of force)

Pounds-force inches (lbf in; lb in)	x 1.152	= Kilograms-force centimetre (kgf cm; kg cm)	x 0.868	= Pounds-force inches (lbf in; lb in)
Pounds-force inches (lbf in; lb in)	x 0.113	= Newton metres (Nm)	x 8.85	= Pounds-force inches (lbf in; lb in)
Pounds-force inches (lbf in; lb in)	x 0.083	= Pounds-force feet (lbf ft; lb ft)	x 12	= Pounds-force inches (lbf in; lb in)
Pounds-force feet (lbf ft; lb ft)	x 0.138	= Kilograms-force metres (kgf m; kg m)	x 7.233	= Pounds-force feet (lbf ft; lb ft)
Pounds-force feet (lbf ft; lb ft)	x 1.356	= Newton metres (Nm)	x 0.738	= Pounds-force feet (lbf ft; lb ft)
Newton metres (Nm)	x 0.102	= Kilograms-force metres (kgf m; kg m)	x 9.804	= Newton metres (Nm)

Power

Horsepower (hp)	x 745.7	= Watts (W)	x 0.0013	= Horsepower (hp)

Velocity (speed)

Miles per hour (miles/hr; mph)	x 1.609	= Kilometres per hour (km/hr; kph)	x 0.621	= Miles per hour (miles/hr; mph)

Fuel consumption*

Miles per gallon, Imperial (mpg)	x 0.354	= Kilometres per litre (km/l)	x 2.825	= Miles per gallon, Imperial (mpg)
Miles per gallon, US (mpg)	x 0.425	= Kilometres per litre (km/l)	x 2.352	= Miles per gallon, US (mpg)

Temperature

Degrees Fahrenheit = (°C x 1.8) + 32   Degrees Celsius (Degrees Centigrade; °C) = (°F - 32) x 0.56

It is common practice to convert from miles per gallon (mpg) to litres/100 kilometres (l/100km), where mpg x l/100 km = 282

This Section provides an easy reference-guide to the more common faults that are likely to afflict your machine. Obviously, the opportunities are almost limitless for faults to occur as a result of obscure failures, and to try and cover all eventualities would require a book. Indeed, a number have been written on the subject.

Successful troubleshooting is not a mysterious 'black art' but the application of a bit of knowledge combined with a systematic and logical approach to the problem. Approach any troubleshooting by first accurately identifying the symptom and then checking through the list of possible causes, starting with the simplest or most obvious and progressing in stages to the most complex.

Take nothing for granted, but above all apply liberal quantities of common sense.

The main symptom of a fault is given in the text as a major heading below which are listed the various systems or areas which may contain the fault. Details of each possible cause for a fault and the remedial action to be taken are given, in brief, in the paragraphs below each heading. Further information should be sought in the relevant Chapter.

1 Engine doesn't start or is difficult to start

- ☐ Starter motor doesn't rotate
- ☐ Starter motor rotates but engine does not turn over
- ☐ Starter works but engine won't turn over (seized)
- ☐ No fuel flow
- ☐ Engine flooded
- ☐ No spark or weak spark
- ☐ Compression low
- ☐ Stalls after starting
- ☐ Rough idle

2 Poor running at low speed

- ☐ Spark weak
- ☐ Fuel/air mixture incorrect
- ☐ Compression low
- ☐ Poor acceleration

3 Poor running or no power at high speed

- ☐ Firing incorrect
- ☐ Fuel/air mixture incorrect
- ☐ Compression low
- ☐ Knocking or pinking
- ☐ Miscellaneous causes

4 Overheating

- ☐ Engine overheats
- ☐ Firing incorrect
- ☐ Fuel/air mixture incorrect
- ☐ Compression too high
- ☐ Engine load excessive
- ☐ Lubrication inadequate
- ☐ Miscellaneous causes

5 Transmission problems

- ☐ No drive to rear wheel
- ☐ Vibration
- ☐ Poor performance
- ☐ Clutch not disengaging completely

6 Abnormal engine noise

- ☐ Knocking or pinking
- ☐ Piston slap or rattling
- ☐ Valve noise (four-stroke engines)
- ☐ Other noise

7 Abnormal frame and suspension noise

- ☐ Front end noise
- ☐ Shock absorber noise
- ☐ Brake noise

8 Excessive exhaust smoke

- ☐ White smoke (four-stroke engines)
- ☐ White/blue smoke (two-stroke engines)
- ☐ Black smoke
- ☐ Brown smoke

9 Poor handling or stability

- ☐ Handlebar hard to turn
- ☐ Handlebar shakes or vibrates excessively
- ☐ Handlebar pulls to one side
- ☐ Poor shock absorbing qualities

10 Braking problems – disc brake

- ☐ Brakes are ineffective
- ☐ Brake lever pulsates
- ☐ Brakes drag

11 Braking problems – drum brake

- ☐ Brakes are ineffective
- ☐ Brake lever pulsates
- ☐ Brakes drag

12 Electrical problems

- ☐ Battery dead or weak
- ☐ Battery overcharged

1 Engine doesn't start or is difficult to start

Starter motor doesn't rotate

- ☐ Fuse blown. Check fuse and starter circuit (Chapter 10).
- ☐ Battery voltage low. Check and recharge battery (Chapter 10).
- ☐ Starter motor defective. Make sure the wiring to the starter is secure. Make sure the starter relay clicks when the start button is pushed. If the relay clicks, then the fault is in the wiring or motor.
- ☐ Starter relay faulty. Check it (Chapter 10).
- ☐ Starter switch on handlebar not contacting. The contacts could be wet, corroded or dirty. Disassemble and clean the switch (Chapter 10).
- ☐ Wiring open or shorted. Check all wiring connections and harnesses to make sure that they are dry, tight and not corroded. Also check for broken or frayed wires that can cause a short to earth.
- ☐ Ignition switch defective. Check the switch according to the procedure in Chapter 10. Renew the switch if it is defective.

Starter motor rotates but engine does not turn over

- ☐ Starter pinion assembly or starter drive defective. Inspect and repair or renew (relevant part of Chapter 2).

Starter works but engine won't turn over (seized)

- ☐ Seized engine caused by one or more internally damaged components. Failure due to wear, abuse or lack of lubrication. On all engines damage can include piston, cylinder, connecting rod, crankshaft, bearings and additionally on four-strokes, valves, camshaft, camchain. Refer to the relevant part of Chapter 2 for engine disassembly.

No fuel flow

- ☐ No fuel in tank.
- ☐ Faulty automatic choke unit (Chapter 5).
- ☐ Fuel hose or tank breather trapped.
- ☐ Fuel filter clogged. Check the in-line fuel filter (Chapter 5).
- ☐ Fuel tap vacuum hose split or detached. Check the hose.
- ☐ Fuel tap diaphragm split. Renew the tap (Chapter 5).
- ☐ Float needle valve or carburettor jets clogged. The carburettor should be removed and overhauled if draining the float chamber doesn't solve the problem.

Engine flooded

- ☐ Float needle valve worn or stuck open. A piece of dirt, rust or other debris can cause the valve to seat improperly, causing excess fuel to be admitted to the float chamber. In this case, the float chamber should be cleaned and the needle valve and seat inspected. If the needle and seat are worn, then the leaking will persist and the parts should be renewed (Chapter 5).

No spark or weak spark

- ☐ Ignition switch OFF.
- ☐ Battery voltage low. Check and recharge the battery as necessary (Chapter 10).
- ☐ Spark plug dirty, defective or worn out. Locate reason for fouled plug using spark plug condition chart at the end of this manual and follow the plug maintenance procedures (Chapter 1). Condition is especially applicable to two-stroke engines due to the oily nature of their lubrication system.
- ☐ Spark plug cap or secondary (HT) wiring faulty. Check condition. Replace either or both components if cracks or deterioration are evident (Chapter 6).
- ☐ Spark plug cap not making good contact. Make sure that the plug cap fits snugly over the plug end.
- ☐ CDI unit defective (Chapter 6).
- ☐ Pulse generator coil or source coil defective. Check the unit, referring to Chapter 6 for details.
- ☐ Ignition coil defective. Check the coil, referring to Chapter 6.
- ☐ Ignition switch shorted. This is usually caused by water, corrosion, damage or excessive wear. Spray switch with electrical contact cleaner. If cleaning does not help, renew the switch (Chapter 10).
- ☐ Wiring shorted or broken. Make sure that all wiring connections are clean, dry and tight. Look for chafed and broken wires (see Wiring Diagrams).

Compression low

- ☐ Spark plug loose. Remove the plug and inspect its threads (Chapter 1).
- ☐ Cylinder head not sufficiently tightened down. If the cylinder head is suspected of being loose, then there's a chance that the gasket or head is damaged if the problem has persisted for any length of time. The head bolts/nuts should be tightened to the proper torque in the correct sequence (Chapter 2 relevant part).
- ☐ Low crankcase compression on two-stroke engines due to worn crankshaft oil seals. Condition will upset the fuel/air mixture. Renew the seals (Chapter 2A or 2B).
- ☐ Improper valve clearance (four-strokes). This means that the valve is not closing completely and compression pressure is leaking past the valve. Check and adjust the valve clearances (Chapter 1).
- ☐ Cylinder and/or piston worn. Excessive wear will cause compression pressure to leak past the rings. This is usually accompanied by worn rings as well. A top-end overhaul is necessary (Chapter 2 relevant part).
- ☐ Piston rings worn, weak, broken, or sticking. Broken or sticking piston rings usually indicate a lubrication or carburation problem that causes excess carbon deposits or seizures to form on the piston and rings. Top-end overhaul is necessary (Chapter 2 relevant part).
- ☐ Cylinder head gasket damaged. If a head is allowed to become loose, or if excessive carbon build-up on the piston crown and combustion chamber causes extremely high compression, the head gasket may leak. Retorquing the head is not always sufficient to restore the seal, so gasket renewal is necessary (Chapter 2 relevant part).
- ☐ Cylinder head warped. This is caused by overheating or improperly tightened head bolts/nuts. Machine shop resurfacing or head renewal is necessary (Chapter 2 relevant part).
- ☐ Valve spring broken or weak (four-stroke engines). Caused by component failure or wear; the springs must be renewed (Chapter 2C, D, E, F or G).
- ☐ Valve not seating properly (four-stroke engines). This is caused by a bent valve (from over-revving or improper valve adjustment), burned valve or seat (improper carburation) or an accumulation of carbon deposits on the seat (from carburation or lubrication problems). The valves must be cleaned and/or renewed and the seats serviced if possible (Chapter 2C, D, E, F or G).

Stalls after starting

- ☐ Faulty automatic choke unit. Check connections and movement (Chapter 5).
- ☐ Ignition malfunction (Chapter 6).
- ☐ Carburettor malfunction (Chapter 5).
- ☐ Fuel contaminated and/or filter blocked. The fuel can be contaminated with either dirt or water, or can change chemically if the machine is allowed to sit for several months or more. Drain the tank and carburettor and renew the filter (Chapter 5).
- ☐ Inlet air leak. Check for loose carburettor-to-inlet manifold connection, loose carburettor top (Chapter 5).
- ☐ Engine idle speed incorrect. Turn idle adjusting screw until the engine idles at the specified rpm (Chapter 1).

1 Engine doesn't start or is difficult to start (continued)

Rough idle

☐ Ignition malfunction (Chapter 6).
☐ Idle speed incorrect (Chapter 1).
☐ Carburettor malfunction (Chapter 5).
☐ Fuel contaminated and/or filter blocked. The fuel can be contaminated with either dirt or water, or can change chemically if the machine is allowed to sit for several months or more. Drain the tank and carburettor and renew the filter (Chapter 5).
☐ Inlet air leak. Check for loose carburettor-to-inlet manifold connection, loose carburettor top (Chapter 5).
☐ Air filter clogged. Clean or renew the air filter element (Chapter 1).

2 Poor running at low speeds

Spark weak

☐ Battery voltage low. Check and recharge battery (Chapter 10).
☐ Spark plug fouled, defective or worn out. Refer to Chapter 1 for spark plug maintenance.
☐ Spark plug cap or HT wiring defective. Refer to Chapter 6 for details on the ignition system.
☐ Spark plug cap not making contact.
☐ Incorrect spark plug. Wrong type, heat range or cap configuration. Check and install correct plug.
☐ CDI unit defective. See Chapter 6.
☐ Pulse generator coil defective. See Chapter 6.
☐ Ignition coil defective. See Chapter 6.

Fuel/air mixture incorrect

☐ Pilot screw out of adjustment (Chapter 5).
☐ Pilot jet or air passage clogged. Remove and clean the carburettor (Chapter 5).
☐ Air bleed hole clogged. Remove carburettor and blow out all passages (Chapter 5).
☐ Air filter clogged, poorly sealed or missing (Chapter 1).
☐ Air filter housing poorly sealed. Look for cracks, holes or loose screws and renew or repair defective parts.
☐ Carburettor inlet manifold loose. Check for cracks, breaks, tears or loose fixings.

Compression low

☐ Spark plug loose. Remove the plug and inspect its threads (Chapter 1).
☐ Cylinder head not sufficiently tightened down. If the cylinder head is suspected of being loose, then there's a chance that the gasket or head is damaged if the problem has persisted for any length of time. The head bolts/nuts should be tightened to the proper torque in the correct sequence (Chapter 2 relevant part).
☐ Improper valve clearance (four-stroke engines). This means that the valve is not closing completely and compression pressure is leaking past the valve. Check and adjust the valve clearances (Chapter 1).
☐ Low crankcase compression on two-stroke engines due to worn crankshaft oil seals. Condition will upset the fuel/air mixture. Renew the seals (Chapter 2A or 2B).
☐ Cylinder and/or piston worn. Excessive wear will cause compression pressure to leak past the rings. This is usually accompanied by worn rings as well. A top-end overhaul is necessary (Chapter 2 relevant part).
☐ Piston rings worn, weak, broken, or sticking. Broken or sticking piston rings usually indicate a lubrication or carburation problem that causes excess carbon deposits or seizures to form on the piston and rings. Top-end overhaul is necessary (Chapter 2 relevant part).
☐ Cylinder head gasket damaged. If a head is allowed to become loose, or if excessive carbon build-up on the piston crown and combustion chamber causes extremely high compression, the head gasket may leak. Retorquing the head is not always sufficient to restore the seal, so gasket renewal is necessary (Chapter 2 relevant part).
☐ Cylinder head warped. This is caused by overheating or improperly tightened head bolts/nuts. Machine shop resurfacing or head replacement is necessary (Chapter 2 relevant part).
☐ Valve spring broken or weak (four-stroke engines). Caused by component failure or wear; the springs must be replaced (Chapter 2C, D, E, F or G).
☐ Valve not seating properly (four-stroke engines). This is caused by a bent valve (from over-revving or improper valve adjustment), burned valve or seat (improper carburation) or an accumulation of carbon deposits on the seat (from carburation or lubrication problems). The valves must be cleaned and/or renewed and the seats serviced if possible (Chapter 2C, D, E, F or G).

Poor acceleration

☐ Carburettor leaking or dirty. Overhaul the carburettor (Chapter 5).
☐ Faulty automatic choke (Chapter 5).
☐ Timing not advancing. The pulse generator coil or the CDI unit may be defective (Chapter 6). If so, they must be renewed, as they can't be repaired.
☐ Engine oil viscosity too high (four-stroke engines). Using too heavy an oil can damage the oil pump or lubrication system and cause drag on the engine.
☐ Brakes dragging. On disc brakes, usually caused by debris which has entered the brake piston seals, or from a warped disc or bent axle. On drum brakes, cable out of adjustment, shoe return spring broken. Repair as necessary (Chapter 8).
☐ Clutch slipping or drive belt worn (Chapter 3).

3 Poor running or no power at high speed

Firing incorrect

☐ Air filter clogged. Clean or renew filter (Chapter 1).
☐ Spark plug fouled, defective or worn out. See Chapter 1 for spark plug maintenance.
☐ Spark plug cap or HT wiring defective. See Chapter 6 for details of the ignition system.
☐ Spark plug cap not in good contact (Chapter 6).
☐ Incorrect spark plug. Wrong type, heat range or cap configuration. Check and install correct plug.
☐ CDI unit or ignition coil defective (Chapter 6).

Fuel/air mixture incorrect

☐ Main jet clogged. Dirt, water or other contaminants can clog the main jet. Clean the in-line filter, the float chamber and the jets and carburettor orifices (Chapter 5).
☐ Main jet wrong size. The standard jetting is for sea level atmospheric pressure and oxygen content.
☐ Air bleed holes clogged. Remove and overhaul carburettor (Chapter 5).
☐ Air filter clogged, poorly sealed, or missing (Chapter 1).
☐ Air filter housing or duct poorly sealed. Look for cracks, holes or loose clamps or screws, and renew or repair defective parts.
☐ Carburettor inlet manifold loose. Check for cracks, breaks, tears or loose fixings.

Compression low

☐ Spark plug loose. Remove the plug and inspect its threads. Reinstall and tighten to the specified torque (Chapter 1).
☐ Cylinder head not sufficiently tightened down. If the cylinder head is suspected of being loose, then there's a chance that the gasket or head is damaged if the problem has persisted for any length of time. The head bolts/nuts should be tightened to the proper torque in the correct sequence (Chapter 2 relevant part).
☐ Improper valve clearance (four-stroke engines). This means that the valve is not closing completely and compression pressure is leaking past the valve. Check and adjust the valve clearances (Chapter 1).
☐ Low crankcase compression on two-stroke engines due to worn crankshaft oil seals. Condition will upset the fuel/air mixture. Renew the seals (Chapter 2A or 2B).
☐ Cylinder and/or piston worn. Excessive wear will cause compression pressure to leak past the rings. This is usually accompanied by worn rings as well. A top-end overhaul is necessary (Chapter 2 relevant part).
☐ Piston rings worn, weak, broken, or sticking. Broken or sticking piston rings usually indicate a lubrication or carburation problem that causes excess carbon deposits or seizures to form on the piston and rings. Top-end overhaul is necessary (Chapter 2 relevant part).
☐ Cylinder head gasket damaged. If a head is allowed to become loose, or if excessive carbon build-up on the piston crown and combustion chamber causes extremely high compression, the head gasket may leak. Retorquing the head is not always sufficient to restore the seal, so gasket replacement is necessary (Chapter 2 relevant part).
☐ Cylinder head warped. This is caused by overheating or improperly tightened head bolts/nuts. Cylinder head skimming or head replacement is necessary (Chapter 2 relevant part).
☐ Valve spring broken or weak (four-stroke engines). Caused by component failure or wear; the springs must be renewed (Chapter 2C, D, E, F or G).
☐ Valve not seating properly (four-stroke engines). This is caused by a bent valve (from over-revving or improper valve adjustment), burned valve or seat (improper carburation) or an accumulation of carbon deposits on the seat (from carburation or lubrication problems). The valves must be cleaned and/or renewed and the seats serviced if possible (Chapter 2C, D, E, F or G).

Knocking or pinking

☐ Carbon build-up in combustion chamber. Use of a fuel additive that will dissolve the adhesive bonding the carbon particles to the crown and chamber is the easiest way to remove the build-up. Otherwise, the cylinder head will have to be removed and decarbonised (Chapter 2 relevant part). On two-stroke engines, the regular service interval for cylinder head decarbonisation should be adhered to.
☐ Incorrect or poor quality fuel. Old or improper grades of fuel can cause detonation. This causes the piston to rattle, thus the knocking or pinking sound. Drain old fuel and always use the recommended fuel grade.
☐ Spark plug heat range incorrect. Uncontrolled detonation indicates the plug heat range is too hot. The plug in effect becomes a glow plug, raising cylinder temperatures. Install the proper heat range plug (Chapter 1).
☐ Improper air/fuel mixture. This will cause the cylinder to run hot, which leads to detonation. Clogged jets or an air leak can cause this imbalance. See Chapter 5.

Miscellaneous causes

☐ Throttle valve doesn't open fully. Adjust the throttle twistgrip freeplay (Chapter 1).
☐ Clutch slipping or drive belt worn (Chapter 3).
☐ Timing not advancing (Chapter 6).
☐ Engine oil viscosity too high (four-stroke engines). Using too heavy an oil can damage the oil pump or lubrication system and cause drag on the engine.
☐ Brakes dragging. On disc brakes, usually caused by debris which has entered the brake piston seals, or from a warped disc or bent axle. On drum brakes, cable out of adjustment, shoe return spring broken. Repair as necessary (Chapter 8).

4 Overheating

Engine overheats – air-cooled engine

☐ Air cooling ducts or engine cowling blocked or incorrectly fitted.
☐ Problem with cooling fan.

Engine overheats – liquid-cooled engine

☐ Coolant level low or system leak (Pre-ride checks).
☐ Water pump failure (Chapter 4).
☐ Thermostat stuck closed (Chapter 4).

Firing incorrect

☐ Spark plug fouled, defective or worn out. See Chapter 1 for spark plug maintenance.
☐ Incorrect spark plug.
☐ CDI unit defective (Chapter 6).
☐ Faulty ignition coil (Chapter 6).

Fuel/air mixture incorrect

☐ Main jet clogged. Dirt, water or other contaminants can clog the main jet. Clean the in-line filter, the float chamber and the jets and carburettor orifices (Chapter 5).
☐ Main jet wrong size. The standard jetting is for sea level atmospheric pressure and oxygen content.
☐ Air bleed holes clogged. Remove and overhaul carburettor (Chapter 5).
☐ Air filter clogged, poorly sealed, or missing (Chapter 1).
☐ Air filter housing or duct poorly sealed. Look for cracks, holes or loose clamps or screws, and renew or repair defective parts.
☐ Carburettor inlet manifold loose. Check for cracks, breaks, tears or loose fixings.

Compression too high

☐ Carbon build-up in combustion chamber. Use of a fuel additive that will dissolve the adhesive bonding the carbon particles to the piston crown and chamber is the easiest way to remove the build-up. Otherwise, the cylinder head will have to be removed and decarbonised (Chapter 2 relevant part). On two-stroke engines, the regular service interval for cylinder head decarbonisation should be adhered to.
☐ Improperly machined head surface or installation of incorrect size cylinder base gasket during engine assembly.

Engine load excessive

☐ Clutch slipping or drive belt worn (Chapter 3).
☐ Engine oil level too high (four-stroke engines). The addition of too much oil will cause pressurisation of the crankcase and inefficient engine operation. Check the specifications in your handbook and drain to proper level (Chapter 1 and Pre-ride checks).
☐ Engine oil viscosity too high (four-stroke engines). Using too heavy an oil can damage the oil pump or lubrication system as well as cause drag on the engine.
☐ Brakes dragging. On disc brakes, usually caused by debris which has entered the brake piston seals, or from a warped disc or bent axle. On drum brakes, cable out of adjustment, shoe return spring broken. Repair as necessary (Chapter 8).

Lubrication inadequate

☐ Engine oil level too low (four-stroke engines). Friction caused by intermittent lack of lubrication or from oil that is overworked can cause overheating. The oil provides a definite cooling function in the engine. Check the oil level (Chapter 1 and Pre-ride checks).
☐ Oil pump delivering insufficient amount of oil (two-stroke engines). Oil pump control unit fault (Chapter 10).
☐ Poor quality oil or incorrect viscosity or type. Oil is rated not only according to viscosity but also according to type. Check the specifications in your handbook and change to the correct oil (Chapter 1). On two-stroke engines, make sure that you use a two-stroke oil which is suitable for oil injection engines.

Miscellaneous causes

☐ Modification to exhaust system. Most aftermarket exhaust systems cause the engine to run leaner, which makes them run hotter. When installing an accessory exhaust system, always obtain advice on rejetting the carburettor.

5 Transmission problems

No drive to rear wheel

☐ Drive belt broken (Chapter 3).
☐ Clutch not engaging (Chapter 3).
☐ Clutch or drum excessively worn (Chapter 3).

Transmission noise or vibration

☐ Bearings worn. Also includes the possibility that the shafts are worn. Overhaul the transmission (Chapter 3).
☐ Gears worn or chipped (Chapter 3).
☐ Clutch drum worn unevenly (Chapter 3).
☐ Worn bearings or bent shaft (Chapter 3).
☐ Loose clutch nut or drum nut (Chapter 3).

Poor performance

☐ Variator rollers worn (Chapter 3).
☐ Weak or broken driven pulley spring (Chapter 3).
☐ Clutch or drum excessively worn (Chapter 3).
☐ Grease on clutch friction material (Chapter 3).
☐ Drive belt excessively worn (Chapter 1).

Clutch not disengaging completely

☐ Weak or broken clutch springs (Chapter 3).
☐ Engine idle speed too high (Chapter 1).

6 Abnormal engine noise

Knocking or pinking

☐ Carbon build-up in combustion chamber. Use of a fuel additive that will dissolve the adhesive bonding the carbon particles to the piston crown and chamber is the easiest way to remove the build-up. Otherwise, the cylinder head will have to be removed and decarbonised (Chapter 2 relevant part). On two-stroke engines, always decarbonise the cylinder head and piston crown at the recommended service interval (Chapter 1).

☐ Incorrect or poor quality fuel. Old or improper fuel can cause detonation. This causes the piston to rattle, thus the knocking or pinking sound. Drain the old fuel and always use the recommended grade fuel (Chapter 5).

☐ Spark plug heat range incorrect. Uncontrolled detonation indicates that the plug heat range is too hot. The plug in effect becomes a glow plug, raising cylinder temperatures. Install the proper heat range plug (Chapter 1).

☐ Improper air/fuel mixture. This will cause the cylinder to run hot and lead to detonation. Clogged jets or an air leak can cause this imbalance (Chapter 5).

Piston slap or rattling

☐ Cylinder-to-piston clearance excessive. Caused by improper assembly. Inspect and overhaul top-end parts (Chapter relevant part).

☐ Connecting rod bent. Caused by over-revving, trying to start a badly flooded engine. Renew the damaged parts (Chapter 2 relevant part).

☐ Piston pin or piston pin bore worn or seized from wear or lack of lubrication. Renew damaged parts (Chapter 2 relevant part).

☐ Piston ring(s) worn, broken or sticking. Overhaul the top-end (Chapter relevant part).

☐ Piston seizure damage. Usually from lack of lubrication or overheating. Renew the piston and cylinder, as necessary (Chapter 2 relevant part). On two-stroke engines, check that the oil pump is functioning correctly.

☐ Connecting rod small or big-end bearing clearance excessive. Caused by excessive wear or lack of lubrication. Renew worn parts.

Valve noise – four-stroke engines

☐ Incorrect valve clearances. Adjust the clearances by referring to Chapter 1.

☐ Valve spring broken or weak. Check and renew weak valve springs (Chapter 2C, D, E, F or G).

☐ Camshaft bearings worn or damaged. Lack of lubrication at high rpm is usually the cause of damage. Insufficient oil or failure to change the oil at the recommended intervals are the chief causes (Chapter 2C, D, E, F or G).

Other noise

☐ Exhaust pipe leaking at cylinder head connection. Caused by improper fit of pipe or loose exhaust flange. All exhaust fasteners should be tightened evenly and carefully. Failure to do this will lead to a leak (Chapter 5).

☐ Crankshaft runout excessive. Caused by a bent crankshaft (from over-revving) or damage from an upper cylinder component failure.

☐ Engine mounting bolts loose. Tighten all engine mount bolts (Chapter 2 relevant part).

☐ Crankshaft bearings worn (Chapter 2 relevant part).

☐ Cam chain worn, tensioner defective or guide blades worn (four-stroke engines). Replace according to the procedure in Chapter 2C, D, E, F or G.

7 Abnormal frame and suspension noise

Front end noise

☐ Steering head bearings loose or damaged. Clicks when braking. Check and adjust or replace as necessary (Chapters 1 and 7).

☐ Bolts loose. Make sure all bolts are tightened to the specified torque (Chapter 7).

☐ Fork tube bent. Good possibility if machine has been dropped. Renew the tube or the fork assembly (Chapter 7).

☐ Front axle nut loose. Tighten to the specified torque (Chapter 8).

☐ Loose or worn wheel or hub bearings. Check and renew as needed (Chapter 8).

Shock absorber noise

☐ Fluid level incorrect. Indicates a leak caused by defective seal. Shock will be covered with oil. Renew the shock (Chapter 7).

☐ Defective shock absorber with internal damage. This is in the body of the shock and can't be remedied. The shock must be renewed (Chapter 7).

☐ Bent or damaged shock body. Renew the shock (Chapter 7).

Brake noise

☐ Squeal caused by dust on brake pads or shoes. Usually found in combination with glazed pads or shoes. Clean using brake cleaning solvent (Chapter 8).

☐ Contamination of brake pads or shoes. Oil, brake fluid or dirt causing brake to chatter or squeal. Clean or renew pads or shoes (Chapter 8).

☐ Pads or shoes glazed. Caused by excessive heat from prolonged use or from contamination. Do not use sandpaper, emery cloth, carborundum cloth or any other abrasive to roughen the pad surfaces as abrasives will stay in the pad material and damage the disc or drum. A very fine flat file can be used, but pad or shoe renewal is advised (Chapter 8).

☐ Disc or drum warped. Can cause a chattering, clicking or intermittent squeal. Usually accompanied by a pulsating lever and uneven braking. Check the disc runout and the drum ovality (Chapter 8).

☐ Loose or worn wheel (front) or transmission (rear) bearings. Check and renew as needed (Chapters 8 or 3).

8 Excessive exhaust smoke

White smoke – four-stroke engines (oil burning)

☐ Piston oil control ring worn. The ring may be broken or damaged, causing oil from the crankcase to be pulled past the piston into the combustion chamber. Renew the rings (Chapter 2C, D, E, F or G).

☐ Cylinder worn, or scored. Caused by overheating or oil starvation. A new cylinder and piston will have to be installed (Chapter 2C, D, E, F or G).

☐ Valve stem oil seal damaged or worn. Renew oil seals (Chapter 2C, D, E, F or G).

☐ Valve guide worn. Inspect the valve guides and if worn seek the advice of a Peugeot dealer (Chapter 2C, D, E, F or G).

☐ Engine oil level too high, which causes the oil to be forced past the rings. Check the specifications in your handbook and drain to proper level (Chapter 1 and *Pre-ride checks*).

☐ Head gasket broken between oil return and cylinder. Causes oil to be pulled into the combustion chamber. Renew the head gasket and check the head for warpage (Chapter 2C, D, E, F or G).

☐ Abnormal crankcase pressurisation, which forces oil past the rings.

White/blue smoke – two-stroke engines (oil burning)

☐ Oil pump control unit faulty (Chapter 10).

☐ Accumulated oil deposits in the exhaust system. If the scooter is used for short journeys only, the oil residue from the exhaust gases will condense in the cool silencer. Take the scooter for a long run in hot weather to burn off the accumulated oil residue.

Black smoke (over-rich mixture)

☐ Air filter clogged. Clean or renew the element (Chapter 1).

☐ Main jet too large or loose. Compare the jet size to the Specifications (Chapter 5).

☐ Automatic choke unit faulty (Chapter 5).

☐ Float needle valve held off needle seat. Clean the float chamber and fuel line and renew the needle and seat if necessary (Chapter 5).

Brown smoke (lean mixture)

☐ Main jet too small or clogged. Lean condition caused by wrong size main jet or by a restricted orifice. Clean float chamber and jets and compare jet size to specifications (Chapter 5).

☐ Fuel flow insufficient. Float needle valve stuck closed due to chemical reaction with old fuel. Restricted fuel hose. Clean hose and float chamber.

☐ Carburettor inlet manifold clamp loose (Chapter 5).

☐ Air filter poorly sealed or not installed (Chapter 1).

☐ Ignition timing incorrect (Chapter 6).

9 Poor handling or stability

Handlebar hard to turn

☐ Steering head bearing adjuster nut too tight. Check adjustment as described in Chapters 1 and 7.

☐ Steering head bearings damaged. Roughness can be felt as the bars are turned from side-to-side. Replace bearings and races (Chapter 7).

☐ Races dented or worn. Denting results from a collision or hitting a pothole. Renew races and bearings (Chapter 7).

☐ Steering stem lubrication inadequate. Causes are grease getting hard from age or being washed out by high pressure car washes. Disassemble steering head and repack bearings (Chapter 7).

☐ Steering stem bent. Caused by a collision or hitting a pothole. Renew damaged part. Don't try to straighten the steering stem (Chapter 7).

☐ Front tyre air pressure too low (*Pre-ride checks*).

Handlebar shakes or vibrates excessively

☐ Tyres worn (*Pre-ride checks*).

☐ Swingarm pivots worn. Renew worn components (Chapter 7).

☐ Wheel rim(s) warped or damaged. Inspect wheels for runout (Chapter 8).

☐ Wheel bearings worn. Worn wheel bearings (front) or transmission bearings (rear) can cause poor tracking. Worn front bearings will cause wobble (Chapter 8).

☐ Handlebar mountings loose (Chapter 7).

☐ Front suspension bolts loose. Tighten them to the specified torque (Chapter 7).

☐ Engine mounting bolts loose. Will cause excessive vibration with increased engine rpm (Chapter 2 relevant part).

Handlebar pulls to one side

☐ Frame bent. Definitely suspect this if the machine has been involved in a collision. May or may not be accompanied by cracking near the bend. Renew the frame.

☐ Wheels out of alignment. Caused by improper location of axle spacers or from bent steering stem or frame (Chapter 7 or 8).

☐ Steering stem bent. Caused by impact damage or by dropping the machine. Renew the steering stem (Chapter 7).

☐ Fork tube bent. Disassemble the forks and renew the damaged parts (Chapter 7).

Poor shock absorbing qualities

Too hard:
a) Fork oil quantity excessive or viscosity too high – conventional forks (Chapter 7).
b) Fork or front shock internal damage (Chapter 7).
c) Suspension bent. Causes a harsh, sticking feeling (Chapter 7).
d) Rear shock internal damage (Chapter 7).
e) Tyre pressure too high (Pre-ride checks).

Too soft:
a) Fork oil quantity too low or viscosity too light – conventional forks (Chapter 7).
b) Fork or shock spring(s) weak or broken (Chapter 7).
c) Shock internal damage or leakage (Chapter 7).

10 Braking problems – disc brake

Brakes are ineffective

☐ Air in brake hose. Caused by inattention to master cylinder fluid level or by leakage (*Pre-ride checks*). Locate problem and bleed brake (Chapter 8).
☐ Pads or disc worn (Chapters 1 and 8).
☐ Brake fluid leak. Locate problem and rectify (Chapter 8).
☐ Contaminated pads. Caused by contamination with oil, grease, brake fluid, etc. Renew pads. Clean disc thoroughly with brake cleaner (Chapter 8).
☐ Brake fluid deteriorated. Fluid is old or contaminated. Drain system, replenish with new fluid and bleed the system (Chapter 8).
☐ Master cylinder internal parts worn or damaged causing fluid to bypass (Chapter 8).
☐ Master cylinder bore scratched by foreign material or broken spring. Repair or renew master cylinder (Chapter 8).
☐ Disc warped. Renew disc (Chapter 8).

Brake lever pulsates

☐ Disc warped. Renew disc (Chapter 8).
☐ Axle bent. Renew axle (Chapter 8).
☐ Brake caliper bolts loose (Chapter 8).
☐ Wheel warped or otherwise damaged (Chapter 8).
☐ Wheel bearings damaged or worn (Chapter 8).

Brakes drag

☐ Master cylinder piston seized. Caused by wear or damage to piston or cylinder bore (Chapter 8).
☐ Lever balky or stuck. Check pivot and lubricate (Chapter 8).
☐ Brake caliper piston seized in bore. Caused by corrosion, wear or ingestion of dirt past deteriorated seal (Chapter 8).
☐ Brake pads damaged. Pad material separated from backing plate. Usually caused by faulty manufacturing process or from contact with chemicals. Renew pads (Chapter 8).
☐ Pads improperly installed (Chapter 8).

11 Braking problems – drum brake

Brakes are ineffective

☐ Cable incorrectly adjusted. Check cable (Chapter 1).
☐ Shoes or drum worn (Chapter 8).
☐ Contaminated shoes. Caused by contamination with oil, grease, etc. Renew shoes. Clean drum thoroughly with brake cleaner (Chapter 8).
☐ Brake lever arm incorrectly positioned, or cam excessively worn (Chapter 8).

Brake lever pulsates

☐ Drum warped. Renew drum (Chapter 8).
☐ Axle bent. Renew axle (Chapter 8).
☐ Wheel warped or otherwise damaged (Chapter 8).
☐ Transmission bearings damaged or worn (Chapter 3).

Brakes drag

☐ Cable incorrectly adjusted or requires lubrication. Check cable (Chapter 1).
☐ Shoe return springs broken (Chapter 8).
☐ Lever balky or stuck. Check pivot and lubricate (Chapter 8).
☐ Lever arm or cam binds. Caused by inadequate lubrication or damage (Chapter 8).
☐ Brake shoe damaged. Friction material separated from shoe. Usually caused by faulty manufacturing process or from contact with chemicals. Renew shoes (Chapter 8).
☐ Shoes improperly installed (Chapter 8).

12 Electrical problems

Battery dead or weak

☐ Battery faulty. Caused by sulphated plates which are shorted through sedimentation. Also, broken battery terminal making only occasional contact (Chapter 10).
☐ Battery cables making poor electrical contact (Chapter 10).
☐ Load excessive. Caused by addition of high wattage lights or other electrical accessories.
☐ Ignition switch defective. Switch either earths internally or fails to shut off system. Renew the switch (Chapter 10).
☐ Regulator/rectifier defective (Chapter 10).
☐ Alternator stator coil open or shorted (Chapter 10).
☐ Wiring faulty. Wiring either shorted to earth or connections loose in ignition, charging or lighting circuits (Wiring Diagrams).

Battery overcharged

☐ Regulator/rectifier defective. Overcharging is noticed when battery gets excessively warm (Chapter 10).
☐ Battery defective. Renew battery (Chapter 10).
☐ Battery amperage too low, wrong type or size. Install manufacturer's specified amp-hour battery to handle charging load (Chapter 10).

Note: *References throughout this index are in the form* **"Chapter number"** • **"Page number"**. *So, for example, 2A•10 refers to page 10 of Chapter 2A.*

Note: *References throughout this index are in the form* **"Chapter number"** • **"Page number"**. *So, for example, 2A•10 refers to page 10 of Chapter 2A.*

Note: *References throughout this index are in the form "Chapter number" • "Page number". So, for example, 2A•10 refers to page 10 of Chapter 2A.*

Note: *References throughout this index are in the form* **"Chapter number"** • **"Page number".** *So, for example, 2A•10 refers to page 10 of Chapter 2A.*

Note: *References throughout this index are in the form* **"Chapter number"** • **"Page number"**. *So, for example, 2A•10 refers to page 10 of Chapter 2A.*

Haynes Motorcycle Manuals – The Complete List

Title	Book No
APRILIA RS50 (99 – 06) & RS125 (93 – 06)	4298
Aprilia RSV1000 Mille (98 – 03) ♦	4255
Aprilia SR50	4755
BMW 2-valve Twins (70 -96) ♦	0249
BMW F650 ♦	4761
BMW K100 & 75 2-valve models (83 - 96) ♦	1373
BMW F800 (F650) Twins (06 – 10) ♦	4872
BMW R850, 1100 & 1150 4-valve Twins (93 – 06) ♦	3466
BMW R1200 (04 – 09) ♦	4598
BMW R1200 dohc Twins (10 – 12) ♦	4925
BSA Bantam (48 – 71)	0117
BSA Unit Singles (58 – 72)	0127
BSA Pre-unit Singles (54 – 61)	0326
BSA A7 & A10 Twins (47 – 62)	0121
BSA A50 & A65 Twins (62 – 73)	0155
CHINESE, Taiwanese & Korean Scooters	4768
Chinese, Taiwanese & Korean 125cc motorcycles	4781
DUCATI 600, 620, 750 & 900 2-valve v-twins (91 – 05) ♦	3290
Ducati Mk III & Desmo singles (69 – 76) ◊	0445
Ducati 748, 916 & 996 4-valve V-twins (94 – 01) ♦	3756
GILERA Runner, DNA, Ice & SKP/Stalker (97 – 11)	4163
HARLEY-DAVIDSON Sportsters (70 – 10) ♦	2534
Harley-Davidson Shovelhead & Evolution Big Twins (70 -99) ♦	2536
Harley-Davidson Twin Cam 88, 96 & 103 models (99 – 10) ♦	2478
HONDA NB, ND, NP & NS50 Melody (81 -85) ◊	0622
Honda NE/NB50 Vision & SA50 Vision Met-in (85-95)	1278
Honda MB, MBX, MT & MTX50 (80 – 93)	0731
Honda C50, C70 & C90 (67 – 03)	0324
Honda XR70/80/100R & CRF50/70/80/100F (85 – 07)	2218
Honda XL/XR 80, 100, 125, 185 & 200 2-valve models (78 – 87)	0566
Honda H100 & H100S Singles (80 – 92) ◊	0734
Honda 125 Scooters (00 – 09)	4873
Honda ANF125 Innova Scooters (03 -12) ♦	4926
Honda CB/CD125T & CM125C Twins (77 – 88) ◊	0571
Honda CBF125 (09 – 12)	5540
Honda CG125 (76 – 07) ◊	0433
Honda NS125 (86 – 93) ◊	3056
Honda CBR125R (04 – 10)	4620
Honda MBX/MTX125 & MTX200 (83 – 93)	1132
Honda XL125V & VT125C (99 – 11)	4899
Honda CD/CM185 200T & CM250C 2-valve Twins (77 – 85)	0572
Honda CMX250 Rebel & CB250 Nighthawk Twins (85 – 09) ◊	2756
Honda XL/XR 250 & 500 (78 – 84)	0567
Honda XR250L, XR250R & XR400R (86 – 03)	2219
Honda CB250 & CB400N Super Dreams (78 – 84) ◊	0540
Honda CR Motocross Bikes (86 – 07)	2222
Honda CRF250 & CRF450 (02 – 06)	2630
Honda CBR400RR Fours (88 – 99) ◊♦	3552
Honda VFR400 (NC30) & RVF400 (NC35) V-Fours (89 – 98) ◊♦	3496
Honda CB500 (93 – 02) & CBF500 (03 – 08) ◊	3753
Honda CB400 & CB550 Fours (73 – 77)	0262
Honda CX/GL500 & 650 V-Twins (78 – 86)	0442
Honda CBX550 Four (82 – 86) ◊	0940
Honda XL600R & XR600R (83 – 08) ♦	2183
Honda XL600/650V Transalp & XRV750 Africa Twin (87 – 07)	3919
Honda CB600 Hornet, CBF600 & CBR600F (07 – 12) ♦	5572
Honda CBR600F1 & 1000F Fours (87 – 96) ♦	1730
Honda CBR600F2 & F3 Fours (91 – 98) ♦	2070
Honda CBR600F4 (99 – 06) ♦	3911
Honda CB600 Hornet & CBF600 (98 – 06) ◊♦	3915
Honda CBR600RR (03 – 06) ♦	4590
Honda CBR600RR (07 -12) ♦	4795
Honda CB650 sohc Fours (78 – 84)	0665
Honda NTV600 Revere, NTV650 & NT650V Deauville (88 – 05) ◊♦	3243
Honda Shadow VT600 & 750 (USA) (88 – 09)	2312
Honda NT700V Deauville & XL700V Transalp (06 -13) ♦	5541
Honda CB750 sohc Four (69 – 79)	0131
Honda V45/65 Sabre & Magna (82 – 88)	0820
Honda VFR750 & 700 V-Fours (86 – 97) ♦	2101
Honda VFR800 V-Fours (97 – 01) ♦	3703
Honda VFR800 V-Tec V-Fours (02 – 09) ♦	4196
Honda CB750 & CB900 dohc Fours (78 – 84)	0535
Honda CBF1000 (06 -10) & CB1000R (08 – 11) ♦	4927
Honda VTR1000 Firestorm, Super Hawk & XL1000V Varadero (97 – 08) ♦	3744
Honda CBR900RR Fireblade (92 – 99) ♦	2161
Honda CBR900RR Fireblade (00 – 03) ♦	4060
Honda CBR1000RR Fireblade (04 – 07) ♦	4604
Honda CBR1100XX Super Blackbird (97 – 07) ♦	3901
Honda ST1100 Pan European V-Fours (90 – 02) ♦	3384
Honda ST1300 Pan European (02 -11) ♦	4908

Title	Book No
Honda Shadow VT1100 (USA) (85 – 07)	2313
Honda GL1000 Gold Wing (75 – 79)	0309
Honda GL1100 Gold Wing (79 – 81)	0669
Honda Gold Wing 1200 (USA) (84 - 87)	2199
Honda Gold Wing 1500 (USA) (88 – 00)	2225
Honda Goldwing GL1800 ♦	2787
KAWASAKI AE/AR 50 & 80 (81 – 95)	1007
Kawasaki KC, KE & KH100 (75 – 99)	1371
Kawasaki KMX125 & 200 (86 – 02) ◊	3046
Kawasaki 250, 350 & 400 Triples (72 – 79)	0134
Kawasaki 400 & 440 Twins (74 – 81)	0281
Kawasaki 400, 500 & 550 Fours (79 – 91)	0910
Kawasaki EN450 & 500 Twins (Ltd/Vulcan) (85 – 07)	2053
Kawasaki ER-6F & ER-6N (06 -10) ♦	4874
Kawasaki EX500 (GPZ500S) & ER500 (ER-5) (87 – 08) ♦	2052
Kawasaki ZX600 (ZZ-R600 & Ninja ZX-6) (90 – 06) ♦	2146
Kawasaki ZX-6R Ninja Fours (95 – 02) ♦	3451
Kawasaki ZX-6R (03 – 06) ♦	4742
Kawasaki ZX600 (GPZ600R, GPX600R, Ninja 600R & RX) & ZX750 (GPX750R, Ninja 750R) (85 – 97) ♦	1780
Kawasaki 650 Four (76 – 78)	0373
Kawasaki Vulcan 700/750 & 800 (85 – 04) ♦	2457
Kawasaki Vulcan 1500 & 1600 (87 – 08) ♦	4913
Kawasaki 750 Air-cooled Fours	0574
Kawasaki ZR550 & 750 Zephyr Fours (90 – 97) ♦	3382
Kawasaki Z750 & Z1000 (03 – 08) ♦	4762
Kawasaki ZX750 (Ninja ZX-7 & ZXR750) Fours (89 – 96) ♦	2054
Kawasaki Ninja ZX-7R & ZX-9R (94 – 04) ♦	3721
Kawasaki 900 & 1000 Fours (73 – 77)	0222
Kawasaki ZX900, 1000 & 1100 Liquid-cooled Fours (83 – 97) ♦	1681
KTM EXC Enduro & SX Motocross (00 – 07) ♦	4629
LAMBRETTA Scooters (58 – 00) ♦	5573
MOTO GUZZI 750, 850 & 1000 V-Twins (74 – 78)	0339
MZ ETZ models (81 – 95)	1680
NORTON 500, 600, 650 & 750 Twins (57 – 70)	0187
Norton Commando (68 – 77)	0125
PEUGEOT Speedfight, Trekker & Vivacity Scooters (96 – 08) ◊	3920
PIAGGIO (Vespa) Scooters (91 – 09) ◊	3492
SUZUKI GT, ZR & TS50 (77 – 90)	0799
Suzuki TS50X (84 – 00) ◊	1599
Suzuki 100, 125, 185 & 250 Air-cooled Trail bikes (79 – 89)	0797
Suzuki GP100 & 125 Singles (78 – 93) ◊	0576
Suzuki GS, GN, GZ & DR125 Singles (82 – 05)	0888
Suzuki Burgman 250 & 400 (98 -11) ♦	4909
Suzuki GSX-R600/750 (06 – 09) ♦	4790
Suzuki 250 & 350 Twins (68 – 78)	0120
Suzuki GT250X7, GT200X5 & SB200 Twins (78 – 83) ◊	0469
Suzuki DR-Z400 (00 – 10) ♦	2933
Suzuki GS/GSX250, 400 & 450 Twins (79 – 85)	0736
Suzuki GS500 Twin (89 – 08) ♦	3238
Suzuki GS550 (77 – 82) & GS750 Fours (76 – 79)	0363
Suzuki GS/GSX550 4-valve Fours (83 – 88)	1133
Suzuki SV650 & SV650S (99 – 08) ♦	3912
Suzuki GSX-R600 & 750 (96 – 00) ♦	3553
Suzuki GSX-R600 (01 – 03), GSX-R750 (00 – 03) & GSX-R1000 (01 – 02) ♦	3986
Suzuki GSX-R600/750 (04 – 05) & GSX-R1000 (03 – 06) ♦	4382
Suzuki GSF600, 650 & 1200 Bandit Fours (95 – 06) ♦	3367
Suzuki Intruder, Marauder, Volusia & Boulevard (85 – 09) ♦	2618
Suzuki GS850 Fours (78 – 88)	0536
Suzuki GS1000 Four (77 – 79)	0484
Suzuki GSX-R750, GSX-R1100 (85 – 92) GSX600F, GSX750F, GSX1100F (Katana) Fours (88 – 96)	2055
Suzuki GSX600/750F & GSX750 (98 – 02) ♦	3987
Suzuki GS/GSX1000, 1100 & 1150 4-valve Fours (79 – 88)	0737
Suzuki TL1000S/R & DL V-Strom (97 – 04) ♦	4083
Suzuki GSF650/1250 (07 – 09) ♦	4798
Suzuki GSX1300R Hayabusa (99 – 04) ♦	4184
Suzuki GSX1400 (02 – 08) ♦	4758
TRIUMPH Tiger Cub & Terrier (52 – 68)	0414
Triumph 350 & 500 Unit Twins (58 – 73)	0137
Triumph Pre-Unit Twins (47 – 62)	0251
Triumph 650 & 750 2-valve Unit Twins (63 – 83)	0122
Triumph 675 (06 – 10) ♦	4876
Triumph 1050 Sprint, Speed Triple & Tiger (05 -13) ♦	4796
Triumph Trident & BSA Rocket 3 (69 – 75)	0136
Triumph Bonneville (01 – 12) ♦	4364
Triumph Daytona, Speed Triple, Sprint & Tiger (97 – 05) ♦	3755
Triumph Triples & Fours (carburetor engines) (91 – 04)	2162
VESPA P/PX125, 150 & 200 Scooters (78 – 12)	0707
Vespa GTS125, 250 & 300 (05 – 10)	4898

Title	Book No
Vespa Scooters (59 – 78)	0126
YAMAHA DT50 & 80 Trail Bikes (78 – 95) ◊	0800
Yamaha T50 & 80 Townmate (83 – 95) ◊	1247
Yamaha YB100 Singles (73 – 91) ◊	0474
Yamaha RS/RXS 100 & 125 Singles (74 – 95)	0331
Yamaha RD & DT125LC (82 – 87) ◊	0887
Yamaha TZR125 (87 – 93) & DT125R (88 – 07) ◊	1655
Yamaha TY50, 80, 125 & 175 (74 – 84) ◊	0464
Yamaha XT & SR125 (82 – 03) ◊	1021
Yamaha YBR125 & XT125R/X (05 – 13)	4797
Yamaha YZF-R125 (08 – 11) ♦	5543
Yamaha Trail Bikes (81 – 00)	2350
Yamaha 2-stroke Motocross Bikes (86 – 06)	2662
Yamaha YZ & WR 4-stroke Motocross Bikes (98 – 08)	2689
Yamaha 250 & 350 Twins (70 – 79)	0040
Yamaha XS250, 360 & 400 sohc Twins (75 – 84)	0378
Yamaha RD250 & 350LC Twins (80 – 82)	0803
Yamaha RD350 YPVS Twins (83 – 95)	1158
Yamaha RD400 Twin (75 – 79)	0333
Yamaha XT, TT & SR500 Singles (75 – 83)	0342
Yamaha XZ550 Vision V-Twins (82 – 85)	0821
Yamaha FJ, FX, XY & YX600 Radian (84 – 92)	2100
Yamaha XT660 & MT-03 (04 – 11) ♦	4910
Yamaha XJ600S (Diversion, Seca II) & XJ600N Fours (92 – 03) ♦	2145
Yamaha YZF600R Thundercat & FZS600 Fazer (96 – 03) ♦	3702
Yamaha FZ-6 Fazer (04 – 08) ♦	4751
Yamaha YZF-R6 (99 – 02) ♦	3900
Yamaha YZF-R6 (03 – 05) ♦	4601
Yamaha YZF-R6 (06 – 13) ♦	5544
Yamaha 650 Twins (70 – 83)	0341
Yamaha XJ650 & 750 Fours (80 – 84)	0738
Yamaha XS750 & 850 Triples (76 – 85)	0340
Yamaha TDM850, TRX850 & XTZ750 (89 – 99) ◊♦	3450
Yamaha YZF750R & YZF1000R Thunderace (93 – 00) ♦	3720
Yamaha FZR600, 750 & 1000 Fours (87 – 96) ♦	2056
Yamaha XV (Virago) V-Twins (81 – 03) ♦	0802
Yamaha XVS650 & 1100 Drag Star/V-Star (97 – 05) ♦	4195
Yamaha XJ900F Fours (83 – 94) ♦	3239
Yamaha XJ900S Diversion (94 – 01) ♦	3739
Yamaha YZF-R1 (98 – 03) ♦	3754
Yamaha YZF-R1 (04 – 06) ♦	4605
Yamaha FZS1000 Fazer (01 – 05) ♦	4287
Yamaha FJ1100 & 1200 Fours (84 – 96) ♦	2057
Yamaha XJR1200 & 1300 (95 – 06) ♦	3981
Yamaha V-Max (85 – 03) ♦	4072

ATV's

Title	Book No
Honda ATC 70, 90, 110, 185 & 200 (71 – on)	0565
Honda Rancher, Recon & TRX250EX ATVs	2553
Honda TRX300 Shaft Drive ATVs (88 – 00)	2125
Honda Foreman (95 – 11)	2465
Honda TRX300EX, TRX400EX & TRX450R/ER ATVs (93 – 06)	2318
Kawasaki Bayou 220/250/300 & Prairie 300 ATVs (86 – 03)	2351
Polaris ATVs (85 – 97)	2302
Polaris ATVs (98 – 07)	2508
Suzuki/Kawasaki/Artic Cat ATVs (03 – 09)	2910
Yamaha YFS200 Blaster ATV (88 – 06)	2317
Yamaha YFM350 & YFM400 (ER & Big Bear) ATVs (87 – 09)	2126
Yamaha YFZ450 & YFZ450R (04 – 10)	2899
Yamaha Banshee and Warrior ATVs (87 – 10)	2314
Yamaha Kodiak and Grizzly ATVs (93 – 05)	2567
ATV Basics	10450

TECHBOOK SERIES

Title	Book No
Twist and Go (automatic transmission) Scooters Service and Repair Manual	4082
Motorcycle Basics Techbook (2nd edition)	3515
Motorcycle Electrical Techbook (3rd edition)	3471
Motorcycle Fuel Systems Techbook	3514
Motorcycle Maintenance Techbook	4071
Motorcycle Modifying	4272
Motorcycle Workshop Practice Techbook (2nd edition)	3470

◊ = not available in the USA ♦ = Superbike

Preserving Our Motoring Heritage

< The Model J Duesenberg Derham Tourster. Only eight of these magnificent cars were ever built – this is the only example to be found outside the United States of America

Almost every car you've ever loved, loathed or desired is gathered under one roof at the Haynes Motor Museum. Over 300 immaculately presented cars and motorbikes represent every aspect of our motoring heritage, from elegant reminders of bygone days, such as the superb Model J Duesenberg to curiosities like the bug-eyed BMW Isetta. There are also many old friends and flames. Perhaps you remember the 1959 Ford Popular that you did your courting in? The magnificent 'Red Collection' is a spectacle of classic sports cars including AC, Alfa Romeo, Austin Healey, Ferrari, Lamborghini, Maserati, MG, Riley, Porsche and Triumph.

A Perfect Day Out

Each and every vehicle at the Haynes Motor Museum has played its part in the history and culture of Motoring. Today, they make a wonderful spectacle and a great day out for all the family. Bring the kids, bring Mum and Dad, but above all bring your camera to capture those golden memories for ever. You will also find an impressive array of motoring memorabilia, a comfortable 70 seat video cinema and one of the most extensive transport book shops in Britain. The Pit Stop Cafe serves everything from a cup of tea to wholesome, home-made meals or, if you prefer, you can enjoy the large picnic area nestled in the beautiful rural surroundings of Somerset.

> John Haynes O.B.E., Founder and Chairman of the museum at the wheel of a Haynes Light 12.

< The 1936 490cc sohc-engined International Norton – well known for its racing success

The Museum is situated on the A359 Yeovil to Frome road at Sparkford, just off the A303 in Somerset. It is about 40 miles south of Bristol, and 25 minutes drive from the M5 intersection at Taunton.
Open 9.30am - 5.30pm (10.00am - 4.00pm Winter) 7 days a week, *except Christmas Day, Boxing Day and New Years Day*
Special rates available for schools, coach parties and outings Charitable Trust No. 292048